D1560174

Language in the Americas

Joseph H. Greenberg

Language in the Americas

Stanford University Press

Stanford, California   1987

Stanford University Press
Stanford, California

© 1987 by the Board of Trustees of the
Leland Stanford Junior University

Printed in the United States of America

Library of Congress Cataloging-in-Publication Data

Greenberg, Joseph Harold, 1915–
  Language in the Americas.

  Bibliography: p.
  Includes indexes.
  1. America—Languages—Classification. I. Title.
P376.G7 1987   497'.012   86-14359
ISBN 0-8047-1315-4 (alk. paper)

To the memory of EDWARD SAPIR (1884–1939)

Preface

All through 1984, the centennial of Edward Sapir's birth, scholars around the world commemorated the man who is recognized as without peer in the field of anthropological linguistics. Much was said of his personal qualities as well as his scholarly achievements. Of those qualities, unfortunately, I cannot speak from first-hand knowledge. In the year 1937, I interrupted my graduate work at Northwestern for a period of study at Yale, then recognized as the foremost center for linguistic studies. For me, the greatest attraction was, of course, the prospect of working with Sapir. But when I arrived, I was told that he was ill and living in New York. I felt that it would have been presumptuous on my part to take up any of his time under these circumstances and thus, to my regret, I never made his personal acquaintance.

One of Sapir's primary and abiding interests was the historical classification of American Indian languages. If he never had the opportunity and the leisure to survey the entire set of indigenous languages from Tierra del Fuego to the Far North, it was because, in his time, the greatest priority was on gathering data for numerous languages that had not even been the subject, in many cases, of cursory vocabulary collection, much less basic grammatical and lexical investigation.

In recent years, scholars have tended to deprecate Sapir's work in the area of historical classification. It will be obvious to any American Indianist reading this volume that in both method and results it is far closer to Sapir than to much current work. Sapir was thoroughly trained in general historical linguistics as well as in Indo-European studies, to which he made lasting contributions, particularly in regard to laryngeal theory. That he did not, out of ignorance, invoke phonological reconstructions as proof of his classifications is, to say the least, implausible. The extent to which I agree with his methods and results is discussed in greater detail in the body of this volume. If the results should be regarded as worthy of his memory, I will have received a more than adequate reward.

In its present form this book is somewhat less extensive than originally planned. A chapter on the Eurasiatic family, which includes Eskimo-Aleut, spoken in North America, and, in the case of Eskimo, in Siberia also, was in an advanced state of preparation when it became clear to me that it was preferable to treat it in a separate volume. That volume, if all goes well, will be published not much later than this one.

Another omission is a contemplated mathematical appendix on the phonological distance among related languages as measured by the recurrence of valid sound correspondences. This project was shelved because it became evident that unique correspondences might reflect either the existence of systems with large numbers of phonemes or a longer period of elapsed time with the consequent divergence of related sounds. Although this difficulty could probably be taken into account by a further elaboration, the topic seemed only obliquely related to the main concerns of the work and hence did not justify the further delays in final publication that would have inevitably resulted. I am particularly indebted to William S.-Y. Wang for collaboration on the mathematical aspects of this problem and to Mary Wang for devising the relevant computer program.

Among the many others to whom I am indebted are all those scholars who have made unpublished material available to me, notably Charles Wagley for data on Trumai and Ernest Migliazza on Yanomama. I am also strongly indebted to various librarians, one of whom, Clara Galvão, helped me obtain materials on languages of Brazil not to be found in libraries in this country. I cannot express in adequate terms my gratitude to all the research librarians and members of the interlibrary loan staff at Stanford for their efforts in my behalf. I particularly wish to mention Ed Rawlings, the research librarian for anthropology and linguistics, and Florence Chu, now retired, who headed the interlibrary loan service. I also wish to mention a librarian in the American Philosophical Library in Philadelphia whose name I do not know. In defiance of all the usual bureaucratic norms, she kept the library open for me beyond regular closing hours so that I could finish copying material in the Boas collection on my last day in Philadelphia.

I also wish to record my deep gratitude to the Stanford Administration, particularly Halsey Royden, former dean of Humanities and Sciences, Norman Wessells, the present dean, and Donald Kennedy, the president. This is no mere perfunctory gesture. All three have encouraged and supported my work in concrete and important ways. Among Stanford institutions my indebtedness includes in no small measure Stanford University Press, especially its past director, Leon Seltzer, who originally contracted with me for this book; I am also indebted to J. G. Bell for his general helpfulness and to Bill Carver for his unfailingly useful advice and constant encouragement.

Finally I wish to express my gratitude to Merritt Ruhlen, himself a linguist of no mean accomplishment, who undertook the arduous task of preparing my manuscript for publication on a word processor. He provided numerous highly useful suggestions and emendations in the course of his labors.

Since the appearance of "The General Classification of Central and South American Languages" (Greenberg 1960), based on a paper given in 1956, I have been engaged in the collection of a truly massive amount of data. The materials on Amerind and Na-Dene alone, for example, occupy 23 notebooks (available from the Stanford University Library; P203/G7/f), each containing information on approximately 80 languages, and each including, so far as the sources permit, a maximum of 400 lexical items for every language. On a rough estimate, these notebooks encompass well over 2,000 sources and contain perhaps a quarter of a million separate entries. An additional Eurasiatic notebook and six grammatical notebooks have not been duplicated.

The present work is in many respects a pioneering one. Although I have exercised great care, it would be miraculous if, in handling such a vast mass of material, there were no errors of fact or interpretation. I will be grateful for any corrections suggested by readers. However, I believe that the work should be judged as a whole. Particularly in regard to etymologies, any user of existing dictionaries, even of intensively studied language families, will encounter numerous instances in which the same form has been assigned to different etymological entries by different scholars, or even in which the same form has erroneously been included in different etymologies. As I note in the first chapter, possible etymological connections are underdetermined by the attested processes of linguistic change, phonological and semantic. Still, while some etymologies are virtually certain or highly probable, others are marginal and will perhaps never be finally decided.

One other remark is in order. I have not despised early sources. For many languages they are the only ones available, and they have been accorded new respect in much recent work. Historical linguistics is a historical discipline, after all, and no worthy historian would ignore relevant sources. All sources are imperfect. It is simply that some are more imperfect than others. But as I seek to show here, the sheer accumulation of relevant material from a vast variety of languages serves to produce a coherent overall picture. If the strength of Indo-European studies is largely based on the existence, in a few instances at least, of very old sources, the strength of Amerindian studies is simply the vast number of languages. Thus synchronic breadth becomes the source of diachronic depth.

J. H. G.

Contents

Maps

References Cited   393

Indexes

Tables

A Note on
Methods of Citation and Notation

In preparing this work, I used a very large number of sources, particularly
for the comparative vocabularies. Listing all these sources in a general bibliography would have added greatly to the length and cost of the work. Hence
only those sources actually referred to in the text—which are far fewer than
those employed in the research—are contained in the References Cited at the
back of the book.

The citation of linguistic forms presents complex problems. Older, and
nonprofessional, sources represent a variety of linguistic backgrounds,
which are often reflected in the transcription: e.g. *que-* in a Spanish source
will generally be *ke-*. For professional sources the phonetics will in general
be reliable, but often subject to phonemicization in accordance with differing theoretical procedures. Under these circumstances, complete accuracy
and consistency are probably an unattainable goal.

In general, I have sought to interpret the existing data and represent
them in a reasonably consistent manner. Phonetic rather than phonemic
choices were made in many instances, but avoiding fine phonetic detail
when it seemed irrelevant. Where, particularly for earlier sources, I was not
reasonably certain of the phonetics, I have either restricted myself to the
original citation, putting it in brackets, or given that citation along with my
own best guess (e.g. *šã* [cham] from an unprofessional Portuguese source).

The phonetic transcription used in the present work is a modified version of the International Phonetic Association's system. An attempt has been
made to provide a uniform transcription for all Amerind citations. Given the
great disparity in transcription systems, which vary considerably from lan-

guage to language, and even sometimes from one generation to the next in the same language, there will inevitably be some inconsistencies in some forms. For example, there is probably some confusion regarding sounds represented by *th,* which may signify a *t* followed by an *h,* or an aspirated *t,* or a voiceless interdental fricative. Since such cases of transcriptional ambiguity almost always involve sounds that are phonetically similar, the value of the etymologies is unaffected.

A further difficulty attends the citation of forms that were accompanied by prefixes or suffixes in the original source. I have sought to be scrupulous in excluding as part of the stem, in etymological entries, those elements for which there was good internal evidence concerning their affixal status. But I have not been entirely consistent in including these in citations. The following general convention has been adopted for morphologically complex forms. Individual morphemes are separated by hyphens. The longest form is assumed to be the stem: e.g. in *i-pe, pe* is the stem and *i-* a prefix. If, however, there is an affix that is of the same length as the stem (or of greater length), then the affix is enclosed in parentheses. Thus in *(no-)pe, pe* is the stem and *no-* is a prefix.

Where reconstructions have been carried out, as is particularly the case in North America, they are often used in lexical entries. They are preceded by asterisks and the source given in the text. However, sometimes the actual form, as given in the original, is modified to conform to the general conventions of this book.

Finally there is the question of language names. I have generally followed Čestmír Loukotka, *Classification of South American Indian Languages* (1968); Norman A. McQuown, ed., *Linguistics,* vol. 5 of *Handbook of Middle American Indians* (1967); and *Linguistics in North America,* vol. 10 of Thomas A. Sebeok, ed., *Current Trends in Linguistics* (1973), for South, Central, and North America, respectively. Where variant forms are merely transcriptions of the same word, using different orthographic conventions, they have in general not been used or mentioned since they are easily recognized. For example, Loukotka's *Mashakali,* a Macro-Ge language, is cited in that form, although in more recent publications there has been a reversion to the Portuguese form *Maxacali.* Loukotka's *Fulnio,* likewise a Macro-Ge language, has often been called *Iate;* hence, when this name is first cited, *Fulnio* is followed by *Iate* in parentheses as a further identification.

Language in the Americas

Chapter 1

The Principles of
Genetic Linguistic Classification

My purpose in this chapter is to discuss genetic classification; but I hope that the discussion will also help to explain and justify a deviation from what has become virtually a compulsory practice among American Indianists: the use of sound correspondence tables and asterisked reconstructed forms.

In proceeding in this manner, this volume will resemble my first published classificational work, namely, that on African languages (Greenberg 1963). In that study I did not use a single asterisk or a single table representing a reconstructed sound system; and although I made occasional reference to particularly striking sound correspondences, these figured in no essential way as part of my method. There were, however, extensive lists of proposed etymologies, both lexical and grammatical, and shared grammatical irregularities. Yet it is reasonable to assert that this classification has won general acceptance and has become the basis for a considerable body of comparative work on African languages.

These aspects of my methodology earned me a fair share of criticisms, of course, even from those who accepted and built on my results in their own investigations. The following are representative quotations. The first are the views of William Welmers (1973: 5, 6, 15, respectively):

> Greenberg has not, to be sure, demonstrated the existence of regular sound correspondences among all of the languages in any of the four language families he posits for Africa, although it has already been implied that such correspondences are the only real proof of genetic relationship. In fact, evidence that falls short of clear demonstration of regular phonetic correspondences may nevertheless be overwhelm-

ing. . . . But the nature of the similar forms with similar meanings which Greenberg cites, and the number of them, is such that the fact of genetic relationship can be considered established. . . . For all practical purposes the validity of the four families can be considered established.

Several years earlier, at a conference held at Aix, Luc Bouquiaux (1967: 156) made the following statement:

I do not assert that I accept the totality of his conclusions, but for the languages of the Jos Plateau in Nigeria which I know, my studies have in every instance confirmed the classification he has proposed. It is possible in fact that his method may not be absolutely correct in regard to the regularity of sound correspondences, but I cannot but pay tribute to his intuition, which was later verified in every instance, although he often had at his disposal materials of very unequal value.

In a general review of the state of African linguistics, Paul Schachter (1971: 34) virtually stumbles on the correct solution in the following statement. (My italics indicate the decisive point.)

Certainly much more work of the kind begun by [J. M.] Stewart will be needed before the same regularity of correspondences as that found within the Bantu family can be claimed for Niger-Congo as a whole, or for that matter for any of its branches, none of which has to date been accorded the kind of scholarly scrutiny with which the Bantu languages have been favored. In the meantime, however, it seems appropriate to ask what conclusions *other* than genetic relationship between Bantu and West African languages can be drawn from an objective examination of the data cited by Greenberg and his supporters; e.g. Greenberg's extensive lists of strikingly similar forms, with shared meanings, attested over the entire Niger-Congo areas, or the detailed morphophonemic similarities noted by Welmers.

But in an empirical science, how much more can be reasonably required than that the evidence be "overwhelming" and "the fact of genetic relationship [be] established" (Welmers), or that there be no "other conclusion than genetic relationship" (Schachter) or that "the classification . . . proposed" be confirmed "in every instance" (Bouquiaux)?

Welmers' mention of demonstration, a term traditionally associated with Euclidean geometry, is appropriate in mathematics and logic, which were once described as consisting of "surprising tautologies." The notion that regular sound correspondences can fittingly be called demonstrative in this sense, although this and similar terms have often been used, will be shown in the course of this chapter to be illusory. As we shall see, what is in question is not just the nature of the truth exhibited by sound correspondences, but the still more basic question of what is *meant* by these and simi-

2

lar expressions, which are often used by linguists as though their meanings were self-evident.

There are indications that some investigators in the field of African languages have begun to realize that my work not only produced certain specific results, but also employed a revolution in methodology, as Edgar Gregersen (1977: 5), for example, has noted. Having made this point, Gregersen then quotes approvingly the following statement by Paul Newman (1970), a Chadic specialist: "The proof of genetic relationship does not depend on the demonstration of historical sound laws. Rather the discovery of sound laws and the reconstruction of linguistic history normally emerge from the careful comparison of languages already presumed to be related." Actually what is involved is not so much a revolution as a return, in certain essential respects, to an earlier point of view, as will be noted later in this chapter. In fact the Neo-Grammarians of the late nineteenth century, the very school that proclaimed the regularity of sound change as their central doctrine, never made the claims for it that have grown up since, and that have been accepted by many linguists as a virtually indisputable dogma— though never, I would add, either stated with clarity or reasonably proved, but simply taken for granted as axiomatic.

In discussing this doctrine critically, let me say at the outset, if it is not obvious, that my remarks are not intended as an attack on the validity of comparative linguistics or on the importance of undertaking reconstruction. Rather, the discussion is meant constructively as a way of taking first steps where the comparative method has not been applied for want of an assured basis in valid genetic classification.

I do not wish to claim that all of the points I shall raise in this discussion are original with me. Several have been made by others, and in the pages below their work will be duly noted. However, as far as I can see, the only persons who have thought along basically similar lines are Sydney Lamb, Aaron Dolgopolsky, and, to a lesser extent, the famous anthropologist Alfred Kroeber and his co-worker Roland Dixon.

Basically, the wrong question has been asked, namely, when are languages genetically related? Sometimes in fact it is phrased as follows: when are two languages genetically related? What should be asked is, how are languages to be classified genetically? Note that in all of the quotations above, the problem is stated in terms of relationship. As Lamb (1959: 33) notes, "To many linguists the classification of languages and the determination of relationships seem almost synonymous."

Consider this example. A linguist proposes the following classification for certain languages of Europe: (1) Swedish, Sicilian, and the Laconian dialect of Greek; (2) Norwegian and Provençal; (3) Bulgarian and Icelandic; and so forth. In every one of these groupings the languages are related, since they are all Indo-European. Moreover, we may credit our hypothetical classifier with caution, for if he proceeds in like fashion a large number of independent stocks will be proposed. What is absurd, of course, is that none of these groups is a valid genetic unit. By a valid genetic unit is meant a group at any level whose members are closer to each other genetically than to any form of speech outside the group. No doubt Bulgarian is related to Icelandic, but we are dealing here with a pseudo-entity from which strange cultural-historical conclusions would be drawn, and which does not constitute a reasonable unit for historical comparative investigation.

The concept of classification into valid genetic units in a hierarchy of various levels is a far richer notion than mere relationships. From such a detailed classification many statements of relationship of differing degrees can be deduced. Statements of relationship are thus mere consequences of classification, but not vice versa.

Note also that the above definition of valid genetic unit contained the phrase "closer to each other genetically than to any form of speech outside the group." The occurrence of "any" in this definition requires that one look exhaustively outside the group, since such external evidence is relevant to determining the validity of the group. Those, therefore, who focus on a limited group determined by accidents of expertise, and anywhere else they just happen to look, are anything but cautious. For what is more incautious than to disregard relevant evidence, as any trained historian will attest?

We may distinguish two kinds of lack of caution in these matters, asserting and denying. In the former, two languages or low-level groupings are compared to the exclusion of other languages at least equally closely related, as would happen if one compared Swedish and Albanian in isolation and asserted their relationship. Equally incautious is to deny a relationship while disregarding relevant evidence, as for example when an expert in a particular Hokan language who is skeptical of its Hokan affiliation, or indeed the existence of a Hokan group at all, looks at only one other Hokan language. A comparable case would be that of an Armenian specialist who, when told that Armenian is an Indo-European language, compared it only with English. With such a procedure, the specialist may well be overwhelmed by the differences, unable to evaluate the similarities for lack of a comprehensive comparative framework, and unaware of important pieces of evidence for Armenian being Indo-European because they happen not to appear in English, a point that will be developed in detail later in this chapter.

In light of the distinction between relationship and classification, the statement sometimes made that you cannot disprove the relationship of two languages becomes uninteresting. No doubt you cannot *disprove* that Nahuatl is related to Swahili, but you can disprove that Nahuatl is closer to Swahili than to Pima. It is to account for such comparative degrees of resemblance that one posits that Nahuatl and Pima must belong to some valid genetic group (in this instance Uto-Aztecan) that does not include Swahili.

We see that from this point of view the problems of subgrouping and classification are closer than has generally been realized. Indeed if all the languages of the world are related, the problems become identical. Classifying the languages of the world becomes simply a matter of subgrouping a single large stock.

But in subgrouping it is once more the distribution of similarities that counts. The significance of a particular similarity, in so far as it bears on classification, becomes apparent only when we know where else it is found. Put another way, the significance of distribution as the essential basis of historical inference is known to all historically oriented anthropologists, and language is merely a special case.

Note that all that has just been said is based on the notion of evaluating resemblances, and the point has sometimes been made that the notion of resemblance is vague. However, what is involved in classification is not the registering of a resemblance, but a noting of the comparative degree of resemblance. Is a form A more like B than it is like C? Given, for example, *pan/fan/ezuk,* who would hesitate? What is meant, moreover, by greater resemblance is diachronic resemblance, that is, the probability that A and B derived by changes from a common source, as compared with C's having derived from a common source at greater remove (e.g. *four/vier/cuatro*) or from a different source altogether (e.g. *hand/Hand/mano*).

We may distinguish synchronic from diachronic resemblance even though they are enough alike that they can be largely equated in the heuristics of classification. Sounds and meanings by and large change to other sounds and meanings that are synchronically similar, e.g. the change from p to b, which involves a single feature difference. But s and h may be said to be diachronically similar because of the frequently attested change $s > h$, whereas in synchronic analysis they differ by a whole series of features.

5

This example also illustrates another characteristic of diachronic resemblance, its frequent asymmetry, since $h > s$ is not known to occur, whereas synchronically, by definition, s is as similar to h as h is to s.

Further, if we find three forms that all look very different from each other, no judgment of differential similarity is required. We base our classification on the strong predominance of similarities in one language, or set of languages, in comparison with another. There will no doubt be marginal cases, but even the most sophisticated techniques of the comparative method cannot decide *all* etymologies, as the reading of even a page or two of standard etymological dictionaries will show.

Also to be taken into account is the fact that as the number of languages ultimately known to belong to a grouping at some level increases, the precision of our judgment increases both in regard to the lower level of decisions, mere cognation, and in regard to at least some higher-level deductions regarding the shape and meaning of the source form.

Now we turn to the question of sound correspondences. Suppose there were a test that, when applied to two or more languages, always gave a definite answer. Let us suppose it is like a litmus test. The paper turns red when the languages are related, blue when they are not. Faced with, say, 1,000 languages in Africa, we begin to apply it. But even with pairwise comparison, there are $1,000 \times 999/2$, or 499,500, pairs we could choose. And even if such a test existed and gave valid results, the vast work of subgrouping would remain.

In fact, probably no one claims that we can devise a classification by regularity of sound correspondence, only that we can test hypotheses that have already been proposed. We therefore need a method of forming hypotheses. The number of ways of classifying n objects into one set, two sets, etc., up to n is called the partitions of n. Even without subgrouping, the number of partitions as a function of n increases astronomically with increasing values of n. The number of ways of classifying merely 20 languages is already $5,172 \times 10^{10}$, i.e. over 51 trillion.* For 1,000 languages, of course, the number is far more staggering. How this is to be dealt with is discussed later in this chapter.

Those who have realized that as an initial step one must first choose some hypothesis in order to test it by regularity of correspondence maintain,

*For a discussion of the mathematics of this function, see Greenberg (1957: 44). I am indebted to George Collier for providing a computer program that calculates the values of this function.

then, that the comparative method is not a method of *arriving* at a classification, but a method of *proving* a classification already hypothesized. What is not taken into account is the truly astronomical number of possible classifications, as just noted. No method is given for choosing a hypothesis except "inspection" or perhaps intuition, as mentioned above by Bouquiaux.

Basically what I am denying is that there really are two separate steps. This possibility has been noted by some well-known philosophers of science. For example, in a discussion of Norwood R. Hanson's theories, Peter Achinstein (1977: 358) states: "Any of the reasons Hanson mentions for suggesting a hypothesis can also be, and often are, reasons for accepting it. Take Hanson's retroductive reasoning, the fact that a hypothesis offers a plausible explanation of the data can be a reason for accepting it once it has been suggested. There is no such thing as a *logic* of discovery as opposed to a logic of justification" (italics in the original).

Returning to our litmus-test analogy, we must, however, ask if any such test exists. Considering that such expressions as proof, demonstration, and certainty constantly recur in the literature, one can reasonably ask for a rigorous procedure. But in fact a variety of versions occur, usually not worked out in any detail, but alluded to as if generally understood, and equated in some fashion with the methodology of comparative linguistics as developed by the nineteenth-century Neo-Grammarians. I shall therefore set up a number of models that can be constructed on the basis of the sorts of statements that are commonly made in the literature. They seem to arrange themselves between two poles, an emphasis on regularity of correspondence at the one pole, and on the reconstruction of an ancestral or proto-language at the other.*

An extreme example of the insistence on the regularity of correspondence is István Fodor's book (1966) on the problems of African linguistic classification. Fodor appears to demand that whenever a particular phoneme *x* is found in one language, we should always find a particular phoneme *y* in the other. But clearly a simple regular merger in one of the languages not occurring in the other, or regular conditioned change resulting in a split in one not occurring in the other, will produce results that do not meet this test. As in virtually all these discussions, it is not clear what the consequence is of discovering an irregularity in correspondence, however defined. There are four possibilities. The most drastic is to deny the relationship; the next most

---

*For a clear statement of this view, see Gleason (1955).

drastic is to reject that particular etymology. A third possibility is to accept the etymology if it seems strong on other grounds, e.g. length of the form, semantic plausibility, and widespread distribution in other languages that display numerous other similarities with the languages under consideration, so that they appear to be, or are accepted as forming, a valid linguistic stock. If the etymology, along with the relationship, is accepted, one may seek to explain what appears to be a discrepancy by employing one of numerous strategies, nine of which are discussed below. The last possibility is to accept the etymology as valid without explaining all the related forms, and simply to admit that certain developments may become clear in the light of subsequent knowledge or may even remain indefinitely inexplicable.

Fodor, it seems, opts for the most drastic: rejection of relationship. But on that basis, we can disprove the relationship of New York City English to Philadelphia English. In New York City $bɔ:d, ɔ:$ corresponds to Philadelphia $ɔr$ in 'board,' but $ɔ:$ in 'bawd.' This is no doubt a straw man, though I believe it is Fodor's doctrine. It does, however, make an important point: we must distinguish between processes and the results of processes. To some extent the distinction is made when the term "sound law" is reserved for instances in which a particular sound changes, either unconditionally or under stated phonetic conditions, in a particular language. Whenever this occurs in two or more languages stemming from a common source, the result will be a regular correspondence, although, as we have seen, it by no means needs to result in the sort of simple situation posited by Fodor. Indeed, it is a commonplace of reconstruction that the same proto-phoneme is reflected by a whole series of different correspondences under varying original phonetic conditions. Moreover, many other processes are admitted by even the strictest comparatists, e.g. metatheses and sporadic distance and adjacent assimilation and dissimilation, very often of liquids, nasals, or sibilants.

The comparative method of reconstruction is essentially the application of what we know about the processes of change in general in order to reconstruct the probable historical course of events, starting from a hypothetical reconstructed original. Of these processes, regular sound change is but one, even in phonology.

A less naïve view than Fodor's is expressed by Franz Boas (1929: 15) when he states that "until definite phonetic shifts can be provided by a sufficient number of parallel forms, the question of relationship must be open." This is, of course, exceedingly vague; for a start, we are not told what is a sufficient number of parallel forms. But Boas's view, if I understand it correctly, is broader than Fodor's, since he would not exclude, for example, an *s* in one language in some instances corresponding to an *s* in another language but in other instances to an *š*, provided they were recurrent (i.e. occur more than once). In the absence of a statement to the contrary, this would presumably not exclude the occurrence of a unique correspondence in a valid etymology, requiring only that any relationship have at least some recurrent ones.

Robert D. Levine (1979), in his critique of Edward Sapir's Na-Dene hypothesis, goes beyond Boas to reject all etymologies in which there is at least one unique correspondence. However, this position fails to take into account the fact that uniqueness and regularity are not necessarily related. A resemblance may be unique but regular. On the other hand, it can be recurrent, yet in one or more of its instances not a genuine correspondence at all. Let us examine both phenomena.

In the first case, a unique correspondence may be regular if it reflects a rare proto-phoneme that happens to survive in one etymology common to the two languages, or if there have been conditional splits in two languages, but in differing environments. In the simplest instance, a single but different split in each language, there will be four correspondences, at least one of which may be under such restricted conditions that only one instance will occur. In addition, a unique correspondence may occur if any of a number of well-attested but sporadic processes is involved, e.g. dissimilation of liquids in one of the languages.

In the second case, consider the phonetically unusual correspondence English *d* = French *f*, as in 'do' and *faire* 'to make,' 'to do' (in fact an established etymology in which the initial consonant is traditionally reconstructed as **dh*, but which appears to be the only etymology containing this correspondence if we confine ourselves to English and French). We may then happily note *head* = French *chef* (*h/š* is in fact recurrent) and thus find a second instance of *d* = *f*. However, the further comparison in Germanic of English 'head' with German *Haupt*, Danish *hoved*, etc., and on the French side with the Rumanian plural *capete*, which preserves the *t* of Latin *caput*, shows us that *d* in English corresponds not to *f* but to **t*, lost in French, while the *f* in French *chef* corresponds to the *p* of *Haupt*, etc., lost in English. This last example is typical in showing how reconstruction is always an approximation, and how, not surprisingly, the approximation becomes more precise as further evidence from other related languages is introduced.

9

Thus far we have cited those whose emphasis is on the regularity of correspondence. At the other pole, and this is characteristic of much recent work in the Amerindian languages, one can emphasize the carrying out of a reconstruction as proof. A straightforward expression of this point of view is found in Henry A. Gleason's workbook for his textbook on descriptive linguistics. After giving a comparative list of 25 words in Swahili, Kikongo, Zulu, Persian, Malay, and Tagalog, he cautions: "Do not attempt to reconstruct. To prove your conclusions this would be necessary, but adequate data have not been provided here" (1955: 58).*

Let us call those who put their trust in sound correspondences strict constructionists and those who emphasize reconstruction as proof, loose constructionists. Then, to put it epigrammatically, the really rigid strict constructionists can never succeed, and the really loose constructionists can never fail. Besides the later Boas, we may cite Harry Hoijer as a strict constructionist who started out believing in a relatively simple theory of sound correspondences and ended up profoundly skeptical of the validity of all except the very lowest level of Amerindian classifications. For those who see reconstruction as proof, there are so many quite legitimate ways of explaining what are apparently irregular correspondences that there is no empirical way of disproving a reconstruction.

Before we consider this topic in more detail, it will be helpful to make a number of distinctions, some of which have been made in previous discussions, but some of which have not. To begin with, we must distinguish sound changes, which when regular are often called sound laws, and their results, which when we compare them in related languages are regular correspondences. Thus if, from a reconstructed proto-phoneme *k (there can of course also be cases historically attested from documents) in language A, there was a regular unconditional change *$k > x$ such that k became x in all instances, whereas in language B k became $č$ regularly before front vowels but otherwise remained k, there would be three sound laws, $k > x$, $k > č$, $k > k$, but two correspondences, $x : č$ (before earlier front vowels) and $x : k$ (everywhere but before front vowels). Since the correspondences result from the changes, there is a tendency to use the terms almost interchangeably, which can lead to confusion.

A further distinction is that between a recurrence and a correspon-

---

*Gleason is also typical here in another respect. Instead of asking the student to classify the six languages, he asks for pairwise judgments of relationship: "For each pair of languages between which vocabulary similarities were found, determine whether they may be considered related by re-examining the pairs of words that are similar" (*ibid.*).

dence. A recurrence is a surface phenomenon. Thus, in our earlier example, the *d* of English 'head' and the *f* of French *chef* are an instance of a recurrence, but not of a correspondence. There is a further distinction between a correspondence in general and a regular correspondence. By a regular correspondence is meant an occurrence in two or more languages, relative to a particular theory of reconstruction, of a set of sounds that came from a common ancestral sound only by regular conditioned or unconditioned sound changes. Thus the *p* of Latin *pater*, the *p* of Sanskrit *pitā*, and the *f* of English 'father' are regular correspondents that derive from Proto-Indo-European **p*. But the *m* of Latin *novem* 'nine,' though it corresponds to the second *n* of English 'nine' because it derives from the same original sound, does so with a change from *n* to *m* owing to the influence of other numerals, such as *septem* 'seven' and *decem* 'ten.' The *m* is in correspondence with the second *n* of 'nine' in the sense that it comes from the same original sound, but it includes a process other than regular change in its derivation, contamination. Hence it is not a regular correspondence. The most common such process, of course, is morphological analogy. Such correspondences will be called non-regular, when it is necessary to distinguish them from regular ones.

Correspondences (both regular and non-regular) are relative to a particular theory of reconstruction. For example, certain recurrences between Germanic, on the one hand, and other Indo-European languages, on the other, were viewed as non-regular correspondences until the late 1870's because they did not accord with Grimm's law. They became regular with the discovery of Verner's law, which showed that they were the result of regular changes under certain conditions statable in terms of the position of the Proto-Indo-European pitch accent as found, basically, in Greek and Sanskrit. Had Verner rejected the forms as unrelated because of the non-regularity or, more drastically, denied the validity of Indo-European, he would never have made his discovery.

These various distinctions will be useful in discussing my thesis that the loose constructionist can never fail. Faced with what looks like a non-regular correspondence, a term that, as just noted, is always relative to a particular reconstruction, the comparatist has at least ten options, all of which can be documented from proposals actually made in the literature of Indo-European studies or that of other linguistic families. Since different solutions to the same problem have often been offered by different linguists, the same examples will in some instances occur under different rubrics.

The first option, often used by the Neo-Grammarians, is to give additional conditioning factors. In this way no new proto-phoneme is postulated, but of course the number of examples of each correspondence is reduced, and the number of distinct regular correspondences associated with the specific proto-phoneme increases. If one makes the conditions fine enough, one can account for all apparent deviations, but some may be improbable on phonetic or other grounds. An example is Fortunatov's law relating to Proto-Indo-European *r and *l. Indic has examples of both l and r recurring in words with either r or l in other languages. In other words there are four sets of recurrences: $r = r, r = l, l = r$, and $l = l$. Fortunatov seeks to show that the distinction of *r and *l survived in Indic. According to him, *r + dental remained unchanged, but *l + dental resulted in the loss of l and the modification of the original dental to a retroflex consonant. There is an alternative and more generally accepted explanation, as we shall see later.

A second option is in a sense the exact opposite of the first. Instead of refraining from further complicating the proto-language and positing new, later changes under differing phonetic circumstances, one attributes the recalcitrant cases to different proto-phonemes that survived only in the given language and merged everywhere else. It is not even always necessary to add a new phoneme to the proto-language. We can attribute the differing sounds to varying sequences of phonemes already posited for the ancestral speech. For example, corresponding to what has usually been reconstructed as Proto-Indo-European *y, Greek has h in some instances and z in others. G. Schulze and others, including Karl Brugmann, attributed this to two different phonemes that merged everywhere except in Greek. Sapir, using the laryngeal phonemes based on Ferdinand de Saussure's original theory and the more recent evidence of Hittite, which seems to preserve them, at least in some instances, as h̥, deduced initial h from a voiceless laryngeal (which he needs anyway) followed by y, with z the result in other environments.

As with the first option, we can always make this one work, but at the cost of constantly adding to the number of proto-phonemes or their combinations. However, a proto-language with, say, 125 phonemes is completely implausible on typological grounds. This shows in any case that if we are to consider a reconstruction proof of relationship, we need tests for the plausibility of the reconstruction itself, in which typological factors will figure prominently.

Suppose we find that in two highly similar tonal languages both have two pitch phonemes, high and low, but that every possible equation is a recurrence: H = L, H = H, L = H, and L = L. Will this prevent reconstruction and thus disprove the relationship? We can simply posit four tonal proto-phonemes as the source of each correspondence, and in this case no typologically cogent objection can be brought, since four-tone languages are well attested.

A third option is not to attribute the apparent irregularity to phonological processes alone, but to resort to what has been called reverse analogy. Suppose there is morphophonemic alternation in the original language as the result of earlier phonetic changes. In each word in which it occurs the alternation can be eliminated by the analogical spread of one of the alternants. However, different words in the same language, and the same original word in different languages, can analogize in different ways.

This form of explanation is well known and constantly resorted to by comparatists dealing with morphologically complex languages. Thus the *e* of Latin *ped-* and the *o* of Greek *pod-*, an example of a non-regular correspondence, are not attributed to a single earlier phoneme. Rather, as part of the Ablaut (vowel alternation) system of Proto-Indo-European, *e* occurred in certain forms of the paradigm and *o* in others. Thus from an original alternation *ped/pod*, Latin generalized *e* and Greek *o*. Many Indo-Europeanists treat *e* rather as a reduced grade that replaces a theoretical zero grade when unaccented or when unacceptable clusters result. The principle, however, remains the same. Evidently reverse analogy can lead to 2^n sets of recurrences across *n* languages. With two languages, as in the foregoing example, *e/e*, *e/o*, *o/o*, and *o/e* are all possible sets of recurrences.

A further example is once more Verner's law in Germanic, according to which one pair of alternating phonemes arising from an earlier change conditioned by the Indo-European accent appear in English and German as *r/z*. In 'hare' English generalized *r*, while in *Hase* German generalized *z*; in 'lose' English generalized *z*, while German generalized *r* in *ver/lieren*. In many other instances *r = r* and *z = z*. Survivals of the original alternation are English 'was'/'were' and 'lose'/'forlorn.' The first alternation is of course lost in *r*-less dialects.

A kindred but distinct source of non-regular correspondence is morphophonemic analogy. Suppose, as a result of earlier changes, two morphophonemic alternations, X ~ Y and Y ~ Z, have survived in parallel fashion in two languages. Because of the equivocal status of Y it will often happen that X replaces Z, or vice versa. The result is a non-regular correspondence, which may well be recurrent, of the type X/Z, or Z/X, respectively, in which the sounds are not reflexes of the same original phoneme. If Z > X or X > Z in both languages, we will reconstruct the wrong phoneme.

A fourth option is somewhat like the preceding except that the condition of the alternation is presumed to be a word-boundary phenomenon ("word sandhi"). In initial or final position it is supposed that phonetic variants depended on the nature of the preceding or following word, respectively. An example of the former is so-called Indo-European s-movable. Roots with an initial consonant often appear with or without a preceding s- in a completely sporadic way, e.g. Greek *tegos* 'roof,' but Lithuanian *stogas* with the same meaning. One commonly espoused theory is that the forms with s- arose in contexts in which the previous word ended in -s, a common final in Proto-Indo-European, with a reinterpretation of the position of the word boundary so that s- was considered part of the following word, giving rise to two variants for each word. These generalized in different ways in different words across languages. A similar phenomenon in word final position is the existence of forms with final long vowels followed by sonants (*n, r, w,* etc.) in some instances and not in others, e.g. Sanskrit *çvā* 'dog' as against Greek *kuōn.* A common explanation is that the sonant was lost before the initial consonant of the next word, and thus sandhi alternants arose that were generalized differently in different instances. Lane (1968) wishes to limit the loss of sonants to instances in which the following word begins in a sonant. There is, of course, a difference in principle between these two examples. In the first an element is transferred to a word as a result of the reinterpretation of the place of the boundary. In the second an element is *lost* at the boundary. They could therefore be considered examples of somewhat different processes.

A fifth option is allied to the preceding two in that in order to account for apparently random variations across languages, two alternants are assumed to have existed in the ancestral language, and individual languages chose one or the other independently in each instance, giving rise once more in n languages to 2^n correspondences, some of which may be unique. But whereas in the preceding type, the origin was phonological, here a formerly meaningful element has "faded" so that it has become a purely conventional element, either devoid of function or with a secondary acquired function.

Some Indo-Europeanists have suggested such a theory to explain the origin of s-movable, namely, that it was a formerly meaningful prefix.* In

*For the literature on this theory, see the references in Szemerényi (1970: 88).

14

an earlier work (Greenberg 1978) I have described the process by which a demonstrative becomes first a definite article, then a combination of definite and indefinite article (stage II article), and finally an empty marker. In the last stage, stage III, instead of always remaining on the noun or adjective, or always disappearing in a specific language, we may have random survival for each individual word. An example of this is a prefixed k- found in random fashion, distributed differently for each word across languages in all nouns that originally began with a vowel in Nilo-Saharan. In Greenberg (1963) it is called k-movable and has from all appearances developed from an old stage II article already in the proto-language. Since this k- did not differ for noun class or gender, it is a marker of nominality as such in its final stages.*

An example closer to hand is the free and semantically empty use of diminutive suffixes in Romance languages resulting in such cognates as Italian *sole* 'sun' < Vulgar Latin *solem,* as against French *soleil* < Vulgar Latin *soliculum,* literally 'little sun,' with of course many examples of the opposite kind. A widespread North American phenomenon of this kind is "diminutive consonantism."

Under the sixth option I include a whole series of sporadic processes that are well known and accepted as explanatory by even the strictest Neo-Grammarians. Some are purely phonetic, e.g. assimilation and dissimilation, which are especially common in liquids and sibilants, or metathesis, the exchange of position of two different sounds. For example, English 'wasp' and Lithuanian *vepsa* are universally recognized as cognates. In English 'wasp' comes from an earlier *waps* (cf. the variants 'ask' and 'axe' in English). Such a change is non-regular, or sporadic, there being no general rule that all earlier *ps* sequences became *sp* in English. Other sporadic changes are generally attributed to semantically related forms, e.g. Vulgar Latin *grevis* 'heavy' as against Classical Latin *gravis* through the influence of *levis* 'light.' Again Latin *-m* in *novem* 'nine,' as against final *-n* elsewhere, is not attributed by anyone to a third proto-nasal besides *m* and *n*. The solution is obvious when one takes into account the inherited final *-m* of *septem* 'seven' and *decem* 'ten.'

A seventh option in dealing with cases that are deviant on the basis of a specific reconstruction is the method Malcolm Guthrie heavily relies on in his important study on comparative Bantu (1967). Faced with the usual

---

*On this point, see Greenberg (1981). The "Penutian Parallel" referred to in the title of this article concerns a suffixed *-s* of similar origin.

deviations, Guthrie, a firm believer in the complete exceptionlessness of sound laws, simply reconstructs numerous variant forms of what are clearly the same word. In a spot check, I found that about 25 percent of the words he reconstructed required at least two variant, and phonetically similar, protoforms. An extreme case is the word for 'day,' which is reconstructed as *cîku, *cûgu, *cûku, *tîku, *tûku, and *tûkû. Guthrie does not, of course, maintain that these six forms are six different words for 'day,' all synonyms that happen to be phonetically similar; instead he calls them "mutations," merely a polite term for irregularities. A resort to this method on a still vaster scale is found in Calvin Rensch's reconstruction of Oto-Manguean (1976). What is posited in these cases is presumably free variation among competing forms in the proto-language. This is sometimes a convincing explanation if we have reason to believe that a particular sound was just in the process of change at the time of the dialectal break-up of the ancestral language.

An eighth option is to explain irregular correspondences by positing dialect mixture. This is a now widely accepted explanation for the Indic liquids r and l, which, as we have seen, Fortunatov explained by positing more conditioning factors. Many now believe that *r and *l merged in earlier Indic, with some dialects taking r for the liquid that resulted, and others l. The dialect represented in literary Sanskrit would, on this view, have taken some of its forms from an r-dialect and some from an l-dialect.

A ninth option is to reject the difficult etymologies altogether as not being valid cognates. W. S. Allen (1953) saw this possibility clearly. One can prove the complete regularity of sound laws simply by eliminating any exceptions, thus tautologically producing regularities. Many believe that lack of conformity to regular correspondences routinely results in the elimination of etymologies. Actually such cases are very rare because of all of the other resources just described. If we resorted to it on a wholesale scale, we would need another theory to account for the existence of so many near misses.

The tenth and final option is frequently the wisest policy. This is neither to reject recalcitrant cases as invalid etymologies nor to accept an explanation where none looks very plausible. It is now recognized that all, or very many, sound changes leave unexplained residues. Perhaps some day an explanation will be found by greater ingenuity or by the discovery of new data. In some cases—for example, Indo-European problems that have not yielded a satisfactory explanation after over a hundred years of intensive effort—we must perhaps simply say *ignorabimus.*

Up to this point we have proceeded as if there were no question that sound changes are regular and have simply discussed the various other processes that could account for apparent exceptions. But in fact the Neo-Grammarians, who at first proclaimed the absence of exceptions to sound laws, soon gave ground and stated this as a mere hypothesis. As Berthold Delbrück (1880), a leading Neo-Grammarian, put it, sound laws without exception are only to be found in heaven. According to both Schachter and Fodor, Carl Meinhof "proved" that the Bantu languages were related by reconstructing Proto-Bantu. But Meinhof himself took the later Neo-Grammarian position, writing (1932: 20) that "there are and always will be a number of exceptions for which no explanations are found."

In fact, although sound changes are largely regular, there are well-attested cases of wholesale violations. An example is that one of the tones of early Chinese, the Ju-Shêng, gave rise to each of the four tones of modern Mandarin under conditions that are not completely understood. R. A. D. Forrest (1950) gives a sort of statistical solution to this problem. For example, after initial unaspirated consonants we find the second tone in 52.1 percent of the cases, whereas after aspirated consonants we find the fourth tone in 62.1 percent, but for both classes all four occur. One could, of course, take the second of the ten earlier options and posit a much more complex proto-Chinese system. But there is no evidence for this. In doing it, ironically, one would have "proved" the relationship of Mandarin to the other Chinese dialects, hardly a necessary exercise, by an invalid reconstruction.

The foregoing example refers to tone, which some linguists may think of as a marginal feature. But no one presumably would deny the centrality of the vowel system. Yet in Finno-Ugric, a family whose comparative treatment is still earlier than that of Indo-European and whose validity is not doubted by even the most conservative, scholars have not been able to reconstruct the ancestral system of vowels. At best they have succeeded only in determining whether vowels of the initial have front- or back-vowel harmony. Joszef Szinnyei (1910) notes that the decision is based mostly on Hungarian, Finnish, Mordvin, Cheremiss, and the Tavda dialect of Vogul. Where they disagree, he simply goes with the majority. For non-initial syllables he concludes that since proto-Finno-Ugric probably did not have vowel harmony, the vowels of the non-initial syllable must have been independent of the initial vowel. But, he adds, "We cannot say anything beyond this in regard to the vowels of the second and subsequent syllables" (p. 52).

The common doctrine thus inverts scientific logic. It purports to prove etymologies that are strong on other grounds by a reconstructed sound system and a set of historical changes, whereas it is rather the success of a particular theory in explaining the best-established etymologies that tests the plausibility of the reconstruction itself. Even in the best-studied families, such as Indo-European, the theories may undergo drastic changes while the main body of etymologies remains unchanged. Edgar Sturtevant (1942: 37) notes in reference to English 'fire,' Greek *pyr*, etc., after seeking to account for all the variations in different Indo-European languages, "These details are in part mere suggestions, but the underlying etymology is beyond question." That great apostle of common sense, Otto Jespersen, was well aware of this point: "Nowhere have I found any reason to accept the theory that sound changes always take place according to rigorous or 'blind' laws admitting no exceptions. . . . It is very often said that if sound laws admitted of exceptions there would be no possibility of a science of etymology. There are, however, many instances in which it is hardly possible to deny etymological connection though the phonetic laws are violated" (Jespersen 1922: 295). After citing some examples, he adds: "All this goes to show (and many more cases might be instanced) that there are in every language words so similar in form and meaning that they cannot be separated, though they break the sound laws."

In fact there is no necessary logical connection between complete regularity of sound change and the possibility of genetic classification. If there were, classification would be largely impossible. All that is required is that the change not be random and/or enormously rapid.

Consider the following conceptual experiment. Suppose that words in languages consisted of sequences of five digits, and that there are two unconnected languages generated by independent random selections of these digits. Let us call these languages A and B. Suppose both split into two languages, C,D and E,F, respectively. Further suppose that after a fixed period, say 1,000 years, the probabilities of changing to the next higher digit is 25 percent, the next lower 25 percent, two higher 15 percent, two lower 15 percent, and three higher 10 percent, three lower 10 percent—in other words, an approximation to a normal probability distribution. It is clear that for an enormous period of time C will resemble D more than it does E or F, and E will resemble F more than it resembles C or D. In fact, as we will see later, reasonable analogues of such a situation occur in other fields in which the genetic branching model applies, and lead to results easily as reliable as those obtained in linguistics.

Regarding changing theories of reconstruction, Georg von der Gabelentz (1891) remarked that in the short period from August Schleicher (1850's) to

Karl Brugmann (1880's) the views on the Indo-European proto-language had changed quite a bit. He could be forgiven for failing to envisage that far greater changes were to come. After more than a century of effort, which has involved the majority of the linguistic community in the nineteenth century and a substantial group of specialists in the twentieth, it is not too much to say that the only matters on which everyone agrees in regard to the sound system of Proto-Indo-European are that there were at least four points of articulation for the stops, including at least labials and dentals or alveolars, at least three manners of articulation for stops, and at least one sibilant and one vowel.

When it was discovered that Hittite had a back fricative ẖ in some of the positions in which de Saussure had posited a *coefficient sonantique* in his famous *Mémoire* (1879), most Indo-Europeanists accepted the existence of one or more laryngeals in Proto-Indo-European that disappeared in all the languages except Hittite and the other Anatolian languages. (Survival has, however, also been asserted for Armenian and Albanian.) But almost every number from zero (Kronasser, Bonfante, and others who reject laryngeal theory) to ten or more has been posited. The most popular have been two and three, but even in respect to these, different phonetic properties and conditioning effects are assumed.

In the last five decades or so, we may note, Hittite, Luwian, Lycian, Palaic, and other Anatolian languages have been universally recognized as Indo-European, as has Tokharian with two dialects, Tokharian A and B. In no case did anyone publish the sorts of articles with tables of correspondences and asterisked forms so common in the pages of the *International Journal of American Linguistics*, which are believed to reflect the methodology of Indo-European comparative linguistics. In the case of Tokharian, one must believe that all three (or four) consonant manners had merged into one, and then each phoneme, now the sole representative of the position of articulation, split into two under phonetic circumstances that no one has been able to state.

Why, then, have all these languages been accepted as Indo-European? The reason is the existence of a considerable number of word-stems resembling those that are widespread in Indo-European, and a number of highly characteristic grammatical formatives involving sound and meaning. Thus the existence of even a few forms such as Hittite *eszi* 'he is' and *asanzi* 'they are' (cf. Latin *est/sunt*, Sanskrit *asti/santi*) is quite sufficient to exclude accident.

It is widely believed that true cognates can be distinguished from bor-

19

Table 1. French-English Correspondences

1 pje = fʊt	29 sæk = fajv	57 lɛ:vr = lɪp
2 pe:r = 'faðər	30 si~sis = sɪks	58 lõ~lõg = lɔŋ
3 pwasõ = fɪš	31 sɛt = 'sɛvən	59 lu:~lu:v = wʊlf
4 plæ~plɛ:n = fʊl	32 sɔlɛ:j = sʌn	60 leš(e) = lɪk
5 pu:r = fɔr	33 sɛl = sɔlt	61 lɛ:n = wʊl
6 frɛ:r = 'brʌðər	34 sã = 'hʌnd(rɪd)	62 rasin = ruwt
7 fɛ:(r) = duw	35 sœ:r = 'sɪstər	63 katr = fɔr
8 fy = bij	36 sa:bl = sænd	64 ki = huw
9 fãd(r) = bajt	37 syœ:r = swɛt	65 kə = hwat
10 vã = wɪnd	38 (rə)səv(wa:r) = hæv	66 kã = hwɛn
11 ve:r = wʌrm	39 šod = hat	67 kœ:r = hart
12 vul(wa:r) = wɪl	40 šjæ~šjɛn = hawnd	68 kɔrn = hɔrn
13 vœ:v = 'wɪdow	41 šef = hɛd	69 ku:r = jard
14 vif~vi:v = kwɪk	42 še:r = howr	70 gɛ:p = wasp
15 vən(ir) = kʌm	43 žɔnu = nij	71 græ = korn
16 vɛt(i:r) = wer	44 žug = jowk	72 ɥi~ɥit = ejt
17 mwa: = muwn	45 nœf~nœ:v = najn	73 œj = aj
18 mɛ:r = 'mʌðər	46 ne = nowz	74 ɔre:j = ir
19 mwajæ = mɪd	47 nɥi = najt	75 õ:gl = nejl
20 trwa = θrij	48 nœf~nœ:v = nuw	76 ø~œf = ɛg
21 etwa:l = star	49 nõ = nejm	77 (a)s(wa:r) = sɪt
22 tɔnɛ:r = 'θʌndər	50 ni = nest	78 æ~yn = wʌn
23 ty = ðaw	51 nɛ:ž = snow	79 žə = aj
24 twa = θæč	52 nõbri = 'nejvəl	80 nu~nuz = ʌs
25 trɛ:r = drɔ	53 ny = 'nejk(əd)	81 mwa = mij
26 dø = tuw	54 nwa = nʌt	82 (sɛ)t = ðə
27 dis = tɛn	55 lã:g = tʌŋ	
28 dã = tuwθ	56 ly(i:r) = lajt	

rowings because they exhibit regular sound correspondences. In Greenberg (1957) I pointed out, and I was not the first to do so, that borrowed words sometimes showed equal or greater regularity. In an otherwise not always favorable review in *Language* (1959), Isidore Dyen, a rigorous comparatist of impeccable credentials, agreed with me, and others have subsequently made the same point.

In Table 1 we have most of the cognates from French and English, taken from etymological dictionaries. French and English are, of course, Indo-European languages of different branches. I do not vouch for the completeness of the list, and there may be a few errors. Still it is hardly deniable that it gives a general view of what these cognates are like. The tables that follow (2–4) break the Table 1 list down by initial and non-initial consonant correspondences and vowel correspondences.

An examination of the initial consonants, the most regular of all, shows for example that *k* in French corresponds to English *f* (once), *h* (three times), *hw* (twice), and *j* (once); and so for all the other initial consonants to a

Table 2. Initial Consonant Correspondences in Table 1

p = f, 1, 2, 3, 4, 5	ž = zero, 43, 79
f = b, 6, 8, 9	ž = j, 44
f = d, 7	n = n, 45, 46, 47, 48, 49,
v = w, 10, 11, 12, 13, 16	50, 51, 52, 53, 54
v = kw, 14	n = zero, 80
v = k, 15	l = t, 55
m = m, 17, 18, 19, 81	l = l, 56, 57, 58, 59, 60, 61
t = θ, 20, 22, 24	r = r, 62
t = t, 21	k = f, 63
t = ð, 23, 82	k = h, 64, 67, 68
t = d, 25	k = hw, 65, 66
s = f, 29	k = j, 69
s = s, 31, 32, 33, 35, 36, 37	g = w, 70
s = h, 34, 38	g = k, 71
š = h, 39, 40, 41, 42	

Table 3. Vowel Correspondences in Table 1

i = ε, 27, 50; zero, 62; uw, 64	œ: = ɪ, 13, 35; ε, 37; a, 67, 73
i~i: = ɪ, 14, 30	ə = ʌ, 15; æ, 38; zero, 43, 79; a, 65
e = zero, 21; ow, 46; ɪ, 60	ā = aj, 9; ɪn, 10; uw, 28; ʌn, 34; εn, 66
ε = ε, 31, 41; ɔ, 33	ā: = ʌ, 55
ε = a, 2, 70; zero, 4, 61, 74; ʌ, 6, 11, 18;	ǣ = ɪ, 19; aj, 29; n, 71
uw, 7; e, 16; ɪ, 57; ə, 22; ɔ, 25; ow, 42, 51	ō = ejm, 49; ej, 52
a = ij, 20; uw, 62; ɔ, 63	ō: = n, 75
a: = æ, 36	wa = ɪ, 3; uw, 17; a, 21; æ, 24; ʌ, 54;
ɔ = ʌ, 22, 32; o, 68; i, 74	ij, 81
u = ɪ, 12; ij, 43; ow, 44; ʌ, 80	jε = aw, 40
u = ɔ, 5; a, 69; ʋ, 59	je = ʋ, 1
y = ij, 8; aw, 23; w, 37; ej, 53; aj, 56; ʌ, 78	ɥi = aj, 47; ej, 72
ø = uw, 26	

Table 4. Non-Initial Consonant Correspondences in Table 1

p = p, 70	ž = zero, 51
b = n, 36; v, 52	k = v, 29
f = d, 41; g, 76	g = k, 44; ŋ, 55, 58; zero, 75
v = zero, 13; v, 38; p, 57; f, 59	r = r, 2, 5, 6, 11, 18, 20, 22, 25,
f~v = k, 14; n, 45; zero, 48	35, 42, 63, 67, 68, 69, 71, 74; t, 37;
t = r, 16; v, 31; zero, 63; t, 72	l, 52; zero, 57
d = t, 9	l = l, 4, 12, 33, 75; r, 21; n, 32
s = š, 3; n, 27; s, 30; t, 62; zero, 70	n = zero, 4; m, 15; n, 22, 40, 43,
z = s, 80	68, 78
š = k, 60	j = zero, 19, 74

Table 5. "Proto-Turco-Arabic" Correspondences

Arabic	Turkish	Proto-Turco-Arabic	Arabic	Turkish	Proto-Turco-Arabic	Gloss
b	b	*b	ʕajiba	ajibe	*ʕajibe	marvel (n)
b	p	*b	ṭālib	talip	*ṭaleb	student
f	f	*f	farāḥ	ferah	*feraḥ	spacious
w	v	*w	dawāʔ	deva	*dɛwaʔ	medicine
m	m	*m	mufaḥḥam	müfahham	*möfaḥḥam	illustrious
t	t	*t	tablīġ	tevlig	*tɛbliġ	communication
d	d	*d	dirham	dirhem	*derhɛm	dirham, a coin
d	t	*d	ʕābid	abit	*ʕabed	worshipper
n	n	*n	ʔajnabī	ejnebi	*ʔejnɛbi	foreign
s	s	*s	sākin	sakin	*saken	stationary
ṣ	s	*ṣ	ṣaff	seff	*ṣeff	row, rank
z	z	*z	ʕazīz	aziz	*ʕaziz	powerful
š	š	*š	kašf	kešf	*kɛšf	exposure
th	s	*th	mathal	masal	*mathal	story
dh	z	*dh	dhamm	zemm	*dhɛmm	blame (n)
ṭh	z	*ṭh	manṭhur	manzur	*manṭhur	considered (a)
ḍh	z	*ḍh	xamiḍh	hamiz	*xameḍh	acid (a)
r	r	*r	raybiya	reybiye	*rɛybiyɛ	skepticism
l	l	*l	lāḥim	lahim	*laḥem	carnivorous
y	y	*y	yābis	yabis	*yabes	dry
j	j	*j	ʔajala	ajele	*ʔajɛlɛ	haste

lesser or greater degree. The vowels are close to statistical randomness, and in this they are rivaled by the final consonants. In the light of the earlier discussion, the reasons should be obvious. Even regular sound change, when conditioned, gives a variety of correspondences. As time goes on these accumulate, along with various sporadic phonetic processes, grammatically induced analogy and new derivational affixes, etc., while lexical replacement reduces the number of cognates. All of these processes work to produce more and more diversity of correspondence and virtually never to reduce it.

In Table 5 I have reconstructed with great ease a pseudo-entity, Proto-Turco-Arabic, based on loanwords in Turkish from Arabic. But how do we know that Turkish is not in fact a Semitic language like Arabic? If anything, much current doctrine would force the conclusion that the case for Turco-Arabic is better than that for French-English.

One obvious consideration, of course, is that these loanwords are not basic vocabulary items. But we do not even need such a hypothesis. The most powerful proof is, once more, distribution across languages. Turkish and Arabic are not mutually intelligible and are obviously distinct languages. Hence, if Turkish were really a Semitic language, it would show some independence within that family. But Turkish never has a Semitic morpheme unless it occurs in close to the same form in Arabic. In the absence of direct historical evidence, which is of course present in this case, this is the most powerful evidence for borrowing.

In Table 6 I have listed just three of the eight Bantu languages Meinhof used for his reconstruction of Proto-Bantu. Among them we see no less than ten correspondences, all representing his reconstructed *g. Coupez subsequently posited two phonemes, *g and *y, and this is now generally accepted, but it will not account for all the facts. The addition of others of the hundreds of Bantu languages will, of course, greatly increase the number of additional and mostly unique correspondences. Recall that Schachter and Fodor both stated that Meinhof had "proved" the validity of Bantu by his reconstructions.

In Table 7 I have listed a few basic words for 25 languages of Europe. The number of ways of classifying 25 languages, even without specifying subgrouping, is $.4639 \times 10^{19}$, that is, over a quintillion. Yet the correct classification and even subgroupings and intermediate groupings (e.g. Balto-Slavic) are apparent from just a cursory glance at two or three words. The power of a method that looks at everything at once, instead of testing isolated hypotheses, is thus immense. This method may be called multilateral comparison.

If, following the arrangement of Table 7, words are listed in the horizontal dimension and languages in the vertical, we may say that the method advocated here is the vertical. The commonly advocated one is horizontal. We are accustomed to looking at a few languages across many words rather than at many languages across a few words. Let us say that the vertical method is synoptic, like scanning an entire forest from the air; then the hori-

Table 6. Bantu Correspondences

Swahili	Konde	Sango	Proto-Bantu (Meinhof)	Gloss	Correspondences
imba	imba	lu-yimbo	*gimba	sing	0/0/y
mw-ona	gɔna	ɔna	*gona	sleep	0/g/0
gumu	uma	yuma	*guma	hard	g/0/y
ganja	iky-anja	li-ganja	*ganja	lake	g/0/g
uki	ul-uki	iny-usi	*guki	sweetness	0/0/0
gawa	ya'ba	—	*gaba	divide	g/y/-
el-eza	gɛla	jela	*gela	measure	0/g/j
gwa	gwa	gwa	*gua	fall	g/g/g
fyag-ia	phyag-ila	fyaj-ila	*piaga	sweep	g/g/j
m-kuyu	u-khuyu	—	*kugu	fig tree	y/y/-

Table 7. Basic Vocabulary of 25 European Languages

Language	One	Two	Three	Head	Eye	Ear	Nose	Mouth	Tooth
Breton	unan, eun	dau	tri	penn	lagad	skuarn	fri	genu, bek	dant
Irish	aon	dau	tri	ceann	súil	au, clúas	srón	béal	fiacal
Welsh	un	do	tri	pen	ligad	klust	truyn	geneu	dant
Danish	en	to	tre	hoved	öje	öre	næse	mund	tand
Swedish	en	to	tre	huvud	öga	öra	näsa	mun	tand
Dutch	e:n	tve:	dri:	ho:ft	o:x	o:r	no:s	mont	tant
English	wən	tuw	θrij	hed	aj	ijr	nowz	mawθ	tuwθ
German	ajns	tsvai	draj	kopf	auga	o:r	na:ze	munt	tsa:n
French	æ, yn	dø	trwa	tɛ:t	œj, jø	orɛ:j	ne	bu:š	dã
Italian	uno, una	due	tre	testa	okkjo	orekkjo	naso	bɔkka	dente
Spanish	un, una	dos	tres	kabesa	oxo	orexa	naso	boka	diente
Rumanian	un, o	doj, dowə	trej	kap	okju	ureke	nas	gure	dinte
Albanian	nji	dy	tre, tri	krye-(t)	sy(ni)	veš(i)	hund(a)	goja	dãmi
Greek	enas	dhyo	tris	kefáli	máti	aftí	míti	stóma	dhóndi
Lithuanian	vienas	du, dvi	trýs	galva	akis	ausis	nosis	burma	dantis
Latvian	viens	divi	tris	galva	aks	auss	deguns	mute	zuobs
Polish	jeden	dva	tši	glova	oko	uxo	nos	usta, geba	zãb
Czech	jeden	dva	tři	hlava	oko	uxo	nos	usta	zup
Russian	ad'in	dva, dv·e	tr'i	galavá	óko	úxo	nos	rot	zĩb
Bulgarian	edin	dva	tri	glava	oko	uho	nos	usta	zub
Serbo-Croatian	jedan	dva	tri	glava	oko	uxo	nos	usta	zub
Finnish	yksi	kaksi	kolme	pää	silmä	korva	nenä	suu	hammas
Estonian	üks	kaks	kolm	pea	silm	korv	nina	sua	hambaid
Hungarian	egy	ket	harom	fö:, fej	sem	fül	orr	sa:j	fog
Basque	bat	bi	iru	buru	begi	belari	sudur	aba	ortz

zontal method can be likened to wandering about in the dark undergrowth, here and there espying a similarity at random without any possibility of understanding the totality.*

Kroeber, using a format he called tabular (identical with that of Table 7) for Uto-Aztecan, whose unity was still in doubt for many, stated (1906–7: 162):

As to the conclusions to be drawn from this table there can be no question. The evidence of the genetic relationship of all the languages represented from Nahuatl to Luiseño is overwhelming and leaves room only for wonder how the fact could have been doubted. Others have perhaps had the experience of comparing some particular Shoshonean dialect with Nahuatl on the strength of relationship currently announced, and of being disappointed at the small number of positive resemblances visible; but the present collocation in compact and unified form from all dialect groups alters the condition thoroughly so that identities, which before could only be suspected and seemed exceedingly doubtful, are revealed with entire certainty.

Confronted by the numerous independent stocks in California posited in the Powell classification, Kroeber himself once told me that after fruitlessly making individual paired comparisons, he one day conceived the notion of looking at all of them simultaneously. He and his co-worker Dixon immediately noted that two major groupings accounted for a large majority of these families, to which they gave the names Penutian and Hokan; and these groupings, later expanded to include many languages outside of California (some subsequently noted by Kroeber himself), have stood the test of time.[†]

Another way of seeing the importance of multilateral comparison, and incidentally showing the weakness of pairwise percentages as used in glottochronology, is the following. Suppose we were to compare in isolation English and Hindi, known to be related since both are Indo-European. As we compared each pair of words, we would often encounter quite dissimilar forms, and this would seem to argue against a connection. But in fact one or the other might be Indo-European, as would be shown from a wider com-

---

*The vertical method has a superficial resemblance to glottochronology, but glottochronology gives us only pairwise percentages. A full-scale critique of glottochronology is not within the scope of this work; on the fundamental weakness of pairwise comparison, see Gleason (1959).

[†] See Dixon (1913: 649) on the Penutian languages of California: "This relationship would have been recognized previously were it not that attention was directed chiefly toward phases of structures, which, while conspicuous, were not very typical of the group in question; and especially because comparisons had been instituted between single languages instead of the whole five." In the first part of this citation, Dixon is clearly referring to typological criteria.

parison, and hence relevant to proving the relationship. We thus see that the evidence for relating two languages may be in only one of them, or indeed in neither but found elsewhere within the larger stock. We may state these considerations in the following way. English is a Germanic language. Hindi is an Indo-Iranian language. Both Germanic and Indo-Iranian languages are Indo-European languages. Hence English is related to Hindi.

The introduction of other languages is also relevant to the evaluation of those resemblances that are found in both languages. Continuing with the English-Hindi example, we might for instance note the somewhat vague resemblance between English 'tooth' and Hindi *dā:t*. Comparison with other Germanic languages, e.g. German *tsa:n* and Dutch *tand* will suggest that there was formerly a nasal consonant before English *-th*. Comparison of Hindi *dā:t*, on the other hand, with Kashmiri and Sindhi *dand* will suggest that the Hindi nasalized vowel reflects a short vowel + nasal consonant. If we introduce other branches, the additional evidence, e.g. of Italian *dente*, Spanish *diente*, makes the connection between the English and Hindi forms a virtual certainty.

Having thus arrived at an approximate source form, **dant* or **dent*, we now turn to the Baltic languages, where we find Lithuanian *dant-is* 'tooth' (*-is* is the nominative singular inflection), and to Modern Greek, where we find *ðondi*, both easily derivable from a form stemming from the initial Germanic-Indic comparison. That all this is accidental is completely improbable. Thus even from this single comparison we will arrive at the hypothesis that Germanic, Romance, Indic, Baltic, and Greek form the nucleus of a genetic group.

Since any form can be replaced, the divergent forms in Slavic (e.g. Russian *zup*, Czech *zub*) do not disprove the affiliation of Slavic. In addition to the numerous other comparisons of the kind just discussed for other lexical items, there is obviously a special resemblance between Baltic and Slavic. Genetic relationship is plainly transitive, so that if Baltic is related to Slavic, and also to Germanic, Romance, and Indic, then Slavic must be related to Germanic, Romance, and Indic.

The addition of evidence from other highly plausible cognates, with varying distributions over the languages, at once serves to define the stock and to add powerful new evidence. We have two dimensions along which probabilities are being simultaneously multiplied. One is that of individual lexical items. Given the basic arbitrariness of the sound-meaning relationship, each word that is semantically dissimilar (e.g. 'tooth' and 'three') gives independent evidence. Using a metaphor based on the arrangement of Table 7, we may call this the horizontal dimension. In the other, vertical dimension we have the constant recurrence of the same set of languages in various combinations.

Two further observations can be made on the foregoing example of 'tooth.' First, we have compared contemporary forms. Yet many eminent comparatists claim that were it not for the existence of early written evidence from languages like Greek, Latin, and Sanskrit it would be impossible to frame or confirm the Indo-European hypothesis. The second observation is that within the etymology for the word 'tooth' there is not a single recurrent correspondence, yet it should be clear that what we have done is the initial step in the comparative method itself. We have compared related forms and posited an approximate original form and subsequent changes. We also have correspondences. Clearly we are comparing the *t* in English 'tooth' with the *d* in Italian *dente* and not with any of the other sounds in that word.

All this runs against the current widely held view that there are two methods of classification (to which glottochronological classification is sometimes added). One is inspection, which is prescientific. By sheer luck, then, many of the classifications we hypothesize turn out to be correct, although, as has been noted earlier, the probability of chance success makes discovering a needle in a haystack a relatively simple task by comparison. Then, to be sure our hypothesis is correct, we must use the comparative method and make a reconstruction. Only with that in hand will we be sure we are correct.

I believe, however, that the preceding discussion shows the superficiality of such a view. One must look at the operations performed and not be led astray by vague terms like inspection and comparative method. To inspect languages pairwise, or at a half-guess, is a different thing from a multilateral comparison undertaken with a consciousness of the types of resemblances that are likely to bespeak common origin. As we have seen, this is the initial and in fact indispensable first step in the comparative method itself. Nor is the comparative method defined by the external, and no doubt impressive, trappings of correspondence tables and asterisks.

The preceding discussion also helps to show that the following frequently adduced negative argument, based on glottochronology, is invalid. The empirically noted fact is that in the 100-word glottochronological list, about 80 percent of the vocabulary remains after 1,000 years. Hence, if loss is independent, the expected resemblance between two languages is .64 at this point. In the next 1,000 years, the loss for each will be $(.80)^2 = .64$ and the expected resemblance $(.64)^2$ or .4096. Continuing in this fashion, we can calculate that after 8,000 years the resemblances will be .0281, and after 10,000 years, approximately .012, which is presumably less than chance. Hence relationships of this degree of depth cannot be discovered.

One obvious flaw in these calculations is that the number of cognates will be larger than the above percentages because certain words will drop off the list owing to semantic change, but will still exist in the language, e.g. English 'hound,' which is cognate with the ordinary German word for 'dog,' namely *Hund*. There is also what is called the "dregs phenomenon." The words in the list are surely not of equal stability. Hence those that have stood the test of 8,000 years of change are far more likely to be retained during the next 1,000 years than the words of the original list during the first 1,000. Martin Joos (1964) has suggested a plausible mathematical modification that will take this factor into account.

But what is far more important, from my point of view, is the fact that through multilateral comparison we can extend glottochronological theory to account for resemblances not between two languages, but among any number of languages. For example, if we compare three languages, A, B, and C, we can ask, for a given time period, how many resemblances will be found between A and B, A and C, B and C, and A, B, and C. Clearly every word found in at least two languages of the stock can be recovered by comparison.

It is possible to combine the Joos function with the calculation of expected recoverable vocabulary by extending glottochronology from two to n languages. For the mathematics of these calculations, and a table of recoverable vocabulary (which is actually even higher since the factor of semantic change is not considered), the reader is referred to Appendix A. From this it can be seen, for example, that with only 10 languages, even after 10,000 years about 42 percent of the original vocabulary is recoverable. More languages will, of course, greatly increase these values.

Since most of the original vocabulary is thus recoverable, it is possible to carry out multilateral comparisons with other, similar stocks. There is, of course, no reason to compare just one large stock with another. As the great principle of uniformitarianism suggests, many of the linguistic stocks of an earlier period, like the present ones, could have had up to 10 or more branches. Consequently, there is no theoretical limit to the depth at which classification can be carried out when the number of languages examined is large. Only at the final stage, if no subgroupings appear, will we have to resort to such considerations as the sheer number of similarities or shared grammatical irregularities.

One reason that linguists have not in general employed the methods discussed here is that in including all the languages for which material is available, much poorly recorded data will be used. This is, of course, what Bouquiaux has in mind when he refers to "materials of unequal value." But, one may ask, if such materials cannot be used, how could the correct and reliable results he mentions have been attained? The fact is, the method of multilateral comparison is so powerful that it will give reliable results even with the poorest of materials. Incorrect material should have merely a randomizing effect. If a clear pattern emerges, the hypothesis is all the more likely to be correct.

Moreover, it is not only possible to classify a language with very poor material; it is often possible to classify one with very little material. For in the context of a broad comparison we can discover the diagnostic items that distinguish each family and grouping, and even a very few resemblances of this sort are highly probative.

Not out of vanity, but because important questions of methodology are at stake, I should like to point to a further example to demonstrate that reliable results can be obtained from desperately poor data. In Greenberg (1953), I briefly outlined a general classification of Australian languages. An examination of the results given there with those obtained by Stephen Wurm (1972), based on far fuller and more reliable data, shows detailed agreement. For example, my general Australian correlates exactly with his Pama-Nyungan. Yet all I had at my disposal were Edward M. Curr's very poorly recorded vocabularies (1886–87) and the two studies of A. Capell (1939–40; 1941–43), which, though more reliable phonetically than Curr, gave only minor lexical information and fragmentary grammatical data, and that for only a relatively small portion of the continent.

In all of the preceding discussion, it has been assumed that resemblances involving sound and meaning simultaneously are the only relevant ones for classification. This would include both lexical items and specific grammatical agreements, e.g. the fact that both English and German use comparative -er and superlative -est for adjective comparison. The choice of basic vocabulary for initial comparison is made for certain practical reasons. It is often the only material available. It involves that aspect of language, next to morphological markers, that is least subject to borrowing, with the advantage of length, relatively easy semantic comparability, and the essential historical independence of each item, whereas morphological systems involve relatively short items and are subject to morphological leveling. There is, however, no opposition between the two. They should and do lead to the same results, and both should be employed.

Agreement in irregularities and evidence from survivals of grammatical markers that have become petrified are worthy of special consideration and are used in the present work. An agreement like that between English 'good'/'better'/'best' and German *gut/besser/best* is obviously of enormous probative value. However, subject as such agreements are to analogical pressure, their absence is not negative evidence, and their presence tells us that there is a relationship, but not at what level. They are psychologically reassuring in showing that we are on the right track and inherently interesting, but not really necessary.

The famous comparatist Antoine Meillet, precisely because he was so aware of all the processes of diversification that give the kind of results we find in Tables 1–4, but who never thought of the simple expedient of mass comparison, believed that if we did not have earlier languages like Latin, Greek, and Sanskrit to work with, we could prove Indo-European only by such agreements in irregularities, e.g. the third person singular and plural of the present tense of the verb 'to be': German *ist/sind,* Spanish *es/son,* Polish *jest/są,* etc.*

If, as I believe, our current ideas are based on a fundamental misunderstanding of Neo-Grammarian doctrine, how did these mistaken ideas arise? Only a few points can be noted here. In Terence H. Wilbur's collection of documents (1977) on the great *Lautgesetz* (sound laws) controversy of the 1880's, one finds not a hint that the genetic relationship of the Indo-European languages is involved or would be shaken if it turned out that sound laws had exceptions. Consider, moreover, the following statement by Delbrück (1880: 121–22) in what is frequently looked on as the basic manifesto of the Neo-Grammarians:

My starting point is that specific result of comparative linguistics that is not in doubt and cannot be in doubt. It was proved [*erwiesen*] by [Franz] Bopp and others that the so-called Indo-European languages are related. The proof [*Beweis*] was produced by juxtaposing [*Nebeneinanderstellung*] words and forms of similar meaning. When one

---

*Resemblances involving sound only, or meaning only, and relations of order are of typological, not genetic relevance. This point is, I believe, generally understood at present and is therefore not discussed here. For previous discussions see Greenberg (1953, 1957, 1963).

considers that in these languages the formation of the inflectional forms of the verb, noun, and pronoun agrees in essentials and likewise that an extraordinary number of inflected and uninflected words agree in their lexical parts, the assumption of chance agreement must appear as absurd.

Nowhere in this whole passage do we find the terms *Lautgesetz* 'sound law' or *Lautentsprechung* 'sound correspondence,' or even *Vergleich* 'comparison,' which would imply something more elaborate than mere *Nebeneinanderstellung* 'juxtaposition,' seemingly the key word. Nor is the *Ursprache*, or reconstructed proto-language, mentioned. The relationship, according to Delbrück, was proved by Bopp in the early nineteenth century before this concept was current, as it later became with the work of Schleicher.

If one considers three major examples of the reconstruction of proto-sound systems of non-Indo-European languages, all undertaken by linguists squarely in the Neo-Grammarian tradition, Carl Meinhof for Bantu, Otto Dempwolff for Austronesian, and Carl Brockelmann for Semitic, the results are the same. As we have seen, Schachter and Fodor, among others, believed that Meinhof demonstrated the relationship of the Bantu languages by his reconstruction. A reasonably careful reading of what Meinhof and the others say shows that this idea never occurred to them. Meinhof simply states (1932: 18): "First of all, the characteristics which were found to be common to a great number of languages in Europe and Asia led to these languages being grouped together as the Indo-European 'family' of languages. Since then we have also recognized the existence of other language families in Europe and Asia as well, e.g. the Semitic, the Malayo-Polynesian, the Bantu." As noted earlier, Meinhof believed there will always be a number of exceptions to sound laws for which no explanation can be found.

In the first volume of his great comparative work on Austronesian, Dempwolff (1934: 17) talks about "sound correspondences that in many cases are regular." When his reconstruction, based on Indonesian languages in the first volume, is applied to Fijian in the second volume, he finds some remarkable deviations. These mostly involve consonants, which are lost in word final position, but reappear when suffixes are present. He notes (1937: 133) that "statistically, if one considers all the words likewise found in proto-Indonesian, there are 59 cases of correct correspondence and 49 deviations." In fact, for two of the consonants the number of exceptions is greater than the number of regular cases. Why does he then call them regular? Because they are phonetically plausible and coincide with correspondences in other word positions. He then states: "On the basis of these facts, these irregularities in Fijian are to be interpreted as false analogy." This term is the equivalent of what is now usually called analogy. That he should abandon the relationship to Indonesian because of this never even occurs to him.

As for Brockelmann, in his comparative Semitic grammar of 1908, far from thinking that he has proved that the Semitic languages are related by means of reconstruction, he denies its very reality. This fictionalist, or conventionalist, view of reconstruction, also found in Meillet, sees reconstruction as merely a convenient set of formulae to show the relations among forms. An allied, but somewhat different, view is that the reconstruction is hypothetical—our best, but provisional, approximation to reality on the basis of present knowledge. It thus approaches the truth with increasing knowledge, but can never be completely certain. As noted by Allen (1953: 70), "This example shows how the addition of fresh languages adds to the comparative formulae."

Even if one were to find documentary evidence of what looks like a candidate for the *Ursprache*, it would surely not coincide exactly with the current reconstruction, showing either that the reconstruction is not entirely correct or that it is not really the *Ursprache*, but some extinct side branch. This is the case with Geez (Classical Ethiopic), earlier viewed as equivalent to the ancestral language of the present Semitic languages of Ethiopia. However, because it shows some innovations not reflected in the modern languages, it is now generally believed not to be ancestral.

That reconstruction is not necessary to prove relationship is shown by the interesting case of Albanian. Its status as an Indo-European language is universally accepted. Earlier, Delbrück was cited as stating that Bopp and other pioneers had proved that the Indo-European languages formed a family. In an immediately preceding passage he lists these and includes Albanian. There had, in fact, been doubt concerning Albanian, but it was agreed that Bopp had proved the case for its Indo-European affiliation in a monograph published in 1854. An examination of this work shows a number of things of interest in the present connection. Bopp rests his case mainly on specific morphological resemblances, although he cites a number of lexical items in the course of his exposition and obviously considers them of great importance too. He does not derive Albanian forms from reconstructed Proto-Indo-European. The notion of family tree and proto-language both originated with Schleicher, but only several years later.

Bopp realizes that Sanskrit has in some instances undergone changes, but evidently considers that it represents the original form in almost all instances, although in etymologies he generally cites Latin, Greek, Gothic, and Lithuanian alongside Sanskrit. He has no term for sound law or sound correspondence. He realizes that there are certain common correspondences, but it is clear that he considers them merely usual and is not disturbed by deviations. In fact, he generally does not even notice them.

In place of regular sound change, he operates with three concepts, all of them value-laden, and none of them implying regularity. If, in comparison with Sanskrit, the Albanian form is longer, then there has been an addition that is *unorganisch* 'inorganic.' If it is shorter it is *verstummelt* 'mutilated'; if it is of the same length, but has a different sound from Sanskrit in some position it is *entartet* 'degenerate,' a term used in plant and animal breeding.

We might expect that given this, to us, quaint conceptual apparatus, Bopp's etymologies would be commonly invalid. Not so. Of the first 25 etymologies I encountered in the text, 23 appear in Walde-Pokorny's etymological dictionary of Indo-European. The other two are not just accidents but borrowings—from Latin in one case, Italian in the other. Actually, Bopp was quite aware of these borrowings and often identifies them correctly.

More than 30 years after Bopp's monograph, Brugmann noted, of Albanian, that "the historical treatment of this language is beset with many difficulties and is still in its infancy" (1886, 1: 7). In the 1880's and 1890's Gustav Meyer began his fundamental work on the historical grammar of Albanian. Yet in Brugmann's *Kurze vergleichende Grammatik* (1902) Albanian appears only in the table listing reflexes of the stressed vowels, largely with unexplained multiple values for each proto-Indo-European vowel, which are neither referred to nor explained in the text. Meillet simply takes no account of Albanian in his well-known *Introduction,* even in the last edition actually prepared during his lifetime, namely, the seventh edition of 1934, just 80 years after Bopp's original study.

Are recurrent correspondences and reconstruction of no value at all, then, as a superficial reading of this chapter might suggest? The answer can be put as follows. The existence of the same correspondence in several different etymologies certainly adds to the probabilities of each being correct. Moreover, such correspondences are our chief methodological tool in reconstruction. However, what many linguists fail to appreciate is that anything approaching a complete and highly convincing reconstruction on the basis of recurrent correspondences is in general possible only with languages so closely related that it is unnecessary anyway. Even here we have cases like Athabaskan in which the reconstructions not only differ, but are confined to initial and non-final consonants. Where the separation is greater, as we have seen, the reconstructions are so underdetermined by the data that deviations from a particular theory of reconstruction can be accommodated by a whole series of strategies. Some etymologies will always remain uncertain. In others the lesser claim of cognation can be maintained, even though the reconstructive explanatory theory remains uncertain or in dispute. A far more convincing refutation is to show an incorrect morphological analysis, not deviation from a predicted phonological outcome.

It will give us a broader perspective on the problems discussed in this chapter if we consider that, whereas linguists have treated the problem of historical classification as unique to linguistics, and have in part at least suggested idiosyncratic solutions, the same basic model occurs in a whole series of other cases in different disciplines; a comparison can prove enlightening.

One of these is biological classification. Both in evolutionary biology and in comparative linguistics, hierarchical classifications are explained by the dynamic process of successive splits from common ancestors of differing degrees of historical depth. This was well recognized in the nineteenth century by Darwin and Lyell on the biological side, and by Schleicher on the linguistic side. In his *Descent of Man* (1871: 20) Darwin notes that "the formation of different languages and distinct species, and the proof that both have developed through a gradual process, are curiously parallel." Since then Otto Jespersen, Raimo Anttila, the present writer, and no doubt others have discussed this similarity.

I do not believe that anyone would argue that biological classification is less advanced than linguistic classification. Yet nothing in biology seems equatable with sound correspondence. Moreover, even in that science common ancestors can be reconstructed only in the most tentative way. The biologist of course has the direct evidence of fossils (though a zoologist of my acquaintance once told me that fossils were always surprising). Beyond that, the biologist, much like the linguist trying to identify an ancestral language from earlier written forms, faces the problem of deciding whether a particular fossil represents the ancestor of a particular taxonomic group or a side branch that is now extinct, a process fraught with the same sorts of difficulties encountered by the linguist.

One may note that biologists are very clear on the distinction between hierarchical classification and genetic relationship, and the primacy of the former. No biologist has yet, to my knowledge, written a treatise directly comparing a beaver to a mackerel in order to prove their genetic relationship, both being vertebrates. Fortunately, Linnaeus, and even his predecessors, got biological classification off on the right foot by boldly surveying and classifying all forms of life as part of the same operation.

Another comparison that might be made is with textual criticism. Henry Hoenigswald even suggests that Schleicher, the first to represent linguistic classifications by a branching tree, was inspired by his training in classical philology under Friedrich Ritschl, who depicted the relationship of manuscripts of the same work as a stemma or family tree. The splitting of a language over time into distinct languages corresponds to the various copies of the same manuscript, which thus form a subgroup defined by this process.

To say that manuscripts are genetically related without specifying their position in the fully worked-out stemma, which corresponds to genetic linguistic classification, is simply to say that they are manuscripts of the same work. A statement parallel to that often made by linguists would be the following. Though they look suspiciously similar, we really have no right to say that two manuscripts of, say, Sophocles' play *Ajax* are really manuscripts of the same play, that is, go back to a common original, until we have reconstructed the original text. But, of course, that they are manuscripts of the same play is so obvious that no one even discusses the question, while the problem is precisely to restore the original text. This is the goal of textual criticism, and one that will probably never reach a completely certain and universally accepted outcome.

One can also make the profound observation that whenever there is an epsilon at a particular position on a particular line of one manuscript, one normally finds one at the corresponding place in the other manuscript. A few very rigorous thinkers would then claim that if this sometimes does not hold, there is an irregular correspondence; and thus we could never prove that they are copies of the same work.

In actual fact, however, it is the classification of manuscripts in the form of a hierarchical tree or stemma, in which those copies from the same earlier manuscript form a subgroup, that is basic to reconstruction. The copies within a subgroup do not give independent witness regarding the original text, and if we happen to have the manuscript from which they were copied, they can be eliminated. Moreover, it is precisely the agreement in random errors of the type unlikely to occur independently that provides the basis for classifying manuscripts in the same group. These errors correspond to arbitrary irregularities in language, not to recurrent regular correspondences.

Another example close to linguistics is writing systems. These can also be classified genealogically. Thus, all alphabets descended from the North Semitic version of the alphabet can be distinguished as a group from those like Minean and Ethiopic, which derive from the South Semitic alphabet, as anyone can see from mere inspection. Yet the arbitrary pairings of sound and visual symbol are very few in number compared with the lexicon of a language, the changes of the letters do not seem to exhibit any recurrent regularities, and the original alphabet cannot be reconstructed.

In fact, even in linguistics, only for *phonological systems* is it claimed that regular correspondence or reconstruction is necessary for proving relationships or verifying classifications. Such requirements are never invoked for morphology, syntax, or semantics, yet in Indo-European it was the numerous points of specific contact in *morphological systems* that played the major role at an early stage in regard to these questions. Although the morphological systems clearly are related and must derive from a common original, probably no one would claim that we have a reliable and detailed reconstruction of the ancestral morphological systems. With the discovery of Hittite, the situation worsened. While, on the one hand, Bedrich Hrozný's original demonstration leaned heavily on both morphology and vocabulary (and most of his morphological equations have stood the test of time), on the other, the addition of Hittite had a devastating effect on the validity of many of the details of the original morphological system as reconstructed at that time.

There has grown up, as a corollary of present doctrine, the notion that one must first reconstruct the proto-language of each lower grouping, thus proving its validity, before proceeding to the reconstruction of the higher-level groupings. Such a stepwise procedure appears to be very virtuous, but in fact is an illusion. The reconstruction will itself be a poorer approximation to the truth if it is confined to a restricted group. In the model case of Indo-European, it was the broader group that was first reconstructed. In fact, many phenomena of narrower groups can only be understood historically by outside evidence from within the broader stock. An example is the Germanic consonant alternations that arose as a result of the change expressed in Verner's law. These alternations require a knowledge of the Indo-European pitch accent that did not exist in Germanic in the historic period. After all, in historical matters, the earlier explains the later. If the earlier is not directly attested, one looks backward by looking sideways, which is precisely the comparative method.

The broad approach advocated here does not require the reckless positing of risky and uncertain etymologies. All that is needed is to show decisively more cognates than those of any rival hypothesis. Actually, it is better to start with a relatively small number of first-rate etymologies. These are the ones that establish the classification. One may then discover others, given a valid initial hypothesis. In such work a wider comparison often invalidates etymologies erected on too narrow a base.

In the absence of a principled theory on how many etymologies are necessary, many comparatists seek to produce as many as possible. I myself have in several instances worked out etymologies for specific groups of Amerindian languages only to find later that someone has compared at least some of these languages and published a set of etymologies, complete with asterisks and tables of correspondences. I have found in every case that I have fewer etymologies, and that almost all, if not all, are contained in the larger list. This is partly because I have not included much in the way of kinship terms or zoological and botanical terms in my word lists, but also because I have excluded many words that I consider too venturesome or im- probable in the light of wider evidence.

Of course, most sound changes are regular, and some competing theo- ries of reconstruction are more plausible than others. Though there is much indeterminacy in reconstructed sound systems, some features do seem quite secure. Besides, for all of these uncertainties, I am by no means saying that comparative linguistics is an idle endeavor. On the contrary, it is an indis- pensable means toward the attainment of two major goals. The first lies at the very heart of linguistics as a scientific enterprise. This is the understand- ing of linguistic change, with the ultimate aim of diachronic generalizations. Without the comparative method, we would be confined to the relatively narrow limits set by the existence of written records and to the here-and-now of internal reconstruction.

The other goal is the contribution that the comparative method can make to nonlinguistic history, a matter of greater inherent interest to lin- guists than might meet the eye. After all, language is our major instrument for dealing with the external world. Such topics as semantic change cannot be fruitfully pursued without a knowledge of this world. But again, though such endeavors as genetic classification are, in a sense, a kind of scientific obligation that we owe to the related historical disciplines, they are not a mere favor to them, but an indispensable part of linguistics itself.

Chapter 2

Unity and Bounds of Amerind

The thesis of this book is that all the indigenous languages of the Americas, except those of the Na-Dene and Eskimo-Aleut groups, fall into a single vast assemblage. The bulk of this volume will be devoted to a demonstration of the genetic unity of what I will call the Amerind family. But it will be useful first, I think, to set that effort in historical perspective and to summon up a few of the most striking pieces of evidence in support of what most Amerindian specialists will no doubt consider a very bold thesis indeed.

Up till now, except for the broader efforts of Morris Swadesh, attempts at classification in North and South America have had virtually separate histories, with Central America apportioned in various ways between the two continents. The most comprehensive studies of South American languages are those of the Czech investigator Čestmír Loukotka. Loukotka (1968), a posthumous work, posited no fewer than 117 independent stocks. A few of these, however, had become extinct before Loukotka carried out his studies, leaving no linguistic trace except for some place-names or statements by early travelers or missionaries about their linguistic resemblance to other groups. I believe that a few of Loukotka's supposedly independent stocks are not valid genetic units at any level.

Loukotka's method was to classify languages by comparing 45 words from each, including such culture words as 'maize' and such animal names as 'tapir.' On this basis Loukotka, a believer in "mixed languages," distinguished three broad categories: (1) mixed languages, or those with more than nine non-native words out of the 45, (2) languages with foreign intrusions (*Einschläge*), or those with a comparatively large number of such words (but evidently fewer than nine), and (3) languages with only traces of non-native sources, i.e., a few loanwords. This "method" hardly requires comment. The work is, however, still valuable for its comprehensive bibliography.

Mason (1950) and Tovar (1961) are basically catalogs of South American families in which the number of independent stocks likewise hovers around 100. McQuown (1955) examined the languages of Mexico, Central America, and South America. His hierarchical taxonomic symbolization included a few hypotheses concerning South American groups considered independent in Loukotka (1968) and similar classifications, e.g. Tupian, Uitoto, and Zaparo as M1, M2, and M3, respectively, but by any count his classification would also involve scores of independent stocks in South and Central America. This work is particularly valuable for its enormously detailed maps giving numerically coded locations for 1,820 languages of South America, Central America, and Mexico.

Along rather different lines is Key (1979), a work on South American languages organized by sections, following Greenberg (1960). It gives much incidental phonological, grammatical, and occasional comparative information, with regional maps and a highly useful bibliography that helps to bring Loukotka's up to date. Matteson et al. (1972) gives comparative reconstructions for five major South and Central American stocks: Chibchan, Mayan, Tucanoan, Guahiban, and Arawakan. In an introductory article, Matteson attempts "by the rigorous application of standard techniques of the comparative method" to demonstrate the genetic relationship of a wide sample of groups of American Indian languages, "determined on the basis of completely recorded data and reliable reconstructions" (p. 21). The 17 groups and three isolates compared range geographically from Algonquian in North America to Ge in South America, though the majority are South American. The precise limits and subgroupings of "Proto-Amerindian," however, are not indicated. Matteson also provides a table of Proto-Amerindian phonemes and a list of 974 etymologies involving two or more of her groups. Many of these coincide, at least in part, with etymologies included in this volume. Matteson also briefly examines Eskimo-Aleut, which I exclude from Amerind, and claims that plentiful similarities appeared on brief inspection but were omitted for lack of data.

For North American languages, we begin with the 1891 classification of J. W. Powell, which was the point of departure for subsequent work. Powell covered North America above Mexico and listed 58 separate stocks.

In a few instances, he separated stocks that had been consolidated by his predecessors. Uto-Aztecan, for example, now universally recognized as a valid unit, he divided into Shoshonean, Piman, and Nahuatlan.

Beginning about the turn of the century, several important hypotheses considerably reduced the number of independent stocks. In particular, Alfred Kroeber and Roland Dixon, chiefly concerned with California languages (for which Powell had posited a considerable number of separate families), distinguished two major new groupings: Hokan and Penutian. Both turned out to have relationships well beyond California. Edward Sapir founded the comparative study of Hokan-Coahuiltecan and also showed that two languages of California, Wiyot and Yurok, whose connection Kroeber had already noted, were in turn connected with Algonquian. The connection between Algonquian, Wiyot, and Yurok, long considered controversial, is now universally accepted. Sapir also was the first to articulate clearly the Na-Dene hypothesis and to present supporting evidence. George Trager and Benjamin Whorf linked Uto-Aztecan with Tanoan and Kiowa, a connection that had already been suggested by J. P. Harrington. These widely accepted hypotheses were summed up and extended in Sapir's famous article in the *Encyclopaedia Britannica* (1929). His classification, with some changes in spelling, is shown in Table 8. (The question marks are his.)

In a number of important respects this classification represented a significant advance. The first three stocks are valid genetic units, though they do not belong on the same level, in my view. The fourth embodies a large portion of my Penutian, a major subgroup of Northern Amerind. Although incomplete, Sapir's enumeration of Penutian contained no languages that do not belong to it. The sixth group, except for Zuni (which Sapir queried), assumes that Kiowa-Tanoan bears a special relationship to Uto-Aztecan, an idea followed up successfully in Whorf and Trager (1937). With the further inclusion of Oto-Mangue, it becomes the Central Amerind branch of Amerind as defined in this study. The main problems with Sapir's classification lie in the fifth group, Hokan-Siouan, which, though it provides some valuable insights, is not the homogeneous group he suggested.

The seminal contributions of Mary R. Haas indicate that there are relationships that cut across Sapir's groupings. In particular, she has shown a special relationship within Hokan-Siouan between Tunican (V.D) and Natchez-Muskogean (V.F.2) in a larger grouping that she calls Gulf and links with Algonquian-Ritwan (II.A). Others whose work challenged Sapir's groupings are William Shipley (1957), who compares Yuki (Sapir's Hokan-

Table 8. Sapir's Classification of North American Indian Languages

I   ESKIMO-ALEUT

II ALGONQUIAN-WAKASHAN
    A Algonquian-Ritwan
      1 Algonquian
      2 Beothuk (?)
      3 Ritwan
        a Wiyot
        b Yurok
    B Kutenai
    C Mosan (Wakashan-Salish)
      1 Wakashan (Kwakiutl-Nootka)
      2 Chemakuan
      3 Salish

III NA-DENE
    A Haida
    B Continental Na-Dene
      1 Tlingit
      2 Athabaskan

IV PENUTIAN
    A California Penutian
      1 Miwok-Costanoan
      2 Yokuts
      3 Maidu
      4 Wintun
    B Oregon Penutian
      1 Takelma
      2 Coast Oregon Penutian
        a Coos
        b Siuslaw
        c Yakonan
      3 Kalapuya
    C Chinook
    D Tsimshian
    E Plateau Penutian
      1 Sahaptin
      2 Waiilatpuan (Molala-Cayuse)
      3 Lutuami (Klamath-Modoc)
    F Mexican Penutian
      1 Mixe-Zoque
      2 Huave

V   HOKAN-SIOUAN
    A Hokan-Coahuiltecan
      1 Hokan
        a Northern Hokan
          (1) Karok, Chimariko,
              Shasta-Achomawi

V   HOKAN-SIOUAN continued
          (2) Yana
          (3) Pomo
        b Washo
        c Esselen-Yuman
          (1) Esselen
          (2) Yuman
        d Salinan-Seri
          (1) Salinan
          (2) Chumash
          (3) Seri
        e Tequistlatecan
      2 Subtiaba-Tlappanec
      3 Coahuiltecan
        a Tonkawa
        b Coahuilteco
          (1) Coahuilteco proper
          (2) Cotoname
          (3) Comecrudo
        c Karankawa
    B Yuki
    C Keres
    D Tunican
      1 Tunica-Atakapa
      2 Chitimacha
    E Iroquois-Caddoan
      1 Iroquoian
      2 Caddoan
    F Eastern group
      1 Siouan-Yuchi
        a Siouan
        b Yuchi
      2 Natchez-Muskogean
        a Natchez
        b Muskogean
        c Timucua (?)

VI AZTECO-TANOAN
    A Uto-Aztecan
      1 Nahuatl
      2 Pima
      3 Shoshonean
    B Tanoan-Kiowa
      1 Tanoan
      2 Kiowa
    C Zuni (?)

Siouan V.B) with Penutian (Sapir's IV), and Stanley Newman (1964), who connects Zuni (tentatively included by Sapir in Azteco-Tanoan, VI) with California Penutian (Sapir's IV.A).

But the fact that Sapir's *Encyclopaedia Britannica* article was incorrect in some respects does not diminish the importance of his work. In my opinion, all the groupings for which he presented concrete etymologies (e.g. Algonquian-Ritwan, Hokan-Coahuiltecan, Na-Dene) are correct, with the single exception that at one point he included Atakapa in his Hokan-Coahuiltecan family, although it hardly appeared in his etymologies. This error he tacitly rectified in his general classification, where Atakapa was correctly included in Tunican (group V.D). Similarly, Kroeber, Dixon, and Harrington, because of the pioneering nature of their work, inevitably covered a broad spectrum of languages in their investigations. Yet I have found that they and some of the other early investigators who worked on an intuitive and common-sense basis, free of the erroneous notions concerning the comparative method discussed in Chapter 1, were invariably correct.

The numerous resemblances among North American languages led Paul Radin (1919) to posit that all North American Indian languages, including many in Mexico, were related. He cited about 60 lexical and 75 grammatical sound-meaning resemblances among various groups, though nowhere did he set forth the exact membership of the stock. His etymologies include citations from Na-Dene languages but do not mention Eskimo-Aleut at all.

Although Sapir's famous essay "Time Perspective in Aboriginal American Culture" (1963: 454–55), originally published in 1916, identified Na-Dene and Eskimo-Aleut as the most recent arrivals in North America, it is clear that he did not see the remaining languages as a single genetic unit. In his view, there had been a whole series of movements of linguistically related peoples, who arrived at different times and from different places, of which the Na-Dene and Eskimo-Aleut speakers were merely the latest. On the other hand, certain of Sapir's remarks about the widespread *n*- 'first person' and *m*- 'second person' of American Indian languages, cited later in this chapter, suggest that as early as 1918 he was entertaining the possibility of Amerind unity.

In 1956, I proposed a tripartite configuration similar, except in some details of subgrouping, to that which forms the thesis of this work. My paper, given at an international anthropological congress, was not published until four years later (Greenberg 1960). Meanwhile, Sydney Lamb independently proposed a very similar hypothesis (1959; personal communication), though his work covered only North America. Having noted the numerous resemblances among Sapir's groups II, IV, V, and VI, he arrived at the conclusion that all North American languages, except Na-Dene and Eskimo-Aleut, were related.*

The last 20 years or so of work in Amerindian classification have been marked by widespread skepticism about entities formerly considered securely established (e.g. Hokan; see Campbell & Mithun 1979). This period has also seen the publication of some important comparative works, the compiling of etymological dictionaries on relatively low-level groupings (e.g. Uto-Aztecan), and extensive reconstructive work on the large Oto-Manguean group. For the most part, however, the published materials have been of limited scope. The articles seeking to prove some relationship or other have typically been two-way comparisons, based to a very large extent on the misguided notions about the necessity of reconstruction as proof, discussed in the previous chapter. There have also been a number of articles seeking to disprove relationships. By far the most important of these is Levine (1979), whose thesis that Haida is not a Na-Dene language has evidently been widely accepted and will be discussed in detail in Chapter 6. I have examined these negative articles in detail and have found them invariably flawed in two ways: they make no alternative suggestions, and they are wrong.

I am therefore well aware that what is attempted in this work runs against the current trends in Amerindian work and will be received in certain quarters with something akin to outrage. Given the investment in time and energy that has led to results different from mine, such a reaction is wholly understandable. Yet as Allan Taylor (1982) suggests in his review of Campbell and Mithun, perhaps the time has come for a fundamental change. Referring to my argument for the genetic unity of the vast majority of American Indian languages (Greenberg 1956, 1979), he cautions: "A rejection of this provocative hypothesis by Americanists is at their own peril, for it is both plausible and testable. Perhaps after Sapir's sweeping claims—now fallen into disrepute—we are jaded. But Greenberg's suggestion rests on a

---

*Physical anthropologists like Christy Turner and Stephen Zegura, pursuing wholly different lines of research (on dentition in the one case and blood types in the other) have turned up data that provide extremely important evidence (to be discussed in Chapter 7) in support of this thesis.

carefully constructed data base and a consistent methodology and as such is far more credible than Sapir's intuitive formulations."

Most of the rest of this chapter is devoted to presenting a few widespread grammatical markers and some lexical evidence, often involving shared irregularities, by way of a preliminary argument in support of the book's main thesis. Each line of evidence will be presented in detail in Chapters 3–5.

As we have seen, early researchers posited as many as 100 independent stocks among the languages of South America. This multiplicity is generally believed to be implausible. Yet, as far as I know, no one has gone beyond suggesting very limited linkages among individual stocks. An exception is the fairly wide acceptance of the notion that the large Ge family must be, as early writers in fact had suggested, a member of a more extensive group, often called Macro-Ge, which would include groups like Puri, Mashakali, Kamakan, and Caraja (all distinct in Loukotka's classification). In my "General Classification" (Greenberg 1960), I suggested that this grouping includes, besides others, Chiquito, a language of Paraguay known almost exclusively from eighteenth-century Spanish sources. Since no one has followed this up, let me set forth some evidence for this proposal, and some of its implications.

Like many Amerind languages, Chiquito has a set of pronominal prefixes that indicate the possessor of a noun, and a similar or even identical set that indicates the person and number of a verb's subject. The forms for a singular possessor of the noun *poo-s* 'house' are as follows:

i-poo	'my house'
a-poo	'thy house'
i-poo-s-tii	'his house'
i-poo-s	'her house'

The suffix -*s*, no doubt an old demonstrative element (see Greenberg 1978), indicates the absolute, or non-possessed, form and also occurs in all forms with third-person possessors. We have then a pattern *i-*/ *a-*/ *i-* for first-, second-, and third-person possession.

There is, however, a complication, for in nouns whose initial consonant is *k*, the *k* (written *c*) is replaced by *ts* (written *z*) after the *i-* of the first-person singular possessor. This is easily understandable as a palatalization of *k* after the high front vowel *i-*. Oddly enough, however, the *i-* of the third person does not cause a similar palatalization. We can illustrate this phenomenon in the Chiquito word for 'ring,' *kuosoko-s:*

i-tsuosoko	'my ring'
a-kuosoko	'thy ring'
i-kuosoko-s-tii	'his ring'
i-kuosoko-s	'her ring'

Similarly, in nouns beginning with *t*, *t* is replaced by *č* after *i-* in the first person, but not after *i-* in the third person.

In Fulnio, another language hitherto considered independent, we have a similar set of prefixes: *i-/a-/e-*. In one of the two major classes of nouns, however, initial *t, d, k,* and *kʰ* (aspirated *k*) are palatalized in the first person, with the *i-* deleted, so once more we have not only a similar prefix pattern, but also a palatalizing action of the first-person prefix.

In Choroti, a language of the Mataco group that belongs to a large subgroup including Panoan, and that I assigned in 1956 to a large Ge-Pano-Carib grouping, we have not only the by-now-familiar pattern *i-/a-/i-*, but once again a palatalization by the first-person *i-*, but not by the third-person *i-*. An example is the word for 'house,' with the stem *wet:*

i-yet	'my house'
a-wet	'thy house'
i-wet	'his, her house'

Likewise in Bororo, another family generally considered independent that I included in Macro-Ge (Greenberg 1960), and that Floyd Lounsbury has long believed to be affiliated with Ge (personal communication), we have the same pattern *i-/a-/i-*, though without palatalization in the first person. (It is, of course, easy to see how such an irregularity is subject to analogical regularization.)

The key to this apparent mystery of a pattern that crosses recognized group boundaries is provided by Ge itself. In one of the very few accounts we have of Ge languages, for Kraho, we find the following set:

i-kwa	'my child'
a-kwa	'thy child'
iʔ-kwa	'his, her child'

In Krenje, another Ge language, a similar set is found. In both cases a glottal stop in the third person has precluded direct contact between *i-* and the stem, thus preventing the palatalization that is widely found, as has been seen, with *i*- of the first person.

The presence of a glottal stop in the third person, moreover, enables us to explain why Fulnio has *e* rather than *i* in the third person. A glottal stop tends to lower a preceding *i* to *e*, as in Biblical Hebrew *lɛ ʔᵉxol* 'to eat' as against *liqtol* 'to kill.' In the Hebrew verb for 'to say,' this process is complete: *lemor* < *lɛ ʔᵉmor* < **liʔmor* is completely parallel to the sequence of changes hypothesized for Fulnio.

This pattern has ramifications beyond those for Macro-Ge and Macro-Panoan. Turning to Carib, another of the major stocks of South America, we again find the *i-* / *a-* / *i-* pattern, but with an interesting complication. In some of these languages, *i-* is the marker for the third-person possessor only for stems beginning with a consonant. When the stem begins with a vowel, we have *i-t-* with an intercalated *-t*. Examples from Pemon are *i-paruči* 'his, her sister,' but *i-t-enna* 'his, her hand.' What we have here is a well-known linguistic process of change by which an irregular unmarked form is interpreted as a zero form to which other markers are then added. In this case, there was first an irregularity in the third-person prefix, with an *i-* before consonants and a *-t* before vowels, and then *i-* was added to the *t-* form by analogy.

As noted earlier, the Mataco language Choroti exhibits the *i-* / *a-* / *i-* pattern. In Mataco proper, we find the expected third-person *t* before vowel stems, e.g. *t-isan* 'his, her body.' But the analogical process has added the *i-* as a first-person prefix: *i-t-isan* 'my body.' Still other South American languages, e.g. Guaicuru, have similar systems.

The historical relatedness of all the South American forms just discussed seems obvious, and the evidence suggests that these forms may in fact represent localized variants of a generalized Amerind pattern. Kroeber, in his study of the language of the Salinan Indians of California, noted that he had detected a "mysterious" *t-* prefixed to nouns, and went on to observe that "the Washo language . . . shows a peculiarity of structure that may be similar to this one in Salinan," namely, an initial *d-* (Kroeber 1904: 46). Later, he discovered a *t-* prefix in the San Luis Obispo dialect of Chumash, which he once more compared to Salinan (Kroeber 1910). Chumash, Salinan, and Washo are all Hokan languages of California.

In 1915, Walter Lehmann published his findings on the close relationship between the Subtiaba language of Nicaragua and the Tlappanec language of Chiapas in Mexico. One item that figured prominently in his discovery was a nominal prefix *d-*, which he connected with *r-* in Tlappanec. By 1920, Lehmann had noted the startling resemblance in form and function between these prefixes in Subtiaba and Tlappanec and the initial *d-* of Washo, an observation he dealt with in his vast work *Zentral-Amerika* in a brief section called "Relations of Subtiaba-Tlappanec to Washo (California)" (pp. 973–78).

A few years later, Sapir proposed that the *d-* prefix of Subtiaba, along with much other evidence, indicated the membership of Subtiaba and Tlappanec in the by now much-enlarged Hokan family. He incorporated Kroeber's and Lehmann's observations on the similarity of the *d-* of Subtiaba, the *t-* of Salinan, the *d-* of Washo, and the *t-* of Chumash, noting the significant additional fact that "in Washo the *d-* is found . . . with a vowel [but] not before consonant stems. This is as in Subtiaba" (Sapir 1925b: 496).

The resemblance to the South American forms discussed earlier now becomes evident, since there, too, as we have seen, the *t-* prefix is confined to vowel stems. The Hokan forms have the characteristics of what I have elsewhere called a stage III article (see Greenberg 1978)—that is, a demonstrative element that has passed through the stages of functioning first as a definite article, then as a combined definite and indefinite article, to finally become a marker of mere nominality. One trait of the stage III article is that it appears with some nouns but not with others in a quite sporadic way that differs from language to language.

A related phenomenon may exist in the Mayan languages, which like very many Amerind languages have a set of prefixes to express pronominal possession. Many Mayan languages have partially or completely different sets for stems beginning in vowels and in consonants. One, Ixil, has the exact pattern for the third person hypothesized here as the original one: *i-* before a consonant and *t-* before a vowel. Kekchí and Quiché have *r-* before vowel stems. The reconstruction of this element as *ʰr* in Proto-Mayan is usual, but on at least one view it would be *t-*. The tendency in Mayan has been for the analogical spread of *i-* (*j-* before a vowel), but Mam has generalized *t-* as the sole third-person marker in the singular.

The story perhaps does not end even here. A well-known characteristic of the Algonquian languages is that when the possessive or verbal subject prefixes precede an initial vowel stem there is an intercalated *-t-*, which shows up in Wiyot as *-d-* (e.g. *ru-d-aluwi* 'my boat') and therefore goes back to Proto-Algic, the ancestral form of Algonquian, Wiyot, and Yurok. (See Sapir's etymological entry for the first-person pronoun in 1913: 633.)

The process is parallel to that noted in certain South American languages, but here the analogical spread of the prefixed person marker to the original $t + V$ of the first person is complete. (V indicates an indeterminate vowel.)

I consider the relatedness of the South American forms to each other to be beyond question, and the connection between these forms and those of Hokan, Mayan, and Algic to be quite probable.

These cases may be considered a first step in reconstructing more completely the pronominal system of Proto-Amerind. To begin with, we may note that the possessive prefixes of the noun are often identical with, or similar to, the agent prefixes in many Amerind languages, in both North and South America. Indeed much that has been said above is equally valid for subject markers of transitive verbs in the languages mentioned. There is considerable evidence that what is involved here is an ergative pronominal pattern, that is, a pattern with two sets of markers, one for the subject of transitive verbs and the other for the subject of intransitive verbs and the object of transitive verbs. For the purposes of this discussion, we may simply call this second type of marker an object.

Whereas the ergative set is also widely used for nominal possession, the objective set is often used for nominal predication. The noun is then treated as a stative verb: 'I am a man' often parallels 'I sleep.' The third-person object marker is commonly zero, as against the $i \sim t$ marker discussed above. We may add a further typological fact. Kinship nouns that have a relational meaning are sometimes treated like transitive verbs when they are predicated—for example, 'she is my mother' is, as it were, 'she mothers me.' Complete agreement in this typological scheme may be found in languages as distant as Salishan in the northwestern United States, Nahuatl in Mexico, and Chiquito in Bolivia.

Although the i- of the first person in the widespread South American pronominal pattern is indeed very common in Amerind, it is more frequently found as an object than as an ergative marker. Even in the South American groups with this pattern, i- occurs as the first-person object of the transitive verb (e.g. Guaicuru). Occurrences of i- as first-person markers are not further considered here, but will be discussed in Chapter 5, which is devoted to the grammatical evidence for Amerind. (Its ergative use is probably an innovation in certain South American groups.)

The most common ergative marker in Amerind languages, as well as the most common independent first-person pronoun, is nV-. Even the South American languages with the i-/a-/i- pattern generally have n in other uses, e.g. Mataco *no* as first-person singular object. Unlike *i-* for the first person, the second-person prefix *a-* is in all probability a specific South American innovation, since it is uncommon elsewhere. The most widespread second-person marker is *mV-*, usually *ma-* or *mi-*. In fact, it would probably be easier to enumerate where *nV-* and *mV-* are not found than where they are.

Of interest in this connection is an aspect of a controversy between Sapir and Truman Michelson concerning the genetic relationship of the Algic languages (Algonquian-Ritwan). Sapir viewed as his most cogent evidence the identity of a set of pronominal prefixes in Algonquian, Wiyot, and Yurok. One of these was *n-* of the first person. He also equated Cree second-person plural, *-mwa*, with the most common marker of the second person in Yurok, *-m*. Michelson (1915: 194) argued that Sapir's examples proved nothing because they were found in so many other North American languages. As one might expect, he had a field day, citing *n-* and *m-* forms from Hokan, Penutian, and Uto-Aztecan languages, often with examples of both from the same language. But this is, of course, the same as claiming that the resemblance between English 'two' and Italian *due* has no significance because Russian has *dva* and Hindi has *do*.

Although Sapir was well aware of the wide distribution of the second-person *m-* in North America, he evidently had very little acquaintance with South American languages. Hence, when he read Benigno Bibolotti's grammar of Moseten, a Macro-Panoan language of Bolivia, he was startled by the marker's appearance there. As he put it in his review of that work (Sapir 1917a: 184), "The curiously widespread second-person singular *m-* meets us here once more (*mi* 'thou')."

Sapir was also aware of the extremely wide distribution of the first-person *n-*. In a letter to Speck in 1918, he used an argument similar to mine above: "Getting down to brass tacks, how in the Hell are you going to explain general American *n-* 'I' except genetically?" (Cited in Darnell & Sherzer 1971: 27.)

How are *n* as a first-person marker and *m* as a second-person marker distributed in Amerind languages, and what conclusions may be drawn from their distribution?

To seek answers to these questions, we may begin in South America with Macro-Ge. In Krenje, a member of the Ge substock and one of the very few languages described in any detail, we find such forms as *i-n-sun* 'my uncle' and *i-n-josō* 'my dog' (cf. *a-josō* 'thy dog'). Evidently *n-* has been prefixed by *i-*, the widespread Amerind first-person singular marker discussed earlier. Here is interesting evidence for the hypothesis that *i-* has spread analogically as a possessive marker in Macro-Ge, Macro-Panoan, and Macro-Carib. Kaingan, the group most closely related to Ge and often included as a branch within it, has both the first-person *n* and the second-person *m*. Examples from Kaingan languages are Dalbergia *nu* and *ma* and Tibagi *in* and *ama*. In other Macro-Ge branches, we find Botocudo *n-*, the first-person singular subject of stative verbs; Opaie *ni-*, the first-person singular (with functions not clear from the existing data); and Kamakan *n-* 'my,' the first-person possessive.

Macro-Panoan, the major stock that is closest genetically to Macro-Ge, consists of Mataco-Guaicuru, Pano-Tacana, and a series of languages that seem to be intermediate between these two groupings. In Mataco, we find *no-* 'my,' *na-* 'our' (exclusive), and *em* 'thou'; in Vejoz and Choroti *am* 'thou'; and in Vejoz *no-* 'our' (exclusive). In Guaicuru languages, we have Toba *am* 'thou' and Pilaga *ina* 'I,' *ien* 'we.' For Proto-Panoan, Olive Shell (1965) reconstructs **no* 'we.' In Key's list of Pano-Tacana cognates (1968: 75), she lists under 'you' (sing.) for the Tacanan subgroup Cavineña *mike*, Tacana *mike, mi-da, mia-da*, Chama *mia*, and Reyesano *mibe;* and for the Panoan subgroup, Chacobo *mi, mia*, Cashinahua *mi*, Cashibo *mii*, Marinahua *mī*, Mayoruna *miβi*, and Shipibo-Conibo *mia*. As examples from other Macro-Panoan languages, we may cite from Guenoa, a member of the extinct Charruan stock and the only one for which we have pronominal data, *empti* 'thou, you,' *an-ti* 'our' (*-ti* is a suffix found in all pronouns); from Vilela, *m-* 'thou' (no plural recorded), *nati* 'we'; from Lule, *mi-l* 'you' (pl.); and from Moseten, *mi* 'thou,' *mi-in* 'you.' The Moseten forms are from Bibolotti (1917). An early source, Andrés Herrero (1834), records first-person singular *nu* instead of Bibolotti's *je*.

We now turn to the Andean group. The Patagon group consists of two main languages, Ona and Tehuelche, with identical forms: *m-* 'thy,' *ma* 'thou,' and *mai, mar* 'you.' Mapuche, sometimes called Araucanian, exhibits both the first-person *n-* and the second-person *m-* in various connections, perhaps most clearly in the possessive pronouns *ta-ñi* 'my' and *ta-mi* 'thy.' In the Aymaran group, Aymara proper has *naja* 'I,' *-ma* 'thy,' and *huma* 'thou.' Jaqaru, the other Aymaran language, has *na* 'I' and *huma* 'thou.' With *huma* we should no doubt equate Gennaken (also called Pehuelche) *kemu*, Quechua *kam*, and Kahuapana *kema*. Quechua also probably shows first-person *n* in *noqa* 'I.' Finally, Cholona has *mi* 'thou,' *m-* 'thy.'

In the Timote languages of the Equatorial group, Timote proper and Cuica have *an* 'I,' and Mocochi has both *an* 'I' and *ma* 'thou.' The first-person pronoun in Zamuco proper is *ñu*. Chamacoco, another language in this group, has *p-* 'thy'; such second-person forms in *p-* for either singular or plural are common in Equatorial and may derive from **m*. The independent pronouns of Guahibo are *hane* 'I' and *hame* 'thou.' In Otomaco, the first-person singular pronoun is recorded variously as *no* and *nu*. Yuracare has *me* 'thou' and *mi-* 'thy,' and a second-person plural pronoun *pa*, both independent and bound. The second-person singular pronoun for the subject of a verb in Cayuvava is *p-*, a type mentioned earlier as characteristic of Equatorial. One of the two largest language groups in Equatorial, Tupian, has no trace of first-person *n-*, though many Tupian languages have a second-person plural *pe*. The other large group, Arawakan, consists of Maipuran and some other small subgroups. Within Maipuran, most of the languages are designated *nu*-Arawak precisely because the first-person singular independent or bound pronoun is *nu* or a similar form. The basic second-person pronoun is *pi*, found almost everywhere in the singular and often in the plural. The non-Maipuran languages of the Arawakan group include Chapacura, which furnishes such examples as Itene *ana-* and *ma-* as first- and second-person singular verb subjects and Abitana *-ma* 'thy'; and Uro, where we find Uro proper *am* 'thou' and Puquina *no-* 'my,' *pa-* 'thou' (verb subject), and *pi-, po* 'thy.' A substock of Equatorial that we may call Jibaro-Kandoshi provides the following examples: Murato (also called Kandoshi) *nua* 'I,' Yaruro *naja* 'my,' Gualaquiza *amue* 'thou,' and Aguaruna *ma* 'thou.' For Esmeralda, an extinct member of the Jibaro-Kandoshi group, no material on the pronominal system is available.

Another major South American stock is Macro-Tucanoan. The Tucano languages of this group all have *m-* forms in the second person (e.g. Wanana *mãi* 'thou,' *mi-* 'thy'). In the second large group of Macro-Tucanoan, Puinave, every language has *am* or a similar form for the second-person singular pronoun (e.g. Papury *am*, Puinave proper *ma*). There are also the first-person plurals *en* in Yehubde and *yn* in Papury. Capixana, another branch of Macro-Tucanoan, has as its second-person singular pronoun *mi*.

The last of the major South American stocks is Macro-Carib. In the Carib branch, the most widespread second-person singular pronoun is *amore, amare*, or the like; *-re* is probably a suffix, as suggested by Bakairí *ama* 'thou' and the widespread first-person singular pronoun *u-re*. First-person plural pronouns commonly contain *n*, e.g. Taulipang *ina*, Cariniaco *naana*, and Galibi and Macusi *ana*. In Uitoto, the only other large substock in Macro-Carib, the western language Uitoto proper has the second-person plural *omo*. In the eastern language Ocaina, the only one for which we have any detailed account of the pronominal system, the second-person dual and plural pronouns have the base *mō*.

In this review of the purely South American stocks it has perhaps struck the reader that the second-person *m* has a somewhat broader distribution than the first-person *n*. Where the first-person *n* is lacking, the first-person singular is frequently *i*. It seems probable that *n*, unlike the basically singular as well as objective *i*, was indifferent to number. In a whole series of South American families, *i* has taken over other functions, thus confining *n* to the plural. This pattern holds for the Macro-Panoan stock, for much of the Andean stock, and for the Ge and Carib substocks.

We now turn to the vast Chibchan-Paezan group—found primarily in South and Central America but with one North American outlier, Timucua, in Florida. Here I will follow a partly geographic and partly genetic ordering of the data, first considering the languages spoken in South America. Among the languages hitherto generally considered Chibchan, we find Chibcha *mue* 'thou,' *m-* 'thy'; Duit *m-* 'thy'; Kagaba *nas* 'I,' *naui* 'our,' *ba* ~ *ma* 'thou'; Bintucua *nan* 'I,' *ma* 'thou'; Chimila *na-* 'my,' *ma-* 'thy'; Guamaca *nerra* 'I,' *nabi* 'we,' *ma* 'thou'; Paez *an* 'I'; and Guambiana *na* 'I.' Chocoan, hitherto not considered Chibchan-Paezan, has Choco *bere* 'thou,' and Catio *by*, *biči* 'thou,' *mare*, *mačia* 'you.' Jirajara, another substock of Chibchan-Paezan, has Ayoman *moh* 'thou'; in Warrau, there is *ine* 'I.'

In Central America, Nuclear Chibchan has Cuna *an* 'I,' *pe* 'thy'; Muoi *ba* 'thou'; Move, Norteño, and Penomeño *nu* 'we,' *mo* 'thou,' *mu* 'you'; Murire, Chumulu, and Gualaca *ba* 'thy'; Terraba *fa* 'thou'; Bribri *ba*, *bo*, *bi*, *ma* 'thou'; Cabecar *ba* 'thou'; Borunca *ba* 'thou'; Rama *na* 'I,' *ma* 'thou' (with bound forms *n-* and *m-*, respectively); and finally Miskito, Sumu, and Ulua *man* 'thou.' Among languages not hitherto reckoned Chibchan, we have Paya *paa* 'thou,' Xinca *ni* 'I,' Lenca (Guajiquero) *am-* 'thy,' and Timucua *ni-* 'I.'

In the group I call Central Amerind I distinguish three major subgroups: Uto-Aztecan, Kiowa-Tanoan, and Oto-Manguean. Uto-Aztecan has the first-person *n-* and the second-person *m-* quite generally. Whorf and Trager (1937) reconstruct only two Azteco-Tanoan pronouns; these are their items 37 **neʔa*, **neʔ* 'I,' and 77, *ʔeme*, *eŋʷe*, *eŋʷ* 'thou' and 'you.' Since the Kiowa-Tanoan branch also belongs in this stock, it is relevant to cite at this point Kiowa *nã* 'I, we' and *am* 'thou, you.' In Oto-Manguean, we have *n* forms used only for the first-person singular in Zapotec and for the first-person singular and the first-person plural exclusive in Mixtec and Popoloca. In Chinantec, however, *n-* is used for both singular and plural with an apparently secondary differentiation of the plural by final vowel for inclusive and exclusive.

We next consider Hokan, one of three major subgroups of my Northern Amerind. Here we can cite Achomawi *mi-* 'thy'; Atsugewi *mi?* 'thou,' *mi-* 'thy'; Shasta *maj?i* 'thou'; Chimariko *no-ut* 'I,' *mam-ut* 'thou,' *-mi* 'thy'; Karok *na* 'I,' *i:m* 'thou'; Washo *mi:* 'thou'; South Yana *ǰi-n* 'our,' *ǰu-m* 'thy'; Pomo *ma* or *a:ma* (dialect variation); Santa Ynez (Chumash) *noi* 'I,' and Santa Barbara, Santa Cruz (also Chumash), etc., *noo* 'I,' *p-*, *pi, pii* second-person singular with varying dialect forms; Salinan *mo?* 'thou'; Esselen *niš-* 'my,' *miš-* 'thy'; in the Yuman group, Mohave *manja* 'thou,' Diegueño *ma* 'thou,' etc.; Seri *me* 'thou, you'; Jicaque *nap* 'I' (*na* in the western dialects noted by Eduard Conzemius); Comecrudo *na* 'I'; Cotoname *na* 'I, we,' and Coahuilteco *na* 'I,' *mai* 'thou.'

In Penutian, another major Northern Amerind subgroup, I include (for reasons to be given later) not only Mexican Penutian, but also Yuki, Wappo, Gulf, Muskogean, and Zuni. The *n* and *m* pronominal forms are widespread here also. Beginning in the north, we may cite Tsimshian transitive subjects *n-* 'I,' *m-* 'thou'; Chinook first-person singular subject *n-*, second-person singular subject and possessive *m-;* Takelma first-person transitive subject pronoun *-n* in aorist and future tenses, *ma* 'thou'; Coos *n*, *nəx* 'I'; Miluk *ənneu* 'I'; Siuslaw *na* 'I'; Alsea first-person verb subject *n-;* Klamath *no:*, *ni* 'I,' *mi* 'thy'; Kalapuya *maha* 'thou'; North Sahaptin second-person singular subject *am;* Nez Perce *na-* 'my' (with kinship terms), *na* 'we,' *im* 'thou'; Molala *?ina* 'I'; Rumsien (Costanoan) *me* 'thou'; Central Sierra Miwok *mi?* 'thou' (with similar forms in other dialects of Miwok); Wintu *ni* 'I,' *mi* 'thou'; Yokuts *na?* 'I,' *ma* 'thou'; Maidu *ni* 'I,' *mi* 'thou'; Yuki *mi* 'thou'; Wappo *mi?* 'thou'; Chitimacha *him?* 'thou'; Natchez *ni-* 'me,' *ba* 'thou, thee'; Creek *une* 'I'; Apalachee *ani* 'I'; Mayan (general) first-person singular subject of transitive verbs *?in*, first-person subject of intransitive verbs *-n;* Zoque *mimič* 'thou'; Sierra Popoluca *miih, miič* 'thou'; Totonac *mi-* 'thy'; and Huave first-person subject *-na-* (future tense), second person *me-* (*-mer-*, *-mir-* in certain verb classes).

As its name suggests, the third Northern Amerind stock, Almosan-Keresiouan, has two branches. One, Almosan, is identical to Sapir's Algonquian-Wakashan, and comprises the Algic, Mosan, and Kutenai languages. We have seen that Sapir put special emphasis on the possessive prefixes of Algonquian, Wiyot, and Yurok—the Algic substocks. The first person in Algonquian is *ne-,* for which corresponding forms exist in the other Algic languages. As noted earlier, Sapir equated the Cree second-person plural, *-mwa,* with the most common second-person marker in Yurok, *-m;* but the prefix marker for the second person in Algic is *k-,* a point to which we will return later.

In Mosan, the Salishan languages in general have *n* in the first person, e.g. Tillamook *n-* and Kalispel *-ən,* both 'my.' Kalispel also has the second-person plural subject *-əm.* Some of these languages lack nasal consonants; the second-person plural *-p* is common. In Wakashan, Nootka has *newa* 'we' and *-ni* for almost all first-person plural forms of the verb; Bella Bella has *-ən* for the first-person singular verb subject. In another branch of Mosan, Quileute, a language without nasal consonants, has *l* < **n* for the first person. In the third subgroup of Almosan, Kutenai, we find the first-person-singular imperative object *-ən* and the second-person singular reflexive imperative *-m.*

As for the other branch of Almosan-Keresiouan, consisting of Siouan, Yuchi, Caddoan, Iroquoian, and Keresan, the only sure trace of these pronominal forms seems to be in Keresan: the first-person singular and plural independent pronoun in Santa Ana is *hinu,* contrasting with the second-person pronoun *hisu.* There is also a series of verbal hortative forms with the suffix *-n* in the first person.

The first scholar, to my knowledge, who was aware of the widespread distribution of *n* and *m* as first- and second-person markers in both North and South America was Morris Swadesh (1954: 311), who noted that "at least two short elements, *n* for the first person and *m* for the second, can be safely added to the list of recurrent elements even though they do not meet the CVC requirement." It was at least a year after he made this statement that I first directed my attention to Amerindian languages. Unaware of Swadesh's observation (which was made very much in passing and without documentation), I myself soon noted the widespread distribution of the *n* and *m* markers. That two scholars should independently make the same basic observation is an interesting sidelight in the argument for the Amerind grouping as I have defined it.

What conclusions can we legitimately draw from the widespread distribution of *n* and *m* alone? The most obvious is that it cannot be simply the result of borrowing. There are few if any authenticated instances of the borrowing of a first- or second-person pronoun. That an utterly improbable event should have recurred more than a hundred times surpasses the bounds of credibility. Another possibility is accident, that is, resemblance by convergent change from originally different elements. Though this is distinctly more probable, such an accident could hardly have occurred spontaneously anything like a hundred or more times. Moreover, it must have occurred for both *n* and *m* in many languages, from Chinook in the far northwest to Araucanian in Chile. Let us allow accidents, but at most, this would lead us to posit conceivably three or four different stocks.

Does the fact that a few Amerind languages have neither *n*- nor *m*- refute their membership in these one or more large groupings? Certainly not. Genetic affinity cannot be disproved on the grounds of specific differences alone, since no aspect of language—not even pronouns—is completely immutable. It is only where the positive evidence is insufficient or the differences point consistently to some other hypothesis that the argument against a grouping can be sustained. This somewhat obvious point is often violated in negative arguments in the literature.

It is the business of science to note non-random phenomena and to explain them. Were we to plot the occurrence of specific first- and second-person markers on a world map, we would not fail to notice a clustering of first-person *m* and second-person *t* (along with *s*) in Europe, northern Asia, and the northern part of North America as far as Greenland, with a second clustering of first person *n* and second person *m* covering the rest of the Americas, outside of the Eskimo-Aleut and Na-Dene areas. In my opinion, this observation alone would suffice to lead any historically minded anthropologist to the view that there must be at least one very large stock to account for the first set and another to account for the second set.

As evidence for the relationship of Algonquian, Yurok, and Wıyot, Sapir cited a set of four person markers: *n*- 'first person,' *k*- 'second person,' *w*- 'third person,' and *m*- 'someone's, indefinite possessor.' We have already seen that first-person *n* occurs throughout Amerind and that *m* occurs as a second-person marker marginally in Algonquian and prominently in Yurok. But what of the *k*- that marks the second person in all of the Algic languages in the above series?

In a discussion of Algonquian, Charles Hockett (1966) noted that in the *k*- so used, there is something like an association of the first and the second person, as shown in its occurrence in markers that express the first-person inclusive plural, the first person acting on the second person, or the second person acting on the first person. Evidence for this *k-* as a first-person inclusive in other Amerind languages is widespread. In particular the Carib languages have a *ki-* prefix for the first-person inclusive (generally dual), for the first person acting on the second person, and for the second person acting on the first person. This *k-*, as will be seen in the discussion of grammatical morphemes of various Amerind subgroups (Chapter 5), has developed in other groups (e.g. Hokan) from an inclusive pronoun into a general first-person plural and then, occasionally, into a singular first-person marker. The only thing lacking is the specialized second-person usage of Algic, which can be recognized in this light as an innovation that developed from a general Amerind *k-* prefix for the first-person inclusive plural (originally more likely dual).

Almost without exception, it is a worldwide typological fact that when there is a distinction between the first-person inclusive and the first-person exclusive in the dual or plural, the inclusive is either a separate element or analyzable as first person plus second person. We shall call such a case the *inclusive person,* giving 1, 2, 1 + 2, and 3. With plural markers, 1 + plural is the first-person exclusive plural ('I and the others'), 1 + 2 in the plural is inclusive ('I and you'), and 2 + plural ('you') and 3 + plural ('they') are second- and third-person plurals, respectively. Such systems are found in various parts of the world (e.g. the Philippines). It is a very common typological development, as in Hokan, for the pluralized inclusive person to develop into a general first-person plural.

There is little at this point to say about the Algic third-person prefix *w-*. It may well be another innovation. As has been seen, *i-* is the most common Amerindian third-person marker, but *w-* and *u-* appear sporadically.

The Algic *m-* as impersonal possessor is less problematical. By a well-known phenomenon within Algic, *m-* becomes a generic noun marker, and the prefix *m-* in petrified form is then reinterpreted as part of the root, to which prefixes are added anew. Thus 'somebody's hand' is reinterpreted as a general abstract word for 'hand' and then receives the usual personal prefixes. Michelson, as we have seen, rejected Sapir's Algic hypothesis, stating that "it is a well-known fact that in Proto-Algonquian times stems with initial **m-* have non-initial cognates lacking this *m-*" (1938: 103). Similarly, in cognates among Algonquian, Wiyot, and Yurok, forms in one language containing *m-* often are related to forms in another without *m-*.

As noted by Haas (1958: 165), and Michelson before her, many Algonquian body parts end in -an. Within Sapir's Algonquian-Wakashan, clear traces of both m- and -an are found in Salish. Aert Kuipers (1967: 116), in his grammar of Squamish, a Salishan language belonging to a non-Algic branch of Algonquian-Wakashan, lists "m- a prefix found on body parts." An example from another Salishan language, Upper Chehalis, is *maqsn* 'nose.' That this word consists of three parts, *ma-qs-n*, is shown by the fact that here and elsewhere in Salish *-qs-* alone means 'nose.' Since this root is not found in Algic, borrowing is out of the question. Moreover, there are other survivals of m-. One involves a series of Salishan cognates with Algonquian: Kalispel *-qin-* 'head,' Musqueam *meqn* 'hair,' Siciatl *maken* 'hair,' and so forth. Compare Proto-Algonquian *mi:kwana* 'quill, feather,' from which we have, for example, Menomini *me:kon* 'feather' and Cheyenne *meʔkon* 'hair.' * There is much additional evidence that Algonquian-Wakashan is a valid grouping. It may turn out that Algonquian-Wakashan is the only one of Sapir's groupings (outside of Na-Dene and Eskimo-Aleut) that is a valid genetic unit at any level—a nice bit of irony, indeed, since of all his overall groupings, this one has probably been greeted with the greatest skepticism.

Thus, in a broader context, each of Sapir's four Algic pronominal prefixes has a different historical status. First-person n- is Amerind; second-person k- derives from an Amerind marker of inclusive person that has become specialized as a second-person marker in Algic; third-person w- is difficult to say anything definite about; and the prefix m-, at least in its indefinite use, is an Almosan innovation (in Chapter 5 we will consider the possibility that it derives from the widespread, and probably Proto-Amerind, distance demonstrative and third-person pronoun m-).

Consider as a final piece of preliminary evidence the forms of the words for 'hand' and for the related ideas of 'give' and 'take' listed in Table 9. The Amerind etymological dictionary (Chapter 4) includes numerous additional instances under etymology no. 137 (HAND$_1$); see also Swadesh (1954: 309). What makes this evidence particularly cogent is the existence of variant forms of a similar type—namely, with the suffix -k or sometimes -ka attached to a base *ma* or the like—appearing both in North and in South America. My own guess is that *ma* was originally a verb, and that -ki is a very old Amerind noun-forming suffix from which a denominative verb occasionally was later formed (compare English 'to hand'). Very common also

---

*The -an body-part suffix occurs elsewhere in Amerind, particularly in North America.

Table 9. The Amerind Etymology 'Hand, Give, Take'

Language	Cognate	Gloss	Language	Cognate	Gloss
	MACRO-GE			EQUATORIAL	
Botocudo	am	give	Proto-Tupi	*me?eŋ	give
Karaho	i-ma	give me! [a]	Timote	ma	bring
Kamakan	ma, mane	give	Taparita	mea	hand
Bororo	mako	give		CENTRAL AMERIND	
	MACRO-PANOAN		Uto-Aztecan	*ma-; *maka,	hand, action
Caripuna	moken	hand		*mika	with the hand;
Amahuaca	maka	hand			give
Lengua	amik	hand	Taos	mān	hand
Payagua	i-mahiar	my hand	Kiowa	mã	hand
	ANDEAN			PENUTIAN	
Alakaluf	merr	arm	Wappo	me?, mɛ	hand [b]
Ona	mar	arm, hand	Maidu	ma; maha	hand; bring
Kahuapana	imira	hand	Central Sierra		
Mayna	mani	arm	Miwok	ammə	give
Quechua	maki	hand	Chinook	m-	to hand
	CHIBCHAN-PAEZAN		Mixe	ma	give
			Totonac	makan	hand
Ayoman	man	hand	Tunica	muhi	carry in the
Itonama	ma-	action with			hand
		the hand		HOKAN	
Chimu	mæča	hand			
Rama	mukuik	hand	Tequistlatec	mane	arm, hand
Xinca	mux	finger	Akwa'ala	man	hand
	MACRO-TUCANOAN		Salinan	maa; ma?a	hand; bring,
					carry
Sara	amo	hand	Yana	moh-	take along
Auake	umē	arm	Chimariko	mai	carry
Puinave	mo	arm	East Pomo	ma	hold
Catuquina	mu	palm of the		ALMOSAN	
		hand	Algonquian	*mi:; *mi:-l	hand; give
			Blackfoot	-mi	hand
			Kwakiutl	maχwa	give a
					potlatch

[a] With first-person *i-* discussed earlier.
[b] Also instrumental prefix.

is a nasal extension, giving forms like *ma-n*, which may well be the body-part suffix *-an* mentioned earlier; for example, Totonac seems to add *-an* to the form *mak-* in *makan* 'hand.'

This narrow survey is intended only to give a certain plausibility to the contention that all of the indigenous languages of the Americas, except the Na-Dene and Eskimo-Aleut families, form a single vast linguistic unit. The material on Amerind proper, to which the bulk of this volume is devoted, is organized in the following fashion. In the next chapter, Chapter 3, the 11 stocks we have been discussing—Macro-Ge, Macro-Panoan, Macro-Carib, Equatorial, Macro-Tucanoan, Andean, Chibchan-Paezan, Central Amerind, Hokan, Penutian, and Almosan-Keresiouan—are treated individually, and a set of etymologies exclusive to each is given. Etymologies found in two or more stocks are presented in the Amerind etymological dictionary (Chapter 4); the entries where these appear are listed in the appropriate section in Chapter 3.

This system is, of course, not entirely satisfactory, but is, I believe, the least of four evils, the other three being (1) repeating the etymologies in both places, (2) including all etymologies in one dictionary, even those found in only one stock, and (3) citing all etymologies found in each stock, regardless of their broader distribution, or lack of it, with the general etymological dictionary consisting only of an index referring to each occurrence of a particular etymology in each of the stocks in which it occurs and thus giving no overall picture of the more widespread etymologies.

Chapter 5 complements the lexical evidence provided in Chapters 3 and 4, presenting grammatical evidence for Amerind and its 11 stocks. The rest of the text is given over to two chapters. Chapter 6 is devoted to what has become known as the Na-Dene problem; and Chapter 7 gives an overview of the work and some of its historical implications, discusses the genetic position of Eskimo-Aleut, and summarizes the current status of world linguistic classification, taking into consideration the results of this volume. The book concludes with two mathematical appendixes, two tables showing the distribution of the Amerind etymologies, a summary of the classification, an index to the etymologies, and an index of language names.

Before we turn to the details of the 11 stocks of Amerind, a few words on their classification and exposition. To begin with, the order of presentation is south to north throughout the book; this has no particular significance, merely reflecting how I assembled my materials. As for the 11 stocks themselves, I consider some well established as valid groupings, others less so. The validity of Amerind as a whole is more secure than that of any of its stocks. This is a familiar situation. For example, there is no doubt concerning just which languages belong to the vast Austronesian family, but subgrouping has proved difficult and has not led to any generally accepted result.

In the case of certain Indo-European languages known only from a limited body of inscriptions (e.g. Venetic), their status as Indo-European is not in doubt, but their precise genetic position within the family is uncertain. After all, more evidence is required to show that a language is Italic than that it is Indo-European.

In the case of Amerind I do not believe we are as badly off as with Austronesian. Some groupings are quite clear. Others are not, and this is so at two very different levels. At the lowest level are instances like Venetic, where the existing material makes the general affiliation certain, but is so sparse that the subgroup assignment is difficult. At a higher level it is often difficult to say whether some large group of, say, 50 languages is closer genetically to one or another comparable grouping, either because of the sheer mass of material or because of factors like those involved in Austronesian. In Appendix B, a mathematical model is proposed that will, I hope, help us understand just why these difficulties do or do not arise in specific classes of instances.

In fact, I do not maintain that the 11 stocks set out in this book are of equal genetic status. On the contrary. Macro-Ge and Macro-Panoan, for example, are particularly close, and together with the somewhat more distant Macro-Carib, form a broader Ge-Pano-Carib branch of Amerind. This agrees in essentials with the grouping proposed in Greenberg (1960). Likewise, Equatorial has a special relationship to Macro-Tucanoan. But where I included both with Andean in an Equatorial-Andean group in 1960, I now believe that Andean is probably a separate stock of Amerind. Chibchan-Paezan and Central Amerind also seem to form separate stocks. On the other hand, Hokan, Penutian, and Almosan-Keresiouan show sufficient exclusively shared traits to justify their consideration as stocks of equal status in a broader Northern Amerind branch.

We can thus aggregate the 11 stocks to six branches: (1) Ge-Pano-Carib, (2) Equatorial-Tucanoan, (3) Andean, (4) Chibchan-Paezan, (5) Central Amerind, and (6) Northern Amerind. It is by no means excluded that some of these branches might be further grouped at a higher level, but provisionally, at least, they are considered coordinate. (For a number of reasons, I have found the 11-stock division better suited to the presentation of etymologies.)

In light of the foregoing, not all the etymologies in the Amerind dictionary can be considered evidence for the unity of Amerind. Obviously, an etymology represented only in Macro-Ge, Macro-Panoan, and Macro-Carib, though it attests to the existence of a Ge-Pano-Carib grouping, cannot be marshaled in support of Amerind as a whole. Such etymologies attest either to intermediate groupings within Amerind (e.g. Ge-Pano-Carib) or to the incompleteness of our data. Despite such problems and ambiguities inherent in a work of this nature, we still have ample evidence (buttressed by the grammatical data in Chapter 5) for a single Amerind family, for the six branches delineated above, for the 11 stocks treated in Chapter 3, and for still lower-level entities. These etymologies succeed, I maintain, on both *qualitative* and *distributional* grounds. On the first ground, let us take, for the sake of comparison, the Indo-European etymology for the number 'four,' in which we find both Germanic and Slavic forms (along with forms from other branches). Obviously, within Germanic, English 'four' and German *vier* are more similar to each other than either is to Russian *četyry,* just as *četyry* resembles Polish *cztery* more than it does either of the Germanic forms. There are many such instances in the Amerind etymologies, for example, the etymology FLEA, in which the Penutian entries show *p-* as against *m-* elsewhere. The distributional factor is illustrated by the existence of a number of Chibchan-Paezan etymologies in which either Chibchan occurs without Paezan or vice versa. Such etymologies clearly strengthen the case for considering each a group in its own right, as proposed in Chapter 3.

Admittedly, some of the etymologies are less convincing than others. It is the truly strong ones that establish the classification, since the links shown require the hypothesis of an Amerind family along the lines proposed. But any examination of etymological dictionaries of well-established families such as Indo-European will reveal the same phenomenon. Moreover, there are many instances of particular entries that are rejected by some scholars or placed under different etymologies by others. This study is a pioneer one; subsequent work will certainly lead to modifications as entries are added, subtracted, or transferred from one etymology to another. For all that, I am confident there is a large enough core of highly probable etymologies in Chapters 3 and 4 to establish the validity of both the Amerind family as a whole and its 11 stocks.

Finally, it should be noted that the exclusion of Na-Dene and Eskimo-Aleut rests simply on the fact that Amerind languages share an enormous common heritage of grammatical and lexical elements not found in either of those families. Of course there are occasional resemblances, attributable either to accident or to common membership in some still deeper grouping. An instructive example is the following. Among the Amerind etymologies is one listed under FINGER, but more accurately reconstructed as ONE in some subgroups (e.g. Karok *ti:k* 'hand, finger,' Yagua *tiki* 'one'). In Na-

Dene, we find an Eyak (Yakutat) form *tikhi* 'one' and a Tlingit root variously reported as *tlexʔ* (Boas) 'one' and *tl'eq* (Velten) 'finger.' We also find that among the etymologies cited by Uhlenbeck for connecting Eskimo with Indo-European is Eskimo *tik-iq* 'index finger' and Indo-European **deik-* 'point' (cf. Latin *digitus* 'finger,' assigned by many to the same Indo-European root). In addition, we have Sino-Tibetan *tik* 'one' (Benedict 1976) and Ainu *tek* 'hand.' And in my own work on African languages, the Nilo-Saharan etymology for 'one' includes such forms as Maba *tek* and Fur *dik*. It may be more widely distributed for aught I know. The few resemblances that I have found between Na-Dene and Amerind tend to be of this sort, and it is likely that some of these reflect a common inheritance from a very extensive family—which may even be proto-Sapiens.

Chapter 3

The Subgroups of Amerind

In this chapter, we begin our study of Amerind, a linguistic stock that embraces most of the New World languages, by examining its 11 subgroups in detail. Evidence for each of these subgroups—Macro-Ge, Macro-Panoan, Macro-Carib, Equatorial, Macro-Tucanoan, Andean, Chibchan-Paezan, Central Amerind, Hokan, Penutian, and Almosan-Keresiouan—is presented in a separate section. Each section is organized along roughly the same lines. First I discuss the languages and language groups in the subgroup and sketch their classificational history; then I give an alphabetical list of the etymologies in the Amerind dictionary where entries for that subgroup appear; and last I present a set of etymologies that are exclusive to the subgroup and thus provide evidence for its validity.

For reasons of space, I have not given the exact source for every citation in the etymologies. As noted earlier, the interested reader will find these in the notebooks on deposit at Stanford University's Green Library. The sources used for reconstructed forms are identified in the text. Citations are given by subgroup in alphabetical order. Where more than one language is involved, both the subgroup name and the language name are given, the subgroup name first. But where the only citation is for a language in a subgroup of the same name, the subgroup name is dropped as redundant. Although I have proposed some intermediate groupings within certain of the 11 Amerind subgroups, as discussed in this chapter (and as shown in the classification in Appendix D), the component groups are listed separately in the etymologies. For example, within the Andean family I have identified both a Northern and a Southern subgroup (as well as other subgroups), but the

families that comprise these two intermediate groupings are listed alphabetically in the Andean etymologies. Similarly, Yukian and Gulf are listed
separately in the Penutian etymologies, even though I consider them a single
group. In the Almosan-Keresiouan etymologies Wiyot and Yurok are listed
separately under Algic, though I am inclined to believe (like Sapir) that the
Ritwan grouping is valid.

Obviously not every etymology represents a lexical item that was
present in the ancestral language of one of the 11 Amerind groups. In a
good number of cases they represent innovations within a particular subgroup. However, since the internal subgrouping of the 11 Amerind groups
remains largely unknown, it is usually not possible to be sure whether an
item derives from the ancestral Proto-language, or is a later innovation in a
specific subgroup. When an etymology is apparently restricted to such a
lower-level subgroup, say, Southern Andean, an abbreviation (in this case,
S) will follow the etymology to indicate this restricted distribution. The abbreviations used are given in the appropriate sections of this chapter. The
same abbreviations are used in the Amerind dictionary, though there the restricted distribution indicates not a later innovation, but rather the apparent
loss of the item in the rest of the family, as the larger Amerind context
demonstrates.

MACRO-GE

Ge has long been recognized as one of the major stocks of South America, comparable in its geographical spread, number of consitituent languages, and obvious unity to such other South American groups as Carib,
Arawak, and Tupi, or to Siouan or Algonquian in North America. Martius,
in his pioneer two-volume work of 1867, was the first to distinguish Ge as a
separate ethno-linguistic group. But he went even further, proposing that this
group belongs to a still larger one, alongside a number of Mashakali languages, forming what is now known as Macro-Ge (Macro-Je). There is no
doubt that Martius considered the connection genetic, since he calls the Ge
and Mashakali languages dialects of the same language and presents a table
comparing 11 basic words in all of them. He also distinguishes another
group, which he calls Cren, containing Botocudo, Puri, Guato, and Malali.
What is curious here is that Malali is actually a Mashakali language, as recognized even by the ultra-conservative Loukotka. This gives a grouping con-

sisting in modern terms of Ge, Mashakali, Botocudo, Puri, and Guato, all of which I consider to be Macro-Ge.

The next to add to our knowledge of this group was Loukotka, who successively considered Mashakali (1931), Kamakan (1932), and Coroado (an alternative name for the Puri group in the 1930's; 1937). In the first of these studies, he talks of a Ge group that includes, besides the closely related Kaingan (often included in Ge itself), Kamakan, Mashakali, Botocudo, Puri, and Opaie. He concludes that these languages (plus Iate [Fulnio], which he includes in his comparisons) "present few resemblances" with "the other languages of Brazil" (1931:34).

All this might lead one to think that the relationship among the languages is genetic, but this is not Loukotka's view, as is evident from his remarks in an unpublished paper given at the International Congress of Americanists in Hamburg in 1930 and cited in the paper on Mashakali: "We are not concerned here with a single linguistic group, but with eight linguistic families that have a certain number of common elements" (p. 22). We must remember that Loukotka believed in mixed languages. Here eight stocks are presumably all mixed with each other. Still, in this study and the subsequent articles, Loukotka's pairwise comparison of these languages makes a useful contribution yielding a considerable number of convicing etymologies. In the view of Irvine Davis, who took up these questions some 30 years later, the similarities Loukotka detected "involve a number of items that can be reconstructed for Proto-Je and are sufficient to establish beyond reasonable doubt that Kamakan, Puri, and Botocudo indeed belong within Macro-Je" (1966: 25).

Davis himself, in this same article, reconstructs 112 Proto-Ge items. Included in his study was Kaingan, the most deviant branch. In the second paper, published in 1968, he compared Ge with Mashakali and Caraja, and reconstructs 71 forms. Here he concludes that Opaie (Ofaye), Kamakan, Mashakali, Caraja, Puri, and Botocudo, like Ge-Kaingan, can be stated with some confidence to be Macro-Ge. In Greenberg (1960), I included all of the languages mentioned, and a few others, in Macro-Ge. When material on Erikbatsa became available for the first time (Christinat 1963), I concluded that it too was Macro-Ge. (An article by J. Bosswood, published in Brazil in 1973 and entitled "Evidence for the Inclusion of Arikpatsa in the Macro-Ge Phylum," has only recently come to my attention. I have not yet been able to obtain it, but it evidently arrives at the same conclusion.) Among others interested in this group, we can add the name of Floyd Lounsbury, who worked on Bororo and noted its relationship to Ge in the mid-1950's.

Macro-Ge may be considered a well-defined grouping at some level, incorporating the following 15 subgroups: Bororo, Botocudo, Caraja, Chiquito, Erikbatsa, Fulnio, Ge, Guato, Kaingan, Kamakan, Mashakali, Opaie, Oti, Puri, and Yabuti. With the exception of Chiquito, Oti, and Yabuti, all these languages have been grouped with Ge by previous investigators. But these three languages are as validly Macro-Ge as the others. We are simply once more dealing with the fact that in this case linguists have not made comprehensive comparisons. That many are unwilling to consider any evidence not collected by well-trained modern investigators only makes the matter worse. Davis's inclusion of languages like Kamakan, based on earlier vocabularies, is a welcome lapse into common sense.

Except for the special relationship of Ge to Kaingan, which are so close that it becomes a mere matter of terminology whether we call Kaingan languages members of the Ge family, I do not find any strong evidence for further subgroupings. In the comparative grammatical discussion in Chapter 5, Ge and Kaingan are treated separately. However, because the etymologies involving only these two groups are very numerous and the special relationship between them is not in dispute, they will not be presented here. Two languages, Yabuti (actually a group consisting of Yabuti, Mashubi, and Arikapu) and Oti, are known only from brief vocabularies and so do not figure frequently in the etymologies. There are enough occurrences that are diagnostically Macro-Ge, however, to support their inclusion in the group.

In this set of etymologies, all Proto-Ge forms are from Davis. In addition to the 123 exclusively Macro-Ge etymologies presented here, there are 103 Macro-Ge entries in the Amerind dictionary under the following etymologies: $ABOVE_1$, $ABOVE_2$, ARM_1, ARRIVE, ARROW, ASHES, ASK_2, $BACK_2$, BAD_1, BE_1, BEE_1, $BELLY_1$, $BELLY_2$, $BELLY_4$, $BITE_1$, $BITTER_1$, $BLACK_2$, $BLACK_3$, TO BLOW, $BODY_1$, $BODY_2$, $BONE_1$, BREAST, BROTHER, $CARRY_1$, CHEST, $CHILD_1$, $CHILD_3$, CLOSE, $CLOUD_1$, COME, DIE_1, DIE_3, DIRTY, $DRINK_1$, $EARTH_3$, EAT_2, $EXCREMENT_1$, EYE, TO FALL, FAR, TO FEAR, $FEATHER_2$, $FINGER_1$, $FIRE_1$, $FIRE_2$, FIREWOOD, FLY (v.), FLY_1, $FOOT_1$, $FOREHEAD_2$, FRUIT, GO_1, GO_2, $GUTS_1$, $HAND_1$, $HAND_2$, $HAND_3$, $HEAD_1$, $HEAD_2$, $HEAVEN_1$, HIT, HUSBAND, KILL, $LARGE_1$, $LEAF_1$, LEG, $LONG_1$, $LOUSE_1$, $MAKE_1$, MAN_3, $MANY_1$, $MEAT_2$, $MEAT_4$, $MOON_1$, MOSQUITO, $MOUTH_2$, NECK, NOSE, $RIVER_2$, SAY_1, SEE_3, $SEED_2$, SEEK, SIT_1, $SKIN_1$,

SLEEP₁, SNAKE₁, STAR₁, STONE₁, SUN₁, TESTICLE, THIN, TONGUE₂, TONGUE₃, WATER₂, WIND, WISH, WOOD₂, WORK₂, YESTERDAY, YOUNG.

MACRO-GE ETYMOLOGIES

1 ALL   Bororo: Umotina *bota*. Botocudo *pota*. Caraja *ibote*. Ge: Kraho *piti*, Ramkokamekran *hipudu* 'full.' Kamakan: Masacara [pautzöh] 'many.'

2 ANT   Botocudo *prik*. Caraja *waθa*. Fulnio *fetaloa*. Ge: Krenje *preme*, Apinage *muruma*. Guato *ma-fara* (Guato *ma-* is a stage III article found with most nouns). Puri *putu*.

3 ARROW   Ge: Ramkokamekran *pænni* 'thorn.' Kaingan: Tibagi *pan* 'to shoot,' Dalbergia *pænū* 'to shoot' (sing. subject). Kamakan *wān*. Mashakali: Mashakali *pahan*, Macuni *paan*. Puri: Coroado *apun*, Coropo *pan*, *fan*.

4 AUNT   Bororo *ituje* 'sister.' Ge: Krenje *tije*, Kradaho *tuia* 'grandmother.' Mashakali: Malali *ate, ita* 'woman,' Capoxo *ataj*. Opaie: Opaie *či-otoje* 'mother,' *taje, teje* 'woman,' Guachi *outie* 'woman.'

5 BACK   Bororo: Bororo *i-puru*, Umotina *i-puru*. Caraja *bra*. Chiquito *i-piri-ki* 'behind.' Ge: Krenje *poti* 'spine,' Ramkokamekran *panjatudu*, *panjonko* 'buttocks.' Guato *ipana* 'tail.' Kaingan: Apucarana *pani*, Tibagi *pani* 'back, behind.'

6 BARK (SKIN)   Guato *(ma)-fæ* 'skin' (Schmidt), *i-fai* (Martius) 'skin.' Puri: Coroado *pe*

7 BEAUTIFUL₁   Ge: Krenje *pej* 'beautiful, good.' Mashakali: Mashakali *epai*, Capoxo *epai*, Malali *epoi*, Macuni *ibai* 'good.'

8 BEAUTIFUL₂   Botocudo *potain* 'good.' Ge: Apinage *baati, pet*, Ramkokamekran *impeid*. Puri *bate*.

9 BELLY   Bororo: Umotina *ɔna* 'abdomen.' Ge: Kradaho *i-nioŋu*, Northern Cayapo *i-ñin*. Mashakali: Mashakali *inioñ*, Macuni *añion*.

10 BITE (v.)   Kaingan: Dalbergia *plɔ* (sing. subject), Tibagi *pra*. Kamakan: Meniens *imbro*.

11 BITTER   Botocudo *korok*. Caraja *i-šøra*. Chiquito *okoro* 'be sour.' Kamakan *kwade* 'be sharp.'

12 BLACK   Botocudo *him, hime*. Oti *hon*.

13 BLOOD   Bororo *ku*. Puri: Coropo *iku*.

14 BONE   Botocudo *kjiæk*. Kaingan *kuka*.

15 BREATHE   Bororo *akke*. Chiquito *at^si* (internal reconstruction: **aki*).

16 BROTHER₁   Ge: Cayapo *itɔ, itoŋ*, Karaho *tõ* (*tõi* 'sister'), Krenje *tõ* 'younger brother.' Kamakan: Meniens *ato*. Cf. AUNT.

17 BROTHER₂   Botocudo *kijak* 'brother, sister.' Kamakan *kejak*.

18 BURN (v.)   Botocudo *pek*. Erikbatsa *okpog-maha* (*-maha* is a verbal suffix). Ge: Karaho *puk*.

19 CALL (v.)   Bororo: Bororo *kie* 'name' (n.), *akɔ, agɔ* 'says,' Umotina *akaro* 'shout.' Ge: Proto-Ge **kɔ(r)*. Guato *okaaje*. Kaingan: Palmas, Tibagi *ke* 'say.'

20 CLEAN   Botocudo *kurĩ* 'to clean.' Kaingan: Tibagi *kyron* 'new.' Kamakan [kekorroh] 'white.'

21 COLD   Caraja *k(e)re*. Ge: Proto-Ge **kry*.

22 COVER (v.)   Bororo: Bororo *mi* 'to close,' Umotina *momi* 'to close.' Ge: Kradaho *emi*.

23 CROCODILE₁   Bororo *amema* 'lizard.' Ge: Proto-Ge **mĩ, *mĩñ*. Mashakali *mãʔãŋ*.

24 CROCODILE₂   Botocudo *čaj*. Kamakan *uhie*. Mashakali: Malali *ae*.

25 CROOKED   Botocudo *ntang, tangtang*. Ge: Krenje *tone*.

26 CRY (v.)   Chiquito *ipu*. Fulnio *fowa* 'shout.' Kaingan: Tibagi *fa, fua*. Mashakali *opo* 'he cries.'

27 CUT (v.)   Bororo *ki, ka*. Botocudo [gyh]. Chiquito *ki* 'to flay.' Cf. Opaie *kijeñi* 'knife.'

28 DAY   Caraja *tiuu* 'day, sun.' Chiquito *t^suu* 'day, sun.' Guato *ma-čuo*. Kamakan [yöçö?] 'day, sun.'

29 DEFECATE   Botocudo *inku* 'excrement.' Caraja *ku*. Ge: Krenje *ikwø*, Kraho *khwy*, Ishikrin *ikoa*, Cayapo *ikuo* 'excrement.'

30 DOG   Caraja *avoa(i)* 'jaguar.' Chiquito *bau* 'animal.' Guato *ma-vii*, *(ma)-væ*. Kaingan: Southern Kaingan *ba, mban*.

31 DRESS   Botocudo *atak* 'to cover' (bedecken). Caraja *deke, deku* 'woman's shirt,' *taku* 'clothing.'

32 DRINK₁ (v.)   Botocudo *žop*. Mashakali *ĩ-čoob*.

33 DRINK₂ (v.)   Bororo: Bororo *kudu(o)*, Umotina *i-kotu*. Fulnio *i-kote*.

34 EAR   Bororo: Bororo *bia, via*, Umotina *(m)bia*. Guato *(ma)-ve, (ma)-vi*.

35 EARTH   Fulnio *fea, fe*. Guato *(ma)-fo*.

36 EGG   Chiquito *čiki* 'egg, testicle.' Fulnio *eska* 'egg, testicle.' Cf. Kamakan: Meniens *sakre*.

37 EYE₁   Botocudo *ketom*. Chiquito [çuto] 'eye, hole, window.' Kamakan:

Kamakan [kodoh], Cotoxo *kitho, kedo.* Mashakali: Malali *keto,*
Hahahay *ačeto.*

38 EYE₂   Fulnio *i-to.* Ge: Proto-Ge **nɔ,* Krenje *to,* Northern Cayapo *into,*
Acroamirim *aintho,* etc.

39 FALL (v.)   Kaingan *kuta, kute.* Kamakan *kičei.* Mashakali: Macuni
gote.

40 FAT   Ge: Proto-Ge **twəm* 'fat, grease.' Kaingan: Came *taimbe* (adj.),
Tibagi *tang* (adj.), etc. Mashakali *-top.*

41 FEMALE   Botocudo *tontan* 'wife.' Kaingan: Palmas *tantā.* Oti *dondu-
ede* (*ede* 'person' inferred from *inuade* 'man' and other forms).

42 FEW   Ge: Krenje *kri,* Crengez *nkrie.* Puri: Coroado *kre.*

43 FINGER   Botocudo *kekri* 'joint.' Bororo: Bororo *kera* 'hand,' Otuke
keara 'hand.' Ge: Krenje *krāʔi,* Cayapo *i-ni-krai.* Kamakan: Kamakan
in-kru 'hand,' Cotoxo *nin-kre* 'hand.'

44 FISH (n.)   Ge: Proto-Ge **tɛp.* Kamakan *topa* 'meat.'

45 FLAT   Botocudo *impa.* Ge: Proto-Ge **pɔ* 'broad.'

46 FLOUR   Mashakali: Malali *kuniæ,* Capoxo *kon.* Yabuti *ukoni* 'ashes,
salt.'

47 FOREST   Ge: Chavante *anta.* Kamakan: Cotoxo *antho,* Meniens *anto.*

48 FRIEND   Bororo *media, meduia, mede.* Fulnio *i-mti.*

49 FROG₁   Ge: Apinage *pri* 'toad,' Kradaho *bri.* Opaie *pera* 'toad.'

50 FROG₂   Bororo *ru* 'toad.' Caraja *ara.*

51 FRUIT   Caraja *te* 'seed.' Chiquito *ita.* Mashakali *-taʔ* (But Davis
compares the Mashakali form with Proto-Ge **rā* 'flower' and Caraja *ra*
'fruit.')

52 GOOD₁   Bororo: Koraveka *ɛmaka,* Otuke *i-maxa-he* 'je vais bien.' Ge:
Proto-Ge **mɛč.* Mashakali *mač.* Puri: Coroado *mɛka* 'beautiful.'

53 GOOD₂   Bororo *akku* 'cleanliness,' *aku-(dda)* 'to clean.' Fulnio *kaka.*
Kaingan: Came *ke.* Kamakan: Cotoxo *koiki.* Cf. WHITE₂.

54 GRANDFATHER   Fulnio *i-ito,* *tʰej.* Ge: Apinage *tui.* Puri: Coroado
anta.

55 GRASS   Bororo: Otuke *oro* 'straw.' Kaingan: Tibagi *are* 'field, grass,'
Apucarana *re* 'field,' Guarapuava *ere* 'field.'

56 HAIR₁   Botocudo *ke.* Chiquito *iki* 'down.' Ge: Proto-Ge **ki,* Kaingan:
Guarapuava *kek.* Kamakan *ka, ke.* Mashakali: Malali *akø* 'head,' *kai*
'hair.' Puri: Puri *ke,* Coroado *ke* 'head, hair.' Yabuti: Arikapu *ši-kaæ*
'head.'

57 HAIR₂   Caraja *ira* 'cabaleira.' Erikbatsa *ka-ari.* Fulnio *li.* Ge: Krenje
ara 'down.'

58 HARD   Chiquito *taio*. Fulnio *t'ea*. Ge: Krenje *tøj* 'hard, strong.' Kaingan: Dalbergia *tuju* 'strong.'

59 HEAD   Bororo: Otuke *i-kita*. Botocudo *kræn, ku*. Caraja *ra(-dʃi)*. Ge: Proto-Ge **krā*. Kaingan: Palmas *krī*, Bugre *akreng*, etc. Kamakan: Kamakan [herrah], Masacara [acharoh]. Opaie *kate, kete, kite*. (Davis connects the Ge and Caraja forms.)

60 HEAR₁   Bororo *mearu, meru*. Ge: Proto-Ge **ma, *mar*. Kaingan: Came *me*, Tibagi *me*.

61 HEAR₂   Botocudo *apa*. Ge: Karaho *pa*.

62 HERE   Botocudo *kre*. Kaingan: Aweikoma *kri*. Puri: Coroado *kara*, Coropo *kra*.

63 HIT (v.)   Bororo *okori-*. Ge: Aponegicran *i-kura* 'kill,' Crengez *gura* 'kill.' Guato *ne-keera*. Opaie *hẽ-gere-xe* 'kill.'

64 HOLE₁   Botocudo *kro*. Ge: Krenje *kre*, Cayapo *kre*, etc. Opaie *igri* (deduced from the word for 'nostril' = 'nose-hole').

65 HOLE₂   Kaingan *doro* (general in Kaingan languages). Puri: Coroado *dore* 'cave.'

66 HOT   Botocudo *kerong* 'burning.' Ge: Northern Cayapo *krenkio*. Kamakan *granka*.

67 HOUSE   Bororo *bai, baa, baha* 'village.' Chiquito *poo*. Kamakan: Masacara *pa*.

68 HOW MANY?   Botocudo *tan*. Kaingan: Palmas *ndena*.

69 KILL   Bororo: Bororo *bi* 'die,' Umotina *bia* 'die, kill.' Fulnio *we*. Ge: Proto-Ge **pī(r)*.

70 KNIFE   Fulnio *kʰeči* 'divide.' Ge: Suya *kodu*. Kamakan *kedia*.

71 LEFT (SIDE)   Ge: Proto-Ge **-kɛ, *kɛč*. Mashakali *čač*.

72 LICK   Kaingan *tuma*. Puri: Coroado *tompe, tope*, Coropo *tupe*.

73 LIE (TELL A LIE)   Botocudo *uwin, avin* (n.). Caraja *ibine* 'bad.' Fulnio *wī*. Kaingan: Palmas *vī* 'language,' Serra do Chagu *wen* 'speak,' Tibagi *vin* 'speak.'

74 LIVER   Caraja *baa*. Ge: Proto-Ge **ma*, Crengez *im-pa*, Chavante *in-pa* 'guts.' Guato *ipe*.

75 LOUSE   Bororo *pipi*. Chiquito *apa*. Erikbatsa *pepe*. Ge: Apinage *bi:* 'flea,' Crengez *wape* 'flea.'

76 MAN   Guato *ma-tai, (ma)-de*. Kaingan: Serra do Chagu, Apucarana *ti*. Mashakali: Mashakali *tik, tihejj*, Monachobm *tehej*. Oti *inuade* (*ede* means 'person'; cf. *tardu-ede* 'boy' and *dondu-ede* 'woman').

77 MANY   Caraja *tede* 'very,' *titire* 'very.' Ge: Krenje *te*, Crengez *titi*. Kaingan: Palmas *ete*, Guarapuava *ititi*.

78 MEAT   Botocudo *čin, ačim*. Kaingan: Came *tini*. Mashakali: Mashakali, Macuni, Kumanasho *tiungin*. Puri: Coroado *čama* 'animal.'

79 MONKEY   Ge: Proto-Ge **kukəz*, Apinage *kukoi*, Crengez *kuxui*, etc. Kaingan: Catarina *ngugn*. Mashakali: Patasho *kuki*. Opaie *kai, kaikā*.

80 MOON   Chiquito *paa*. Fulnio *fea* 'star.' Ge: Geico *paang*. Guato *mabeu* 'star,' *upina*. Kamakan *piong* 'star,' Meniens *pinia* 'star,' Cotoxo *peo, piao* 'star.' Mashakali: Mashakali, Patasho *pua*. Puri: Coroado *ope* 'sun.'

81 MOSQUITO   Botocudo *kook* 'fly.' Caraja *ahæ*. Ge: Chavante *kuku* 'fly.' Guato *(ma-)ka*. Kaingan (general) *ka* 'mosquito, fly.' Opaie *kaka* 'fly.'

82 MOUTH   Kaingan: Tibagi *jentky*. Kamakan: Meniens *iniatago*. Mashakali: Malali *ajatako*, Hahahay *ajatoko*.

83 NECK   Caraja *θau*. Chiquito *tii*. Guato *(ma-)to*. Kaingan: Came, etc. *ndui*. Opaie *towe* 'nape,' *toe-hi, tou-ñi*. Puri *thong*, Coroado *tong, ton*.

84 NEW   Botocudo *orang*. Puri: Coroado *oron* 'new moon.'

85 NOSE   Bororo *eno*. Chiquito *i-nja*. Ge: Proto-Ge **ñi-ña-krɛ*, Krenje *nja*. Kaingan: Came, Tibagi *niñe*. Puri: Puri, Coroado *ñe*. Yabuti *ninikokne* (*kokne* = 'aperture'; cf. *ši-šambi-kokne* 'mouth').

86 OLD   Bororo *kuri* 'large.' Chiquito *a-tˢiri-bo* (*tˢ*< **k*). Fulnio *efe-kla* 'old man,' *ke-kla* 'ancestors.' Oti *ekeri*.

87 OTHER   Botocudo *ihoen*. Ge: Krenje *ʔnō*. Kaingan *hon, om*, Dalbergia *on, un*. Yabuti: Mashubi *no*.

88 PAIN   Bororo: Umotina *ori* 'it hurts.' Chiquito *s-ura-k* 'I am sick.'

89 PRESS   Botocudo *atom* 'to squeeze.' Chiquito *tume*.

90 PUT   Fulnio *ne* 'make.' Kaingan: Dalbergia *nɛ* 'to place.'

91 RIVER   Bororo: Otuke *ouru*. Botocudo *aranko* 'lake, swamp.' Caraja *bero*. Kaingan: Palmas *war* 'swamp,' Apucarana, etc. *ore* 'lake.'

92 ROAD   Botocudo *brom, emporong, mporo*. Caraja *rɨi*. Ge: Proto-Ge **prɨ*, Cayapo *pru*.

93 RUN   Botocudo *apron*. Ge: Kraho *apron* (imp.), Cayapo *pron*, etc.

94 SALIVA   Ge: Kadurukre *išu*. Kamakan *jašo*.

95 SHARP (TASTE)   Botocudo *areu*. Chiquito *ari* 'chile, pimiento.'

96 SHARPEN   Botocudo *angrak* 'sharp.' Ge: Southern Cayapo *ži-angro* 'wetstone,' *ñagrø*.

97 SICK   Botocudo *māumāu*. Ge: Kraho *meo-ti* 'I am sick.' Kaingan: Southern Kaingan *amao*. Yabuti: Mashubi *mai* 'bad.'

98 SING   Botocudo *angrin*. Ge: Kraho *nkrɛr* 'song,' Kradaho *ngrere* 'song,' etc. Kaingan: Came *angra* 'dance,' Dalbergia *gringe* 'dance.'

Kamakan: Masacara *aggreamu*. Puri: Coroado *gangre* 'song,' Coropo *gangre*.

99 SIT Bororo: Umotina *imo* 'rest,' Bororo *ammu, ammi* 'rest.' Botocudo *men*. Ge: Crengez *moinj*. Mashakali: Capoxo *moinjam*, Macuni *muingniam*.

100 SKIN Botocudo *kat*. Yabuti: Mashubi *či-kati* 'lip.'

101 SMALL Bororo *-rogo* (diminutive suffix). Opaie *eri, erig*.

102 SMOKE Botocudo *khum* 'tobacco smoke.' Ge: Proto-Ge **kūm*. Mashakali *ŋōñ*. (Davis equates the Ge and Mashakali forms.)

103 STONE Chiquito *kaā*. Ge: Proto-Ge **kɛn*. Guato (*ma-*)*ku*. Kamakan: Kamakan *kiñia*, Cotoxo *kēa, kiang*. Puri: Puri *ukhua*, Coroado *uka, høka*. Yabuti: Arikapu *kra*.

104 SWALLOW (v.) Bororo: Otuke *oaketa* 'eat.' Botocudo *(nun-)kot* 'eat, swallow.' Kaingan *god*.

105 SWIM Caraja *adobu*. Chiquito *topi* 'bathe.' Ge: Chavante *darbi*.

106 TAKE OUT Fulnio *ki*. Ge: Krenje *ake* 'apanhar.' Kaingan: Tibagi *ge, gi*.

107 TEAR (DROP) Chiquito *kukii*. Ge: Krenje *nto-kako* (*nto* = 'eye'), Cayapo *no-kāgo*.

108 THIN Bororo *aru* 'be thin.' Chiquito *aruboz* 'narrow.' Ge: Apinage *iræ*, Cayapo *ire*.

109 THROW Bororo: Umotina *mi* 'throw earth.' Botocudo *amak* 'shove.' Ge: Kraho *mēmen*, Crengez *ame*, Northern Karaho *me* 'lose, throw away.'

110 THUS Botocudo *han-han* 'c'est ainsi.' Kaingan *han* 'c'est ainsi.' Mashakali: Patasho *han* 'thus.'

111 TIRED Bororo: Umotina *kari* 'lazy.' Kaingan: Southern Kaingan *kere*.

112 TODAY Fulnio *łe* 'now.' Kaingan: Tibagi *ori*, Guarapuava *hori*. Puri: Coropo *hora*.

113 TOOTH Bororo *ito*, Otuke *itio*. Caraja *tǰu*. Chiquito *tˢoo*. Ge: Proto-Ge **tˢwa*. Guato *djio* 'mouth.' Kaingan: Tibagi *ža*, Catarina *nǰa*, etc. Kamakan: Kamakan *ko, čo*, Cotoxo *dio*, Masacara *thjo*. Mashakali: Macuni *tsioi*, Monachobm *tšooi*, etc. Puri: Coroado *če*, Coropo *ǰe*. Yabuti *(hi)-do*.

114 TORTOISE Botocudo *ankut*. Caraja *katu* 'land tortoise.'

115 WALK Botocudo *pa* 'go, tread.' Ge: Apinage *pa*. Cf. FOOT₁ in the Amerind dictionary.

116 WASH Bororo *kabi*. Guato *kuafu*. Kaingan: Came, Tibagi, etc. *kupe*.

117 WASP   Bororo *miau, muiawo* 'bee.' Ge: Northern Cayapo *amiu,* Apinage *amju,* Crengez *amčy.*

118 WATER   Ge: Proto-Ge *ŋo, *ŋočj,* Krenje *ko,* Chicriaba *ku,* etc. Guato *ma-gūng, ma-guen.* Kaingan *goi, ngo,* etc. Kamakan: Coropo *kuang* 'river.'

119 WEAK   Botocudo *niñok, ñeñok.* Mashakali: Capoxo *ñiña.*

120 WHITE₁   Caraja *dora, taroite.* Chiquito *turasi.*

121 WHITE₂   Bororo *kiga.* Ge: Cayapo *aka,* Krenje *aka.* Opaie *oka.*

122 WOMAN₁   Ge: Chavante *piko* 'woman, girl,' Cherente *pikō.* Yabuti: Mashubi, Arikapu *pakuhe* 'wife,' Yabuti *pako.*

123 WOMAN₂   Fulnio *de, dea.* Ge: Krenje *jiti.* Kaingan: Catarina *t⁵i* 'female.' Mashakali: Capoxo *ti,* Macuni *ati* 'woman, wife.'

MACRO-PANOAN

The Panoan languages constitute one of the major low-level groups in South America in terms of territory and number of languages. The group's special relation to Tacanan, long recognized, has been worked out in detail by modern researchers. In 1965, Olive Shell did a comparative study of Panoan languages and gave 512 Proto-Panoan reconstructions. In 1968, Mary Key, in what was basically a comparative Tacanan work, added a consideration of the Pano-Tacana relationship and cited a considerable number of comparisons, some with reconstructions and some without. And in 1971 Victor Girard presented 504 reconstructed Proto-Tacanan forms and 116 Pano-Tacana reconstructions. Since it is clear that Tacanan is the most closely related family to Panoan and forms a group with it, forms exclusive to these two families are not included in this section.

As early as 1901–2 S. A. Lafone y Quevedo suggested in a study of Moseten that it was connected with Tacanan. This suggestion was finally followed up in 1969 by Jorge Suárez, who cites 121 comparisons in which Moseten figures with either Tacanan, or Panoan, or both. He does not present any reconstructed forms.

In Greenberg (1960) I suggested that as part of a large Ge-Pano-Carib grouping, Pano-Tacana, Moseten, and a whole series of other languages formed a Macro-Panoan group. Among the other languages were Mataco and Guaicuru. In 1939, Jules Henry noted some significant resemblances between Ashluslay, a Mataco language, and Pilaga, a Guaicuru language. Even the most cursory examination will show that these two groups are indeed closely related, perhaps even more closely than Panoan and Tacanan.

In fact Loukotka (1968) includes Payagua, a Mataco language, in the Guaicuru family. For this reason, as with Pano-Tacana (and Ge-Kaingan earlier), etymologies involving only these two groups, which probably run in the hundreds, are not included here.

According to Longacre (1968: 354), Benigno Ferrario first proposed a relationship between Mataco and Charruan, a group of three sparsely documented extinct languages (Charrua, Chana, and Guenoa). José Rona, in his 1964 study, on the other hand, argues rather for a connection between Charruan and Lule-Vilela. As is so often the case, they were both right. It may be added that though Lule and Vilela are listed as separate stocks by Loukotka, their special connection has long been recognized, and Key (1979) simply lists them in hyphenated form as Lule-Vilela. These are two distinct languages, but so closely related that, again, etymologies found exclusively in them are not included in this section.

If we combine the two chains of suggested relationships, we have, then, Panoan, Tacanan, and Moseten on the one hand and Mataco, Guaicuru, Charruan, Lule, and Vilela on the other. There is still another stock, Lengua (also called Mascoy), that belongs here. It appears to be somewhat more distantly related to the remaining Macro-Panoan languages. In the etymologies that follow, the poorly attested Charruan languages figure only infrequently. Proto-Tacanan forms are from Girard, Proto-Panoan from Shell (S) and Girard (G). In addition to the 63 exclusively Macro-Panoan etymologies presented here, 78 Macro-Panoan entries will be found in the Amerind dictionary under the following etymologies: ABOVE$_2$, ARM$_1$, ASHES, ASK$_1$, AUNT, BACK$_1$, BAD$_2$, BE$_1$, BEE$_1$, BEHIND, BELLY$_1$, BELLY$_4$, BITE$_1$, BITE$_2$, BITTER$_1$, BLACK$_2$, BLOOD$_2$, BLOW, BREAST, BROTHER, CALL$_2$, CARRY$_1$, CHEST, CHILD$_1$, CHILD$_3$, CLOSE, CLOUD$_1$, COME, COOK, COVER, CRY, DEER$_1$, DIE$_1$, DIG$_2$, DRINK$_1$, EAT$_1$, EYE, FEATHER$_2$, FINGER$_2$, FIRE$_1$, FLEA, FOOT$_1$, FOOT$_2$, FOREHEAD$_1$, GO$_1$, GO$_4$, GOOD$_1$, GUTS$_1$, HAND$_1$, HAND$_2$, HEAD$_2$, HIT, HOUSE, KNEE$_1$, LARGE$_1$, LEG, LIP, LOUSE$_1$, MAKE$_1$, MEAT$_1$, MOUTH$_1$, MOUTH$_2$, NIGHT$_1$, NOSE, OLD, ONE$_1$, PERSON, RAIN, SEE$_2$, SEE$_3$, SEED$_2$, SIT$_1$, STAR$_1$, SUN$_1$, TESTICLE, WHITE$_1$, WISH, WOMAN$_2$.

MACRO-PANOAN ETYMOLOGIES

1 BE ABLE Lengua *wan(-či), wan(-kje)*. Mataco: Chulupi *ha-wanaia*.
2 ANIMAL Guaicuru: Toba-Guazu *sigiak*. Lengua *askok*. Mataco: Vejoz *łokue*.

3 ANSWER (v.) Mataco: Choroti *kamtini* 'speak.' Panoan: Cazinaua *kØma*. Tacanan: Cavineña *kiema.*

4 ANUS Guaicuru: Caduveo -*auio* 'buttocks.' Mataco: Choroti *i-we,* Vejoz *wex.* Moseten *jive* 'buttocks, anus.' Panoan: Caripuna *wahaa* 'open.' Tacanan: Huarayo *wexa* 'opening,' Chama *wexa* 'hole.'

5 AWAKE Charruan: Chana *inambi.* Guaicuru: Toba-Guazu *tom* 'awake, dawn.' Mataco: Vejoz *nom* (intransitive). Cf. Panoan: Proto-Panoan (S) **nama* 'to dream.'

6 BACK Lengua *ak-puk, (eja-)puk* 'behind.' Panoan: Shipibo *puika.* Tacanan: Cavineña *ebebakwa,* Chama *kiibaaxaxe* 'behind.'

7 BAD Guaicuru: Guachi [oetcho] 'devil.' Mataco: Nocten, Vejoz *čoi,* Vejoz *tsoi* 'devil.' Moseten *ači-tui* 'make dirty.' Tacanan: Tacana *ači.* Cf. Lule *ičelo* 'devil.'

8 BAT Guaicuru *kahit* (*h* < *s*). Panoan: Proto-Panoan (S) **kaši.*

9 BE Lengua: Mascoy *h-.* Mataco *ihi, hi.*

10 BEAR (v.) Guaicuru: Mocovi *koo,* Toba-Guazu *koe.* Lule *kaa* 'born.' Mataco *ko,* Vejoz *ko.* Panoan: Proto-Panoan (S) **kai* 'to bear, mother,' Chacobo *ko* 'born.' Tacanan: Chama *kwaja* 'be born.'

11 BEFORE Lengua: Lengua, Mascoy *nanič,* Lengua *nahno, nahtu* 'mucho anteo.' Mataco: Chulupi *naxeš* 'forward,' Payagua *inahi.* Moseten [yno], *xinoje.*

12 BLOOD Guaicuru: Toba *t-auo.* Lule *ewe.* Mataco: Chunupi *woi.* Tacanan: Chama *woʔo* 'red.'

13 BODY Lule *toip.* Mataco *tape.* Tacanan: Cavineña *etibo* 'trunk.' (Lule *toip,* however, may contain a suffix -*p.)*

14 BREAK Lengua: Mascoy *pok-* (intransitive). Mataco: Mataco *puhʷoje,* Suhin *poktoče* (intransitive). Moseten *fok.*

15 BREAST Lengua: Lengua *namankuk,* Kaskiha *neme* 'nipple.' Lule *ineme* 'milk.'

16 BROTHER Charruan: Charrua *inčala.* Lule *kani* 'younger brother.' Mataco: Mataco *čila* 'older brother,' *činix* 'younger brother,' Choroti *kiili* 'older brother,' *kiini* 'younger brother.' Vilela *ikelebepe.* (Perhaps two related roots for older and younger brother.)

17 CLOSE (v.) Mataco: Choroti *pone, pione* 'close, cover,' Vejoz *ponhi* 'imprison,' Towothli *aponik* 'cover.' Tacanan: Cavineña *pene.*

18 COLD₁ Lengua *math(-kaiyi)* 'be cold.' Panoan: Proto-Panoan (S) **matˀi* 'be cold.'

19 COLD₂ Lule *kei.* Mataco: Enimaga *koija,* Chunupi *kui.*

20 CUT   Lengua: Guana čečet 'cut up.' Mataco: Suhin siči, Choroti esita, ešita. Panoan: Proto-Panoan (S) *šaʔti.

21 DARK   Guaicuru: Toba, Mocovi epe, pe 'night.' Mataco: Choroti pe 'shadow.' Tacanan: Chama kea-apo 'night,' Tacana apu- 'dark.'

22 DIG   Mataco: Vejoz tih, Mataco tiho. Tacanan: Chama teo.

23 DOG   Mataco: Suhin nuu, Choropi nuux. Panoan: Proto-Panoan (S) *ʔino, *ʔinaka.

24 DOOR   Lule atʸiki- [aciqui-p] 'hole.' Panoan: Proto-Panoan (G) *šikʷi 'doorway.' Tacanan: Proto-Tacanan *tʸekʷe 'door, doorway.'

25 DRESS (v.)   Lule tala 'clothing,' talaks. Mataco tula 'clothing.'

26 DRY   Lengua jima(-gjaji) 'be dry.' Mataco: Mataco jɨm 'dry up,' Suhin, Chulupi jim, Macca iim. Moseten jiñ 'bone.'

27 EMPTY   Lule em-p. Mataco: Vejoz jim, Chulupi jimši.

28 FEAR₁ (v.)   Guaicuru: Toba-Guazu nahi. Mataco: Vejoz nowai. Moseten nojii 'frighten.' Panoan: Cashibo noo 'frighten,' Nocaman no 'enemy,' Panobo, Shipibo nawa 'enemy.'

29 FEAR₂ (v.)   Lule lako 'be ashamed.' Panoan: Proto-Panoan (S) *rakʷi.

30 FINISH   Lule tum-p 'be finished.' Mataco: Choroti temi, Suhin timš. Cf. Tacanan: Cavineña tupu 'enough.'

31 FLY (v.)   Moseten naj. Panoan: Proto-Panoan (S) *noja.

32 GREEN   Lule [za]. Moseten [za]. Panoan: Proto-Panoan (G) *šoo 'green, not ripe.' Tacanan: Proto-Tacanan *zawa.

33 HANG   Moseten pina 'hammock.' Panoan: Conibo panea 'be hung,' pani 'hang up,' Shipibo panni 'hang up.'

34 HATE   Guaicuru: Abipone n-paak 'hated.' Moseten fakoj, fakin 'be angry.'

35 HORN   Lengua: Guana taša. Moseten daš [dasc].

36 KNEAD   Mataco pʔon. Moseten puñe 'knead mud.'

37 KNOW   Mataco: Vejoz hanex, Choroti hane 'know, be able.' Moseten (am)-xeñ '(no) se puede.' Panoan: Proto-Panoan (S) *onā 'know, be able,' Shipibo huna.

38 LEAF   Guaicuru: Toba l-awe. Lengua wa.

39 LEAVE (ABANDON)   Guaicuru: Toba-Guazu jane. Lengua: Mascoy jiño. Panoan: Proto-Panoan (S) *ini. Vilela jane.

40 LOOK   Charruan: Chana sola. Guaicuru: Pilaga čelage, Toba-Guazu silaha.

41 LOSE   Moseten moñi 'perish, lose, err.' Panoan: Cashibo mano 'forget,' Cashinahua manu 'miss.' Tacanan: Proto-Tacanan *manu 'die.'

42 MAKE   Guaicuru: Toba-Guazu *uo*. Panoan: Proto-Panoan (S) **wa*,
*ʔa. Tacanan: Proto-Tacanan **a* 'make, say.'

43 MANY   Guaicuru: Toba-Guazu *lamai*. Lengua *ɬamo*. Mataco: Payagua
lehmi 'all.'

44 MEAT   Guaicuru: Pilaga *niiak* 'fish.' Lengua *nohak* 'wild animal.'
Tacanan: Chama *noe*, Tiatinagua, Huarayo *noči*. Vilela *nuhu* 'fish.'

45 MOSQUITO   Lengua: Mascoy *p-aija*. Mataco: Choroti *eji*, Suhin *ija*.

46 MOTHER   Mataco: Macca *nana*. Tacanan: Proto-Tacanan **nene* 'aunt.'
Vilela *nane*.

47 MOUSE   Guaicuru: Toba-Guazu *mekahi* 'bat.' Moseten *meče* 'rat.'
Panoan: Proto-Panoan (S) **maka* 'rat, mouse.' Cf. Mataco: Mataco,
Suhin, Chulupi *ama*, Vejoz *ma*.

48 NECK₁   Moseten *tetˢ* [tez]. Panoan: Proto-Panoan (S) **tɨšo*.

49 NECK₂   Lule *u(-p)*. Mataco: Mataco, Choroti, etc. *wo*. Moseten [huh]
'throat.'

50 OLD   Guaicuru: Guachi *seera*. Mataco: Payagua *aheri* 'old woman.'
Panoan: Proto-Panoan (S) **šɨni*. Tacanan: Proto-Tacanan **ziri*.

51 RED   Guaicuru: Toba, Mocovi *tok*. Lengua *eteig-ma*. Mataco: Macca
tek 'blood,' Payagua *čiaka*.

52 RIB   Guaicuru: Mocovi [emeneh]. Moseten *mana*.

53 ROTTEN   Lengua *abik*. Lule *poko* 'to rot.' Moseten *fokoi*.

54 SHOUT   Lule *se* 'cry.' Panoan: Shipibo *sei*, Conibo *sije*, Cashinahua
sa. Tacanan: Proto-Tacanan **ʈˢea*.

55 SIDE   Guaicuru: Toba-Guazu *ai, aji*, Mocovi *ai* 'side,' Abipone *uii*.
Lule *je*.

56 SMALL   Lengua: Mascoy *etkok*. Mataco: Churupi *tikin*, Suhin *tika*,
Towothli *taake* 'short.' Panoan: Culino *tukuča* 'short.'

57 SON   Charruan: Chana, Guenoa *ineu*. Guaicuru: Guachi *inna*. Vilela
ina-hmi (Pelleschi), *ina-kc* 'son, daughter' (Gilij), *hina-kis* (Fontana).

58 SOUR   Mataco: Choroti *paši* [paxhi]. Moseten *pase*. Panoan: Proto-
Panoan (S) **paṣa* 'sour, raw, uncooked,' Tacanan: Proto-Tacanan
*paʈˢe.

59 SWIM   Guaicuru: Pilaga *ubogai*. Moseten [vigi]. Tacanan: Proto-
Tacanan **betˢa*.

60 THIN   Lule *kam*. Moseten *kum*. Cf. Mataco: Vejoz *čemsa-* 'small.'

61 URINE   Lengua *jis(-weji)* 'urinate.' Lule [ys] 'urinate.' Mataco: Suhin
juɬ, Churupi [yius, yiusl] 'urinate' (*sl* probably represents the voiceless
lateral fricative *ɬ*). Panoan: Proto-Panoan **isõ, *istõ*.

62 WEAK   Lengua: Mascoy *jil, jel-k*. Mataco: Mataco *jel* 'weak, tired.'
63 WOMAN   Moseten *pen*. Tacanan: Proto-Tacanan **e-pona*.

MACRO-CARIB

Carib is another one of the major low-level stocks of South America. The following families in Loukotka's classification are considered here to form a group that includes Carib: Andoke, Bora (sometimes called Miranya), Kukura, Uitoto, and Yagua (also called Peba). Apparently my only predecessor here is Paul Rivet, who in a paper on Peba (1911a) points to a series of important resemblances between Peba and Carib, concluding that "the Peba languages must have formerly been dialects of Carib." In his paper on Miranya, published the same year, he states that Bora (Miranya) is closest to Tupi-Guarani; but he also includes comparisons with Peba and Uitoto that are much more convincing evidence of its connection to those languages. Because it is clear that Bora and Uitoto have a special relationship, etymologies exclusive to those two groups are not included in this section.

Kukura is known from a single very short wordlist, and its assignment to Macro-Carib is therefore tentative. It figures relatively infrequently in the etymologies. There has been no overall reconstruction of Proto-Carib. The most extensive work is the 1946 study of C. H. de Goeje, which gives "approximate" forms rather than reconstructions. These are occasionally cited as Carib (G). In 1973, Marshall Durbin did a reconstruction based on a small group of related Carib languages—Guaque, Carijona-Hianacoto, and Umaua—under the name Proto-Hianacoto. These forms are cited as Carib (D).

There are two languages called Muinane in the literature. One belongs to the Bora and the other to the Uitoto subgroup. Each is cited under its appropriate subgroup.

In addition to the 79 exclusively Macro-Carib etymologies presented here, 64 Macro-Carib entries will be found in the Amerind dictionary under the following etymologies: $ABOVE_1$, $ABOVE_2$, ANGRY, ARM_1, ARRIVE, ASK_1, $BACK_1$, $BELLY_3$, $BELLY_4$, $BITE_1$, $BLOOD_1$, $BODY_1$, BREAK, BROTHER, $CALL_1$, $CARRY_1$, CHEW, $CHILD_3$, $COLD_1$, COME, DIE_3, DRY_2, $EARTH_4$, EYE, $FEATHER_1$, $FEATHER_2$, $FINGER_1$, $FINGER_2$, $FIRE_2$, $FOOT_1$, GO_2, $GOOD_3$, $GUTS_1$, $HAND_3$, $HARD_1$, KILL, $LEAF_3$, LEG, LIP, $LONG_1$, $MAKE_1$, $MANY_1$, $MEAT_4$, $MOON_1$, $MOUTH_2$, OLD,

ONE₁, PAIN, RAIN, RED, RIVER₂, ROAD₁, SEE₁, SEE₂, SING, SLEEP₁,
SMALL, SNAKE₁, SUN₁, TESTICLE, TONGUE₁, TREE₁, TREE₂,
WATER₁.

MACRO-CARIB ETYMOLOGIES

1 ANT   Kukura *tain.* Yagua: Yameo *ɔtenua.*
2 BEAUTIFUL   Carib: Proto-Carib (D) **kuule* 'good,' Accawai *kure*
   'good,' Bakairí *kxura* 'good,' etc. Uitoto: Ocaina *xarooga.*
3 BEHIND   Uitoto: Muinane *moi-,* Ocaina *muun* 'de atras.' Yagua: Yameo
   mowe.
4 BLACK   Bora: Miranya *mukohørike* 'blue.' Carib: Cariniaco, Galibi
   mekoro, Trio *meker,* Bakairí *ta-maɣeneng.* Uitoto: Uitoto-Kaimo
   mokoreti 'blue,' Coeruna *mokorø* 'blue.' Yagua: Peba *mixalaj*
   [michalay]. (The Cariniaco, Galibi, and Trio forms are said to be from
   Spanish *negro.*)
5 BOW (n.)   Carib: Proto-Carib (G) **taku.* Uitoto: Uitoto *tikuiña,* Orejone
   otaki 'arrow.' (The Carib languages Goeje cites are geographically
   distant from Uitoto.)
6 BRANCH   Carib: Galibi *ipolire,* Surinam *poriri,* Hianacoto *pɔli.* Uitoto
   iforo.
7 BREAST   Carib: Galibi *manate,* Jaricuna *manati,* Arara *mangu,*
   Palmella *emate* 'chest,' etc. Uitoto: Uitoto *mono,* Muinane *monoi,*
   Nonuya *omonyhy,* Coeruna *munia* 'milk,' Ocaina *monnø.*
8 BUTTOCKS   Uitoto: Muinane *tirao.* Yagua *teli.*
9 CHEEK   Carib: Palmella *paxo,* Motilon *ipæpok.* Uitoto: Ocaina *faʔxon.*
10 CHEST   Bora: Faai *mex-pikua.* Uitoto: Ocaina *bagooʔja,* Uitoto (Erare)
   ogob. Yagua *upeko* 'neck.'
11 CLOSE (v.)   Carib: Wayana *apu,* Chayma *ot-apu-raz,* Surinam *apuru.*
   Uitoto *ipua.*
12 DEER   Bora: Miranya [göhsu]. Carib: Proto-Carib (D) **kaha,* Galibi
   kosari, Cumanogoto [coze], Bakairí *kxose-ka.* Uitoto: Uitoto *kyto,*
   kiddo, Ocaina *keto, xooʔtjo.*
13 DOG   Bora: Muinane *høku* 'dog, jaguar.' Carib: Apiaca *okori,*
   Azumara *kule,* Diau *jeki.* Uitoto: Erare *eikø,* Ocaina *oko, hoʔxo.*
14 DREAM (v.)   Carib: Hishcariana *nik* 'sleep,' Chayma [gu-enequi-az]
   'sleep,' etc. Uitoto: Uitoto *neka-ide,* Ocaina *noʔxaajo* 'dreamed.'
15 EARTH   Andoke *ñohe.* Bora: Bora *jinioxee,* Imihita *injuhe.* Uitoto:
   Ocaina *naʔaaxo,* Uitoto *nanexe.*

16 ENTER   Andoke *dia-to*. Carib: Galibi *eta, ida* 'inside,' Hishcariana *eta, ta* 'inside.' Uitoto *du* 'penetrate.'

17 EVENING   Andoke *nejejma*. Uitoto: Muinane *naiio* 'night.' Yagua: Yameo *ñuwa*.

18 EXCREMENT   Bora: Bora *namee*, Imihita *ma-name*. Uitoto: Uitoto *nemu*, Ocaina *nemoon?in*. Yagua *domet'ina* 'latrine.' Cf. Andoke *umahe-həh* 'I defecate' ('I' = *ohəh*).

19 EYE   Bora: Imihita *tha-njemi* 'forehead.' Yagua: Peba *vi-nimi-ši*, Yameo *we-nin-se*.

20 FAT (OIL)   Andoke *kehə* 'oil.' Uitoto: Nonuya *kwi, kwihi*, Ocaina *kwahihi* 'oil.'

21 FOOT   Carib: Proto-Carib (G) **tapu* 'heel,' Jaricuna *utapo* 'footprint,' Opone *idebu*. Uitoto: Andoquero *ko-itebo*, Orejone *etaiboi*, Ocaina *topuuxo* 'heel.'

22 FOREHEAD   Bora: Miranya Oira Assu-Tapuya *tha-iimi*, Faai *(me-)mi*, Muinane *?ime* 'face.' Yagua: Yagua *mwɔ*, Peba *(vi-)mo*.

23 GIVE   Carib: Galibi *i* 'put,' Surinam *i-(ri)* 'put, give,' Tamanaco *i*. Uitoto *i*.

24 GO   Andoke *ta-boe* 'he goes.' Bora: Miranya *pe(-ku)* 'go!,' *me-pei* 'let's go.' Uitoto *yfo* 'let's go.' (*-ke* and *-ko* are common imperative suffixes in Carib languages.)

25 GRANDFATHER   Andoke *japitah*. Bora: Miranha Oira Assu-Tapuya *pathoa*. Carib: Nahugua *apit'i*.

26 HAND   Carib: Proto-Carib (D) **-ñali*, Trio *ji-njadi*, Accawai [*entzarri*], Nahugua *ui-ñatore*, etc. Yagua: Peba *vi-niteli*.

27 HEAVY   Carib: Taulipang *ame?ne*, Macusi *amunine*, Apalai *t-eeme*. Uitoto: Muinane *mee* 'weight,' Ocaina *maaji* 'weight.'

28 HOT   Bora: Miranha Oira Assu-Tapuya *kogoro*, Muinane *?aigukunu*. Carib: Proto-Carib (G) **uka* 'burn.' Uitoto: Coeruna [*äocke*] 'sun.'

29 HOUSE   Bora: Bora *ha*, Miranya *ha, xa*, Imihita *(mee-)ha*, Muinane *ixa*. Carib: Bakairí *eka* 'sit,' Motilon *aga* 'seat,' Taulipang *kə* 'stay.' Uitoto: Muinane *-ko* (suffix) 'house.'

30 HUSBAND₁   Carib: Kaliana, Chayma *wane*. Yagua *wanū* 'men,' *rai-wano* 'my husband.'

31 HUSBAND₂   Carib: Proto-Carib (G) **ino*. Uitoto: Uitoto *inuj, iñi*, Ocaina *oonna*.

32 LARGE   Andoke *mə(ks)nio-həh*. Carib: Proto-Carib (D) **moonomi*, Oyana *mon-me* 'thick,' Gimanoto [*hu-emanupi-aze*] 'grow.' Uitoto: Uitoto *moni* 'grow,' Ocaina *aamon* 'grow.'

33 LEG₁   Bora: Imihita *(mex-)tea* 'foot,' Muinane *idɨ, (mex-)tia* 'foot.'
Carib: Opone *ite*, Macusi *čɨ*. Uitoto *idaɨ* 'foot.'

34 LEG₂   Uitoto: Coeruna *oemana*. Yagua *wi-mana*.

35 LICK   Carib: Proto-Carib (G) **ame*. Uitoto *me*.

36 LIGHTNING   Carib: Arara *imere* 'thunder, lightning,' Pimenteira
mørury 'thunder,' Trio *imemuru*, etc. Uitoto *bor(-ide)* 'to lightning.'
Yagua: Peba *malajere* 'thunder.'

37 MAKE   Bora *(me-)ne*. Uitoto: Ocaina *nuu*. Yagua *ne* 'be occupied
with,' *nane, nene* 'make.'

38 MAN   Bora: Miranya *thimae*. Kukura *tieme*. Yagua: Yameo *atin*. Cf.
Motilon *tama* 'boy.'

39 MONKEY₁   Bora: Imihita *nome* 'howler monkey. Yagua *nymni* 'howler
monkey.'

40 MONKEY₂   Uitoto: Uitoto *homa*, Orejone *ame*. Yagua: Peba *amu*.

41 MOON₁   Kukura *malahan*. Yagua: Yagua *aremane, alimani*, Peba
remelane, Yameo *arremelen*.

42 MOON₂   Carib: Proto-Carib (D) **nuuna*, Carib (G) **nunuø*. Uitoto:
Ocaina *nəhna, nēna* 'sun.'

43 MOUTH   Andoke *mətⁱewi* 'lip.' Carib: Wayana *j-emtala*, Cumanogoto
mtar, Arekuna *mda*, etc.

44 NEPHEW   Andoke *opitu*. Carib: Apalai *poito*, Macusi *paito* 'son-in-
law.'

45 NOSE   Carib: Proto-Carib (D) **onali*, Bakairí *j-enari*, Azumara *unari*,
etc. Yagua: Yagua *y-niru*, Peba *vi-nerro*.

46 NOW   Carib: Galibi *ereme, erome*, Barama River *erome* 'today.' Yagua:
Yameo *errama*.

47 OUT   Uitoto *maña(-ha)* 'go outside' (*ha* = 'go'). Yagua: Yameo *mans*
'go out.'

48 PENIS   Carib: Arara *opengo*, Apɪaca *enpen*. Yagua: Yagua *hapwē*,
Yameo *wi-pinši*.

49 PERSON   Uitoto: Uitoto *komoene* 'people,' Orejone *kome* 'person.'
Yagua: Peba *komolej*. Cf. Carib personal plural *-komo*.

50 PIERCE   Carib: Taulipang *po, pə*, Pauishana *axpe*. Uitoto *fefo*.

51 RAIN   Uitoto: Nonuya *tomonahi* 'rainy season.' Yagua *tomara*.

52 RED   Bora: Muinane *texbueʔno*, Faai *me-tibani*. Kukura *tipoil*. Cf.
Carib: Chayma *t-apire*, Barama River *t-apide*, etc.

53 RIB   Carib: Maiongom *korori*, Tamanaco *čurari*. Uitoto *kiraike* (sing.),
kiraie (pl.).

54 ROAST   Uitoto: Uitoto, Muinane *rui*. Yagua *rujē* 'fry.'

55 ROPE   Carib: Surinam *kapuja*, Chayma *kabuja;* Galibi *kabuia*. Uitoto: Ocaina *oʔkaape*.

56 RUN   Carib: Roucouyenne *ta-kane*, Galibi *ta-kani*, Surinam *ekanumi*, etc. Uitoto *ekain-ite* 'walk fast.'

57 SHADOW   Carib: Trio *amali-li*, Galibi *t-imue-re*, etc. Uitoto *manaide*.

58 SHORT   Andoke *tofitu*. Yagua *tapuse*.

59 SHOULDER   Carib: Proto-Carib (D) **mootali*, Apalai *e-motari*, Bakairí *umata*, etc. Uitoto: Muinane *emodo* 'back.' Yagua: Peba *vi-omote*, Yagua *namatɔ*.

60 SPEAK   Carib: Carib *ura*, Accawai *j-uro*, etc. Uitoto *uʔurii-*.

61 SPIDER   Andoke *todə*. Yagua: Yagua *tetiu* 'spider web.'

62 STEAL   Carib: Surinam *mona*, Galibi *maname*, Yabarana *mərə* 'take!' Uitoto: Muinane *meri-de*, Ocaina *muuro*.

63 STONE   Carib: Proto-Carib(G) **topu*, Maquiritare *taho*, Bakairí *toxu*. Kukura *tatahy*. Uitoto: Nonuya *tahihə*. Yagua: Yameo *tao* 'mountain.'

64 SUN   Carib: Macusi *winai* 'day,' Galibi *uanu* 'sunlight,' Tamanaco *ano* 'day,' etc. Yagua: Yagua *ini, iñi*, Peba *wana*.

65 SWAMP   Carib: Proto-Carib (G) **(š)akoro* 'scum,' Northern Wayana *ikalitao*, Apalai *ikulipato*, Taulipang *kuliža*. Uitoto *ikare*.

66 THIGH   Bora: Miranya *ma-pateri* 'lower leg.' Carib: Surinam *peti*, Galibi *i-piti*, Yabarana *petti*, etc.

67 TIE (v.)   Carib: Surinam *mɨ*, Waiwai *mi*, Taulipang *mē*. Uitoto: Uitoto *ma*, Muinane *maɨ-*.

68 TODAY   Andoke *ñeahpə*. Yagua *nibia*.

69 TOMORROW   Bora: Imihita *bexkore* 'morning,' Faai *pekore*. Carib: Surinam *koropo*, Apalai *kokoro*, Arara *kogorone*, etc. Uitoto *ukoro*.

70 TOOTH   Carib: Proto-Carib (G) **je*. Yagua: Yameo *e*.

71 TREE   Andoke *doapa* (Tastevin) 'forest,' *hodeefah* (Warrin) 'forest.' Yagua: Peba *tapasej* 'tree,' Yagua *toha, tox* 'forest.'

72 TWO   Bora: Muinane *minoke*, Imihita *minjekə*. Carib: Bakairí *meni* 'twin.' Uitoto: Uitoto *mena*, Andoquero *inama*, Ocaina *hanama*. Yagua: Peba *nomoira*, Yameo *naramue*.

73 UNDER   Bora: Miranya Oira Assu-Tapuya *paa* 'low,' Muinane *baaβi*. Carib: Kaliana *popo* 'low,' Surinam *poxpo* 'low,' Taulipang *po* 'come down,' Galibi *paapo* 'descent.' Uitoto *bu-* 'to sink.' Yagua: Yameo *popo* 'earth.'

74 VAGINA   Carib: Proto-Carib (G) **eni* 'vase' (with meanings such as 'interior, sheath' in various languages). Uitoto *iani*.

75 WAIT   Carib: Chayma *mueke,* Accawai *mogo,* Surinam *momoki* 'wait for,' etc. Uitoto (Las Cortes) *mače* 'aguarde.'

76 WAX   Carib: Tamanaco *moropo,* Taulipang *morombe.* Uitoto: Ocaina *mara* 'gummy.'

77 WHITE   Carib: Cariniaco *t-amune,* Jaricuna *amona,* etc. Uitoto *mone-ide* 'clear.'

78 WISH (v.)   Uitoto *iraine.* Yagua *-rūūj* (desiderative suffix).

79 WOMAN   Carib: Carib (G) *puiti* 'wife,' Bakairí *i-witi* 'my wife.' Yagua: Peba *watoa,* Yameo *wato,* Yagua *huitarynia.*

EQUATORIAL

In Greenberg (1960), I proposed an Equatorial-Andean grouping as one of the two major subfamilies of Amerind confined to South America. Subsequent investigation showed that, in considerable conformity to the subgrouping outlined there, there are three groups—Equatorial, Macro-Tucanoan, and Andean. Each will be treated in a separate section, beginning here with Equatorial. Under that name, I put the following families: Arawa, Cayuvava, Chapacura, Coche, Cofan, Esmeralda, Guahibo, Guamo, Jibaro, Kandoshi, Kariri, Katembri, Maipuran, Otomaco, Piaroa, Taruma, Timote, Tinigua, Trumai, Tupi, Tusha, Uro, Yaruro, Yuracare, and Zamuco. Within the group, I see Cofan, Esmeralda, Jibaro, Kandoshi, and Yaruro as a subgroup that will be called Jibaro-Kandoshi.

As far as I can see, I have had no predecessors in regard to defining an Equatorial grouping except in one respect, namely, the proposed grouping of Maipuran and certain families that are particularly close to it. This is the work of Paul Rivet and numerous collaborators. As defined by him, such a grouping—called Arawakan—would contain Maipuran, Arawa, Chapacura, and Uro (including Puquina). To it, I would add at least provisionally Guamo, an extinct language of Venezuela known only from vocabularies of two dialects (Santa Rosa and San José) made up almost entirely of nouns. I treat all five as separate subgroups in the etymologies below, but identify those etymologies restricted to this group with an (A) at the end of the entry. (The same practice is followed in the Amerind dictionary for this and other abbreviations defined in this chapter.) Similarly, because Otomaco, Tinigua, Guahibo, and Katembri seem especially close to Arawakan, I group them with the Arawakan families under the name Macro-Arawakan, and etymologies restricted to this group are followed by (MA).

Although Loukotka (1968) includes Guahibo in Arawakan proper, I consider it one of the groups closest to Arawakan within Equatorial, but not Arawakan as such. Loukotka includes Esmeralda, Cofan, and Yaruro in Chibchan. I consider this an error and place these languages in the Jibaro-Kandoshi group of Equatorial, as indicated above. Loukotka separates Uro (spelled Uru by most writers) from Puquina. But their close relationship is evident, as noted by Olson (1964, 1965), as well as earlier writers; I simply include Puquina in the Uro group. Loukotka is similarly in error in listing Purubora as a separate stock, for even the most casual examination shows that it belongs to Tupi in the broader sense. Olson has proposed that Uro is related to Mayan, but apart from the fact that both are Amerind, I see no special relationship between them. Uro is clearly closer to Maipuran and other languages of the Arawakan group than to Mexican Penutian, the family to which Mayan belongs.

In the citations below, Proto-Tupi forms are cited from Lemle (1971). However, her reconstruction is based on a single subgroup of Tupian, the one containing Tupi proper. Kariri is probably closest to Tupi. Tusha is known only from a brief list but shows significant resemblances to Katembri, which is clearly Equatorial.

In addition to the 134 exclusively Equatorial etymologies presented here, 95 Equatorial entries will be found in the Amerind dictionary under the following etymologies: $ABOVE_3$, ANT_1, ARM_1, ASHES, ASK_2, AUNT, $BACK_2$, BARK, BE_1, BEAR (v.), $BEARD_1$, $BELLY_1$, $BELLY_2$, $BELLY_3$, $BLACK_3$, $BLOOD_1$, $BLOOD_2$, $BODY_2$, BREAST, BROTHER, BURN, CHEST, $CHILD_2$, CLEAN, $CLOUD_1$, COME, DARK, DIE_1, DIE_2, DIG_1, DIRTY, $DRINK_1$, $DRINK_2$, DRY_1, EAR, $EARTH_1$, $EARTH_2$, $EARTH_4$, EGG_2, EYE, FAR, $FEATHER_1$, $FINGER_1$, FLY_1, FLY_2, $FOOT_1$, FORE-$HEAD_1$, GO_1, $GOOD_1$, $GOOD_2$, GRASS, $HAND_1$, $HARD_1$, HATE, $HEAD_1$, HOUSE, HUSBAND, KILL, $KNEE_1$, $LARGE_1$, $LEAF_1$, $LEAF_2$, LEG, LIP, LIVER, LIZARD, MAN_3, $MEAT_2$, $MOUTH_1$, NAVEL, $NIGHT_4$, PENIS, RED, $ROAD_2$, ROOT, SALIVA, SAY_1, SEE_1, SHORT, $SLEEP_1$, $SLEEP_2$, $SNAKE_2$, STRONG, SUN_1, THIN, $TONGUE_3$, $TREE_1$, VAGINA, $WHITE_1$, $WOMAN_1$, $WOMAN_2$, $WORK_1$, $YELLOW_1$, YESTERDAY, YOUNG.

EQUATORIAL ETYMOLOGIES

1 ABOVE   Arawa: Yamamadi, Jarua *neme* 'heaven,' Paumari *nama* 'heaven,' Culino *meme* 'heaven.' Kandoshi *-mona*. Piaroa: Saliba *mena, mumea* 'heaven.'

2 ALL₁ Piaroa: Saliba *sina*. Tinigua *tʲana*. Tupi: Guayaki *tana* 'much.'
Uro: Caranga *šina* 'each.'

3 ALL₂ Guahibo *daxi-ta*. Jibaro: Shuara *tuke*, Upano *tuki*. Maipuran:
Wapishana *teki* 'much.'

4 ANT₁ Tupi: Tupi *taebihi*, Kawahib *taəp*, Pawate *tabuni*. Timote: Cuica
tsipa.

5 ANT₂ Arawa: Culino *mehi* 'ant,' Paumari *manei* 'large ant.' Guahibo
amai. Maipuran: Mandauaca *amai*, Yucuna *mai*, Adzaneni *ame*,
Machiguenga *manihi*, etc. (MA)

6 ARM Kariri: Sapuya [tz-aneh], Kamaru *aena*. Maipuran: Baniva *-anu*,
Marawa *-ana*, *anī*, etc. Piaroa: Saliba *añoa* 'shoulder,' Piaroa *tsa-nane*
'upper arm.' Tupi: Arikem *na*, *nã*, Makurape *onæne*. Zamuco:
Chamacoco *os-unnere* 'shoulder.'

7 BACK Chapacura: Quitemo *šipara-či* 'shoulder.' Guahibo *pe-tabui-to*
'buttocks.' Guamo: San José *očepe* 'shoulder.' Kandoshi: Murato
supuan-ič. Kariri *sebi* 'back, kidney.' Maipuran: Goajiro *sape* 'spine,'
Campa *sapi-či* 'buttock,' Bare *-sepa* 'shoulder.' Tupi: Yuruna *sabu*,
Kawahib *aseap* 'shoulder,' Kuruaya *ašebia* 'shoulder.' Uro: Callahuaya
čupa 'tail.'

8 BAD Cofan *vaho* 'devil.' Guahibo *abexe*. Kariri: Dzubucua *buaga*.
Katembri *boš*. Maipuran: Arawak *aboa* 'bad, sick.' Otomaco *ababa*.
Tupi: Siriono *-aba* 'ugly,' Guaraní *vai* 'ugly.' Tusha *boše* 'ugly person.'

9 BEAR (v.) Maipuran: Ipurina *n-amarite* 'child.' Tupi: Purubora *meroa*
'infant, small,' Ramarama *merimit* 'child,' Guayaki *mita* 'child,'
Yuruna *matiu* 'pregnancy.' Uro: Chipaya *mače* 'pregnant,' Caranga *mat*
'be in labor.' Zamuco: Tumraha *mate* 'pregnant.'

10 BELLY₁ Chapacura *ketet* 'sein.' Guahibo *koto* 'abdomen.' Maipuran:
Piapoco *ukuta* 'chest,' Curipaco *kuda* 'chest.' Piaroa: Saliba *iktebo*
'intestines,' *iktego* 'guts.' Timote: Mocochi *kito*. Uro: Caranga *kata*
'chest.' Zamuco: Ebidoso *-xoto*.

11 BELLY₂ Jibaro: Aguaruna *ik(-ič)*. Piaroa: Saliba *iko* 'stomach.' Yaruro
ak. Zamuco *ika*.

12 BITE Jibaro: Aguaruna *esa-t*. Tupi: Proto-Tupi *tsuʔu*. Zamuco:
Ebidoso *-ies*, Tumraha *-is*.

13 BLACK₁ Coche *singa*. Cofan *singu*, *singo*. Jibaro: Shuara *šunga*. Uro
sinki 'dark.'

14 BLACK₂ Kariri [goh] 'Negro.' Timote: Cuica *kue*.

15 BLACK₃ Arawa: Culino *sowe* 'darkness.' Guamo: Santa Rosa *di-siaku*,
San José *di-sau*. Maipuran: Terena *šexa-iti*, Wachipairi *wasix*,

Wapishana *išawak* 'night,' Amarakaeri *sik^nda* 'black,' *sikio* 'darkness,'
Toyeri *sikia* 'night.' Uro: Caranga *saxwa* 'brown,' Uro *saxwa* 'green,
grass.' (A)

16 BLADDER   Chapacura: Itene *kurupi*. Uro *korro*. (A)

17 BLOOD$_1$ Maipuran: Carutana *irai*, Campa *iraha*, Karro *irrai*, etc.
Tupi: Oyampi *iruwi*, Pawate *aru*, Kawahib *aeru*.

18 BLOOD$_2$ Chapacura: Chapacura [ahui], Itene [hui], Quitemo
[ahueiche], Tora *wi*. Guamo: Santa Rosa *xue*. Kariri: Dzubucua *(be-)he*.
Tupi: Proto-Tupi **uwɨ*, Kamayura *wɨ*.

19 BONE   Guahibo *taha* 'hard.' Guamo: Santa Rosa, San José *di-tanku*.
Maipuran: Campa *tonki*, Machiguenga *toniʔ*, etc. Otomaco *takta*
'hard.' Piaroa *tiweka* 'hard.' Uro: Callahuaya *čuku*, Uro *sixi*, Chipaya
tˤih.

20 BREAK   Kariri *pete*. Piaroa: Saliba *pataga*. Zamuco: Zamuco *peto*,
Ayoré *pero*.

21 BROAD   Jibaro *waŋga-ram*. Taruma *wakana*.

22 BROTHER   Maipuran: Ipurina *-piri* 'younger brother,' Baure *ri-piri*,
Black Carib *-beri* 'younger brother,' etc. Uro *pali-tak* (for the suffix,
cf. *kontrario-tik* 'enemy' < Spanish). (A)

23 BURN$_1$ Arawa: Culino *itabiše* 'roast.' Cayuvava *tɔpɔ*. Kariri: Kamaru
toppo 'roast.' Piaroa *čufua*. Tupi: Yuruna *tivou* 'roast,' Amniapa
tawyra 'roast.' Uro: Chipaya *thap*.

24 BURN$_2$ Kandoshi *kora*. Maipuran: Wapishana *karimet* 'roast,' Baure
-aharow, Yucuna *karaʔa*, Arawak *akkurran* 'bake,' Kozarini *kera*. Piaroa: Saliba *igara*. Yuracare *kula* 'cook.'

25 CALF   Katembri *ila*. Maipuran: Cauishana *na-yla* 'foot.' Zamuco:
Zamuco *iri* 'calf, foot,' Chamacoco *p-øhrø* 'calf, foot,' Tumraha *p-iri*
'foot.'

26 CHIEF   Guahibo: Guahibo *peruhu-ni* 'old man,' Cuiva *peru-wa-jo* 'old
man.' Maipuran: Kuniba *pəre*, Bare *si-bure-ne*, Tariana *ho-aferi*
'grandfather,' Piapoco *beri* 'old man,' etc. Otomaco *apurura* 'large.'
Uro: Puquina *apurej*. (MA)

27 COLD$_1$ Maipuran: Toyeri *dohina*. Piaroa: Saliba *duha*.

28 COLD$_2$ Taruma *siwa*. Yaruro *čiwah*.

29 COLD$_3$ Maipuran: Yucuna *ipee-ni*, Tariana *hape*, Karutana *hape-ri*,
etc. Uro *xipu*. (A)

30 COOK (v.)   Chapacura *khenoči-na*. Guamo: Santa Rosa *kinehwa*, San
José *es-kino*. Kariri: Dzubucua *kine* 'be cooked.' Maipuran: Piro *xima*
'roast,' Apurina *kimi* 'roast,' Bare *akani* 'burn.'

31 DAY   Coche *bonete*. Esmeralda *pine*. Kariri *i-hine* 'light.' Yuracare *puine* 'light, sun.'

32 DRESS (v.)   Cayuvava *rɔ* 'carry' (for the semantics, cf. French *porter).* Chapacura: Wanyam *iri* 'bark-clothing.' Maipuran: Maypure *arruti* 'clothing.' Tupi: Oyampi *raa* 'carry,' Guaraní *araha* 'carry,' etc. Uro: Caranga *ira* 'men's shirt,' Uro *irs* 'poncho, covering.'

33 EAGLE   Chapacura *kawi*. Maipuran: Ipurina *kokoi*, Paresi *kukui* 'harpy,' Siusi *kakue* 'large falcon.' Uro *gawi* 'condor.' (A)

34 EAR   Maipuran: Moxo *nu-kiña*, Ipurina *ne-kena-ko*, Guana *geno*, etc. Uro *kuñi, kunni*. (A)

35 EAT₁   Jibaro *hura*. Yaruro *hura*.

36 EAT₂   Jibaro: Shuara *iu*, Aguaruna *ju*. Tinigua *io*.

37 EAT₃   Cayuvava *ni*. Cofan *añe*. Esmeralda *ene*. Kariri: Dzubucua *ñu* 'eat, chew.'

38 EGG   Guamo *tinue*. Maipuran: Yavitero *itiniko, teniko*, Bare *ne-sinaxa*. Uro *siñe, zini*. (A)

39 EYE   Arawa: Culino *nokʰo*, Paumari *nukui* (for Arawa *n* < **t*, see WOMAN₁ below). Chapacura: Itene *tok*, Tora *tok*, Abitana *teki-si*, etc. Guamo: Santa Rosa *tuxua*. Uro *čuhki*, Caranga *čukˀi*. (A)

40 FAT₁ (n.)   Kariri: Dzubucua *niadi* 'oil.' Tupi: Oyampi *jandɨ*, Guaraní *ñandɨ*.

41 FAT₂ (n.)   Chapacura: Itene *imika*. Uro: Callahuaya *makha* 'obesity.' (A)

42 FEATHER   Cayuvava *pote*. Chapacura: Quitemo *ipati-ko*. Maipuran: Ipurina *ipiti*, Piro *-piti*, etc. Piaroa *uotse*. Yuracare *pusi*. Zamuco: Tumraha *vuešo*.

43 FIRE   Chapacura: Chapacura *ise*, Abitana *itsæ*, Yaru *isi*. Guahibo *iso*. Kariri: Kariri *usu*, Kamaru *isu*. Maipuran: Kustenau *tsei*, Baniva *asi*, Amuesha *soʾ*, etc. Tupi: Yaruna *aši* 'fire, firewood,' Shipaya *aši* 'fire, firewood.' Yuracare *soto-i* 'kindle.'

44 FISH   Chapacura: Quitemo *ixam*, Tora *hoam*, Urupa, Yuva *iham*. Chapacura *ĩšuam*. Maipuran: Arawak *hime*, Campa *šima*, Piro *čima*, Moxo *himo*, etc. (A)

45 FLEA₁   Piaroa *nãnē*. Tupi: Kuruaya *nong*, Digüt *nom* 'foot flea.' Yaruro *enini, eni*. Zamuco *unna-*.

46 FLEA₂   Arawa: Paumari *kadjapa* 'tick.' Chapacura: Quitemo *koʎapi*, Tora *hujipi*. Maipuran: Bare *kudiba*, Mandauaca *kutiha*, Baniva *otsipa*, etc. Timote: Timote *kits*, Maripu *kis*. Uro: Chipaya *kˠuti*.

47 FOREST   Jibaro: Gualaquiza, Aguaruna *numi*. Maipuran: Toyeri

nemba 'forest, mountain.' Otomaco: Taparita *arapa* 'mountain.' Piaroa: Saliba *rampo*. Zamuco: Ebidoso *eremi*, Zamuco *ērāp* 'forest, mountain.'

48 GO   Coche *wajo* 'walk.' Jibaro: Aguaruna *wə*. Kariri: Dzubucua *wa*, *owa*, Kamaru *wi*. Maipuran: Wachipairi *wa*, Toyeri *iwaj*, Amarakaeri *waʔ*, Amuesha *aawoʔ*. Piaroa: Saliba *wa*.

49 GO OUT   Cayuvava *βɔrɔ*. Kariri: Kariri *pere*, Dzubucua *pele*. Yuracare *porere*.

50 GOOD   Jibaro: Shuara, Aguaruna *aju*. Maipuran: Toyeri *ajo-ajo*.

51 GRANDMOTHER   Cayuvava *tætæ*. Chapacura *čiči*. Maipuran: Bare *čeče*, Yavitero *n-ači*, etc. Trumai *atsets*. Uro: Uro *ačiči*, Callahuaya *čiči*.

52 GRASS   Cofan *nūnpasi*. Jibaro: Aguaruna *dupā*, Shuara *nupa*. Timote: Cuica *numbu*, *nunbu* 'pasture.' Tupi: Proto-Tupi *jū*, Guaraní *ñu*. Zamuco: Chamacoco *nemi*.

53 GUTS   Kariri: Kamaru *he*. Trumai *-xe* 'belly.' Zamuco: Zamuco *ahe*, Ayoré *j-axei*.

54 HAIR₁   Chapacura: Chapacura *čumi-či*, Quitemo *čumi-če*. Uro: Caranga *čuma*. (A)

55 HAIR₂   Chapacura: Wanyam *tini-či*, Tora *tuni*. Maipuran: Chamicuro *ux-čeno*, Paresi *tani-ti* 'feather,' Piapoco *čona* 'hair, feather.' Uro: Chipaya *čara*, Uro *čer-s*, *čir-s*. (A)

56 HAND   Arawa: Culino *dʼepe*, Yamamadi *jefe*. Chapacura *kapi* 'ring finger.' Guahibo: Cuiva *kobe* 'arm.' Guamo: San José *očepe* 'arm.' Katembri *kifi*. Maipuran (general) *kapi*. Otomaco *gibi*. Piaroa *čufo* 'arm.'

57 HEAD   Cofan *tsobe*, *sube*. Kariri: Kariri *tsabu*, Dzubucua *tsebu*, Kamaru *tsambu*. Katembri *ki-tipa-ti*. Yaruro *tobe:h*. Zamuco: Ebidoso *a-tibi* 'nape.'

58 HEAR   Esmeralda *ofisa*. Tupi: Guaraní *apysa*, etc. Yuracare *a-vese-i*.

59 HEAVEN   Guahibo: Guayabero *fato*. Timote *ki-veuč* 'cloud.' Zamuco: Ebidoso *pod*.

60 HEAVY   Otomaco *pare*. Zamuco: Chamacoco *peluppa*.

61 HONEY₁   Maipuran (general) *mapa* 'bee, honey.' Uro: Callahuaya *mapa* 'pitch, tar'. (A)

62 HONEY₂   Kariri: Dzubucua *kati*. Trumai *kot* 'wax.' Tupi: Mekens *ekwɨit*, Kepkiriwate *euit*, Sanamaika *ivit*, Yuruna *kadega* 'wax.' Zamuco: Zamuco *kuten*, Ayoré *kutere*.

63 KNEE   Piaroa: Saliba *nopui, nohai.* Tupi: Proto-Tupi **enɨpɨʔa.*

64 LAKE   Chapacura: Kitemoka *su-huaiše,* Itene *huče* 'swamp.' Guamo *du-agiš* 'river.' Uro *koasi* 'water.' (A)

65 LAUGH (v.)   Jibaro: Shuara *višir-,* Zamora *višuai.* Piaroa: Saliba *ibeči* (n.).

66 LEG   Arawa: Paumari *kapahei* 'thigh.' Chapacura *kaima-či.* Cofan *kupati-ču* 'thigh.' Katembri *ko-kibi* 'thigh.' Maipuran: Atoroi *ikub,* Wapishana *kubu,* Amuesha *čip* 'leg, thigh.' Tupi: Kabishiana *ukibie-i,* Mekens *o-kɨp,* Arara *ičap.* Uro: Caranga *kˣomi* 'thigh.'

67 LIE (TELL A LIE)   Kariri: Kariri *upre,* Sapuya *uple, me-peli* 'slander.' Maipuran: Arawak *mull-,* Wapishana *malidin,* Manao *obota* 'tell a lie, deceive.' Piaroa: Saliba *ubade.* Tupi: Sanamaika *awerote,* Oyampi *iwarite* 'false.'

68 LIVER₁   Cayuvava *čaβe.* Esmeralda *kobin-sa* 'belly.' Jibaro: Aguaruna *akap.* Kandoshi *šip-ič.* Maipuran: Apurina *akipa* 'heart,' Wapishana *keba, kuba.*

69 LIVER₂   Guahibo *ape-to.* Tupi: Proto-Tupi **pɨʔa,* Mekens *o:pita, u:piza,* Kawahib *pia.* Yuracare *ipisa.* Zamuco: Ebidoso *ipete.*

70 LONG   Chapacura: Itene *čikna.* Guahibo *tahe* 'far.' Maipuran: Wapishana *duku* 'high,' Ipurina *itaku* 'far,' Baure *tiči.* Trumai *athukh.* Uro: Caranga *čukˣu.* Yuracare *teče.*

71 LOUSE₁   Arawa: Yamamadi, Jarua, Culino *kama-ti,* Paumari *kuma-ʔi.* Maipuran: Ipurina *kimičitu.* Uro: Callahuaya *koma.* (A)

72 LOUSE₂   Piaroa: Saliba *iwewe.* Timote *wi.*

73 LOUSE₃   Chapacura *okuaapi* 'puce pénétrante.' Maipuran: Arawak *kaiaba* 'flea,' Wapishana *kwaib* 'flea.' Tupi: Wirafed *kib,* Cocama *kiwa,* etc.

74 LOVE   Cayuvava *čo* 'wish.' Esmeralda *iso.* Tupi: Guaraní *ajsu,* Chiriguano *asu.*

75 MAKE₁   Tupi: Guayaki *japo* 'work,' Guaraní *japo.* Uro: Callahuaya *japa-na.*

76 MAKE₂   Jibaro: Aguaruna *na- ~ n-.* Kandoshi *ina.* Kariri: Kariri *ñio,* Dzubucua *niño.*

77 MAN   Maipuran: Arawak *lukku,* Kariay [lhuxü-müry] 'husband.' Uro *luku.* (A)

78 MANY₁   Coche *butˢa* 'large.' Kariri *pečo.* Trumai *pux.* Yuracare *puče* 'surpass.' Zamuco: Ayoré *pis* 'very.'

79 MANY₂   Arawa: Culino *wapi,* Paumari *apoi-ki.* Cofan *bu,boe.* Piaroa

buio 'large.' Tupi: Guayaki *ipo* 'very,' Sanamaika *pui* 'large.' Zamuco: Chamacoco *apube* 'more.'

80 MONKEY   Maipuran: Campa *kočiro, koširi,* Piro *kesiri,* Amuesha *kuč,* etc. Uro *kusiʎo.* (A)

81 MOON   Esmeralda *čabla* 'star.' Kandoshi *tsoopi.* Piaroa *itsefa* 'star.' Yuracare *subi.*

82 MORNING   Guamo: Santa Rosa, San José *čuna* 'evening.' Maipuran: Adzaneni *teuena,* Ipurina *otana* 'tomorrow.' Otomaco: Taparita *tuna.* (MA)

83 MOUNTAIN   Cofan *t'ampo* 'mountain, forest.' Esmeralda *mo-topa.* Yuracare *teme* 'summit.' Cf. Jibaro: Shuara *ikiam(a)* 'forest.'

84 MOUSE   Chapacura: Quitemo *pitijaho* 'rat.' Otomaco: Otomaco *potea,* Taparita *botoa.* Tupi: Purubora *bado* 'rat.' Zamuco: Chamacoco *apeti.*

85 MOUTH   Guahibo *kuibo.* Timote: Mocochi *kabo.* Tinigua: Pamigua *kiwa.* Trumai *xop.* Tupi: Ramarama *ogopu* 'chin,' Kepkiriwate *kape,* Digüt *gopepoa,* etc. Yuracare *kubu* 'put in mouth.'

86 NAIL   Trumai *fi.* Tupi: Proto-Tupi **pwã-pē* 'fingernail,' Mekens *opu-ape* 'fingernail.'

87 NAME   Tupi: Proto-Tupi **er.* Zamuco: Zamuco *ireo,* Ayoré *iri.*

88 NIGHT   Chapacura *paitin.* Coche *ibita.* Tupi: Cocama *ipit'a,* Guaraní *pĩtu,* Tupi *pitun.*

89 NOSE   Kariri: Kariri *nebi,* Kamaru *nabi, na:mbi,* Dzubucua *nabid'e.* Maipuran: Toyeri *e-nimpe* 'hear.' Otomaco: Otomaco *nima,* Taparita *nipa.* Tupi: Proto-Tupi **nami* 'ear,' Kuruaya *numbi* 'ear.' Yaruro *napaa, nopee.* (For the semantic connection between 'nose' and 'ear' [i.e. aperture in the head], see HOLE₁ in the Amerind dictionary.)

90 OLD   Jibaro: Gualaquiza *ašand,* Zamora *assand.* Kandoshi: Kandoshi *sinap-či,* Murato *t'erab-či.* Yuracare *suñe* 'man,' *suñe-i* 'grow.'

91 OLD MAN   Guahibo *uamu.* Tupi: Proto-Tupi **amõj* 'grandfather.' Yuracare *eme* 'chief.'

92 PLACE   Cayuvava *βi.* Tupi: Arikem *-βa,* Shipaya *apa.*

93 PULL   Arawa: Yamamadi *huka,* Culino *hoka.* Uro: Caranga *joka, jaka.* (A)

94 RAIN   Maipuran: Chamicuro *timili* 'wind,' Machiguenga *tampia* 'wind,' etc. Cayuvava *daba.* Timote: Maguri *šimbu* 'water,' Cuica *šombeuč,* etc. Tupi: Mekens *at'oab,* Awety *tompa* 'storm.' Uro: Chipaya *thami* 'wind.' Yuracare *sama* 'water.'

95 RIVER   Coche *boiše, buiš* 'river, water.' Guahibo *baswe.* Jibaro:

Gualaquiza *muetsan.* Trumai *misu* 'river, water.' Yuracare *masi* 'to rain.'

96 RUN   Cayuvava *βe(-re).* Kariri *bi.* Maipuran: Baure *-pi-* 'flee' (cf. Uainuma *pipina* 'go away!').

97 SHADOW   Kariri: Dzubucua *kaja* 'night.' Piaroa: Saliba *kajo.*

98 SHIN   Guahibo *pesi-ta.* Kandoshi: Murato *poaš-ič.* Yuracare *pisisi.*

99 SMALL₁   Kariri: Dzubucua *bupi.* Maipuran: Arawak *ibi-li.* Tupi: Guayaki *pe* 'small, flat, young,' *papi* 'short, small,' Oyampi *e-api* 'short.' Zamuco *abi.* Cf. Saliba *-ap* (diminutive).

100 SMALL₂   Esmeralda *-ku* (diminutive). Jibaro: Aguaruna *ekeu.*

101 SMALL₃   Kandoshi: Kandoshi *kaniaši* 'new,' Murato *kaniači* 'young.' Maipuran: Kozarini *kirani,* Guana *kali,* Amuesha *kuñič.* Tupi: Tupi *kan,* Arikem *kenin,* Tupari *t'in,* Maue *kūnīn* 'smallness.' Uro: Callahuaya *kani* 'new.'

102 SMELL   Piaroa: Saliba *ome* 'sense of smell.' Yuracare *umei* 'stink.'

103 SMOKE (n.)   Maipuran: Toyeri *t'iuvi.* Piaroa *it'efofa.* Zamuco: Ebidoso *gi(j)ep,* Tumraha *kiebo,* Chamacoco *čiebo.*

104 SNAKE₁   Katembri *angiu.* Otomaco: Taparita *ingea.* (MA)

105 SNAKE₂   Chapacura *amani-či* 'worm.' Maipuran: Ipurina *imini,* Piapoco *manu.* Uro: Callahuaya *amaru.* (A)

106 STONE   Cofan *pote, paate.* Guahibo *iwoto.* Kariri: Dzubucua *boedo* 'mountain.' Tupi: Guaraní *iwïtrï,* Tupi *ewete* 'mountain.'

107 SUN₁   Chapacura: Urupa *kumen,* Yaru *komem.* Esmeralda *hime, hieme* 'moon.' Guahibo: Guahibo *huame-to,* Cuiva *home-to.* Maipuran: Kustenau *kama,* Marawa *kamu* (general in Arawakan). Piaroa: Piaroa *gama* 'moon,' Macu *gama* 'sun.' Timote: Cuica *kumben, kumbeu* 'month.' Tupi: Emerillon *koeme* 'day,' Oyampi *koem* 'day, to dawn.' Uro: Callahuaya *kaman* 'day,' *kamañito* 'sun,' Puquina *gaman* 'day.'

108 SUN₂   Arawa: Jarua *massiku* 'moon,' Paumari *massiku.* Maipuran: Chamicuro *mosoxko.* (A)

109 SUN₃   Guahibo *ikatia.* Maipuran: Goajiro *kači* 'moon,' Cauishana *keesi* 'moon,' Ipurina *kasuri* 'moon,' etc. Piaroa *uxkude* 'fire.' Timote: Cuica *kuči* 'day.' Tupi: Monde, Digüt, etc. *gati* 'moon.' Zamuco: Ayoré *gede,* Guaranoco *gedodia* 'star,' Siracua *gete.*

110 TAIL₁   Cayuvava *eñe.* Maipuran: Paresi *inihu,* Island Carib *t-ili.* Piaroa: Saliba *inea.*

111 TAIL₂   Kariri: Kamaru *kru.* Zamuco *kari.*

112 THIGH   Guahibo *pe-sito* 'lower leg.' Katembri *bo-titi*. Yuracare *oteta* 'hip.' Zamuco *p-ithet*.

113 THORN   Cofan *nuxa*. Zamuco: Guaranoco *onak*.

114 THROAT₁   Esmeralda *kola* 'neck.' Maipuran: Wapishana *kono*, Piapoco *kanapi* 'neck,' Uarakena *kane* 'neck.' Uro *kʾora* 'neck.' Yaruro *goro* 'neck.' Cf. Zamuco *potogoro*.

115 THROAT₂   Maipuran: Toyeri *jera* (Oppenheim), *-ari* (Aza). Tupi: Proto-Tupi **ajur*.

116 TOOTH₁   Jibaro: Gualaquiza *naj*, Aguaruna *ñai*, etc. Maipuran: Toyeri *ine*. Tupi: Mekens *iñai*, Shipaya *aña*, Kuruaya *naī*, etc.

117 TOOTH₂   Chapacura: Pawumwa, Urupa, Yaru *iti(-či)*, Tora *jat*. Maipuran: Apolista *asi*, Achagua *esi*, Maypure *n-ati*, Arawak *d-ari*, etc. Uro: Uro *atse* (Polo), *atta*, Chipaya *atta*, Callahuaya *iti* 'bite.' (A)

118 TREE   Arawa: Paumari, Culino, etc. *awa*. Maipuran: Bare *jawa, ijawa* 'forest,' Uarakena *aua(-kapi)* 'forest,' Yavitero *awa-bo* 'forest.' Uro *wa* [hua]. (A)

119 UGLY   Kandoshi: Murato *mančer* 'bad,' Kandoshi *mantʾeri*. Tupi: Kepkiriwate *moenena* 'ugly, black.' Yuracare *emne-te*. Zamuco: Ebidoso, Tumraha *mene*.

120 URINE   Jibaro: Shuara *šiki*. Kariri: Kamaru *sako*, *tʾako* 'urinate.' Piaroa *tʾaxkuelia*. Zamuco: Chamacoco *tyče*.

121 VAGINA   Maipuran: Campa *šibiče*, *šibiči* 'penis,' *sibiči* 'vulva,' Jumana *sopo*, *sapuh* 'vulva,' Siusi *tʾupote*, Baniva *tʾibehe*. Uro *šapsi* 'genital organ.' (A)

122 VEIN   Maipuran: Wapishana *pararu*, Atoroi *wariru*. Yuracare *bala*.

123 WATER₁   Arawa: Culino *unin* 'river,' Paumari *waini* 'river.' Esmeralda *una* 'rain.' Maipuran (general, sometimes meaning 'river') *wini, uni*. Uro: Chipaya *unu* (according to Rivet this word has been borrowed into Cuzco Quechua; this statement is supported by the fact that other dialects have *jaku*, and that *unu* is not Andean).

124 WATER₂   Maipuran: Guinau *hija* 'water, rain,' Bare *hija* 'rain,' Tariana *ija, iia* 'water, rain.' Otomaco: Otomaco, Taparita *ia*. Piaroa: Saliba *ia, ahija*.

125 WATER₃   Guahibo: Guahibo, Cuiva *ema* 'rain.' Jibaro: Gualaquiza *jumi*, Aguaruna *jumi* 'water, rain,' Shuara *jumi* 'rain.' Maipuran: Wachipairi *mahe* 'drink,' Toyeri *meei*, Amarakaeri *māīʔ*. Timote *meu*, *meuč* 'to drink.' Tupi: Tapute *ama* 'rain,' Tupi (general) *aman* 'rain.' Yuracare *jumijumi*. Zamuco: Siracua *mama*.

126 WING   Chapacura: Urupa *tiñi*. Maipuran: Arawak *d-adøna* 'arm,
    shoulder,' Bare *dana* 'arm.' (A)

127 WISH₁   Maipuran: Yucuna *no-ata*, Maypure *nu-jasa*. Uro: Puquina
    ata, Callahuaya *hata*. (A)

128 WISH₂   Timote: Mocochi *ea*. Yaruro *ea*.

129 WOMAN₁   Arawa: Culino *inin* (for Arawa *n* < *t*, see EYE).
    Cayuvava *torene*. Chapacura: Itene, Mure *tana*. Esmeralda *tīn, tiōna*.
    Maipuran: Marawa *tanan*, Mehinacu *tene-ru*, Baure *eteno*. Piaroa *te-
    tireku* 'my wife.' Uro: Chipaya *tˣuna*, Caranga *tʰun* 'wife.'

130 WOMAN₂   Arawa: Paumari *gamu* 'wife, woman' (general in Arawa).
    Guamo: Santa Rosa *di-kime*. (A)

131 WORM₁   Arawa: Culino *somi*, Jarua *tˢome*, Yamamadi *sume*. Guahibo
    homo 'snake.' Jibaro: Aguaruna *sumai*. Tupi: Proto-Tupi *čeboʔi*,
    Sanamaika *sobo* 'snake.'

132 WORM₂   Cayuvava *naiñi*. Kariri: Dzubucua *nieñi* 'snake.' Otomaco
    wiñea.

133 YELLOW   Chapacura: Itene *sakene*. Maipuran: Paresi *tˣike-le*, Passe
    šikje 'green.' Uro *čakni, čakña*. (A)

MACRO-TUCANOAN

I am unaware of any recognition of the Macro-Tucanoan stock prior to
my article in 1960. I now assign the following families to this stock: Auake,
Auixiri, Canichana, Capixana, Catuquina, Gamella, Huari, Iranshe, Kaliana, Koaia, Maku, Mobima, Muniche, Nambikwara, Natu, Pankaruru,
Puinave, Shukuru, Ticuna, Tucano, Uman, and Yuri. Since Loukotka
(1968) uses Máku and Makú for two of these groups, I have chosen to replace his Makú with the name Puinave (often found in the literature) in one
case, and to drop the accent in the other (i.e. my Maku is his Máku).

Auake, Kaliana, and Maku seem to form a subgroup, and Ticuna and
Yuri another. Beyond this, I see no obvious subgrouping. A number of these
languages are known only from sparse vocabularies and hence do not figure
frequently in the etymologies. These are Auixiri, Gamella, Koaia, Natu,
Pankaruru, Shukuru, and Uman. Their assignment to Macro-Tucanoan is
therefore somewhat tentative. Proto-Nambikwara forms are from Price
(1978).

In addition to the 107 exclusively Macro-Tucanoan etymologies presented here, 85 Macro-Tucanoan entries will be found in the Amerind dic-

tionary under the following etymologies: ABOVE$_2$, ANT$_1$, ARROW, AUNT, BATHE, BEAR (v.), BEARD$_2$, BEE$_2$, BELLY$_1$, BELLY$_2$, BITE$_1$, BITE$_2$, BLACK$_1$, BLACK$_3$, BLOOD$_2$, BONE$_1$, BREAST, BROTHER, BURN, CHEST, CHILD$_2$, CHILD$_3$, COVER, DIE$_1$, DIG$_2$, DIRTY, DRINK$_1$, DRY$_1$, EAR, EARTH$_4$, EAT, EAT$_2$, EGG$_1$, EXCREMENT$_2$, EYE, FEATHER$_2$, FIRE$_3$, FLY$_1$, FLY (v.), FOOT$_1$, FOREHEAD$_2$, FRUIT, GO$_1$, GOOD$_2$, GOOD$_3$, HAND$_1$, HAND $_2$, HEAR$_2$, HEAVEN$_2$, HOLE$_2$, HUSBAND, KNEE$_1$, LARGE$_1$, LEAF$_2$, LEG, LIGHT, LONG$_1$, MEAT$_2$, MEAT$_3$, MOON$_2$, MOSQUITO, MOUTH$_1$, NAVEL, ONE$_2$, PENIS, ROAD$_1$, SIT$_1$, SLEEP$_2$, SMALL, SNAKE$_2$, STAR$_1$, STRONG, SUN$_1$, SUN$_2$, TONGUE$_1$, TONGUE$_2$, TONGUE$_3$, TWO, WATER$_1$, WATER$_2$, WHITE$_1$, WOMAN$_1$, WOOD$_1$, WORK$_2$, YESTERDAY.

MACRO-TUCANOAN ETYMOLOGIES

1 ARM   Huari: Masaka *ki-taka*. Muniche *xtaaše* 'hand.' Ticuna *take* 'elbow.'

2 ASHES   Huari *noeka*. Maku *nuhē-nakuči* 'charcoal' (*nuhē* = 'fire'). Tucano: Tucano, Waikina *noha*, Wanana *nuha*.

3 AUNT   Kaliana *teke*. Ticuna *tege*.

4 BARK (SKIN)   Iranshe *aʔ-kuri* 'tree-skin.' Nambikwara: Proto-Nambikwara *kəlǝu*. Tucano: Dyurema *(hihekamu-)ekari* 'lip' (= mouth-skin).

5 BAT   Auake *jõ*. Tucano: Coto *ojo*, Yahuna *odjo*, Yupua *odje*, Wanana *dʼo*.

6 BEAUTIFUL   Puinave: Ubde-Nehern *nao*, Tiquie *nau*. Tucano *noa* 'beautiful, good.'

7 BEE   Auake *akoatso*. Canichana *xe* 'fly.' Iranshe *iki-hī*. Kaliana *iko* 'bee, honey.' Ticuna *aku*.

8 BIRD$_1$ Canichana *mela, melu*. Tucano: Yupua *mira*, Curetu *mira, mila*, etc.

9 BIRD$_2$ Iranshe *itʲi*. Nambikwara: Proto-Nambikwara *ʔaikʾ*. Ticuna *goe* 'to fly.'

10 BLACK   Kaliana *tçãē*. Mobima *tuni*. Nambikwara: Proto-Nambikwara *ton*, Southern Nambikwara *tʼun*.

11 BLOOD$_1$ Auake *kãinje*. Capixana *inkoni*. Nambikwara *hǝin*. Yuri *ukonia*.

12 BLOOD$_2$ Mobima *donʔi*. Puinave: Tiquie *(d)jeu*, Curiariai *jeu*, etc. Ticuna *du* 'bleed.' Tucano (general) *di*.

13 BODY₁   Puinave: Nadobo *ibø* 'corpse.' Tucano: Bara *uxpə*, Tucano *øxpø*, etc. Yuri *su-upi, ta-obi.*

14 BODY₂   Puinave: Querari *(m)baka*, Curiariai *bək* 'skin,' Papury *bok* 'skin.' Tucano: Wanana *pagə*, Bara *paga* 'belly,' Tucano *paga* 'belly,' etc.

15 BONE   Kaliana *uina, uino.* Tucano *uani.* Yuri *-ino, -uino.*

16 BOW (n.)   Iranshe *poku.* Nambikwara: Proto-Nambikwara **pok.* Puinave: Curiariai *bitço(γ)*, Puinave *heg*, Dou *bičog.* Cf. Capixana *mā-pika*, but *(mā-)pi* 'arrow'.

17 BREAST₁   Kaliana *wi.* Puinave: Curiariai *pu(e)n*, Tiquie *podn*, Hubde *pwun, pu:n*, Parana Boaboa *ibi*, Papury *pun* 'milk.' Tucano: Uasona, Uaiana *ope*, Wanana *peno*, Yahuna *opea*, Cubeo *ope* 'nipple.'

18 BREAST₂   Capixana *njānō* 'bosom.' Huari *nini.* Nambikwara: Proto-Nambikwara **nūnk.* Ticuna *nonnon* 'suckle.'

19 BRING   Auake *mañan* 'bring!' Puinave: Nadobo *umana* 'bring!' Tucano *mian* 'carry.'

20 BURN   Puinave: Tiquie *hō(e)*, Papury *hooi.* Tucano: Wanana *həa*, Siona *eho:*, Yeba *ǒhǒo*, Buhagana *əhəa*, etc.

21 CHEEK   Maku *tse-mune.* Mobima *mora* 'face.' Puinave: Querari *mō(d).*

22 CLOSE (v.)   Puinave: Papury *bibi* 'close, cover.' Tucano *biʔa.*

23 COOK   Puinave *a-kag.* Tucano: Siona *kwako.*

24 DANCE₁   Catuquina *uaigpa* 'sing.' Puinave *wag.* Tucano: Tucano *baksa* 'dance, sing,' Wanana *baxsa.*

25 DANCE₂   Canichana *au-dahdara, a-tatra.* Mobima *telo.* Yuri *tarøhene* 'I dance.'

26 DEEP   Tucano: Wanana *kəa(-nina)*, Waikina *kəa(-line)*, Tucano *əka-ne.* Yuri *kaa.*

27 DEER   Iranshe *jāma, iamantᶜi.* Puinave: Curiariai *jam* 'dog,' Tiquie *jambe* 'dog.' Tucano: Siona, Wanana, etc. *jama.*

28 DIG   Iranshe *ohu.* Nambikwara: Proto-Nambikwara **ʔuh.*

29 DOG   Huari *ajua.* Nambikwara: Proto-Nambikwara **janal* 'jaguar.' Puinave: Querari *hiu* 'jaguar.' Ticuna *aj* 'dog, jaguar.' Tucano: Siona, Sara, etc. *jaj*, Coto *hoje.*

30 DRY   Auake *amaiai, mo* 'bone,' *omamo* 'bone.' Maku *a:mu* 'bone.' Puinave: Papury *hammai.*

31 EARTH₁   Iranshe *bata* 'ground.' Maku *boʔte.* Puinave *(m)baγtçi.*

95

32 EARTH₂ Auixiri *okake*. Canichana *čix, čixiči, čeče*. Capixana *kekeke* 'land.' Puinave: Curiariai, Dou *čax*, Hubde *čia*. Tucano: Tama *čiha*, Coreguaje *čoa*.

33 EGG Canichana *em-če*. Pankaruru *aži*. Puinave: Tiquie *de,dø* (probable borrowing from Tucanoan). Tucano: Coto *dja*, Tucano *dee*, Coreguaje *čia*, Desana *diu*, etc.

34 EYE₁ Auixiri *atuka*. Canichana *tokhe* (cf. Iranshe *kutake?i*).

35 EYE₂ Koaia *etoim, etoini*. Puinave: Curiariai *tem*, Dou *tubm*.

36 EYE₃ Capixana *i-kīi, i-kaē*. Catuquina: Parawa, Bendiapa *iku*. Maku *ku* 'see.' Nambikwara: Proto-Nambikwara *eika*. Puinave: Papury *keøi* 'see.'

37 FACE Ticuna *čiwe* (no *s* in Ticuna). Tucano: Pioje *sia*, Amaguaje, Siona [zia].

38 FAT (n.) Kaliana *mian* 'meat.' Koaia *maneni* 'fish.' Nambikwara: Proto-Nambikwara *panēit*. Puinave *minā*.

39 FATHER Kaliana *pan*. Maku *me*. Nambikwara: Proto-Nambikwara *mī:n*. Tucano: Waikina, Wanana *mai*.

40 FEAR (v.) Puinave: Hubde *(o)mõi*, Papury *joomoi*. Ticuna *mu*.

41 FIREWOOD Auake *a?ne* 'fire.' Capixana *inī* 'fire, firewood.' Huari *ine* 'fire, firewood.' Iranshe *āina* 'fire.' Maku *nyhē* 'fire,' *ni?* 'burn' (pl. subject). Nambikwara: Northern Nambikwara *niw?*. Ticuna *naj* 'firewood, wood, tree.'

42 FISH Pankaruru *kami-jo* (*jo* probably means 'water'; cf. *joo* 'lake'). Puinave: Dou *hāmb*, Tiquie *homp*, etc.

43 FLOUR Puinave: Nadobo *uhi*, Yehubde *tegn-oi* 'ashes' (*tegn* = 'fire'). Ticuna *ui*. Tucano: Buhagana *ohoa* 'ashes,' Yahuna *ua* 'ashes,' Tuyuka *hua* 'ashes,' etc.

44 FLY (n.) Capixana *mokō* 'kind of wasp.' Huari: Masaka *manšɯ* 'pium.' Pankaruru *moka*. Ticuna *mu?k* 'gnat.' Tucano: Wanana *miki-ro* 'bee.'

45 HAIR Capixana *ii*. Huari: Huari *jii, ži*, Masaka *ji* 'hair, beard.' Yuri *ii*.

46 HAND₁ Catuquina [poghy]. Puinave: Papury *mbake*, Tiquie *(m)bake* 'arm,' etc.

47 HAND₂ Canichana *ripha, rep*. Mobima *dimpa* 'finger.' Puinave *lab*.

48 HEAD Auake *kakoati*. Capixana *i-kuta*. Huari *kača* 'face.' Maku *tsi-gate*. Ticuna *katu, kati* 'forehead.'

49 HEAR Huari *niu* 'ear.' Iranshe *ēna, ana*. Nambikwara: Proto-Nambikwara *ain, *n?a* 'ear.' Ticuna *ine*.

96

50 HERE   Catuquina: Canamari *tih*. Nambikwara: Proto-Nambikwara **ti*.

51 HONEY   Puinave: Querari *belu*. Ticuna *berure* 'honey, wax.' Tucano:
Sara *beroa*, Buhagana *belua*, etc. (The Querari form is probably
borrowed from Tucanoan.)

52 HOUSE   Maku *mine*. Muniche *ime, imed*. Puinave: Puinave *mō, mu*,
Tiquie *mōi, moin*, Querari *mē*, etc.

53 JAGUAR   Catuquina *pytha, pida*. Kaliana *puǰin, buǰin*.

54 LARGE   Canichana *mara*. Mobima *merehe*.

55 LEAF   Capixana *ijy*. Huari: Masaka *ji:*.

56 LEG   Iranshe *īnā*. Mobima *d-inohi*. Tucano: Yupua *noa*.

57 LIP   Puinave: Marahan *-no* 'lip, mouth,' Curiariai, Dou *nō* 'mouth.'
Yuri *ane, anæ*.

58 LIZARD   Capixana *tare*. Kaliana *tulei* 'crocodile.' Tucano: Coreguaje,
Siona *toro*.

59 LONG   Iranshe *məʔi*. Puinave *mōnōā* 'deep.' Ticuna *ma* 'be long.'
Tucano: Wanana *məa* 'high,' Tuyulu *əmə-alope* 'high.' Yuri *mæhæ,
meje, maee*.

60 LOUSE   Iranshe *inim*. Maku *ine*. Mobima *damʔi*. Puinave: Papury
dum, Tiquie *num*, Yehubde *nem*, Nadobo *tum*, Puinave *daam* 'nigua.'

61 MAN₁   Canichana *kohti* 'husband.' Gamella *katu*. Puinave: Dou *hude*,
Curiariai *xot* 'person.' Uman *katu*.

62 MAN₂   Capixana *miaʔ*. Iranshe *mija*.

63 MAN₃   Natu *pikoa*. Pankaruru *porkia*. Uman *porkia*.

64 MANY   Puinave *ibag*. Tucano: Uasona *paʔə* 'many, all,' Tucano *pehe*
'abundance, more,' Yupua *paxha*, etc. Yuri *bæxo*.

65 MOUNTAIN₁   Kaliana *ūaīkū*. Maku *wike*.

66 MOUNTAIN₂   Auake *piʔa*. Iranshe *poʔi*. Puinave: Hubde *paa*, Papury
paχ. Tucano: Yupua *fo*, Tuyuka *po, pu* 'forest,' Sara *hoa* 'forest.' Yuri
poa.

67 MOUTH   Auake *komē*. Canichana *čene*. Capixana *ikanjō* 'beak.' Huari
kan 'beak.' Mobima *kuana*.

68 NAIL₁   Ticuna *patai, pati*. Yuri *ču-ubati, su-pety*.

69 NAIL₂   Capixana *piko*. Huari *ka-peka*. Puinave: Curiariai *bok*, Tiquie
boɣ.

70 NOSE   Auake *koa*. Capixana *i-kaīū*. Iranshe *kāmī*. Kaliana *īku*.
Mobima *čini*. Puinave: Puinave *goe*, Querari *uəɣna*. Tucano: Wanana
keno, Wiriana *engenu*. Yuri *kane, ugone*.

71 PENIS   Auixiri *ko-thaka*. Kaliana *ku-tuka*.

72 PULL   Mobima *man*. Ticuna *mina* 'drag.'

73 PULL OUT   Iranshe *opu*. Ticuna *pu*.

74 RAIN   Maku *yly* 'storm.' Mobima *luʔluʔu, luʔtiʔiʔ* 'it is raining.'

75 ROAD   Catuquina: Canamari *to-* (prefix of motion). Maku *te* 'walk.'
Mobima *toba, towanel*. Puinave: Papury *tiw*, Hubde *teew, teu*, Curiariai
təu.

76 ROOT₁   Puinave *di*. Yuri *ti*.

77 ROOT₂   Nambikwara: Proto-Nambikwara **nəik* 'leg, root.' Tucano:
Uaiana *neko*, Waikina *neko-li*, Wanana *n(ə)ako*, etc.

78 ROPE   Huari: Masaka *ambæ* 'liana, fiber.' Nambikwara: Proto-
Nambikwara **ēp*.

79 SEE   Mobima *de*. Ticuna *dau*.

80 SEED   Canichana *(nem)-ka*. Catuquina: Canamari *akong*. Iranshe *kəhi
~ məhi*. Nambikwara: Proto-Nambikwara **ki*. Puinave: Papury
køwang. Tucano: Amaguaje *ka*, Yupua *go*, etc.

81 SKIN   Maku *čimo*. Ticuna *čame* 'skin, bark.'

82 SLEEP   Maku *we* (v.). Tucano: Siona *weo* (n.), Tucano *weha* (n.).

83 SNAKE   Catuquina: Catuquina, Bendiapa *ixpang*. Puinave *pen* 'large
water snake.' Tucano: Tucano, Uaiana, Tuyuka, Sara, etc. *pino*.

84 STAND   Auake *kara*. Puinave: Hubde *kere*.

85 STICK   Auake *šapi* 'tree.' Mobima *čaʔpa*. Muniche *čapue*.

86 STONE₁   Ticuna *nota, nuta*. Tucano: Sara *nəxta*, Tucano *ēxta*, Waikina
etã.

87 STONE₂   Nambikwara: Proto-Nambikwara **tʾapal*. Tucano: Uasona
ətape, Uaiana *etape*.

88 STONE₃   Capixana *aki*. Huari *aži*. Koaia *aki*.

89 STRING   Huari: Masaka *nai*. Nambikwara: Proto-Nambikwara **nu*.

90 TELL   Capixana *wararaæere* 'speak.' Iranshe *wala* 'talk.' Ticuna *ore*
'word, story.' Tucano *uere* 'say.'

91 TESTICLE   Kaliana *katukuba* 'scrotum.' Maku *kote*. Puinave *katəyp*
'scrotum, testicle.'

92 TODAY   Canichana *unexe*. Mobima *nokoa*. Ticuna *nokowa* 'now.'
Tucano: Tucano *nika*.

93 TOOTH   Capixana *i-pe*. Tucano: Uaiana, etc. *opi*.

94 TREE₁   Canichana *ni-jiga*. Tucano: Sara *juxkə-kə*, Erulia *juxkə*, etc.

95 TREE₂   Kaliana *taba*. Maku *taba* 'tree, firewood.' Puinave: Tiquie
temba 'firewood.'

96 URINE   Puinave: Puinave *akan*, Curiariai *çinɔx*. Tucano: Amaguaje, Uasona, etc. *kone.*

97 VULVA₁   Maku *ts-e?ne.* Tucano: Uasona *jane*, Yahuna *ja?na*, etc.

98 VULVA₂   Puinave: Querari *(n)de.* Ticuna *de.*

99 WASP   Iranshe *ači.* Tucano: Coto, Piojeuti, Uasona *utia*, Waikina *uxti-ro* (general in Tucanoan).

100 WATER   Muniche *ide.* Pankaruru *žai, ža.* Puinave: Puinave *ɔd* 'water, river,' Ubde-Nehern *de.* Shukuru *teu.* Ticuna *de?a.* Tucano: Yeba, Sara, Buhagana, etc. *ide.*

101 WAX   Canichana *ni-kme* 'beeswax.' Iranshe *kjamā.* Tucano: Wanana *komape* 'pitch.'

102 WIND₁   Catuquina *wani* [huany]. Tucano: Bara, etc. *uino*, Yahuna *uinoa.*

103 WIND₂   Huari *ywo.* Kaliana *oua.* Yuri *ooa.*

104 WISH   Iranshe *ītaku.* Puinave: Papury *tukui*, Puinave *-ziug* (desiderative).

105 WOMAN₁   Iranshe *ikipu.* Kaliana *kapaj.*

106 WOMAN₂   Koaia *etal.* Puinave: Tiquie *tain*, Puinave *tehen.*

107 YELLOW   Auake *pišio.* Canichana *nem-bese, nim-bit'i* 'red.' Catuquina: Catuquina *puixni* [puichny] 'red,' Parawa *apanig* 'red,' Canamari *pahning* 'red.' Kaliana *pusia.* Puinave: Querari *(m)bu(x)ni.*

ANDEAN

The following languages are here classified as Andean: Alakaluf, Araucanian, Aymara, Catacao, Cholona, Culli, Gennaken (Pehuelche), Itucale (Simacu), Kahuapana, Leco, Mayna (Omurana), Patagon (Tehuelche), Quechua, Sabela (Auca), Sechura, Yamana (Yahgan), and Zaparo.

Loukotka (1968) lists Aksanas as a separate stock, but it is similar to, and perhaps only dialectally different from, Alakaluf. Catherine Peeke, in her grammar of Auca (1973), rightly criticizes me for listing Sabela (i.e. Auca) as Zaparoan. However, as she notes, the term Auca has been very loosely used, and this is simply a matter of a confusion of names. The Auca that she treats, though unquestionably Andean, is entirely distinct from Zaparo.

There are two well-marked subgroupings within Andean. Despite very limited material, the languages Catacao, Cholona, Culli, Leco, and Sechura clearly form a Northern subgroup. Since this relationship has not been hitherto recognized, I have included etymologies exclusive to this subgroup, which probably represent innovations within the subgroup rather than a heritage from Proto-Andean. These exclusively Northern Andean etymologies are followed by (N) in the list below. The other clear grouping, in the extreme south, consists of Alakaluf, Araucanian, Gennaken, Patagon, and Yamana and may be called Southern Andean. Etymologies found only in these languages are followed by (S).

The two most widespread language groupings, Quechua and Aymara, have often been compared. There are of course numerous borrowings, particularly from Quechua into Aymara. However, I do not believe that they have a special relationship within Andean. Zaparoan appears to be closest to Kahuapana; and if we had more data, Itucale, Mayna, and Sabela would probably turn out to form a subgroup. Aymara appears relatively isolated within Andean.

In addition to the 129 exclusively Andean etymologies presented here, 85 Andean entries will be found in the Amerind dictionary under the following etymologies: $ABOVE_3$, ANT_2, ARM_1, ASK_1, BE_2, $BEARD_2$, BEE_1, $BELLY_2$, $BELLY_3$, $BITE_1$, $BITTER_1$, $BLACK_1$, $BLACK_2$, $BLOOD_1$, $BODY_1$, BREAST, BROTHER, $CALL_1$, $CALL_2$, $CARRY_1$, $CHILD_1$, $CHILD_4$, $CLOUD_1$, $COLD_1$, $COLD_3$, COME, COOK, COVER, DIE_1, DIE_2, DIG_3, $DRINK_1$, $DRINK_2$, DRY_1, DRY_2, $EARTH_1$, EAT_2, EGG_1, $FEATHER_1$, $FEATHER_2$, $FIRE_3$, FIREWOOD, GO_1, GO_4, GRASS, $GUTS_2$, $HAND_1$, $HAND_3$, HATE, $HEAR_2$, $HOLE_1$, HOUSE, $LARGE_2$, LAUGH, MAN_2, $MANY_1$, $MEAT_1$, MOUSE, $MOUTH_1$, NEAR, NOSE, PAIN, PERSON, $RIVER_2$, $ROAD_1$, ROOT, ROUND, SALIVA, SAY_1, $SEED_1$, SEEK, SHINE, SHORT, SIT_3, $SKIN_1$, $SNAKE_1$, $STONE_1$, $STONE_2$, SUN_2, $TREE_2$, TWO, WIND, WISH, $WOMAN_1$, $WORK_1$.

ANDEAN ETYMOLOGIES

1 ALL_1 Araucanian: Pehuenche *fil*. Patagon: Tehuelche *wilom*. Yamana *wølaii-ama*. (S)

2 ALL_2 Kahuapana *ipa* 'enough.' Sabela: Auca *baa*.

3 ANGRY   Araucanian: Pehuenche γ*yd* 'be angry,' *yd-* 'be angry.' Patagon: Tehuelche *ihot-* 'be angry.' (S)

4 ANUS   Alakaluf *kioot-pe*. Gennaken *oqoti* 'anus, large intestines.' Quechua: Lamisto *okote* 'buttocks,' Santiagueño *oqoti* 'guts.' Yamana *guta* 'hole.'

5 ARM Alakaluf *appail.* Aymara *ampara.* Kahuapana *ipølli-lalla* 'armpit'
(*lalla* = 'hollow'). Patagon *fan* 'hand.'

6 ARROW₁ Cholona *ujuk* [ulluc]. Gennaken *aeke* 'bow.' Yamana *ajaku.*
Cf. Quechua: Yanacocha *ʎaki* 'thorn'.

7 ARROW₂ Leco *uela.* Patagon: Ona *el.*

8 ASHES Itucale *auxe* 'charcoal.' Patagon: Tsoneka *ahe.* Yamana *øxwa.*

9 AUNT Cholona *pan* 'mother.' Patagon: Tehuelche *epan,* Ona *poon*
'maternal aunt.'

10 BACK Gennaken *ja-sače.* Patagon: Manekenkn *eškun,* Ona *ešk*
'shoulder.' Yamana *iski.* (S)

11 BAD Cholona *išivax.* Leco *čepe.* Cf. Quechua: Cochabamba *supaj*
'devil'.

12 BAT Gennaken *čexčux.* Kahuapana: Jebero *išok, išiq.* Quechua:
Ancash *tˢiktˢi,* Huanuco *siksi.*

13 BATHE Kahuapana *ama.* Sabela *āa.*

14 BE Araucanian *x(-en)* [gen]. Kahuapana: Jebero *-k-* (nominal
predicator). Patagon: Ona *ke.* Quechua (general) *ka* (*ser* rather than
estar). Zaparo: Iquito *iikii,* Arabela *ki* 'be, remain.'

15 BEARD Alakaluf *af-* (in various compounds 'mouth,' 'beard,' 'chin,'
etc.). Itucale *mami.* Kahuapana *amu-kujula.* Patagon *ma.* Zaparo *amu.*

16 BEAUTIFUL Aymara *kʔača.* Kahuapana *kša-.* Patagon: Tehuelche
ket-. Quechua *kʔača* (Aymara borrowing from Quechua?).

17 BIRD Cholona *kumkoči.* Leco *kaču.* (N)

18 BLOOD Patagon: Tehuelche *unake* 'menstruation.' Zaparo *nanaka,*
unaka.

19 BOY Kahuapana: Kahuapana *vila, wila* 'boy, child, son,' Jebero *wila.*
Quechua: Wanka *walas.* Sabela *wɨɨñæ, wēī* (Sabela has no liquids).

20 BREAST Itucale *maxkui* 'nipple.' Kahuapana: Jebero *muyi.* Patagon:
Tehuelche *maka* 'milk, breast,' Ona *max* 'milk.'

21 BROTHER Catacao [aszat] 'man.' Cholona *azot.* (N)

22 BURN Kahuapana *ukølje, ukøra.* Quechua: Wanka *kaña.* Sabela
gō(-te) 'be burned.' Yamana *ki:nia.*

23 COLD Alakaluf *turra-jerra.* Patagon: Teuesh *taal* 'ice,' Tehuelche *tharr*
'ice,' Manekenkn *tal* 'ice.' Yamana *tørri.* (S)

24 COME₁ Araucanian *aku* 'arrive.' Kahuapana *kwa.* Patagon: Tehuelche
ague 'comes.' Zaparo: Zaparo *ikwa* 'go,' Andoa *ekwa* 'go.'

25 COME₂ Cholona *(či-)pza-n* 'they come.' Leco *busa.* (N)

26 DANCE   Aymara: Lupaca *toqʔo*, Aymara *thokʔo*. Quechua: Cochabamba *taki* 'sing.' Zaparo *siki*.

27 DARK   Alakaluf: Kaueskar *ksapaj* 'night.' Kahuapana *kašišø*. Yamana *akuš, kuški*.

28 DIE₁   Cholona *mi-kol*. Culli *koni* 'dead.' Kahuapana: Kahuapana *kalloi-li* 'sick,' Jebero *kaluwi* 'sick.'

29 DIE₂   Catacao: Catacao *lakatu*, Colan *dlakati*. Sechura *laktuk*. (N)

30 EARTH₁   Alakaluf *wiš, weš*. Yamana *uši*. (S)

31 EARTH₂   Alakaluf *toltol* 'mud.' Itucale *axtani*. Patagon: Ona *tarw*. Yamana *tøn*.

32 EARTH₃   Cholona: Hivito *puts*. Culli *pus*. Cf. Quechua: Chinchaysuyu *patsa* 'ground.'

33 EAT   Cholona *a-mok*. Quechua: Santigueño *miku*, Cochabamba *mikhu*, etc.

34 EYE   Alakaluf *tʲell, teɬ*. Araucanian *thol* 'forehead.' Gennaken *trol* 'forehead.' Patagon: Tehuelche *otel*. Yamana *tella*. (S)

35 FATHER   Cholona: Cholona *kuč*, Hivito *kotk*. Itucale *kiča* 'man.' Leco *ač*. Sechura *kuč*. Zaparo: Iquito *kati*.

36 FIGHT₁   Araucanian: Pehuenche *kajo*. Patagon: Ona *kekej-en*. (S)

37 FIGHT₂   Alakaluf *toks*. Aymara *tokʔe* 'to quarrel.' Kahuapana *an-čiokma*.

38 FISH   Kahuapana: Kahuapana, Jebero *samer*. Sechura *šum, šuma*.

39 FLAT   Yamana *panuš*. Zaparo *pana*.

40 FLOWER₁   Catacao *čukču(m)*. Culli *čuču*. (N)

41 FLOWER₂   Gennaken *akeše*. Patagon: Tsoneka *akeše*, Ona *košpe*. (S)

42 FLY (v.)   Araucanian *lev-, lef-*. Yamana *alapa*. (S)

43 FOOD   Cholona *sak*. Leco *sokoč*. (N)

44 FREEZE   Alakaluf [ghesas], *kizas, kisak*. Patagon: Ona *košek* 'winter,' Manekenkn *koheš* 'cold.' Quechua: Santigueño *qasa*, Yanacocha *qasei* 'cold.'

45 FROG   Alakaluf: Kaueskar *walap* 'toad.' Kahuapana *waulla*. Patagon: Tehuelche, Teuesh *ualuel*.

46 GALL   Aymara *hipʰiʎa* 'guts.' Yamana *hipa* 'liver.' Zaparo *hipa-ka, hipa-no* 'bitter.'

47 GO UP   Araucanian *eko-n* 'climb.' Patagon *kea-n*. Yamana *ukeia*. (S)

48 GOOD₁   Araucanian *kothy*. Aymara *kʔača*. Kahuapana *kaassi* 'sweet.' Patagon: Tehuelche *ket-en*. Quechua: Cochabamba *kʔača*.

49 GOOD₂   Alakaluf *laplap, laip* 'beautiful, good.' Araucanian: Moluche
   lepu- 'to clean.' (S)

50 GRANDFATHER   Gennaken *baja.* Patagon: Tehuelche *bai.* (S)

51 GUTS   Itucale *ðidi.* Kahuapana *luʎi, ruʎi.* Patagon: Tehuelche *le.*
   Sabela: Sabela *ōnōnē,* Auca (phonemic) *ōdōdō.*

52 HAIR   Patagon: Ona *aal.* Yamana *ali* 'feather.' (S)

53 HAND   Patagon: Tehuelche *oš.* Yamana *još.* (S)

54 HARD   Araucanian *læk-an* 'strong.' Aymara *ñaqʰo* 'rough.' Itucale
   nuxue. Patagon: Ona *unker.* Quechua: Chinchaysuyu *anak* 'be hard.'
   Zaparo: Iquito *niiki.*

55 HEAVEN   Catacao: Colan *kutuk-nap.* Leco *kaut.* Patagon: Tehuelche
   koč. Sechura *kučuk-jor.*

56 HUNGER   Aymara *mačča.* Quechua: Santiagueño *mučú* 'famine.'
   Yamana *amaš-agu* 'be hungry.'

57 HURT₁   Cholona *kama* 'sick.' Quechua: Santiagueño *kami* 'injure.'

58 HURT₂   Kahuapana *ike, ikø.* Sabela: Tuwituwey *kæ-* 'hurt in the . . . '

59 INSIDE   Araucanian *minu.* Aymara *mankxa.* Cholona *-man* 'in.'
   Quechua *-man* (dative).

60 JAGUAR   Kahuapana: Kahuapana, Jebero *amana.* Sabela: Auca *mēnē.*

61 KILL   Leco *kis.* Patagon: Tehuelche *ikeš,* Ona *kečer* 'beat.'

62 KISS   Kahuapana *muša.* Quechua: Santiagueño *muča.*

63 KNEE   Alakaluf: Kaueskar *taltal.* Kahuapana: Kahuapana *tula* 'thigh,'
   Jebero *tula* 'leg.' Patagon: Ona *tolke* 'calf, ankle.' Yamana *tula-pur.*

64 LARGE   Leco *umun.* Zaparo: Iquito *uumaana.*

65 LAUGH   Cholona: Hivito *kolxam.* Culli *kankiu.* Zaparo *kora.*

66 LEAF   Araucanian: Mapuche *lupi, lipi* 'feather.' Aymara: Aymara
   lapʰi, Jaqaru *napʰra.* Zaparo: Iquito *nam.* Cf. Kahuapana: Kahuapana
   lalumo, Jebero *lalumok.*

67 LEFT   Kahuapana: Jebero *amøng-nang* (cf. *inči-nang* 'right'). Zaparo:
   Arabela *mwenikja* 'left hand.'

68 LEG   Alakaluf *kal, kalt, kath* 'thigh.' Aymara *čara* 'leg, thigh.' Cholona
   a-čel. Leco *be-sel* 'foot.' Patagon: Tsoneka *kel* 'foot,' Patagon *keal*
   'foot.' Yamana *kalaka* 'hip.'

69 LONG   Kahuapana: Kahuapana *šin,* Jebero *šin* 'tall.' Patagon: Ona
   šinke, šemkaj 'deep.' Quechua: Santiagueño *suni.* Cf. Kahuapana *sama*
   'deep'; Sabela *ðaema.*

70 MALE   Alakaluf: Alakaluf *arak, arek,* Kaueskar *arak* 'husband.'

Araucanian *alka*. Patagon: Ona *xork*. Quechua: Santiagueño *orqo*
'husband,' Yanacocha *oloqo* 'husband.'

71 MAN   Cholona: Cholona *num, non,* Hivito *nam, nun.* Sechura *non.*
(N)

72 MEAT   Catacao *kʾol.* Gennaken *kalul* 'flesh.' Sabela: Auca *-kā* 'flesh,
animate.' Sechura *kolt.* Cf. Alakaluf *alkæɫ.*

73 MOON   Itucale *axteni.* Mayna *thnṇ* 'star.' Patagon: Ona *tel* 'star,'
Teuesh *teruč.*

74 MOUTH₁   Cholona *lol.* Kahuapana *lala.*

75 MOUTH₂   Leco *kollo.* Sechura *bo-korua.* (N)

76 NAVEL   Alakaluf *kupu* 'belly.' Yamana *kup(f)u.* (S)

77 NECK   Aymara: Lupaca *aru* 'voice, speech.' Culli *uro* 'neck.' (For the
semantics, cf. Aymara *kunka* which means both 'voice' and 'neck.')

78 NEW   Aymara *mačakʾa.* Patagon: Tehuelche *mago* 'young, fresh,'
Teuesh *maak.* Quechua: Santiagueño *mosox,* Wanka *mušu,* etc. Zaparo
maka 'raw.'

79 NOSE   Cholona *čul-nik* 'snotty.' Leco *bi-činua.* Sechura *čuna.* (N)

80 OLD   Aymara *ačači* 'old man.' Gennaken *ietˀa.* Patagon: Teuesh *aačn,*
Manakenkn *ača.* Yamana *wata.*

81 ONE   Kahuapana: Jebero *saka* 'only.' Quechua: Ecuadorean *sux* 'one,
other,' Lamisto *sok.* Patagon: Ona *sus, suš.*

82 OTHER₁   Araucanian *ka.* Patagon: Tehuelche *kajuko.* Yamana *haku:.*
(S)

83 OTHER₂   Quechua: Cochabamba *wah.* Sabela: Auca *wa.*

84 PAIN   Culli *pillač.* Sechura *punuk.* (N)

85 PENIS   Itucale *laxe.* Quechua: Santiagueño *laka* 'vagina.' Yamana
lakač.

86 PIERCE   Itucale *oxku* 'needle.' Sabela: Auca *ko* 'pierce, make a hole.'

87 PLAY   Gennaken *makinga.* Yamana *miku.* (S)

88 RAIN₁   Alakaluf *pere, apera.* Gennaken [furfurgey]. Mayna *baal* 'sky.'
Quechua: Santiagueño *para.* Sechura *purir.* Yamana *balaka.*

89 RAIN₂   Itucale *ixlo.* Kahuapana: Kahuapana *øla, uɫa,* Tschaahui
uˀlang.

90 RAIN₃   Mayna *athn.* Patagon: Tehuelche *ten* 'shower,' Manekenkn *oten*
'water.' Quechua: Ecuadorean *tamia.*

91 RED   Alakaluf *keplaik* 'blood.' Patagon: Tehuelche *kapenk,* Teuesh
kapen. Yamana *kapi* 'a red face.' (S)

92 RETURN   Araucanian *kut-un.* Quechua: Cochabamba, Caraz *kuti.*

93 RIB   Mayna *ana-baani*. Patagon: Tehuelche *parr*, Ona *par*.

94 ROTTEN   Kahuapana *taokulli*. Patagon *tokhon* 'be rotten.'

95 RUN   Aymara *t'ikta*. Kahuapana: Kahuapana *tøka-lk*, Jebero *tək'k'a*.

96 SAY   Quechua: Santiagueño, Chinchaysuyu, Cochabamba *ni*. Sabela *ā*. Zaparo *ana, na* (quotative).

97 SEA   Catacao: Catacao *amum*, Colan *amaum*. Cholona *omium* 'wave.' (N)

98 SEE₁   Alakaluf *luk*. Quechua: Cochabamba *ruk*. Yamana *urruksi*. Zaparo: Zaparo *noki*, Arabela *nunikjaj*.

99 SEE₂   Aymara: Jaqaru *iʎa*. Kahuapana: Kahuapana, Jebero *ʎi*.

100 SEE₃   Cholona: Cholona *a-mnajč-an* 'watch,' Hivito *montˢa, mantˢa* 'eye.' Leco *mini*. (N)

101 SISTER   Cholona *akiñiu*. Culli *kañi*. (N)

102 SKIN   Kahuapana: Jebero *pi* 'body.' Mayna *-pa*. Yamana *api* 'skin, body.'

103 SLEEP   Aymara: Aymara, Jaqaru *iki*. Yamana *aka*.

104 SMALL   Araucanian *piči* 'few, small.' Aymara *pisi*. Quechua: Cochabamba *pisi*. Yamana *paači* 'weak.' Zaparo [picckara] 'weak.'

105 SMELL₁   Aymara *mukhi*. Zaparo *moka* 'fetid.'

106 SMELL₂   Itucale *asi* 'nose.' Patagon *os*. Quechua: Chinchaysuyu *asia* 'stink.'

107 SOFT   Patagon: Teuesh *apoi*. Quechua: Ecuadorean *apija* 'become soft.'

108 STAR₁   Alakaluf *fualas*. Cholona *pel* 'moon.' Leco *polea*. Yamana *aporea-n*.

109 STAR₂   Catacao: Colan *čupčup* (pl.). Culli *čuip*. Sechura *čupčup* (pl.). (N)

110 SUN   Leco *heno*. Mayna *hena*.

111 SWEET   Cholona *aʎhi* 'sweet thing.' Kahuapana: Jebero *jali* 'tasty.' Quechua: Chinchaysuyu *ali* 'well,' Cochabamba *aʎin* 'well.'

112 THORN   Patagon: Ona *meč*. Yamana *umoš*. (S)

113 THREE   Araucanian *kyla*. Kahuapana: Kahuapana *kara*, Jebero *kala*. Patagon: Hongote *čalas*, Tehuelche *kaaš*.

114 THROW   Aymara *aha*. Zaparo *aha*.

115 TOMORROW   Mayna *baoeni*. Sabela: Sabela *baana*, Tuwituwey *bauna*.

116 TREE   Itucale *eneγa*. Zaparo: Zaparo *naku* 'forest,' Iquito *naki* 'forest.'

117 TRUNK   Patagon: Ona *korke*. Quechua: Cochabamba *kurku*.

118 TWO   Patagon: Ona *soki*, Patagon *xeukaj*. Quechua: Santiagueño, Chinchaysuyu *iškaj*.

119 UNCLE   Aymara *lari*. Zaparo *nari*.

120 VOMIT   Quechua: Santiagueño *čuña*. Zaparo *činiaka* (n.).

121 WATER   Cholona: Cholona *kot, køta*, Hivito *kači*. Sechura *xoto*. (N)

122 WHITE   Alakaluf: Kaueskar *jeraxia*. Araucanian *ajary-en* 'be whitish.' Quechua: Cochabamba *jurah*, Yanacocha *jurax*, Lamisto *jurak*.

123 WIND₁ (n.)   Alakaluf *kel*. Zaparo: Iquito *akira*.

124 WIND₂ (n.)   Catacao *vik*. Sechura *fik*. (N)

125 WISH   Kahuapana: Jebero *-ʔina* (desiderative). Leco *ra, era*. Quechua: Ecuadorean *-naja* (desiderative); Junin, Huanuco *-naa* (desiderative). Sabela: Auca *ā*. Yamana *jana*. Zaparo *-ira* (purposive).

126 WORM   Aymara *laqʾo*. Cholona *laua* 'larva.' Kahuapana: Kahuapana *laua* 'snake,' Tschaahui *rawan* 'snake,' Jebero *daua* 'snake.'

127 YELLOW   Alakaluf *tal(-kar)*. Patagon: Ona *tool*. (S)

128 YESTERDAY   Araucanian: Araucanian *uja*, Moluche *wija*. Kahuapana: Jebero *jaʔ*, Kahuapana *ija, ja*.

129 YOUNG   Itucale *enamana*. Quechua: Huanuco *malwa*, Ancash *maʎwa*, Caraz *malqo*. Sabela: Auca *mīī* 'new.' Zaparo: Zaparo *manino*, Iquito *manini*.

CHIBCHAN-PAEZAN

The Chibchan-Paezan branch of Amerind consists of the following families: Allentiac, Andaqui, Antioquia, Aruak, Atacama, Barbacoa, Betoi, Chibcha, Chimu, Choco, Cuitlatec, Cuna, Guaymi, Itonama, Jirajara, Lenca, Malibu, Misumalpan, Motilon, Mura, Paez, Paya, Rama, Talamanca, Tarascan, Timucua, Warrau, Xinca, and Yanoama. It falls into two clearly marked groups, one of which will be called Chibchan and the other Paezan. In the first are Antioquia, Aruak, Chibcha, Cuitlatec, Cuna, Guaymi, Lenca, Malibu, Misumalpan, Motilon, Paya, Rama, Talamanca, Tarascan, Xinca, and Yanoama. What might be called the nuclear Chibchan group consists of Antioquia, Aruak, Chibcha, Cuna, Guaymi, Malibu, Motilon, Misumalpan, Rama, and Talamanca. Correspondingly, within Paezan—Allentiac, Andaqui, Atacama, Barbacoa, Betoi, Chimu, Choco, Itonama, Jirajara, Mura, Paez, Timucua, Warrau—we might call Andaqui, Barbacoa, Choco, and Paez nuclear Paezan.

Naturally enough, it was the existence of these two nuclear groups, and their connection, that was first recognized. For the Chibchan group, we are largely indebted to the pioneer work of Max Uhle, published in 1890; for Paezan, and for the connection between certain Paezan and Chibchan languages, we are indebted to Paul Rivet and his collaborators. Unfortunately, Rivet excluded Choco from Paezan, though he was aware of its numerous and fundamental resemblances to other languages in the group, especially Paez-Coconuco and the Barbacoa languages. For this, he was criticized by Walter Lehmann (1920). Rivet also erroneously included Coche, Esmeralda, and Yaruro, all Equatorial languages, in Chibchan, as did Loukotka (1968). Clearly, Loukotka's Chibchan, which includes its Central American extensions, is not on the same level as his other stocks, consisting as it does of subgroups whose genetic rank is more nearly equivalent to supposedly independent stocks in the rest of his classification.

Lehmann correctly noted the special relationship of Guaymi and Dorasque (i.e. Changuena, Chumulu, and Gualaca), as well as that of Rama, Guatuso and two members of the group now generally called Misumalpan (Miskito and Matagalpa). All these are listed as distinct subfamilies by Loukotka. Although Loukotka lists Mura and Matanawi as independent South American stocks, they are so closely related that I include Matanawi in the Mura family. What I found most surprising with regard to Chibchan-Paezan were the affiliations of Allentiac far to the south in northern Argentina; Tarascan and Cuitlatec, hitherto considered isolated languages of Mexico; and above all Timucua, an extinct language of Florida. As regards the last, Julian Granberry, after comparing Timucua with every stock in the Gulf and Caribbean area, found it closest to Warrau of Venezuela and Guyana (as cited in Crawford 1979). But Warrau is a Paezan language, and further comparison, particularly with Paez-Coconuco, the Barbacoa languages, and Choco, strongly confirms its membership in that family.

In the following etymologies, those exclusive to nuclear Chibchan, which are very numerous, are omitted, since there seems to me no question of the validity of that group. Nuclear Paezan etymologies, however, *are* included because of the doubts concerning Choco. Under Chibcha, I include the closely related Tunebo group, and under Paez the Coconuco languages. Catio, a Chocoan language, is arbitrarily distinguished by spelling from Katio, a language of the very poorly attested Antioquia group. Etymologies exclusive to the Chibchan and Paezan subgroups are followed by (C) and (P), respectively.

In addition to the 226 exclusively Chibchan-Paezan etymologies pre-

sented here, Chibchan-Paezan entries will be found in the Amerind diction-
ary under the following 98 entries: ABOVE₁, ABOVE₂, ANGRY, ANT₁,
ARM, ASHES₁, BE₂, BELLY₂, BITE₁, BITTER₁, BITTER₂, BLOOD₂,
BOIL, BONE₃, BREAK, BROTHER, CALL₂, CHEW, CHILD₁, CLEAN,
CLOSE, CLOUD₁, CLOUD₂, COLD₁, COLD₂, COME, COVER, CRY,
DARK, DEER₁, DIE₁, DIG₁, DOG, DUST, EARTH₂, EGG₂, EXCRE-
MENT₁, FAR, FEATHER₂, FIRE₁, FIREWOOD, FLY₂, FOREHEAD₁,
FOREHEAD₂, GO₁, GO ₃, GOOD₂, GOOD₃, HAND₁, HAND₃, HARD₁,
HARD₂, HEAR₁, HOUSE, KILL, KNEE₁, KNEE₂, LAUGH, LIGHT,
LIVER, LIZARD, LONG₁, LONG₂, LOUSE₁, MAKE₂, MANY₂, MANY₃,
MOON₂, MOSQUITO, MOUSE, NARROW, NIGHT₁, NIGHT₄, RIVER₂,
ROUND, SAY₁, SEED₁, SNAKE₁, SNAKE₂, STAR₂, STONE₂, SUN₁, SUN₂,
SUN₃, SUN₄, TONGUE₁, TREE₃, TWO, WATER₁, WATER₂, WHITE,
WIND, WISH, WOMAN ₃, WOOD₁, WOOD₂, WORK₁, YELLOW₁.

CHIBCHAN-PAEZAN ETYMOLOGIES

1 ABOVE   Allentiac: Allentiac *kleu*, Millcayac *qleu, qlu.* Guaymi: Move
   koin 'heavens,' Penomeño *kokoin* 'heavens.' Itonama *kʼana-no* 'top.'
   Motilon: Dobocubi *kanu.* Talamanca: Bribri *kā*, Terraba *-kin*, Cabecar
   kī-ga.
2 ANT   Mura *ibohū.* Warrau *mu(h)a.* (P)
3 ANUS   Aruak: Bintucua *gase.* Paez *kuts* 'anus, vagina.' Talamanca:
   Borunca *kas* 'ravine.' Warrau *akoho* 'cave, hueco' (Warrau *h < s*).
4 ARM   Aruak: Kagaba, Guamaca *gula*, Bintucua *guna* 'arm, hand.'
   Choco: Catio *ekara* 'shoulder.' Chibcha: Tegria, Pedraza *ikara* 'back.'
   Cuna *ankala.* Guaymi: Murire *kana*, Chumulu *kulgalu*, Gualaca *kula*
   'hand.' Lenca: Opatoro *gulala* 'hand,' Guajiquero *gwala* 'hand.'
   Misumalpan: Cacaopera *kari-ka.* Paez: Totoro, Guambiana *kwal.* Paya
   kara 'arm, shoulder.'
5 ARROW   Motilon: Dobocubi *kani* 'bow.' Malibu: Chimila *kan(-gra).*
   Rama: Rama *kani* 'shoot,' Guatuso *karu.* Warrau *ikare* 'shoot an arrow.'
   Cf. Allentiac: Allentiac *čaly*, Millcayac *čali.*
6 AUNT   Barbacoa: Cayapa *manggu*, Colorado *māku.* Jirajara: Ayoman
   moγo [mogho]. (P)
7 AWAKE₁   Barbacoa: Cayapa *tenga-.* Chimu *tˢok* (intransitive). Paez
   tengg- 'see.' Talamanca: Bribri *tina.*
8 AWAKE₂   Atacama *kʼep-ni.* Itonama *kupux-na.* (P)
9 AXE   Andaqui *boxo-(ka).* Chibcha: Tunebo *baxi-ta* 'machete.'
   Talamanca: Cabecar, Chiripo *bak.* Cf. Cuitlatec *navaxo* 'knife.'

10 BAD   Chimu: Eten *piss.* Cuitlatec *baɫa* 'sin.' Paez *patˢ(-kue)* 'ugly.'

11 BATHE   Cuna *oka.* Paya *ok(-ka).* Talamanca: Bribri *ku* ~ *uk* (different tenses). (C)

12 BEAR (v.)   Allentiac *tau.* Choco: Catio *to.* Paez *do.* (P)

13 BEE   Guaymi: Gualaca *ala* 'honey,' Muoi *uli.* Misumalpan: Matagalpa *ala* 'honey.' Talamanca: Tirub *or* 'bee, honey,' Terraba *or.* Xinca: Xinca *uwaɫ* (Maldonado), Chiquimulilla *uilua.* (C)

14 BEHIND   Allentiac: Allentiac *punak,* Millcayac *punar.* Barbacoa: Colorado *bene,* Cayapa *beneša.* Chimu: Eten *fenčep, feneng* 'back.' Choco: Darien *barrea.* (P)

15 BELLY   Barbacoa: Cayapa, Colorado *bi* 'inside.' Choco: Citara, Catio, Tucura *bi.* Misumalpan: Sumu, Ulua *ba,* Matagalpa *pu.* Talamanca: Terraba *bu(-wo).* Tarascan *-va-* 'inside.'

16 BIRD   Allentiac: Millcayac [zure]. Aruak: Guamaca, Atanque *suri,* Bintucua *turi.* Chibcha: Margua *mua-sira,* Pedraza *dua-sira,* Boncota *rugue-sira,* Manare *ruba-sira,* Tegria *roa-sira* (the first element in these Chibcha examples means 'flesh, animal'). Lenca: Guajiquero *sira.* Yanoama: Sanema *tˢalo.*

17 BITE   Cuitlatec *eʔla.* Chimu *rr(-an).* Malibu: Chimila *erau.* Tarascan *ara* 'eat.'

18 BLACK₁   Cuitlatec *puluši-li, puruši.* Cuna *polea* 'be dark.' Itonama *bola* 'shadow.' Misumalpan: Ulua *bara.* Tarascan *vera-* 'dark.'

19 BLACK₂   Choco: Chami *tauri* 'shadow.' Guaymi: Move *tra,tro.* Talamanca: Bribri *dororoi,* Chiripo *dorona,* Borunca *turinat.* Paya *tersu* 'Negro.' Tarascan *tuli* 'black, charcoal.' Cf. Mura: Matanawi *torupi* 'shadow.'

20 BLOOD   Lenca: Chilanga *ala.* Misumalpan: Cacaopera *arru.* Paya *uri.* (C)

21 BODY   Choco: Waunana, Urıbe, etc. *kakua.* Paez *kakue.* (P)

22 BOIL (v.)   Aruak: Bintucua *su.* Cuitlatec *iɫe.* Yanoama: Sanema, Yanomam *īši* 'burn,' Sanema (Wilbert) *iiš.* (C)

23 BONE₁   Barbacoa: Colorado *čide.* Chimu *čotti.* Itonama *čədəkə.* Motilon: Barira *kada.*

24 BONE₂   Cuitlatec *dihta.* Misumalpan: Miskito *dusa.* Paez *dith, dʲiʔtx.* Talamanca: Borunca *det(-kra),* Bribri *diča.*

25 BOY   Chibcha *ča* 'male.' Chimu: Eten *čoh* 'boy, child.' Cuitlatec *ču, čuʔu.* Paez *uču* 'small.' Tarascan *ača* 'child.'

26 BROTHER   Chimu *čang.* Cuitlatec *ɫø̃.* Guaymi: Changuena *sin.*

Talamanca: Terraba *ši* 'older brother.' Xinca (Maldonado) [szuya] 'older brother.'

27 BURN₁ Cuitlatec *tul(-wakaši)* 'dried beef' (analyzed by Escalante Hernandez as 'burn-cow'). Tarascan *tʰiri*. Xinca *tala, taraɬa* 'to toast.' (C)

28 BURN₂ Allentiac *čaps*. Barbacoa: Colorado *čiba-na, čiba-ge* 'heat.' Chimu: Chimu [xllep]. Cuitlatec *čibe*. Guaymi: Chumulu *keba* 'fire.' Paez *šaβʲ* 'burn oneself.' Tarascan *čuhpi,čpʰi-ri*. Yanoama: Sanema *tˢopi, čɔɔbi* 'hot.'

29 BURY Choco: Catio *ugga*. Cuitlatec *ake* 'dig.' Paez *akkue* 'grave.'

30 CHEST Chimu *axtærr*. Cuitlatec *ixtaloja*. Lenca: Guajiquero *thala* 'neck.' Tarascan *teru(-nhe-kua)*. Xinca: Yupultepec, Chiquimulilla *taɬi*.

31 CHEW Choco: Catio *biaka*. Paez *peki*. (P)

32 CHIN Atacama *takˀil* 'jaw.' Lenca: Intibucat *tixe* 'face,' Guajiquero, Opatoro *amp-tiga* 'face.' Motilon: Dobocubi *daka* 'chin, beard.'

33 CLOUD Cuitlatec *kunā, kumā*. Tarascan *xuma* 'cloud, fog.' Xinca: Yupultepec *kunu* 'cloud, fog.' (C)

34 COME₁ Barbacoa: Colorado *fua* 'arrive.' Motilon: Dobocubi *abaj*. Mura *abe* 'let's go.' Paez: Paez *pa* 'arrive,' Guambiana *pu* 'arrive.' Tarascan *-pe-* 'do while coming.' Timucua *po(-no)*. Xinca (Maldonado) *pe* 'future.'

35 COME₂ Cuitlatec *iti*. Cuna *-ta-* 'go' (verbal auxiliary). Itonama *tˀo, tˀe* 'arrive.' Talamanca: Bribri *do:* ~ *dæ* (different tenses). Xinca *taa*.

36 COME₃ Cuna *taka*. Paya *tek*. (C)

37 COME₄ Barbacoa: Colorado, Cayapa *ha*. Atacama *hau*. (P)

38 COOK₁ Barbacoa: Colorado *nija* 'burn,' Colorado, Cayapa *ni* 'fire.' Chibcha: Uncasica *ani* 'to boil,' *anina* 'cooked,' Tegria *ani(-ndro)* 'cook.' Chimu: Eten *nin* 'cook, boil.' Guaymi: Move, Norteño *ñio (-kwa)* 'fire.' Paez: Guambiana *nenin* 'working.' Tarascan *nini-rha-ni*.

39 COOK₂ Tarascan *hiri*. Yanoama: Yanoam, Yanomam *hari*. (C)

40 COVER (v.) Chibcha: Tunebo *teka-ra* 'poncho.' Cuna *tukusii* 'be hidden.' Misumalpan: Sumu *sakawaki* 'hide.' Rama *al-taku-ai* 'be hidden.' Tarascan *šuku-ta-hpe-ni*. (C)

41 CROCODILE Andaqui *rapae*. Aruak: Atanque *lobu* 'lizard.' Barbacoa: Colorado *lampa(-lo), lumpa(-lo)* 'lizard.' Guaymi: Move *lapa*.

42 DANCE₁ Guaymi: Muoi *ubra*, Norteño, Penomeño *prare* (n.). Jirajara *prarara* (n.). Tarascan *vara-ni*. Yanoama: Yanomam *praia*.

43 DANCE₂ Barbacoa: Colorado *terake-de*. Itonama *tuluke*. (P)

44 DAUGHTER   Aruak: Guamaca *busi*. Lenca: Guajiquero *peza, upeša*.
Misumalpan: Sumu *basan*. Paya *pača* 'female.' (C)

45 DAY   Aruak: Bintucua *juia*. Barbacoa: Colorado *jo* 'day, sun.' Jirajara
juau 'sun.' Misumalpan: Miskito *ju* 'day, sun,' *jui* 'sun.' Warrau *ja*
'day, sun.'

46 DEER   Barbacoa: Colorado, Cayapa *mana*. Cuna *immala* 'animal.'
Motilon: Barira *maana* 'meat.' Mura: Matanawi *manjo*. Paez:
Guambiana *pan*. Cf. Betoi *ubadoi* 'animal.'

47 DIG   Barbacoa: Colorado *mena* 'bury,' Cayapa *meng* 'bury.' Guaymi
moin.

48 DIRTY₁   Barbacoa: Colorado *toa*. Chimu: Eten *toixeiñ*. Itonama
tjaxna?ke. (P)

49 DIRTY₂   Cuna *oli* 'mud.' Lenca: Chilanga *ulang*. Rama *ula*.
Talamanca: Terraba *uriurie*. (C)

50 DOG   Jirajara: Ayoman *warhen* 'fox.' Paez: Guambiana, Totoro,
Moguex *wera*. Xinca: Jutiapa *wilaj* 'jaguar.' Cf. Cuna *wasa* 'deer' and
Allentiac: Millcayac *waza* (a different root?).

51 DRINK₁   Barbacoa: Colorado *kuči*, Cayapa *kuš*, Cuaiquer *kuase*
'water.' Itonama *kasi-(?na)*. Timucua *okut*. (P)

52 DRINK₂   Cuitlatec *oł*. Misumalpan: Ulua *uas* 'water.' Mura: Matanawi
iši. Paya *aso* 'water.' Talamanca: Cabecar, Terraba *iše*. (The Cuitlatec
voiceless lateral seems to derive regularly from a sibilant.)

53 DRINK₃   Choco: Catio *do*, Napipi *itua* 'chicha.' Paez: Paez *tungʲ*,
Moguex *tong*, Panikita *tui*. (P)

54 EAR₁   Lenca: Similaton *jan*, Chilanga *jam*. Yanoama: Yanomam,
Yanomamï *jimɔ*. (C)

55 EAR₂   Barbacoa: Cuaiquer *kail*. Choco: Sambu, Waunana *kuru*, Chami
guru. Paez: Guambiana, Totoro, Moguex *kalo*. Rama: Corobisi *kur*
'hear.' Tarascan *kurha-ngu-ni* 'hear.'

56 EAR₃   Aruak: Kagaba *kuka*, Guamaca *kukua, kuhkua*, Atanque
kukkua. Chibcha: Margua *kugexio*, Pedraza *kukača*, Boncota *kukasa*.
Choco: Nonama *katji*, Waunana *kači*. Cuitlatec *kuhčidi*. Guaymi:
Chumulu, Gualaca *kuga*. Malibu: Chimila *kutˢa(-kra), kuusu(-ka)*,
kutˢaka 'hear.' Motilon: Barira *kutˢi-nje*. Talamanca: Tirub *kuzung*
'hear.' Tarascan *kutˢu(-kwa)*. Timucua *okoto* 'hear.'

57 EARTH₁   Aruak: Bintucua *kasi(-ke)* 'under.' Chibcha *guanza*. Itonama
kus- 'down' (v. prefix). Talamanca: Chiripo *kaša*. Tarascan *ketˢe-kwa*
'under.' Timucua [qisa]. Warrau *kahu* 'underside.'

111

58 EARTH₂   Barbacoa: Cuaiquer *piʎ* [pill], Cara *buala* 'field.' Guaymi:
   Muoi *ubar* 'sand.' Mura *bere*. Paez: Totoro *pir-d*, Guambiana *pire*.
   Tarascan *viras* 'white earth.' Timucua *pile* 'field.' Cf. Aruak: Atanque
   avarin 'under,' Guamaca *auariga* 'under.'

59 EARTH₃   Aruak: Kagaba *kagi*, Bintucua *ka, kaa*. Chibcha: Manare
   kakka 'world.' Cuitlatec *kuʔ-li*. Paya *kuka*. Rama: Guetar *ko*.
   Talamanca: Borunca *kak*, Tirub *kok* 'country,' Terraba *kok*. (C)

60 EARTH₄   Allentiac *tawe, te*. Aruak: Kagaba *čui* 'mud.' Barbacoa:
   Cayapa *tu*, Colorado *to*. Guaymi: Murire *čiwa* 'mud.' Malibu: Chimila
   iti. Motilon: Dobocubi *ita*. Timucua *uti*. Cf. the Chibchan-Paezan
   entry for EARTH₂ in the Amerind dictionary.

61 ELBOW   Chibcha: Sinsiga *kuika*, Tegria, Boncota, Manare *kuika*
   'arm.' Paya *kokisa* 'knee.' Tarascan *kukui-si*. (C)

62 EVENING   Barbacoa: Colorado *kebi, kebina*. Choco: Catio *kebara*,
   Tucura *kebura* 'night.' Timucua [qibo] 'yesterday.' (P)

63 EXCREMENT   Choco: Catio *ami* 'diarrhea.' Jirajara: Gayon *moi*
   'dirty.' Paez *ime*. (P)

64 EYE   Andaqui *sifi*. Atacama *ikepe, kepi*. Barbacoa: Colorado *kapa-ka*,
   Cayapa *kapu-kua* (for *-kua* as suffix, note *kapuʔpihi* 'eyebrow'; see also
   item 40 in Chap. 5). Jirajara: Ayoman *a-kibaux*. Paez: Guambiana,
   Totoro, Moguex *kap*. (P)

65 FACE   Allentiac *pakat* 'forehead.' Aruak: Kagaba *uaka* 'face, cheek.'
   Betoi *fuka*. Chibcha: Sinsiga *aka* 'cheek.' Cuna *wakala* 'cheek.'
   Jirajara: Ayoman *buki*. Yanoama: Yanomam *wiik*.

66 FAR   Cuitlatec *jo, jaj-*. Tarascan *io-* 'high, long.' (C)

67 FAT₁ (n.)   Motilon: Dobocubi *tota*. Paez *totʰ*. Warrau *toi, atoi* 'oil.'

68 FAT₂ (n.)   Cuitlatec *kuji*. Talamanca: Terraba, Tirub *kio*, Bribri *kioʔ*.
   Timucua *uke*.

69 FEATHER₁   Mura: Matanawi *jaa*. Paez *ja(-kue)*. (P)

70 FEATHER₂   Aruak: Bintucua *kui* 'feather, wing.' Chibcha [quye] 'leaf.'
   Cuitlatec *kuwa(-li)*. Guaymi: Murire *ga*. Motilon *oka* 'banana leaf.'
   Rama *ka:* 'leaf.' Talamanca: Terraba *(du-)kvo* (*du* = 'bird,' *kvo* =
   'leaf'), similarly Estrella *(du-)ka*, etc. Xinca: Yupultepec *kaja*. (C)

71 FEMALE   Chibcha: Margua *maringa*. Choco: Andagueda *mwajra*.
   Guaymi: Norteño, Penomeño *meri*, Move *møre*. Misumalpan: Miskito
   mairin 'female, woman.'

72 FINGER   Cuitlatec *axpal(-koja)* 'toe' (*koja* = 'foot'). Xinca: Jutiapa
   pere. (C)

73 FINISH   Chimu: Eten *siaip.* Itonama *so?p.* (P)

74 FIRE   Allentiac: Millcayac *ketek.* Chibcha *gata.* Cuitlatec *kuhtə* 'fire, light.' Motilon: Dobocubi *kadø.* Tarascan *kata* 'firewood.'

75 FLEA   Chimu: Eten *čuka.* Motilon: Dobocubi *čexe* 'to delouse.' Warrau *sika.*

76 FLOUR₁   Barbacoa: Colorado *(ni-)fu* 'ashes' (*ni* = 'fire'). Chimu *æp* 'salt.' Choco: Chami *fu,* Catio *fo.* Timucua *api* 'ashes, dust, salt.' (P)

77 FLOUR₂   Itonama *uka?tje.* Jirajara: Ayoman *kač* 'cinders.' Paez *koč.* (P)

78 FLOWER   Cuitlatec *tuxtu, tutul.* Cuna *tutu.* Cf. Tarascan *tˢitˢi.* (C)

79 FLY (n.)   Cuitlatec *iɬi?i, øɬi.* Xinca: Yupultepec *usu* 'fly, wasp.' (C)

80 FLY (v.)   Atacama *heu.* Barbacoa: Colorado *he?.* (P)

81 FOOT   Aruak: Tairona, Kagaba *kasa,* Atanque *køsa,* Bintucua *katte.* Atacama *k?uči* [kh'oche]. Chibcha: Pedraza *kesa.* Cuitlatec *kuɬa.* Malibu: Chimila *kotˢa, katˢa.* Motilon: Dobocubi *kitu* 'leg, foot.' Paez: Coconuco *kaatˢi,* Guambiana *kasik.*

82 FRONT (IN FRONT OF)   Atacama *k?onni* 'before.' Itonama *kanu* 'before.' Misumalpan: Miskito *kan-ra.*

83 FULL   Allentiac *topata* 'be full.' Barbacoa: Colorado *tua,* Cayapa *tuwa.* Guaymi: Move *debe* 'enough.' Motilon *tow* 'all.' Talamanca: Terraba *tue* 'all.' Warrau *tobo.* Xinca: Chiquimulilla *tumuki* 'all.'

84 GIRL   Aruak: Atanque *kuima* 'young man,' Kagaba *akumi.* Jirajara: Gayon *kobas,* Ayoman *kob-pa.* Rama *kuma* 'wife, young woman.'

85 GIVE   Andaqui *fi.* Antioquia: Katio *be* 'give!' Barbacoa: Colorado *epe.* Chimu: Eten *poi.* Paez: Moguex *pe,* Guambiana *pe* 'lend.'

86 GOOD₁   Antioquia: Katio *avi-ra* 'very good, God.' Choco: Waunana *pia,* Catio *pia* 'well,' Citara *bua.* Guaymi: Gualaca *ape.* Itonama *pu-* (benefactive prefix). Motilon: Dobocubi *baj.* Mura *baha* 'beautiful.' Talamanca: Bribri *buai,* Cabecar *boe,* Chiripo *bui.*

87 GOOD₂   Barbacoa: Cayapa *uwa.* Paez: Paez *ew,* Moguex *eu-t* 'well.' (P)

88 GRASS   Chimu: Chimu, Eten *pe.* Cuitlatec *bejo?o* 'grass, stubble.' Paez: Guambiana *pu* 'roof straw, grass.'

89 GUTS   Paya *suku.* Yanoama: Yanam, Yanomam *šik,* Yanomamï *siikɨ.* (C)

90 HAIR   Andaqui *(un-)so(-xo)* 'beard.' Aruak: Kagaba *sai, saí,* Guamaca *sa, ša,* Atanque *ša.* Chibcha *zye.* Lenca: Similaton *aša,* Guajiquero

asa. Rama: Guatuso *iisa, iza*. Talamanca: Borunca *se(-kwo)*, Terraba *zo* 'body hair,' Bribri *t°ā*. Xinca: Yupultepec *susi* 'beard.'

91 HALF   Allentiac *ker*. Chimu: Eten *ken*. Warrau *akari*. Xinca (Maldonado) *t°ar(-gua)* 'cosa separada.'

92 HAND₁   Chibcha: Manare *kus-kara* 'finger joints.' Guaymi: Norteño *kuse*, Penomeño *kuse, kis-e*, Move *kise*. Jirajara: Ayoman *a-kosi-kega* 'finger.' Paez: Paez *kose, kus*, Panakita *kuse*, Moguex *koze*. Talamanca: Borunca *i-kus(-kua)* 'finger.'

93 HAND₂   Andaqui *saka-a*. Chibcha: Tunebo *azka-ra*, Chibcha *yta-saka* 'back of hand.' Talamanca: Tiribi *sak-wo* 'finger,' Chiripo *sku* 'finger.'

94 HARD   Atacama *t°araba* 'harden.' Chimu: Eten *t°urr, č°urr*. Choco: Catio *čare* 'strong.' Itonama *č°al-i°na*. (P)

95 HEAD₁   Barbacoa: Cayapa *mišu*, Colorado *misu*. Atacama *musa* 'hair.' Choco: Waunana *paru, pudu*, Catio *poru*. Jirajara: Gayon *besa* 'feather.' Paez: Totoro *pušu*, Moguex *pusro*. (P)

96 HEAD₂   Aruak: Kagaba *sankala*, Bintucua *saku-ku* 'skull.' Betoi *ro-saka*. Chimu: Eten *sak* 'hair.' Cuna *sagila, sakla*. Guaymi: Move *thokua*, Chumulu *duku*. Paez: Guambiana *isix* 'wool.' Xinca: Jutiapa *usaxle*, Yupultepec *hysaxli*.

97 HEART₁   Chibcha *ie* 'belly.' Cuitlatec *ɔjə°*. Misumalpan: Miskito *aia* 'stomach.' Paya *ja, jaa* 'belly.' (C)

98 HEART₂   Allentiac *zaha*. Choco: Sambu *izo, zo*, Citara *zoo*. Misumalpan: Ulua *asung* 'liver.' Motilon: Dobocubi *ši, iši* 'belly.'

99 HEAVEN   Barbacoa: Colorado *nan* 'above.' Itonama *nano*. Jirajara: Ayoman *ñiña*. (P)

100 HEAVY   Atacama *nul-ir*. Chimu: Eten *norr-em*. (P)

101 HIDE   Barbacoa: Cayapa *dišu* 'hidden.' Warrau *dihisa*. (P)

102 HOLE₁   Chibcha *pihigua*. Misumalpan: Ulua *paxka*, Miskito *pakni* 'excavation.' Yanoama: Yanam *paka*, Yanomamï *pəka*. (C)

103 HOLE₂   Allentiac *huru* 'door.' Barbacoa: Colorado *foro*, Cayapa *horo*. Cuitlatec *palałeli*. Talamanca: Terraba *fre* 'cave.' Tarascan *poro* 'cave.' Timucua *pali* 'to open.'

104 HORN   Barbacoa: Cayapa *kaču*. Chimu: Eten *kači*. (P)

105 HOT   Motilon: Dobocubi *bočon* 'heat.' Paez: Paez *bač* 'become hot,' Guambiana *pačig*.

106 HOUSE   Barbacoa: Colorado, Cayapa *ja*. Paez: Paez *jat^h*, Panikita *ja*, Moguex *jaatk*. Paya *uja* 'nest.'

107 KIDNEY   Paya *sakka* 'spleen,' *sukka* 'back.' Talamanca: Estrella,
Cabecar *sokko*. (C)

108 KILL   Barbacoa: Colorado *piti*. Choco: Catio *bata*. Mura *batai*.
Talamanca: Bribri *fto*.

109 KINDLE   Barbacoa: Cayapa *bextsu* 'toasted.' Misumalpan: Sumu
buswi 'burn.' Paez *apaz* 'burn' (transitive). Paya *pas*. Talamanca:
Bribri *patˤe*.

110 LARGE   Andaqui *fi*. Barbacoa: Colorado *ave*. Chibcha: Duit *oba*.
Itonama *bɨ*. Lenca: Chilanga *buj*. Misumalpan: Ulua *baj* 'long.'

111 LAUGH   Allentiac: Millcayac *alau*. Cuna *ale-*. Lenca: Chilanga *jolo-*.
Motilon: Dobocubi *aru*. Tarascan *erhe-*.

112 LEAF   Andaqui *maso(-xo)*. Barbacoa: Colorado *apišu*. Itonama *mas-*
(classifier). (P)

113 LEG₁   Betoi *moka*. Choco: Saija *makara*, Catio *bakara*. Itonama
mukaka 'hip, thigh.' (P)

114 LEG₂   Andaqui *sona-so*. Jirajara: Gayon *senan*, Ayoman *sangan*
'foot,' *a-sagan-ipipo*. Cf. Timucua [secah]. (P)

115 LIE DOWN   Aruak: Bintucua *a-pass-an*. Lenca: Similaton *piax*
[piaq]. Paya *apiš*, *apis*. Talamanca: Terraba *pozung* 'sleep.' (C)

116 LIVE (v.)   Barbacoa: Cayapa *su*. Cuna *sii* 'sit, be.' Itonama *si* 'be.'
Talamanca: Terraba *se*, Tirub *si*. Tarascan *tˤi(-pe)*. Xinca: Yupultepec
iši.

117 LOUSE₁   Barbacoa: Colorado, Cayapa *mu*. Chimu: Eten *moh*. Paez:
Guambiana *miu*, *mui*. Warrau *ami*. (P)

118 LOUSE₂   Cuitlatec *nimȭʔo* 'flea.' Lenca: Guajiquero *tem*. Paez:
Guambiana *itˤimbi* 'flea.' Xinca: Chiquimulilla, Yupultepec *tuma*.
Yanoama: Yanomamï, etc. *noma*.

119 LOVE   Aruak: Kagaba *lun*, Bintucua *duna* 'aimable.' Xinca:
Yupultepec *ulan*. (C)

120 MAKE   Cuna *imake*. Guaymi: Move *mike*. Itonama *matˤihi* 'work.'
Lenca: Guajiquero *mangiar* 'work' (n.), *mangin* 'work' (v.). Paez *maši*
'work.' Xinca (Maldonado) *myka* 'work' (n. and v.).

121 MAN₁   Cuitlatec *ʔele-li*. Misumalpan: Ulua *al*. (C)

122 MAN₂   Andaqui [miszihi]. Betoi *umasoi*. Choco: Saija *mukina*, Tado
mukira, etc. Lenca: Chilanga *mišu*. Misumalpan: Matagalpa *misa*,
Cacaopera *misil*. Paez: Guambiana *møx*, Panikita *pis*, Totoro *mux-el*,
etc.

123 MOSQUITO   Andaqui *tunihi*. Aruak: Bintucua *čun*, Guamaca *tun*,
Kagaba *sungulu*. Barbacoa: Cayapa *tanda* 'bee,' Colorado *čina* 'bee.'
Chimu: Eten *sinu, senu*. Cuitlatec *čile, šilega* 'wasp.' Guaymi:
Changuena *suerit*, Chumulu *siiru* 'fly.' Lenca: Guajiquero *sira* 'bee.'
Misumalpan: Miskito *tairri*. Talamanca: Terraba, Borunca *serung* 'fly.'
Tarascan *t²iri* 'wasp.' Timucua: Tawasa *čena* 'bee.'

124 MOUNTAIN   Atacama *k²abur* 'high hill.' Chibcha: Manare *kupara*.
Cuitlatec *kɨmɨ, kōmō*. Guaymi: Sabanero *xuma*. Paez: Moguex *guape*
'snowy mountains.' Xinca (Maldonado) *goma*.

125 MOUTH   Chimu *sap*. Cuitlatec *šuxpi*. Paya *sapa*.

126 NAIL   Barbacoa: Colorado *(tja-)ki*, Cayapa *(fia-)ki* (literally
'hand-nail'). Itonama *(me?-)k²e* (*me?* = 'hand'). Jirajara: Jirajara
(a-)gi(-guse) (*guse* = 'hand'), Ayoman *ki(-gua)*. (P)

127 NAME   Chibcha: Chibcha [hyca], Margua *aka*. Chimu: Eten *ok*.
Guaymi: Move *ko*. Malibu: Chimila *kaka* 'be called.' Rama *ak*.
Talamanca: Terraba, etc. *ko*. Tarascan *het⁵(-nga-rha-qua)*.

128 NEAR   Atacama *k²ol* 'with.' Barbacoa: Cayapa *kale*, Colorado
kolo-i-no 'approach.' Guaymi: Move *ken*. Malibu: Chimila *keera*.
Talamanca: Borunca *kuret*.

129 NECK₁   Andaqui *san-guaka*. Chibcha *guikin*. Talamanca: Bribri *uako*
'armpit.'

130 NECK₂   Itonama *pakas-* '(incorporated object) front of. . . .' Jirajara:
Ayoman *apuesiu*, Gayon *apaxiguo*. Paez: Paez *peti*, Panikita *peč*. (P)

131 NECK₃   Choco: Catio *osorro* 'throat.' Chimu: Eten *ajtærr, altærr*.
Lenca: Guajiquero *thala*, Similaton *šala*. Misumalpan: Ulua *salaχ*
'shoulder.' Xinca (Maldonado) *taɬi*.

132 NEW   Misumalpan: Ulua *ali* 'young.' Timucua *ele* 'young.' Xinca
(Maldonado) *eɬa*, Yupultepec *ila* 'fresh' (of meat). Yanoama: Sanema
lie 'raw,' Yanam, Yanomam, Yanomamï *rie* 'raw.'

133 NOSE₁   Cuna *asu, azu(-gua)*. Guaymi: Murire, Sabanero *se*. Paez *asa*
'stink.' Talamanca: Chiripo *ču*. Warrau *aha* 'to smell.'

134 NOSE₂   Andaqui *kifi*. Atacama *sepe, sipe*. Barbacoa: Cuaiquer *kimpu*,
Colorado *kifu, kimfu*, Cayapa *kiho*. Chimu *xione*. Choco: Citara
kembu, Catio *keambue*, etc. Jirajara: Ayoman *a-kin*, Gayon *kin*,
Jirajara *a-kingans*. Paez: Guambiana, Totoro *kim*, Moguex *kind*.
Timucua *čini*. (P)

135 NOW₁   Misumalpan: Cacaopera *ira* 'today.' Talamanca: Terraba *eri*
'now, today.' Xinca: Chiquimulilla *raj*. (C)

136 NOW₂   Allentiac *maan*. Barbacoa: Colorado *aman*, Cayapa *ama*
'today.' Chimu: Eten *molun* 'today.' Cuna *emi*. Warrau *ama* 'today.'

137 OLD   Cuna *sele*, *sere*. Guaymi: Chumulu, Gualaca *tare*, Norteño,
Penomeño *turua* 'grandfather.' Lenca: Guajiquero *toolo* 'old man.'
Misumalpan: Miskito *tara* 'large.' Talamanca: Terraba, Tirub *ter*
'grandmother.' Tarascan *thare-pe-ti*. (C)

138 OLD MAN   Allentiac *tomal*. Antioquia: Nutabe *tobe*. Chibcha *tiba-ra*, *tiba-ča*. Choco: Nonama *tumbela* 'large.' Cuna: Cueva *tiba* 'king.'
Jirajara: Ayoman *tum*. Misumalpan: Miskito *dama* 'grandfather.' Paez
tēē 'adult.' Talamanca: Cabecar *dabai* 'father-in-law.' Tarascan *tama-pu*. Warrau *idamo*.

139 ONE₁   Lenca: Chilanga *pis*, *bis*. Misumalpan: Matagalpa *bas*. Paya
pes 'only.' (C)

140 ONE₂   Choco: Catio, Citara, Chami, etc. *aba*. Warrau *ba* (deduced
from 'five' = *moxo-ba* 'hand-one.' Timucua *wa* (deduced from 'five'
= *mar-wa*; cf. 'six' *mar-eka*). (P)

141 ONE₃   Chibcha: Tegria *at-uba* 'finger,' Chibcha *ata*, *yta* 'hand,' Duit
atia. Guaymi: Move *-ti*. Lenca: Guajiquero *etta*. Malibu: Chimila
aatta-kra 'hand.' Motilon: Dobocubi *atu* 'finger.' Talamanca: Bribri *et*.
Paez *ias*. Paya *as*. Tarascan *to(-mu)*. Warrau *isa*.

142 ONE₄   Allentiac: Millcayac *negui*. Aruak: Atanque *eingui* 'other,'
Bintucua *ingui* 'other.' Chimu: Chimu *onæk*, Eten *oneke*.

143 OPEN (v.)   Atacama *pai* 'uncover.' Barbacoa: Cayapa *be?* 'denude.'
Choco: Catio *ebaja*. (P)

144 PAIN   Aruak: Atanque *sana* 'wound' (n.). Misumalpan: Miskito
saura. Motilon *sala*. Rama *sliba* 'wound' (n.). Talamanca *suro* 'sick.'
Warrau *ahera*.

145 PERSON   Cuna *tule*. Misumalpan: Cacaopera *tali*. Yanoama: Yanam,
Yanomam, Yanomamï *tɨli* 'inhabitants.' (C)

146 PUSH   Cuna *epike*. Tarascan *phaka*. (C)

147 RAIN₁   Paez *nus*. Warrau *naha(p)*.

148 RAIN₂   Barbacoa: Colorado, Cayapa *šuwa*. Paez: Guambiana *šebu*.
Warrau *sebo* (v.). (P)

149 RAIN₃   Aruak: Kagaba *ni-mue* 'rainy season,' Bintucua *manje*
'storm.' Talamanca: Cabecar *mo*. Tarascan *emen-da* 'rainy season.'
Yanoama (general) *maa*. (C)

150 RAW   Barbacoa: Cayapa *tˢana*, Colorado *sana*. Itonama *u-čʼaʔna*. (P)

151 RIVER₁   Cuna *ti-wala* (*ti* = 'water'). Lenca: Chilanga *uarra*,
Guajiquero *wara*. Misumalpan: Miskito *awala*. (C)

152 RIVER₂   Aruak: Guamaca *kañaa*. Cuitlatec *kuni* 'sea.' Malibu: Chimila *koono*. Paez *kɨna* 'irrigation canal.'

153 ROPE   Barbacoa: Colorado *čili, sili*. Chibcha: Manare *čita-ra*. Motilon *sita* 'belt, liana.' Paez: Moguex *čit*. Rama *sira* 'thread.' Talamanca: Terraba *(kor-)sreng* 'root' (*kor* = 'tree'), Tirub *seren*. Tarascan *sira(-ngua)* 'root.' Warrau *ahutu* 'rope' (*h* < *s*). Yanoama: Yanomamï *ašitʰa*.

154 ROTTEN   Barbacoa: Cayapa *pete* 'to spoil.' Cuitlatec *paʔdeʔe*. Warrau *boto* 'be rotten.'

155 RUN   Aruak: Bintucua *koreni*. Misumalpan: Sumu *kiri*. Motilon: Dobocubi *kuri* 'flee.' (C)

156 SALT   Antioquia: Nutabe *naku*. Aruak: Bintucua *nagu*, Kagaba *naku*, Atanque *nøngui*. Chibcha *nigua*. Paez *nenga*.

157 SAY   Aruak: Bintucua *j(-an)*. Cuitlatec *e*. Lenca: Chilanga *aj(-on)*. Tarascan *aj-* 'inform, tell.' (C)

158 SCRATCH   Choco: Catio *byr-*. Itonama *buruʔtje*. (P)

159 SEE₁   Allentiac: Millcayac *tene(-kina)*. Guaymi: Norteño *teen*. Misumalpan: Sumu, Ulua *tal*. Paez *teng*. Xinca: Yupultepec *tili*. Yanoama: Yanomam *tara* (pl. subject).

160 SEE₂   Atacama *mini*. Barbacoa: Cayapa *mi*, Colorado *mi* 'knowledge, learn.' Misumalpan: Cacaopera *bi*. Paez *βia* 'appear.' Tarascan *mi, miu* 'see, count.' Yanoama (general) *mɨ*.

161 SEED₁   Barbacoa: Colorado *ni*, Cayapa *ñi*. Paez *ñin*. (P)

162 SEED₂   Chibcha: Chibcha *uba* 'flower,' Uncasica *uba* 'fruit.' Choco: Chami *fa* 'fruit.' Itonama *u-pawe*. Mura *ubai, iobai* 'flower.' Paez *ɸiw*. Paya *wa* 'seed, eye.' Talamanca: Bribri *va, wo*, Cabecar *we* 'fruit,' Borunca *ua* 'fruit.'

163 SEEK₁   Atacama *kʼip* 'love.' Cuitlatec *kab*. Misumalpan: Cacaopera *kapai*.

164 SEEK₂   Jirajara: Ayoman *bakami*. Paez *pakae*. (P)

165 SEW   Chibcha: Tegria *kesk(-indro)*. Itonama *kesi*. Paez *katˢ*.

166 SHADOW   Atacama *minas*. Itonama *manis-* 'be in the shadow.' (P)

167 SHIN   Andaqui *sa-sagua-na* 'tibia.' Chibcha *tsa-sagua-ne* 'kneecap.' Talamanca: Chiripo *so-saue* 'kneecap.'

168 SHOOT   Aruak: Kagaba *teia*. Barbacoa: Cayapa *tjaʔ-ke* 'throw.' Chibcha *ta* 'throw.' Paya *tung*. Talamanca: Bribri *ite, te*. Timucua *iči-ki, eče-so* 'throw.' Warrau *toa, tia* 'throw.'

169 SHOULDER₁   Allentiac *palen, palem*. Barbacoa: Cayapa *pala*. (P)

170 SHOULDER₂ Andaqui [fasziyunichini] 'back.' Barbacoa: Colorado
behči 'back.' Cuitlatec *pułke* 'back.' Itonama *pacu-kaka,*
ux-pača-čano 'your upper back.' Tarascan *pešo.*

171 SHOUT (v.) Andaqui *fifi* 'call.' Choco: Catio *bia.* Cuitlatec *baʔbe*
'sing.' Motilon: Dobocubi *iba, ibo* (n.). Paez *paja* 'call, shout, sing.'

172 SIDE Choco: Catio *kida.* Itonama *kas-* '(incorporated object) body
part.' Mura *kisi* 'rib.' Paez *kate.* (P)

173 SING Allentiac *namia.* Cuitlatec *ɨmi, imaxma* 'dance.' Cuna
namake. Misumalpan: Miskito *nong* 'dance.' Paez: Paez *nemgaʔ,*
Moguex *nemeh.* Xinca: Xinca (Maldonado) *mymy,* Yupultepec *myne.*
Yanoama: Sanema *amamo.*

174 SIT Barbacoa: Cayapa, Colorado *ču.* Itonama *čaʔu.* (P)

175 SKIN Aruak: Bintucua *kutiru.* Atacama *kʾati.* Barbacoa: Colorado,
Cayapa *kido.* Cuitlatec *kuti.* Guaymi: Move *kuata.* Misumalpan:
Cacaopera *kʾuta.* Paez *kati.* Talamanca: Terraba, Tirub *kwota.* Tarascan
čes. Timucua *ukwata* 'body, flesh.' Yanoama: Yanam, Yanomam,
Yanomamï *kasi* 'lip.'

176 SLEEP₁ Itonama *puʔ* 'lie down.' Lenca: Chilanga *pa.* Misumalpan:
Miskito *jap-.* Talamanca: Terraba *pi.*

177 SLEEP₂ Aruak: Kagaba *kaba,* Bintucua *kama.* Atacama *kʾip-ti* 'bed.'
Barbacoa: Colorado *kepe* 'night,' *kapi-ana* 'be sleeping.' Chibcha:
Chibcha [quyby], Tegria *kamaria,* Boncota *kamaja.* Choco: Catio
kebu-ra 'night,' Chami *kaimbej* 'lie down.' Cuna *kape.* Guaymi:
Gualaca *kabi-gal,* Sabanero *gabede.* Motilon: Dobocubi *koba.* Rama
kami. Talamanca: Bribri *kipue,* Chiripo *kepu.* Tarascan *kuvi-kua.*

178 SMOKE (v.) Atacama *tʾoj* 'to steam.' Choco: Saija *doi.* (P)

179 SNAKE₁ Misumalpan: Cacaopera *jarra.* Paez: Guambiana, Panikita
uʎ, Totoro *oʎ.* Timucua *jola.* Xinca: Chiquimulilla *ara* 'worm.'
Yanoama: Yanomamï *oru.*

180 SNAKE₂ Choco: Chami *he* [ge], Nonama *ihi* 'kind of snake.' Jirajara:
Ayoman *uhi* [ugi], Gayon *huhi.* (P)

181 STAR Antioquia: Nutabe *papa.* Barbacoa: Cuaiquer *ufa* 'light' (n.).
Chibcha: Margua, Manare *upa,* Boncota, Sinsiga *uba,* Chibcha
fa(-gwa). Rama *pi(-up).* Talamanca: Bribri *be(-kwo),* Cabecar
be(-kwe), etc.

182 STEAL₁ Chibcha [ze] 'take!' Cuitlatec *ɨłi.* Paez [zee]. Warrau *isa.*

183 STEAL₂ Chimu *omor* 'thief.' Choco: Catio *mera.* (P)

184 STONE Atacama *kʾatu* 'rock.' Paez *kuet, kuetʰ.* (P)

185 STRONG₁   Chibcha: Tegria *te(-kro)* 'brave.' Cuitlatec *ahte* 'be able.'
Guaymi: Move *di* 'strength.' Malibu: Chimila *taje.* Tarascan *atie-ti*
'hard.' Warrau *ta.* Cf. STRONG₂.

186 STRONG₂   Barbacoa: Cayapa *dera.* Chimu: Eten *tarr.* (P)

187 SUN₁   Chimu: Eten *kæss.* Lenca: Similaton, Guajiquero *kaši.*
Misulmalpan: Miskito *kati* 'moon.' Tarascan *kutˢi* 'moon.'

188 SUN₂   Atacama *lalakˀ-un* 'shine.' Chimu: Eten *lun* 'day.' Misumalpan:
Cacaopera *lan* 'sun, day,' Matagalpa *lal.*

189 TAIL₁   Cuitlatec *dihta.* Tarascan *theta(-kwa)* 'buttocks.' (C)

190 TAIL₂   Barbacoa: Colorado *me, meh.* Misumalpan: Ulua *umax-ka,*
Sumu *mamaxne.* Paez *menz.*

191 TAKE   Cuitlatec *wiˀɨ* 'buy.' Paez *uwe* [ugue]. Timucua *uwa* [uba,
ubua]. Warrau *oa.*

192 TALK   Cuitlatec *oxmele* 'chat.' Lenca: Similaton *molo,* Intibucat
malmal. (C)

193 THORN₁   Barbacoa: Cayapa *pu,* Colorado *pu.* Chimu: Eten *fu*
'needle.' (P)

194 THORN₂   Chibcha: Margua, Boncota *sikara* 'needle,' Manare *sakara*
'needle,' Uncasica *sikira* 'needle.' Paya *siki.* Xinca: Chiquimulilla
šikaji [xicayi], *sakajał* (Maldonado). (C)

195 THREE   Aruak: Kagaba, Guamaca *mai(-gua),* Bintucua *mai(-kane).*
Chibcha: Chibcha *mi(-ka),* Duit *meia,* Margua *mai, bai.* Cuna *pa(-gwa).*
Guaymi: Move *mon.* Jirajara: Ayoman *mo(-ngaña), ma-(gana).* Malibu:
Chimila *ma(-xana).* Paez: Guambiana, Coconuco *puen.* Talamanca:
Borunca *ma-n,* Terraba *(kra-)mia* (cf. *kra(-bu)* 'two,' etc). (The basic
root is *mai,* with survivals of various numeral classifiers.)

196 THUNDER   Choco: Saija, Baudo, etc. *pa,* Catio *ba.* Mura: Matanawi
api, Mura *pia.* (P)

197 TIE₁   Atacama *takˀal.* Chibcha: Tegria *tak* 'attach,' Manare *tataka*
'attach.' Motilon: Dobocubi *døk* 'tie a knot.'

198 TIE₂   Atacama *kˀoijo* 'fasten.' Warrau *koja.* Cf. Xinca (Maldonado)
kawi [cagui] 'to lasso.'

199 TOMORROW   Antioquia: Nutabe *ma-čiki* 'morning.' Aruak:
Guamaca *sigi, šigi,* Atanque *šigi,* Bintucua *sige, sigi.* Lenca: Similaton
šiga. Talamanca: Borunca *seek.* (For *ma-* as prefix in Nutabe, see the
Chibchan entry for NIGHT₄ in the Amerind dictionary.) (C)

200 TONGUE₁   Andaqui *sonae, šonae.* Warrau *hono.* (P)

201 TONGUE$_2$ Cuitlatec *ehti^{2}i*. Misumalpan: Ulua, Sumu, Cacaopera, Miskito *tu*. (C)

202 TOOTH$_1$ Atacama *enne*. Cuna *nu(-kala)*. Lenca: Chilanga *ne*. Malibu: Chimila *ne*. Misumalpan: Cacaopera *nini*, Sumu, Ulua *ana*. Yanoama: Yanam, Yanomamï, Sanema *na*.

203 TOOTH$_2$ Choco: Waunana, Tado *kida*, Chami *gida*, Catio *čida*. Paez: Paez *ki^{2}t^h*, Panikita *kit*. (P)

204 TOUCH Chibcha: Boncota *kato*. Tarascan *kat^{s}i(-ku-ni)* 'squeeze.' Warrau *kata* 'press.'

205 UNDER Chibcha: Tegria *kama*. Xinca: Sinacatan *šama* [xama]. Yanoama: Yanam, Yanomam, Sanema *komo*. (C)

206 UNTIE Misumalpan: Miskito *lauks*, Sumu *uluk-ta*. Paez *lakja^2* 'it is loose.'

207 URINE$_1$ Barbacoa: Cayapa *šiipi*. Choco: Chami *sjifana*. Paez: Guambiana *t^{s}uvi*. Warrau *ahibo*. (P)

208 URINE$_2$ Aruak: Kagaba *wisi*. Chibcha: Chibcha [hysu], Manare *jisa*. Choco: Catio *sia* 'urinate.' Cuitlatec *wiłi* 'urinate.' Misumalpan: Miskito *is(-ka)*, Sumu, Ulua *usu*. Talamanca: Borunca *wiš(-ku)*. Tarascan *jaz(-ka-ta)*.

209 VAGINA Aruak: Bintucua *sisi* 'vulva.' Barbacoa: Cayapa *su*, Colorado *so*. Cuna *sisi*. Misumalpan: Matagalpa *su*. Motilon: Dobocubi *ču*. Mura: Matanawi *sa*.

210 VEIN Malibu: Chimila *tøø*. Paya *taūwa* 'rope.' Warrau *tao, tau* 'vein, rope.'

211 WATER$_1$ Cuitlatec *^{2}umə*. Tarascan *-ma-* 'action on water.' (C)

212 WATER$_2$ Antioquia: Nutabe *ni*. Aruak: Bintucua *ria* 'liquid,' Kagaba *ni*. Atacama *(pu-)ri* 'water,' *(la-)ri* 'blood.' Chibcha: Tegria *ria, lia*, Pedraza, Margua, Tairona *dia*, Boncota, Manare *ria*, Uncasica *li*. Guaymi: Gualaca *ti*, Move *-rı, -lı, -ni* 'liquid.' Misumalpan: Miskito, Matagalpa, Cacaopera *li*. Paya *uri* 'blood.' Rama *ari* 'liquid.' Talamanca: Terraba *ti*, Bribri *di*, etc. Tarascan *juri-ri* 'blood'; in Tarascan the suffix *-ri* is found in many words for liquids, e.g. *p^{h}i-ri* 'a small amount of liquid,' *sindu-ri* 'a thick liquid,' *čut^{h}u-ri-kua* 'a drop' (cf. *čut^{h}utora* 'to drip'). On the suffix *-kua*, see Chap. 5, item 40.

213 WAX Barbacoa: Cayapa *amuja* 'beeswax.' Itonama *obovo* 'wax, bee.' Mura: Matanawi *mawi* 'bee.' Warrau *abi*. (P)

214 WET Betoi *ofaku* 'rain.' Choco: Tucura *bek(-eai)* 'to water, sow.' Cuitlatec *bıhkı* 'to wet.' Talamanca: Terraba *puk*.

121

215   WHITE₁   Atacama *tara, tarar.* Choco: Nonama, Chami *torroa,* Tucura
torro. (P)

216   WHITE₂   Chibcha: Margua *kuas(-airo),* Pedraza *kuasea,* Boncota
kuasuga, Manare *kuasaja.* Guaymi: Muoi *xusa,* Murire *xutha.* Malibu:
Chimila *guača* 'white man.' Paez: Panikita *guas,* Moguex *guass.*

217   WIND (n.)   Aruak: Kagaba *mulkala.* Cuna *proa.* Guaymi: Move
murue, Penomeño *moru,* Murire, Sabanero *mlie.* Rama: Rama *pulkat,*
Guatuso *puru.* Talamanca: Terraba *feruk, pruk.* Yanoama: Yanomam
iproko. (C)

218   WING₁   Aruak: Kagaba *gekala* 'wing, fin.' Chibcha *gaka.* Guaymi:
Chumulu *kek.* Talamanca: Borunca *ika.* Tarascan *ak(-s-kua).* Xinca:
Yupultepec *kaha.* (C)

219   WING₂   Misumalpan: Cacaopera *pik-ka.* Talamanca: Bribri, Cabecar
pik. Xinca: Yupultepec *paha.* Yanoama: Yanoam, Yanomam *fako.* (C)

220   WISH   Allentiac: Millcayac *-pia* 'in order to,' *-pa-, -paj-* (future).
Cuna *apea-* 'want, desire,' *pia-, bia-* (desiderative, future).
Misumalpan: Misquito *-bia-* (future). Paya *-pa* (first person future),
-pia, -pi (third person future). (What is given as the second person
is apparently an imperative.) Rama: Rama *pe,* Guatuso *-pe* (future).
Talamanna: Borunca *beja-.* Xinca *-pe* (future).

221   WOMAN₁   Choco: Sambu *wara,* Saija *wera.* Misumalpan: Cacaopera
jora, Sumu *jal* 'female, woman.' Talamanca: Terraba *ware.* Tarascan
uarhi-ti. Xinca: Chiquimulilla *ajal,* Sinacatan *ajala* (but also Jutiapa
aja, etc.).

222   WOMAN₂   Barbacoa: Colorado *sona, suma* 'wife,' Cuaiquer *asamba,*
Cayapa *supu* 'wife.' Chimu: Eten *sonang* 'wife.' Cuitlatec *łønø*
'female.' Cuna *sanwa* 'wife.' Jirajara: Ayoman *sempa, seña* 'woman,
female.' Paez: Guambiana *išumbur.* (Possibily two roots with *-m, -n;*
Cuna *sanwa* would be a suitable source for both.)

223   WORK₁ (v.)   Atacama *kʼemp* 'use.' Chimu: Eten *kaf* (n.). Paya *kappa*
'be concerned with' (ocuparse).

224   WORK₂ (v.)   Aruak: Bintucua *nina* 'activity.' Guaymi *noaine* 'do.'
Jirajara: Ayoman *no* 'make.' Rama *uni* 'make.' Timucua *inoni* 'work,'
ini(-so) 'cause to work.'

225   WORM   Guaymi: Chumulu, Gualaca *kisi.* Paez *ges.*

226   YELLOW   Lenca: Chilanga *šuninga.* Malibu: Chimila *sunsuru* 'green.'
Misumalpan: Tawaska *sang-ni* 'green.' Tarascan *šunga-peti, šušungas*
'green.' (C)

CENTRAL AMERIND

Central Amerind has three apparently coordinate branches: Kiowa-Tanoan, Uto-Aztecan, and Oto-Mangue. Amerindian specialists have long been aware of the relationship of the first two, thanks to the work of Benjamin Whorf and George L. Trager (1937). The third branch, Oto-Mangue, is a stock of great internal diversity, but its validity as a group is evident. In Greenberg (1960), I did not specifically associate it with any other Amerind stock, and even expressed some reservation about its Amerind status. Since then, what seemed the daunting prospect of a general internal comparison of Oto-Mangue has been made unnecessary by a series of studies of specific branches culminating in Calvin Rensch's comparative phonology, published in 1976 (based on his 1966 dissertation). In fact, as soon as I added Rensch's reconstructions to a notebook in which I had already entered etymologies from Na-Dene and all branches of Amerind except Oto-Mangue, it immediately became clear that Oto-Mangue was not only Amerind, but that it had a special connection with Uto-Aztecan and Kiowa-Tanoan, as evidenced by such fundamental etymologies as TWO and FIRE.

Because of the work of Rensch, Whorf and Trager, Wick R. Miller, Kenneth Hale, and others, we can largely dispense with citations from individual languages in the Central Amerind etymologies cited here. However, although some work has been done with Kiowa-Tanoan, especially by Hale (1962, 1967), following earlier studies by Trager and Harrington, no one has compared Kiowa with Uto-Aztecan. Since Rensch's Oto-Mangue phonology is fundamental to this study and is far from being a conventional type of analysis, a brief discussion of the work is in order. The reader interested in further details should, of course, consult the book itself. For Oto-Mangue languages, Rensch assumes a basic CV (consonant-vowel) structure and one of three tones. However, more often than not, he leaves the tone unreconstructed or gives alternative tones. They are omitted in the citations. In addition to the CV structure, there may be, and often are, preposed and/or postposed elements. The preposed elements are Y for palatalization, n for nasalization, and a laryngeal element— $\textipa{P}$, h, or, when it is not possible to decide between them, the cover symbol H. The order in which these elements occur is conventional and has nothing to do with the phonetic order. The postposed elements are laryngeals (the same as the preposed set) and nasalization. Here also the order is conventional.

These elements are often parenthesized, indicating that they occur in more than one, but not in all of the seven branches of Oto-Mangue assumed in Rensch's analysis. If an element appears in a single branch, it is given only in the reconstruction for that branch. It should further be noted that postposed *n,* when not accompanied by a postposed laryngeal, has oral reflexes in a large majority of the languages.

In addition, there are consonantal alternations, of which *t/j/n* is the most important, such that two or more of these may appear in the same etymology in different languages. The set just mentioned is entered as *t* in Proto-Oto-Mangue. All things considered, I am inclined to think that though almost all of Rensch's etymologies are valid, not all the forms from the different branches are necessarily related, so that some etymologies cited for five branches may in fact only occur in three, or may represent two or more different etymologies.

As an example, let us consider Rensch 123, *(h)ka(h).* Under this form we find citations of first-person pronouns, most of which actually have initial *n.* This is based on a *k/n* alternation found only in a few instances. The *k*- forms of Otomi-Pame indicate first-person plural inclusive, in complete agreement with the general Amerind pattern, whereas the *n*- forms are either first-person singular, first-person indifferent to number, or first-person singular and first-person plural exclusive. Once again, this conforms to general facts about Amerind. If, as posited by Rensch, the *n*- and *k*- forms have a single origin within Oto-Mangue, it is indeed a remarkable coincidence that they have differentiated, by an internal process, to give rise to two separate forms that agree perfectly with the general Amerind pattern.

A few further remarks will clarify how I have used Rensch's results in compiling the etymologies. First, his *k^w* corresponds to *p* in Uto-Aztecan and Kiowa-Tanoan, as can be seen in a number of the etymologies below. In Oto-Mangue itself, *p* actually occurs in Zapotec, Chiapanec-Mangue, and Otomi-Pame, and Longacre (1967: 133) notes that " **p* could be reconstructed rather than *$*k^w$*." Second, Rensch's **k* corresponds to Uto-Aztecan *k* and *k^w*. And finally, his *nw* is formulaic and actually occurs as *m* almost everywhere; it corresponds to *m* in Uto-Aztecan and Kiowa-Tanoan. In the citations in the etymologies, R stands for Rensch, M for Miller, and WT for Whorf and Trager. Since Rensch does not reconstruct meanings, I give a selection, often exhaustive, of the glosses he uses for the accompanying citations. Miller, on the other hand, though he gives a reconstructed meaning for most etymologies, often does not attempt a phonological reconstruction; in these cases the actual forms are cited. A further problem arises in Whorf

and Trager, where we find a considerable number of etymologies for
Azteco-Tanoan reconstructed forms without citations from individual languages. For these, it has almost always been possible to discover the intended Uto-Aztecan cognate in Miller, but for Kiowa-Tanoan I have usually
had recourse to my own collection of Tanoan vocabularies and Harrington's
dictionary of Kiowa. I am indebted to the late Edward Dozier for some Hopi
Tewa forms not found in the existing literature.

In addition to the 90 exclusively Central Amerind etymologies pre-
sented here, 45 Central Amerind entries will be found in the Amerind dic-
tionary under the following etymologies: AUNT, BE$_2$, BEHIND, BELLY$_4$,
BITE$_1$, BITTER$_2$, BLACK$_3$, BLOOD$_2$, BLOW, BODY$_1$, BROTHER,
CARRY$_2$, CHILD$_3$, CLOUD$_1$, CLOUD$_2$, DEER$_2$, DIE$_3$, DIG$_1$, DUST,
EARTH$_4$, EYE, FEATHER$_2$, FIRE$_1$, FOOT$_1$, GIRL, GO$_1$, GO$_3$, HAND$_1$,
HARD$_1$, HOUSE, LARGE$_1$, LEAF$_2$, LEG, MAKE$_1$, NARROW, NECK,
RIVER$_1$, ROAD$_2$, SEE$_1$, STAR$_1$, TONGUE$_3$, TREE$_1$, WATER$_2$, WOMAN$_3$,
YELLOW$_2$. An additional 22 entries, apparently restricted to a single
branch of Central Amerind, are given under the following Amerind ety-
mologies: ANT$_2$, ASK$_2$, BEARD$_1$, BEE$_2$, CALL$_1$, CHILD$_1$, CHILD$_4$,
COLD$_1$, COVER, DIE$_1$, EXCREMENT$_2$, FOREHEAD$_2$, GOOD$_2$, HEAR$_1$,
KNEE$_2$, LARGE$_2$, MAKE$_2$, MEAT$_3$, SMALL, STAR$_2$, TWO, VAGINA.

CENTRAL AMERIND ETYMOLOGIES

1 AUNT   Uto-Aztecan: M 502 *pa* 'aunt.' Oto-Mangue: R 236 *k^{w}a(H)(n)*
'aunt, grandmother, mother-in-law.'

2 BACK (n.)   Kiowa-Tanoan: Kiowa *dæ̃-n* 'shoulder blade'; Tanoan: Jemez
tø 'neck.' Oto-Mangue: R 51 *(Y)(n)ta(h)(ʔ)* 'back, shoulders and
neck, neck.'

3 BARK   Kiowa-Tanoan: Kiowa *k^{h}ɔ-e* 'skin, cloth, mat'; Tanoan: Jemez *hɨ*
'clothing.' Uto-Aztecan: M 21 *ko* 'bark of tree.'

4 BELLY   Kiowa-Tanoan: Kiowa *se* 'intestines'; Tanoan: Tewa *si:*, Jemez
k^{j}iʔ-š. Oto-Mangue: R 278 *(n)(ʔ)se(h)(n)* 'belly, intestines, heart,
liver.' Uto-Aztecan: Mono *sihi* 'intestines,' Tarahumara *siwa*
'intestines,' Hopi *siihi* 'intestines,' Yaqui *siiwa-m* 'intestines,' Opata
siwa-t.

5 BIRD   Kiowa-Tanoan: Tanoan: Taos *tˢiwju-*, Jemez *sejiw*, San Ildefonso
tˢi-. Oto-Mangue: R 90 *(Y)(h)tu(ʔ)(n)* 'turkey, road-runner, hen.' Uto-
Aztecan: M 41 *tˢutu* (= WT 5).

6 BOIL (v.)   Kiowa-Tanoan: Kiowa *sa-l* 'be hot'; Tanoan: Taos *ɬəja*. Oto-

Mangue: R 295 *nsah, *ntah 'warm, fever.' Uto-Aztecan: M 352 *sa 'to roast.' (Azteco-Tanoan: WT 77 *ɬəʔa 'to boil'; without citations.)

7 BOY   Kiowa-Tanoan: Kiowa tʰæ-ɬ-iæ, (iæ 'child,' diminutive). Uto-Aztecan: M 54 *tu, M 53 *ti, *tiʔo.

8 BREAK   Kiowa-Tanoan: Kiowa tʰa- (pl. object); Tanoan: Taos tʰə, Santa Clara tha, Jemez šo. Oto-Mangue: R 302 *sa(n).

9 BREAST   Kiowa-Tanoan: Tanoan: Taos pia-na, Tewa pī, Jemez pado. Oto-Mangue: R 144 *kʷi(ʔ)(n) 'breast, rib, back.' Uto-Aztecan: M 58 *pi.

10 BUFFALO   Kiowa-Tanoan: Tanoan: Taos kon-, San Ildefonso kō, San Juan kōʔōng. Uto-Aztecan: WT 16 *ku-, *kutˢu (not found in M).

11 BURN   Kiowa-Tanoan: Tanoan: Taos xa 'roast,' Tewa xoʔtogeh. Oto-Mangue R 119 *ka 'burn.' Uto-Aztecan: M 170 *ku, *koʔ 'fire.'

12 BURY   Oto-Mangue: R 407 *ʔja. Uto-Aztecan: M 132 *ja 'die' (also 'grave' and 'kill' in some languages).

13 BUY   Azteco-Tanoan: WT 92 *ty (without citations). Oto-Mangue: R 13 *te 'buy, sell.'

14 CLOSE₁ (v.)   Oto-Mangue: R 400 *je(h)(n) 'fence.' Uto-Aztecan: M 91a *je 'to close.'

15 CLOSE₂ (v.)   Kiowa-Tanoan: Tanoan: Taos kʷi-l, Jemez gile. Oto-Mangue: R 135 *ku 'close, cover.'

16 COLD₁   Kiowa-Tanoan: Kiowa kˀa; Tanoan: Taos kˀo, Tewa kˀo, Jemez kˀe. Oto-Mangue: R 141 *kʷi(n). Uto-Aztecan: M 307a *kʷin 'north,' M 307b *kʷi 'north, cold.'

17 COLD₂   Kiowa-Tanoan: Tanoan: Taos tˢia-, Isleta tˢi(-im). Uto-Aztecan: M 94a *se, *sep. (Azteco-Tanoan: WT 2 *tˢija, *tˢi.)

18 COLD₃   Kiowa-Tanoan: Kiowa tˀo 'be cold'; Tanoan: Tewa tˀi, Jemez (we-)tˀe. Uto-Aztecan: M 467 *tome. (Azteco-Tanoan: WT 90 *toŋʷi 'winter.')

19 COME   Kiowa-Tanoan: Tanoan: Tewa kɛ̃ʔ. Uto-Aztecan: M 96 *kim.

20 COUNT   Kiowa-Tanoan: Kiowa pe-l 'think'; Tanoan: Taos pia- 'think.' Oto-Mangue: R 160 *kʷe(n).

21 COVER (v.)   Oto-Mangue: R 386 *nʔwa 'to hide.' Uto-Aztecan: M 108 *ma.

22 CRUSH   Oto-Mangue: R 426 *ʔju(ʔ) 'break, cut, burst.' Uto-Aztecan: M 112 *ju.

23 CUT   Kiowa-Tanoan: Kiowa tˀa 'knife'; Tanoan: Taos tˀẽ, Towa tˢˀaʔ. Oto-Mangue: R 63 *Htaʔn 'break, cut, knife.'

126

24 DANCE   Kiowa-Tanoan: Kiowa *da* 'sing'; Tanoan: Jemez *čỹ*. Oto-Mangue: R 68 *(n)(h)ta(h)(n)* (includes Proto-Otomi-Pame *nahn*, Proto-Chinantec *nja*). Uto-Aztecan: M 378 *na* 'sing.'

25 DEER₁   Kiowa-Tanoan: Kiowa *tʾa-p;* Tanoan: Taos *tʾo-na.* Oto-Mangue: R 39 *(Y)(n)te(H)(n)* 'fox, wolf, dog.' Uto-Aztecan: M 123 *te*.

26 DEER₂   Kiowa-Tanoan: Tanoan: San Juan *pā*, Tewa *pɛ*, Piro *pije.* Oto-Mangue: R 203 *(Y)kʷa(h)* 'animal, deer, horse.'

27 DIE   Kiowa-Tanoan: Kiowa *pe* 'dead'; Tanoan: Piro *piwe* 'dead,' Taos *piu* 'dead,' San Juan *pe-nī* 'dead person,' Jemez *pæ* 'be dead.' Oto-Mangue: R 157 *(h)kʷeH* 'finish.' Uto-Aztecan: M 385 *pei* 'sleep.' (Azteco-Tanoan: WT 83 *pəwa* 'cease, die'; without citations.)

28 DOG   Kiowa-Tanoan: Tanoan: Tewa *tʾeh*, Piro *tʾue.* Uto-Aztecan: M 137 *tʾu.* (Azteco-Tanoan: WT 71 *tʾiju;* without citations).

29 EARTH   Oto-Mangue: R 99 *ki* 'under, earth.' Uto-Aztecan: M 151 *kʷi (*kʷijaʔ).*

30 EGG   Kiowa-Tanoan: Tanoan: Hopi Tewa *wa*, Jemez *wæ.* Oto-Mangue: R 389 *(ʔ)wa(H)²* 'round, egg, ball.'

31 FALL   Kiowa-Tanoan: Tanoan: Santa Clara *wāh* 'go down.' Oto-Mangue: R 379 *we(ʔ)(n)* 'come down, arrive.' Uto-Aztecan: M 163 *we.*

32 FAT   Oto-Mangue: R 397 *ʔji(n)* 'heavy, fat, sick.' Uto-Aztecan: M 166 *wi* (no *ji* is reconstructed for Uto-Aztecan).

33 FATHER   Kiowa-Tanoan: Kiowa *ta;* Tanoan: Jemez *tā-e*, Taos *tō.* Oto-Mangue: R 4a *Yta(h)* 'father, grandfather.' Uto-Aztecan: M 273a *tawa.* (Azteco-Tanoan: WT 89 *taŋʷa* 'man, father.')

34 FEAR (v.)   Kiowa-Tanoan: Kiowa *pe.* Oto-Mangue: R 186 *(Y)(h)kʷe(h)(ʔ)(n)* 'fear, frighten.'

35 FEATHER   Oto-Mangue: R 138 *(n)(h)kʷi* 'hair, beard.' Uto-Aztecan: M 168 *pi.*

36 FIRE   Kiowa-Tanoan: Kiowa *pʰiæ;* Tanoan: Tewa *fa*, Piro *faje*, Isleta *pʰāi-de.* Oto-Mangue: R 197 *(n)(h)kʷa* 'warm, hot, sun.'

37 FLOUR   Kiowa-Tanoan: Tanoan: Taos *tʰɔo-.* Oto-Mangue: R 96 *(ʔ)tu(h)(ʔ)(n)* 'powder, sand, ashes.' Uto-Aztecan: M 206c *tu* 'grind.' (Azteco-Tanoan: WT 52 *tʰəho* 'flour, grind.')

38 FLOWER   Kiowa-Tanoan: Tanoan: Taos *ɬi-* 'grass,' Isleta *ɬi* 'grass.' Oto-Mangue: R 272 *(H)se(n)* 'grass, hay.' Uto-Aztecan: M 178a *se*, M 178b *si.* (Azteco-Tanoan: WT 30 *ɬi* 'flower, herb, grass.')

39 FRUIT   Kiowa-Tanoan: Tanoan: Tewa *t^oo*, Taos *t^oow-* 'nut, pine-nut.'
   Oto-Mangue: R 89 *(h)tu(n)* 'fruit, egg.' Uto-Aztecan: WT 50 *teva*
   (probably the same as M 319 *tepa* 'pine nut').

40 GATHER   Kiowa-Tanoan: Tanoan: Taos *t^suwi.* Uto-Aztecan: M 194
   t^supa. (= WT 4).

41 GRANDMOTHER   Kiowa-Tanoan: Tanoan: Taos *łi-tu* 'maternal
   grandmother.' Uto-Aztecan: M 497 *su.* (= WT 29).

42 GRIND   Kiowa-Tanoan: Kiowa *sō-m* 'grind.' Oto-Mangue: R 332
   su(ʔ) 'stone, grindstone.'

43 GROW   Oto-Mangue: R 423 *ju* 'grow, large.' Uto-Aztecan: M 208 *ja.*

44 HAIR₁   Oto-Mangue: R 336 *(Y)su(n)* 'hair of the head, fur, feathers.'
   Uto-Aztecan: M 219c *t^soni* 'hair of the body.'

45 HAIR₂   Kiowa-Tanoan: Tanoan: Taos *p^ho-*, Isleta *p^ha-*, Jemez *fwola.*
   Uto-Aztecan: M 212b *po* 'hair of the body.' (= WT 44)

46 HEAR   Oto-Mangue: R 412 *(ʔ)ja(n)* 'hear, see, know'; Proto-
   Chiapanec-Mangue *Ynan*, *jan.* Uto-Aztecan: M 148b *na*, *nam*
   'hear, ear.'

47 HIT   Oto-Mangue: R 202 *(n)(h)k^wa(h).* Uto-Aztecan: M 231 *pa.*

48 HOUSE   Oto-Mangue: R 131 *(n)ka(H)(n)* 'nest, house.' Uto-Aztecan:
   M 240 *ki.*

49 LARGE   Oto-Mangue: R 367 *nʔwi(h)(n)* 'wide, thick.' Uto-Aztecan:
   M 276 *mui* 'many.'

50 LEG   Kiowa-Tanoan: Tanoan: Taos *xu*, Jemez *ho*, San Ildefonso *k^hū.*
   Uto-Aztecan: M 435 *kasi* 'thigh.' (= WT 20)

51 LIE (DOWN)   Kiowa-Tanoan: Tanoan: Taos *kʔuo*, Tewa *kʔo,kʔuʔu* 'put.'
   Uto-Aztecan: M 381b *ka* 'sit down.' (= WT 18)

52 LIZARD   Oto-Mangue: R 28 *(Y)te(n).* Uto-Aztecan: M 267 *t^sana.*

53 LOOK   Kiowa-Tanoan: Kiowa *pō* 'see'; Tanoan: Tewa *pū-* 'see.' Oto-
   Mangue: R 228 *(Y)k^wa(h)(n)* 'look, know, see.'

54 MAN   Kiowa-Tanoan: Tanoan: Taos *səonena*, Isleta *səoni-*, Jemez *šoł*,
   San Ildefonso *sē.* Oto-Mangue: R 254 *sin* 'father, man.' Uto-Aztecan:
   M 273 *tiho.* (Cf. Azteco-Tanoan: WT 53 *thəho.*)

55 MOTHER   Kiowa-Tanoan: Tanoan: Tewa *jia*, Jemez *jia.* Oto-Mangue: R
   405 *ja* 'female.' Uto-Aztecan: M 486 *je* 'mother.'

56 MOUNTAIN   Kiowa-Tanoan: Tanoan: Tewa *pʔî-ng*, Taos *pʔian.* Oto-
   Mangue: R 167 *(h)k^wen* 'mountain, hill, high.' Uto-Aztecan: M 229
   pan 'high.'

57 NAIL   Kiowa-Tanoan: Tanoan: Taos -tˢe-, Isleta -tˢi-, Jemez -sō. Oto-
Mangue: R 325 *su 'fingernail.' Uto-Aztecan: WT 1 *su-, *suta, *sutu,
M 298a *sut. (Azteco-Tanoan: WT 1 *tˢə-.)

58 NET   Oto-Mangue: R 388 *(n)(H)wa(h) 'thread, weave, net'; Proto-
Chinantec *nwan; Proto-Mixtecan *hnan. Uto-Aztecan: M 304 *wana.

59 ONION   Kiowa-Tanoan: Tanoan: Tewa si. Oto-Mangue: R 1 *Hti. Uto-
Aztecan: M 301 *siwi.

60 RABBIT   Kiowa-Tanoan: Kiowa polāji; Tanoan: Tewa pu:, Taos piwe-.
Oto-Mangue: R 193 *kʷa. Uto-Aztecan: M 336 *pa 'jackrabbit.'

61 RAISE   Kiowa-Tanoan: Tanoan: Tewa ša 'arise.' Oto-Mangue: R 294
*saʔ 'raise, get up.'

62 RAT   Oto-Mangue: R 143 *(n)kʷi(n) 'bat, rat.' Uto-Aztecan: M 292
(no reconstruction), Mono puwetˢi, Southern Paiute puʔitˢa, Hopi pøsa.

63 RIPE   Kiowa-Tanoan: Kiowa ta 'be ripe, cooked'; Tanoan: San Juan tˢi
'be cooked.' Oto-Mangue: R 27 *(n)(ʔ)te(n) 'ripe, tender, cooked.'

64 RUB   Kiowa-Tanoan: Kiowa (mān-)sep-ga. Oto-Mangue: R 266 *(Y)se
'to dry, clean, wipe.' Uto-Aztecan: M 364 *sipa 'scrape.'

65 SALT   Oto-Mangue: R 5 *tin. Uto-Aztecan: M 404 'sour' (no
reconstruction), Huichol tˢinaa 'sour,' -tˢiiwi 'salty,' Cora tˢinah.

66 SAND   Oto-Mangue: R 283 *(Y)(n)(h)se(h)(n). Uto-Aztecan: M 362
*se.

67 SEE   Kiowa-Tanoan: Tanoan: Taos, Isleta, Jemez mū, San Ildefonso
muu. Uto-Aztecan: M 249 *ma, *mai, *mati, *matˢi. (= WT 34)

68 SEED   Kiowa-Tanoan: Kiowa ʔe-tā 'wheat, wheat flour'; Tanoan: San
Ildefonso tā, Hopi Tewa tang. Oto-Mangue: R 35 *(n)(h)te(h)(n) 'seed,
coconut, palm tree.'

69 SEVEN   Kiowa-Tanoan: Tanoan: Santa Clara tˢeh, San Ildefonso tˢe,
Taos tˢu. Oto-Mangue: R 2 *(n)ti (with note "could as well be
reconstructed *(n)te").

70 SHORT   Oto-Mangue: R 18 *(ʔ)te 'short, little.' Uto-Aztecan: M 388
*te 'small.'

71 SIBLING   Oto-Mangue: R 387 *(n)(ʔ)wa(ʔ) 'sibling of opposite sex,
brother, husband.' Uto-Aztecan: M 493 *wa 'younger sister,'
Tarahumara [waye] 'younger sister (man speaking).'

72 SMALL   Kiowa-Tanoan: Kiowa sjā-n. Oto-Mangue: R 258
*(Y)(n)(H)si(ʔ)(n).

73 SOFT   Kiowa-Tanoan: Kiowa to-l 'be soft.' Oto-Mangue: R 42 *ta.

74 SPEAK   Kiowa-Tanoan: Kiowa *tō;* Tanoan: Taos *tū.* Uto-Aztecan: M
300a **tew* 'name' (n.). (= WT 48)

75 STAND   Kiowa-Tanoan: Tanoan: Taos *wīnē,* Isleta *wi,* Piro *-wien,*
Jemez *kʷi.* Oto-Mangue: R 357 **wi(n)* 'become, be, exist, be able' (for
the semantics, cf. Spanish *estar* 'be' < Latin *stare* 'stand'). Uto-
Aztecan: M 411 **we, *wene.* (= WT 12)

76 STONE   Oto-Mangue: R 4 **ta.* Uto-Aztecan: M 354b **te.* Cf. Tanoan:
Jemez *tota* 'mountain' (Gatschet).

77 TEN   Kiowa-Tanoan: Kiowa *-tʰā-* '-teen'; Tanoan: Taos *tē.* Oto-Mangue:
R 21 **(n)te(h).*

78 THREAD   Kiowa-Tanoan: Kiowa *jæ-e-ba* 'string, rope,' *ʔæl-jæ-da*
'bow string.' Oto-Mangue: R 388 **(n)(H)wa(h)* 'weave, thread.' Uto-
Aztecan: M 419 **wi* 'string.' (Kiowa has no *w.)*

79 THREE   Kiowa-Tanoan: Tanoan: Taos *pojuo,* Isleta *pačo,* San Ildefonso
poje. Uto-Aztecan: M 510 **pahi.* (= WT 39)

80 TIE   Kiowa-Tanoan: Kiowa *pʰo* 'trap, snare'; Tanoan: Jemez *fo:* 'rope,
snare.' Uto-Aztecan: M 437 **pul.* (Azteco-Tanoan: WT 87 **pʰəɬa*
'wrap, tie'; without citations).

81 TOMORROW   Kiowa-Tanoan: Tanoan: Hopi Tewa *thadi,* Jemez *sedali,*
Santa Clara *tʰandi.* Oto-Mangue: R 316 **(ʔ)sa(h)(n).*

82 TONGUE   Kiowa-Tanoan: Tanoan: Santa Clara *hɛng,* Jemez *ē-il,* Isleta
jē. Oto-Mangue: R 419 **ja(H)(n).*

83 TOOTH   Oto-Mangue: R 26 **(n)te(n)* 'chew.' Uto-Aztecan: M 422
*tam.

84 TREE₁   Kiowa-Tanoan: Tanoan: Taos *ko-* 'plant,' Tewa *ka* 'leaf,' *kōng*
'efflorescence.' Uto-Aztecan: M 170f **kui.* (= WT 17)

85 TREE₂   Kiowa-Tanoan: Tanoan: Taos *ɬo-* 'wood,' Isleta *ɬa* 'wood,'
Jemez *tʲiš* 'wood.' Uto-Aztecan: M 104 **so* 'cottonwood.' (= WT 32)

86 TWO   Kiowa-Tanoan: Tanoan: Taos *wi-,* San Ildefonso *wije,* Jemez
wiš. Oto-Mangue: R 359 **(h)wi(n)* 'two, twins.' Uto-Aztecan:
M 509a–d **wo, *woka, *woj, *wa.* (Cf. WT 58.)

87 UGLY   Kiowa-Tanoan: Tanoan: Piro *foije.* Oto-Mangue: R 207 **kʷan*
'bad, dirty.'

88 WASH   Kiowa-Tanoan: Tanoan: Hopi Tewa *ʔo* 'bathe,' Taos *o.* Oto-
Mangue: R 363 **(ʔ)we(ʔ)(n)* 'rub, wash clothes.'

89 WHITE   Kiowa-Tanoan: Tanoan: Hopi Tewa *tˢɛʔi,* San Ildefonso *tˢæ,*
Jemez *čei.* Oto-Mangue: R 46 **Yta.*

90 WOLF   Kiowa-Tanoan: Kiowa *kue,* Taos *kol,* Isleta *kar-.* Uto-Aztecan:
M 110a *$k^w a$* 'coyote.' (= WT 23)

HOKAN

The term Hokan was introduced by Roland Dixon and Alfred Kroeber
in a brief note in *Science* in 1913 in which they also coined the term Penutian: both terms are based on the word for 'two' in those languages. Faced
with a large number of supposedly independent stocks in California in the
then-standard Powell classification, they assembled about 200 words from all
the known indigenous languages of California and discovered that outside
of the obvious intrusions of Athabaskan languages in the north and Uto-
Aztecan in the south, most of the languages fell into these two groups. The
languages they identified as Hokan were Shasta, Chimariko, Karok, Pomo,
Esselen, and Yuman. Later that same year, in a more detailed article (1913),
Dixon stated his suspicion that Iskoman, consisting of Chumash and Salinan, would be found to be Hokan also.

   Not surprisingly, neither Hokan nor Penutian turned out to respect state
or even national boundaries. In particular, Hokan showed further relationships to the south. Kroeber proposed in 1915 that Seri and Tequistlatec in
Mexico were Hokan languages, and in 1920 Sapir presented etymologies
linking Hokan to Coahuiltecan, a group of languages in Texas and north-
eastern Mexico.

   Even more startling was Lehmann's discovery (1920, 2: 973–74) that
Subtiaba, a language of Nicaragua, had a prefixed *d-* in nouns (which he
called an article) that was very similar to the *d-* in Washo, a language of
Nevada generally accepted as Hokan. He noted other resemblances and realized that more languages must be involved in the same genetic group. This
suggestion was taken up by Sapir, who in an important article published in
1925 presented a large number of etymologies involving Subtiaba, and the
very closely related Tlappanec, and several Hokan languages farther to the
north. Earlier, in 1917, he had published an article containing numerous
Hokan etymologies based on a comparison of Yana with other Hokan languages. These two articles, focusing on Yana and Subtiaba, have remained
the basis of comparative Hokan studies.

   In 1953, Morris Swadesh and I offered evidence for the inclusion of
Jicaque in the Hokan stock. As defined here, Hokan is identical with Sapir's

Hokan-Coahuiltecan (see Table 8 in Chap. 2), with the addition of Jicaque, whose affiliation is generally recognized, and Yurumangui, an extinct language of Colombia that is the most distant outlier of all.*

The present work has profited from several studies, notably Jacobsen (1958) on Washo and Karok; Silver (1964) on Shasta and Karok; McLendon (1964) on Eastern Pomo and Yana; and Oltrogge (1977) on Jicaque, Subtiaba, and Tequistlatec. But despite these and numerous other two- or three-way comparisons of Hokan languages published since Sapir's day, the etymologies presented below, and the Hokan entries in the Amerind dictionary, contain a considerable number of new items or new entries under already published ones. Here, as clearly as anywhere, do we see the limitations of starting from one particular language or comparing only a few languages. By such a procedure, even the most obvious etymology involving Pomo, Chumash, and Tequistlatec would not appear in any published study because it does not involve Yana (Sapir), Subtiaba (Sapir), Jicaque (Swadesh and Greenberg), and so on.

The languages and language groups that figure in the following etymologies are Achomawi (including Atsugewi), Chimariko, Chumash, Coahuilteco, Comecrudo, Cotoname, Esselen, Jicaque, Karankawa, Karok, Maratino, Pomo, Quinigua, Salinan, Seri, Shasta (including Konomihu, probably a distinct language), Subtiaba (including Tlappanec), Tequistlatec (sometimes called Chontal of Oaxaca), Tonkawa, Waicuri, Washo, Yana, Yuman, and Yurumangui. Waicuri is an extinct language of Lower California known only from a few forms, but these appear to be decisive for its Hokan affiliation. Pomo reconstructions are from McLendon (1973).

In addition to the 168 exclusively Hokan etymologies presented here, 100 Hokan entries will be found in the Amerind dictionary under the following etymologies: ABOVE$_2$, ARM, ARRIVE, ASHES, BAD$_1$, BARK, BATHE, BEARD$_2$, BEE$_2$, BEHIND, BITTER$_1$, BLACK$_1$, BLACK$_2$, BLACK$_3$, BODY$_1$, BOIL, BONE$_2$, BONE$_3$, BREAK, BREAST, BROAD, BROTHER, BURN, CALL$_2$, CHILD$_2$, CHILD$_4$, CLOSE, COLD$_2$, COLD$_3$, COME, COOK, DIE$_1$, DIG$_2$, DOG, DRINK$_1$, DRINK$_3$, DRY$_1$, EARTH$_3$, EXCREMENT$_1$, EYE, FEAR, FEATHER$_1$, FINGER$_1$, FLY (v.), FLY$_1$, FOOT$_1$, FOOT$_2$, GIRL, GO$_3$, GOOD$_1$, GOOD$_2$, GUTS$_2$, HAIR, HAND$_1$,

*It was Paul Rivet who first suggested the Hokan affinity of Yurumangui, a hypothesis, broached way back in 1942, that has generally been ignored by Hokanists. Rivet was a brilliant but erratic scholar. He was frequently wrong, as was earlier noted in regard to Choco as a member of Paezan. But my examination of the evidence shows that he was right in this case.

132

HAND₃, HARD₁, HEAVEN₁, HEAVEN₂, HOLE₁, HOLE₂, HUSBAND, KILL, KNEE₂, LARGE₁, LEAF₃, LIVER, LONG₂, LOUSE₂, LOUSE₃, MAKE₁, MAN₁, MAN₂, MANY₂, MEAT₃, MOUTH₁, NIGHT₂, NIGHT₃, ROUND, SAY₁, SAY₃, SEED₂, SHOULDER, SING, SIT₂, SKIN₂, SMELL₁, SMELL₂, SOUR, STAR₁, STAR₂, STONE₂, SUN₁, THIN, THROAT, VA- GINA, WHITE₂, WING, WISH, WOOD₁, WOOD₂.

HOKAN ETYMOLOGIES

1 ABOVE   Achomawi *he:wis* 'on top.' Karok *ʔavah.* Washo *ʔiwiʔ* 'on.' Yana: North, South *-wa-, -waa-* 'over.'

2 ALL   Jicaque *pʰɯ.* Subtiaba *ba:.* Waicuri *pu.*

3 ANIMAL   Chimariko [a-ah] 'meat.' Karok *ax* 'small animal.' Tequistlatec *-aga.*

4 ARM₁   Karok *(at-)ra:x.* Washo *alng* 'arm, wing.'

5 ARM₂   Pomo: Clear Lake *šal,* Southeast *xal.* Shasta *a:čar.* Tequistlatec *-ašaɬ.* Yana *galu.* Yuman: Diegueño *esaʎ,* Cocopa *išaʎ* 'hand,' etc.

6 ARMPIT   Pomo: North, Northeast *dam,* East *da:ma.* Tequistlatec *-nama.*

7 ARROW   Chimariko *saʔa.* Yana: Central, North *sawa.*

8 ASHES   Karankawa *tap* 'earth.' Karok *am-ta:p* 'ashes, dust.' Salinan: San Miguel *ṭapai* (but *ṭ-* may be a prefix). Washo *tˢʔapu.* Yana: North *tʔabʔla:wi* 'dust.'

9 AUNT   Achomawi *hamut* 'paternal aunt.' Chimariko *mu:ta-la-i* 'paternal aunt.' Chumash: San Buenaventura *mok* 'father's older sister.' Coahuilteco *mičal.* Esselen *meččix.* Karok *mi:th* 'paternal aunt.' Pomo: South *mutˢʔ* 'paternal aunt,' North *muʔ* 'paternal aunt.' Yana: North *muxdi* 'paternal aunt,' Yahi *musdi.*

10 BACK₁   Comecrudo *semi* 'after.' Salinan: San Miguel *t-ičʔoʔm,* San Antonio *t-ičʔoʔmoʔ.* Cf. Tequistlatec *-išpulaʔ* 'behind,' *-ašpulaʔ.*

11 BACK₂   Comecrudo *wamak* 'behind.' Yana *makʔi.* Cf. Karok *vasih,* and Washo *ašg.*

12 BEAR (v.)   Seri *-iket* 'be pregnant.' Tonkawa *katwe.*

13 BEHIND   Chimariko *h-imina* 'back,' *h-imina-če* 'behind, outside.' Coahuilteco *malkum* 'afterwards,' *wamalet* 'after.' Pomo: Southeast *man-* 'in back of.' Yana: North *-mmina-kʔi* (locative suffix).

14 BELLY   Chumash: Santa Ynez *qoax* 'chest,' San Buenaventura *p-køwø,* etc. Coahuilteco *kʔuax.* Cotoname *kox.* Pomo: Kashaya *ʔuhqʰa,*

133

Southeast *xa* 'belly, guts,' East *xo*. Salinan: San Miguel *ika*. Waicuri *(ma-)ka* (for *ma-* as prefix, cf. *ma-bela* 'tongue'). Cf. Seri *jaax*.

15 BLACK   Comecrudo *bai* 'black, night.' Karankawa *ma*. Quinigua *pa* 'black, red.' Tequistlatec *umi*. Yurumangui *mai-sa* 'night.'

16 BLOOD   Coahuilteco *kuas, huat*. Comecrudo *kuis* 'red.' Jicaque *kat*, *ʔas*. Karok *ʔa:x*. Salinan: San Antonio *a:katʰ*. Seri *avat*. Shasta *ʔaxta*. Subtiaba *ɛdʔi*. Tequistlatec *l-ahwatsʔ*. Washo *ašang* 'blood, to bleed.' Yuman: Yuma *-i:xʷet*, Diegueño *axwat* 'blood.'

17 BLOW (v.)   Comecrudo *pasekiau*. Seri *-ispx*. Tequistlatec *fušk-*. Yuman: Cocopa *psux*.

18 BODY   Comecrudo *met*. Salinan: San Antonio, San Miguel *matʰ* 'meat, animal.' Yuman: Walapai *mata* 'body, flesh,' Cocopa *hi-ma:č* 'body, flesh.'

19 BOIL₁ (v.)   Jicaque *molk*. Tequistlatec *-mul*.

20 BOIL₂ (v.)   Chimariko *potpot*. Salinan: San Antonio *(k-)opototna*. Yana: North *pidʔ-*.

21 BONE   Esselen *ija*. Pomo: North, Central *ja*, East *hija*.

22 BREAD₁   Chimariko *čeneu*. Karok *sara*.

23 BREAD₂   Jicaque *las* 'food.' Washo *wa:laš*.

24 BREAST₁   Achomawi: Atsugewi *atsiska*. Shasta *ʔi:tsi:k*. Tonkawa *jatsax*. Yana *tsikʔi*. Yuman: Diegueño *ičix* 'breast, heart.'

25 BREAST₂   Chimariko *huʔsiʔ*. Chumash: San Luis Obispo *s-čwø*. Karok *ʔu:čič* 'teat, breast.' Salinan: San Antonio *išoʔ*, San Miguel *išuʔ*. Shasta *ʔičwat* 'breast.' Washo *šu:* 'chest, breast.'

26 BURN₁   Achomawi *malis* 'fire.' Pomo: North *mali*, South *ma:li*, Central *mlej*. Salinan: San Miguel *maltintak*. Tequistlatec *epał*. Washo *meli* 'make a fire.' Yana *maʔlak* 'bake.'

27 BURN₂   Jicaque *pwe*. Tequistlatec *bi*.

28 CHEEK   Jicaque *pʰok*. Tequistlatec *bege*.

29 CHILD   Chimariko *kač* 'son.' Chumash: Santa Cruz *kučo*. Coahuilteco *kʔui* 'daughter, daughter-in-law.' Cotoname *kot* 'son' (man speaking). Jicaque *kukus* 'daughter.' Pomo: Clear Lake *qus* 'baby.' Shasta *ʔa:kwiʔ* 'son.' Subtiaba *-ku*.

30 CLIMB   Coahuilteco *mao* 'go up.' Subtiaba *g-ima*. Yana *maa*. Yuman: Yuma *aman*.

31 COVER₁   Karok *-čak* 'closing up.' Pomo: Northeast *ši:kʔo* 'blanket,' East *ši:ts* 'blanket.' Washo *i:tsʔig* 'close, obstruct.'

32 COVER₂   Karok *sap* 'close.' Yana: North *sabʔli*. Yuman: Mohave *sapet*

'close,' Maricopa *špetam* 'close,' Yuma *šapet.* Yurumangui *sipa-na* 'hat.'

33 CRY₁ Chumash: Santa Barbara *miš.* Maratino *mimɨyi.* Pomo: East *maxar.* Salinan: San Antonio *ʔames,* San Miguel *amas* 'shouts.' Tonkawa *maka.* Yana *mi.* Yuman: Cocopa, Maricopa *mi,* Walapai, Havasupai *mi:ka.*

34 CRY₂ Jicaque *pija.* Karok *ʔivūr* 'weep for.' Subtiaba *mbi:ja.* Washo *iʔb.*

35 DAY Subtiaba *bii.* Tequistlatec *biʔi.* Washo *ebe.* Yana *ba* 'sun moves.' Yuman: Cochimi *i:bi* 'today.' Yurumangui *ba(-isa).*

36 DEER Chimariko *a:ʔa.* Chumash: San Luis Obispo *tˀ-awø* 'dog.' Tonkawa *ao.* Yuman: Cochiti *awi.*

37 DENT (v.) Achomawi *-qol-.* Chimariko *kxol.*

38 DIE Comecrudo *kamau.* Seri *-ʔakxmi.*

39 DIG Chimariko *po.* Subtiaba: Tlappanec *ma-mbɔʔ.* Tequistlatec *bu.*

40 DIRTY Comecrudo *papeleple.* Yana *pun-na* 'red paint, dirt.' Yuman: Tipai *xpɨɬ,* Mohave *hapel.*

41 DOG Coahuilteco *keš.* Karankawa *keš.* Salinan: San Antonio *xuč,* San Miguel *xučai.* Seri *xees* 'fox.' Washo *gušu.* Yuman: Cocopa, etc. *xaṭ.*

42 DREAM₁ (v.) Chimariko *maka.* Jicaque *hami.* Seri *-omooš-.* Yuman: Diegueño *xemač.*

43 DREAM₂ (v.) Pomo: East *xadum.* Yana *xahdai.*

44 DRINK Achomawi: Achomawi *iss,* Atsugewi *iǰ.* Karok *ʔis.* Seri *isi:.* Tequistlatec *čwa.* Yana: North *sii,* Central *tˀii.* Yuman: Mohave *ithi,* Tipai *si,* Akwa'ala *ʔasi,* etc. Yurumangui *si.*

45 DUST Chimariko *(matre-)pa.* Jicaque *ʔipʰɨ* 'ashes.' Tequistlatec *-abi* 'ashes, dust.' Tonkawa *pa.*

46 EAT Achomawi: Achomawi *a:m, amm,* Atsugewi *jam, wam.* Chimariko *-ama-, -ma-.* Chumash: San Buenaventura *uma.* Coahuilteco *ha:m.* Cotoname *hahame* 'eat, food.' Esselen *am.* Karankawa *ama* 'fish.' Karok: Karok *av̄,* Arra-Arra *am.* Pomo: Proto-Pomo **maʔa.* Quinigua *ama* 'eat fish.' Salinan: San Antonio *ama, amma,* San Miguel *amoʔ.* Yana *ma.* Yuman: Yuma *ama,* Havasupai *mama.*

47 EGG₁ Jicaque *pue, pehej.* Seri *iipx.* Tequistlatec *-biʔe* 'egg, testicle.'

48 EGG₂ Chimariko *ano:qai.* Karok *ʔuruh* 'egg, round.' Yuman: Diegueño *ʔur* 'egg, testicle,' Yuma *oraʔor.*

49 ENTER Achomawi *uilu.* Yana: North, Yahi *wul-* 'in, entering.'

50 EXCREMENT Achomawi: Atsugewi *wehki.* Chimariko *h-iwax-ni.* Seri *ooxø.* Yana: North, Yahi *wakˀi* 'defecate.'

51 EXTINGUISH Coahuilteco *ča:p* 'kill.' Karok *ˀišip.* Salinan: San Antonio, San Miguel *šap.* Seri *xop.* Yuman: Tipai *we-sip,* Diegueño *ta:-sip* (*ta:* = causative).

52 FALL Chimariko *-man-.* Comecrudo *mel.* Pomo: Southeast *ban* 'put round object, throw round object.' Yuman: Walapai *mana.*

53 FAT Comecrudo *pak* (n.). Seri *k-ipkø,* pl. *k-ipøkø* (adj.).

54 FATHER Chumash: Santa Ynez, Santa Barbara *qoqo;* Santa Rosa *ukaka.* Karok *ˀakah.* Salinan: San Antonio *ˀek.* Washo *goˀj.* Yuman: Yuma *ko.*

55 FEATHER$_1$ Chumash: Santa Barbara *asah.* Karok: Karok *ˀi:thka,* Arra-Arra *a-isk.*

56 FEATHER$_2$ Jicaque *pom.* Tequistlatec *bimi.*

57 FIGHT Jicaque *palan.* Tequistlatec *fulu.*

58 FINISH$_1$ Comecrudo *itakuak* (intransitive). Tonkawa *to:xa* 'finish, destroy.' Yana: North *dikˀau.*

59 FINISH$_2$ Esselen *amomuths* 'it is finished.' Seri *k-eme* 'finished.' Washo *mama.*

60 FIRE$_1$ Cotoname *manex.* Seri *ˀamak.* Tequistlatec *unkwa.*

61 FIRE$_2$ Chimariko *hau-na* 'tinder.' Esselen *a(-nix).* Jicaque *aua.* Karok *ˀa:ha, ˀa:h* 'carry, handle fire.' Pomo: Kashaya *ˀoho,* North *ho,* East xo, etc. Salinan: San Antonio *ṭ-aˀauh.* Shasta *kw-a:x-ik* 'fire spreads.' Subtiaba *a:gu.* Yana *ˀau-na.* Yuman: Campo *aˀaux,* Kiliwa *ˀaau,* Havasupai *oˀoˀ,* etc. Yurumangui *anga(-fa)* 'ashes.'

62 FLEA Jicaque *pel.* Pomo: Proto-Pomo **ˀimela* (Oswalt). Salinan: San Antonio *ṭ-a:jiɬ.* Tequistlatec *-ˀiɬ.* Yuman: Diegueño *ˀewiɬ.*

63 FOG Comecrudo *milio.* Jicaque *mol* 'fog, cloud.' Cf. Yuman: Yavapai *motha.*

64 FOOT$_1$ Chumash: Santa Ynez *t-em.* Comecrudo *emi, lemi,emi* 'travel.' Pomo: Proto-Pomo **mi-* (instrumental prefix). Tequistlatec *la-ˀmis.* Yuman: Cocopa, etc. *imi* 'foot, leg.'

65 FOOT$_2$ Chumash: San Luis Obispo *pøløwø* 'leg above knee.' Seri *ipeɬ* (Kroeber; not found in Moser's dictionary).

66 FOREHEAD Comecrudo *apel* 'face.' Jicaque *barra.* Karok *jupin.* Seri *ˀaapni.* Tequistlatec *ɬa-bali.* Yuman: Akwa'ala *impul,* etc.

67 FORGET Chimariko *xome:.* Coahuilteco *-(a)xaman.* Cf. Yuman: Yavapai, etc. *šumi* 'lose.'

68 FULL₁   Comecrudo *pakam*. Seri *ka-pok-t*. Shasta *k-upakna?*. Tonkawa *nes-petˢe* 'to fill' (*nes* = causative). Yuman: Kiliwa *ipakal* 'I am full.'

69 FULL₂   Pomo: Clear Lake *minam*. Salinan: San Miguel *epʰena:tɬ* (pl.). Tequistlatec *imanna*. Yana: North *ba?ni* 'be full.' Yurumangui *pini-ta* 'empty' (-*ta* is negative).

70 GIVE₁   Coahuilteco *?ax*. Jicaque *kaja*. Karok *?akih* (pl. subject). Pomo: Southeast *?qa* 'give round object.' Seri *k-ike*. Tequistlatec *kuj*. Tonkawa *?eke*. Yuman: Havasupai *?eka*, Akwa'ala *e:k*.

71 GIVE₂   Jicaque *?oja*. Subtiaba -*aja:a*. Yuman: Yuma *a:ja*.

72 GO₁   Achomawi: Atsugewi *i?w* 'walk.' Chimariko -*owa*-,-*wam*-. Cotoname *awojo* 'let's go.' Karok *var*. Pomo: East *wa*-, *wal*-, North *wa*-, Kashaya *w*-. Quinigua *wame*, *wan*. Tequistlatec *wa*. Yuman: Akwa'ala *vo:* 'walk.' Yurumangui [ne-gua-i] 'go away!' (*ne*- is 'you,' -*i* is imperative, and *gua* = *wa* in Spanish orthography).

73 GO₂   Chimariko *a*. Yana: North *ha* 'woman goes.' Yuman: Walapai *a* 'move,' Cocopa *?ax*.

74 GO OUT   Achomawi: Achomawi -*da* 'out of,' Atsugewi -*ta* 'out of.' Chimariko *tap* 'out of.' Tonkawa *ta* 'come.'

75 GOOD   Cotoname *kenax*. Tonkawa *henex*. Yuman: Walapai *ahan*, Akwa'ala *xan*, etc.

76 GRIND   Karok *?ikrav*. Pomo: Southeast *knil-it* 'pound.' Salinan: San Antonio *exwaɬ*. Shasta *?iknu?* 'flourhopper.' Subtiaba *na-hnu*.

77 HAND₁   Chimariko -*teni*, *h-itanpu*. Pomo: South *tʰa:na*, Southeast *?tan*, etc. Salinan: San Miguel *ita?l* 'shoulder,' San Antonio *etaɬ* 'shoulder.'

78 HAND₂   Karok *muut* 'carry in hand.' Yana: North *muut*- 'reach out, hand.'

79 HEAD₁   Achomawi: Achomawi *laħ*, Atsugewi *naxa*. Comecrudo *elax*. Shasta *?innax*.

80 HEAD₂   Chimariko *hima* 'hair, head.' Karok *axva:h*. Washo *iheb*.

81 HEAR   Achomawi: Atsugewi *kuka*. Chimariko -*ke:*-. Coahuilteco *xo* 'know.' Quinigua *kawi*, *kawa* 'ear.' Shasta *ri-kjaw:a?* 'he heard it.' Tequistlatec -*gjeh*-. Yana: North *go*. Yuman: Kiliwa *kwe:*. Cf. Seri *k-keokɬ*.

82 HEART   Achomawi: Achomawi *sulqa* 'lungs,' Atsugewi *skəkar* 'lungs.' Pomo: East *tˢukun*, Southwest *tˢʼukul*. Salinan: San Antonio *škʼo?il* 'lungs,' San Miguel *šukaiel* 'lungs.' Seri *?askt* 'lungs.' Yana: North, Central *dᶻugutˢʼi*.

83 HEAVY   Achomawi: Atsugewi *mi:jas?i.* Chimariko *ču-midan* (*ču* = 'round object'). Karok *ma:th.* Salinan: San Antonio *k-met'o,* San Miguel *šmot.* Seri *motet.* Yana: North *mi:dʲas?i.*

84 HILL   Esselen *ausai* 'above.' Pomo: South *wišša* 'ridge,' Northeast *wiša:* 'mountain,' etc. Yana: North *wasa* 'over, above,' Yahi *wasdʲa* 'over, above.'

85 HIT   Pomo: East *ol* 'throw at.' Yana *hal.*

86 HORN   Chimariko *huwes, huwis.* Karok *ve:šura.* Washo *mesu?, mesu* 'antler, horn.' Yana *weeju* (Yana *j* < *s, š*).

87 HOUSE   Chimariko *awa.* Chumash: Santa Ynez *mam.* Esselen *aua.* Jicaque *wa.* Karok *?i:v.* Salinan: San Antonio *ṭ-a:m.* Shasta *amma.* Subtiaba *k-a:mo* 'sit.' Washo *d-anga-l; anga-l* 'dwell.' Yuman: Yavapai *uwa,* Diegueño *uwa:,* etc. Yurumangui *a-umi-ssa* 'sit down!' a-uma-sa 'chair.' (Cf. the Hokan entry for SIT$_2$ in the Amerind dictionary.)

88 KNEE   Achomawi: Achomawi *pullutˢ,* Atsugewi *pulludᶻ.* Seri *?afɬk.* Yana: Yahi *purutˢʔi,* etc.

89 LARGE$_1$ Jicaque *-po* (augmentative). Subtiaba *-mba* (augmentative).

90 LARGE$_2$ Quinigua *ki.* Salinan: San Miguel *kʔʷaka* 'long, high, tall.' Seri *k-aakoh.* Shasta *?ukkʷaxu:(h)i?* 'long.' Subtiaba *d-agu.* Tequistlatec *agwega?.* Yana *kʔu-* 'be long' (inferred from compounds). Yuman: Diegueño *?iikuu.*

91 LARGE$_3$ Coahuilteco *apna:n.* Jicaque *pøne.* Waicuri *panne.*

92 LAUGH   Salinan: San Antonio *ilikʔ.* Subtiaba *na-ndiɛgu.* Yana *halai* (pl. subject). Cf. Achomawi *le:jo?.*

93 LEAF   Achomawi: Atsugewi *ku-tara.* Chimariko *tahalwi.* Comecrudo *sel.* Jicaque *tˢulo.* Pomo: Kashaya, etc. *si?ṭʔal.*

94 LEFT (SIDE)   Chimariko *xuli.* Salinan: San Antonio *o?kel,* San Miguel *okel.*

95 LIGHTNING   Achomawi *-amet-* (v.). Comecrudo *met* 'lightning flash.' Tonkawa *m?etan.*

96 LIVE   Seri *-i?* 'sit, live.' Subtiaba *ja.* Yana *jai* 'stay' (pl. subject).

97 MANY   Jicaque *pɨlɨk.* Tequistlatec *?ašpela?.*

98 MIDDLE   Chumash: San Buenaventura *s-mak-tinuč* 'half (in length).' Comecrudo *imak.* Seri *imak.*

99 MOSQUITO   Chimariko *tˢele:je.* Karok *tˢanna:kkat.*

100 MOTHER   Achomawi *tatʰi:.* Coahuilteco *tai.* Comecrudo *te.* Karok *ta:t.* Pomo: North, East, etc. *-ṭʰe.* Seri *?ita.* Shasta *atxi.* Subtiaba *-udu.* Yuman: Yavapai *titi,* Walapai *čit,* Mohave, Maricopa *ntaj.*

101 MOUNTAIN   Chimariko *awu*. Comecrudo *waj*. Quinigua *ai, aje*.
Yuman: Cocopa *wi* 'mountain, rock,' Tipai *wij* 'stone,' Kiliwa *wej*
'mountain, stone,' etc.

102 MOUTH   Comecrudo *xal*. Karok *-kara* 'into the mouth.' Tonkawa
kala. Washo *-a:gal* 'into or in the mouth.'

103 NAVEL   Chimariko *hi-nabu*. Karok *arup*. Shasta *ʔe:raw*. Yuman:
Diegueño *miɬipo:*, Mohave *hilʲpu*.

104 NEAR   Karok *ʔu:mukič*. Pomo: East *imak* 'in company with.' Shasta
ʔammax, umme. Yana: North *matˢʔu* 'soon, near.'

105 NECK   Chumash: San Buenaventura *paktamus, pakløwø* 'throat.'
Seri *k-iphk* 'hang on neck.' Subtiaba: Tlappanec *apuh*, Subtiaba *ha:pu*.
Tequistlatec *(ɬa-)hokʔ*. Washo *i:bu*.

106 NEW   Achomawi *palawi*. Comecrudo *pelex*.

107 NOSE   Chimariko *hɔχu*. Comecrudo *jaχ*. Karok *jufiv, juph* (Powers).
Seri *ʔaaf*. Washo *šujeb*. Yuman: Yuma *i:xu:*, Kiliwa *api, pʰi*. Cf.
Achomawi *jammi* and Karankawa *emai*.

108 OLD   Achomawi: Atsugewi *pe:ǰu*. Comecrudo *pat*. Yuman: Walapai
pataj 'old man.'

109 ONE₁   Chumash: Santa Ynez, Santa Barbara *paka*. Esselen *pak*. Yana:
Yahi, North *-pgu-* 'each.'

110 ONE₂   Chimariko *pun*. Coahuilteco *pil*. Jicaque *pani*.

111 PENIS   Salinan: San Antonio *enoʔol*, San Miguel *noɬ*. Tonkawa *ne:l*
'sexual organs.'

112 PULL   Karok *-ju:n*. Yana *jun*.

113 PULL OFF   Achomawi *pil*. Chimariko *pul*.

114 RABBIT   Achomawi: Achomawi *kenek*, Atsugewi *kiniʔiki*. Chumash:
Santa Ynez *qun*. Quinigua *kun*. Salinan: San Antonio *kol* 'hare.'
Yuman: Walapai *i:kuʎ*, Diegueño *kuñaw*.

115 RAIN   Achomawi: Atsugewi *kwaji:t* 'to rain.' Chumash: La Purisima
aka 'cloud.' Tequistlatec *-agwi*. Yuman: Mohave *ikwe* 'cloud,'
Diegueño *ekwi*.

116 RAW   Pomo: South *kahšo* 'raw, alive,' Northeast *kašoj*, etc.
Tequistlatec *ikʔašwi* 'green.' Yana: North, Yahi *-xsui-*.

117 RIPE   Subtiaba *nægo*. Tonkawa *naxo* 'ripen.'

118 ROAD   Jicaque *kampa* 'long.' Subtiaba *gamba*.

119 ROAST   Jicaque *sar*. Seri *sil*. Yuman: Cocopa *wašil*, Walapai, Campo
sil.

120 ROOT   Comecrudo *jemo*. Pomo: Kashaya, South *ʔima* 'sinew,'

Northeast *jima* 'sinew.' Shasta *ʔimmi* 'sinew,' *ʔummaj* 'pine root.'
Subtiaba *u:ñu* 'string' (Subtiaba *ñ* < *m*).

121 ROPE   Achomawi *asli*. Pomo: Kashaya *sul*, Central *slimet* 'string.'
Salinan: San Antonio *asoł*. Shasta *ʔassa* 'string.'

122 RUN   Coahuilteco *kuino*. Pomo: East *gadi* (pl. subject). Subtiaba
d-agal-ni 'runner.' Washo *igelu* (pl. subject). Yuman: Yuma *kono*,
Diegueño *ganau*.

123 SALT   Chimariko *aqai*. Pomo: East *kʰe:ʔe*, Northeast *čeʔe*. Salinan:
San Antonio, San Miguel *ţ-akai*.

124 SEE₁   Seri *ʔaʔo*. Subtiaba *ajo*. Yuman: Diegueño *ʔuwow*, Mohave
ʔija-m, Yavapai [o-o].

125 SEE₂   Achomawi *-imm*. Coahuilteco *maš, mas*. Comecrudo *max*.
Karok *imus, mah*. Salinan: San Antonio *iam, iem*, San Miguel *ia:m*,
me- 'go to see.' Shasta *im*. Cf. Pomo *ma-bi, ma-jap* 'face, look,' *maga*
'look for.'

126 SHOOT   Jicaque *ni*. Subtiaba *di:na-lu* 'hole.' Tequistlatec *na*
'perforate.'

127 SINEW   Achomawi: Achomawi *pim*, Atsugewi *ippiw*. Karok *ʔipam*.
Yana *baama* 'sinew.'

128 SIT₁   Seri *-ix-*. Subtiaba *-iʔiguʔ*.

129 SIT₂   Karok *ikriv*. Washo *g-i:gel* (sing. subject). Yana: Yahi *kʼuʔla*.

130 SKIN   Tequistlatec *l-išmi*. Tonkawa *-som-*.

131 SLEEP₁   Karok *ʔasiṽ*. Pomo: Kashaya *simaq-*, South *si:ma*, etc. Seri
sim. Shasta *r-itˢmasa:kaʔ* 'he is sleeping.' Tequistlatec *-sma-*. Washo
elšɨm. Yana: Central *sam*, North *sab*, etc. Yuman: Mohave *isma*,
Havasupai *sma:ka*, etc.

132 SLEEP₂   Chimariko *po, poi*. Chumash: Santa Cruz *k-opok* 'dead.'
Esselen *poko*. Salinan: San Miguel *p-apa* 'copulate.' Subtiaba *g-ap* 'lie
sleeping.' Waicuri *pibikiri* 'he died,' *tibikiu* 'dead ones.' Yuman:
Cocopa *patχ* 'lie down,' Kiliwa *pi* 'die,' Maricopa *epuik* 'dead,' etc.

133 SMALL   Jicaque *tˢikwaj*. Seri *-iteoøko* 'weak.' Shasta *atʔuk*. Subtiaba
taxū.

134 SMOKE   Esselen *čaxa*. Pomo: East *saha*, Southeast *tˢaxa*. Subtiaba
na-si:xa 'to smoke.' Yana: North, Central *tˢʼe:kʔau*.

135 SMOOTH   Jicaque *lalakʔon*. Tequistlatec *łukʔ*. Cf. Yuman: Diegueño
xeleqaj, Tipai *xalkat*.

136 SNOW₁   Pomo: North, Central *ju:*, Southeast *ju-l, ju*, East *hju-l*,

North *ʔi:hu.* Shasta *ʔijuʔai* 'ice.' Yana: Central, Yahi *dʸu-ri* 'to snow' (*-ri* = 'down').

137 SNOW₂   Chimariko *hi-pui, pa-nna* 'snowshoes.' Chumash: Santa Barbara *poi.* Yana: North *paǰa, pa:-* 'snow lies on ground.' Cf. Yuman: Mohave *upaka,* Tonto *paka.*

138 STONE₁   Comecrudo *pak-mat, paknax* 'high.' Jicaque *pe.* Quinigua *pixa.* Shasta: Konomihu *pakwai* 'high.' Tequistlatec *ɬ-abik.* Yana: North, Yahi *baa* 'stone-like object lies.'

139 STONE₂   Chumash: Santa Ynez, Santa Barbara *xøp,* San Buenaventura *xøp, køp.* Esselen *šiefe.* Pomo: Kashaya *qʰaʔbe,* East *xa:be,* etc. Salinan: San Miguel *šxap,* San Antonio *šxaʔ.* Shasta: Konomihu *kip* 'mountain.' Tonkawa *kapow* 'hard, stale.' Yuman: Yuma, Maricopa, etc. *axpe* 'metate.'

140 STRING   Jicaque *nulu* 'maguey.' Subtiaba *-u:ñulu:.* Tequistlatec *-ajnuɬ* 'fiber.'

141 SUN₁   Achomawi *tˢul.* Shasta *tˢʔuwar.*

142 SUN₂   Jicaque *lak-sak* 'sun, day' (*lak* = 'glowing'). Yurumangui *siko-na.*

143 SWEAT   Karok *astu:k.* Shasta *-u:stukʔ.*

144 SWIM   Comecrudo *akikete.* Seri *akat.* Tonkawa *koxoxwa.*

145 TESTICLE   Salinan: San Antonio *solo,* San Miguel *sola:xo.* Tequistlatec *la-šʔuɬ* 'penis.' Tonkawa *tˢa:l.* Cf. Karok *thirixo:n.*

146 THORN   Comecrudo *tet.* Yuman: Yavapai *tat,* Mohave *ʔatat.*

147 THROW₁   Coahuilteco *tʔam.* Comecrudo *tap.* Yuman: Tipai *atap,* Yavapai *tami.*

148 THROW₂   Karok *path* (sing. object). Seri *afit.* Washo *beš.* Cf. THROW₁, above; metathesis?

149 THROW₃   Comecrudo *aka.* Tonkawa *ka:.*

150 THROW₄   Chimariko *hi-ssumat.* Washo *šuʔm.*

151 TONGUE   Achomawi: Achomawi *ipʰle, iplaʔtaj* 'lick,' Atsugewi *apʰli.* Chimariko *hi-pen, pen* 'lick.' Comecrudo *expen.* Jicaque *berang, pelam.* Karok *aprih.* Pomo: East, Southeast *bal.* Salinan: San Antonio *epa:l,* San Miguel *ipaɬ.* Seri *ʔapɬ.* Tequistlatec *-apaɬ, beɬ* 'lick.' Waicuri *ma-bela.* Yuman: Maricopa *hipaʎ,* Walapai *ipaal,* etc.

152 TOOTH   Achomawi: Achomawi *iǰa,* Atsugewi *iʔdʸaw* ~ *iʔtˢaw.* Chimariko *h-utˢʔu.* Chumash: Santa Ynez, Santa Barbara *sa.* Shasta *ičʔo, itˢau.* Yana: Central, Yahi *ki-tˢʔau-na* (according to Sapir, *ki-* is a prefix, probably the third-person possessive).

153 TWO   Achomawi: Achomawi *ha?aq, haq*, Atsugewi *hoqi*. Chimariko *xoku*. Karok *?axak*. Salinan: San Antonio *kakšu*, San Miguel *xakiš*. Tequistlatec *kook^h*. Tonkawa *haikia*. Yuman: Cocopa *xawak*, Yuma *xavik*, etc.

154 UNDER   Cotoname *eta*. Seri *itis* 'bottom.' Yana: Yahi *(?i-)ri(-k'u)*. Washo *-iti?* ~ *iti* 'down.'

155 UP   Chumash: Santa Ynez, etc. *alapa* 'above, heaven.' Comecrudo *apel* 'above, heaven.' Jicaque *arpa* 'above.' Karok *?ipan* 'end, top.' Yana: North, Yahi *-bal-* 'up from the ground.'

156 UPON   Achomawi *wina* 'top.' Pomo: East *wina:* 'on top of,' Northeast *wi:nal* 'straight up.' Waicuri *aena* 'above, heaven.'

157 WASH₁   Chimariko *pok*. Comecrudo *pak* 'wet.' Jicaque *pat^s*. Karok *pithxah* (inanimate object). Yuman: Kiliwa *pas?il* (reflexive).

158 WASH₂   Comecrudo *pawapel* 'bathe,' *pellap* 'wash.' Tonkawa *panxo*. Yurumangui *punpun* 'bathe.'

159 WEAVE   Karok *vik*. Shasta *-ik'j-*. Yana *waga-* 'twine a basket.'

160 WHITE   Chimariko *mata?i* 'clean.' Cotoname *mesoi*. Salinan: San Antonio *mataɬ*. Tonkawa *maslak*. Yuman: Kiliwa *?amasap*, Cocopa *xamaɬ*, etc. (Sapir cites Subtiaba *miša*, but *m-* is probably a prefix; cf. *t-i:ču* 'white,' *di-g-i:ša* 'white hair.')

161 WIFE   Achomawi *ta* 'woman.' Coahuilteco *ta:jagu:* 'man marries, wife.' Esselen *ta-* 'woman.' Pomo: Proto-Pomo **-d?* 'feminine,' East *da*. Tonkawa *ta-e* 'marry.' Yurumangui *ita(-asa)*.

162 WIND (n.)   Pomo: Kashaya, South *?ihja*, North *ja*. Seri *?ai*. Tequistlatec *awa?*.

163 WISH   Salinan: San Antonio *k'unip* 'desire.' Yana: Central, Yahi *k'un* 'want, like,' North *k'ud*. Cf. Tonkawa *ta:kona* 'seek for, hunt.'

164 WOMAN₁   Comecrudo *kem*. Jicaque *kep*. Seri *kuāam* (Kroeber *kmam*). Tequistlatec *ɬ-aga?no*. Tonkawa *k^wa:n*.

165 WOMAN₂   Jicaque *kek*. Subtiaba *a:gu* 'female, wife.' Yuman: Kiliwa *keko*.

166 WOMAN₃   Pomo: North, Central *mata*, Kashaya *?ima:ta*. Salinan: San Miguel *hemuč*. Yana: North, Central *mari?mi* (< *madi?mi*).

167 WORM   Achomawi: Atsugewi *amoq*. Karok *vakaj*. Tequistlatec *mo:xa*. Washo *ma:ki* 'rattlesnake.'

168 YELLOW   Comecrudo *jalu*. Jicaque *lu*. Seri *k-oil* 'blue, green.'

PENUTIAN

As with Hokan, the nucleus of a much larger stock was first established by the work of Dixon and Kroeber in California (as enunciated in Dixon 1913). They defined Penutian as consisting of Yokuts, Maidu, Wintun, and Miwok-Costanoan. This set of languages may even today be considered a valid grouping and is called here California Penutian. The first important extensions were to the north and were chiefly the work of Sapir, especially his publication of 1921. He added Oregon and Plateau Penutian as well as Chinook and Tsimshian even farther north. The pioneer work on the southern extension was done by Lucy Freeland, who in 1930 linked California Penutian to Mixe, a language of Mexico. In this she built on the work of Paul Radin, who had proposed in 1916 that Huave was related to the Mixe group (Mixe-Zoque), and in 1924 that Mayan was related to both.

Sapir, in his famous classification of 1929, included in Penutian a Mexican substock consisting of Mixe-Zoque and Huave, but he excluded Mayan, to which he assigned independent status. In 1942, Norman A. Mc-Quown pointed to important resemblances between Totonac (and the closely related Tepehua), Mayan, and Mixe-Zoque. This group he called Macro-Mayan. Huave, however, was omitted.* The view presented here is that Huave, Mayan, Mixe-Zoque, and Totonac-Tepehua form a well-defined subgroup of Penutian.

The classification of Yukian (Yuki and Wappo) has also been problematical over the years. Though it is a language group of California, Dixon and Kroeber did not include it in Penutian, Hokan, or any of their other California stocks. Kroeber, as early as 1906, had compared it with Yokuts, later included in Penutian, but he drew no genetic conclusions. In 1957 William Shipley compared Yukian with California Penutian, suggesting 32 possible lexical cognates between the two groups. Though he did not accept genetic connection as the explanation, he left it open as a possibility. Eight years later Karl-Heinz Gursky (1965) sought to connect Yukian with Hokan, as Sapir had done.

The case for Yukian as part of a larger Penutian grouping appears sound, however. It is also clear that it is not California Penutian. The far greater resemblance, say, of Yokuts to Maidu or Wintun as compared to

---

*That language has been much discussed in recent years. It might well be called a meta-mystery. That is, it is a mystery why it should be a mystery.

Yukian is immediately clear. Hence Yukian must be part of some other group of Penutian or form a substock by itself. At the same time, as noted by William Elmendorff (1968), Yuki and Wappo are more closely related to each other than to any language outside of Yukian.

Once I had assembled sufficient comparative evidence on all the major groupings of the Americas, I compared Yukian with each of them. The result was as clear as it was startling. Yukian is a geographically distant subgroup of the Gulf family. It shows close and obvious cognates with such languages as Atakapa, Chitimacha, and the Muskogean group. In fact, it is as close genetically to, say, Atakapa as Chitimacha and Natchez are.

The existence of a Gulf group consisting of Atakapa, Chitimacha, Tunica, Natchez, and the Muskogean languages, first hypothesized by Mary R. Haas (1951, 1952, 1956), is widely accepted. Hence if Yuki is both a Gulf language and a Penutian language, then Gulf must be Penutian. Haas (1956) has proposed instead a relationship of Gulf to Algonquian. I do not argue that Gulf is unrelated to Algonquian, only that its affinity with Penutian seems to me decisively closer.

Since the Yuki-Gulf hypothesis is likely to be controversial, etymologies exclusive to Yukian and the rest of Gulf are included both when they are found in other branches of Penutian and when they are not. In addition, the Amerind dictionary entries for FIRE$_3$ and LEG cite forms found in Yuki-Gulf but not, as far as I can determine, in the rest of Penutian. Etymologies exclusive to Yuki-Gulf are followed by (YG) both below and in the Amerind dictionary. There remains the question of Zuni. In 1964, Stanley Newman connected Zuni with California Penutian. This seems to me correct, but to imply no more than that both belong in the larger grouping. Because I find Sapir's subgrouping of Penutian, except for its incompleteness in regard to the Mexican branch and its omission of Zuni and Yuki-Gulf, entirely correct, the etymologies in this section, unlike those in the preceding sections, are cited in terms of nine subgroups: California, Chinook, Gulf, Mexican, Oregon, Plateau, Tsimshian, Yukian, Zuni. As noted earlier, Yuki-Gulf is really a single group, but the languages are cited separately as explained above.

The Proto-Muskogean reconstructions cited are from Haas (1956, 1958a) and the Proto-California Penutian reconstructions from Pitkin and Shipley (1958). I have also cited some Proto-Mayan reconstructions from Campbell (1977) and Fox (1978). I use a (C) to distinguish Campbell's forms from Fox's.

144

In addition to the 288 exclusively Penutian etymologies presented here, 106 Penutian entries will be found in the Amerind dictionary under the following etymologies: ABOVE$_2$, ANT$_2$, ARM$_2$, ASHES, BACK$_2$, BATHE, BE$_2$, BEE$_2$, BELLY$_2$, BITE$_1$, BITTER$_1$, BLACK$_1$, BLOOD$_1$, BLOW, BODY$_1$, BOIL, BONE$_2$, BREAK, BREAST, BRING, BROAD, BROTHER, BURN, CALL$_1$, CALL$_2$, CARRY$_2$, CHEST, CHILD$_4$, CLEAN, CLOUD$_2$, COLD$_2$, COME, DARK, DIG$_3$, DIRTY, DRINK$_1$, DRINK$_3$, DRY$_1$, EARTH$_3$, EARTH$_4$, EAT$_1$, EGG$_2$, FAR, FEATHER$_1$, FIRE$_3$, FLEA, FLY (v.), FLY$_1$, FOOT$_1$, FOOT$_2$, GIRL, GO$_1$, GO$_3$, GO$_4$, HAND$_1$, HARD$_1$, HEAR$_1$, HOLE$_1$, HORN, KNEE$_1$, KNEE$_2$, KNOW, LARGE$_1$, LARGE$_2$, LEG, LIGHT, LONG$_1$, LONG$_2$, LOUSE$_3$, MAKE$_2$, MAN$_1$, MAN$_3$, MANY$_3$, NEAR, NECK, NIGHT$_2$, ONE$_2$, RIVER$_1$, ROAD$_1$, ROAD$_2$, ROUND, SAY$_2$, SEE$_1$, SEE$_2$, SEED$_2$, SHINE, SKIN$_2$, SLEEP$_1$, SMELL$_1$, SMELL$_2$, SNAKE$_1$, SOUR, STAR$_2$, SUN$_3$, SUN$_4$, SWALLOW, THIN, THROAT, TREE$_1$, TREE$_3$, TWO, WATER$_2$, WING, WISH, WOMAN$_3$, WORK$_1$.

PENUTIAN ETYMOLOGIES

1 BE ABLE   California: Costanoan: Rumsien *tuman;* Miwok: Lake *temma.* Mexican: Huave *ndom;* Mayan: Quiché *etamax* 'know.' Oregon: Takelma *t$^{s^2}$am-x* 'strong'; Coos *dæmił* 'strong, male.'

2 ABOVE   California: Maidu *ʔəlləm* 'up over'; Miwok: Lake *liile;* Wintun: Wintu *ʔol,* Patwin *olel* 'heaven.' Oregon: Iakon *la:ʔ* 'heaven.' Plateau: Klamath *lalli-s* 'hill.'

3 ALL$_1$ Gulf: Atakapa *kuš.* Mexican: Mayan: Uspantec, Quiché *k^{2}is* 'finish,' Tzeltal *k^{2}aš* 'very'; Mixe-Zoque: Tetontepec *kuš* 'finish (a meal),' Sayula *kíš* 'finish.' Oregon: Coos *go:s.*

4 ALL$_2$ California: Miwok: Lake *muʔe.* Gulf: Muskogean: Choctaw *moma.* Mexican: Mixe-Zoque: Mixe *maj* 'many.'

5 ALL$_3$ California: Costanoan: Santa Clara *emen,* San José *hemen;* Maidu *ma:no.* Gulf: Atakapa *man, mon;* Muskogean: Creek *amali, amalga.* Tsimshian *məła* 'each.' Yukian: Wappo *muli.* (Cf. ALL$_2$, above.)

6 ANGRY   Mexican: Mixe-Zoque: Tetontepec *akaʔa* 'anger.' Zuni *ʔika* 'be angry.'

7 ARM   California: Costanoan: Mutsun *isu* 'hand'; Wintun *se,sem* 'hand.' Gulf: Atakapa *wiš* (Eastern), *woš* (Western) 'finger'; Chitimacha *waši;* Natchez *ʔi:š* 'arm, hand'; Tunica *(tir-)waš* 'fingernail'; Muskogean: Creek *wešaku* 'fingers, hand,' Choctaw *iši,eši* 'take.' Mexican: Huave

owiš, viš; Mayan: Quiché *iš(-kʾaq)* 'nail.' Plateau: Nez Perce *ʔe:se* 'nail,' North Sahaptin *a:sa* 'nail.' Yukian: Yuki *hyss,* Coast Yuki *heʔs,* etc. Zuni *ʔasi.*

8 ARRIVE ́   California: Miwok: Bodega *wila* 'come!'; Wintun: West Wintu *wǝr* 'come.' Gulf: Natchez *ala* 'come.' Mexican: Mayan: Yucatec *hul-el,* Mam, Kakchiquel, Kekchí *uli* 'come, arrive,' Kekchí *wulatˢ,* Tzeltal *hul-el* 'come from,' etc. Oregon: Yakonan *wi:l,* Kalapuya *wal.*

9 ARROW   California: Maidu *nokʾo;* Yokuts: Yaudanchi *nukʾon* 'bow,' Gashowu *nekʾ-, nukʾ* 'bow.' Gulf: Natchez *onoxk* 'thorn'; Muskogean: Alabama *nakɨ,* Koasati *ɫaki.* Mexican: Proto-Mayan **la(:)h* 'nettle.' Oregon: Kalapuya *enuk.* Yukian: Wappo *luka* 'bow.'

10 ASHES   California: Maidu *pʾidusi;* Wintun: Patwin *put;* Miwok: Lake *pootel.* Mexican: Mixe-Zoque: Sierra Popoluca *potpot* 'dust.' Yukian: Yuki *pʾotil* (probable borrowing from Miwok).

11 BACK   Gulf: Muskogean: Alabama *wakh.* Tsimshian *waxɫ* 'beaver's tail.'

12 BAD   Chinook *qʾatxal* 'badness.' Gulf: Atakapa *katˢe* 'ugly.' Oregon: Kalapuya *kuske, kasq.* Plateau: Lutuami *qoitˢ.* Yukian: Yuki, Huchnom *kačum.*

13 BARK (SKIN)   Gulf: Chitimacha *suʔu* 'bark, skin.' Mexican: Totonac *šuwaʔ.* Yukian: Yuki *ol-šo* (*ol* = 'tree').

14 BEAT   California: Yokuts: Yokuts, Calavera *bok* 'kill'; Maidu *bok-* (as first member of compounds meaning 'knock, beat'); Wintun: South Wintu *buktu.* Gulf: Natchez *pa:k;* Tunica *pɛka;* Atakapa *pak.*

15 BEAUTIFUL   California: Wintun: North Wintu *čal* 'good'; Miwok: Central Sierra *kǝlli* 'healthy.' Gulf: Atakapa *šili, šiling.* Mexican: Mayan: Huastec *kul(-bel)* 'happy,' Jacaltec *čʾul* 'good.'

16 BITE   California: Miwok: Central Sierra *kasǝt.* Chinook *qš.* Gulf: Chitimacha *kʾušt* 'eat'; Tunica *kɛhča.* Mexican: Mayan: Quiché *katˢ;* Mixe-Zoque: Zoque *kuʔt* 'eat,' Sierra Popoluca *kǝʔš* 'eat.'

17 BLACK   California: Wintun *ku:ta.* Gulf: Natchez *kaʔahs* 'blue, bruised,' *kasa:ht* 'gray'; Tunica *kɔta* 'gray'; Chitimacha *katʾi* 'blue, green.' Oregon: Iakon *kajtet.*

18 BLOOD₁   California: Costanoan: Monterey *paččan;* Yokuts *pajčikin* 'red.' Gulf: Atakapa *poš, pošk.* Oregon: Yakonan *poutˢ.* Plateau: Lutuami *pojtˢ.* Tsimshian *misk* 'red.'

19 BLOOD₂   Gulf: Natchez *ʔitˢ;* Muskogean: Choctaw *issiš,* Koasati *ičikči.* Yukian: Yuki, Huchnom *ãš,* Coast Yuki *es.* Zuni *ʔate.*

20 BLOOM   Gulf: Proto-Muskogean *pak*. Mexican: Mixe-Zoque: Ayutla *pux* 'flower,' Tetontepec *puk* 'flower'; Huave *mbah* 'flower.'

21 BODY   Gulf: Atakapa *iwal* 'shell.' Yukian: Wappo *wil*. (YG)

22 BOIL₁   California: Yokuts *šuṭušuṭu*. Gulf: Chitimacha *šoxt*. Mexican: Mixe-Zoque: Sierra Popoluca *seʔt* 'to cook.'

23 BOIL₂   Gulf: Atakapa *uk*. Yukian: Wappo *kʰohkʰoh*. (YG)

24 BOY   Gulf: Muskogean: Muskokee *eppuče* 'son' (man speaking). Yukian: Huchnom *(iwi-)peč* (*iwi* probably = 'male'; cf. Wappo *ʔew* 'husband'). (YG)

25 BREAST₁   Gulf: Tunica *ʔuču*. Mexican: Mayan: Huastec *ičič*, Chorti *ču*.

26 BREAST₂   California: Proto-California Penutian *mu* 'milk'; Miwok: Tuolumne *musu;* Costanoan: Monterey *muš* (pl.). Tsimshian *muš*, *maš*, *mas-x*.

27 BRING₁   Gulf: Tunica *u:i*. Yukian: Yuki *u*. (YG)

28 BRING₂   California: Maidu *maha*. Gulf: Tunica *muhi* 'carry in hand.' Mexican: Mixe *mah* 'bring water.'

29 BRING₃   Gulf: Natchez *i:x*. Mexican: Mayan: Quiché *eq* 'carry'; Huave *ahan* 'bring (people)' (cf. Mayan: Tzeltal, Tzotzil *ičʔ-el* 'take'; Totonac *čiʔj* 'take').

30 BROAD   California: Maidu: Northeast *dapdape*. Gulf: Muskogean: Creek *tapʰe*.

31 BROTHER (OLDER)   California: Maidu *ʔeti*; Miwok: Lake *ʔatta*. Gulf: Tunica *-hta-* 'sibling.' Mexican: Mayan: Quiché *atˢik*, Kekchí *asˀ*, Mam *itˢik*, *itˢi* 'younger brother'; Mixe-Zoque: Sayula *axč*, Zoque *atˢi*. Oregon: Alsea *haʔt*.

32 BURN   California: Miwok: Bodega *hulih*, Central Sierra *həltə* 'blaze,' Lake *həlsi*. Gulf: Muskogean: Koasati *heɬi* 'take fire.' Mexican: Mayan: Quiché *xul* 'scorch.' Yukian: Wappo *hel* 'fire.'

33 BURY   Gulf: Atakapa *moš*. Mexican: Mayan: Proto-Mayan (C) *muk*, *muq*, Yucatec *mak*, Tzotzil *mukej*, etc.

34 CHEEK   Gulf: Atakapa *al*. Mexican: Mayan: Huastec *alwiʔ* 'jaw.' Oregon: Takelma *al-* 'face' (instrumental prefix), Coos *ila* 'in front of.'

35 CHEST   California: Wintun *tu:n;* Miwok: Lake, Bodega *tena*. Oregon: Kalapuya *təmpo* 'belly.' Plateau: North Sahaptin *-tm-*, *təmna* 'heart,' Nez Perce *tiʔmi:ne*. Yukian: Yuki *tunan*, Coast Yuki *tome*.

36 CHILD₁   Gulf: Atakapa *ška* 'child, boy.' Yukian: Yuki *sak*, Huchnom *sax*. (YG)

37 CHILD₂   Mexican: Mayan: Mam *kual,* Tzutuhil *ak²ual,* etc.; Huave
    kwa:l. Oregon: Alsea *kʲi:la* 'son.' Yukian: Yuki *kil* 'son, daughter.'
38 CHILD₃   Chinook *ka.* Gulf: Tunica *ɔka, -ehku* 'offspring.' Yukian:
    Wappo *-eka* 'son,' *ekaiji* 'child.'
39 CLOSE (v.)   California: Maidu *ban* 'cover.' Gulf: Atakapa *pan;* Natchez
    pala. Mexican: Huave *apal* 'cover.' Yukian: Wappo *pɔn.*
40 CLOUD   Plateau: Yakima *pasčit* 'fog,' North Sahaptin *pastˢ²at* 'fog.'
    Yukian: Coast Yuki *po²tit.*
41 COLD   Chinook *tˢəs.* Gulf: Chitimacha *tatu* 'freeze'; Tunica *to:* 'ice.'
    Plateau: North Sahaptin [toah]. Tsimshian *dau* 'ice.' Yukian: Wappo
    tˢatˢ, tˢa 'become cold.'
42 COME   Gulf: Muskogean: Koasati, Hitchiti *onti,* Alabama *ati.*
    Mexican: Mayan: Jacaltec *toji* 'go'; Huave *andəj.* Yukian: Wappo *t²ɔ*
    'arrive.'
43 COOK₁   Gulf: Tunica *juki.* Yukian: Wappo *joko.* (YG)
44 COOK₂   Gulf: Atakapa *am.* Mexican: Mixe-Zoque: Sierra Popoluca
    ju:m 'boil,' Zoque *jum* 'boil'; Mayan: Yucatec *om* 'boil.'
45 COOK₃   California: Miwok: Central Sierra *hinna* 'roast.' Gulf:
    Muskogean: Choctaw *hona.*
46 COVER   California: Costanoan: Mutsun *ese* 'to dress.' Gulf: Chitimacha
    šax; Muskogean: Choctaw *iši.* Oregon: Siuslaw *aswiti* 'blanket.'
    Yukian: Wappo *sah, sɔ.*
47 CRY₁   California: Maidu *wak;* Yokuts *wa:xal;* Wintun *watˢ.* Gulf: Tunica
    waha. Mexican: Mixe-Zoque: Sierra Popoluca *wex.* Plateau: Klamath
    swaqč.
48 CRY₂   Chinook: Wasco *ajaw.* Gulf: Atakapa *jau;* Muskogean: Choctaw
    jaija. Tsimshian *au.*
49 CUT₁   California: Wintun *pʰi:la* ~ *pʰi:le;* Costanoan: Rumsien *wal.*
    Gulf: Natchez *bala* 'cut up.'
50 CUT₂   Gulf: Natchez *topʰ* 'cut off.' Yukian: Wappo *tˢipu.* (YG)
51 DANCE₁   California: Yokuts *wotej.* Chinook *na-wetˢko* 'I dance,'
    Wishram *wičk.* Gulf: Tunica *wahsa* 'jump, *wesa* 'dance' (Haas);
    Chitimacha *owaš* 'jump.' Mexican: Mixe-Zoque: Mixe *otˢ,* Sayula *eč,*
    Zoque *²ehts.* Plateau: North Sahaptin *waša,* Nez Perce *we:še:.*
52 DANCE₂   Gulf: Muskogean: Koasati *bit.* Mexican: Mayan: Quiché *bis,*
    Huastec *bišom,* Mam *bišan,* Kekchí *bič* 'sing.'
53 DIE₁   Gulf: Chitimacha *tuw* (pl. subject), Natchez *wata.* Yukian: Wappo
    ɔta 'be dead,' *ɔtɛwi* 'be dead.' (YG)

54 DIE₂   California: Maidu: Northeast *heno*. Oregon: Takelma *he:n* 'be used up, consumed.'

55 DIE₃   Plateau: Klamath *čoːq* (pl. subject). Tsimshian *t$^{s^2}$ak* 'be extinguished.'

56 DIVE   Gulf: Tunica *muču*. Mexican: Mayan: Quiché *mušix* 'swim.' Oregon: Siuslaw *mi:x* 'swim.'

57 DOG   California: Maidu *sɨ*. Gulf: Tunica *sa*. Cf. Tsimshian *ha:s*.

58 DUST   California: Costanoan: Santa Cruz *pirren* 'earth.' Oregon: Takelma *p^{2}ol*. Yukian: Wappo *pɔl*.

59 EAR   California: Wintun *mat*. Mexican: Mixe-Zoque: Sierra Popoluca *matɔng* 'hear'; Huave *gašmata*. Plateau: Nez Perce *mut^{s}aiu, mat$^{s^2}$i* 'hear,' North Sahaptin *mət$^{s^2}$iu, mət^s* 'hear,' Klamath *mača:* 'hear.' Tsimshian *amuks* 'listen.'

60 EAT   Mexican: Huave *əet;* Mayan: Uspantec *ti*, Jacaltec *ita* 'food'; Mixe-Zoque: Sayula *toʔ*. Zuni *ʔito*.

61 ELBOW₁   Gulf: Atakapa *temaːk* 'knee.' Yukian: Wappo *t^{s}aima*. (YG)

62 ELBOW₂   Gulf: Atakapa *šuk;* Muskogean: Choctaw *šūkani*. Mexican: Mayan: Tzotzil *šukub*, Uspantec *čuk*.

63 ELBOW₃   California: Yokuts: Yaudanchi *k^{h}ošoji*. Gulf: Muskogean: Creek *ekuče:*. Mexican: Mixe-Zoque: Mixe *kɔš* 'knee,' Sierra Popoluca *ko:su* 'knee'; Huave *kos* 'knee.' Plateau: North Sahaptin *k^{2}ašinu*.

64 ENTER   California: Miwok: Northern Sierra, Central Sierra *ʔu:k;* Costanoan: Mutsun *akku*. Gulf: Tunica *ʔaka* 'come in'; Muskogean: Creek *eku*. Mexican: Mayan: Uspantec, Kakchiquel *ok*, Jacaltec *oki*, etc.

65 EXCREMENT   California: Wintun: Patwin *t^{2}ena*, Wintu *t$^{s^2}$ina*. Mexican: Mixe-Zoque: Sierra Popoluca *t^{j}iñ*, Zoque *tin*, Tetontepec *ti^{2}ing*.

66 EYE   Gulf: Muskogean: Koasati, Alabama, etc. *hiša*, Muskokee *heš* 'see.' Yukian: Wappo *hut$^{s^2}t^{s^2}$i*. (YG)

67 FALL₁   California: Miwok: Central Sierra *peta*. Gulf: Tunica *pata*.

68 FALL₂   Gulf: Natchez *t^{j}i:*. Yukian: Wappo *t^{s}ɛ* 'drop.' (YG)

69 FALL₃   Gulf: Natchez *tot*. Yukian: Yuki *tot*. (YG)

70 FAR₁   Gulf: Atakapa *ja*. Mexican: Mixe-Zoque: Zoque *jaʔaj, jeʔngu* 'high.'

71 FAR₂   California: Yokuts *waʔat* 'long.' Gulf: Chitimacha *wet$^{s^2}$i*. Plateau: Nez Perce *wajat*, Yakima *wiet*. Tsimshian *wajto*. Yukian: Yuki *wič*.

149

72 FATHER   California: Miwok: Central Sierra *əpə;* Wintun: Kope *pajse.*
     Gulf: Natchez *ʔipis.*

73 FEAR₁   California: Maidu *mole.* Gulf: Muskogean: Proto-Muskogean
     maɫ.

74 FEAR₂   California: Maidu: Nisenan *bʔyk;* Yokuts: Yaudanchi *bax.*
     Mexican: Mayan: Chol *bʔuknian* (n.), *muh-buknam* 'frighten.'

75 FEATHER   Gulf: Atakapa *li;* Muskogean: Choctaw *ɬi* 'wing.' Plateau:
     Lutuami *laː-s.* Tsimshian *li.* Zuni *la.*

76 FIELD   California: Maidu *sopʼo.* Gulf: Muskogean: Chickasaw *osepaʔ.*

77 FIRE₁   Gulf: Atakapa *jim* 'lightning.' Yukian: Yuki *jim,* Huchnom
     jehum. (YG)

78 FIRE₂   Gulf: Muskogean: Koasati *heɬi* 'ignite' (intransitive). Yukian:
     Wappo *hel.* (YG)

79 FIRE₃   Gulf: Natchez *hak* 'afire.' Mexican: Mixe-Zoque: Texistepec
     hugut, Sierra Popoluca *huktə,* Zoque *hukətək.*

80 FISH   California: Maidu *mako;* Miwok: Southern Sierra *mičeːma*
     'meat.' Gulf: Chitimacha *makš.* Oregon: Kalapuya *muːkw* 'meat.'
     Plateau: Modoc *mehe-s.*

81 FLEA   Gulf: Chitimacha *tˤat* 'louse.' Yukian: Wappo *čote.* (YG)

82 FLY₁ (v.)   Gulf: Chitimacha *peš.* Oregon: Lower Umpqua *pxuš,* Miluk
     ɬpaš.

83 FLY₂ (v.)   California: Maidu *kaj.* Chinook *ka.* Gulf: Atakapa *kaʔu*
     'wing, to fly.' Tsimshian *qai* 'arm, wing.'

84 FLY₃ (v.)   Gulf: Muskogean: Hitchiti *jaka.* Yukian: Wappo *jɔkkɔ.* (YG)

85 FRUIT   California: Miwok: Bodega *ʔalla* 'nuts'; Yokuts *ʔelaw* 'flower.'
     Gulf: Tunica *elu;* Natchez *unu* 'berry'; Muskogean: Choctaw *ani,*
     Alabama, Koasati *aɬi.* Plateau: Klamath *leːw* 'flower.'

86 FULL₁   California: Maidu *pe.* Gulf: Atakapa *puː;* Natchez *pi* 'to swell.'
     Oregon: Coos *paa* 'to fill.'

87 FULL₂   California: Maidu *ʔopitpe.* Chinook *patˡ.* Gulf: Tunica *pixči*
     'be full'; Chitimacha *piski* 'be swollen.' Mexican: Mixe-Zoque: Sayula
     patˢ-ik. Oregon: Takelma *byːkʔ.* Zuni *potti.*

88 GIRL   Gulf: Atakapa *kiš;* Chitimacha *kiča.* Mexican: Mixe-Zoque:
     Mixe *kiiš;* Mayan: Tzeltal *ačʔiis.*

89 GIVE₁   Gulf: Natchez *kus;* Muskogean: Koasati *kus.* Mexican: Mayan:
     Quiché *koč* 'gift.'

90 GIVE₂   California: Miwok: Marin *to(-wis).* Chinook *tʼoː.* Oregon:

Takelma *tu:*. Plateau: North Sahaptin *taˀtˢ*, Nez Perce *tautˢ*, *taus*. Yukian: Yuki *tat*. Zuni *ˀutˢˀi*.

91 GO DOWN   Gulf: Muskogean: Choctaw *kaha* 'fall.' Mexican: Mayan: Tzeltal *keh-el*, Uspantec *kexik*, Pokomchi *kax-*.

92 GRANDMOTHER   California: Maidu *koto*. Plateau: Yakima *katla*. Zuni *hotta*.

93 GRASS   California: Proto-California Penutian **po*, **pu*. Gulf: Chitimacha *po* 'grass, herb'; Muskogean: Creek *puhe*, Chickasaw *abawaa*. Zuni *pe*.

94 GRIND   California: Wintun: Patwin *kuri*. Gulf: Tunica *kiri*.

95 GUM   Gulf: Atakapa *ni:kš*; Chitimacha *ni:ki* 'gum, sap.' Mexican: Mayan: Quiché *noox* 'pine gum.'

96 GUTS   California: Maidu: Nisenan *kə*; Miwok: Bodega *kee* 'excrement.' Gulf: Atakapa *kui*; Chitimacha *ˀaki*. Mexican: Mayan: Chontal *ak*. Plateau: Klamath *qˀaje*.

97 HAIR₁   Chinook *qšo*. Gulf: Atakapa *kueš*; Muskogean: Muskokee *kise*. Plateau: Nez Perce *kukux*. Tsimshian: Tsimshian *gaus*, Nass *qe:s*. Yukian: Yuki *(noho-)kuš* 'beard,' *kes* 'feather.'

98 HAIR₂   Gulf: Muskogean: Creek *esse* 'feather, hair,' Choctaw *hiši* 'feather,' Koasati *hisi* 'feather, hair.' Mexican: Mayan: Quiché *is* 'feather, hair,' Huastec *ši* 'hair,' Mam *iši-matˢl* 'beard.' Zuni *tˢi*.

99 HAND   California: Costanoan: Monterey *putˢ*; Maidu [bee-che]; Yokuts *pʰutʰɔng* 'hand, arm.' Chinook *pote* 'arm.' Gulf: Muskogean: Choctaw *potoli* 'handle, feel, touch.' Oregon: Kalapuya *putukwi* 'arm.' Yukian: Yuki *mippat*.

100 HARD₁   California: Wintun *ˀa:l-*. Mexican: Huave *el* 'difficult.' Tsimshian *a:l-x* 'brave.'

101 HARD₂   Gulf: Atakapa *tiˀu*. Yukian: Wappo *tˀɔˀɛ*. (YG)

102 HARD₃   California: Miwok: Central Sierra *katta:ky*. Chinook *qotˢo* 'bone' (Bella Bella *kˀodˀo* is probably a borrowing from Chinook). Gulf: Chitimacha *katˢi* 'bone.' Oregon: Lower Umpqua *qasqas*. Yukian: Wappo *tˢiti* 'bone,' Yuki *kˀiˀt* 'bone.' Zuni *kˀusa* 'be hard.' Cf. HARD₂ in the Amerind dictionary.

103 HAVE   Gulf: Muskogean: Choctaw *iši*, Creek *ose*, Hitchiti *hič*. Mexican: Mayan: Quiché *eč* 'possess.'

104 HEAD   California: Miwok: Plains *tolo* 'hair'; Maidu: South *tˢol*; Yokuts **šiliš* 'hair.' Gulf: Tunica *-esini*; Atakapa *tol*. Oregon: Miluk

151

šel, Takelma *se:n* 'hair.' Plateau: Cayuse *talš*, Yakima *tel-pi*. Yukian: Yuki *tʾol* 'hair,' Wappo *tʾol* 'hair,' Huchnom *tol.*

105 HEAR₁ Gulf: Atakapa *pax* 'listen'; Muskogean: Creek *pox*, Koasati *poh*. Oregon: Kalapuya *pokta* 'ear.' Yukian: Wappo *pikakhiʔ* 'listen.'

106 HEAR₂ Gulf: Muskogean: Choctaw *ikhana*. Yukian: Yuki *hāl*. (YG)

107 HEART Gulf: Atakapa *šo* 'seed, heart'; Chitimacha *ših* 'belly.' Yukian: Yuki, Huchnom, Coast Yuki *tʾu* 'belly.' Zuni *tʾu* 'stomach.'

108 HIDE₁ (v.) California: Wintun: Patwin *ɫom*. Gulf: Muskogean: Chicasaw *loma*. Plateau: North Sahaptin *ɫama.*

109 HIDE₂ (v.) California: Miwok: Central Sierra *ʔokoj* 'cover.' Gulf: Chitimacha *ʔiki;* Natchez *kʷeje:*. Mexican: Mayan: Quiché *kʾuj*. Plateau: Yakima *ik* 'to close.'

110 HIT Gulf: Natchez *ta*. Oregon: Coos *to:h*, Takelma *toj-kʾ*. Yukian: Wappo *tɔh, to,* 'kill,' *tohe* 'kill.'

111 HOLE₁ California: Miwok: Marin *hoppa*. Gulf: Atakapa *ho:p*. Mexican: Mayan: Tzotzil *hap*.

112 HOLE₂ California: Costanoan: Mutsun *lupu-s* 'anus.' Oregon: Coos *tlpi* 'door.' Plateau: Klamath *lbo* 'tunnel.' Tsimshian *ɫab*.

113 HOLE₃ California: Proto-California Penutian **tuk*. Plateau: North Sahaptin *tqu-* 'be a hole.'

114 HOLE₄ California: Proto-California Penutian **holoq*. Gulf: Atakapa *hal* 'buttock'; Tunica *helu* 'hollow out.' Mexican: Mayan: Yucatec *hol*, Huastec *hol*, etc. Yukian: Wappo *hɛl* 'anus.'

115 HOLE₅ California: Miwok: Lake *talokʰ*. Gulf: Atakapa *tol* 'anus.' Mexican: Totonac *tan* 'buttocks'; Mayan: Tzotzil *tiʔil*. Oregon: Takelma *telkan* 'buttocks.'

116 HOT₁ California: Yokuts *hajal* 'summer.' Gulf: Muskogean: Hitchiti *haji* 'hot, ripe,' Muskokee *hije:*. Yukian: Yuki [hi-uh-hoh].

117 HOT₂ California: Maidu *ləp* 'to heat.' Gulf: Muskogean: Alabama *lahpa* 'to heat,' Choctaw *lohbi*.

118 HOT₃ Gulf: Chitimacha *čʰa*. Mexican: Mayan: Aguacatec, Ixil *tˢa*. Cf. Yukian: Wappo *šɔija*.

119 HOUSE₁ Gulf: Chitimacha *hana*. Yukian: Yuki *han, hā* 'build.' (YG)

120 HOUSE₂ California: Wintun: South Wintu *kel*. Chinook *qutˡ*. Plateau: Molala *helim*. Yukian: Wappo *hile* 'build a house.'

121 HUNGRY California: Maidu *ʔok*. Gulf: Atakapa *kaʔu*. Mexican: Mayan: Huastec *kʾa(-il)* 'be hungry.'

122 HUSBAND₁ California: Wintun: South Wintu *naiwi*. Mexican: Mixe-

Zoque: Texistepec *nā*, Western Mixe *naʔu;* Totonacan: Tepehua *noh.*
Plateau: Cayuse *inaiu.* Yukian: Huchnom *i-na.*

123 HUSBAND₂ Gulf: Tunica *haji.* Mexican: Mixe-Zoque: Zoque *hajah.*
Cf. Chinook *xajal* 'commoner.'

124 JUMP Gulf: Atakapa *tˢat.* Mexican: Mixe-Zoque: Sayula *tˢut;* Mayan:
Yucatec *sitʔ.*

125 KEEP Gulf: Tunica *pala* 'catch.' Yukian: Wappo *pihne.* (YG)

126 KILL₁ California: Proto-California Penutian **tˡe, *tˡo.* Gulf:
Muskogean: Hitchiti *ili,* Choctaw *ile* 'do.' Mexican: Totonac *ni:* 'die.'
Yukian: Wappo *li,* Coast Yuki *li.*

127 KILL₂ California: Costanoan (general) *nimi,* San Francisco *mimi.*
Gulf: Atakapa *nima.* Cf. Chinook *čim,* Miwok *čam-, čem-* 'die.'

128 KILL₃ Gulf: Tunica *rapa.* Yukian: Wappo *lipu.* (YG) Cf. KILL₂.

129 KILL₄ Oregon: Miluk *tˢu:, tˢxau.* Yukian: Wappo *tˢʔaɛ.*

130 KILL₅ Gulf: Natchez *ox;* Muskogean: Alabama *oksi.* Mexican: Mixe-
Zoque: Sayula *oʔk* 'die,' Tetontepec *ɔ:ʔk* 'die.' Tsimshian *oks* 'hit.'

131 KNEE California: Costanoan: Monterey *kulluš* 'elbow,' Santa Cruz
kullališ 'elbow.' Chinook: Chinook *o-qʔoxtˡ,* Wishram *qʔoxɬ.* Gulf:
Tunica *čina.* Mexican: Mayan: Huastec *kʔʷalal.* Plateau: Lutuami
qolens, Klamath *qolinč.* Yukian: Yuki *kank, kan* 'kneel,' Coast Yuki
kʔenk.

132 KNOW₁ California: Yokuts *hutu.* Mexican: Mixe-Zoque: Sierra
Popoluca *hoʔdong.* Yukian: Wappo *hata.*

133 KNOW₂ California: Maidu *jakkit.* Oregon: Kalapuya *jukʰ,* Takelma
jokʰj-.

134 LARGE₁ Gulf: Atakapa *hetˢ.* Yukian: Yuki, Huchnom *hot.* (YG)

135 LARGE₂ California: Miwok: Lake *ʔade* 'be large.' Gulf: Chitimacha
ʔati; Tunica *tˢɛ.* Plateau: Klamath *ʔadi* 'long, deep, broad.' Yukian:
Wappo *taʔɛja* 'heavy.'

136 LAUGH₁ Gulf: Tunica *amax* 'make fun of.' Plateau: North Sahaptin
-msa- 'laugh at.' Tsimshian *hmaməx* 'smile.' Yukian: Yuki *mus,*
Huchnom *musel.* Cf. Costanoan: Santa Cruz *majsi,* but root is
probably *maj* (Mutsun *mai*).

137 LAUGH₂ California: Miwok: Northern Sierra *həja,* Central Sierra
həjak; Yokuts *ha:jʔa.* Gulf: Atakapa *haju;* Muskogean: Hitchiti *haja.*

138 LEAF₁ California: Costanoan: Rumsien *is,* Monterey *o:š* (pl.). Gulf:
Atakapa *waš;* Muskogean: Creek *ose,* Koasati *assi.*

139 LEAF₂ California: Yokuts: Gashowu *tˢap,* Yawelmani *dapdap;*

Costanoan: Santa Cruz *tapa-š,* Santa Clara *tap* 'feather.' Gulf:
Muskogean: Creek *tafə* 'feather.' Plateau: Klamath *t'apaq.*
140 LEG₁   Gulf: Atakapa *mal.* Yukian: Coast Yuki, Huchnom *mil.* (YG)
141 LEG₂   California: Maidu *lul.* Yukian: Wappo *lulu* 'shin bone'
(possible borrowing).
142 LIE DOWN   Gulf: Atakapa *joxt* (pl. subject). Yukian: Wappo *jɔke.*
(YG)
143 LIE₁ (TELL A)   California: Miwok: Central Sierra *male:p;* Yokuts:
Gashowu *molel* 'dupe, deceive.' Yukian: Yuki *min.*
144 LIE₂ (TELL A)   California: Maidu *hal, holabe.* Gulf: Muskogean:
Choctaw *holabi.* Mexican: Mayan: Mam *hal.*
145 LIGHT (n.)   California: Maidu *ʔeki* 'day'; Costanoan: Mutsun *akke*
'day'; Miwok *ʔoko* 'day.' Mexican: Proto-Mayan (C) **qʔi:xʲ* 'day, sun.'
Oregon: Coos *kʔʷiʔi-s,* Alsea *qe, qai* 'be light,' Siuslaw *qai* 'to dawn.'
Yukian: Wappo *kʲεu, kʲε* 'be daylight.'
146 LIGHTNING   California: Proto-California Penutian **wV₁lV₂p,* where
V₁ = i or u and *V₂* = e or o; Maidu *wipʔil* (metathesis?). Gulf: Natchez
pulu. Plateau: Klamath *wlepʔlʔ.* Tsimshian *liplib* 'thunder.'
147 LIVE₁ (v.)   Gulf: Tunica *laka.* Mexican: Mayan: Quiché *laq-* 'dwell.'
148 LIVE₂ (v.)   Gulf: Atakapa *nun* 'sit.' Yukian: Wappo *nɔmi* 'live,
dwell.' (YG)
149 LIVER   California: Wintun: Patwin *kosol* 'lungs.' Gulf: Chitimacha
kesi; Atakapa *ketˢ, ketˢk.* Mexican: Mayan: Kekchí *čʔočel,* Quiché *kuš*
'heart,' Mam *kuh* 'heart,' etc. Plateau: Lutuami *kas* 'belly.' Yukian:
Huchnom *kʔoč* 'lungs.'
150 LOOK₁   California: Maidu *tˢʔen.* Mexican: Mixe-Zoque: Zoque *tuʔn*
'look at.' Oregon: Takelma *tˢʔelei* 'eye.' Plateau: Nez Perce *tˢilu* 'eye.'
Zuni *tuna* 'eye, look at.'
151 LOOK₂   Gulf: Tunica *po.* Mexican: Mixe-Zoque: Sayula *eʔp,* Oluta
epe 'see.' Yukian: Wappo *pε, pεhε.*
152 MAKE₁   California: Costanoan: Mutsun *kam* 'do, make.' Chinook
kʲim 'say.' Oregon: Takelma *kemei-,* Coos *kʔe:m* 'practice,' Yakonan
tˢimx- 'work.' Yukian: Wappo *tˢamiʔ* 'do.'
153 MAKE₂   California: Miwok: Central Sierra *ʔiččə.* Gulf: Chitimacha
ʔuči 'do'; Muskogean: Choctaw *ʔiši.* Plateau: Klamath *sʔ-.* Tsimshian
sə-. Zuni *ʔaša.*
154 MEAT₁   California: Maidu *symi* 'meat, deer.' Oregon: Takelma *si:m*
'animal.' Tsimshian: Tsimshian *sami,* Nass *smaxʲ.*

155 MEAT₂   California: Wintun *nope*. Gulf: Muskogean: Koasati, Alabama
nipu, Choctaw *nipi*. Mexican: Huave *onih*.

156 MORNING   California: Wintun *ʔol-tik-al* 'to dawn'; Costanoan *tuxi*
'day.' Gulf: Muskogean: Chickasaw *čiiki* 'early.' Mexican: Mayan: Chol
[zuka] 'to dawn.' Oregon: Siuslaw *tˢʼuxti:tˢ* 'early.'

157 MOUNTAIN₁   California: Costanoan: San Francisco *ani* 'stone.' Gulf:
Muskogean: Choctaw *nanih*. Plateau: Nez Perce *ne:n* 'hill.'

158 MOUNTAIN₂   California: Wintun *kodo* 'stone.' Gulf: Atakapa *katt*.
Mexican: Mixe-Zoque: Sierra Popoluca *kotˢək*; Mayan: Yucatec *kaaš*.
Oregon: Iakon *kwotˢ*.

159 MOUSE   California: Maidu *sapa* 'rat.' Oregon: Takelma *tˢʼamāl*.

160 MOUTH   Gulf: Natchez *ihi*; Muskogean: Alabama *iči*, Choctaw *ihi*.
Mexican: Proto-Mayan (C) *čiiʔ*.

161 MUCH₁   Gulf: Muskogean: Choctaw *laua*. Yukian: Wappo *lɛa*. (YG)

162 MUCH₂   California: Maidu *heli-m*. Oregon: Iakon *hol* 'many.'
Tsimshian *he:lt* 'very.' Yukian: Huchnom *hile* 'all.'

163 MUCH₃   Gulf: Chitimacha *ʔowi*. Plateau: North Sahaptin *wi-*.
Tsimshian *wi-*.

164 NAIL   California: Yokuts *kesik*. Gulf: Muskogean: Choctaw *čus*, *čuš*.
Mexican: Mixe-Zoque: Zoque *čus*, Sierra Popoluca *tˢəs*; Mayan: Proto-
Mayan (C) *(iš-)kʼaq*, Huastec *itsikʼ*, Chontal *ičʼok*, etc. Plateau:
Lutuami *stak-s*, Molala *suk-s*. Tsimshian: Tsimshian *łaxs*, Nass *łaqs*.

165 NAVEL   Gulf: Tunica *čika*. Mexican: Mixe-Zoque: Zoque *tˢek* 'belly';
Mayan: Proto-Mayan (C) *tˢu:k*. Plateau: Klamath *tʔoɢ*.

166 NEAR₁   California: Miwok: Central Sierra *haje:*; Maidu: Nisenan *hoj*.
Gulf: Tunica *hija*.

167 NEAR₂   California: Proto-California Penutian *-nek* (allative); Maidu:
naka; Miwok: Lake *nakah* 'reach, end.' Gulf: Atakapa *nak;* Tunica
naxk; Chitimacha *nakš;* Muskogean: Creek *unaku*, Choctaw *naha*
'almost, nearly.' Mexican: Mayan: Aguacatec *nax*, Mam *nakaku*, etc.;
Mixe-Zoque: Sierra Popoluca *noko*, Totonac *lakatsu*.

168 NEW   California: Maidu *di* 'young'; Costanoan: Monterey *iitti*.
Mexican: Mayan: Huastec *it*.

169 NIGHT₁   Gulf: Muskogean: Choctaw *ninak*. Yukian: Yuki *nāk*. (YG)

170 NIGHT₂   Gulf: Natchez *tuwa*, *tewa*. Yukian: Wappo *učuwa*. (YG)

171 OLD   Gulf: Atakapa *waši;* Muskogean: Muskokee *ahase;* Natchez
haš. Yukian: Yuki *wes*, Wappo *hasi*. (YG)

155

172 OPEN₁   Gulf: Tunica *hax;* Chitimacha *hakin.* Mexican: Mayan: Mam *hakon,* Quiché *xaq.*

173 OPEN₂   Oregon: Lower Umpqua *qunh-.* Plateau: North Sahaptin *kuł.* Yukian: Wappo *kʾine.*

174 OPEN₃   California: Maidu: Nisenan *pe.* Gulf: Atakapa *pai;* Tunica *ʾɛpa.*

175 PENIS   California: Wintun: Patwin *jot.* Mexican: Mayan: Tzeltal *jat,* Tzotzil *jat* 'genitals.'

176 PEOPLE   Gulf: Tunica *ʾoni.* Yukian: Wappo *oni* 'people' (also third-person pl. pronoun). (YG)

177 PERSON₁   Chinook *i-kala* 'man.' Gulf: Muskogean: Choctaw *kana.* Oregon: Iakon *kalt,* Yakonan *qaalt* 'man.' Yukian: Wappo *kʲaniʾ.*

178 PERSON₂   California: Costanoan: Rumsien *ama,* Soledad *mue;* Miwok: Central Sierra *-me* (agentive); Yokuts: Yaudanchi *mai.* Oregon: Coos *ma,* Kalapuya *amim* (pl.).

179 PERSON₃   California: Wintun: Wintu *wintʰuːh,* Patwin *win.* Mexican: Proto-Mayan (C) **winaq* 'man, person.' Plateau: North Sahaptin *wintˢ* 'man.'

180 PLACE   California: Miwok: Western *ʾawa.* Plateau: North Sahaptin *-awa-s.*

181 PLAY   California: Miwok: Lake *ʾeela;* Yokuts: Gashowu *luʾu.* Oregon: Coos *aləš* 'toy,' Takelma *loːux.* Plateau: Klamath *leːʾwa.*

182 PULL₁   Gulf: Atakapa *išul* 'pull out'; Muskogean: Choctaw *šełi* 'pull out.' Yukian: Yuki *čʾal.* (YG)

183 PULL₂   California: Yokuts *tuxu.* Gulf: Muskogean: Koasati *tex.* Oregon: Yakonan *txu,* Coos *tˢɐyiː(t).* Tsimshian *sakʾ.*

184 PUT₁   California: Miwok *pongngu.* Gulf: Muskogean: Choctaw *bołi.* Mexican: Mayan: Huastec *balij-al* 'put in,' Quiché *pal.* Yukian: Yuki *pɛn.*

185 PUT₂   Oregon: Takelma *masg.* Plateau: Yakima *mač* 'lay.' Tsimshian: Nass *maɢ.*

186 RED   California: Miwok: Central Sierra *kičawi* 'blood.' Gulf: Atakapa *kutˢ;* Muskogean: Creek *čate,* Hitchiti *kitisči,* Mikasuki *kitiski.* Mexican: Proto-Mayan **kikʾ.* Plateau: Nez Perce *kiket.*

187 RETURN₁   California: Proto-Maidu **joʾkʰe* (Ultan). Gulf: Tunica *jaka.*

188 RETURN₂   Gulf: Tunica *maru.* Mexican: Mayan: Mam *mel,* Jacaltec *meltˢoji.* Oregon: Takelma *moloʾmala* 'turn over.'

189 RETURN₃   Plateau: Nez Perce *toq*, North Sahaptin *tuχ*. Tsimshian *adək* 'turn back.'

190 RIB   California: Wintun *wehut*. Gulf: Atakapa *wext*.

191 ROAD   Gulf: Chitimacha *miš*. Yukian: Wappo *mitˢ*. Cf. Central Sierra Miwok *mukku*.

192 ROAST   California: Proto-California Penutian **tu* 'burn,' **ʔitV* 'roast.' Gulf: Atakapa *tiu* 'broil.' Plateau: North Sahaptin *tʾawa*.

193 ROOT₁   Oregon: Yakonan *łiqaju*. Yukian: Wappo *luki*. Zuni *łakʷi*.

194 ROOT₂   Gulf: Atakapa *wi:l*. Mexican: Mayan: Huastec *ibil*, Tzotzil *ibelal*.

195 ROPE   California: Yokuts *čʾik*. Mexican: Mayan: Huastec *tˢʾah*. Oregon: Takelma *tˢuk*.

196 ROTTEN   California: Maidu *hissa*. Gulf: Atakapa *i:š* 'rotten, stink.' Tsimshian *i:s* 'smell.'

197 RUN₁   Gulf: Muskogean: Hitchiti *palak* (dual subject). Yukian: Wappo *puli* 'run away.' (YG)

198 RUN₂   California: Miwok: Plains *taige;* Maidu: Nisenan *dok*. Gulf: Tunica *taka* 'chase.'

199 RUN₃   California: Maidu *wele*. Plateau: Nez Perce *wele*, North Sahaptin *wile*. Cf. Tsimshian *ulloban*.

200 SALIVA   California: Miwok: Marin *tuka* 'to spit.' Gulf: Chitimacha *tux* 'to spit'; Natchez *tˢuh-;* Tunica *čʾuhu;* Proto-Muskogean **tuxʷ*. Mexican: Mixe-Zoque: Tetontepec, Sayula *tˢux;* Totonac *čuhut*. Oregon: Yakonan *tˢak*.

201 SAY₁   California: Miwok: Bodega *ʔona*, Central Sierra *-ene:-* 'tell to, do.' Gulf: Tunica *ni;* Muskogean: Alabama *ni*. Oregon: Coos *na* 'say, do.' Plateau: North Sahaptin *ən* 'speak.'

202 SAY₂   Gulf: Natchez *hi*. Plateau: Nez Perce *hi*. Tsimshian: Nass *he*. Yukian: Wappo *hai, ha*.

203 SAY₃   California: Yokuts *wili* 'say, make, do.' Chinook *o:lχ*. Gulf: Natchez *weł* 'speak'; Tunica *wali* 'call'; Chitimacha *wan* 'speech.' Mexican: Totonac *wan*. Oregon: Coos *iil*, Yakonan *iil*. Yukian: Wappo *wilɛ* 'tell,' *wale* 'call.'

204 SAY₄   California: Maidu *ʔa*. Gulf: Muskogean: Koasati *a*.

205 SEEK₁   Gulf: Muskogean: Choctaw *hojo*. Mexican: Mayan: Mam *hojon*.

206 SEEK₂   California: Yokuts: Calavera *wanin* 'love, desire'; Miwok: Central Sierra *wel-si*, Lake *welle*, Bodega *welak* 'want, like.' Gulf:

Atakapa *wen;* Tunica *wana* 'wish'; Muskogean: Creek *bana,*
Chickasaw, Koasati, Alabama, Choctaw *banna.* Mexican: Mixe-Zoque:
Sayula *waʔn.* Oregon: Siuslaw *winu* 'be willing.'

207 SELL   Gulf: Atakapa *jik.* Mexican: Mixe-Zoque *ˀjəʔk.*

208 SEW   Gulf: Natchez *bo:x.* Zuni *pik(-ɬa)* (passive).

209 SHADOW   Gulf: Atakapa *išk.* Plateau: Molala *iskai* 'night.'
Tsimshian: Tsimshian *atk* 'night,' Nass *axkʷ* 'night.'

210 SHINE   Chinook *wax* 'light, to shine.' Gulf: Tunica *wɛha.*

211 SHORT₁   Chinook *mənxʲka.* Gulf: Atakapa *ming* 'weak'; Chitimacha
mun, min.

212 SHORT₂   Gulf: Atakapa *mok.* Yukian: Yuki *puh-ič.* (YG)

213 SHOOT   California: Miwok: Bodega *tuwe,* Lake *tˀuw;* Costanoan:
Rumsien *tio,* San Juan Bautista *tio-s* 'arrow'; Yokuts *tʰuju.* Mexican:
Mixe-Zoque: Zoque *tuh,* Mixe *tuh,* Sayula *tux* 'weapon.' Oregon:
Kalapuya *tˀuwan, tˀiuwiš* 'arrow.' Plateau: North Sahaptin *tuχwən,*
Modoc *tewi.* Zuni *towo.*

214 SHOULDER   Gulf: Muskogean: Alabama *apakha.* Mexican: Totonac
pak-an 'wing.' Oregon: Yakonan *ɬpax* 'shoulder, shoulder blade.'

215 SHOW   California: Costanoan: San Francisco *-hima* 'see,' Santa Clara
xima; Miwok: Mutsun *ima.* Chinook *xomem.* Oregon: Coos *hem*
'be visible,' Yakonan *kʲim.* Plateau: Nez Perce *himtekse* 'teach.' Cf.
Chitimacha *ʔam* 'see'; Mutsun *amiu, amo* 'teach.'

216 SIT₁   California: Proto-California Penutian **tˡakwa.* Oregon: Coos
tˡokʷ.

217 SIT₂   Chinook *š-* 'be.' Mexican: Mayan: Kakchiquel *ša* 'be,' Quiché
uš 'become.' Oregon: Kalapuya *siju.* Plateau: Klamath *či ~ ča.*
Yukian: Yuki *šai* 'live.'

218 SKIN₁   California: Miwok: Central Sierra *ṭalka.* Gulf: Atakapa *tal, til;*
Natchez *toloks.* Oregon: Miluk *tˀeɬi-s.* Plateau: Klamath *čˀelg.*

219 SKIN₂   Gulf: Atakapa *uk.* Mexican: Mixe-Zoque: Mixe *ʔak.*

220 SKY   Gulf: Tunica *ʔaparu* 'heaven, cloud.' Mexican: Mayan:
Kakchiquel *paruwi* 'above,' Tzotzil *-bail* 'above,' Huastec *ebal* 'above.'

221 SMALL₁   California: Maidu: Northeast *nu:si* 'short.' Chinook *nukstx*
'smallness.' Gulf: Chitimacha *nahtˢʔi.*

222 SMALL₂   Gulf: Atakapa *išol.* Yukian: Yuki *ollisel, unšil,* Huchnom
unsel, olsel. (YG)

223 SMOKE   California: Proto-California Penutian **kal.* Oregon: Miluk
qwullə. Yukian: Wappo *hɛlɛ* 'steam.'

224 SMOOTH   Gulf: Tunica *hina*. Mexican: Mixe-Zoque: Zoque *heen*.

225 SNAKE   Plateau: North Sahaptin *pju-š*, Nez Perce *paju-s*. Yukian: Huchnom *poj*, Coast Yuki *beʔi* 'rattler.'

226 SNOW₁   California: Yokuts *pʰonpʰon*. Plateau: Molala *peng*. Yukian: Wappo *pel*, Huchnom *pi:l*. Zuni *ʔu-pinna* 'snow, frost, hail.'

227 SNOW₂   California: Maidu: Nisenan *killi:t* 'icicle'; Miwok: Central Sierra *ke:la* 'to snow,' Bodega *killi* 'ice,' Lake *ki:wil* 'ice'; Yokuts: Yawelmani *kelkel* 'icicle.' Gulf: Natchez *ko:wa*. Oregon: Siuslaw *kuwini* 'ice,' Coos *kwilau* 'ice.' Plateau: Nez Perce *ken*, Klamath *kena* 'it snows.'

228 SPIDER   Gulf: Atakapa *lam*. Mexican: Mayan: Yucatec *leum*. Oregon: Takelma *do:m*.

229 SQUIRREL   California: Maidu *hilo*. Gulf: Muskogean: Creek *iɫu*, Hitchiti *hĩ:ɬi*. Oregon: Yakonan *xaɬt*.

230 STAND₁   California: Miwok: Bodega, Lake *talah*, Central Sierra *talngi* 'arise.' Gulf: Muskogean: Choctaw *tani*, Chickasaw *ta:ni*. Mexican: Mixe-Zoque: Tetontepec *tena*, Zoque *tenaj*.

231 STAND₂   Mexican: Mayan: Quiché *takʔiik* 'stand up.' Oregon: Coos *ti:k*, Yakonan *tkʲ-*. Plateau: Klamath *tg-*.

232 STAND UP₁   Gulf: Muskogean: Koasati *juko*. Yukian: Wappo *joka*, *jokal*. (YG)

233 STAND UP₂   California: Maidu *ʔoto, tə* 'stand.' Gulf: Tunica *to*; Atakapa *to*.

234 STEAL   California: Miwok: Central Sierra *wəla:ng*. Chinook *ʔolou* 'thief.' Oregon: Coos *wi:n* 'cheat.' Yukian: Wappo *ʔɛlu* 'keep hold of.' Zuni *ʔilli* 'have.'

235 STICK   California: Miwok: Lake *tumaj* 'stick, wood,' Bodega *tumaj* 'wood.' Gulf: Atakapa *tˢom*. Mexican: Mayan: Quiché *čamij* 'staff.'

236 STONE₁   California: Maidu: Northeast *ʔo*, Nisenan *ʔo:*. Gulf: Atakapa *wai*. Yukian: Huchnom *wai* 'obsedian,' Wappo *we* 'obsedian, knife.' Zuni *ʔa*.

237 STONE₂   Gulf: Proto-Muskogean *tali*. Yukian: Wappo *ɔtˢɔla* 'rock.' (YG)

238 SWALLOW₁   Gulf: Muskogean: Creek *lok*. Mexican: Huave *lax*. Yukian: Wappo *lɛkɛ, lik*.

239 SWALLOW₂   Chinook: Wishram *məlq*. Gulf: Proto-Muskogean *mil*; Tunica *milu* 'get choked,' *miru* 'swallow'; Atakapa *mol* 'gargle.' Oregon: Takelma *mylkʔ*, Kalapuya *milq*.

240 SWEEP   California: Maidu *he-bas*. Gulf: Proto-Muskogean **pas;*
Natchez *pes*. Mexican: Mayan: Yucatec *mis*, Kekchí *mes*, Quiché *mes*,
etc.

241 SWIM₁   California: Miwok: Central Sierra *mɨ:ng*. Oregon: Coos *mil*.

242 SWIM₂   California: Maidu: Northeast *me:*. Gulf: Muskogean:
Alabama *moi*, Creek *omij*.

243 TAKE   Gulf: Muskogean: Alabama *pota*. Yukian: Wappo *pita*. (YG)

244 TASTE   California: Costanoan: San José, Mutsun *lase* 'tongue,'
Rumsien *las*, etc. 'tongue.' Gulf: Tunica *lisa;* Muskogean: Alabama
lasap (sing. subject), Creek *las*. Oregon: Takelma *lat$^{s^2}$ag*.

245 TELL₁   Gulf: Muskogean: Natchez *wit^s;* Tunica *wiš* 'talk.' Yukian:
Yuki *wač*. (YG)

246 TELL₂   California: Miwok: Central Sierra *kojo:w;* Maidu *kai*. Gulf:
Proto-Muskogean **ka* 'talk.' Mexican: Mayan: Pokomchi *ki* 'say,'
Huastec *kau* 'speak.' Zuni *ka* 'make.'

247 TELL₃   Oregon: Takelma *malg^j*. Tsimshian: Nass *maɫ*.

248 TEN   California: Maidu *mačum*. Gulf: Tunica *miču*. Mexican: Mixe-
Zoque: Mixe *mak*.

249 TESTICLE   Gulf: Tunica *-htolu*. Plateau: North Sahaptin *tala*, Nez
Perce *ta:lo*.

250 THIN   Gulf: Atakapa *pax;* Muskogean: Choctaw *fahko*. Mexican:
Mixe-Zoque: Sayula *pexaj*, Tetontepec *pehi;* Mayan: Kekchí *bak*.
Oregon: Kalapuya *puučak* 'small.'

251 THROW₁   Gulf: Muskogean: Hitchiti *piɫ* 'throw away,' Choctaw *pila*.
Mexican: Mayan: Yucatec *pul*.

252 THROW₂   Mexican: Huave *wiič*. Yukian: Yuki *wit*.

253 THUNDER   California: Proto-California Penutian **tʰim, *tʰum*.
Plateau: Molala *timiun*. Tsimshian *t$^{s^2}$amti* 'lightning.'

254 TIE₁   Mexican: Huave *ol*. Plateau: North Sahaptin, Nez Perce *wala*.
Yukian: Wappo *leo, ilɛ*.

255 TIE₂   California: Miwok: Central Sierra *topo:n*. Oregon: Coos *t^{s}imx*.
Tsimshian: Nass *t$^{s^2}$eip*.

256 TONGUE₁   California: Maidu: Nisenan *ʔal* 'action with tongue.' Gulf:
Tunica *-lu*. Oregon: Coos *ela*.

257 TONGUE₂   California: Yokuts: Proto-Yokuts **thalxaṭh*. Gulf:
Muskogean: Alabama *t^{s}ula:ksi*, Creek *tulaswə*. Oregon: Iakon *tulela*.
Tsimshian: Tsimshian *dula*, Nass *de:lix*.

258 TOOTH₁   California: Maidu: Maidu *t$^{s^2}$iki*, Nisenan *t$^{s^2}$ik*. Chinook

ačx. Mexican: Totonac *tatˢ-an;* Mixe-Zoque: Mixe *totˢ*. Oregon: Siuslaw *tʔix*. Yukian: Coast Yuki *sekʔ*, Yuki *sek*, Huchnom *sunk*.

259 TOOTH₂   California: Yokuts: Proto-Yokuts **tʰe:lij*. Oregon: Yakonan *təli:l*.

260 TOUCH   Gulf: Proto-Muskogean **put*, **puč-k*. Plateau: Klamath *apsk* 'taste.' Yukian: Wappo *pito*.

261 TREE   Gulf: Muskogean: Hitchiti *abi* 'tree, stem'; Natchez *pa* 'plant.' Yukian: Huchnom *ipo*. (YG)

262 TURN   California: Maidu *kʔot* 'turn one's body.' Gulf: Natchez *kitip;* Chitimacha *kutʔiht*.

263 UNCLE   Gulf: Chitimacha *kan* 'paternal uncle.' Mexican: Mayan: Kekchí, Quiché *ikan*, etc.

264 URINE   Chinook *wiuš*. Mexican: Mayan: Yucatec *iš*. Yukian: Yuki *aš* 'urinate.'

265 VAGINA   Gulf: Chitimacha *neʔe:s*. Mexican: Mayan: Quiché *nus*.

266 VEIN   California: Maidu *paka* 'sinew'; Proto-Yokuts **pʰikil* 'sinew'; Miwok: Central Sierra *pasu:ka* 'muscle.' Gulf: Atakapa *poš;* Muskogean: Creek *fuku* 'rope.' Mexican: Mixe-Zoque: Sayula *pox*, Zoque *poʔk* 'rope'; Mayan: Mam *ibokš*, Quiché *ibočʔ*.

267 WALK   California: Maidu *wije;* Miwok: Plains *wə* 'go,' *wən* 'walk.' Gulf: Tunica *wa* (sing. subject) 'go'; Natchez *we* (pl. subject); Atakapa *wang*. Oregon: Takelma *wi:* 'go about, travel.'

268 WASH₁   Mexican: Mixe-Zoque: Sierra Popoluca, Zoque *tʼeʔ*. Oregon: Coos *tʼou*. Yukian: Wappo *tˢɔ*.

269 WASH₂   California: Miwok: Southern Sierra *heka*. Yukian: Yuki *hukol*.

270 WASH₃   California: Wintun *joq*. Tsimshian *jaks*.

271 WASP   California: Miwok: Central Sierra *šuššu* 'bee.' Mexican: Mayan: Tzeltal *šuš*.

272 WATER   Gulf: Tunica *wiši*. Yukian: Wappo *isɛ* 'dig for water.' (YG)

273 WET₁   Gulf: Atakapa *patˢ* 'wash'; Natchez *patˢak* 'wet.' Mexican: Mayan: Kekchí *pučʔ* 'wash' (cf. Huastec *pakul* 'wash'). Tsimshian *pʔakʰpʔakʰ* 'wash.'

274 WET₂   California: Yokuts *ʔilik* 'water'; Maidu: Nisenan *likopʔ* 'mud.' Gulf: Tunica *lihča*, *wis-loki* 'puddle' (*wis* = 'water'); Muskogean: Choctaw *lača*, Creek *lučpe*. Mexican: Mayan: Quiché *ločix* 'dampen,' Huastec *lukuk* 'mud'; Mixe-Zoque: Tetontepec *nik*, Texistepec *nog*

'water.' Oregon: Coos *t'aq*, Siuslaw *t'aq-t*. Tsimshian *la?k* 'mud,' *logaks* 'wet.'

275 WHITE   California: Miwok: Central Sierra *kelelli*. Oregon: Siuslaw *qut'qut'*. Yukian: Yuki *č'al*, Wappo *k'ajil*.

276 WIND₁ (n.)   Chinook *ikxala*. Gulf: Tunica *huri*. Oregon: Takelma *kwalt*. Plateau: Yakima *xuli*.

277 WIND₂ (n.)   Gulf: Atakapa *patˢ*. Yukian: Yuki *p'ans*, Huchnom *puntˢ*. (YG)

278 WING₁   Gulf: Muskogean: Choctaw *əɬi*. Plateau: Lutuami *la-s*. Tsimshian: Tsimshian *li:* 'feather,' Nass *lae*.

279 WING₂   California: Miwok: Central Sierra *tappa*. Chinook *tupe:* 'feather.' Oregon: Yakonan *tap-s*.

280 WISH₁   California: Wintun *-ska* (desiderative). Mexican: Mayan: Chol *suklan* 'seek,' Pokomchi *sik* 'seek,' etc. Tsimshian *saga*.

281 WISH₂   Mexican: Mixe-Zoque: Sierra Popoluca *su:n*, Zoque *sun* 'love.' Plateau: Lutuami *sanal*, Klamath *san?a:whawli*.

282 WISH₃   Gulf: Atakapa *ko:*. Yukian: Huchnom *kau* 'like.' (YG)

283 WOMAN   California: Maidu *kyle;* Miwok: Marin *kulejis;* Yokuts *kaina*. Chinook *o?okwil*. Plateau: Lutuami *kulu* 'female of large animals.' Tsimshian: Tsimshian *hanax*, Nass *hanaq*.

284 WOOD₁   California: Yokuts [koi-ukh]. Gulf: Atakapa *kak* 'wood, tree, forest.' Oregon: Siuslaw *kauxu*. Plateau: Molala *kux*.

285 WOOD₂   California: Wintun: Colouse *tok*, Sacramento River *doče*, etc. Oregon: Takelma *do:k* 'log.'

286 YELLOW   Chinook *k'æs*. Oregon: Takelma *gwasi*. Plateau: Molala *kaskaswe*.

287 YOUNG₁   Oregon: Kalapuya *amuii*. Yukian: Huchnom *mu*.

288 YOUNG₂   Gulf: Atakapa *šom;* Chitimacha *šoma* 'new'; Muskogean: Choctaw *himmita, himmona* 'new.' Mexican: Totonac *tˢu?ma?t;* Mixe-Zoque: Zoque *home* 'new.' Plateau: North Sahaptin *čmti* 'new,' Lutuami *tˢimanka* 'young man.' Tsimshian *šupuš*.

ALMOSAN-KERESIOUAN

Almosan-Keresiouan consists of two major groups, clearly distinct from each other, but sharing so many lexical and grammatical innovations that they must be considered a single subgroup of Amerind. These two groups are Keresouian and Almosan. The first consists of Caddoan, Iroquoian,

Keresan, and Siouan-Yuchi. The second is identical with Sapir's Algonquian-Wakashan, both in membership and in subgrouping. The term Mosan
was introduced by Morris Swadesh for the subgroup consisting of
Wakashan, Chemakuan, and Salish, and is based on the common term for
'four' in these languages. The term Almosan seems appropriate, combining
as it does Algic and Mosan, two of the three basic divisions of the stock, the
third being Kutenai. Robert G. Latham seems to have been the first to suggest a Keresiouan group by linking Caddoan to Iroquoian in 1846 and to
Siouan in 1860. In 1929, Sapir classified Iroquoian and Caddoan as one subgroup and Siouan-Yuchi as another within his large Hokan-Siouan assemblage. The first real comparison of any of these languages was made in
1931 by Louis Allen, who linked Siouan to Iroquoian. In 1964, Wallace
Chafe returned to this connection, basing his comparative data essentially
on Winnebago and Seneca. Later, in 1973, he added Caddoan to the group,
which he now called Macro-Siouan. In the same paper, he mentions Yuchi
as a possible member, but says nothing of Keresan. In 1967, Swadesh made
a three-way connection among Keresan, Caddoan, and Iroquoian. This was
subsequently taken up by David Rood (1973), a specialist in Caddoan, who,
though critical of some of Swadesh's comparisons, thought those showing a
connection between Caddoan and Keresan encouraging but inconclusive.
Meanwhile, by the early 1960's, my own independent examination of the
evidence had led me to conclude that Keresan, Siouan, Yuchi, Caddoan, and
Iroquoian formed a valid grouping, to which I gave the name Keresiouan. In
this work, Adai, an extinct language whose affiliation to Caddoan has been
doubted by some, is considered a separate branch of that family (see Taylor
1963: 131 for a similar conclusion).

As for Almosan, although a Mosan grouping was noted by Franz Boas
and other early scholars, the only systematic studies are Swadesh (1953a,b).

In 1913, Sapir, in a famous and long-controversial paper, linked Algonquian to Wiyot and Yurok, two languages of northern California. The dispute over this relationship is considered to have been settled by Mary Haas's
persuasively entitled article "Algonkian-Ritwan: The End of a Controversy"
(1958a). In the early 1950's, I examined this problem myself, using the additional material on Wiyot published by Gladys Reichard (1925); her data
made the case for Sapir's original thesis even more obvious. In the present
work, I have adopted Karl Teeter's convenient term Algic for Algonquian,
Wiyot, and Yurok. I am inclined to think that Wiyot and Yurok form a subgroup despite their considerable divergence from each other. Such a group,

163

first noted by Dixon and Kroeber in 1913, is called Ritwan. Finally, I consider the extinct Beothuk language to be Algonquian (see Hewson 1968).

The notion of a stock consisting of Algic, Mosan, and Kutenai, as advanced by Sapir in 1929, has generally been greeted with great skepticism. Only Haas has treated it at all, but even then, this was not her major concern. In a 1960 paper she presents a few comparisons between Algonquian and Mosan (particularly Chemakuan); and in a 1965 article she considers some evidence pointing to a relationship between Algonquian and Kutenai.

Not only has an overall comparison of Algic, Kutenai, and Mosan led me to definitely positive results in respect to an Almosan grouping, but once I began to delve deeper into grammatical details and to assemble the Amerind dictionary, I was virtually forced into the conclusion that there is a special relationship between that group and Keresiouan. On the grammatical side, a number of Almosan characteristics are found in Keresiouan as well. The most telling of these is an *s second-person marker. The lexical evidence is equally persuasive. For one thing, we find 77 etymologies exclusive to these two groups and there are often "cross-resemblances," that is, an etymology that is widespread in one group appears in a single subgroup of the other.

The etymologies below give only those forms that appear in two or more of the following subgroups: Algic, Caddoan, Iroquoian, Keresan, Kutenai, Mosan, and Siouan-Yuchi. Etymologies exclusive to Algic, Mosan, or Siouan-Yuchi are not included. Etymologies found only in Almosan are followed by (AM); those restricted to Keresiouan by (KS).

In assembling the etymologies, I have made certain assumptions because some Almosan-Keresiouan languages have typologically unusual gaps in their consonant system. Various Mosan languages (Quileute of Chemakuan; Nitinat of Wakashan; and several in the Salish group) have no nasal consonants. It is clear that they have become the corresponding voiced oral consonants. Iroquoian has no labial obstruents. I have adopted Chafe's suggestion that $*p > k^w$ and $*m > n$. In Caddoan, except for Caddo itself, there is no *m. It evidently appears as w. The Kutenai voiceless lateral (ł) derives from an earlier n and, somewhat less certainly, n comes from l. This appears in a number of etymologies. In Algonquian, Arapaho has no p; it has become č, and m has become b. The classification is sufficiently clear without such assumptions, as can be seen from the early recognition of Arapaho as Algonquian and of the unity of Chemakuan, Salish, and Wakashan. They are important, of course, in relation to certain etymologies.

164

Except as otherwise noted, Proto-Algonquian forms are from Siebert (1941, 1975), Proto–Central Algonquian forms from Bloomfield (1925, 1946) and Hockett (1957; marked with an H), Proto–Central-Eastern Algonquian forms from various publications by Haas, especially Haas (1958), Proto-Salish forms from Kuipers (1970), Proto-Siouan forms from Wolff (1950–51) and Chafe (1964; marked with a C), and Proto-Keresan forms from Miller and Davis (1963). In addition to the 209 exclusively Almosan-Keresiouan etymologies presented here, 81 Almosan-Keresiouan entries will be found in the Amerind dictionary under the following etymologies: ABOVE₂, ARM₂, ARROW, ASHES, AUNT, BACK₁, BAD₂, BE₂, BEARD₁, BEE₂, BELLY₂, BITE₁, BITTER₁, BLACK₂, BLOOD₂, BONE₂, BREAST, BRING, BROAD, BURN, CHEST, CLEAN, TO CLOSE, COLD₁, COLD₂, COME, DARK, DEER₂, DIG₁, DIRTY, DRINK₁, EARTH₂, EARTH₃, EAT₁, EXCREMENT₁, EXCREMENT₂, FALL, FIRE₁, FLEA, FLY (v.), FOOT₂, FOREHEAD₁, GIRL, GO₁, GO₃, GRASS, HAIR, HAND₁, HAND₂, HARD₂, HEAD₂, HIT, HOLE₁, HORN, HOUSE, KNOW, LARGE₁, LARGE₂, LONG₂, LOUSE₂, MAKE₁, NIGHT₃, SAY₂, SAY₃, SEE₁, SEED₂, SHOULDER, SIT₂, SIT₃, SKIN₂, SMALL, SMELL₁, SMELL₂, STONE₂, SWALLOW, WHITE₂, WING, WISH, WOOD₁, WORK₁, YELLOW₂.

ALMOSAN-KERESIOUAN ETYMOLOGIES

1 BE ABLE   Algic: Algonquian: Arapaho *nonaxe* 'possibly'; Yurok *rakw-*. Caddoan: Adai *olaek* 'strong.' Iroquoian: Seneca *nõʔkow.* Mosan: Wakashan: Kwakiutl *enox*ʷ 'professional,' Nootka *-nuk* 'expert.'

2 ALL₁   Algic: Algonquian: Blackfoot *akap* 'much,' Ojibwa *kabe.* Kutenai *kʾæpe.* Mosan: Chemakuan: Quileute *xaba:ʔ.* (AM)

3 ALL₂   Algic: Algonquian: Blackfoot *auk* 'completely.' Kutenai *o:kʷe.* Mosan: Salish: Pentlatch *aukx*ʷ, Squamish *ʔiʔiχ*ʷ. (AM)

4 ALL₃   Algic: Algonquian: Proto-Algonquian **ket* 'eats all of it'; Wiyot: Wiyot *qat*ˢ 'be many,' Wishosk *kat*ˢ*a*; Yurok *ko:s-i* 'everybody.' Caddoan: Kitsai *akwat*ˢ, Pawnee *kitu, kitawi* 'be most.' Mosan: Salish: Thompson *hwet,* Bella Coola *xs.*

5 ANSWER   Algic: Algonquian: Proto-Algonquian **naxkw.* Iroquoian: Cherokee *-negə̃* 'speak.' Mosan: Wakashan: Kwakiutl *nʔek* 'say,' Bella Bella *ne:k*ʲ 'say.'

6 ARM₁   Algic: Algonquian: Blackfoot *-kinist*ˢ 'hand.' Kutenai *-kin* 'hand' (suffix). Mosan: Salish: Kalispel *axən* 'arms,' Tillamook *kun* 'take' (*-ən* in Kalispel may be a body-part suffix). (AM)

7 ARM₂   Algic: Algonquian: Proto-Algonquian *nexkee, Northern
Arapaho nes, Shawnee neʔki; Yurok -rkow 'armpit.' Iroquoian:
Cherokee -noge, Seneca nēša, Mohawk nə̃č, etc. Mosan: Chemakuan:
Quileute, Chemakum (hii-)naq(-sit); Salish: Squamish naqč; Wakashan:
Nootka nʔokʷ 'hand,' -inkʷ 'at, on the hand.' Siouan-Yuchi: Yuchi ɔki.

8 ARRIVE   Algic: Yurok nes. Mosan: Salish: Tillamook niš; Wakashan:
Bella Bella laka. (AM)

9 ARROW   Algic: Algonquian: Proto–Central Algonquian *ka:wi 'thorn.'
Kutenai ka. Mosan: Chemakuan: Quileute ki-. (AM)

10 ASK   Algic: Wiyot kɬæl–. Kutenai akɬeɬ. Mosan: Salish: Proto-Salish
*kʔʷanʔ. (AM)

11 BAD   Algic: Algonquian: Beothuk ašei 'sick.' Caddoan: Adai ašawe.
Siouan-Yuchi: Siouan: Proto-Siouan *xi, Hidatsa išia; Yuchi šiʔɛ̃.

12 BATHE   Iroquoian: Seneca ata-wē. Siouan-Yuchi: Siouan: Proto-
Siouan *(ni-)wā (*ni- = 'water'). (KS)

13 BE   Caddoan: Wichita ʔi. Iroquoian: Cherokee i. (KS)

14 BEAR (v.)   Algic: Wiyot we:j, we:t, wi:t 'be pregnant.' Iroquoian:
Seneca wij, Cherokee o-wiiraʔ 'child.' Keresan: Proto-Keresan
*-wʔɪ 'child.' Mosan: Salish: Tillamook wijatˢ 'stomach.'

15 BEAR₁ (n.)   Algic: Algonquian: Proto–Central Algonquian *maxkwa;
Wiyot makʷ 'black bear.' Mosan: Salish: Coeur d'Alene -maχiʔčən
'grizzly bear,' Columbian mexaɬ, Squamish mičaɬ 'black bear.' (AM)

16 BEAR₂ (n.)   Caddoan: Caddo nuwitˢseh. Siouan-Yuchi: Siouan:
Catawba nume. (KS)

17 BEAVER   Algic: Algonquian: Proto-Algonquian *amethkwa,
Proto–Central Algonquian *amexkwa. Kutenai moqʔune 'young
beaver.' (AM)

18 BEGIN   Algic: Wiyot kowa (inceptive particle). Siouan-Yuchi: Siouan:
Mandan ka- (inceptive prefix); Yuchi kɛ . . . (ɬa) (ɬa = 'to go').

19 BEHIND   Algic: Yurok hinoj. Iroquoian: Cherokee o:ni 'behind, late,'
(cf. Seneca ʔnowa 'back'). Kutenai iɬ (Kutenai ɬ < *n).

20 BELLY₁   Algic: Algonquian: Proto-Algonquian *tohša 'breast.' Mosan:
Wakashan: Nootka taača, Nitinat ta:č; Salish: Twana tʔʔa:ʔč, Upper
Chehalis tʔʔč, etc. (AM)

21 BELLY₂   Algic: Algonquian: Proto–Central Algonquian *-ink 'inside,'
Ojibwa unakiš 'entrails.' Iroquoian: Seneca nēkē:ʔ-t 'stomach, tripe,'
Mohawk nekwə̃ʔ-t. Keresan: Santa Ana -načʔai 'stomach.' Mosan:

Salish: Shuswap, etc. *-enk;* Wakashan: Nootka *inqi* 'in the belly,' *nak^je.*
Cf. Siouan: Dakota *nixe.*

22 BIRD₁   Algic: Algonquian: Proto–Central Algonquian **ši:ši:pa* 'duck,
fowl, large bird.' Mosan: Wakashan: Bella Bella *t^sit^sipe;* Salish: Shuswap
spju?, Thompson *spəzuzu,* Nisqualli *spekoh.* (AM)

23 BIRD₂   Caddoan: Pawnee *ri(-kut^ski)* (cf. *ri-piku* 'bird's egg'). Iroquoian:
Seneca *d^ri?t-.* Siouan-Yuchi: Siouan: Proto-Siouan (C) **ri?t ~ *rī?t.*
(KS)

24 BITE   Algic: Algonquian: Ojibwa *(tek-)kom(-a:t)* 'he bites him,'
Abenaki *gu-kwom-uš* 'I will bite you,' Arapaho *ka?āb.* Mosan:
Wakashan: Bella Bella *k^?imta* 'bite off'; Salish: Bella Coola *k^?m,*
Squamish *č^?m,* Coeur d'Alene *χæm* 'bite, eat,' etc. (AM)

25 BITTER   Algic: Algonquian: Proto–Central Algonquian **oxkuni*
'liver,' Cree *oskon* 'liver,' etc.; Yurok *sken* 'be bitter.' Mosan: Salish:
Lkungen *sæxən,* Upper Chehalis *sat^{s?}* 'liver.' (Semantic connection:
liver → bile → bitter) (AM)

26 BLOW   Algic: Algonquian: Proto-Algonquian **po:tatamwa* 'he blows
it,' Natick *putau* 'he blows.' Keresan: Santa Ana *pu:t^sa,* etc. Mosan:
Salish: Pentlatch *po:t,* Nisqualli *opud.*

27 BODY   Algic: Algonquian: Proto–Central Algonquian **wiijawi* 'his
body.' Iroquoian: Seneca *ja?-t.* Siouan-Yuchi: Siouan: Proto-Siouan
*ja? ~ *jo? 'meat, body.'

28 BOIL   Kutenai *-nmuk^w.* Mosan: Wakashan: Nootka *mox^w,* Kwakiutl
mex^j 'kindle,' Bella Bella *bek^ja* 'light a fire.' (AM)

29 BONE   Kutenai *t^{s?}əma:k* 'hard.' Mosan: Kwakiutl *t^?əmk^w* 'hard';
Salish: Proto-Salish **s-t^{s?}um? ~ *s-t^{s?}am?.* (AM)

30 BREAK₁   Algic: Yurok *tepoh* 'be hit.' Mosan: Wakashan, Kwakiutl
təpa. (AM)

31 BREAK₂   Algic: Algonquian: Kowilth *tik* 'cut through'; Wiyot *deg;*
Yurok *tik^wohs.* Caddoan: Pawnee *takit* 'be broken.' Mosan: Salish:
Proto-Salish **t^?aq^{?w},* Tillamook *tq.*

32 BREAST₁   Algic: Algonquian: Proto–Central Algonquian **- then-,*
Arapaho *(be-)then,* Gros Ventre *ten;* Wiyot *sar.* Mosan: Chemakuan:
Quileute *tał* 'heart'; Salish: Musqueam *t^sɛlɛ?,* Snohomish *s-t^{s?}ali?*
'heart.' (AM)

33 BREAST₂   Keresan: Acoma *(ka-)si.* Siouan-Yuchi: Siouan: Hidatsa *at^si*
(< **a-si).* (KS)

34 BROAD   Algic: Algonquian: Natick *puk* 'thin and flat,' Blackfoot
apakiu. Keresan: Proto-Keresan **pisč²a-zi* 'is flat.' Mosan: Wakashan:
Bella Bella *pa:q* 'lie flat,' Kwakiutl *p²əs* 'flatten'; Salish: Siciatl *pek,*
Pentlatch *pe:kʲ.* Siouan-Yuchi: Siouan: Mandan *pši* 'flat,' Biloxi *ptča.*

35 BROTHER   Algic: Algonquian: Kickapoo *tota:ma* 'sibling,' Cheyenne
tatan- 'older brother'; Yurok *tˢitˢ.* Caddoan: Pawnee *tat* 'sister' (man
speaking). Kutenai *tat²* 'older brother.'

36 BURN₁   Algic: Algonquian: Arapaho *-tana-* 'action by fire.' Kutenai
tohoł 'to char.' Mosan: Salish: Tillamook *t²un.* (AM)

37 BURN₂   Keresan: Santa Ana *ha:-k²a-ni* 'fire.' Kutenai *ko.* Mosan:
Salish: Tillamook *ku* 'to light.'

38 BUTTOCKS₁   Algic: Algonquian: Proto-Algonquian **čjexki;* Yurok
tˢək 'bird's tail,' *tu:k* 'fish's tail.' Iroquoian: Mohawk *tahs* 'tail,' Cherokee
ka-toxka 'tail.' Mosan: Salish: Nisqualli *t²ukʷ,* Snohomish *tˢəqʷ.*

39 BUTTOCKS₂   Iroquoian: Seneca *ō²ša.* Siouan-Yuchi: Siouan: Proto-
Siouan (C) **ūse.* (KS)

40 BUY   Algic: Algonquian: Proto–Central Algonquian **ata:wæwa* 'he
trades.' Mosan: Salish: Shuswap *tew,* Kalispel *teu* 'buy, sell'; Wakashan:
Kwakiutl *da* 'take.' Siouan-Yuchi: Siouan: Quapaw *dā* 'take.'

41 CALL   Iroquoian: Mohawk *jat* 'to name,' Seneca *jas.* Kutenai *at* 'to
name.' Mosan: Wakashan: Bella Bella *a:t* 'shout.' Siouan-Yuchi: Proto-
Siouan (C) **jaš* 'name'; Yuchi *jada* 'be called.'

42 CARRY   Algic: Algonquian: Ojibwa *nika:* 'carry on shoulder'; Yurok
negem. Iroquoian: Seneca *nēhkwi-* 'haul away, pull out.' Mosan:
Wakashan: Nitinat, Bella Bella *nku-la.*

43 CHEST   Algic: Algonquian: Shawnee *²paleewa* 'breast,' Miami *apalewi*
'breast.' Mosan: Wakashan: Kwakiutl *-p²əla.* (AM)

44 CHILD   Iroquoian: Seneca *-ksa-.* Siouan-Yuchi: Siouan: Proto-Siouan
(C) **kši* 'boy.' (KS)

45 CLOSE (v.)   Algic: Algonquian: Proto–Central Algonquian (H) **kašk.*
Caddoan: Pawnee *kaiku* 'covering.' Siouan-Yuchi: Siouan: Assiniboin
kaxka.

46 CLOUD₁   Algic: Algonquian: Ojibwa *a:nekkwat,* Micmac *aluk,*
Shawnee *alikatwi.* Mosan: Wakashan: Bella Bella *anqʷ.* Siouan-Yuchi:
Siouan: Quapaw *načči.*

47 CLOUD₂   Algic: Algonquian: Chippewa *awan* 'fog,' Abenaki *awan*
'air,' Arapaho *ba²anā* 'fog'; Wiyot *we²n* 'sky'; Yurok *won* 'sky.'
Kutenai *ał.* Mosan: Wakashan: Kwakiutl *anwe,* Bella Bella *²nwi.* (AM)

48 COLD   Caddoan: Wichita *ki-t˟tiije*. Keresan: Santa Ana *staja* 'be cold.'
(KS)

49 COME₁   Algic: Algonquian: Cheyenne *ho;* Yurok *ho:* 'go'; Wiyot *how.*
Siouan-Yuchi: Siouan: Proto-Siouan **hu* ~ **hi* 'arrive, come back';
Yuchi *hi* 'arrive having come.'

50 COME₂   Algic: Wiyot *wa* 'go.' Iroquoian: Mohawk *-w-* 'arrive.' Kutenai
w- 'arrive.' Siouan-Yuchi: Yuchi *wi.*

51 COOK   Algic: Yurok *skeʔwoj*. Mosan: Wakashan: Nootka *si:qa.* (AM)

52 CROOKED   Algic: Algonquian: Shawnee *kotekwi* 'turn, wind.'
Iroquoian: Mohawk *aʔktu,* Seneca *ašaʔ(-)ktō* 'become crooked.'
Mosan: Salish: Squamish *kʔʷutˢun.* Siouan-Yuchi: Siouan: Biloxi, Ofo
keči; Yuchi *kota.*

53 DEER   Algic: Algonquian: Proto−Central Algonquian **atehkwa*
'caribou,' Natick *ahtuk* 'deer.' Caddoan: Pawnee *ta:k* 'meat, flesh.'
Mosan: Wakashan: Kwakiutl *təkʲo:s;* Salish: Nisqualli *tˢikʰ.*

54 DIE₁   Algic: Algonquian: Proto−Central-Eastern Algonquian **-up-.*
Kutenai *-ip-.* (AM)

55 DIE₂   Algic: Algonquian: Proto−Central Algonquian **nepw.* Mosan:
Chemakuan: Quileute *lob-.* (AM)

56 DOG   Caddoan: Wichita *ki-t˟ijee.* Iroquoian: Seneca *dˢija.* Keresan:
Proto-Keresan **dija.* (KS)

57 EAR₁   Algic: Algonquian: Blackfoot, Gros Ventre *-itæn-.* Mosan:
Salish: Tillamook *tʔni,* Spokane *tenme,* Kalispel *tʔene.* (AM)

58 EAR₂   Keresan: Santa Ana *sʔ-i:pe* 'my ear.' Siouan-Yuchi: Siouan:
Hidatsa *apa* 'animal's ear.' (KS)

59 EAT   Algic: Algonquian: Proto−Central Algonquian **-am-* 'eat small
inanimate object.' Mosan: Salish: Kalispel *ʔem* 'feed,' Coeur d'Alene
æm 'share food,' Shuswap *m(-t)* 'feed.' (AM)

60 EGG₁   Caddoan: Pawnee *pi:ku* 'testicle,' Arikara *nipi:ku* 'bird's egg,'
Wichita *rikwiikaʔ.* Keresan: Acoma *nʔa:wʔi:kʔa,* etc. (KS)

61 EGG₂   Algic: Wiyot *me-lak* 'testicle.' Caddoan: Adai [oolaken]. Mosan:
Chemakuan: Chemakum *łaqʔu.*

62 EVENING   Algic: Algonquian: Chippewa *a-nago(-šig),* Micmac *uelag*
'this evening,' Munsee *ulakwe* 'yesterday'; Yurok *nahstˢewen* 'night.'
Kutenai *wałkwa* 'yesterday.' Mosan: Wakashan: Kwakiutl *dˢa:qwa.*
(AM)

63 EYE   Algic: Yurok *kʷəł* 'see'; Wiyot *tu-kł* 'watch.' Caddoan: Pawnee
kiri:ku, Wichita *kirikʔa.* Iroquoian: Mohawk *kə̄,* Seneca *kē.* Kutenai

169

qⱡiⱡ. Mosan: Chemakuan: Quileute *qaⱡ* 'look'; Wakashan: Nitinat *qaliʔ;* Salish: Songish *qəl(-əng),* Musqueam, Cowichan *qəl-əm.*

64 FAR   Algic: Wiyot *ⱡawi, ⱡow* 'long.' Mosan: Salish: Coeur d'Alene *lun,* Upper Chehalis *le:ʔ* 'far away,' Nisqualli *lel,* etc. (AM)

65 FAT   Iroquoian: Seneca *sē* 'be fat.' Siouan-Yuchi: Siouan: Proto-Siouan (C) **šī.* (KS)

66 FEAR   Algic: Algonquian: Proto–Central-Eastern Algonquian **kweʔ,* Proto–Central Algonquian **kuʔthæwa* 'he fears him.' Mosan: Salish: Squamish *qʷaiqʷaiʔəχ* 'shy,' Lkungen *qaiaqa* 'shame.' Siouan-Yuchi: Siouan: Hidatsa *kie,* Quapaw *kxi* 'anger.'

67 FEATHER   Algic: Algonquian: Menomini *(me:-)kon,* Ojibwa *mi-gwan.* Mosan: Salish: Siciatl *m-ake:n* 'hair,' Kalispel *(kam-)kan* 'hair,' Squamish *qin* 'hair.' Siouan-Yuchi: Siouan: Proto-Siouan **kʲū.*

68 FEEL   Algic: Algonquian: Arapaho *bæsæ,* Fox *ne-peʔšena* 'I feel it.' Mosan: Salish: Shuswap *mu:s,* Coeur d'Alene *mus* 'fumble, feel about.' (AM)

69 FIELD   Caddoan: Pawnee *atˢiʔuʔ.* Keresan: Proto-Keresan **ʔaṣa-nih* 'grass, wheat.' Siouan-Yuchi: Siouan: Proto-Siouan **sʾa.* (KS)

70 FINISH   Kutenai *hu.* Mosan: Wakashan: Nootka *hawi;* Chemakuan: Quileute *hijo-do;* Salish: Squamish *hu:* (transitive), Snohomish *huju* 'finish, make, do.' (AM)

71 FIRE₁   Kutenai: *-kap* 'by fire.' Mosan: Wakashan: Kwakiutl *qʷap,* Proto-Salish **kup.* (AM)

72 FIRE₂   Caddoan: Caddo *na-bahn* 'catch fire.' Keresan: Santa Ana *ʔu:-baja-ni* 'fire place,' Acoma *baja* 'make fire,' etc. Siouan-Yuchi: Siouan: Osage *poe* 'flames,' Catawba *impi;* Yuchi *pa* 'flame, to burn.' (KS)

73 FIRE₃   Algic: Algonquian: Proto–Central Algonquian **-s, *-su* 'by heat,' Northern Arapaho *isei.* Mosan: Salish: Squamish *tm-iʔis* 'summer' (*tm* = 'season'), Nisqualli *sa(-dub)* 'summer' (analysis similar to Squamish). (AM)

74 FIRST   Algic: Algonquian: Blackfoot *is* 'ahead.' Kutenai *-us-.* Mosan: Chemakuan: Quileute *sisaʔwa* 'in front of.' (AM)

75 FISH₁   Algic: Algonquian: Ojibwa *-ame:,* Blackfoot *mamiu,* Arapaho *bi(-thi).* Mosan: Wakashan: Bella Bella *memaʔe:mas, me:a,* Kwakiutl *me.* (AM)

76 FISH₂   Caddoan: Wichita *kaatˢʾa,* Pawnee *katˢixi.* Keresan: Proto-Keresan **skʾaašɨh,* Santo Domingo *kʾaašɨh.* (KS)

77 FLOAT   Mosan: Wakashan: Nootka *pux,* Kwakiutl *pxwa,* Bella Bella

$p^{\eta}xwa;$ Chemakuan: Quileute *puxwal* 'drift'; Salish: Bella Coola *p$^{\eta}$ixla*, Squamish *p$^{\eta}$ak^w*. Siouan-Yuchi: Siouan: Quapaw *pxa* 'swim.'

78 FLOWER   Algic: Algonquian: Proto–Central Algonquian **paQk* (Q = consonant other than *n*, *s*, or *š*). Mosan: Salish: Musqueam *s-pεq$^{\eta}$εm$^{\eta}$*, Twana *s-p$^{\eta}$q$^{\eta}$ab*. (AM)

79 FLY (n.)   Algic: Algonquian: Micmac *msusok*, Natick *mosuhq*, Ojibwa *mesisa:kk* 'horsefly.' Mosan: Wakashan: Nootka *ma:t^{s}k^{w}in;* Salish: Bella Coola *mamis*, Thompson *muza*, etc. Cf. BEE$_2$ in the Amerind dictionary. (AM)

80 FOG   Algic: Algonquian: Ojibwa *-a:pu*. Caddoan: Pawnee *pihu* 'be foggy,' Arikara *pju* 'mist.' Siouan-Yuchi: Siouan: Hidatsa *pue*, Santee *p$^{\eta}$o*, Mandan *pi:* 'smoke.'

81 FOLLOW   Algic: Algonquian: Proto-Algonquian **no:t^s*. Mosan: Chemakuan: Chemakum *lata* 'run.' Siouan-Yuchi: Siouan: Quapaw *nūse* 'chase.'

82 FOOT   Algic: Algonquian: Blackfoot *-kin* 'by means of the foot.' Kutenai *-ikin* 'by means of the foot.' Mosan: Salish: Proto-Salish **xin, **xən* (Haas). (AM)

83 FULL$_1$ Mosan: Proto-Salish **p$^{\eta}$ər* 'overflow.' Siouan-Yuchi: Siouan: Catawba *pā, parā* 'completely,' Quapaw *panā* 'all.' Cf. Yuchi *$^{\eta}$opa* 'all.'

84 FULL$_2$ Algic: Algonquian: Proto–Central Algonquian **mo:t^{s}ki* 'fill,' Cheyenne *moxkoh* 'very much.' Iroquoian: Seneca *-nōke* 'abound' (*n < *m*). Mosan: Proto-Salish **məq$^{\eta}$* 'eat one's fill,' Squamish *məq$^{\eta}$* 'full from eating'

85 GIVE$_1$ Caddoan: Pawnee *u, uh*. Keresan: Proto-Keresan **-$^{\eta}$u* 'give flat long thing.' Iroquoian: Seneca *awi* ~ *$^{\eta}$o*, Mohawk *u:* 'give away.' (KS)

86 GIVE$_2$ Algic: Wiyot *łaγ-* 'give present.' Mosan: Salish: Proto-Salish **næq* 'potlatch,' Thompson *naq*. (AM)

87 GO   Algic: Yurok *le$^{\eta}$-m* (pl. subject). Iroquoian: Seneca *-ine-* 'go, proceed.' Kutenai *n-*. Mosan: Wakashan: Kwakiutl *la;* Chemakuan: Chemakum *la*. Siouan-Yuchi: Siouan: Proto-Siouan **le, *re*.

88 GOOD$_1$ Algic: Algonquian: Proto-Algonquian **kan* 'beautiful.' Iroquoian: Mohawk *akarite* 'be healthy.' Mosan: Salish: Tillamook *k$^{\eta}$unək* 'beautiful.' Siouan-Yuchi: Siouan: Catawba *kəri*.

89 GOOD$_2$ Algic: Algonquian: Blackfoot *sokapiu*, Delaware *si:ki* 'be good'; Yurok *skoje*. Kutenai *sok*. Siouan-Yuchi: Siouan: Hidatsa *t^{s}aki*.

90 GRANDFATHER$_1$ Algic: Algonquian: Cree *muso-m*, Ojibwa *ne-*

miššomis 'my grandfather,' Cheyenne *na-mše-m* 'my grandfather';
Wiyot *biǰotek, bičatker;* Yurok *pit⁵owas*. Mosan: Chemakuan:
Chemakum *amaas*. Siouan-Yuchi: Siouan: Chiwere *wāsa* 'old man.'

91 GRANDFATHER₂ Caddoan: Pawnee *ikani*, Caddo *ika*. Siouan-Yuchi:
Siouan: Proto-Siouan *kū*, Biloxi *ikoni*, Osage *iko*. (KS)

92 GUTS Algic: Algonquian: Proto-Algonquian *tempi* 'brains' (for the
semantics, see Shuswap below), Cheyenne *ma-tʰap* 'brains,' Arapaho
be-teč 'brains' (*č < *p*). Mosan: Wakashan: Nootka *t⁵ʔijip*, Kwakiutl
t⁵ʔijim; Salish: Shuswap *-t⁵ʔm-qin* 'brains' (literally 'guts [of] head'),
Snohomish *s-t⁵ʔəb-qid*. Siouan-Yuchi: Siouan: Proto-Siouan *kⁱipe*.

93 HAND₁ Algic: Algonquian: Blackfoot *-kit⁵-* 'finger'; Wiyot *kisan;*
Yurok *-ketew* 'little finger.' Mosan: Salish: Squamish *čis*, Thompson
akst, etc. (AM)

94 HAND₂ Caddoan: Caddo *sik*, Adai *seku-t*, Pawnee *iks*, Wichita *ʔiska*
'arm.' Siouan-Yuchi: Siouan: Proto-Siouan (Matthews) *šaki*, Tutelo
ksa, Catawba *iksa*. (KS)

95 HARD Keresan: Laguna *ni*. Iroquoian: Seneca *nij ~ ni* 'be hard.' (KS)

96 HEAD₁ Iroquoian: Cherokee *u-sko-li, -sk-*. Mosan: Salish: Nisqualli
šuk, šišuk 'above'; Wakashan: Kwakiutl *səqʔa* 'over.' Siouan-Yuchi:
Siouan: Catawba *-skā*, Tutelo *sako* 'above.'

97 HEAD₂ Caddoan: Pawnee *paksu*, Arikara *paxu*. Siouan-Yuchi: Siouan:
Proto-Siouan *pa*. (KS)

98 HEART Algic: Algonquian: Proto–Central Algonquian *-teehi*,
Arapaho *be-tee*. Caddoan: Pawnee *e:t*. Siouan-Yuchi: Siouan: Catawba
taʔ 'breast'; Yuchi *ta*.

99 HEAVY Algic: Wiyot *laʔy*. Kutenai *anikʔe*. Siouan-Yuchi: Siouan:
Biloxi *nakhe*.

100 HIT Kutenai *moχune* 'hit, fall into,' *maqʔne* 'slap.' Mosan:
Wakashan: Kwakiutl *məxⁱa*. (AM)

101 HOLD Algic: Algonquian: Mohegan *ne-kunu* 'I catch'; Wiyot *kul*
'take hold of'; Yurok *ʔekonem*. Kutenai *qun* 'touch.' Mosan: Proto-
Salish *kinʔ* 'hold, touch,' Tillamook *kun* 'catch.' (AM)

102 HOLE Caddoan: Pawnee *hata < *jata*. Iroquoian: Seneca *jata*. (KS)

103 HOT Algic: Algonquian: Proto–Central Algonquian *kešj-*, Cree,
Shawnee *kis*, Natick *kussitau* 'it is hot,' Blackfoot *ksistosiu;* cf. Yurok
ket⁵ojn-hego 'sun.' Mosan: Proto-Salish *kʔʷas* 'hot, 'scorch.' (AM)

104 HUNT Iroquoian: Seneca *-ora-*. Siouan-Yuchi: Siouan: Proto-Siouan
(C) *ore*. (KS)

105 ICE   Algic: Algonquian: Proto–Central Algonquian (Michelson) *mexkwami*, Ojibwa *-kkomi*. Mosan: Chemakuan: Quileute *xabi:č;* Salish: Squamish *čim* 'cold,' Lillooet *kemalič* 'freeze.' (AM)

106 INSIDE   Caddoan: Pawnee *huk*. Siouan-Yuchi: Siouan: Catawba *huk*. (KS)

107 KINDLE₁   Iroquoian: Seneca *ō(-t-hw)*. Siouan-Yuchi: Siouan: Proto-Siouan (C) **ū*. (KS)

108 KINDLE₂   Kutenai *tˢukʷ* 'start a fire.' Mosan: Wakashan: Kwakiutl *tˢexʲa;* Salish: Lkungen *čukku* 'burn.' (AM)

109 LAKE   Iroquoian: Seneca *(njota)-re*. Siouan-Yuchi: Siouan: Proto-Siouan **re*. (KS)

110 LARGE   Algic: Algonquian: Proto–Central Algonquian **keqt-*, Ojibwa *kečči;* Yurok *ketʾul* 'to form large . . . .' Caddoan: Pawnee *ku:tˢu*, Arikara *kusu*. Mosan: Salish: Kalispel *kʷtun*, Spokane *kʷuttunt*.

111 LEAF   Algic: Algonquian: Ojibwa *pak*, Shawnee *pakw-* 'leaf-shaped,' Abenaki *wanibakw*. Mosan: Wakashan: Kwakiutl *pa:q;* Salish: Pentlatch *pʾaqan*. (AM)

112 LEFT (SIDE)   Algic: Yurok *kes(-omewet)* (cf. *neko-omewet* 'right'). Mosan: Wakashan: Nootka *qatˢ-* 'on the left'; Salish: Proto-Salish **tˢʾiqʷ-* (metathesis; cf. Kalispel *čʔtˢi* < **ktˢi*). (AM)

113 LEG   Algic: Algonquian: Proto-Algonquian **ne-xkaači* 'my foot,' pl. *ne-xkaatali*, Fox *-ska-* 'with the foot'; Wiyot *čkač;* Yurok *tˢka* 'foot.' Kutenai *saqʾ*. Mosan: Salish: Tillamook *suq* 'jump,' Snanaimuk *sqəna* 'foot' (but is *s-* a prefix?). (AM)

114 LIE (TELL A)   Keresan: Acoma *seʔ-ibe* 'I am a liar.' Siouan-Yuchi: Siouan: Biloxi *pxi* 'deceive.' (KS)

115 LIE DOWN₁   Algic: Algonquian: Shawnee *šekšinawa* 'he lies down.' Kutenai *saq*. Mosan: Proto-Salish **tˢq(-al)* 'lie on back.' (AM)

116 LIE DOWN₂   Iroquoian: Seneca *-jē-* 'set down.' Siouan-Yuchi: Siouan: Proto-Siouan (C) **jã* 'sleep, lie down.' (KS)

117 LIP   Iroquoian: Seneca *skwa-r*. Siouan-Yuchi: Siouan: Proto-Siouan (C) **špa*. (KS)

118 LIVE   Iroquoian: Mohawk *ha* 'dwell, live.' Siouan-Yuchi: Yuchi *ha*. (KS)

119 LIVER   Algic: Algonquian: Proto-Algonquian **we-thkwani* 'his liver'; Yurok *ɬkun;* Wiyot *(wat-)war*. Caddoan: Pawnee *kari:ku*, Caddo *kanku*. Mosan: Salish: Lillooet *kal*, Twana *s-čal-ab*, etc.

120 MAN   Algic: Yurok *peg-iɬ* 'make,' *peg-ək*. Mosan: Wakashan: Kwakiutl *bekʷ-*. (AM)

121 MANY₁   Iroquoian: Cherokee *hilə ~ hila* 'many, far.' Siouan-Yuchi: Yuchi *hɛlɛ, hilɛ* 'all.' (KS)

122 MANY₂   Caddoan: Arikara *kari.* Iroquoian: Cherokee *kali* 'full.' Siouan-Yuchi: Siouan: Mandan *kerere, -kere* (pl. suffix), Catawba *kre.* (KS)

123 MANY₃   Caddoan: Wichita *asse:ha* 'all,' Caddo *asi:ha* 'all.' Iroquoian: Seneca *eso.* Keresan: Proto-Keresan **sai* 'all.' Mosan: Chemakuan: Chemakum *ʔi:sa,* Quileute *ʔiša.* Siouan-Yuchi: Siouan: Catawba *šoji.*

124 MEAT   Kutenai *łak.* Mosan: Salish: Nisqualli *nqʔ* 'animal.' (AM)

125 MIDDLE   Iroquoian: Mohawk *assenen,* Seneca *ahsənō-* 'be in the middle.' Keresan: Proto-Keresan **sənʔa.* (KS)

126 MOON   Iroquoian: Seneca *ē:niʔtaʔ* 'month,' Cherokee *nāto* 'sun, moon.' Siouan-Yuchi: Siouan: Catawba *nūti, nunti* 'sun, moon' (loan?). (KS)

127 MOSQUITO   Keresan: Keres *tˢa:p* 'fly.' Siouan-Yuchi: Siouan: Dakota *čapāka,* Biloxi *čamaki,* etc. (KS)

128 MOTHER   Algic: Algonquian: Proto-Algonquian **ne-kjaʔšiwa* 'my mother,' Ojibwa *(nen-)kašši* 'my mother,' Delaware *okasu,* Cheyenne *na-kahe* 'my mother'; Wiyot *gwač.* Iroquoian: Cherokee *asagi* 'aunt.' Mosan: Chemakuan: Chemakum *ʔukisima;* Salish: Spokane *eskui,* Twana *skʔuj.* Siouan-Yuchi: Siouan: Catawba *juksu.*

129 MOUNTAIN   Caddoan: Caddo *anehko* 'stone.' Kutenai *nukʷ* 'stone.' Mosan: Wakashan: Kwakiutl *ni:kʲe,* Nootka *nəgʲe.* Siouan-Yuchi: Siouan: Woccon [erroco] 'peak.'

130 MOUSE   Algic: Algonquian: Miami *kosia;* Wiyot *ge:š.* Mosan: Proto-Salish **kʔʷatʔan,* Lillooet *xʷuz.* Cf. Keresan: Santa Ana *sga:waši* 'rat.'

131 MOUTH   Algic: Algonquian: Proto–Central Algonquian **-m-, *-mu-* 'by speech or thought,' Chippewa *-am* 'by mouth'; Yurok *mu-m* 'say.' Caddoan: Arikara *wa* 'say,' Wichita *wa* 'say.' Mosan: Wakashan: Nootka *mʔa* 'hold in mouth.'

132 MUCH₁   Keresan: Santa Ana *nʔau* 'many.' Kutenai *a:n-* 'more.' Mosan: Wakashan: Nootka *ʔana* 'this much.'

133 MUCH₂   Iroquoian: Seneca *-aʔte.* Siouan-Yuchi: Siouan: Proto-Siouan (C) **aʔte ~ *oʔta;* Yuchi *aode* 'abundance,' *a . . . de* 'to abound.' (KS)

134 NAME₁   Algic: Algonquian: Cree *senika,* Natick *we-suonk,* Ojibwa *ižinik,* Micmac *we-son.* Caddoan: Pawnee *asar* 'be named,' Caddo

hisaar. Iroquoian: Seneca *hsē:nõ²*, Mohawk *hsə̃n*, Onandaga *hak-šinna* 'my name.' Mosan: Salish: Nootsack *sna*, Lkungen *sna*, Musqueam *snɛ* (but *s-* is probably a prefix).

135 NAME₂   Algic: Algonquian: Proto–Central Algonquian *we:;* Yurok *hew.* Mosan: Salish: Proto-Salish *²aw-t*, Shuswap *wew* 'to call.' (AM)

136 NEAR   Algic: Algonquian: Proto–Central Algonquian (H) *ketaw* 'I see him nearby.' Caddoan: Wichita *kata* 'next to.' Iroquoian: Seneca *-kt-* 'be next to,' Mohawk, Onandaga *akta.* Kutenai *akatak.* Mosan: Wakashan: Nootka *k²ač;* Salish: Proto-Salish *k²it.* Siouan-Yuchi: Siouan: Proto-Siouan *kkʲa* ~ *kʲta*, Tutelo *īktei.*

137 NECK   Algic: Algonquian: Proto–Central Algonquian *- hkweeka-ni. Kutenai *-o:kak.* (AM)

138 NEW   Algic: Algonquian: Proto–Central Algonquian *weški* 'new, young.' Mosan: Wakashan: Nootka *wa:stk* 'fresh, undried.' (AM)

139 NOSE₁   Iroquoian: Seneca *kõswa* 'snout.' Kutenai *qsaɬa.* Mosan: Salish: Proto-Salish *(ma-)qs(-ən)*, Tillamook *-qs.*

140 NOSE₂   Algic: Algonquian: Cheyenne *-e:s-*, Arapaho *be-iš, be-²is.* Iroquoian: Cherokee *ka-jāsa, ka-jaso-li.* Mosan: Chemakuan: Chemakum, Quileute *-o:s.*

141 NOW   Caddoan: Pawnee *we.* Iroquoian: Mohawk *u:wa.* Keresan: Acoma *w²ai* 'today,' Santa Ana *hiw²a* 'today.' (KS)

142 OLD   Iroquoian: Seneca *kē(-hji).* Siouan-Yuchi: Siouan: Proto-Siouan (C) *kā.* (KS)

143 ONE₁   Caddoan: Pawnee *asku*, Arikara *axku*, Wichita *ass*, Caddo *wistˢi.* Iroquoian: Seneca *ska*, Mohawk *ə̃ska*, Huron *eskate.* Keresan: Acoma, Santa Ana *²iska.* (KS)

144 ONE₂   Algic: Algonquian: Proto–Central Algonquian *nekotw*, Cheyenne *-nokæ, nočo;* Wiyot *gotˢ;* Yurok *koht.* Mosan: Proto-Salish *nak²*, *nək²u* (*nV-* seems to be a prefix; it appears also in the Algonquian numerals 'two' and 'three'). (AM)

145 OPEN₁   Algic: Algonquian: Arapaho *kāne;* Yurok *kæn.* Kutenai *uk²un, hukʷen* 'be open.' (AM)

146 OPEN₂   Iroquoian: Seneca *tõ.* Keresan: Santa Ana *t²a.* Siouan-Yuchi: Yuchi *tʰa* 'uncover.' (KS)

147 PAIN   Algic: Algonquian: Shawnee *-tka.* Mosan: Wakashan: Kwakiutl *t²əxʲ* 'have pain'; Salish: Upper Chehalis *t²ak²ʷ.* (AM)

148 PENIS   Algic: Algonquian: Proto–Central Algonquian *thak.* Mosan: Wakashan: Nootka *saqo:;* Chemakuan: Quileute *-sko.* (AM)

149 PERSON₁   Iroquoian: Seneca -ōkwe. Mosan: Wakashan: Kwakiutl -okʷ (numeral classifier for persons). Siouan-Yuchi: Siouan: Proto-Siouan (C) *wōkwe, Biloxi āngkwa.

150 PERSON₂   Kutenai nikˀ. Mosan: Wakashan: Kwakiutl, Bella Bella enoq; Salish: Coeur d'Alene nikʷ 'tribe.' Siouan-Yuchi: Siouan: Osage nika 'man.'

151 PERSON₃   Caddoan: Caddo haja:nuˀ. Keresan: Proto-Keresan *hanU 'people.' (KS)

152 PLANT (v.)   Iroquoian: Cherokee ka. Keresan: Santa Ana, Acoma kiˀwa (n.). Siouan-Yuchi: Siouan: Proto-Siouan *kˀe 'dig, scratch.' (KS)

153 POUND   Caddoan: Caddo daˀ 'pound corn.' Kutenai tˀa:- 'knock.' Mosan: Salish: Shuswap tˀ, Coeur d'Alene tiˀ 'pound, hit,' Kalispel te. Siouan-Yuchi: Siouan: Mandan (ka-)tɛ (ka = 'by striking'); cf. Hidatsa ta 'kill,' Quapaw teje 'kill,' Yuchi twa 'kill.'

154 POUR   Algic: Algonquian: Ojibwa sikenank 'he pours it out.' Mosan: Salish: Tillamook sǝx 'spill,' Kalispel, Coeur d'Alene sixʷ. (AM)

155 RAIN   Iroquoian: Seneca sta, Onandaga ho-sta. Mosan: Salish: Columbian staˀu. Siouan-Yuchi: Yuchi šta 'snow.' Cf. Algonquian: Cheyenne hestas 'snow.'

156 RED₁   Algic: Algonquian: Mohegan skwaio; Wiyot saɣ-. Mosan: Chemakuan: Chemakum suˀuqʷa; Salish: Proto-Salish *tˢaqʷ, *tˢiqʷ 'blood, red,' Bella Coola six 'blood.' Siouan-Yuchi: Siouan: Catawba skeˀ.

157 RED₂   Algic: Algonquian: Proto-Algonquian *meçkwi 'blood,' Proto–Central Algonquian *meçkweewi 'it is red,' Blackfoot mik 'blood.' Caddoan: Wichita wa:tˢ 'blood.' Keresan: Santa Ana mˀaˀatˢˀi 'blood,' Acoma mˀa:tˢˀi 'blood.' Mosan: Salish: Bella Bella mukʷ; Chemakuan: Quileute piˀči.

158 RIB   Kutenai nokak. Mosan: Salish: Nisqualli lukh, Lkungen lukwukh, Squamish lǝwx. (AM)

159 ROAST   Iroquoian: Seneca (ta-)kiriˀ. Mosan: Chemakuan: Chemakum qaɫii-lii; Salish: Shuswap qʷl-, Nootsack kˀʷl 'cook.' Siouan-Yuchi: Siouan: Proto-Siouan (C) *ra-xere.

160 SALIVA₁   Keresan: Acoma šupǝ, Laguna šupšup 'to spit.' Siouan-Yuchi: Siouan: Catawba (Speck) čǝpā. (KS)

161 SALIVA₂   Mosan: Wakashan: Nootka ta:xʷ 'to spit'; Chemakuan: Quileute tux-al 'to spit.' Siouan-Yuchi: Siouan: Teton tʰaxe, ɔsage tatoxe; Yuchi tɛko.

162 SEE₁   Algic: Algonquian: Blackfoot *api.* Mosan: Chemakuan: Chemakum *hu:paʔa.* Siouan-Yuchi: Siouan: Proto-Siouan **pʰa* 'meet, find'; Yuchi *pʔa* 'look.'

163 SEE₂   Iroquoian: Cherokee *(ha-)ga(-ta)* 'look,' Seneca *kē,* Mohawk *kā.* Keresan: Santa Ana *ga* 'look.' Siouan-Yuchi: Siouan: Hidatsa *ika* 'see, look,' Crow *ikʲa* 'look,' Ofo *eke* 'know'; Yuchi *kʔa* 'watch.' (KS)

164 SEEK   Algic: Algonquian: Proto–Central Algonquian **kwat, *kot* 'try.' Mosan: Chemakuan: Quileute *kwat* 'try.' Siouan-Yuchi: Siouan: Hidatsa *kidi* 'try,' Santee *akita.*

165 SHADOW   Algic: Algonquian: Natick *onkauaht,* Miami *alakwaki;* Yurok *loʔogej* 'black.' Kutenai *ɬo:kwa.* Mosan: Wakashan: Bella Bella *ne:kk* 'night'; Salish: Songish *nəqix,* Lkungen *nukʲeeq.* (AM)

166 SHINE   Kutenai *maaka* 'flicker.' Mosan: Wakashan: Nootka *moqʔ* 'glowing.' (AM)

167 SIDE   Kutenai *maɬ* 'sideways.' Mosan: Salish: Squamish *minʔ* 'side, half.' (AM)

168 SING₁   Algic: Algonquian: Proto–Central Algonquian **ne-kamowa* 'I sing.' Mosan: Wakashan: Kwakiutl *kmta.* (AM)

169 SING₂   Keresan: Santa Ana *či:ni* 'dance.' Siouan-Yuchi: Siouan: Mandan *kana;* Yuchi *kɔ.* (KS)

170 SING₃   Iroquoian: Seneca *wē* 'voice.' Siouan-Yuchi: Siouan: Proto-Siouan (C) **wā.* (KS)

171 SIT₁   Caddoan: Pawnee, Arikara *ku.* Keresan: Santa Ana *ku* 'be in a place.' Kutenai *qa* 'be.' Siouan-Yuchi: Siouan: Proto-Siouan **amā-ki* 'sit on ground' (**amā* = 'ground'); Yuchi *kʔu* 'dwell.'

172 SIT₂   Algic: Algonquian: Proto–Central Algonquian **pemaatesiwa* 'he lives,' Cheyenne *ametanen* 'he lives,' Beothuk *meotik* 'house.' Mosan: Salish: Shuswap *mut* 'be at home,' Songish *ʔəmət,* Bella Coola *mʔt.* (AM)

173 SLEEP   Iroquoian: Mohawk *itaʔ,* Seneca *itaʔw ~ ita,* etc. Siouan-Yuchi: Siouan: Proto-Siouan **tʔe* 'die.' (KS)

174 SMALL   Algic: Algonquian: Blackfoot *as* 'small, young,' Cheyenne *-es.* Mosan: Wakashan: Nootka *-is.* (AM)

175 SMELL   Iroquoian: Seneca *ʔosē:nōʔ* (n.). Siouan-Yuchi: Siouan: Chiwere *sīnge,* Catawba *sūw* 'stink.' (KS)

176 SMOKE   Algic: Algonquian: Abenaki *ahsokʷ* 'cloud,' Blackfoot *soksistˢiko* 'cloud.' Caddoan: Wichita *istqaak.* Keresan: Proto-Keresan **tˢʔekə* 'to smoke.' Mosan: Salish: Upper Chehalis *šq* 'cloud.' Siouan-Yuchi: Siouan: Ofo *ošigwe* 'cloud.'

177 SNAKE   Algic: Algonquian: Mohegan *nato* 'black snake.' Caddoan:
Arikara *nu:t,* Pawnee *ratki.*

178 SNOW₁   Algic: Yurok *ror-* (v.). Iroquoian: Seneca *-nija-.* Kutenai *ɬu.*
Mosan: Wakashan: Kwakiutl *nae:, na?ja.* Siouan-Yuchi: Siouan: Proto-
Siouan (C) **nije.*

179 SNOW₂   Keresan: Proto-Keresan **hawe,* Santa Ana *ha:m?e* 'ice.'
Siouan-Yuchi: Siouan: Proto-Siouan **wa,* Hidatsa *ma,* Catawba *wɔ?.*
(KS)

180 STAND   Iroquoian: Mohawk *ta?* 'stand up,' Oneida *de.* Siouan-Yuchi:
Yuchi *ta.* (KS)

181 STEAL   Algic: Algonquian: Proto–Central Algonquian **kemot,*
Blackfoot *aikamosi;* Yurok *kemol;* Wiyot *kemar.* Mosan: Wakashan:
Nootka *k?imk²ima.* (AM)

182 STICK   Algic: Yurok *meɬ-kʷeɬ.* Mosan: Salish: Bella Coola *mila,*
Lillooet *mulič* 'wood.' (AM)

183 STONE₁   Iroquoian: Seneca *nēj,* Cherokee *nāja.* Siouan-Yuchi:
Siouan: Proto-Siouan (C) **mīj.* (KS)

184 STONE₂   Algic: Algonquian: Proto–Central Algonquian **aqsenja,*
Shawnee *sæni,* Mohegan *suen.* Mosan: Chemakuan: Chemakum *čaala;*
Salish: Tillamook *šanš,* Upper Chehalis *sown* 'boulder,' etc. Siouan-
Yuchi: Yuchi *sɛnɛ, sɛ̄* 'iron.'

185 SWALLOW   Algic: Algonquian: Proto-Algonquian **kwentakaa-ni*
'throat,' Proto–Central Algonquian **kwan-, *kon-.* Mosan: Wakashan:
Bella Bella *q?oq?one* 'throat'; Salish: Squamish *qənax* 'throat';
Chemakuan: Quileute *k?a?das.* Siouan-Yuchi: Yuchi *k?ɛnɛ.*

186 SWEET   Iroquoian: Seneca *ænn-,* Mohawk *oniete.* Keresan: Proto-
Keresan **?an?e:za* 'be tasty.' (KS)

187 SWELL   Algic: Algonquian: Cheyenne *epeohotˢ* 'be swollen'; Wiyot
pe:š. Mosan: Chemakuan: Quileute *ap* 'grow'; Salish: Cowichan
p?a-m, Upper Chehalis *pos,* Thompson *pau,* Shuswap *pew-t* 'swollen.'
Siouan-Yuchi: Siouan: Proto-Siouan **po, *pu.*

188 SWIM   Kutenai *naq-.* Mosan: Salish: Columbian *naq?əram,* Coeur
d'Alene *nuxʷ* 'frog floats,' Lillooet *?nkailič,* Thompson *nkaiχʷ.* (AM)

189 TASTE   Algic: Algonquian: Blackfoot *-poko,* Ojibwa *-ippokosi.*
Keresan: Santa Ana *p?ak?atˢa* 'touch.' Mosan: Wakashan: Kwakiutl
p?aq.

190 TELL   Caddoan: Pawnee *rihku,* Arikara *rairika.* Siouan-Yuchi:
Siouan: Winnebago *rak* 'story,' Osage *oðage.* (KS)

191 TESTICLE   Kutenai *maqʾən* 'egg.' Mosan: Wakashan: Kwakiutl
məkʷ- 'round thing is somewhere'; Salish: Squamish *mačʾn*, Pentlatch
məčin, etc. (AM)

192 THICK   Algic: Algonquian: Natick *kuppi*, Ojibwa *keppaka:mekat* 'it
is thick.' Keresan: Keres, Acoma *kaba-*.

193 THUNDER   Algic: Algonquian: Arapaho *baxaʔā*. Mosan: Quileute
beʔex 'to thunder.' Cf. Keresan: Santa Ana *mu:tˢa*. (Arapaho and
Quileute *b* < **m*; Keres *tˢ* < **k*).

194 TOOTH   Algic: Algonquian: Cheyenne *-onen* '-toothed.' Kutenai
una:n. (AM)

195 TREE₁   Algic: Algonquian: Proto–Central Algonquian **meʔtekwi*,
Micmac *musi*, Blackfoot *mistˢis*. Mosan: Wakashan: Kwakiutl, Bella
Bella *-mis*. (AM)

196 TREE₂   Algic: Wiyot *-ałat*. Mosan: Chemakuan: Quileute *-lat* 'wood.'
(AM)

197 TURTLE₁   Caddoan: Wichita *niwot* 'mud turtle.' Iroquoian: Mohawk
anowara, Seneca *ʔnowa*. (KS)

198 TURTLE₂   Caddoan: Wichita *kikʾi:s* 'tortoise,' Caddo *čia*. Siouan-
Yuchi: Siouan: Biloxi *akisi*, Catawba *kaija*, Santee *keja*. (KS)

199 TWO   Algic: Algonquian: Proto–Central Algonquian **n-iišwi* (**n-* is
prefixed to numerals in Algonquian). Kutenai *as*. Mosan: Salish:
Squamish *čʾiui* 'twins,' Tillamook *dʾu*, Columbian *seja*. (AM)

200 URINE   Algic: Algonquian: Proto–Central Algonquian **šeki*,
Blackfoot *isksini*. Mosan: Salish: Musqueam *səχʷa* 'urinate,' Nisqualli
osahwa 'male urinates.' (AM)

201 WASP   Caddoan: Pawnee *patˢ* (< **watˢ*). Iroquoian: Catawba *wuss*
(Lieber), *wos* 'bee.' Keresan: Santa Ana *bi:su* 'bee.' (KS)

202 WIND (n.)   Algic: Wiyot *ro:kʷ*. Mosan: Salish: Proto-Salish **-alaq*.
(AM)

203 WING   Algic: Algonquian: Proto-Algonquian **na-xpeto-ni*, Abenaki
u-pedi-n 'his arm.' Caddoan: Pawnee *pi:d, pi:ru* 'arm,' Arikara *wi:nu*
'arm.' Mosan: Wakashan: Bella Bella *pʾətˡ-am*.

204 WISH   Algic: Wiyot *ragʷ*. Mosan: Wakashan: Nitinat *-naq* 'fond of
eating . . . ,' Kwakiutl *nʔe:q*, Nootka *nʔa:ħ* 'seek.' (AM)

205 WOMAN   Iroquoian: Seneca *-ihō-*. Siouan-Yuchi: Siouan: Proto-
Siouan (C) **wīhā*. (KS)

206 WOOD   Caddoan: Caddo *nako* 'fire,' Pawnee *laktit* 'fire,' Arikara

nač. Kutenai *ɬukʷ*. Mosan: Salish: Tillamook *-alaq;* Wakashan: Nootka *ɬoʔok* 'board.'

207 WORM₁   Keresan: Proto-Keresan *ṣu:wi:*. Siouan-Yuchi: Siouan: Catawba (Speck) *čūwi*. (KS)

208 WORM₂   Algic: Algonquian: Ojibwa *ukkwe* 'maggot,' Natick *ohk;* Yurok *jekʷɬ* 'maggot.' Mosan: Wakashan: Kwakiutl *jaqʷe:ʔ* 'woodworm.' (AM)

209 YELLOW   Algic: Algonquian: Blackfoot *otaxku*. Mosan: Wakashan: Bella Bella *te:x, tixa*. (AM)

Chapter 4

Amerind Etymological Dictionary

This chapter contains 281 etymologies common to two or more of the 11 Amerind groups treated in Chapter 3. Etymologies exclusive to certain subgroups (e.g. Arawakan, Chibchan, Yuki-Gulf) are identified at the end of the entry for the group by the same abbreviations used in Chapter 3. Likewise, the same policy is followed here as there in the ordering of the subgroups and the use (or non-use) of their names. For particulars, see p. 63.

The unidentified reconstructed forms are drawn from the following sources:

Proto-Algonquian: Siebert (1941, 1975)
Proto-Caddoan: Taylor (1963)
Proto–Central Algonquian: Bloomfield (1925, 1946)
Proto-Ge: Davis (1966)
Proto-Hianacoto: Durbin (1973)
Proto-Keresan: Miller & Davis (1963)
Proto-Mayan: Campbell (1977)
Proto-Nambikwara: Price (1978)
Proto-Panoan: Shell (1965)
Proto-Pomo: McLendon (1973)
Proto-Siouan: Wolff (1950–51)
Proto-Tacanan: Girard (1971)
Proto-Tupi: Lemle (1971)
Proto-Yokuts: Pitkin & Shipley (1958)
Proto-Yuman: Langdon (1979)

Other reconstructed forms are cited either by the author's name or by the following abbreviations: Oto-Mangue, R, Rensch (1976); Uto-Aztecan, M, Miller (1967); Azteco-Tanoan, WT, Whorf & Trager (1937); Proto-Siouan, C, Chafe (1964); Proto-Siouan, M, Matthews (1958).

1 ABOVE₁

Macro-Ge HEAD. Chiquito *ta, ita* 'top of.' Fulnio *etai* 'on top.'
Mashakali: Monosho *toi.*

Macro-Carib HEAD. Andoke *tai.* Uitoto *aite* 'high' (Kinder), *aise* 'high'
(Las Cortes). Yagua: Peba *saj* 'head, hair.'

Chibchan-Paezan ABOVE. Barbacoa: Colorado *du* 'hill.' Choco: Chami
itare, Catio *utu* 'peak.' Malibu: Chimila *itta, ita* 'heaven.' Motilon *adu*
'high.' Paez *ete.* Warrau *(j)ata.*

Cf. HEAD₂. The relationship between these two etymologies may be the
same as in ABOVE₂, which has forms with and without *-k.* This *k* may
be an old locative.

2 ABOVE₂

Macro-Ge ABOVE. Botocudo *pok, pawi* 'high.' Chiquito *ape, j-aapi* 'up,'
ape-z 'heaven.' Fulnio *efua, fua, foa* 'hill.' Mashakali *apoxo, pokox*
'heaven,' *pæpii* 'up.' Opaie *pi* 'heaven.'

Macro-Panoan ABOVE. Mataco: Chulupi *apee* 'action above' (Susnik
1968: 48), Mataco *-pe, pa.* Moseten *fan(-če)* (*-če* is a locative marker,
cf. *tas-če* 'in front of'). Panoan: Panobo *buespa,* Shipibo *bušiki,*
Mayoruna *abo* 'heaven.' Tacanan: Proto-Tacanan **ba.*

Macro-Carib ABOVE. Carib: Macusi *-epoi,* Trio *epoe,* Wayana *-po,* etc.
Uitoto: Uitoto *afei-ne* (cf. *tuiri-ne* 'below'), Muinane *ipo* 'head,'
Ocaina *ooʔfo* 'head.'

Macro-Tucanoan ABOVE. Huari: Huari *ananu-pui* 'heaven.' Iranshe *poku*
'go up.' Puinave: Papury *poχ* 'above, heaven,' Hubde *po* 'sky,' Tiquie
bui. Tucano: Tucano *bui,* Waikina *pui* 'upon,' Coreguaje *suka-pue*
'heaven,' etc.

Chibchan-Paezan ABOVE. Barbacoa: Cayapa *faka,* Colorado *feeči.* Chimu:
Eten *fok* 'upward.' Choco: Empera *baxa* 'heaven,' Saija *paxa* 'heaven.'
Jirajara: Jirajara *pok* 'hill.' Timucua *abo.* (P)

Hokan ABOVE. Jicaque *-pʰuk.* Salinan: San Miguel *oːpʰak.* Tequistlatec
-hwak.

Penutian ABOVE. California: Wintun *pʰoj* 'head.' Gulf: Chitimacha *pek-,*
pokta 'heaven, cloud'; Natchez *aboː* 'head'; Muskogean: Chickasaw
paknaʔ 'top,' Choctaw *pakna, aba* 'up, high, heaven,' Koasati *aba* 'up.'
Oregon: Kalapuya *am-efo* 'mountain.' Tsimshian *bax* 'up.'

Almosan-Keresiouan ABOVE. Algic: Algonquian: Proto-Algonquian
(Haas) *umpi 'high,' Arapaho api 'stand up,' -ap 'standing.' Caddoan:
Pawnee pe 'erect, but humped.' Mosan: Wakashan: Nootka -api 'up in
the air, erect, standing.' Siouan-Yuchi: Siouan: Ofo iphi, Hidatsa apahi
'heaven,' Catawba haap, [wahpee] 'sky' (Gallatin 1836); Yuchi pe.

3 ABOVE₃

Equatorial ABOVE. Jibaro: Shuara arak 'higher,' Upano arakani. Kariri:
Dzubucua arake 'heaven,' Kamaru arakie, aranče.

Andean ABOVE. Alakaluf: Alakaluf arka(u), Kaueskar arqa-tal, arqa-tas
'above, on top.' Aymara arqa, arja. Patagon: Ona ink. Quechua:
Santiagueño orqo 'mountain,' Cochabamba orqo 'hill.'

4 ANGRY

Macro-Carib ANGRY. Carib: Surinam erexko 'be angry,' Waiwai riwo,
Trio əire 'fierce.' Uitoto: Uitoto riie, Muinane riino 'strong.'

Chibchan-Paezan ANGRY. Allentiac: Millcayac irrim. Chimu iri 'be
afraid.' Itonama jari-ʔna 'be angry.' Rama juli-ni 'anger.' Warrau jari.
Timucua juru 'be angry, afraid.'

5 ANT₁

Equatorial ANT. Trumai taj. Tupi: Guaraní tahii, Guayaki taie.

Macro-Tucanoan ANT. Capixana tij. Huari: Masaka di:. Mobima tuwe.
Puinave: Nadobo atⁱoho, Querari (n)dury(e)e.

Chibchan-Paezan ANT. Aruak: Kagaba isa, Atanque iče, Bintucua izø.
Chibcha: Chibcha [ize]. Guaymi: Gualaca is. Lenca: Guajiquero
sizi, Chilanga tˢʼitˢʼi. Talamanca: Terraba son-gwo, Bribri tˢa(-vak),
ša(-vak), etc. (C)

6 ANT₂

Andean ANT. Quechua: Cochabamba čʰaka. Patagon: Tehuelche čakon.

Penutian ANT. Gulf: Atakapa tˢak; Muskogean: Choctaw šúkani. Mexican:
Mixe-Zoque: Tetontepec tˢokun; Huave čok; Totonac: Papantla čakan.
Oregon: Siuslaw tˢaʔkʾitˢ.

Additional: Uto-Aztecan: M 5 (no reconstruction), Tarahumara sikuwi,
Varohio sekwi, Mejicano Azteco aaska-t.

7 ARM₁

Macro-Ge ARM.   Chiquito *i-pa*. Erikbatsa *-čipa*. Ge: Proto-Ge **pa*. Guato *(ma-)po*. Kaingan: Apucarana *pe*, Tibagi *pen*. Opaie *(či-)pe*.

Macro-Panoan ARM.   Charruan: Charrua *is-bax*. Guaicuru: Toba *apige*, Mocovi *ava*. Mataco: Payagua *iva(-čaga)* 'shoulder.' Moseten *bibi* 'elbow.' Panoan: Cashibo *ba-* 'elbow' (instrumental prefix), *baboṣo* 'elbow,' Chacobo *baṣ-* 'elbow, forearm' (instrumental prefix). Tacanan: Proto-Tacanan **bai*.

Macro-Carib ARM.   Carib: Surinam *apo:-ri*, Tamanaco *j-apa-ri*, Pauishana *j-ape*, etc. Uitoto: Coeruna *ko-ipai*.

Equatorial HAND.   Guahibo *-pi*. Kariri: Dzubucua, Kamaru *bo* 'arm.' Maipuran: Amuesha *apa* 'give,' Apolista *apaj* 'give,' Baure *(ni-)po* 'I give,' Toyeri *mpe, upi* 'arm.' Tupi: Proto-Tupi **po*. Yuracare *popo*.

Andean HAND.   Culli *pui*. Itucale *bixi, bihi*. Kahuapana: Jebero *-pi* 'action with palm.' Leco *bueu, biui* 'finger.' Patagon: Tehuelche *paje*. Sabela: Auca *po* 'hand, times.'

Chibchan-Paezan ARM.   Barbacoa: Cayapa *pexpex*. Choco: Waunana *piu*. Cuitlatec *pəja, poxja*. Jirajara: Ayoman *apa(-pušan)*. Mura: Mura *apixi, apiæ*, Matanawi *api-ji*. Xinca: Yupultepec *pu* 'arm, hand,' Jutiapa *paxa*, Chiquimulilla *pux* 'hand.' Yanoama (general) *poko*.

Hokan ARM.   Chimariko *tanpu*. Chumash (general) *pu*. Salinan: San Antonio *puku*. Shasta *ʔa:pxujʔ* 'shoulder.' Subtiaba: Subtiaba *paxpu*, Tlappanec *pahpu*.

8 ARM₂

Penutian ARM.   Gulf: Atakapa *nokʔ* 'arm, wing'; Muskogean: Creek *enke:* 'hand.' Plateau: Nez Perce *nik:-* 'hand' (instrumental prefix). Tsimshian: Nass *næiq* 'fin.' Yukian: Wappo *nɔkʔo* (Radin), *nokʰa* (Sawyer) 'armpit.'

Almosan-Keresiouan ARM.   Algic: Algonquian: Proto-Algonquian **nexkee*, Northern Arapaho *nes*, Shawnee *neʔki;* Yurok *-rkow* 'armpit.' Iroquoian: Cherokee *-noge*, Seneca *nēša*, Mohawk *nɔ̃č*, etc. Mosan: Chemakuan: Chemakum, Quileute *(hii-)naq(-sit);* Salish: Squamish *naqč;* Wakashan: Nootka *nʔokʷ* 'hand,' *inkʷ* 'at, on the hand.'

9 ARRIVE

Macro-Ge ARRIVE.   Erikbatsa *(is-)pik(-maha)*. Ge: Apinage *pok*.
Mashakali: Capoxo *abuj* 'come!,' Macuni *abuih* 'come here!'
Macro-Carib COME.   Carib: Barama River *pui* (sing. subject), Galibi
obwi, Cumanogoto *epu*, etc. Uitoto *bi*.
Hokan COME.   Karok *ʔip*. Maratino *apam* 'walk.' Seri *ifp*. Tequistlatec
paʔpa. Washo *ibi*. Yuman: Mohave *obi, opi* 'return,' Kiliwa *pija*.
Yurumangui *ipi, opi* 'come, go.'

10 ARROW

Macro-Ge ARROW.   Opaie *māa, māe*. Yabuti: Mashubi *mu*.
Macro-Tucanoan THORN.   Iranshe *amiuʔu*. Puinave: Papury, Tiquie *mu*
'arrow.' Tucano: Siona *mio*, Pioje *miu-ñangka*.
Almosan-Keresiouan ARROW.   Caddoan: Caddo *baʔ*. Kutenai *wo* 'bow.'
Mosan: Chemakuan: Quileute *pa* 'bow.' Siouan-Yuchi: Siouan: Proto-
Siouan *mā*.

11 ASHES

Macro-Ge ASHES.   Botocudo pram 'charcoal.' Caraja *bri(-bɨ)*. Ge: Proto-
Ge *mrɔ(tˢ)*, Krenje *pro*, Cayapo *pra* 'embers.' Guato *(ma-)fora(-ta)* (*ta*
= 'fire'). Kaingan: Apucarana *mreje*, Tibagi *brene, mrene*.
Macro-Panoan ASHES.   Mataco: Mataco *(itax-)mok* 'ashes' (= '[fire-]
powder'), Suhin *mak* 'dust, powder,' Vejoz *muk* 'dust, flour.' Moseten
čim (probably cognate with Tacana *e-timu* in which *ti* = 'fire' and *mu*
< *muru* 'ashes'). Tacanan: Proto-Tacanan *muru*, Chama *kwaki-maxo*
(*kwaki* = 'fire').
Equatorial ASHES.   Esmeralda *(mu-)bul* (*mu* = 'fire'). Jibaro: Aguaruna
pušuĵin. Kandoshi *poša či*. Maipuran: Goajiro *paɾi*, Wapishana,
Carutana *pali*, Toyeri *palo*. Zamuco: Chamacoco *peitˢa*. Cf. Timote:
Timote, Cuica *nabuš*.
Chibchan-Paezan ASHES.   Aruak: Kagaba *muli*, Guamaca *bun*. Chibcha:
Uncasica *bura*. Cuna *puru*. Guaymi: Muoi *mono*. Lenca: Guajiquero
poggo. Malibu: Chimila *mukne*. Motilon: Barira *emukn*. Rama *pluŋ*.
Xinca: Yupultepec *maɬi*, Chiquimulilla *mali*. (C)
Hokan ASHES.   Pomo: Northeast Pomo *mal*. Seri *emaɣ* (Kroeber), *anti-
mak* (Moser) (*anti* = 'earth'). Shasta *ma(h)awa* 'dust, ashes.' Yana

mari-p'a 'covered with ashes.' Yuman: Kiliwa *muwag* 'powder,'
Cocopa *mwa:r* 'powder,' etc.

Penutian ASHES.   California: Wintun *pu:k*. Gulf: Tunica *hahpuši;* Natchez
pokah 'make dusty'; Muskogean: Hitchiti *po:k* 'pulverize,' Choctaw
muki 'smoke, dust.' Mexican: Totonac *pu ʔqš-ni;* Mayan: Proto-Mayan
(C) **po(:)k-os* 'dust,' **poqs* 'dust.'

Almosan-Keresiouan ASHES.   Algic: Algonquian: Proto–Central
Algonquian **penkwi*. Mosan: Chemakuan: Chemakum *pu ʔu:sčʾit,*
Quileute *puxusu*. (AM)

12 ASK₁

Macro-Panoan ASK.   Lengua: Lengua *math-,* Mascoy *matˢ-*. Panoan:
Panobo *mašai* 'pray.'

Macro-Carib WISH.   Bora: Miranya *miče, mejĕ*. Yagua: Yagua *amaseo*
'greedy,' Yameo *basei*.

Andean ASK.   Kahuapana *muča*. Quechua: Santiagueño, Ecuadorean, etc.
maska 'seek.' Yamana: Yahgan *amušu* 'ask for.' Zaparo: Iquito *masəə-
jaa*.

Cf. WISH.

13 ASK₂

Macro-Ge LOVE.   Bororo: Umotina *atabɛ* 'seek.' Mashakali: Capoxo
(ma-)tema 'pleasure.' Puri: Puri *tamathi,* Coroado *tima*.

Equatorial WISH.   Cayuvava *dopa*. Guahibo *itomba* 'I wish.' Maipuran:
Baniva *nu-sapeta* 'I wish,' Bare *sambi*. Piaroa: Saliba *ka-indapi* 'seek.'

Additional: Uto-Aztecan: M 12 **tep* 'ask.'

14 AUNT

Macro-Panoan AUNT.   Mataco: Macca *nana* 'mother.' Tacanan: Proto-
Tacanan **nene*. Vilela *nana, nane* 'mother.'

Equatorial AUNT.   Guahibo *ena* 'mother.' Kariri *aña*. Kandoshi *aniari*
'mother.'

Macro-Tucanoan AUNT.   Auake *anaiʔo*. Catuquina *inai*. Kaliana *īnoī*
'grandmother.' Maku *nō* 'mother, aunt.' Nambikwara: Sabane *nau*
'mother,' Mamainde *nat* 'mother.' Puinave: Puinave *aiña,* Querari *nã*
'mother.' Ticuna *ngeʔe, niai* 'woman.' Yuri *wine, aino* 'female.' Cf.
Mobima *-ne* ~ *-ni,* feminine affix.

Central Amerind MOTHER.   Oto-Mangue: R 350 *(n)(ʔ)na(h)(n) 'mother,
woman.' Uto-Aztecan: M 472b *na.

Almosan-Keresiouan MOTHER.   Algic: Algonquian: Gros Ventre -inā,
Blackfoot naʔa. Caddoan: Caddo ʔi-naʔ 'my mother,' Wichita (ati-)naʔ
'my mother.' Iroquoian: Huron anan 'aunt.' Siouan-Yuchi: Siouan:
Biloxi ōni 'aunt,' Ofo ina 'aunt,' Osage ina 'aunt.'

15 BACK₁ (n.)

Macro-Panoan BACK.   Mataco: Choroti keji. Moseten eki 'behind,' kai
'kidney.' Panoan: Cashinahua ka- 'spine,' Cashibo, Chacobo ka-.
Tacanan: Huarayo ekia 'bird's tail.'

Macro-Carib TAIL.   Carib: Macusi -akə, Pauishana axke. Uitoto kaj.

Almosan-Keresiouan BACK.   Algic: Algonquian: Blackfoot -ik. Mosan:
Wakashan: Kwakiutl -igʲ-; Salish: Thompson -ik(-ən), Tillamook
-ič(-ən), etc. (-ən is a body-part suffix). (AM)

16 BACK₂ (n.)

Macro-Ge SHOULDER.   Bororo kana 'wing, upper arm.' Botocudo
knão,kinaon. Opaie (či-)kā.

Equatorial ARM.   Maipuran: Piro, Paresi kano, Canamari kano 'shoulder.'
Uro: Chipaya kʔara 'hand, arm,' Caranga kˣara 'hand.' (A)

Penutian BACK.   California: Miwok: Central Sierra kinatta 'buttocks' (but
kinat 'defecate'). Gulf: Atakapa hal. Oregon: Yakonan xuntˢ. Plateau:
Nez Perce he:lex. Yukian: Wappo han 'behind.'

17 BAD₁

Macro-Ge BAD.   Botocudo eklek 'ugly,' krang 'hateful.' Kaingan: Tibagi
kore, Palmas korende.

Hokan BAD.   Chimariko xuli. Karok: Karok ka:rim, Arra-Arra karip.
Tonkawa kalan 'curser.' Yuman: Yavapai kalepi, Campo kaʎev.

Cf. BLACK₂.

18 BAD₂

Macro-Panoan BAD.   Mataco: Towothli oɬak, Payagua ɬak 'ugly,' Macca
usax. Moseten seki. Panoan: Chacobo šikɨ, Capanahua šakabo,
Cashinahua čakabo. Tacanan: Tacana čiki 'plague.'

Almosan-Keresiouan BAD.   Algic: Wiyot: Wiyot, Wishosk saks. Kutenai

sahan. Mosan: Wakashan: Bella Bella *sχ.* Siouan-Yuchi: Siouan:
Assiniboin *čexi,* Mandan *xik,* Winnebago *šišika,* Dakota *šiča.*

19 BARK (n.)

Equatorial SKIN.   Chapacura: Quitemo *pari-če,* Tora *tu-para.* Guahibo:
Guahibo *pera-bo,* Cuiva *pera-i.* Kariri *buro* 'bark.' Maipuran: Karif
bura. Otomaco *ae-par.* Tupi: Guaraní *pire,* Sheta *ipire,* etc. Yuracare
pele.
Hokan SKIN.   Jicaque *pʰolok.* Tequistlatec *-bił.*

20 BATHE

Macro-Tucanoan SWIM.   Kaliana *pə.* Tucano *ba* (general, except in
Western Tucanoan).
Hokan BATHE.   Achomawi: Achomawi *ehpa,* Atsugewi *-ap-* 'swim.'
Chimariko *-xu:-* 'swim.' Karok *ik-puh* 'swim' (sing. subject), *ith-puh*
'swim' (dual subject). Shasta *kʷi:pukʷ* 'swim, bathe.' Tequistlatec
(di-)bo(-ʔma). Yana *puu* 'swim.'
Penutian BATHE.   California: Yokuts *e:pʰi* 'bathe, swim'; Maidu *pe ~ py
~ pi* 'swim'; Miwok: Central Sierra *ʔyp(-šy),* Bodega *pačče* 'rinse.'
Gulf: Atakapa *patˢ* 'wash'; Tunica *ʔahpu;* Chitimacha *ju:pʰ;* Muskogean:
Alabama *abox* 'wash.' Mexican: Mixe-Zoque: Mixe *puh* 'wash'; Mayan:
Tzotzil *pok* 'wash,' Huastec *pakul* 'wash,' Kekchí *pučˀ* 'wash.' Oregon:
Takelma *pˀagai.* Plateau: Klamath *pew* 'bathe, swim.'

21 BE₁

Macro-Ge BE.   Bororo: Umotina *bo.* Kaingan: Tibagi *be* 'happen.'
Kamakan [phuih] 'live.' Puri: Coropo *pa* 'have,' Coroado *baj* 'live.'
Macro-Panoan BE.   Mataco: Vejoz, Choroti *pa* 'sit,' Nocten *papa* 'sit!'
Moseten *bei* 'be, sit, live.' Panoan: Chacobo *ubia* 'there is.' Tacanan:
Chama *baʔe* 'live at, remain.'
Equatorial BE.   Kariri: Dzubucua *pi* 'dwell.' Otomaco: Otomaco *upo*
'live,' Taparita *ipe* 'he is.'

22 BE₂

Andean BE.   Aymara: Jaqaru *uta,* Aymara *utta* 'sit.' Quechua:
Cochabamba, Ecuadorean, etc. *tija.* Zaparo: Zaparo *ta, ata ~ ati,*
Iquito *tə.* Cf. Leco *ten;* Sabela: Tuwituwey *ta* 'stand' (for the semantics
cf. Spanish *estar).*

Chibchan-Paezan BE.   Allentiac *ti* 'have.' Aruak: Kagaba *ta-i, te-i* 'be
in a place,' Guamaca *te*. Barbacoa: Cayapa *ti* 'become,' Colorado *ta*
'have.' Cuitlatec *ahti* 'sit.' Guaymi: Move *ta*. Malibu: Chimila *ate*.
Misumalpan: Cacaopera *da*. Paez: Panikita *to*. Warrau *ta*.

Central Amerind BE.   Kiowa-Tanoan: Kiowa *tʾa* 'stay, live'; Tanoan: Tewa
tha: 'stay, live.' Oto-Mangue: R 69 **(Y)ta(h)(n)* 'be in a place, be
seated.'

Penutian SIT.   California: Miwok: Central Sierra *toʔ(-nge)* 'sit down,'
Northern Sierra *uču* 'stay.' Gulf: Atakapa *to*, Chitimacha *tej* (sing.),
ten (pl.). Mexican: Mixe-Zoque: Sayula *it* 'exist,' Zoque *iht* 'live.'
Oregon: Siuslaw *tai, ti*. Plateau: Klamath *č-* (sing. subject), Lutuami
tˀi. Tsimshian *tʾa*.

Almosan-Keresiouan HAVE.   Algic: Algonquian: Proto–Central
Algonquian **-a:t* 'way of being, character.' Kutenai *-aʔt-*. Mosan:
Chemakuan: Quileute *ti;* Wakashan: Kwakiutl *-ad*. Siouan-Yuchi:
Siouan: Quapaw *ta*, Biloxi *ite*, Mandan *tu* 'be.'

23 BEAR (v.)

Equatorial BEAR.   Tupi: Proto-Tupi **ʔa*. Zamuco: Zamuco *a*, Ayoré *a:*,
Ebidoso *e*.

Macro-Tucanoan BEAR.   Iranshe *ə(pa)*. Ticuna *ʔo* 'bear fruit.'

24 BEARD₁

Equatorial BEARD.   Arawa: Paumari *bodi* 'mouth.' Cayuvava *ra-poto*.
Guahibo *bixi* 'chin.' Tupi: Guajajara *amutai*, Cocama *muta*. Yuracare
pose.

Almosan-Keresiouan BEARD.   Algic: Yurok *-pʾos*. Keresan *-muša-*.
Mosan: Salish: Bella Coola *(sko-)poč*, Shuswap *epeʔs-qn* 'chin,' etc.

Additional: Uto-Aztecan: M 214 'hair, facial.' Miller comments: "It is
difficult to reconstruct a prototype from these words, but perhaps
something like **motˢ, *mos, *mus*."

25 BEARD₂

Macro-Tucanoan BEARD.   Canichana *čaga*. Puinave: Tiquie *čuγn*, Dou
šugn. Cf. Ticuna *čin*.

Andean BEARD.   Alakaluf: Kaueskar *af-sajok*. Aymara: Lupaca *sunkʰa*.
Patagon: Tsoneka *šeken* 'chin,' Tehuelche *a:šg*. Zaparo: Iquito *mo-
šiga*.

Hokan CHIN.   Chimariko *tˢu(-na)*. Chumash: San Luis Obispo *suks* 'beard.' Jicaque *sek*. Karok *šva:k*. Shasta *čˀawa:k* 'chin, jaw.' Tonkawa *taxˀakan* 'chin, jaw.' Yana *dˀawdtˢʼi*. Yuman: Mohave *ja-tukuθa* (*ja* = 'mouth'), Tipai *tekesa*.

26 BEE₁

Macro-Ge HONEY.   Botocudo *pã* 'bee, honey.' Ge: Proto-Ge *meñ 'bee, honey.' Kaingan: Dalbergia *mong*, Palmas *mãng*, etc., all 'bee, honey.' Mashakali: Macuni *pang*. Opaie *peg*.
Macro-Panoan BEE.   Mataco: Vejoz *pinu*, Mataco *apina* 'mosquito,' Choroti *wona* 'wasp.' Panoan: Cashinahua *buna*, Cashibo *wuna* 'honey,' Amahuaca *wina* 'bee, wasp.' Tacanan: Proto-Tacanan *wini 'wax,' Chama *wini* 'bee, honey.'
Andean BEE.   Alakaluf *wilelele* 'fly.' Mayna *wane* 'honey.' Zaparo: Zaparo *iwana* 'honey,' Iquito *iwuana* 'honey.' Yamana *wi:na* 'flies.'

27 BEE₂

Macro-Tucanoan BEE.   Tucano: Sara *momia*, Tucano *mumi*, Wanana *mĩ*, etc. 'bee, honey.' Maku *mime*.
Hokan BEE.   Esselen *mumirux* 'fly' (pl.). Salinan: San Antonio, San Miguel *le-meˀm* 'bee, wasp.'
Penutian BEE.   California: Costanoan: Santa Cruz, etc. *mumuru* 'fly' (pl.); Maidu *amilalu* 'fly.' Gulf: Natchez *mom;* Chitimacha *(hih)mu;* Atakapa *miŋ, muŋ.* Mexican: Huave *muam;* Mixe-Zoque: Tetontepec *omon* 'fly.' Plateau: Klamath *mem*, Molala *mumu-s* 'fly,' Lutuami *maŋk* 'fly.'
Almosan-Keresiouan BEE.   Algic: Algonquian: Proto–Central Algonquian *amoa. Mosan: Chemakuan: Quileute, Chemakum *muumuuma;* Salish: Siciatl *ma:malwe.* (AM)
Additional: Uto-Aztecan: M 31 *mumu, *meme 'bee,' M 180 *mu 'fly.'

28 BEHIND

Macro-Panoan BEHIND.   Guaicuru: Toba-Guazu *vi* 'back, side.' Lule *va*. Mataco: Choroti *pe*. Moseten *abia* 'afterward.' Tacanan: Tacana *be-* 'back.'
Central Amerind BEHIND.   Kiowa-Tanoan: Tewa *pu*. Uto-Aztecan: M 17 *pi.
Hokan TAIL.   Achomawi *ippi*. Comecrudo *ep*. Karok *apvu:j*. Pomo:

190

Kashaya *hiba*, Central Pomo, Southeast Pomo *ba*. Quinigua *apino*
'deer's tail.' Seri *ʔiip*. Tequistlatec *ifpo*. Washo *apʼil*.

29 BELLY₁

Macro-Ge BELLY.   Erikbatsa *kaše*. Ge: Geico *aejussi* 'breast.' Mashakali:
    Macuni *inkiča* 'heart,' Malali *akešo* 'heart.' Puri: Coropo *kše* 'inside.'
Macro-Panoan HEART.   Guaicuru: Pilaga *kiikate*, Toba-Guazu *kidiakate*.
    Mataco: Chulupi *kači*. Moseten *koči*. Vilela *gose*.
Equatorial BELLY.   Chapacura *ketet* 'bosom.' Guahibo *pe-kototo*, *koto*
    'abdomen.' Maipuran: Karutana *kuta* 'chest,' Chiriana *kuda* 'chest.'
    Piaroa: Saliba *iktebo* 'intestines,' *iktego* 'guts.' Timote: Mocochi *kito*.
    Uro *keto*. Zamuco: Ebidoso *xoto*.
Macro-Tucanoan BELLY.   Maku *gote*. Tucano: Erulia, Tsoloa, Palanoa
    geda, Siona *kata-mea* 'guts' (*mea* = 'rope').

30 BELLY₂

Macro-Ge BELLY.   Bororo: Umotina *upuru* 'thorax.' Fulnio *epatio* 'upper
    abdomen.' Ge: Apinage *pitãn* 'body,' Crengez *patu* 'belly, chest.'
    Kaingan: Serra do Chagu *(idfe-)paro* 'chest.' Puri: Coroado *puara*
    'chest.'
Equatorial NAVEL.   Kariri *biro* 'belly.' Maipuran: Passe *pori*, Siusi *pure*,
    Karif *bare*, Uainuma *pare* 'heart.' Tupi: Shipaya *parua* 'belly,' Arikem
    pera, Guayaki *punua*, *purua*, etc.
Macro-Tucanoan BELLY.   Nambikwara: Proto-Nambikwara **pil* 'liver.'
    Puinave: Tiquie *pedn*. Tucano: Wanana *paro*, Desana *paru*.
Andean GUTS.   Araucanian *ponon* 'lungs.' Patagon: Ona *panhe*, *pahank*.
    (S)
Chibchan-Paezan BELLY.   Guaymi: Move *bule*. Itonama *uh-bunu*
    'abdomen.' Lenca: Guajıquero *palan* 'chest.' Malibu: Chimila *muuna*
    'chest.' Misumalpan: Miskito *biara*. Warrau *obono*. Yanoama:
    Yanomamï *bariki* 'chest,' Yanam, Yanomam *parɨk* 'chest.'
Penutian BELLY.   Chinook *wan*. Mexican: Totonac *paan;* Mayan:
    Kakchiquel *pan*, Pokomchi *pam*. Oregon: Takelma *pʼa:n* 'liver.'
    Plateau: Klamath *balla* 'liver.' Tsimshian *ban*. Zuni *pali* 'liver.'
Almosan-Keresiouan BELLY.   Algic: Algonquian: Shawnee *apani* 'lungs.'
    Caddoan: Caddo [ben-no], *da-bina*. Mosan: Salish: Columbian *pənink*.
    Siouan-Yuchi: Siouan: Catawba *-pā*.

31 BELLY₃

Macro-Carib CHEST.   Carib: Palmella *mate* 'chest, breast,' Cumanogoto *matir,* Tamanaco *matiri.* Yagua *mtʲa.*

Equatorial BELLY.   Katembri *mudo.* Kariri: Dzubucua *mudu.* Tupi: Digüt *bata, mata* 'chest.' Zamuco: Tumraha *pa-mat.*

Andean BELLY.   Aymara *murka* 'rectum.' Itucale *maudi.* Kahuapana: Kahuapana *møtpɯ, mørpi,* Jebero *mørpi.* Mayna *(ana-)muto* 'navel.' Zaparo: Zaparo *marama,* Arabela *marata.*

32 BELLY₄

Macro-Ge BELLY.   Fulnio *diua* 'intestines.' Ge: Krenje *tu,* Suya *tiu,* Cayapo *tu.* Kaingan: Dalbergia *du, dun,* Guarapurava *indu* 'stomach.' Mashakali: Patasho *e-tæ.* Opaie *(či-)ta* 'chest, belly.' Oti *etiu.*

Macro-Panoan INSIDE.   Guaicuru: Komlek *-tovi* 'chest,' Mocovi [otogue] *otowe* 'chest.' Mataco: Choroti *teowe,* Towothli *-towi* 'inside, belly.' Tacanan: Proto-Tacanan **du-* 'inside, deep.'

Macro-Carib BELLY.   Carib: Nahugua *utevui,* Maiongom *ido-re* 'chest,' Galibi *ida, eta* 'inside.' Uitoto: Nonuya [odoh].

Central Amerind BELLY.   Oto-Mangue: R 81 **tuʔ* 'breast, milk.' Uto-Aztecan: M 417 **to* 'stomach.'

33 BITE₁ (v.)

Macro-Ge EAT.   Bororo *kø.* Caraja *ki.* Ge: Proto-Ge **ku, *kur.* Kaingan *ko.* Kamakan: Cotoxo, Meniens *kua.* Yabuti: Mashubi *ko, či-koko* 'bite.'

Macro-Panoan EAT.   Guaicuru: Guachi *iik,* Mocovi *kee,* Abipone *l-aka* 'food.' Lule *kai.* Mataco: Choroti *okie* 'bite,' Vejoz *okua* 'bite.' Panoan: Cashibo *ko,* Cashinahua, Marinahua *kɨju* 'bite,' Caripuna *kɨ* 'bite.' Tacanan: Proto-Tacanan **ika, *ikia* 'eat, bite.'

Macro-Carib EAT.   Bora: Miranya *me-ikoi* 'bite.' Carib: Surinam *e:ka,* Taulipang *eku,* Waiwai *oku* 'eat bread.' Uitoto: Uitoto *eka* 'feed,' *kai* 'to gnaw,' Muinane *eka* 'feed,' Ocaina *ʔooxo, oxooxa* 'food.'

Macro-Tucanoan BITE.   Auake *ake* 'tooth.' Auixiri *aka* 'tooth.' Catuquina *he, hi* 'tooth.' Huari: Masaka *kaukæwi.* Iranshe *kāka.* Kaliana *ka* 'tooth.' Mobima *kaiki* 'eat.' Puinave: Papury *koχjøi,* Puinave *ko(e)hei.* Tucano: Coto *uxe* 'tooth.' Cf. Ticuna *či* 'sting.'

Andean BITE.   Aymara: Jaqaru *aka*. Itucale *ki* 'eat.' Kahuapana *kaki* 'eat.'
Sabela *kǣi* 'bite!,' *-ga* 'tooth.' Zaparo: Iquito *ka* 'tooth.'
Chibchan-Paezan BITE.   Aruak: Guamaca *kaka* 'tooth.' Betoi *xoki* 'tooth.'
Chibcha: Chibcha *ka* 'eat,' Margua *ko* 'eat.' Choco: Catio, Saija *ko*
'eat.' Cuitlatec *ehka*. Malibu: Chimila *koko* 'swallow.' Misumalpan:
Sumu, Matagalpa *ka*. Motilon: Dobocubi *ko,koa* 'food.' Mura: Mura
kau(-assa) 'eat.' Paez *koja* 'food.' Paya *ki:* 'tooth.' Rama: Guatuso *oka*
'teeth.' Talamanca: Bribri *iku*, Chiripo, Estrella, etc. *ka* 'tooth.'
Timucua *ukwa* 'eat.' Yanoama (general) *koa* 'drink.'
Central Amerind BITE.   Kiowa-Tanoan: Kiowa *kʼɔ*. Oto-Mangue: R 132
*ku 'swallow, stomach, bite.' Uto-Aztecan: M 152d **ku, *ko* 'eat,' M
84 **ko* 'chew.' Cf. Kiowa-Tanoan: Kiowa *kʼɔ* 'knife'; Tanoan: Jemez *kʼi*
'sharp.'
Penutian BITE.   California: Miwok: Bodega *kawwu;* Costanoan: Rumsien
ka 'eat.' Mexican: Mayan: Yucatec *ko* 'tooth,' Quiché *ka* 'tooth.'
Plateau: Klamath *gʷ-*. Tsimshian *qʼai*.
Almosan-Keresiouan BITE.   Iroquoian: Mohawk, Oneida *k-* 'eat.' Keresan:
Santa Ana *kʊ*. Kutenai *-χa-* 'action with teeth.' Mosan: Wakashan:
Kwakiutl *-(s)xʲa* 'tooth' (*-s-* only after vowels).

34 BITE₂ (v.)

Macro-Panoan BITE.   Lengua: Kaskiha *-takse-*. Mataco: Choroti *-tek*
'prick,' Vejoz *čak* 'stab.' Moseten *itˤaksi*. Panoan: Panobo *tuku-i*
'chew.' Tacanan: Proto-Tacanan **tekwa* 'pierce, kill.'
Macro-Tucanoan TOOTH.   Koaia *toko* 'tongue, tooth.' Puinave: Curiariai
taki, Marahan *tog*, Parana Boaboa *i-tig*. Yuri *ča-tikou* (Wallace), *su-
seko* (Spix).

35 BITTER₁

Macro-Ge BITTER.   Bororo *pogo-ddo* 'sour.' Chiquito *piča-ka-s* (n.).
Macro-Panoan BITTER.   Moseten *bikka*. Panoan: Proto-Panoan **moka*,
Shipibo *pag* 'sour.' Tacanan: Proto-Tacanan **patˤe*.
Andean ROTTEN.   Alakaluf *paskešše*. Aymara *pokʼota* 'ripe.' Patagon:
Tehuelche *poskš* 'to rot.' Quechua: Santiagueño *pošqo* 'become rotten.'
Zaparo *upaka* 'ripe.'
Chibchan-Paezan SOUR.   Aruak: Atanque *pøganjia* 'bitter.' Atacama
pučkʼur. Chibcha: Manare *pasi-gui* 'sweet.' Chimu: Chimu *pol*

'spleen,' Eten *poj* 'spleen.' Cuitlatec *behči.* Lenca: Guajiquero *pasa* 'bitter,' Membreno *posina* 'bitter.' Paez *pos.* Rama *pakaska* 'bitter.' Talamanca: Borunca *baaka* 'bitter.'

Hokan RIPE. Tequistlatec *imagi.* Yuman: Maricopa, Walapai *mak,* Havasupai *ma:ka,* Yavapai *ma:,* etc.

Penutian SOUR. Plateau: Klamath *m²eq²* (v.). Tsimshian: Nass *mæx.*

Almosan-Keresiouan BITTER. Mosan: Wakashan: Kwakiutl *p²eq* 'rotten,' Bella Bella *p²eqa* 'rotten'; Salish: Musqueam *məsən* 'gall, rotten.' Siouan-Yuchi: Siouan: Proto-Siouan **p²a,* Biloxi *paxka* 'sour'; Yuchi *paka.*

36 BITTER₂

Chibchan-Paezan BITTER. Barbacoa: Cayapa *sa,* Colorado *sā(-ba).* Chimu: Eten *tˢaj.* Choco: Catio *sa, ča* 'sour.' (P)

Central Amerind BITTER. Kiowa-Tanoan: Tanoan: Hopi Tewa *sɛ:,* Tewa *sǽ* 'taste hot.' Oto-Mangue: R 298 **(H)saH* 'chili pepper.'

37 BLACK₁

Macro-Tucanoan BLACK. Capixana *vorone, woronæræ.* Gamella *katu-braho* 'Negro' (*katu* = 'man'). Huari: Masaka *wiʔri.*

Andean BLACK. Alakaluf *pal.* Araucanian *pun* 'night.' Kahuapana: Kahuapana *øk-piʎi* 'night,' Jebero *ðək-piʎ* 'night,' *-wiʎi* 'action at night.' Patagon: Patagon *apula* 'night,' Tehuelche *pulnek, epoln,* Ona *parn.*

Hokan BLACK. Comecrudo *pal.* Karankawa *pal.* Quinigua *pan.* Seri *ko-opoł.* Yana *pal.* Yuman: Tipai *palsaṭ* 'charcoal.'

Penutian BLACK. California: Miwok: Central Sierra *moli* 'shade,' Miwok: Lake *mulumulu.* Gulf: Atakapa *mel;* Tunica *meli.* Mexican: Huave *mbeor.* Tsimshian *metᶥkʷ* 'shade.'

38 BLACK₂

Macro-Ge BLACK. Bororo *čoreu.* Fulnio *klai.* Ge: Cherente *kran,* Cayapo *kotu.* Kamakan: Kamakan *kuada,* Meniens *koata* 'black man.' Opaie *kāora, kōra, ōkaorae.*

Macro-Panoan BLACK. Lule [cele]. Mataco: Mataco *čalax,* Vejoz *čalax* 'blue.'

Andean BLACK. Alakaluf *tirre-kal, hakar* 'dark, black.' Araucanian *kuru.* Aymara: Lupaca *č²iara,* Jaqaru *tˢ²irara.* Cholona *čal.* Gennaken *ačula.*

Kahuapana *peñ-akiʎa* 'charcoal' (*peñ* = 'fire'). Patagon: Ona *kar*
'charcoal.' Quechua: Santiagueno *kiʎu* 'firebrand.' Cf. Yamana: Yahgan
lakar 'night.'

Hokan DARK.   Karok *ikxaram* 'night,' *ikxurara* 'evening.' Subtiaba:
Tlappanec *kina* 'dark, night.' Yana: North Yana *xal . . . lu*, Yahi *xamlu*
'pitch dark.' Yuman: Tipai *xunn.*

Almosan-Keresiouan DARK.   Algic: Wiyot *kʰuʔn* 'get dark,' *kunar* 'be
dark.' Caddoan: Wichita *ka:rʔi* 'black.' Iroquoian: Mohawk *akara.*
Mosan: Salish: Squamish *ginqnʔxni;* Wakashan: Kwakiutl *kʲanut^l*
'night.' Siouan-Yuchi: Siouan: Catawba *kare.*

Cf. BAD₁.

39 BLACK₃

Macro-Ge GREEN.   Caraja *uitira* 'green, blue.' Fulnio *čičia* 'black.' Ge:
Krenje *teted* (v.), Crengez *ntetete.* Kaingan: Dalbergia *či* 'dark brown.'
Kamakan: Kamakan *hittu*, Cotoxo *itił.*

Equatorial BLACK.   Otomaco *teoteo.* Piaroa: Saliba *tanda.* Taruma *daitwi-k*
'blue.' Trumai *date.* Tupi: Manitsawa *diadia.* Yaruro *tottua* 'blue.'
Zamuco *utata* 'black, dark.'

Macro-Tucanoan BLACK.   Huari *ǰyǰyi.* Kaliana *čāē.* Puinave: Curiariai
ča, Dou *čawa*, Puinave *tetaa*, Querari *tetāu* 'black, charcoal,' Tiquie
d(ə)u 'charcoal' (*toa* = 'fire'). Tucano: Hehenawa *toa-teči* 'charcoal'
(*toa* = 'fire'). Yuri *čuhi, suj, tuji.*

Central Amerind BLACK.   Kiowa-Tanoan: Kiowa *to(-e-gja)* 'blind';
Tanoan: Jemez *ⁿdahu*, San Ildefonso *nakʰū* 'night, darkness.' Oto-
Mangue: R 94 *(n)(h)tu(h)(n)* 'black, soot, dark, blind.' Uto-Aztecan:
M 45a *tu*, *tuhu*, M 45b *tuk* 'night.'

Hokan BLACK.   Jicaque *te.* Subtiaba *ida(-gina).*

40 BLOOD₁

Macro-Carib BLOOD.   Carib: Surinam *menu*, Galibi *munu*, Jaricuna
umane, etc. Yagua *mɔna.*

Equatorial BLOOD.   Kariri: Kariri *pri*, Dzubucua *pli.* Tupi: Proto-Tupi
pirang, Guayaki *pira.*

Andean BLOOD.   Aymara *wila.* Leco *bile.* Patagon: Ona *vuar*, [huaarr].

Penutian RED.   Gulf: Tunica *mili.* Oregon: Yakima *mareš*, Takelma *mołit*,
Kalapuya *meenu* 'blood.'

41 BLOOD₂

Macro-Panoan BLOOD.   Lengua *eme.* Panoan: Proto-Panoan **imi.*
Tacanan: Proto-Tacanan **ami.*

Equatorial BLOOD.   Arawa: Yamamadi, etc. *ama.* Chapacura: Itene
mem-je, memena 'red,' Tora *memnu* 'red.' Maipuran: Palicur *omi-ra,*
Wachipairi, Toyeri *mimi.* Otomaco: Otomaco, Taparita *imma.* (MA)

Macro-Tucanoan BLOOD.   Catuquina [mimy]. Iranshe *mĩʔĩ.* Maku *tabe-memu* 'sap' (*tabe* = 'tree'). Puinave: Puinave *ãmã,* Querari *mē* 'red.'
Tucano: Amaguaje, Coto *ma* 'red.' Cf. Southern Nambikwara *ja:mija.*

Chibchan-Paezan BLOOD.   Aruak: Kagaba *abi.* Chibcha: Chibcha *yba;*
Margua, Tegria, Boncota, Manare *aba.* Cuna *api.* Guaymi: Chumulu
have. Motilon *abi.* Mura: Mura *be,* Matanawi *mĩ.* Paez *be* 'red.'
Talamanca: Bribri *pe,* Chiripo *api.*

Central Amerind BLOOD.   Kiowa-Tanoan: Kiowa *ʔõ-m;* Tanoan: Santa
Clara *ũʔ,* Jemez *ʔĩ,* Isleta *ũa.* Oto-Mangue: R 371 **we* 'red.' Uto-
Aztecan: M 47b **ʔew* (with note "perhaps better **ʔem*").

Almosan-Keresiouan BLOOD.   Algic: Algonquian: Arapaho *beʔ, ba,*
Cheyenne *mae.* Caddoan: Caddo *bahʔuh.* Siouan-Yuchi: Siouan:
Dakota *we,* Tutelo *waji, waʔih.*

42 BLOW (v.)

Macro-Ge BLOW.   Botocudo *paori* 'air.' Mashakali: Macuni *paepi* 'wind,'
Capoxo *abu* 'wind.' Puri: Coroado *pui.*

Macro-Panoan BLOW.   Lule *pʰu.* Mataco: Mataco *fwo* 'wind blows,' Suhin
fuji. Moseten *fifi.* Panoan: Proto-Panoan **paja* 'to fan.' Tacanan: Proto-
Tacanan **pei.*

Central Amerind BLOW.   Kiowa-Tanoan: Kiowa *pʰo(-le);* Tanoan: Jemez
ɸo(-se). Uto-Aztecan: M 49a **putˢ,* M 49b **puhi.* Azteco-Tanoan: WT
45 **pʰu.*

Penutian BLOW.   California: Miwok: Central Sierra *puše:l;* Maidu *pɨ.*
Oregon: Alsea *pu,* Coos *pəš.* Tsimshian *pu.*

43 BODY₁

Macro-Ge BELLY.   Bororo: Bororo *uabo* 'heart,' Umotina *uapo* 'heart.'
Chiquito *po.* Ge: Geico *aepu,* Chavante *(im-)pa* 'guts.' Guato *ipo.*
Kaingan: Palmas, Tibagi, Guarapuava *fe* 'heart.'

Macro-Carib BODY.   Bora: Imihita *(mex-)pi.* Uitoto: Muinane *abɨ.*

Andean BODY.   Kahuapana: Jebero *pi*. Mayna *pa* 'skin.' Yamana: Yamana *api* 'body, skin,' Yahgan *api*.

Central Amerind MEAT.   Kiowa-Tanoan: Tanoan: Hopi Tewa *pivih*, San Ildefonso *piβi*. Oto-Mangue: R 153 *k^we* 'meat, body.'

Hokan FAT.   Achomawi *ipħa:w* (adj.). Chimariko *phi:ʔa* (n.). Pomo: North Pomo *pu:i:* 'be greasy.' Salinan: San Miguel *upi(-nit)* (n.). Yana *pʰuih* 'be fat.'

Penutian MEAT.   Oregon: Takelma *pʾiji-n* 'deer.' Yukian: Wappo *pʾih* 'be fat,' *piʔɛ* 'fat' (adj.).

44 BODY₂

Macro-Ge BODY.   Caraja *uma*. Ge: Karaho *am-kahøg* 'animal,' *am-kin* 'harmful animal.' Kaingan: Tibagi *me, mein* 'animal.' Puri *imi*.

Equatorial MEAT.   Arawa: Culino *ime*. Otomaco *aem* 'body.' Yuracare *eme*.

45 BOIL (v.)

Chibchan-Paezan BURN.   Atacama *lokʾ* (intransitive). Itonama *i-lax*. (P)

Hokan COOK.   Subtiaba: Tlappanec *nik* 'burn.' Tonkawa *naxo*.

Penutian BOIL.   Gulf: Atakapa *łok;* Chitimacha *lahi* 'burn'; Natchez *luk;* Muskogean: Choctaw *luak*. Mexican: Mayan: Chol *lok*. Oregon: Coos *lo:qʷ*, Siuslaw *laqʷ*, Yakonan *tʾq-*. Plateau: Klamath *loloq-s* 'fire.' Tsimshian *lak* 'fire.'

46 BONE₁

Macro-Ge BONE.   Caraja *dʕii* (Davis), *te, ti*. Chiquito *tˢii*. Ge: Proto-Ge **zi*, Apinage *ji*, Cayapo, Cherente *hi*. Kaingan: Tibagi, Palmas *hø* 'body.' Kamakan: Cotoxo *huj* 'body.'

Macro-Tucanoan BONE.   Huari: Huari *tu, tˢu*, Masaka *tˢu*. Nambikwara: Proto-Nambikwara **soh*. Cf. Catuquina: Canamari *tˢoampadˢa*.

47 BONE₂

Hokan BONE.   Pomo: Kashaya *ʔihja*, Northeast Pomo *hija*, etc. Salinan: San Antonio *axa:k*, San Miguel *axak*. Seri *itak*. Shasta *ak*. Yuman: Maricopa *ša:k, iša:k*, Akwa'ala *čiaka*, Kiliwa *hak*, Tipai *ʔa:k*, Campo *ʔak*. Cf. Karok *sakri:v* 'hard.'

Penutian DRY.   Gulf: Tunica *sihu;* Atakapa *tˢak;* Natchez *tˢo:x;* Muskogean: Hitchiti *suku:*. Mexican: Mayan: Uspantec *čak-ex*, Kekchí *čeki*, Chol *tixiniš* 'to dry' (transitive), Tzeltal *taki-n.* Tsimshian *ziak* 'become dry.'

Almosan-Keresiouan BONE.   Algic: Algonquian: Proto-Algonquian *oxkani* 'his bone,' Cree *osk-an* (*-an* body-part suffix), Cree *sok* 'strong,' Cheyenne *hekon* 'strong'; Yurok *seki* 'strong,' *sekejow* 'hard.' Keresan: Acoma *(ha:-)ska(-ni),* Santa Ana *(ha:-)sga(-ni).* Siouan-Yuchi: Siouan: Osage *thagi* 'hard,' Hidatsa *tˢoki* 'hard.'

48 BONE₃

Chibchan-Paezan DRY.   Barbacoa: Colorado *fu* 'be dry.' Choco: Chami *pɔɔ.* Mura: Mura *pe(-ase)* 'summer,' Matanawi *api-ranū.* (P)

Hokan BONE.   Karok *ʔipih.* Washo *i:biʔ.*

49 BREAK (v.)

Macro-Carib CUT.   Carib: Chayma *akete,* Surinam *ako:to* 'cut down' etc. Uitoto: Uitoto *kaita,* Uitoto-Kaimo *koaiti,* Muinane *kodʔa.*

Chibchan-Paezan BREAK.   Atacama *kʔura.* Chimu: Eten *korr.* Cuitlatec *kilu.* Misumalpan: Miskito *kilkaja.* Paez *kond* (Paez *nd* < **r).* Warrau *kare.* Yanoama: Shiriana *krɘja.*

Hokan BREAK.   Achomawi *kati.* Karok *ikvit* 'cut.' Seri *k-kašx.* Tonkawa *kesʔatˢe* 'be broken.' Yuman: Yuma *akʲeṭ* 'cut.'

Penutian BREAK.   California: Miwok: Central Sierra *koṭitˢu.* Gulf: Atakapa *ketˢ* (Eastern), *kutˢ* (Western); Tunica *kahču;* Natchez *ketˢ;* Muskogean: Creek *koče,* Hitchiti *kos* 'cut.' Mexican: Mixe-Zoque: Sierra Popoluca *kitʲ;* Mayan: Tzotzil *kʔas,* Mam *kat-um.* Plateau: Klamath *kattʔ* (sing. object). Yukian: Wappo *kʔɛše* 'cut.'

50 BREAST

Macro-Ge INSIDE.   Botocudo *kuā, kuaŋ* 'belly.' Ge: Cayapo *kamaŋ,* Krenje *kamā.* Kaingan: Tibagi *ka, kan,* Palmas *kamme.* Mashakali: Mashakali, Capoxo *it-kematan,* Macuni *i-kematahi,* Patasho *e-kæp.*

Macro-Panoan INSIDE.   Guaicuru: Toba *kom.* Lengua *kañi.* Moseten *kañ* 'in.'

Equatorial BREAST.   Chapacura: Itene *kima,* Tora *ikimā,* etc. Cofan *ixamate* 'chest.' Kariri: Kamaru *kummamang* 'milk.' Maipuran: Machiguenga, Campa *tˢomi.* Piaroa: Piaroa *txu-xkuamū* 'belly,' Saliba *xomexe* 'chest.' Tupi: Proto-Tupi **kam.*

Macro-Tucanoan CHEST.   Canichana *gameni* 'breast.' Kaliana *kamīhī.*

Tucano: Buhagana *egame* 'heart.' Yuri *ču-ukomæ* (Wallace), *su-oyome* (Spix). Cf. Puinave: Hubde *čab* 'chest.'

Andean BELLY.   Cholona *kulu* 'guts.' Kahuapana *ikin-ək* 'middle' (*-ək* is locative). Patagon: Patagon *kim,* Tsoneka *kin.* Yamana *ikimik* 'be inside.'

Hokan BREAST.   Comecrudo *kene* 'chest.' Cotoname *kenam.* Karankawa *kanin.*

Penutian BELLY.   California: Maidu *k^{2}ami.* Gulf: Atakapa *kom, kōp* 'stomach'; Chitimacha *kipi* 'body.' Oregon: Siuslaw *qo:mi,* Yakonan *k^{j}ipl* 'navel.' Zuni *k^{2}o:ppan.*

Almosan-Keresiouan BREAST.   Algic: Algonquian: Cree *na-skikum* 'chest,' Ojibwa *ni-ka:n* 'in front,' Blackfoot *mo-kekin;* Wiyot *k^{w}ar;* Yurok *k^{w}en.* Mosan: Wakashan: Kwakiutl *k^{2}in* 'front of body.' (AM)

51 BRING

Penutian BRING.   California: Yokuts *taxa.* Gulf: Atakapa *tuk.*

Almosan-Keresiouan BRING.   Keresan: Santa Ana *tigu* 'remove' (pl. object). Kutenai *t^{s}ukw-.* Mosan: Wakashan: Bella Bella *tx;* Salish: Lillooet *tukən,* Kalispel *tix^w* 'get.' Siouan-Yuchi: Siouan: Mandan *du-tak* 'take away' (*du-* = 'action with hand').

52 BROAD

Hokan BROAD.   Comecrudo *poskam* 'broad, large.' Esselen *putuki* 'large.' Pomo: North Pomo *bado:* 'flat.' Quinigua *patama.* Seri *k-apt-h* (sing. subject), *k-apt-ałka* (pl. subject). Tequistlatec *spat$^{s?}$.* Yana: North Yana, Yahi *-d^{2}pal* 'flat.' Yuman: Kiliwa *pataj,* Cocopa *putej* 'large.'

Penutian BROAD.   California: Maidu *batbatpe* 'flat, planar.' Gulf: Natchez *^{2}epet, pet* 'spread'; Muskogean: Alabama, Koasati *pat^{h}a.* Mexican: Huave *apal* 'cover.' Tsimshian: Nass *bat^l.*

Almosan-Keresiouan BROAD.   Algic: Wiyot *bel* 'flat, wide'; Yurok *pel, pelin, pleli* (the last two from Kroeber). Mosan: Proto-Salish **pət^l,* **pt^{l}at^l,* **pt^{l}ut^l* (note agreement of Yurok and Salish on partial reduplication). Siouan-Yuchi: Proto-Siouan **pra* 'flat, broad.'

53 BROTHER

Macro-Ge BROTHER.   Botocudo *po.* Kaingan: Palmas *ve* 'sibling,' Tibagi, Guarapurava *ve* 'sister.'

Macro-Panoan BROTHER.   Moseten *voji* 'sister,' *voji-t* 'brother.' Panoan:

Proto-Panoan *poi 'sibling of opposite sex.' Tacanan: Proto-Tacanan
*bu-, *bui, *bue 'son, daughter of mother's sister.'

Macro-Carib BROTHER. Carib: Roucouyenne, Trio pipi, Surinam pɨri
'younger brother,' Hishcariana pepe 'older brother.' Yagua rai-puipuin
'brother' (woman speaking), pwɨ̄ (vocative) (Powlison).

Equatorial BROTHER. Guahibo piauwo. Guamo: San José (di-)pe, Santa
Rosa (di-)pia. Kariri popo 'older brother.' Tupi: Shipaya upa, Oyampi
paa 'older brother.' Yuracare pe 'younger brother.'

Macro-Tucanoan BROTHER. Puinave: Papury pui 'younger brother,'
Tiquie epaja 'brother-in-law' (Koch-Grünberg), pē(-nā) 'brother-in-
law' (Brüzzi). Tucano: Waikina baī(-ga), baū(-ga) 'sister.'

Andean BROTHER. Araucanian peñi. Catacao: Catacao, Colan pua.
Quechua: Chinchaysuyu pani 'sister' (man speaking), Santiagueño
pana 'sister' (man speaking). Sabela: Tuwituwey bibi 'younger
brother.'

Chibchan-Paezan BROTHER. Allentiac pera 'older brother,' piña 'younger
brother.' Choco: Catio amba 'sister.' Guaymi: Chumulu pava.
Misumalpan: Cacaopera pai 'older brother.' Mura: Matanawi upi, opi.
Talamanca: Terraba, Tirub bau 'brother-in-law.' Yanoama: Shiriana aba
'older brother.'

Central Amerind BROTHER. Kiowa-Tanoan: Kiowa pabi; Tanoan: Taos
popo 'older brother,' pʼōj 'younger brother,' Isleta papa 'older brother,'
pʼai 'younger brother,' San Ildefonso pare 'older brother,' etc. Uto-
Aztecan: M 489a *pa 'brother,' M 489b *patʼi 'brother,' M 489c *papi
'older brother,' M 490 *po 'younger brother.'

Hokan BROTHER. Achomawi apo. Salinan: San Miguel ape:u, pepeʔ,
San Antonio peʔ 'older sister.' Shasta ʔapu 'older brother.'

Penutian BROTHER. California: Proto-California Penutian *be: 'older
brother.' Yukian: Wappo ʔepa 'older brother.' Zuni papa 'older
brother.'

Additional: Almosan: Algic: Yurok pa 'brother.'

54 BURN (v.)

Equatorial HOT. Guahibo atahu. Kariri: Dzubucua uduhe. Maipuran:
Wachipairi ta:x, Amarakaeri taʔak 'fire,' Marawa tikiti 'fire,' Campa
taka 'burn,' Baniva adəhe, etc. Piaroa: Piaroa nduae, Saliba duada
'heat.' Timote: Mocochi tˢuhe 'sun.' Zamuco: Tumraha ərehu 'fire,'
Chamacoco ørugu 'fire.'

Macro-Tucanoan BURN. Canichana *čuku, čuko.* Kaliana *djoko.* Natu
tika. Puinave: Nadobo *tøgø,* Querari *təkə(d).* Shukuru *itoka.* Cf.
Muniche *čuse.*

Hokan BURN. Coahuilteco *ti:xam(ko:).* Yuman: Tipai, Akwa'ala *tux,*
Havasupai, Walapai *tuka.*

Penutian COOK. Gulf: Chitimacha *tu:č.* Mexican: Mayan: Huastec *tek²,*
Tzotzil *tok²on* 'cooked,' etc.

Almosan-Keresiouan BURN. Iroquoian: Seneca, Mohawk -*atek-.* Mosan:
Wakashan: Bella Bella *t²i²k²il;* Salish: Shuswap *t²ik* 'fire.' Siouan-
Yuchi: Siouan: Proto-Siouan **arax* (C), **atʰex* ~ **atʰax,* Hidatsa
adaxa.

55 CALL₁ (v.)

Macro-Carib CALL. Carib: Waiwai *añiki,* Hishcariana *añek.* Uitoto *nokoj*
'invite him!'

Andean CRY. Patagon: Manekenkn *uunuk.* Sechura *nik, ñik.* Zaparo
naketa-no.

Penutian CALL. Gulf: Natchez *²inu;* Chitimacha *nuj-t* 'call by name';
Atakapa *eng.* Mexican: Mixe-Zoque: Sierra Popoluca *nəji,* Zoque *nəj.*
Plateau: North Sahaptin *wanik* 'to name.' Tsimshian *wan.*

Additional: Uto-Aztecan: M 432a **niok, *neok²* 'talk.'

56 CALL₂ (v.)

Macro-Panoan SPEAK. Lengua: Mascoy *pawa.* Moseten *peja-ki.*

Andean CALL. Araucanian *pi* 'say, be named.' Sabela: Auca *pe.*
Zaparo *pi.*

Chibchan-Paezan CALL. Andaqui *fifi.* Cuitlatec *ehpɨ* 'call, say.'
Misumalpan: Miskito *paiu-.* Motilon *iba-r* 'shout.' Paez *paja.*

Central Amerind CALL. Oto-Manguc: R 198 **(h)kʷa(²)* 'make noise,
weep, shout, say.' Uto-Aztecan: M 74 **pai.*

Hokan SAY. Chimariko -*pa-.* Karok *pi:p, ipe:r̄* 'tell, name.' Pomo: East
Pomo *ba-* (prefix in verbs of telling). Yana *ba-* 'call.'

Penutian CALL. Gulf: Muskogean: Choctaw *pāja.* Mexican: Mayan:
Yucatec *paj.*

Additional: Keresiouan: Keresan: Keres *be* 'tell.'

57 CARRY₁

Macro-Ge CARRY. Botocudo *pe* 'take.' Ge: Krenje *apø* 'load' (v.).
Kaingan: Tibagi *ba* 'carry, bring.'

Macro-Panoan TOWARD. Moseten -*ve*. Panoan: Proto-Panoan *βɯ*
'bring.' Tacanan: Proto-Tacanan **be* 'bring.' Vilela -*be* 'in.'

Macro-Carib TAKE. Carib: Wayana *apoi*, Galibi *apwi*, Chayma *apue*, etc.
Uitoto: Uitoto *iba* 'buy,' Erare *upa* 'buy.'

Andean CARRY. Aymara: Jaqaru *apa*. Kahuapana: Jebero *ək-paʔ*.
Quechua: Cochabamba, etc. *apa*.

58 CARRY₂

Central Amerind CARRY. Kiowa-Tanoan: Kiowa *kʰɔ-* (prepound 'get');
Tanoan: Tewa *xɔ̃-ng*. Oto-Mangue: R 126 **(h)ka(n)* 'take, carry.' Uto-
Aztecan: M 76 **kʷe*.

Penutian TAKE. California: Maidu *kə* 'have.' Chinook: Wishram *ga*
'seize.' Gulf: Atakapa *ko:* (sing. subject). Tsimshian *go:u* (sing.
subject).

59 CHEST

Macro-Ge CHEST. Chiquito *tutˢi-s*. Ge: Apinage *itko*. Kaingan:
Apacurana *dugn* 'belly.' Mashakali *itkonatan*. Puri: Coroado *teke*
'belly.'

Macro-Panoan CHEST. Charruan: Charrua *itax*. Mataco: Nocten, Vejoz
tokue. Panoan: Mayoruna *takua*, Cashinahua *taka* 'belly.' Tacanan:
Chama *taxo* 'breast.'

Equatorial CHEST. Chapacura: Itene *toko* 'belly,' *tukure* 'heart.' Guamo:
Santa Rosa *duexu* 'belly.' Maipuran: Bare *nduku*, Wapishana *duku-li*,
Atoroi *du-kudi*, etc. Uro: Uro *tuk-si* 'stomach, heart,' Chipaya *tuč-si*,
tuši 'heart.' (A)

Macro-Tucanoan BELLY. Capixana *itakua*. Iranshe *tʲuku*. Kaliana *tukuj*.
Nambikwara: Southern Nambikwara *tʔih* 'abdomen.' Puinave: Marahan
tok, Papury *tok* 'bosom,' Querari *taka*, *daka* 'chest.' Ticuna *tugai*.

Penutian CHEST. California: Costanoan: San Juan Bautista *tukai*, San
Francisco *itok*. Chinook *atˢx*. Gulf: Tunica *čihki* 'belly'; Chitimacha
ših 'belly.' Mexican: Mixe-Zoque *tˢek* 'belly.'

Almosan-Keresiouan BELLY. Algic: Algonquian: Shawnee *ʔseʔki*,

202

Montagnais *škate;* Wiyot *ǰayiɬ.* Mosan: Wakashan: Kwakiutl *tikʔi,*
Bella Bella *tkʔi,* Nitinat *ta:čʔ;* Salish: Nootsack *tⁱʔač,* Twana *tⁱʔa:ʔč.*
(AM)

60 CHEW

Macro-Carib TOOTH.   Andoke *kone.* Bora: Miranya Oira Assu-Tapuya
ma-ɣynieng. Yagua *ixiana, oxana.*
Chibchan-Paezan CHEW.   Aruak: Bintucua *gan* 'chew, bite.' Atacama *kʔin*
'gnaw.' Warrau *kani* 'chew, bite.'

61 CHILD₁

Macro-Ge BEAR (v.). Botocudo *nin.* Ge: Crengez *anin, ani* 'copulate,'
Cayapo *ni* 'copulate.'
Macro-Panoan CHILD.   Charruan: Chana, Guenoa *ineu* 'son.' Guaicuru:
Guachi *inna* 'son.' Mataco: Vejoz *anax,* Choroti *i-nuwe* 'be born,'
naijihi 'bear' (v.), Macca, Towothli *enani* 'girl.' Moseten *nana-t* 'boy,'
nana-s 'girl.' Tacanan: Arasa *nana,* Tacana *e-anana,* Cavineña *nana-*
'small, tender.'
Andean DAUGHTER.   Alakaluf *anne.* Cholona: Cholona *añu, ñu,* Hivito
noo. Mayna *ni-* 'child' (deduced from *ni-thawaa* 'boy,' *ni-pai* 'girl').
Yamana: Yahgan *inia, inni.* Zaparo *nia* 'child.' Cf. Araucanian:
Pehuenche *ñu-* 'bear' (v.).
Chibchan-Paezan CHILD.   Barbacoa: Cayapa, Colorado *na* 'child, small.'
Choco: Catio *niu* 'boy, son.' Jirajara: Jirajara *unu, unujo* 'boy,' Ayoman
unu 'boy.' Paez: Paez *nu(-kue)* 'small,' Guambiana *une.* Timucua *ano*
'young of animals.' Cf. Atacama *pauna* 'boy.' (P)
Additional: Uto-Aztecan: M 389 **no* 'small.'
Cf. CHILD₄.

62 CHILD₂

Equatorial BOY.   Arawa: Paumari *makinaua.* Maipuran: Araicu *emyite*
'child,' Kariay [ymuky]. Tinigua: Pamigua *mekve.* Uro: Caranga,
Chipaya *mač* 'son.' (MA)
Macro-Tucanoan CHILD.   Auake *makuamē* 'son.' Nambikwara: Proto-
Nambikwara **mɔitˢ.* Ticuna *maakan.* Tucano: Yahuna, Waikina, etc.
make 'son'; Dyurumawa, etc. *ma-maki* 'child' (on *ma-,* see the Macro-
Tucanoan entry under SMALL, below).

Hokan BOY.   Chumash: Santa Barbara *mičamo*. Tequistlatec *ɬa-mihkano*.
Washo *mehu*. Yuman: Walapai *mik*, Maricopa *maxaj*.
Cf. SEED₁.

63 CHILD₃

Macro-Ge CHILD.   Botocudo *pu-i* 'to ferment.' Chiquito *ai-bo*. Fulnio *fe*
'grow.' Ge: Krenje *pom* 'born.' Kaingan: Catarina, etc. *po* 'be born.'
Macro-Panoan BORN.   Mataco: Vejoz *pu* 'be born.' Panoan: Proto-Panoan:
*βaki 'child,' Cashinahua *ba* 'beget.' Tacanan: Proto-Tacanan **βakwa*
'child,' Guarayo *poj* 'be born (of plant).'
Macro-Carib CHILD.   Carib: Surinam *pa:ri* 'grandchild,' Cumanogoto *par*
'grandchild,' Tamanaco *par* 'nephew,' etc. Yagua *porii*.
Macro-Tucanoan CHILD.   Mobima *pʾampʾan* 'bear' (v.). Puinave:
Marahan *apuhudn* 'pregnant.' Ticuna *buʔɨ*. Tucano *po(-na)* 'children,'
pini 'sprout.' Yuri *abje* 'daughter.'
Central Amerind NEW.   Oto-Mangue: R 225 **(n)(ʔ)kʷa(h)(n)*. Uto-
Aztecan: M 305 **pa*.

64 CHILD₄

Andean BEAR (v.).   Alakaluf *alla*. Araucanian *jall-*. Zaparo: Arabela *ra*.
Cf. Aymara *juri* 'be born.'
Hokan CHILD.   Pomo: Northeast Pomo *u:la-* (in compounds). Yana *ʔala:*,
with diminutive consonantism in compounds *-ʔana*.
Penutian CHILD.   California: Wintun: Wintu *ila*, *ela*, Patwin *ʔila:j*. Gulf:
Tunica *ʔelu* 'bear fruit.' Mexican: Mayan: Maya *ʔal* (general), Kekchí
al 'bear' (v.), Quiché *alax* 'bear' (v.). Oregon: Coos *a:la*. Tsimshian
o:li-s 'great-grandson.'
Additional: Uto-Aztecan: M 387 **ʔali* 'small.'
Cf. CHILD₁.

65 CLEAN (v.)

Equatorial WASH.   Arawa: Jarua *suku-ke*, Culino *sukumane*, Paumari
sokoi. Maipuran: Wapishana *ske* 'wash,' Goajiro *šixawa* 'wash.' (A)
Chibchan-Paezan WASH.   Allentiac *čok*. Aruak: Bintucua *ačukua*, Kagaba
ižukue 'clean.' Atacama *čʾekʾati-n* 'wash,' *čʾekʾu-n* 'baptize.' Chibcha:
Tegria *suka-* 'bathe,' *suk-ro* 'bath.' Chimu: Eten *tˢuk* 'clean.' Choco:
Catio *sygyja*. Lenca: Chilanga *tˢʾik*, Similaton *sagi*. Misumalpan:
Cacaopera *saka*, Miskito *sik*. Paez *søkak* 'caress, knead.' Rama *suki*.

Tarascan *t^sika* 'rub.' Warrau *siko-, seke-* 'rub.' Yanoama: Sanema
tikukai 'wash.'

Penutian CLEAN (v.). California: Maidu *t^{s²}uku* 'wash.' Gulf: Atakapa *t^sak*
'clean, wash'; Chitimacha *sahči* 'wash'; Tunica *sihi-na* (adj.);
Muskogean: Hitchiti *ok-sax* 'wash' (cf. *uki* 'water'). Mexican: Totonac
t^{s²}a²qa-²ni; Mayan: Proto-Mayan (C) *č²ax.* Tsimshian *saksg* (adj.).
Yukian: Wappo *tak²ɛ.*

Almosan-Keresiouan CLEAN. Mosan: Salish: Squamish *šuk^w* 'bathe,'
Shuswap *sex^w-m* 'bathe,' Pentlatch *t^suχ* 'wash,' Upper Chehalis *t^{s²}x^w*
'wash,' etc. Siouan-Yuchi: Siouan: Proto-Siouan *ska* 'white,'
Winnebago *ske* 'be clean.'

<h2 style="text-align:center">66 CLOSE (v.)</h2>

Macro-Ge CLOSE. Ge: Krenje *kapi* 'bolt.' Puri: Coroado *kapo-em.*

Macro-Panoan COVER. Lengua: Mascoy *kjab-,* Moseten *sup, sipi.* Panoan:
Panobo *kepui* 'close,' Shipibo *kepu* 'close.' Tacanan: Proto-Tacanan
t^sipi.

Chibchan-Paezan HIDE. Atacama *k²aba* (transitive). Cuna *akapa* 'close
one's eyes.'

Hokan ALL. Chimariko *kumičin.* Salinan: San Antonio *xam, xap* 'finish.'
Subtiaba: Tlappanec *kamba.* Tonkawa *kapa* 'shut.'

Almosan-Keresiouan CLOSE. Algic: Algonquian: Proto–Central
Algonquian *kep;* Wiyot *k^wapł* 'be covered.' Mosan: Wakashan: Nootka
hop-ta 'in hiding'; Chemakuan: Chemakum *hap²ilii* 'cover'; Salish:
Squamish *qəp²,* Kalispel *čep* 'lock a door.' Siouan-Yuchi: Siouan:
Dakota *akaxpa,* Mandan *iaxawe,* Catawba *kəpa.*

<h2 style="text-align:center">67 CLOUD₁</h2>

Macro-Ge SKY. Bororo: Umotina *otalu* 'lightning.' Botocudo *taru* 'sky,
day.' Guato *(ma-)tari* 'thunder,' *(ma-)(kvia-)tar* 'lightning.'

Macro-Panoan THUNDER. Lule *til-p.* Mataco: Macca *tetelun.* Panoan:
Conibo *tirin,* Marinahua *tiriłi.* Tacanan: Proto-Tacanan *tiri.*

Equatorial CLOUD. Esmeralda *mu-sala* 'smoke' (*mu* = 'fire'). Maipuran:
Wapishana *iši²ir,* Goajiro *siruma,* Atoroi *išaira.* Uro: Uro *siri,* Chipaya
ziri. Zamuco: Chamacoco *essela* 'fog.'

Andean CLOUD. Alakaluf *tullu.* Kahuapana *tālua.*

Chibchan-Paezan HEAVEN. Barbacoa: Cuaiquer *čillo.* Choco: Sambu
čirrua. (P)

Central Amerind DAY.   Kiowa-Tanoan: Kiowa *dēn* 'sun'; Tanoan: San
Ildefonso *tʰān*, Hopi Tewa *thang*. Oto-Mangue: R 6 **tin*. Uto-Aztecan:
Proto-Uto-Aztecan: M 238a **ton* 'hot,' Nahuatl *tona-tⁱ* 'sun.' (Cf.
Proto-Uto-Aztecan: M 423a **ta-* 'sun.')

68 CLOUD₂

Chibchan-Paezan CLOUD.   Barbacoa: Colorado *pojo*. Chibcha: Chibcha
faoa 'fog,' Tegria *aba*. Choco: Saija *paxa* 'sky,' Citara *baxa* 'sky.' Cuna
poo 'mist.' Mura *pe*. Paez *ipia, ipa* 'smoke.' Talamanca: Terraba *poŋ*
'cloud, fog.' Cf. Timucua *litˢa-faja* 'cloud.'
Central Amerind CLOUD.   Kiowa-Tanoan: Kiowa *pʰan*, Taos *phē-na*. Oto-
Mangue: R 208 **(n)kʷa(n)* 'cloud, smoke, damp, dew, fog.' Cf. Uto-
Aztecan: M 186 **pak* 'fog' (possibly containing **pa-* 'water').
Penutian CLOUD.   California: Miwok: Central Sierra *ʔopa*. Gulf: Atakapa
po, pox, pux 'smoke,' Chitimacha *pok* 'smokey.' Mexican: Mayan:
Huastec *pauh* 'smoke,' Yucatec *buʔ* 'smoke'; Totonac *pukɬ-ni*. Plateau:
Klamath *pʾaj-s*. Yukian: Yuki *i:p*, Wappo *pohi* 'fog.' Zuni *pokɬi*
'smoke.'

69 COLD₁

Macro-Carib COLD.   Carib: Surinam *i:sana* (n.), Kaliana *ti-sano-le*,
Cariniaco *tu-sano-ri*, etc. Yagua *sanora* (Marcoy), *sanehe* 'rainy season'
(Fejos).
Andean COLD.   Kahuapana *sanøk-li*. Zaparo *sǝnǝ*.
Chibchan-Paezan COLD.   Aruak: Guamaca *seanximi*. Atacama *sera-r*.
Chibcha: Tegria *sero*, Pedraza *seroa*. Chimu: Eten *tˢan*. Lenca:
Chilanga *tˢʾana*, Similaton *sani* 'freeze.' Malibu: Chimila *sohnikote*.
Misumalpan: Sumu *sang* 'cold weather.' Motilon: Dobocubi *tero(-kwa)*.
Paya *sainista* 'be cold.' Talamanca: Borunca *tˢaara* 'be cold,' Terraba
sen. Tarascan *tˢira*. Xinca *saraɬtⁱi* 'to cool,' *sarara* 'frost' (Maldonado),
Chiquimulilla *sarara*. Yanoama: Yanam, Yanomam *sāi*.
Almosan-Keresiouan COLD.   Algic: Yurok *sa:won* 'be cold.' Siouan-
Yuchi: Proto-Siouan **sni*, Catawba *čī* (Speck 1934: 370).
Additional: Oto-Mangue: R 279 **(n)(ʔ)si(h)(n)*.   Almosan: Salish: Proto-
Salish **tˢʾutⁱ*, **tˢʾatⁱ*.

70   COLD₂

Chibchan-Paezan WIND.   Paez: Guambiana *isix*. Warrau *ahaka*. (P)

Hokan COLD.   Jicaque *tˢoix* 'ice.' Karok *ʔathi:k*. Shasta *ʔissikʔ*. Tonkawa *sa:x* 'cool, fresh air.'

Penutian COLD.   California: Yokuts *čʔečʔeka*. Gulf: Chitimacha *čʔaki*. Mexican: Mixe-Zoque: Sierra Popoluca *suksuk*; Mayan: Tzotzil *sik*. Plateau: Cayuse *tok* 'ice.'

Almosan-Keresiouan COLD.   Algic: Proto-Algonquian **tahk* 'cool.' Kutenai *-itʔkʔo*. Mosan: Salish: Squamish *(təm-)tʔiqʷ* 'winter' (*təm* = 'season'). (AM)

71   COLD₃

Andean COLD.   Alakaluf [ghesas], [kizas]. Patagon: Ona *košek* 'winter.' Quechua: Santiagueño *qasa* 'freeze.'

Hokan COLD.   Achomawi *aščʔa-siwi* 'it is cold.' Chimariko *xatˢa*. Pomo: East Pomo *katˢil*, South Pomo *katˢʰi*. Yana *xatˢʔitʔ* 'it feels cold.' Yuman: Tipai, Diegueño, Campo *xtˢur* 'winter,' Yuma *xatˢu:r*.

72   COME

Macro-Ge COME.   Botocudo *nī*. Caraja *anakre*. Kamakan: Meniens *ni* (imperative). Mashakali: Mashakali *nūn*, Patasho *nanæ*.

Macro-Panoan COME.   Charruan: Charrua *na* 'bring,' Chana *na*. Guaicuru: Toba *anak*. Lule *ne*. Mataco: Mataco *nam*, Choroti *nek*. Tacanan: Cavineña *ba-na* 'visit, come' (probably *ba* 'see' + *na* 'come'). Vilela *na, no, ne*.

Macro-Carib COME.   Andoke *pa-nænæu* 'he comes,' *i-na-powa* 'he came.' Yagua: Yameo *ana*.

Equatorial COME.   Chapacura: Quitemo *nia* 'come here.' Kandoshi *naa* 'go,' *nani* 'come.' Maipuran: Mashco *ena*, Curipaco *no*, Achagua *ina*. Otomaco *ana* 'travel.' Tupi: Arikem *an* 'go.' Yuracare *-ni-* 'go to do something,' future. Zamuco *no* 'go.'

Andean COME.   Aymara *-ni-* 'go to do something.' Cholona *a-na-n*. Patagon: Ona *enn-en* 'go.' Quechua: Huanacucho *eina* 'go.' Yamana: Yamana *-i:na* 'do while walking,' Yahgan *aina* 'walk.' Zaparo: Iquito *ani*, Arabela *ni*.

Chibchan-Paezan COME.   Allentiac *neñe* 'road.' Aruak: Kagaba *na, nai*, *nei* 'go.' Barbacoa: Colorado *nena* 'walk.' Choco: Catio *nenu.* Cuna *noni, nene, nae* 'go.' Malibu: Chimila *noŋ.* Tarascan *-no-.* Warrau *nao.* Some of these forms may belong under ROAD₁ below.

Hokan GO.   Chumash: La Purisima *nana* 'walk.' Esselen *neni* 'go, walk.' Pomo: East Pomo *negi, nek* 'go to.' Yana *ni* (sing. male subject).

Penutian COME.   California: Costanoan *-na* (future), *ina-* 'go to'; Maidu: Maidu *-no* 'go to,' Nisenan *ʔo:no* 'come, reach'; Miwok: Lake *ʔoni,* Central Sierra *ʔynny,* etc. Gulf: Muskogean: Koasati *ono* 'climb,' Creek *onna.* Mexican: Totonac: Papantla *aʔn* 'go.' Yukian: Wappo *na* 'come up.'

Almosan-Keresiouan COME.   Algic: Algonquian: Arapaho *naʔ* 'come to, arriving'; Wiyot *row* 'come from' (*r* < **n*). Iroquoian: Oneida *-ine-* 'go, proceed.' Keresan: Santa Ana *ni* 'walk, go.' Kutenai *ił.* Mosan: Wakashan: Nootka *nʔi;* Salish: Songish *ənʔɛ,* Lkungen *enæ.* Siouan-Yuchi: Siouan: Proto-Siouan **-ni* 'walk,' usually *ma-ni* 'ground walk,' but Mandan, Quapaw *ni* 'walk.'

73 COOK (v.)

Macro-Panoan COOK.   Lengua *makhit-kʲi* 'cooked, ripe.' Moseten *mak.* Panoan: Caripuna *muexoa* 'roast,' Panobo *muši* 'burn.'

Andean COOK.   Araucanian: Pehuenche *mokomuk.* Patagon: Ona *amk-en* 'burn.' Quechua: Santiagueño *amkaj* 'roast.' Yamana *amux-puka.* Zaparo *mahi* (Peake), *maiki* 'roast' (Martius).

Hokan COOK.   Chimariko *maq* 'roast.' Comecrudo *met* 'burn.' Pomo: Kashaya *mtʔaw* 'be cooked,' *matˢ* 'burn,' Southeast Pomo *mtʔa.* Seri *ka-motni.* Tequistlatec *imagi* 'cooked,' *di-makʔe-ʔma, de-miš-ʔma* 'roasted over hot coals.' Yana *maasi* 'be cooked, ripe.'

74 COVER (v.)

Macro-Panoan FINISH.   Lule *tump-s.* Mataco: Choroti *tipoi* 'be full.' Panoan: Cashinahua *dəbo.* Tacanan: Tacana *tupu* 'it reaches.'

Macro-Tucanoan CLOSE.   Iranshe *tepa.* Tucano: Siona *tapi-see* 'closed,' Tucano *tubia* 'stop up.'

Andean COVER.   Aymara: Jaqaru *tʰapa.* Quechua: Ecuadorean *tapa* 'close.' Yamana: Yahgan *tapa* 'cover oneself.'

Chibchan-Paezan FINISH.   Cuitlatec *timpa* 'all.' Xinca *tumu.* (C)

Additional: Uto-Aztecan: M 90 **tem* 'close.'

Cf. DIE₂.

75 CRY (v.)

Macro-Panoan CRY.   Lengua *wuneji*. Panoan: Proto-Panoan **wini*.
Chibchan-Paezan CRY.   Malibu: Chimila *oni*. Misumalpan: Miskito *ini*.
Paez *une*. Warrau *ona*.

76 DARK

Equatorial NIGHT.   Chapacura: Urupa *etim*, Itene *issim*. Uro: Callahuaya
thami, Caranga *sumči* 'dark,' Chipaya *somči* 'dark.' (A)
Chibchan-Paezan NIGHT.   Jirajara: Ayoman *tem* 'black.' Lenca: Chilanga
tˢuba. Misumalpan: Miskito *timia*. Xinca *syma* 'night, black'
(Maldonado), Chiquimulilla *suʔmax* 'black,' Yupultepec *tˢyøma*, etc.
Penutian NIGHT.   California: Yokuts *či:mʔe:k* 'get dark'; Wintun: Patwin
sunol. Gulf: Chitimacha *tˢʔima*; Atakapa *tem, teng*; Muskogean:
Choctaw *tampi* 'dark,' Koasati *tamoxga*, Natchez *tamuja:* 'yesterday.'
Mexican: Mixe-Zoque: Tetontepec *tˢoʔm* 'midnight'; Huave *tim*
'yesterday'; Mayan: Huastec *tˢamul*. Oregon: Yakonan *tˢaʔmasiju*
'shadow.' Plateau: Klamath *čʔmog* 'dark.' Tsimshian *gʲi:-tˢʔi:p*
'yesterday.' Yukian: Yuki, Huchnom *su:m* 'yesterday,' Clear Lake *somi*
'yesterday,' Wappo *sum* 'evening.'
Almosan-Keresiouan DARK.   Algic: Yurok *tˢmej* 'be evening.' Keresan:
Laguna *tˢamištʲ*. Kutenai *tamoxu-intˢ* 'be dark.' Mosan: Wakashan:
Nootka *tom-, tomi:s* 'charcoal.'

77 DEER₁

Macro-Panoan DEER.   Lengua: Guana *nsenok*, Sanapana *sienak*, Angaite
łonak. Mataco: Mataco *asinax* 'dog,' Vejoz *sinax* 'dog,' Choroti *sona*
'red deer.'
Chibchan-Paezan DEER.   Misumalpan: Sumu *sana, sulu* 'dog,' Ulua *sana*,
solo 'dog,' Matagalpa *sulo*. Rama: Rama *sula, suli* 'animal,' Guetar
suri. Talamanca: Terraba *šuring*, Bribri, Estrella *suni*, Cabecar *sunri*.
(C)

78 DEER₂

Central Amerind DEER.   Kiowa-Tanoan: Kiowa *tʔa-p*; Tanoan: Taos
tʔo(-na). Oto-Mangue: R 39 **(Y)(n)te(H)(n)* 'fox, wolf, dog, etc.' Uto-
Aztecan: M 123 **te, *tek* 'deer.' Azteco-Tanoan: WT 96 **tʔyna*
'antelope.'

209

Almosan-Keresiouan DEER.   Caddoan: Proto-Caddoan *ta?, Caddo da?.
Siouan-Yuchi: Proto-Siouan *ta.

79 DIE₁

Macro-Ge SLEEP.   Mashakali: Mashakali, Monosho *monon;* Macuni
moñung; Capoxo, Kumanasho *mono.* Opaie *moje* 'die.' Puri: Coropo
mamnon.

Macro-Panoan DIE.   Guaicuru: Mocovi *omma* 'bed,' *ommakte* 'finish,'
Abipone *la-amači* 'finish,' Guachi *amma* 'sleep.' Lengua *mašeji,mašoj*
'sleep.' Mataco: Choroti *j-ome* 'extinct,' *me* 'sleep,' Chulupi *wo-miš*
'finish,' Mataco *mo* 'sleep,' Choropi *imak* 'sleep,' Enimaga *ma* 'sleep.'
Moseten *moñi* 'perish, lose.' Panoan: Culino *jamai,* Cashinahua *mawa,*
Shipibo *mama* 'dream,' Caripuna *makø.* Tacanan: Proto-Tacanan
manu, Cavineña *maho.*

Equatorial SLEEP.   Guahibo: Guahibo *mahi-ta,* Guayabero *moxitan.*
Maipuran: Apurina *maka,* Machiguenga *magʲe,* Chana *makasi,* Piapoco
maaku, etc. Timote: Cuica *muu* 'fall asleep.' Tupi: Oyampi *mahē*
'dream.' Uro: Callahuaya *mexana.* Yaruro *mūa.* Zamuco: Zamuco *amo,*
Ebidoso *omog,* Guaranoco *amo* 'lie down.'

Macro-Tucanoan DIE.   Capixana *moa* 'spirits of the dead.' Huari: Huari
ime, Masaka *aimæ.* Puinave: Puinave *možei, možoi* 'dead,' Papury
mehoi 'kill,' Tiquie *memiei* 'kill.' Tucano: Uasona *madʸegǝ* 'kill.'

Andean DIE.   Araucanian [umaugh] 'desire to sleep,' *umaq* 'dream.'
Aymara *amaja* 'corpse.' Patagon: Tehuelche *ma* 'kill,' Ona *mašenk* 'be
sleepy.' Quechua: Santiagueño, Cochabamba *maqa* 'hit.' Sabela:
Tuwituwey *mu* 'sleep.' Yamana *mamaia, umamaia* 'kill,' *maki* 'hit.'
Zaparo: Zaparo *maki* 'sleep,' Andoa *maki* 'sleep,' Iquito *amuhe* 'kill,'
makǝ 'sleep,' Arabela *mo* 'kill.'

Chibchan-Paezan SLEEP.   Chibcha *mujsua* 'dream.' Cuna *ma, mai* 'lie
down.' Misumalpan: Ulua, Sumu *ami.* Yanoama: Shiriana *mi.* (C)

Hokan DIE.   Comecrudo *n-ome-t* 'sleep.' Esselen *moho* 'he died.' Jicaque
maha 'sleep' (n.). Karankawa *mal* 'dead,' *im* 'sleep.' Salinan: San
Antonio *me* 'sleep,' *ema:-tʰ* 'kill' (with causative *-tʰ*). Seri *-iim* 'sleep.'
Subtiaba *ami* 'sleep.' Tequistlatec *ma* 'die,' *ma?a* 'kill.' Yana: Central
Yana *?am?dʸi* 'kill.' Yuman: Diegueño *melaj.* Yurumangui *umu, uma*
'he is lying down,' *ima-sa* 'kill.'

Additional: Uto-Aztecan: M 128a *muk, *muki* 'die' (sing. subject), M 128c

*mu (no reconstructed meaning; glosses 'be sick, kill, die, etc.'),
M 128d *mek, *me (no reconstructed meaning; glosses 'die, kill, be
sick, etc.').

80 DIE₂

Equatorial DIE.   Guahibo *tipa*. Kandoshi: Kandoshi *t'ipaa*, Murato *čipoa*
'kill.' Maipuran: Resigaro *tabana-ki* 'you (pl.) kill.' Tupi: Uruku *topava*
'is dead,' Mekens *tsumpatn, zumba* 'kill.' Yuracare *tubi*. Zamuco:
Ebidoso *dābio* 'corpse.'

Andean DIE.   Alakaluf *taf* (*f* < *m; cf. BEARD). Gennaken: Pehuelche
team 'dead.' Kahuapana *timini*.

Cf. COVER.

81 DIE₃

Macro-Ge DIE.   Caraja *ituæ* 'finish.' Fulnio *tʰo*. Ge: Proto-Ge *ty, *tyr,
tyk, Karaho *ty ~ tyk*, Cayapo *tu*. Kaingan: Tibagi *tere*, Southern
Kaingan *nde*. Kamakan *dau* 'death, kill.'

Macro-Carib DIE.   Uitoto: Muinane *dʔii*. Yagua *ndɨi*.

Central Amerind DIE.   Oto-Mangue: R 7 *ti(m)* 'die, kill.' Uto-Aztecan:
M 131 *te*.

82 DIG₁

Equatorial HOLE.   Maipuran: Kustenau, Mehinacu *ako* (deduced from
'nostril' = 'nose hole'), Guana *aka* 'nostril,' Toyeri *(ua-)he*. Piaroa:
Saliba *aha* 'mouth.' Trumai *-xu* (deduced from nostril). Tupi: Yuruna
kwa, Shipaya *ikua*. Cf. Jibaro: Gualaquiza [hua] (probably *wa)*.

Chibchan-Paezan DIG.   Aruak: Bintucua *kui* 'dig up.' Chibcha: Pedraza
kui, Manare *kaja* 'hole.' Cuna *kwisa*. Guaymi *gu* 'hole.' Motilon *oka*
'hole.' Paez *uxw*.

Central Amerind DIG.   Kiowa-Tanoan: Tanoan: Taos *ko*, Towa *koʔ*, Jemez
ke. Oto-Mangue: R 122 *(ʔ)ka(h)* 'dig, break.' Uto-Aztecan: Proto-
Uto-Aztecan (Hale) *kVₗ* 'to plant' (*Vₗ* represents a correspondence for
which no proto-sound is given).

Almosan-Keresiouan HOLE.   Iroquoian: Seneca *oka-* 'make a hole.'
Kutenai *kʾa* 'hole, pit.' Mosan: Salish: Tillamook *kuji* 'dig.' Siouan-
Yuchi: Siouan: Proto-Siouan (C) *oka*, Catawba *ka*.

83 DIG₂

Macro-Panoan DIG.   Mataco: Choroti *tei, tehi,* Vejoz *tix,* Suhin *tuku* 'to plant.' Tacanan: Chama *teo.*

Macro-Tucanoan DIG.   Iranshe *toʔu.* Ticuna *to.* Tucano: Tucano *ʔoteʔe* 'I dig,' Wanana *toa-ha* 'I plant.'

Hokan DIG.   Chimariko *tˢik.* Jicaque *tok.*

84 DIG₃

Andean DIG.   Aymara *aʎi.* Kahuapana *iwalo-tøčok, iwalo-lallu* 'hollow.' Quechua: Cochabamba, Ecuadorean *aʎa.* Yamana *wøn-.*

Penutian DIG.   California: Miwok: Central Sierra *ʔo:lu,* Northern Sierra *ole.* Yukian: Wappo *ɛli* 'dig a hole.'

85 DIRTY

Macro-Ge DIRTY.   Chiquito *tuki-s.* Ge: Proto-Ge *tɨk* 'black,' Cayapo *tuk.*

Equatorial EXCREMENT.   Kandoshi: Murato *tˢiki.* Maipuran: Arawak *tiki,* Machiguenga *tiga,* Piro *čki,* Ipurina *itike,* etc. Piaroa *tekē.*

Macro-Tucanoan BLACK.   Auake *asikē.* Canichana *takitixe* 'night.' Catuquina [tekniny]. Puinave: Hubde *teča,* Tiquie *tesa,* Yehubde *tuičaa.* Shukuru *taka* 'Negro.'

Penutian GREEN.   California: Costanoan: Monterey *šiex* 'grass,' Rumsien *čuktuk;* Wintun: Patwin *seka.* Mexican: Huave *tek;* Mixe-Zoque: Zoque *tˢuhtˢuh;* Mayan: Tzeltal *itax* 'verdure,' Kekchí *ičax* 'grass.' Plateau: North Sahaptin *tˢəktˢək,* Nez Perce *tˢʔixtˢʔix,* Yakima *seksek* 'grass.' Yukian: Yuki *siek* 'blue,' Huchnom *siex* 'blue,' Wappo *šikatis* 'blue.'

Almosan-Keresiouan BLACK.   Algic: Algonquian: Natick [sucki], Blackfoot *sik-.* Iroquoian: Mohawk *atek* 'dark in color.' Keresan: Proto-Keresan *skɨ* 'green.' Mosan: Salish: Bella Coola *skʔx,* Musqueam *tˢʔqʔix.*

86 DOG

Chibchan-Paezan DEER.   Lenca: Similaton *aguingge,* Guajiquero, Opatoro *ahuingge,* Chilanga *akʔuan.* Tarascan *axuni* 'deer, animal.' (C)

Hokan DOG.   Achomawi *kuan* 'silver fox.' Tonkawa *ʔekuan.* Yana: North Yana *kuwan-na* 'lynx.' Yurumangui *kwan.*

87 DRINK₁

Macro-Ge DRINK.　Bororo: Bororo *ku* (n.), Koraveka *ako* (imperative).
Ge: Kraho *kʰo* 'to smoke.' Kamakan *kwa, ko* 'to smoke.'

Macro-Panoan DRINK.　Guaicuru: Guachi *euak* 'water.' Lule *uk*. Mataco:
Suhin *joke*, Towothli *ijake*, Payagua *uejak, uoejak* 'water.'

Equatorial WATER.　Chapacura: Chapacura *akum*, Urupa, Itene *kom*, etc.
Guamo *kum*. Maipuran: Yaulapiti *(mapa-)kuma* 'honey' (*mapa* =
'bee'), Guana *uko* 'rain.' Otomaco: Taparita *kuema* 'lake.' Tupi: Proto-
Tupi **akɨm* 'wet.'

Macro-Tucanoan WATER.　Auake *okõã* 'water, river.' Capixana *ikunī*,
kuni. Tucano: Tucano (general) *oko* 'water, rain,' Wanana *koneme*
'rain,' Pioje *kono* 'fermented drink,' Bahukiwa *uku-mi* 'he is drinking.'

Andean DRINK.　Araucanian *ko* 'water.' Aymara *oqo* 'swallow.' Catacao:
Colan *kum*. Culli *kumu*. Patagon: Tsoneka *komahi*, Tehuelche *kam-an*,
koi 'lake.' Yamana *aka* 'lake.'

Hokan WATER.　Chimariko *aqa*. Chumash: La Purisima *aho*, Santa Ynez,
Santa Barbara *a:*. Comecrudo *aχ* 'juice.' Cotoname *aχ*. Esselen
asa(-nax). Karok *ʔa:s* 'water, juice.' Pomo: Kashaya *ʔahqʰa*, North
Pomo *kʰa*, East Pomo *xa*, etc. Quinigua *ka*. Salinan: San Antonio *t̮saʔ*.
Seri *ʔax*. Shasta *ʔat'̮t'̮a*. Subtiaba: Tlappanec *ihja*. Tequistlatec *l-axaʔ*.
Tonkawa *ʔa:x*. Washo *a:šaʔ*. Yana *xa(-na)*. Yuman: Yuma *axa*, Cocopa
xa, Mohave *aha*, etc.

Penutian DRINK.　California: Costanoan: Rumsien *uk;* Yokuts *ukun*.
Gulf: Natchez *kun* 'water'; Chitimacha *kuʔ* 'water,' *ʔak-* 'water' (in
compounds); Atakapa (Eastern) *ak* 'water,' *akonst* 'river'; Muskogean:
Chickasaw *okaʔ* 'water,' Koasati, Hitchiti, etc. *uki* 'water.' Mexican:
Mixe-Zoque: Tetontepec *uuʔk*, Sayula *uʔk*, Zoque *ʔuhk*, etc.; Mayan:
Yucatec *ukʾ* 'be thirsty,' Tzeltal *uč'-el*, Tzotzil *uč*, Mam *ukam*, Kekchí
uʔka, etc. Oregon: Takelma *ukʷ*. Plateau: Nez Perce *k'u*, Molala
okuna. Tsimshian: Tsimshian *aks*, Nass *akʲ-s* 'water.' Yukian: Yuki
ukʾu 'water,' Huchnom *ʔu:k* 'water,' Wappo *ʔuki*. Zuni *k'a* 'water.'

Almosan-Keresiouan WATER.　Algic: Algonquian: Proto–Central
Algonquian **akwa:* 'from water'; Yurok *-kʷ* in verbs referring to
movement in or on water, third-person singular (Robins). Kutenai *-qʷ*
'in water.' Mosan: Salish: Songish *qʷaʔ*, Tillamook *qiw*, Musqueam
qaʔ, etc. (AM)

88 DRINK₂

Equatorial DRINK. Maipuran: Campa *iriie*, Yucuna *ira*, Amuesha *ur*, etc.
Zamuco: Chamacoco *ary*. Cf. Yaruro *hara*.
Andean DRINK. Alakaluf *lai*. Yamana *øla*. (S)

89 DRINK₃

Hokan WATER. Achomawi: Atsugewi *jume:* 'river.' Chumash: San
Buenaventura *ma* 'stream.' Esselen *imi-la* 'sea.' Subtiaba: Subtiaba
(na-)ña (Subtiaba *ñ* often derives from **m*), Tlappanec *iña*. Washo
ime. Yurumangui *jo-ima* 'saliva' (= 'mouth-water').
Penutian WATER. California: Wintun *mem;* Maidu *mo* 'drink.' Plateau:
Klamath *ambo*. Yukian: Yuki *mi* 'drink,' Wappo *meʔ*.

90 DRY₁

Equatorial HARD. Guahibo *penehewa* 'bone.' Maipuran: Jumana *pina*
'bone,' Yavitero *feniji*. Piaroa: Saliba *pango* 'bone.' Tupi: Pawate
panga, Amniapa *pen*, Yuruna *panka* 'bone,' Shipaya *pāki* 'bone.'
Macro-Tucanoan HARD. Puinave: Parana Boaboa *mbagn* 'hard, unripe.'
Tucano: Yupua *bə(x)ka*, Curetu *bikadⁱa*.
Andean DRY. Cholona *paxo-let* 'dry season' (*let* = 'season'). Yamana *paka*
'be dry.'
Hokan STRONG. Achomawi: Achomawi *ipa:ži*, Atsugewi *i:paki*. Yuman:
Akwa'ala *paʔxᵂaj* 'fierce.'
Penutian BONE. California: Wintun *bak, baka* 'tough.' Mexican: Mayan:
Proto-Mayan **bʼaq;* Mixe-Zoque: Zoque *pak, paki* 'hard,' Mixe *pahk*,
etc.; Huave *pak* 'hard.'

91 DRY₂

Macro-Carib HARD. Carib: Kaliana *ti-ana-le*, Surinam *jaʔna* 'hardness.'
Uitoto: Muinane *ane-de* 'to harden.'
Andean DRY. Araucanian *angk-yn* 'become dry.' Itucale *hana*. Kahuapana
añi, ana-pa-ʎi.

92 DUST

Chibchan-Paezan DUST. Barbacoa: Colorado *fu*. Choco: Chami *fu* 'flour,'
Catio *po, fo* 'flour.' (P)

Central Amerind DUST. Kiowa-Tanoan: Kiowa *pʰǽ-ē*. Oto-Mangue: R
154 **kʷe*.

93 EAR

Equatorial EAR. Maipuran: Moxo *sama* 'hear,' Piro *xema* 'hear,' Tereno
kamo 'hear,' Apurina *kema* 'hear,' etc. Timote: Timote *ki-kumeu*,
Cuica *kumen, kumeu*. Cf. Guahibo *hometa* 'hear.'
Macro-Tucanoan EAR. Canichana *komete, komeh*. Kaliana *kaūhī*.
Puinave: Dou *kumaē*. Tucano: Bahukiwa *kamuka*, Waikina *kamono*,
etc.

94 EARTH₁

Equatorial EARTH. Guahibo *ira*. Yuracare *ele* 'earth, mud, under.'
Andean UNDER. Kahuapana *wili*. Quechua: Cochabamba *ura* 'down,'
Chinchaysuyu *ula* 'be under,' Santiagueño *ura* 'lower part,' etc. Sabela:
Auca *wǣ* (Auca has no liquids). Yamana: Yahgan *ilu*. Cf. Alakaluf:
Kaueskar *čarakte alalatal* 'lower teeth' (*čarakte* = 'tooth').

95 EARTH₂

Equatorial EARTH. Kandoshi: Kandoshi *tˢaapo*, Murato *tˢabo*, Shapra
tˢapo. Timote *ki-tapo*. Yaruro *dabo* 'sand.'
Chibchan-Paezan EARTH. Aruak: Atanque *simoru* 'sweepings.' Barbacoa:
Cayapa *tumajii* 'dirty.' Betoi *dafi-bu*. Chimu: Mochica *tum* 'mud,' Eten
tumo 'muddy.' Chibcha: Chibcha *tum* 'mud,' Uncasica *tamara* 'mud,'
Tegria *tami* 'mud,' Margua *tabo-ra*. Cuitlatec *ixtame, tamelo* 'field.'
Guaymi: Move *thobo*, Sabanero *debbi*, Chumulu *savi-ru*. Jirajara:
Ayoman, Gayon *dap*. Talamanca: Borunca *tap*, Cabecar *tamā* 'dirty.'
Tarascan *atˢimo* 'mud.' Warrau *hobo-to* 'earth, mud' (Warrau *h* < **s*).
Yanoama: Shiriana *čami* 'mud.' Through a semantic change 'dirty' >
'bad,' the following may also be connected: Choco: Citara *tumia*
'devil'; Motilon *atan, atam* 'bad.'
Almosan-Keresiouan UNDER. Algic: Algonquian: Proto–Central
Algonquian **athaam*, Cree *taːmi* 'underneath.' Mosan: Salish: Proto-
Salish **timixʷ*, Shuswap *temʔ* 'bottom.' (AM)

96 EARTH₃

Macro-Ge EARTH. Botocudo *am* 'island, forest,' *am-tap* 'dew' (*tap* =

'wet'). Mashakali: Mashakali *ahaham*, Capoxo, Macuni *am*, Malali *am*, Patasho *aham*.

Hokan EARTH.   Chimariko *ama*. Chumash: Santa Barbara *matak* 'mud.' Comecrudo *amat* 'village, town.' Esselen *mathra*. Jicaque *ma*, *?ama* (Oltrogge). Karok *am-ta:p* 'dust.' Pomo: Proto-Pomo **?a(h)ma:* (Oswalt), **?a(h)mat̪* (McLendon). Quinigua *ama*, *aba*. Seri *amt*. Subtiaba *mbah*, *u:mba* 'dust, earth.' Tequistlatec *amat^s?*. Washo *ŋawa*, *ŋowa* (Washo *ŋ* < **m*). Yuman: Proto-Yuman **?-mat*.

Penutian EARTH.   Plateau: Yakima *uma*, *ima* 'island,' Nez Perce *uma* 'island,' North Sahaptin *-ma-*, *-mɔ-* 'ground, world.' Yukian: Wappo *ɔma*.

Almosan-Keresiouan EARTH.   Algic: Algonquian: Shawnee *aamki*, Cheyenne *-oma-* 'ground,' Beothuk *emer* 'under.' Iroquoian: Seneca *-wē-*. Keresan: Santa Ana *m?e:wa* 'mud.' Kutenai *amma:k*, *ume:* 'underneath.' Mosan: Salish: Pentlatch *me:i*, Nootsack *mix^w*. Siouan-Yuchi: Siouan: Proto-Siouan **mā*.

97 EARTH₄

Macro-Carib EARTH.   Carib: Carib (general) *nono*, Nahugua *noro*. Uitoto: Uitoto *enerwe*, *enie*, Coeruna *noynae*, Miranya Carapana Tapuya *nanyny*. Yagua *nūnī* 'field.'

Equatorial UNDER.   Esmeralda *nuane* 'go down.' Jibaro: Aguaruna *nunga*, Upano *nungači*.

Macro-Tucanoan UNDER.   Huari: Masaka *numaj*. Kaliana *inūbɔ* 'earth.' Puinave *anuma*.

Central Amerind EARTH.   Kiowa-Tanoan: Kiowa *dãm;* Tanoan: Isleta *nan*, Taos *nãm*, Tewa *nang*. Oto-Mangue: R 408 **(n)ja* 'dirty, mud, earth, dust.'

Penutian EARTH.   Gulf: Atakapa *ne;* Natchez *?inoo* 'under'; Chitimacha *nej*, *neh* 'down.' Oregon: Kalapuya *anu*. Plateau: Yakima *neno* 'sand.' Yukian: Yuki *nu* 'sand, gravel,' Wappo *nui* 'sand.'

98 EAT₁

Macro-Panoan EAT.   Lule *apoo*. Panoan: Proto-Panoan **pi*. Tacanan: Guariza *bobi* 'feed.'

Macro-Tucanoan EAT.   Catuquina: Canamari *pu* 'bite.' Kaliana *pa*. Tucano: Tucano, Bara, etc. *ba*. Cf. Pankaruru *vovo* 'tooth.'

Penutian EAT.   California: Wintun: Patwin *ba;* Maidu *pe*, *pa*. Gulf:

Muskogean: Proto-Muskogean *impa, Hitchiti pa (pl. subject). Plateau: Klamath pʾa, pʾan, North Sahaptin ip. Yukian: Wappo paʔ, paʔɛ.

Almosan-Keresiouan EAT.   Algic: Algonquian: Proto–Central Algonquian *pw- 'bite, eat,' *po 'eat,' Arapaho bi-n. Caddoan: Pawnee tut-pawa 'I eat.' Keresan: Proto-Keresan *bə. Siouan-Yuchi: Siouan: Hidatsa pe 'eat, swallow,' Crow apɛ, apa 'chew'; Yuchi wawa 'chew.'

99 EAT$_2$

Macro-Ge EAT.   Botocudo ni-kore. Ge: Macro-Ge *krẽ, *krẽr. Kamakan: Masacara (inthug-)kryng. (Davis connects Ge with Caraja (rə-)thə̃ and Mashakali -tˢit).

Macro-Tucanoan EAT.   Iranshe kalidi 'gnaw.' Shukuru kri(-ngo) 'food, eat.' Tucano: Yupua kuli 'chew,' Desana kuriri 'bite.'

Andean TOOTH.   Cholona kulu. Leco bi-kiri. Patagon kurr. Quechua: Yanacocha, Lamisto, etc. kiru, Chinchaysuyu kilu. Zaparo ikare.

100 EGG$_1$

Macro-Tucanoan EGG.   Capixana inaī. Nambikwara: Proto-Nambikwara *nau.

Andean EGG.   Mayna uun. Patagon: Teuesh na, Tehuelche na 'ostrich egg.'

101 EGG$_2$

Equatorial EGG.   Guahibo: Guahibo, Cuiva tobi. Maipuran: Curipaco topi. Trumai taf.

Chibchan-Paezan EGG.   Choco: Waunana neman, Nonama neuma, Catio nemu. Warrau onomo. (P)

Penutian EGG.   Oregon: Takelma doum 'testicle.' Plateau: North Sahaptin, Nez Perce tamam, Kalapuya atəmp. Cf. Mexican Penutian: Mayan: Tzotzil ton.

102 EXCREMENT$_1$

Macro-Ge EXCREMENT.   Bororo: Bororo pe, epe 'defecate,' Umotina opthi. Ge: Chavante (im-)pa 'guts.'

Chibchan-Paezan EXCREMENT.   Barbacoa: Cayapa, Colorado pe. Cuitlatec bo, biʔi. Jirajara: Ayoman apoo 'guts.' Misumalpan: Sumu, Ulua ba.

Hokan EXCREMENT.   Chimariko (hi:-)pxa 'guts.' Karok ʔa:f. Pomo:

South Pomo *ʔihpʰa* 'guts,' North Pomo, East Pomo *pʰa*. Salinan: San
Miguel *pʰxat* 'guts, excrement.' Seri *ʔapxikaap*. Shasta *ʔi:pxaj* 'guts.'
Subtiaba: Subtiaba *amba*. Tequistlatec *faj*. Yana: Central, North Yana
pʰa-tˢʔi. Yuman: Cocopa, Tipai *pxa* 'guts,' Kiliwa *pʰaʔ* 'guts,' etc.
Yurumangui *-fa* in *anga-fa* 'ashes' (= fire-excrements')
Almosan-Keresiouan EXCREMENT.   Algic: Algonquian: Proto-Algonquian
mo:wi. Mosan: Chemakuan: Quileute *ba:(-do:)* (< *ma:(-no:))*
'defecate.' (AM)

103   EXCREMENT₂

Macro-Tucanoan EXCREMENT.   Auake *atˢi*. Catuquina *to* 'defecate.'
Puinave: Parana Boaboa *taja*. Tucano: Yahuna *ita*, Tucano *eeta*, Bara
əxta, Wanana *tə*.
Almosan-Keresiouan EXCREMENT.   Caddoan: Caddo *idah*. Iroquoian:
Seneca *iʔta*. Siouan-Yuchi: Proto-Siouan (C) *īre*. (KS)
Additional: Oto-Mangue: R 10 *(ʔ)ti(ʔ)(n)* 'defecate, intestines, manure.'

104   EYE

Macro-Ge EYE.   Fulnio *to*. Ge: Krenje *to*, Crengez *nto*, Cherente *to*, *toi*,
etc.
Macro-Panoan EYE.   Guaicuru: Guachi *jataja*, Pilaga *ite*, etc. Mataco:
Macca *toi*, Vejoz *te*. Tacanan: Proto-Tacanan *tuka*, Tacana *e-tua*,
Huarayo *etoxa*.
Macro-Carib EYE.   Andoke *doa*. Uitoto *etoj*.
Equatorial EYE.   Cofan *tʰaʔtʰaʔ* 'look.' Esmeralda *tu*. Guahibo *tae* 'see,'
ta 'look.' Jibaro: Zamora *ti*, Shuara *hi*. Kandoshi: Kandoshi *k-ači-č*,
Shapra *k-ači*. Taruma *a-tˢi*. Timote *tiji* 'see.' Yaruro *da* 'see.'
Macro-Tucanoan EYE.   Puinave: Parana Boaboa *tu*. Ticuna *etu*, *ete*. Yuri
æti, iti.
Central Amerind SEE.   Kiowa-Tanoan: Kiowa *tʰɔ́-n* 'find'; Tanoan: Jemez
ši. Oto-Mangue: R 14 *te* 'learn, teach.' Uto-Aztecan: M 365 *te*.
Azteco-Tanoan: WT 95 *tʰewa* 'see, find.'
Hokan EYE.   Achomawi: Atsugewi *uji*. Chimariko *h-uso-t* (cf. *hi-su-ma:*
'face,' *h-uso:-xa* 'tear'). Comecrudo [u-i] *uʔi*. Karok *ju-p*. Pomo:
North, Northeast, East, Southeast Pomo *ʔuj*. Seri *ʔa:to* (Kroeber *ito*).
Shasta *uwi*. Subtiaba: Subtiaba *s-i:tu* (cf. *i:tu* in *inji:tu* 'tear'),
Tlappanec *iðu*. Tequistlatec *(la-)ʔu*. Yuman: Maricopa *hiðoʔ*, Cocopa
ijuʔ, Walapai *juʔ*, etc. Yurumangui *(ko-)u(-na)*.

105 FALL (v.)

Macro-Ge DESCEND.   Botocudo *čik*. Ge: Cherente *čikraman*, Krenje *tok* 'stumble.'

Almosan-Keresiouan FALL.   Caddoan: Wichita *tak* 'fall one after the other,' Pawnee *itik* 'go down.' Kutenai *takχaχou*. Mosan: Wakashan: Bella Bella *tekwa*, Kwakiutl *tix;* Chemakuan: Quileute *tuku?;* Salish: Nootsack *ti?č*, Tillamook *tč*. Siouan-Yuchi: Siouan, Catawba *(huk-)tuk* 'fall down' (*huk* = 'down').

106 FAR

Macro-Ge FAR.   Bororo *bari* 'distance.' Kaingan: Southern Kaingan *bra*.

Equatorial FAR.   Coche *ibanoj*. Kandoshi *imori* 'deep.' Kariri *mani*. Tupi: Pawate *amuin*, Kawahib *omohī* 'it is far.'

Chibchan-Paezan LONG.   Atacama *pera* 'stretch.' Barbacoa: Cayapa, Colorado *bara* 'long, far.' Chibcha: Duit *ebre* 'high.' Misumalpan: Sumu *malix* 'high.' Talamanca: Viceyta *boruk* 'high.' Warrau *bari*.

Penutian FAR.   Gulf: Atakapa *pel*. Oregon: Takelma *bal-s* 'long.'

107 FEAR

Macro-Ge ANGRY.   Bororo *kurig(-oddo)* 'be angry.' Botocudo *akran* 'anger,' *krak* 'shame.' Ge: Krenje *kryg* 'be angry.'

Hokan FEAR.   Chimariko *xul* 'bad.' Pomo: East Pomo *kul*. Salinan: San Antonio *šxalo*. Yana *kʰul-* 'bad.'

108 FEATHER₁

Macro-Carib HAIR.   Carib: Chayma *ipot*, Galibi *ipotu*, Wayana *pot* 'feather,' etc. Uitoto: Uitoto *ifatie, ifatre*, Nonuya *ofotar*. Yagua *popεjty* 'feather.'

Equatorial FEATHER.   Chapacura: Quitemo *ipatiko*. Kandoshi *poro* 'hair, feather.' Maipuran: Campa *biti* 'feather, hair,' Ipurina *piti*, Carutana *ti-pitˢ* 'eyelashes' (*ti* = 'eye'), etc. Otomaco *paro* 'hair.' Uro: Caranga, Chipaya *pʰasi* 'wing.'

Andean WING.   Araucanian *maln*. Kahuapana: Kahuapana *anpullo-na* 'feather,' Jebero *ambolu* 'feather,' Tschaahui *amporo* 'crown of feathers.' Patagon: Tehuelche [melh]. Quechua: Cochabamba *pʰuru* 'feather.'

Hokan LEAF.   Tequistlatec *li-bela*. Yana: North Yana *tʾaapal-la*. Yuman: Maricopa *xamaʎ*, Tipai *xu?mał*.

Penutian FEATHER.   California: Maidu: Northeast *butu* 'hair'; Yokuts
pada; Wintun: Colouse *pote* (probably a borrowing from Yukian: Clear
Lake, below). Gulf: Tunica *-puli* 'plummage, hair.' Oregon: Alsea
pǝlupǝlu. Tsimshian *pʾǝlkʾwa* 'bird down.' Yukian: Wappo *pučaja,*
puči:š 'hair,' Clear Lake *pʾoti.*

109 FEATHER₂

Macro-Ge FEATHER.   Bororo: Bororo *bo,* Umotina *bo* 'plumage.'
Botocudo *papa* 'leaf.' Kaingan: Palmas *fei* 'leaf,' Tibagi *fe,feie* 'leaf.'
Mashakali: Malali *poe.*
Macro-Panoan FLY (v.).   Guaicuru: Toba *vajo.* Mataco: Mataco *fwija,*
Chulupi *faija.* Moseten *pañ* 'feather.' Panoan: Proto-Panoan **piʔi*
'feather, leaf.' Cf. Lule [pyly] 'feather.'
Macro-Carib FEATHER.   Andoke *byweh* 'he flies.' Bora: Miranya Oira
Assu-Tapuya *abukwa.* Uitoto: Uitoto *ibbe,* Muinane *pee* 'fly.'
Macro-Tucanoan FEATHER.   Kaliana *-upa.* Tucano *poa* (general in
Eastern Tucanoan).
Andean HAIR.   Aymara *phuu, phuju.* Cholona *pe.* Yamana *api* 'short hair.'
Chibchan-Paezan FLY (v.).   Chimu: Eten *up.* Cuitlatec *pa(-ga).* Itonama
a-pihe. Mura *ipoai* 'wing.'
Central Amerind FEATHER.   Oto-Mangue: R 138 **(n)(h)kʷi* 'hair, beard.'
Uto-Aztecan: M 168 **pi.*

110 FINGER₁

Macro-Ge ONE.   Botocudo *po-čik* (*po* = 'finger'), *ǰik* 'alone.' Ge: Proto-
Ge **pi-tˢi, *pi-tˢit,* Kradaho *po:ǰi,* Gorotire *pydʲi,* Kraho *pučite.*
Mashakali *pičet.*
Macro-Carib ONE.   Carib: Trio *tinki, tinkini,* Accawai *tegina,* Chayma
teukon, etc. Kukura *tikua* 'finger.' Yagua *tiki, tikilo,tekini.*
Equatorial FINGER.   Chapacura: Itene *taka* 'one.' Guamo: Santa Rosa
dixi. Jibaro: Zamora *čikičik* 'one,' Aguaruna *tikiǰi* 'one.' Katembri
tika 'toe.' Tupi: Purubora *(wa-)toka* (*wa* = 'hand'). Yuracare *teče*
'thumb.'
Hokan FINGER.   Karok *ti:k* 'hand, finger.' Pomo: North Pomo *kowal-tek*
'ten,' *kowal-šom* 'nine' (*šom* = 'minus'; parallel forms in some other
Pomo dialects).

111 FINGER₂

Macro-Panoan FINGER.   Lule [ys] 'hand.' Mataco: Churupi *-ič* 'hand'

(from *i-t^sami-ič* 'my left hand,' *i-faa-ič* 'my right hand'). Tacanan:
Chama *sisi*, Huarayo *eme-sisi* (*eme* = 'hand'). Vilela *isi-p* 'hand.'
Macro-Carib FINGER.   Andoke *(ka-)t^si-dome* (*dome* = 'hand'). Bora:
Miranya Oira Assu-Tapuya *ma-ugt^si* 'hand,' Miranya [dau-tseh] 'my
hand,' Imihita *(tha-)usi* 'my hand.'

112 FIRE₁

Macro-Ge FIRE.   Caraja *eatu, hæote, eoti*. Fulnio *to* 'burn,' *towe* 'fire,
light.' Guato *(ma-)ta.*
Macro-Panoan FIRE.   Charruan: Charrua *it*, Chana *dioi* 'sun.' Mataco *ita-x*.
Moseten *t^si*. Panoan: Proto-Panoan **či²i*. Tacanan: Proto-Tacanan **ti*.
Chibchan-Paezan BURN.   Chibcha: Boncota *etera* 'fire (a weapon).' Paez
ot^s. Tarascan *ete, et^s(-ku-ni)* 'set on fire.'
Central Amerind FIRE.   Oto-Mangue: R 295 **nsah, *ntah* 'warm, fever.'
Uto-Aztecan: M 423d **tai, *tahi* 'fire, burn.'
Almosan-Keresiouan FIRE.   Algic: Algonquian: Blackfoot *ototo* 'burn'
(transitive); Wiyot *ad, do:w* 'burn.' Iroquoian: Seneca *a²ta*. Keresan:
Proto-Keresan **²iri* 'be hot,' Acoma *idi*.

113 FIRE₂

Macro-Ge FIRE.   Ge: Krenje *kyhy*, Cayapo *kuə, kui*, Cherente *kuzi*,
Chicriaba *kuče*, etc. Guato *kiši*. Kamakan *kaš* 'firewood, wood.'
Mashakali: Mashakali *kešmam*, Capoxo *kešam*, Monachobm *kičau*.
Macro-Carib TREE.   Andoke *koit^se*. Uitoto *ogode* 'plant.' Yagua *iguntia*.

114 FIRE₃

Macro-Tucanoan TREE.   Catuquina: Catuquina *oma*, Parawa *uma*. Maku
o:ba. Mobima *-bo* 'classifier for trees.' Puinave: Ubde-Nehern *ñium*,
ɪum 'plant, vine,' Dou *bæ* 'tree, vine.'
Andean FIRE.   Cholona *a-mo-n* 'burn.' Culli *mu*. Leco *moa*. Patagon:
Ona *am-* 'burn' (intransitive). Yamana *ama* 'burn' (intransitive).
Penutian BURN.   Gulf: Tunica *²ɛma*. Yukian: Wappo *ma, maha*. (YG)
Cf. LIGHT.

115 FIREWOOD

Macro-Ge FIREWOOD.   Bororo *po* 'tree.' Chiquito: Chiquito *ipi*, Churapa
pee-s 'fire.' Ge: Proto-Ge **pī* 'tree, firewood.' Kaingan: Dalbergia *pɛ̃*,
Tibagi *pin* 'fire, firewood,' *pon* 'burn.' Mashakali *baai, abooi* 'tree.'
Puri: Coroado *bo, ambo* 'tree.'

Andean FIRE.   Alakaluf *appel* 'it is hot.' Araucanian: Pehuenche *pio*.
Aymara *pari* 'hot.' Kahuapana: Kahuapana *pan*, *pəŋ*, Jebero *pəŋ*.
Quechua: Santiagueño *paru-ja* 'be roasted.' Patagon: Tehuelche *poon*,
pohon. Yamana: Yahgan *apuru* 'roast,' *apun* 'fireplace.'
Chibchan-Paezan BURN.   Aruak: Kagaba *pula*. Itonama *ubari* 'fire.'
Tarascan *apare*. Yanoama: Yanomamï *fraa*.

116 FLEA

Macro-Panoan FLEA.   Lengua *miše*. Moseten *musi*. Panoan: Capanahua
miuš, Cashinahua *masā*.
Penutian FLEA.   California: Yokuts *pˀa:kˀil*. Gulf: Atakapa *pux*.
Almosan-Keresiouan LOUSE.   Algic: Yurok *mohkoh*. Mosan: Wakashan:
Nootka *mačˀasin* 'flea'; Salish: Lillooet *məkin*, Pentlatch *mačn*, etc.
(AM)

117 FLY (v.)

Macro-Ge FLY.   Bororo *(tou-)udo*. Caraja *taa* 'wing.' Ge: Proto-Ge **tɔ*,
*tɔr. Mashakali *to(-paha)*.
Macro-Tucanoan WING.   Maku *ide*. Ticuna *atɨ* 'shoulder.' Tucano:
Amaguaje *ete* 'shoulder.' Yuri *mæ-ati* 'shoulder.'
Hokan FLY.   Achomawi *ataˀ*. Chimariko *tu, tudu* 'jump.' Pomo: Southeast
Pomo *di*. Yana: North Yana, Yahi *da*, Central Yana *daa* 'jump, fly.'
Penutian FLY.   California: Wintun: Wintu *tʰew*, Patwin *tewe;* Miwok:
Central Sierra *tu:ja:ng* 'jump.' Gulf: Atakapa *ti*. Oregon: Takelma
dawi. Yukian: Yuki *ti* 'fly, jump.'
Almosan-Keresiouan FLY.   Iroquoian: Seneca *tē*, Mohawk *-tie-*. Siouan-
Yuchi: Proto-Siouan **tˀā* (C); Yuchi *tɛ*. (KS)

118 FLY₁ (n.)

Macro-Ge FLY.   Botocudo *kap*. Ge: Krenje *kob*, Chavante *kube*, etc.
Equatorial FLY.   Jibaro: Aguaruna *kāāp*. Tupi: Amniapa, Mekens *kap*
'wasp,' Arikem *ngaba* 'wasp,' Guaraní *kava* 'wasp.'
Macro-Tucanoan FLY.   Puinave: Puinave *kepa* 'bee,' Nadobo *kob*. Tucano:
Waikina *komana*, Wanana *kumana*.
Hokan FLY.   Karankawa *kamex*. Pomo: Kashaya *sˀamo:*, North Pomo
tˢˀammu, etc. Seri *x-komo-h, x-komo-ɬk* (pl.).
Penutian FLY.   California: Yokuts: Proto-Yokuts **kˀama:šiˀ*. Mexican:
Mayan: Tzeltal *čab* 'bee, honey,' Yucatec, Mam *kab* 'honey.' Oregon:
Siuslaw *kˀupi* 'mosquito.' Yukian: Yuki *čap*. Zuni *ˀohha:pa*.

119 FLY₂ (n.)

Equatorial FLY. Arawa: Paumari *marī* 'pium mosquito.' Maipuran: Amuesha *mure*, Wachipairi *morox*, Amarakaeri *mōrōk*, Toyeri *morok*, *jamoro* 'bee.' Tupi: Guajajara, Oyampi *meru*, Cocama *miru*, Guayaki *mberu*, Arikem *maramo* 'mosquito,' Tembe *meru-i* 'mosquito' (= 'fly-small').

Chibchan-Paezan FLY. Atacama *pairi* 'fly, mosquito.' Guaymi: Chumulu, Gualaca *mulmulu*, Penomeño *mun*, Move *mora* 'bee, wasp.' Itonama *pururu*. Misumalpan: Cacaopera *maramara*. Mura *abari* 'bee.' Paez: Guambiana *pulem*. Talamanca: Bribri, etc. *bur* 'bee.' Yanoama: Yanomamï *mroo*, Yanomam *mroro*.

120 FOOT₁

Macro-Ge FOOT. Bororo: Bororo *bure*, Umotina *apu* 'knee,' Botocudo *po* 'foot, hand.' Caraja *waa*. Chiquito *ipope* 'foot,' *piri* 'leg.' Erikbatsa *pørø*. Fulnio *fe*. Ge: Proto-Ge **par*. Guato *apoo*. Kaingan: Palmas *fa* 'leg,' Tibagi *fa* 'leg,' Dalbergia *pe, pen* 'foot.' Mashakali: Malali *apao*. Opaie *(či-)para*. Oti *fum*. Yabuti: Yabuti *u-pa*, Arikapu *(ši-)pra*.

Macro-Panoan FOOT. Guaicuru: Toba, Mocovi *pia*. Mataco: Mataco *pa*, Suhin *fo*, Enimaga *fe*, Payagua *ivo*. Vilela *ape*.

Macro-Carib LEG. Andoke *pa*. Carib: Macusi *upu* 'foot,' Pariri *upe*. Uitoto: Muinane *eiba* 'foot.'

Equatorial FOOT. Chapacura: Itene *ipi* 'thigh.' Kariri: Kariri, Dzubucua *bui*. Katembri *popu* 'ankle.' Maipuran: Uainuma *api*, Achagua *ipa*, Chamicuro *uxpei*, Baure *poj*, etc. Otomaco: Otomaco *bava* 'leg,' Taparita *ipua* 'thigh.' Piaroa *hepui*. Taruma *pa*. Tupi: Arikem *pi*, Guarayo *ipɨ*, Oyampi *pwi*. Yuracare *(te-)bebe*.

Macro-Tucanoan SHIN. Maku *tˢe-peči*. Puinave: Puinave *a-ped*. Ticuna *para* 'tibia.' Tucano: Coreguaje *api* 'foot,' Waikina *pu(-pama)* 'foot.'

Central Amerind LEG. Kiowa-Tanoan: Kiowa *pɔ* 'thigh'; Tanoan: Taos *po* 'thigh,' San Ildefonso, Hopi-Tewa *po*, etc. Oto-Mangue: R 161 **(ʔ)kʷe(n)*.

Hokan FOOT. Chimariko *h-upo*. Quinigua *boi* 'deer's foot.' Yana *bu-i* 'kick' (probably *-i* verbalizer), *bu-ri* 'dance' (= 'foot down').

Penutian FOOT. California: Maidu *paji;* Costanoan: Santa Clara *(či-)pai*, Mutsun *paja* 'run'; Miwok: Central Sierra *pujja* 'move.' Gulf: Muskogean: Choctaw *api*. Mexican: Mixe-Zoque: Tetontepec *poohi* 'leg,' *pa-* (instrumental prefix), Sierra Popoluca *puj*. Plateau: Lutuami *pat^s*, Nez Perce *peju* 'hoof,' Klamath *peč*, Modoc *pet^s*. Tsimshian *ba* 'hip.' Yukian: Wappo *pɛʔ*, *pɔi* 'kick,' *pek* 'track.' Zuni *pačči* 'sole.'

121 FOOT₂

Macro-Panoan TREAD.   Lule *ise* 'leg.' Mataco: Vejoz *t-ose* 'kick, tread,' Chulupi *t-osee* 'kick, tread.'

Hokan FOOT.   Achomawi *saʔje*. Karok *ap-si:h* (*ap* = body-part prefix). Washo *sə-* 'pertaining to the foot.'

Penutian FOOT.   Oregon: Yakonan *sijaʔ*. Tsimshian *asi:*.

Almosan-Keresiouan FOOT.   Algic: Algonquian: Proto–Central Algonquian **sit*. Caddoan: Wichita *ʔas*, Pawnee *asu*, Arikara *axu*. Iroquoian: Seneca *siʔ-t*. Keresan: Proto-Keresan **ʔaši* 'knee,' Santa Ana, etc. *ha-sdiʔ-ni*. Siouan-Yuchi: Proto-Siouan (C) **si*.

122 FOREHEAD₁

Macro-Panoan FOREHEAD.   Guaicuru: Toba *pi*. Lule *upe*. Moseten *afi* 'eyebrow, eyelid, forehead.'

Equatorial FOREHEAD.   Kariri *beba, bebate* 'temple.' Otomaco: Taparita *ipa*. Piaroa: Saliba *pae*.

Chibchan-Paezan EYE.   Aruak: Kagaba *uba*, Atanque, Bintucua *uma*. Chibcha: Chibcha *up(-kwa), uba* 'face,' Margua, Pedraza, Sinsiga *uba*. Cuna *ibia*. Motilon *oo*. Paya *wa*. Rama *u:p*. Talamanca: Bribri *uo(-bra)*, etc. (C)

Almosan-Keresiouan FOREHEAD.   Keresan: Proto-Keresan **pi*. Siouan-Yuchi: Proto-Siouan (M) **pʰe*. (KS)

123 FOREHEAD₂

Macro-Ge FOREHEAD.   Bororo *ak-kai* 'in front' (= 'face-to'). Caraja *ikoke* 'facing toward.' Ge: Cayapo, Karaho *kuka*, Krenje *kuka* 'face,' Acroamirim *ai-kua*. Kaingan: Apucarana *kaka* 'face,' Southern Kaingan *koko* 'face,' etc. Kamakan: Kamakan *aku*, Cotoxo *ake*, Masacara *ky*. Mashakali: Malali *hake*, Macuni *ikoi*. Oti *kua*.

Macro-Tucanoan HEAD.   Canichana *kuku*. Catuquina: Bendiapa *ky*, Parawa *ke*. Muniche *oke*. Tucano: Yahuna *koa* 'forehead.'

Chibchan-Paezan FACE.   Jirajara: Ayoman *ki*. Itonama *ka-* (incorporated object). (P)

Additional: Uto-Aztecan: M 190 **kowa* 'forehead.'

224

124 FRUIT

Macro-Ge FRUIT.   Bororo: Umotina *tokwa*. Ge: Chavante *udekæ*,
Chicriaba *dekran*. Kamakan *dako*.

Macro-Tucanoan FRUIT.   Puinave: Tiquie *teynde*, Yehubde *teegn*. Tucano:
Tucano *dixka*, Uaiana *deka*, etc.

125 GIRL

Central Amerind CHILD.   Kiowa-Tanoan: Kiowa *t^h ɔ-n* (diminutive). Oto-
Mangue: R 87 **tun*. Uto-Aztecan **tana* 'son, daughter' (Hale &
Voegelin).

Hokan SMALL.   Achomawi *-t^san* (diminutive). Coahuilteco *atiut²an, šan*.
Chumash: Santa Barbara *taniw* 'small, child.' Karok *tunue-ič*. Yana
t²ini: 'be small,' *t²ini:-si* 'child.'

Penutian DAUGHTER.   California: Miwok: Central Sierra *tu:ne*, Plains
tele; Costanoan: Soledad *suri-s*. Gulf: Atakapa *teŋ* 'mother, daughter.'

Almosan-Keresiouan GIRL.   Algic: Algonquian: Proto–Central
Algonquian **ta:na* (Michelson), Blackfoot *tunna;* Mosan: Wakashan:
Nootka *t²an²a* 'child.' (AM)

126 GO₁

Macro-Ge GO.   Bororo: Bororo *me(-ru)* 'walk,' Umotina *a-menu*. Botocudo
mū. Chiquito *imi* 'go out,' *amee* 'walk.' Ge: Proto-Ge **mõ, *mõr* 'go,
walk.' Kaingan: Catarina *mū* 'go out,' Dalbergia *mū* (pl. subject).
Kamakan: Kamakan *emang*, Cotoxo *man*, Meniens *niamu* 'let's go.'
Mashakali *mõng*. Puri: Coroado *gamu* 'go away!,' Puri *ma* 'outside.'

Macro-Panoan GO.   Lengua: Lengua *amai* 'road,' Mascoy *mi, mij,amai*
'road.' Mataco: Vejoz, Chulupi *ma*. Moseten *mii* 'go, walk,' *mi, mu*
'walk,' *mami* 'road.'

Equatorial COME.   Piaroa: Saliba *oome*. Timote: Cuica *mah*. Yuracare
ama 'come!'

Macro-Tucanoan ROAD.   Auake *ma* 'walk,' *a²ma, āmā*. Kaliana *mu*.
Tucano (general) *ma*.

Andean GO.   Araucanian: Araucanian *miau-* 'go along,' *-me-* 'go to . . . ,'
Pehuenche *amu* 'walk.' Aymara: Jaqaru *muju* 'wander.' Gennaken:
Gennaken *me(-t^suk)*, Pehuelche *mu*. Quechua: Cochabamba *mu* 'go to
. . . .'

Chibchan-Paezan GO.   Barbacoa: Colorado *mai*, Cayapa *mi* 'go away.'

Choco: Chami *mai*. Cuitlatec *jume* 'walk.' Itonama *mama*. Mura:
Matanawi *amī* 'go!' Paez: Paez *mee* 'go!,' Guambiana *mai* 'road.'
Rama *mang* 'go!' Talamanca: Bribri *mi:* ~ *mina*.
Central Amerind GO.   Kiowa-Tanoan: Kiowa *bæ;* Tanoan: Taos *mē*, Tewa
mã, Jemez *mī:* 'bring.' Uto-Aztecan: M 197 **mi*, **mija*.
Penutian GO.   Chinook *-am* 'go to . . .' (completive suffix). Gulf:
Chitimacha *ʔami* 'go, go away'; Atakapa *mo:* 'arrive.' Oregon:
Kalapuya *maʔa* 'come.' Tsimshian *amia:(t)* 'come from,' *amo:-s* 'one
who comes.' Yukian: Wappo *mi*.
Almosan-Keresiouan ROAD.   Algic: Algonquian: Proto–Central
Algonquian **mjew,* Cheyenne *meeoʔo*. Keresan: Santa Ana *mə* 'leave,'
i:ma 'go!' Mosan: Kutenai *ma* 'trail.'

127 GO₂

Macro-Ge GO.   Bororo: Umotina *a-tī* 'go!' Ge: Kraho *tē* ~ *tēm*. Kaingan:
Dalbergia *teng* (sing. subject).
Macro-Carib GO.   Carib: Maquiritare *uten*, Waiwai *wto* ~ *wtom*, Jaricuna
etamete, Chayma *itamue*. Yagua *s-itamana* 'he arrives.'

128 GO₃

Chibchan-Paezan ROAD.   Chibcha *ie*. Motilon *ja* 'walk.' Rama: Guatuso
ju. Timucua *eje*.
Central Amerind ROAD.   Kiowa-Tanoan: Tanoan: Tewa *ja* 'bring.' Oto-
Mangue: R 413 **(n)ja(n)*. Uto-Aztecan: M 97 **je* 'come' (sing.
subject), M 98 **ja* 'come' (pl. subject), M 79 **ja* 'carry.' Azteco-
Tanoan: WT 90 **ja* 'go, carry.'
Hokan GO.   Karankawa *je*. Salinan: San Antonio *ia, ie*. Tonkawa *jaʔa*
'several move.' Washo *ijeʔ* ~ *ije* (sing. subject). Yana *aja*.
Penutian GO.   Chinook: Wishram *ja*. Gulf: Muskogean: Choctaw *ia*,
Hitchiti *aj, iji* 'leg,' Alabama *iji-api* 'leg' (*api* = 'foot'), Apalachee *ia*,
ja 'leg.' Mexican: Mayan: Chol *ja* 'leg,' Tzeltal *jaʔ* 'hip.' Oregon:
Alsea *jax*. Tsimshian *je:*. Yukian: Wappo *-ja-*.
Almosan-Keresiouan ROAD.   Algic: Algonquian: Proto–Central
Algonquian **ja:* 'go.' Keresan: Proto-Keresan **(hi-)ja:(-ni)*. Mosan:
Salish: Upper Chehalis *ja*. Siouan-Yuchi: Siouan: Woccon *jɔ*, Catawba
jã.

129 GO₄

Macro-Panoan GO.   Guaicuru: Toba, Mocovi, Abipone, etc. *ik.* Mataco:
Nocten, Choroti *ik,* Chunupi *ič,* Towothli *ikʲi.* Panoan: Shipibo,
Conibo, etc. *ka,* Chacobo *ko.* Tacanan: Proto-Tacanan **kwa.*

Andean GO.   Patagon: Tsoneka *oki* 'go!' Sabela: Auca *go.* Zaparo *oku.*

Penutian GO.   California: Wintun: Wintu *qʾaja,* Patwin *kʾaji;* Maidu *koj;*
Miwok: Northern Sierra *uku.* Mexican: Mayan: Kekchí *ko* 'go away,'
Quiché *qʾoj* 'walk.' Plateau: Klamath *g-,* Nez Perce *ikwi.* Yukian:
Yuki *ko.*

130 GOOD₁

Macro-Panoan GOOD.   Lengua *atʾi* 'be sweet.' Lule [eci] 'be good.'
Mataco: Nocten, Vejoz, Chunupi, etc. *is;* Suhin, Chulupi *is* 'beautiful.'
Tacanan: Proto-Tacanan **sai.*

Equatorial GOOD.   Piaroa: Saliba *saja* 'beautiful.' Timote: Cuica *saj.*

Hokan BEAUTIFUL.   Chimariko *(hi-)si(-ta),* cf. *ha-li-ta* 'bad.' Jicaque
isis 'good, beautiful.' Subtiaba *-uːsu* 'good, pretty.' Yana: North Yana
isii 'right.' Yuman: Diegueño *ʾešaš.*

Additional: Chibchan-Paezan: Chibchan: Cuitlatec *is* 'good.   ' Almosan-
Keresiouan: Iroquoian: Cherokee *osi* 'good.'

131 GOOD₂

Equatorial GOOD.   Chapacura: Urupa *wasabna, asapuna.* Coche
čaba,čabe, saba. Maipuran: Manao *sabi,* Tariana *ma-tʾiama* 'beautiful,'
Apolista *suma.* Trumai *tʾipom.* Tupi: Mekens *i-tʾame* 'beautiful,'
Amniapa *tʾamentʾin* 'beautiful.'

Macro-Tucanoan GOOD.   Canichana *ni-čemači* 'beautiful.' Puinave:
Nadobo *čabe,* Curiariai *jəm.*

Chibchan-Paezan GOOD.   Chimu: Eten *tʾup.* Xinca: Chiquimulilla *tʾama*
'good, beautiful,' *čama* (Maldonado).

Hokan GOOD.   Chumash: Santa Ynez, Santa Barbara *šuma.* Karok *jeːšiːp*
'best.' Pomo: Southeast Pomo *tʾama.* Salinan: San Miguel *tˢʾep.* Yana
tˢʾupʾ 'be good.'

Additional: Uto-Aztecan: M 200 **tˢam* 'good.' Siouan-Yuchi: Siouan: Biloxi
čema 'good'; Yuchi *sē.*

132 GOOD₃

Macro-Carib GOOD.   Bora: Bora *imine*, Muinane *imino*. Carib: Jaricuna *mori*, Galibi *mori* 'clean.' Uitoto: Uitoto *mari*, *mano-dʔe* 'healed,' Erare *mare*. Yagua: Yameo *maringre* 'healthy, good,' Masamae Yameo *marī-neea*.

Macro-Tucanoan GOOD.   Capixana *moræra*. Puinave: Puinave *morō* 'right (hand).'

Chibchan-Paezan GOOD.   Barbacoa: Colorado *mira, mera*. Chimu: Eten *man* 'agreeing with,' *moraiñ* 'certainly.' Itonama *ux-mala* 'good, beautiful.' Mura: Matanawi *amori, amuri*. Rama *mali*. Talamanca: Borunca *moren*.

133 GRASS

Equatorial GREEN.   Arawa: Paumari *kuriki*. Kariri: Dzubucua *kraku* 'blue.' Maipuran: Wapishana *kuli* 'green, blue,' Bare *γuling* 'blue.' Tupi: Cocama *ikira*, Guarayo *iakrɨ*. Zamuco: Ebidoso *xār, xārhu* 'green, yellow,' Chamacoco *kuaržo* 'yellow.'

Andean GRASS.   Araucanian *kary* 'green.' Aymara *kʼora*. Catacao: Catacao *taguakol*, Colan *aguakol*. Patagon: Tehuelche *kor*. Sechura *unñiokol*.

Almosan-Keresiouan GREEN.   Kutenai *haq-ɬojit* (*ɬ < *n*; probably to be analyzed as *haq-* [absolutive] + *ɬojit*). Mosan: Wakashan: Nootka *kinʔitˢ* 'blue'; Salish: Proto-Salish *kʷur*, *kʷar*, Kalispel *kʷin*. (AM)

134 GUTS₁

Macro-Ge GUTS.   Bororo *peguru, appagao* 'inside.' Ge: Ramkokamekran *pajalko*.

Macro-Panoan GUTS.   Lule *epoko*. Moseten *voxko, vokko* 'belly.' Panoan: Proto-Panoan *poko*.

Macro-Carib GUTS.   Bora: Miranya *(maγ)-bohu*, [ga-bohguh]. Carib: Proto-Hianacoto *wakulu* 'stomach, intestines,' Aparai *waku*. Uitoto *hebego*. Yagua: Yameo *buo*.

135 GUTS₂

Andean BELLY.   Cholona *kulu* 'guts.' Kahuapana: Jebero *ikin-ək* 'middle' (*-ək* is locative). Patagon: Tsoneka *kin*, Patagon *kim*. Yamana: Yamana, Yahgan *ikimia* 'be inside.'

Hokan GUTS.   Cotoname *kuwela*. Jicaque *kol* 'guts, stomach.'
Tequistlatec *gu*ʔ*u* 'abdomen.'

136 HAIR

Hokan HAIR.   Jicaque *tˢi* 'hair, root.' Pomo: Kashaya *sime*, North Pomo
tˢime, etc. Subtiaba: Tlappanec *tˢūng* 'hair, root.' Yuman: Cocopa
išma, Mohave *sama* 'root,' Kiliwa *esmok*, etc.
Almosan-Keresiouan HAIR.   Caddoan: Pawnee *uːs*, *ošu*. Keresan: Santa
Ana *haː-ẓa-n*. Siouan-Yuchi: Siouan: Proto-Siouan *kʼū 'feather,'
Dakota *šū* 'feather,' Woccon *summe;* Yuchi *tˢɛ̄*. (KS)

137 HAND₁

Macro-Ge GIVE.   Bororo *mako*. Botocudo *am*, *um*. Ge: Crengez *mango*,
Sakamekran *amu*, Karaho *i-ma* 'give me!' Kaingan: Tibagi *ma*, *ba*
'bring.' Kamakan *min*, *mane*, *ma*.
Macro-Panoan HAND.   Guaicuru: Abipone, Pilaga *imak* 'left hand.'
Lengua: Lengua *amik*, Kaskiha *hemik*. Mataco: Payagua *i-mahiar*,
Macca *imaxi* 'left hand.' Panoan: Proto-Panoan *mɨkɨnɨ, Amahuaca,
Cashinahua *maka*, Caripuna *moken*. Tacanan: Proto-Tacanan *e-me,
Arasa *imiatˢa*.
Equatorial HAND.   Jibaro: Aguaruna *am* 'give,' *umu* 'take.' Kariri:
Dzubucua *mu* 'take.' Maipuran: Ignaciano *-ama* 'take away,' Baure
e-mo 'take.' Otomaco: Taparita *mea*. Timote: Mocochi *ma* 'bring,'
Maguri *me* 'take!' Tupi: Proto-Tupi *meʔeŋ. Uro: Caranga *maka*
'receive.' Zamuco: Ebidoso *mɛ*, Chamacoco *umme*.
Macro-Tucanoan ARM.   Auake *umē*. Catuquina [paghi-mu] 'palm' (*paghi*
= 'hand'). Iranshe *mimā*. Maku *(tabu-)ime* 'branch' (*tabu* = 'tree').
Puinave: Parana Boaboa, etc. *mo*, Ubde-Nehern *mummui*. Ticuna *mi*
'hand.' Tucano: Dyurumawa, etc. *amue*, Sara, etc. *amo* 'hand.'
Andean ARM.   Alakaluf *merr*. Kahuapana *imira* 'hand.' Mayna *mani*.
Patagon: Ona *mar* 'arm, hand.' Quechua *maki* 'hand.'
Chibchan-Paezan HAND.   Aruak: Guamaca *eme* 'take!' Atacama *mut(-sma)*
'five' (*sema* = 'one'). Barbacoa: Cayapa *manda*, Colorado *manta*.
Chimu: Chimu *mæča*, Eten [mechs]. Itonama *ma-* (instrumental
prefix). Jirajara: Ayoman *man*, Gayon *a-mant*. Misumalpan: Miskito
miχta. Rama *mukuik*. Xinca: Sinacatan *mux* 'finger.' Yanoama: Yanam
imɨ 'seize, catch,' Yanomam *imik*, *imi* 'finger,' Sanema *ami* 'finger.'

Central Amerind HAND.   Kiowa-Tanoan: Kiowa *mã, mẽ-ga* 'give';
Tanoan: Proto-Tanoan **ma-n*, Taos *mãn*, Isleta *man*, San Ildefonso
mãng, Jemez *ma(-te)*, Hopi Tewa *mɛ*, *mɛgeh* 'give.' Oto-Mangue: R
382 **wa* 'right hand,' Proto-Chinantec **nwan*. Uto-Aztecan: M 215
*ma, **moʔ*.

Hokan HAND.   Achomawi *-mu-* 'carry.' Chimariko *mai* 'carry.'
Coahuilteco *maux*, *mi* 'have.' Jicaque *mas*. Karankawa *makuel* 'five.'
Pomo: East Pomo *ma* 'hold' (sing. object). Salinan: San Miguel *maa*,
maʔa 'bring, carry.' Tequistlatec *mane* 'hand, arm,' *mage* 'five'
(Angulo & Freeman), *amakeʔ* 'five' (Turner). Tonkawa *mam* 'bring.'
Yana *moh-* 'take along, fetch' (*mah-* passive). Yuman: Yuma *i:mi*, *ami*
'bring,' Akwa'ala *man* 'arm.'

Penutian HAND.   California: Maidu *ma;* Miwok: Central Sierra *ammə*
'give,' *-ma* 'hand' (deduced from 'left hand' and 'right hand').
Chinook *m-* 'to hand.' Gulf: Muskogean: Choctaw *ima* 'give;' Tunica
muhi 'carry in the hand.' Mexican: Mixe-Zoque: Mixe *ma* 'give';
Totonac *makan* 'hand.' Yukian: Wappo *meʔ*, *mɛ* (also, instrumental
prefix).

Almosan-Keresiouan HAND.   Algic: Algonquian: Proto–Central
Algonquian **mi:*, **mi:-l* 'give,' Blackfoot *-mi*. Keresan: Santa Ana
ha-mʔasdiʔi-ni. Mosan: Wakashan: Kwakiutl *maχwa* 'give potlatch.'

138 HAND₂

Macro-Ge HAND.   Botocudo *ni*, *nika* 'arm.' Ge: Apinage *ni-kral*, Suya
ñi-(ko), Cherente *ni(-krai)*, Proto-Ge **ñĩ-kra*. Kaingan: Came, Palmas
ningge, Tibagi *ninge*, *nin*, *ne*. Kamakan: Cotoxo *nin(-kre)*. Opaie
ni(-nje). Yabuti: Yabuti *ni(-ku)*, Mashubi *ni(-ka)*, Arikapu *nu(-hu)*.

Macro-Panoan GIVE.   Guaicuru: Pilaga *na*, Mocovi *an*, Toba *ane*. Lule *ni*.
Panoan: Proto-Panoan **ʔinã*.

Macro-Tucanoan FINGER.   Huari: Masaka *inæ*. Ticuna *-naa*. Yuri *-unoo*
(Wallace), *-enoo* 'hand' (Spix).

Almosan-Keresiouan HAND.   Algic: Algonquian: Proto–Central
Algonquian **-en-*, Micmac, Potowotami *-in* 'by hand.' Iroquoian:
Tuscarora *-ʔohn*. Kutenai *(ahq-)ʔa:n* 'handle.'

139 HAND₃

Macro-Ge BRING.   Bororo: Bororo *to*, Umotina *ta* 'take.' Ge: Krenje *to*.

Macro-Carib GIVE.   Carib: Proto-Carib *utu* (Goeje 1735). Yagua: Yameo
   ti.
Andean TAKE.   Araucanian: Pehuenche *tu*. Yamana: Yahgan *ata*. Zaparo
   ata.
Chibchan-Paezan TAKE.   Aruak: Kagaba *tei* 'carry.' Barbacoa: Cayapa *taʔ*.
   Choco: Catio *ata*, Chami *do*. Yanoama: Yanomamï *te*.
Hokan HAND.   Chimariko *tu-* 'with the hand.' Pomo: East Pomo *du-* 'with
   the hand.' Washo *d-adu*, *du-* 'with the hand.'

140 HARD₁

Macro-Carib HARD.   Uitoto *keriire-ide* 'strong.' Yagua *čøra*, *søra*.
Equatorial HARD.   Arawa: Culino *kʰara* 'be hard.' Kariri: Kariri *kra* 'dry,'
   Dzubucua *kro-dʼe* 'strong.' Maipuran: Anauya *korokoroni* 'bone,'
   Amuesha *ičaš*. Tupi: Mekens *i-kere* 'savage,' Purubora *kirī*, *kirīng*
   'dry.' Zamuco: Tumraha *karo* 'dry, empty, waterless.'
Chibchan-Paezan BONE.   Aruak: Guamaca *kakala*, Bintucua *akana* 'joint.'
   Chibcha: Chibcha [quyne], Tegria *korara*, Manare *kus-kare* 'finger
   joints.' Cuna *kala*. Guaymi: Move *kro*, Gualaca *kone*. Motilon:
   Dobocubi *akara*. Paya *kwakwana* 'hard.' Rama: Guatuso *kora*. (C)
Central Amerind HARD.   Kiowa-Tanoan: Tanoan: Taos *kʷē*. Oto-Mangue:
   R 103 *(n)(h)ki(n)* 'hard, metal, stone.' Uto-Aztecan: M 1 *kʷi*, *kʷini*
   'acorn.' Azteco-Tanoan: WT 22 *kʷenga*.
Hokan BONE.   Jicaque *kʰele*. Tequistlatec *-egaɬ*.
Penutian HARD.   Chinook *qəlqəl*. Gulf: Natchez *ʔekʷele* 'bone';
   Muskogean: Hitchiti, etc. *funi*. Oregon: Yakonan *xulxus* 'strong,'
   Takelma *kʼalʼ-s* 'sinew.' Plateau: Lutuami *kuli-s* 'strong,' Yakima
   klɔ-ei. Yukian: Wappo *kali* 'be strong.' Cf. California: Maidu *kulu*
   'wrist, ankle.'

141 HARD₂

Chibchan-Paezan DRY.   Chimu: Eten *koč* (transitive). Itonama *kʼosa*
   (intransitive). (P)
Almosan-Keresiouan HARD.   Caddoan: Pawnee *kasis* 'be hard,' Arikara
   kaħš, Wichita *kasɪ* 'hard, loud.' Keresan: Santa Ana *skʼasɪ*. (KS)

142 HATE

Equatorial BAD.   Guahibo *bole* 'bad omen.' Kariri: Dzubucua *bule*. Tupi:
   Purubora *bere*. Yuracare *bene-ti*.

231

Andean HATE.   Araucanian: Pehuenche *piʎ-an* 'no quiero.' Cholona
a-puʎu-an.

143 HEAD₁

Macro-Ge HEAD.   Mashakali: Macuni *epotoi*, Patasho *patoi* 'head, hair.'
Puri: Coropo *pitao.*
Equatorial HEAD.   Coche *butᵉe* 'cabecilla.' Guamo *puti, pute.* Maipuran:
Piapoco *nu-puta* 'my forehead,' Adzaneni *nu-ihitu* 'head.' Otomaco
putta.

144 HEAD₂

Macro-Ge HEAD.   Fulnio *tka*. Guato *dokeu*. Puri: Coroado *takuen*
'above.'
Macro-Panoan HEAD.   Charruan: Chana *tuk* 'mountain.' Guaicuru: Toba-
Guazu *-ligi* 'above,' Abipone *alge, elge* 'on top' (Guaicuru *l* < **t*).
Lengua *takhe* 'above.' Lule [tocco]. Mataco: Choroti *atak*, Chulupi
utex 'hill,' Macca *utex* 'hill.' Moseten [tacche] *takke.*
Almosan-Keresiouan ABOVE.   Algic: Algonquian: Blackfoot *-itoxk*,
Cheyenne *ta:xe*. Mosan: Chemakuan: Chemakum *tekʲˀ* 'head,' Quileute
(oˀ)tˀeqʷ 'head'; Salish: Lillooet *təqa*, Shuswap *-tk* 'on top of,' Upper
Chehalis *teč* 'upon,' etc. (AM)
Cf. ABOVE₁.

145 HEAR₁

Chibchan-Paezan HEAR.   Aruak: Kagaba *nuka*, Guamaca *naku*, Bintucua
nokou. Chimu: Eten *nok* 'recognize' (*reconecer).* Malibu: Chimila
nongi. Warrau *noko.*
Penutian HEAR.   Gulf: Atakapa *nak*. Mexican: Huave *o-laag* 'ear.'
Oregon: Coos *nixt* 'touch,' Takelma *latˢˀag* 'touch.' Tsimshian
nˀaxnˀo. Cf. Mayan: Quiché *nakˀax* 'touch.'
Additional: Uto-Aztecan: M 148a **naka* 'ear.'

146 HEAR₂

Macro-Tucanoan EAR.   Capixana *i-tēĩũ*. Ticuna *čin, sinu*. Yuri *tinæho.*
Andean HEAR.   Cholona *a-sinn-an*. Leco *asoni-čiki*. Patagon: Patagon
šene 'ear,' Tsoneka *sane* 'ear,' etc.

147 HEAVEN₁

Macro-Ge ABOVE.   Fulnio *kili* 'go up.' Kaingan: Catarina, Tibagi *kri*, Dalbergia *klẽ* 'on top.'

Hokan ABOVE.   Pomo (general): *kali* 'heaven,' South Pomo *kali* 'heaven, up.' Seri *koła* 'upward' (perhaps *k* is not part of the root). Tonkawa *tˢʔel*.

148 HEAVEN₂

Macro-Tucanoan ABOVE.   Puinave *ma*. Tucano: Amaguaje, Siona *emue*, Tsoloa *emea*, Coto *mwi* 'go up,' etc.

Hokan HEAVEN.   Quinigua *imi* 'hill.' Salinan: San Antonio *l-ema*. Seri *ʔamime*. Subtiaba: Subtiaba *d-ema-lu*, Tlappanec *d-e:hma*. Tequistlatec *le-maʔa*. Yuman: Yuma *ʔame* 'high,' Tipai *maj*, Mohave *ammaja*, etc.

149 HIT (v.)

Macro-Ge HIT.   Botocudo *čik*. Kaingan: Tibagi *taik*.

Macro-Panoan HIT.   Lengua: Mascoy *tik*. Moseten *-tak* in *pak-tak* 'to nail,' etc. (Bibolotti, lxvi, 'hitting action'). Lule *tak-* 'wooden instrument or effect produced by it.' Panoan: Cashinahua *ta-*, *tas-* (instrumental prefix for hitting action).

Almosan-Keresiouan HIT.   Algic: Wiyot *tik*, *tokʷan* 'slap'; Yurok *tikʷohs*. Caddoan: Wichita *ti:kʷi*, *takʷi*, Arikara *takit* 'be broken.' Kutenai *tʼikʔ* 'destroy.' Mosan: Chemakuan: Chemakum *ta:q*, Quileute *tˢex*; Wakashan: Nootka *tˢoqʷ*; Salish: Squamish *tˢəxʷ* 'be hit,' Snohomish *tˢaqʔ*, Lillooet *tˢikən* 'beat, whip,' Tillamook *tq*.

150 HOLE₁

Andean MOUTH.   Aymara: Jaqaru *šimi*. Patagon. Ona *šem*, Tehuelche *šam*. Quechua: Cochabamba *šimi*, other dialects *simi*.

Hokan EAR.   Achomawi: Atsugewi *asmak*. Chimariko *hi-sam*, *šem* 'listen.' Comecrudo *somi* 'cave.' Karok *ʔa:siv* 'cave.' Pomo: Proto-Pomo **šima* (Oswalt). Tequistlatec *la-šʔmas*. Yuman: Proto-Yuman **smaʎ(k)*. Cf. Washo *d-amal* 'hear'; Yana: Central, North *malʔgu*.

Penutian EAR.   Chinook: Chinook *čam* 'hear,' Wishram *čmaq* 'hear.' Mexican: Mayan: Yucatec *čen* 'listen.' Tsimshian: Nass *tˢəm-mux*. Yukian: Wappo *tˢema*, Huchnom *tˢum*, Coast Yuki *tˢem*.

Penutian MOUTH.　California: Proto-Yokuts *sama?, Maidu *simi.* Oregon:
Coos *tsˀma* 'chin,' Lower Umpqua *tˀamitˀəm* 'chin.' Plateau: Klamath
som, Molala *similk.*

Penutian NOSE.　California: Maidu: South *suma;* Yokuts *šen* 'smell.' Gulf:
Natchez *šamatˢ;* Tunica *šimu* 'blow nose.' Mexican: Mayan: Quiché
tˀam, Mam *čam,* Kakchiquel *tˀan.* Oregon: Coos *si:n,* Takelma *xin*
'sniff.' Yukian: Wappo *šina, šima.*

Evidently a root meaning 'hole' was applied especially to the apertures of
the head.　Compare the following Almosan-Keresiouan etymology.

Almosan-Keresiouan HOLE.　Mosan: Wakashan: Kwakiutl, Bella Bella
sms 'mouth'; Chemakuan: Chemakum *simu:sit* 'nose.' Siouan-Yuchi:
Siouan: Catawba *somō.*

151 HOLE₂

Macro-Tucanoan HOLE.　Auake *-muje* (deduced from 'nostril' = 'nose-
hole'). Puinave: Puinave *moi,* Curiariai *māi* (deduced from 'nostril').

Hokan HOLE.　Esselen *imu(-sa).* Pomo: Northeast Pomo, Southeast Pomo
mo, South Pomo *hi:mo.* Yana *mukˀula* 'round hole, pit' (*kˀula* possibly
= 'sit'; Sapir).

152 HORN

Penutian HORN.　California: Miwok: Southern Sierra *killi;* Wintun:
Nomlaki *kˀili;* Costanoan: Rumsien *čirx.* Tsimshian *xaxan-s.* Yukian:
Yuki *hin* 'antler,' Huchnom *hine.*

Almosan-Keresiouan HORN.　Algic: Algonquian: Blackfoot *-ixkin,* Ojibwa
nen-t-e:škan 'my horn.' Kutenai *(akuh-)qɬe* (*ɬ* ~ *n*). (AM)

153 HOUSE

Macro-Panoan HOUSE.　Moseten *tii* 'nest.' Panoan: Shipibo *ati.* Tacanan:
Huarayo, Tiatinagua *eti,* etc.

Equatorial HOUSE.　Arawa: Culino *uza.* Chapacura: Urupa *asa,* Itene *asi.*
Piaroa: Saliba *ito.* Tupi: Guayaki *eiti* 'nest,' Yuruna *atia* 'nest,' etc.
Zamuco *idai.*

Andean HOUSE.　Alakaluf *ata, at.* Aymara: Aymara, Jaqaru *uta.* Zaparo
ita.

Chibchan-Paezan HOUSE.　Allentiac *utu, uti.* Barbacoa: Colorado *toh*
'village.' Chibcha [uze] 'nest.' Choco: Nonama, Saija, Tucura *te,* Catio

te 'house, nest,' Andagueda *taj*, etc. Lenca: Similaton *tou*, Guajiquero *thau*, etc. Mura: Mura-Piraha *ataj*.

Central Amerind HOUSE.   Kiowa-Tanoan: Kiowa *to;* Tanoan: Taos *tʰə-*. Oto-Mangue: R 83 *(ʔ)tu(h)*.

Almosan-Keresiouan HOUSE.   Algic: Algonquian: Proto–Central Algonquian *teewa* 'be,' Ojibwa *ta* 'dwell, live.' Mosan: Chemakuan: Quileute *-ti, te:-;* Salish: Squamish *taʔ* 'be.' Siouan-Yuchi: Proto-Siouan *ti* 'dwell, house.'

Additional: Macro-Carib: Carib: Maiongom *ato*, Chayma *ata*, Bakairí *ɔta*, Barama River *owto*, etc. (all = 'house').

154 HUSBAND

Macro-Ge HUSBAND.   Ge: Cayapo *miæn*. Kaingan: Guarapuava *eibene*. Mashakali: Macuni *et-pen*.

Equatorial HUSBAND.   Guahibo: Guahibo *amona*, Guayabero *amul-t*. Piaroa: Saliba *mure* 'boy.' Uro: Callahuaya *mana* 'person.'

Macro-Tucanoan MAN.   Kaliana *mīnō* 'man, person.' Puinave *mbon, mbodn*. Tucano: Chiranga *imīgno*, Wanana *meno*, Desana *emenge*, Waikina *emeno*, etc.

Hokan HUSBAND.   Chumash: San Luis Obispo *smano*, *ɬmano* 'man.' Karok *ʔavan*. Subtiaba *ambin*. Washo *bu-me:liʔ* (*bu-* is a dual prefix as in 'son-in-law').

155 KILL

Macro-Ge KILL.   Bororo: Bororo *bi* 'die,' Umotina *bia* 'die, kill.' Botocudo *paog*. Fulnio *pa* 'hit.' Ge: Proto-Ge *pī(r)*. Opaie *pie* 'die.'

Macro-Carib KILL.   Carib: Surinam *wo* 'hit, kill,' Taulipang *we*, Pauishana *ipo(-ke)* 'kill!' Uitoto *fa* (Kinder), *pa* (Minor).

Equatorial KILL.   Cochc *obana* 'dead.' Cofan *pa* 'die, dead.' Esmeralda *uba-le* 'died,' *uba-nege* 'assassin.' Kariri: Kariri *pa*, Kamaru *pa* 'be dead.' Maipuran: Toyeri *bei* 'die.' Trumai *fa*. Yuracare *bobo*.

Chibchan-Paezan DIE.   Barbacoa: Cayapa *pe, peja*, Colorado *pu(-jae)*. Chibcha: Manare *paja-gui* 'kill.' Choco: Chami *piuee*. Cuna *ipjoa* 'kill.' Tarascan *ahpe* 'kill.'

Hokan HIT.   Tequistlatec *ba(ʔma)*. Yana *baa*.

156 KNEE₁

Macro-Panoan KNEE.   Lule *akt^s*. Mataco: Suhin *akwis*, Towothli *kooit^s*. Moseten *kat^ege*.

Equatorial KNEE.   Kariri: Dzubucua, Kamaru *kudu*. Maipuran: Kustenau *kati* 'leg,' Waura *kate* 'leg,' Wapishana *kudura*, Mapidiana *kuduru*. Tusha *kudu* 'shin.' Uro: Uro, Chipaya *kut^s*, *kut^si*. Zamuco: Chamacoco *os-ikketi*, Tumraha *kažete*.

Macro-Tucanoan KNEE.   Iranshe *īnā-kati* (*īnā* = 'foot'). Nambikwara: Proto-Nambikwara **kat^?*. Shukuru *gati* 'shin.'

Chibchan-Paezan SHIN.   Guaymi: Move *ngurie*. Misumalpan: Ulua, Sumu *kal*. Tarascan -*kari*- (incorporated). (C)

Penutian KNEE.   Chinook: Wishram *iqxwit*. Gulf: Atakapa *ikat*.

157 KNEE₂

Chibchan-Paezan KNEE.   Aruak: Guamaca *buka* 'knee, elbow.' Betoi *re-moka* 'foot.' Choco: Napipi *makara* 'thigh.' Itonama *muka-kano* 'hip, thigh.' Misumalpan: Sumu *kalas-mak* (cf. *kal* 'foot'). Warrau *muku*. Yanoama: Yanomamï *makoke*.

Hokan KNEE.   Chimariko *h-itxan-imaxa* (*h-itxan* = 'leg'). Chumash: Santa Barbara *sibuk* 'elbow,' Santa Cruz *šipuk* 'elbow,' etc. Pomo: Southwest Pomo *moko*. Washo *moko*. Yuman: Walapai *mipuk*, Tipai *mi:pok, ma-pok* (pl.), etc.

Penutian KNEE.   Gulf: Chitimacha *mo:ku;* Tunica *muhki* 'to bow.' Mexican: Mixe-Zoque: Zoque *muhkehk* 'crouch,' *muknaj* 'crouch'; Huave *mohkeh* 'crouch.' Zuni *mokči* 'elbow.'

Additional: Uto-Aztecan: M 436 **mat^s* 'thigh.'

158 KNOW

Penutian KNOW.   California: Costanoan: San Francisco *hima* 'see,' Santa Clara *xima-i* 'see' (Costanoan *h* and *x* probably derive from **k); Wintun *q^?omiha* 'understand, answer.' Gulf: Chitimacha *kimi* 'think.' Mexican: Mayan: Kekchí *kam* 'answer.' Yukian: Wappo *kɔm* 'think.'

Almosan-Keresiouan KNOW.   Algic: Yurok *kom(t^sum)*. Iroquoian: Seneca *hõ*. Mosan: Wakashan: Nootka *kamat^?ap*, Nitinat *ka^?bat^?p*. Siouan-Yuchi: Proto-Siouan **x^?ū*.

159 LARGE₁

Macro-Ge LONG.   Caraja *titi* 'many.' Chiquito *tii.* Ge: Kraho *-ti*
(augmentative), Krenje *ti* 'many,' Ramkokamekran *ti* 'large.' Kaingan:
Catarina *taie* 'long, high,' Tibagi *teie,* Palmas *tei* 'long, high.'
Mashakali: Capoxo *itoita,* Macuni *itʰoitʰa.* Opaie *ta* 'large.' Puri *tahe*
'large.'

Macro-Panoan LONG.   Lengua *towa-nji* 'deep.' Mataco: Choroti *tiohi, to,
tu* 'high, long.' Panoan: Caripuna *tētē,* Chacobo *titika* 'deep.' Tacanan:
Proto-Tacanan **du-* 'deep,' Tacana *due-da* 'deep,' Cavineña *de(-da)*
'deep.'

Equatorial LARGE.   Jibaro: Zamora *unda.* Maipuran: Toyeri *-da, -nda.*

Macro-Tucanoan LARGE.   Huari *watæa.* Nambikwara: Northern
Nambikwara *aat.* Puinave: Puinave *wotwot* 'long,' Papury *wotji*
'broad.' Ticuna *ta.* Yuri *tihi* 'large, broad' (Wallace), *tij* (Spix).

Central Amerind LARGE.   Kiowa-Tanoan: Kiowa *tʰɔ* 'far.' Oto-Mangue: R
76 **tu* 'large, long, far.'

Hokan MANY.   Chimariko *eta, itat.* Comecrudo *sekua.* Cotoname *ata:*
'very.' Karok: Karok *taj,* Arra-Arra *tai, taikh.* Seri *-atxo.* Tequistlatec
ataxu. Tonkawa *tek.* Washo *tʼekju.* Yana *datʼ-.* Yuman: Yuma *ʔataj,*
Kiliwa *taj,* Walapai *teka.*

Penutian LARGE.   California: Miwok: Lake *ʔadi.* Gulf: Chitimacha *ʔati.*
Plateau: Klamath *ʔa:di* 'long.'

Almosan-Keresiouan LARGE.   Mosan: Wakashan: Nootka *ta:-* 'long
object'; Salish: Tillamook *tan.* Siouan-Yuchi: Proto-Siouan (C) **tʰã.*

160 LARGE₂

Andean ALL.   Cholona: Cholona *mek,* Hivito *maxal* 'much.' Patagon: Ona
meheš, makes. Yamana: Yamana *maagu* 'many,' Yahgan *mu:ka* 'large,
long.'

Penutian LARGE.   California: Yokuts *metʼ;* Costanoan: Mutsun, San Juan
Bautista *matili;* Maidu: Nisenan *mukʼ.* Gulf: Tunica *maka* 'fat' (n.);
Atakapa *metˢ.* Oregon: Siuslaw *mekšt* 'fat' (n.), *mi:xt* 'fat' (adj.), Coos
mitˢi-s 'fat' (n.). Plateau: Nez Perce *imeke-s.*

Almosan-Keresiouan LARGE.   Algic: Algonquian: Proto–Central
Algonquian **meʔθ, *meʔši,* Delaware *imanki* 'it is large,' Natick
mogki, Blackfoot *imaxk.* Keresan: Santa Ana *mʼe:ziči.* Mosan:

Chemakuan: Chemakum *ma:t'ča,* Quileute *me'ši;* Salish: Lkungen
mukku 'all,' Nootsack *mq'w* 'all,' Songish *məkw* 'all,' etc. Cf.
Kutenai *-ma-* 'long object.'
Additional: Uto-Aztecan: M 165 **meka* 'far.'

161 LAUGH (v.)

Andean LAUGH.   Culli *kankiu.* Cholona: Hivito *kolxam.* Zaparo *kora.*
Chibchan-Paezan LAUGH.   Barbacoa: Colorado *kari, kakari.* Chimu: Eten
kall. Misumalpan: Matagalpa *kari.* Yanoama: Shiriana *īka, īkara.*
Additional: Oto-Mangue: R 127 **(n)kan* 'laugh.'

162 LEAF₁

Macro-Ge LEAF.   Bororo *aro.* Caraja *iru.* Kamakan: Kamakan, Cotoxo
ere.
Equatorial LEAF.   Cayuvava *ene.* Jibaro: Shuara *uri* 'feather.' Kariri *era.*
Yuracare *ele.* Zamuco: Tumraha *ingju.*

163 LEAF₂ ˙

Equatorial LEAF.   Arawa: Yamamadi, Culino *apani.* Chapacura: Itene,
Wanyam *pana* 'tree,' Chapacura *pane* 'firewood.' Maipuran: *pana,*
general as 'leaf,' but Uainuma *abana* 'tree,' Ipurina *amana* 'tree,'
Jumana *awana* 'tree.' Uro *parna, para* 'firewood.' (A)
Macro-Tucanoan LEAF.   Catuquina: Canamari *ba.* Puinave *puniohn.*
Tucano: Wanana *poni,* Desana *pū,* Wanana *poli,* etc.
Central Amerind LEAF.   Kiowa-Tanoan: Tanoan: Taos *baane,* Jemez *fōja*
'leaf, grass.' Oto-Mangue: R 232 **(n)kʷa(h)(ʔ)n* 'leaf, bush-plant,
herb.'

164 LEAF₃

Macro-Carib LEAF.   Bora: Muinane *aame.* Carib: Pimenteira *uma.* Uitoto:
Uitoto *ibe,* Miranya Carapana Tapuya *ame.* Yagua *mi.*
Hokan FEATHER.   Chimariko *himi.* Tequistlatec *imi.*

165 LEG

Macro-Ge LEG.   Bororo *tori.* Caraja *ti.* Chiquito *i-ča-s.* Erikbatsa
(ka-)it(-ma). Ge: Proto-Ge **tɛ.* Kaingan: Catarina *(in-)tˢo* 'my leg.'
Kamakan: Cotoxo *tie.* Cf. Oti [taz], [tazh], [etage].
Macro-Panoan LEG.   Charruan: Charrua *atit.* Guaicuru: Mbaya *itti,* Pilaga

iče, Toba *ači*, Komlek *iči*. Mataco: Suhin *atoi*, Vejoz *če*. Panoan: Proto-Panoan **taʔɨ*. Tacanan: Proto-Tacanan **ta-, *tiɨ*.

Macro-Carib LEG.   Andoke *ka-dekkhe* 'foot.' Bora: Bora *take*, Imihita *me-taxki*.

Equatorial LEG.   Cofan *tˢei* 'foot.' Esmeralda *taha, ta* 'foot.' Guahibo: Guahibo *taxu* 'foot,' Cuiva *taxo* 'foot.' Piaroa *tˢiha* 'thigh.' Trumai *da*. Yaruro [tahuh].

Macro-Tucanoan FOOT.   Koaia *toʔa, toha*. Puinave: Marahan *doi*. Yuri *uti*.

Central Amerind LEG.   Kiowa-Tanoan: Kiowa *tʰū*. Uto-Aztecan: M 187 **ta, *to* 'foot.'

Penutian LEG.   Gulf: Natchez *ʔat*. Yukian: Wappo *ṭaʔ*, Clear Lake *tˀa*. (YG)

166 LIGHT (n.)

Macro-Tucanoan LIGHT.   Iranshe *maʔa* 'day, light.' Ticuna *omɨ*. Tucano: Desana *ame*, etc., Amaguaje *mea-gi* 'shines.'

Chibchan-Paezan SUN.   Aruak: Kagaba *mama*. Barbacoa: Colorado, Cayapa *ma* 'day.' Misumalpan: Ulua, Sumu *ma* 'day, sun.' Paya *maa*.

Hokan BURN.   Chimariko *maa*. Jicaque *ʔim*. Karok *im-* 'action by heat or fire.' Shasta *ʔimma* 'fire.' Washo *ng-*. Yana *maa-* 'action by fire.'

Penutian SUN.   California: Yokuts *me* 'sun, moon.' Oregon: Takelma *bē* 'sun, day.' Cf. Mexican: Mixe-Zoque: Tetontepec *poʔɔ*, Sierra Popoluca *poja*, etc.; Totonac *papa;* Mayan: Kekchí *po*, Pokomchi *po, poh*, all meaning 'moon.'

Additional: Uto-Aztecan: M 286a **meja, *mea*, M 286b **metˢa* 'moon, month.'

167 LIP

Macro-Panoan MOUTH.   Guaicuru: Pilaga, Toba-Guazu *ap*, Guachi *iape* 'lip, mouth.' Mataco *(le-)pe* 'door.' Vilela *jep*.

Macro-Carib MOUTH.   Andoke *(ka-)fi*. Bora: Bora *(me-)he*, Imihita *me-ehe*. Carib: Taulipang *ipi* 'lip,' Accawai *epi* 'lip,' etc. Uitoto: Nonuya *ofwe*, Ocaina *poi*, Uitoto *fue*. Yagua: Yameo *ipe* (Tessman), *po* (Espinosa Perez).

Equatorial LIP.   Arawa: Culino *ipou*. Guamo *du-fpa*. Maipuran: Baniva *api*, Marawa *beu, biu* 'mouth.' Otomaco *jopo*. Piaroa *(tˢe-)he*. Tupi: Mundurucu *ubi* 'mouth,' Kuruaya *bi* 'mouth.' Zamuco: Zamuco *aho*, Tumraha *ho*.

168 LIVER

Equatorial LIVER. Chapacura: Itene *fotofoto* 'lungs.' Guahibo *apeto* (but
-*to* may be a suffix). Tupi: Mekens *opita*. Yuracare *ipasa*. Zamuco:
Ebidoso *ipete*.

Chibchan-Paezan LIVER. Allentiac: Millcayac *počok* 'belly.' Aruak:
Guamaca, Atanque *pešu* 'chest.' Barbacoa: Cayapa *pešu* 'stomach.'
Chibcha: Manare *pučira* 'belly,' Boncota *beča* 'chest.' Chimu: Eten
počak. Jirajara: Ayoman *apox* 'belly.' Lenca: Chilanga *mutˢʔu-na*.
Misumalpan: Sumu *pas* 'chest.' Mura: Matanawi *miši-ta* 'heart.' Paez:
Paez *meʔkʲ*, *meeki*, Moguex *mik-t* 'belly,' Guambiana *patˢe, pathe*.
Tarascan *mintˢi-ta* 'heart.' Warrau *amahi*. Yanoama: Yanam, Yanomam
amok, Yanomamï, Sanema *amokɨ*. (Some forms may be borrowed from
Spanish *pecho.)*

Hokan LIVER. Achomawi: Atsugewi *opsi, upsi*. Chumash: San
Buenaventura *pał*. Karok *vafiš*. Shasta *ʔeːpsiʔ*. Yuman: Mohave
hipasa, Tipai *tapsi*, Akwa'ala *čuposi*, etc. Cf. Washo *pʼaːpʼɨš* 'lungs';
Chimariko *(hu-)si*.

Additional: Mosan: Wakashan: Kwakiutl *mas* 'bile'; Salish: Cowichan,
Musqueam *məs-ən* 'gall,' Chilliwak *məs-əl* 'gall.'

169 LIZARD

Equatorial LIZARD. Chapacura: Itene *ira*. Tupi: Kepkiriwate *ira,era*
'crocodile.' Yuracare *uri* 'alligator.'

Chibchan-Paezan LIZARD. Guaymi: Penomeño *ru*. Malibu: Chimila *ari*
'iguana.' Paya *uri* 'alligator.' Yanoama: Shiriana *ueli* 'crocodile.' (C)

170 LONG₁

Macro-Ge LONG. Bororo *raire*. Botocudo *orore* 'long, high.' Caraja
irɛhɛ. Fulnio *ule* 'be long.' Ge: Proto-Ge **ri*. Kaingan: Southern
Kaingan *ri* 'be high.' Kamakan *iroro*. Puri: Coroado *oron* 'on high.'
Cf. Opaie *randa* 'tall man.'

Macro-Carib LONG. Carib: Arara *ari* 'large.' Uitoto: Uitoto *are* 'long,
high, far,' Nonuya *arə* 'large, long,' Muinane *are* 'long, far.' Cf.
Kukura *lar* 'long.'

Macro-Tucanoan FAR. Catuquina: Canamari *inu*. Nambikwara: Proto-
Nambikwara **uːl*. Puinave *hen*.

Chibchan-Paezan LARGE. Aruak: Bintucua *vari-n* 'high.' Cuitlatec *iwili*.

Cuna *wila* 'deep.' Mura *uri*. Paez: Paez *wala*, Moguex *wala*. Paya
uruha 'deep.' Tarascan *era-ka-ta* 'tall.' Warrau *wari*. Xinca: Yupultepec
ura.

Penutian DEEP.   California: Miwok: Central Sierra *ʔala-kan* 'below.' Gulf:
Tunica *halu* 'below, under.' Yukian: Wappo *ɛla*.

171 LONG₂

Chibchan-Paezan FAR.   Chibcha: Tegria *karo*. Paya *kara*. Talamanca: Tirub
kronge. (C)

Hokan LONG.   Chimariko *hi-čun, xu-ičul-an* 'short.' Coahuilteco *čan*
'beyond, farther.' Karok *xara*. Pomo: North, Central Pomo *kol*, South
Pomo *aʔkon*, etc. Tequistlatec *igulwo* 'deep,' *aguliʔ* 'far.' Yuman:
Cocopa *kul*, Diegueño *koɫ*, Tonto *ikule*, etc.

Penutian LONG.   California: Wintun: North Wintu *kelela*. Gulf: Chitimacha
kˀama. Oregon: Coos *qatˡ*. Yukian: Yuki *kāi*, Wappo *kˀɛna*, Huchnom
kaiji:n.

Almosan-Keresiouan LONG.   Algic: Algonquian: Proto–Central
Algonquian **kenw*, Micmac *kunek* 'far'; Yurok *knew*. Mosan:
Wakashan: Kwakiutl *-kən* 'too much.' (AM)

172 LOUSE₁

Macro-Ge TICK.   Botocudo *tuk, tum* 'flea, sandfly.' Chiquito *o-itori-s*. Ge:
Chavante *ti*, Cayapo *tære*. Mashakali: Monosho *toktao* 'flea.' Opaie
tei. Yabuti: Mashubi *čičika*.

Macro-Panoan LOUSE.   Lule [cey] *sej*. Moseten *tˢii*.

Chibchan-Paezan LOUSE.   Mura: Matanawi *iši, isi, išo* 'flea.' Paez: Paez
es. (P)

173 LOUSE₂

Hokan LOUSE.   Chimariko *tˢina* 'wood tick.' Pomo: Southeast Pomo *tˢin*.

Almosan-Keresiouan LOUSE.   Keresan: Proto-Keresan **šina:* 'louse, flea.'
Iroquoian: Cherokee *tina*, Seneca *dˢiiʔnoh*, Mohawk *otˢinon*. (KS)

174 LOUSE₃

Hokan LOUSE.   Achomawi: Atsugewi *k-ači*. Comecrudo *ak* 'black louse.'
Karok *ači:č*. Pomo: North, Central Pomo *či:*, South Pomo *ači:*.
Salinan: San Antonio *t-ikˀeʔ*, San Miguel *ike*. Seri *ʔaixak* 'nit.' Shasta

ʔikʾaj 'flea.' Subtiaba: Subtiaba *ia:χa*, Tlappanec *jaxa*. Yana: North Yana *ǰi(-na)*.

Penutian LOUSE.   Mexican: Maya: Yucatec *uk*, Huastec *utˢ*. Yukian: Huchnom *i:k*, Coast Yuki *ikʾe*.

175 MAKE₁

Macro-Ge MAKE.   Bororo *to*. Ge: Karaho *twy, to ~ ton*.

Macro-Panoan MAKE.   Lule *ti*. Mataco: Mataco, Vejoz *ti* 'put, place, cause.' Panoan: Panobo *atte* 'work' (n.), Shipibo *tehe* 'work.' Tacanan: Tacana *ti*.

Macro-Carib BUILD.   Andoke *i-tooitihe* 'he builds.' Carib: Bakairí *itɔ* 'build,' Accawai *idu* 'make.' Uitoto *tu*.

Central Amerind WORK.   Kiowa-Tanoan: Tanoan: Tewa *tʾo*. Oto-Mangue: R 43 **ʔta*.

Hokan MAKE.   Salinan: San Miguel *eta, ti:* 'do,' San Antonio *etaʔ*. Subtiaba *(na-)da*.

Almosan-Keresiouan MAKE.   Algic: Wiyot *a:t-* (causative). Kutenai *it*. Mosan: Salish: Squamish *ti, taʔ-s*. Siouan-Yuchi: Siouan: Catawba *taʔa*.

176 MAKE₂

Chibchan-Paezan MAKE.   Itonama *ju-* (causative). Paez *jo*. Cf. Allentiac *ju-tuk* 'work.' (P)

Penutian MAKE.   California: Maidu *ja*. Gulf: Tunica *ja* 'make, do.' Yukian: Yuki *ju* 'do, happen.'

Additional: Uto-Aztecan: M 271 **ju* 'make, do.'

177 MAN₁

Hokan MAN.   Achomawi *is* 'person.' Chimariko *iči, itri*. Pomo: Southwest Pomo *ača*, North Pomo *ča*, South Pomo *ačai*, Central Pomo *čač*. Shasta *ʔis* 'person.' Tequistlatec *ašans* 'person.' Yana: North, Central Yana *hisi* 'man, male, husband.'

Penutian MAN.   California: Wintun *siw-ij* 'male'; Miwok: Plains Miwok *sawwe* 'male.' Gulf: Chitimacha *ʔasi;* Tunica *ši* 'male'; Atakapa *ša, ši* 'male.' Mexican: Huave *na-šej* 'man'; Mayan: Quiché *ačij*.

242

178 MAN₂

Andean MAN.   Alakaluf *hekaje*. Aymara: Aymara *hake*, Jaqaru *haqi*.

Hokan MAN.   Chumash: Santa Barbara *oxoix*, Santa Ynez *uyuiɣ*.
Coahuilteco *xagu* 'man, male.' Karankawa *ahaks*. Pomo: East Pomo
ka:kʰ 'person, man.'

179 MAN₃

Macro-Ge MAN.   Bororo *boe* 'people.' Caraja *abu*. Chiquito *poo*. Fulnio
efo 'husband.' Ge: Chavante *ambi*, Chicriaba *amba* 'person.' Kaingan:
Dalbergia *mbæ* 'husband.'

Equatorial MAN.   Arawa: Paumari *baii* 'penis.' Coche *boja*. Guahibo:
Guahibo *pebi*, Churuya *pevi*. Katembri *fofi* 'married man.' Maipuran:
Mehinacu, Kustenau *pei* 'penis,' Baure *pepe* 'penis,' Manao *pjia*
'penis.' Piaroa *uʔbe, ovo*. Tupi: Proto-Tupi **aba* 'man.' Yuracare *ba*
'husband, to marry.'

Penutian MAN.   California: Maidu *jepʔi;* Miwok: Lake *miiw-;* Wintun:
Noema *puewe* 'husband.' Gulf: Atakapa *hipa, ipa* 'husband.'

180 MANY₁

Macro-Ge MANY.   Bororo: Umotina *uri*. Botocudo *uruhu*. Ge: Chicriaba
eruhu.

Macro-Carib FILL.   Carib: Galibi *ali*, Cumanogoto *ar*, Chayma *ara*, Trio
ari 'contents,' Arara *t-ori-g* 'many,' Pauishana *t-ure-eke* 'many.' Uitoto:
Uitoto *orui* 'be full,' Miranya Carapana Tapuya *rahu* 'many.'

Andean MANY.   Araucanian *alli* 'all, each.' Mayna *alema*. Quechua:
Ecuadorean *jali*, Junin-Huanca *ali*. Yamana: Yahgan *jela*.

Cf. LONG₁.

181 MANY₂

Chibchan-Paezan MANY.   Barbacoa: Cayapa *tun*. Chimu *tuni*. (P)

Hokan ALL.   Achomawi *to:lol*. Chumash: Santa Cruz *talakeč* 'much.'
Salinan: San Antonio *k-i:sileʔ*. Tequistlatec *dalaj* 'very much.' Tonkawa
-tana-.

182 MANY₃

Chibchan-Paezan MANY.   Aruak: Guamaca *bini*. Barbacoa: Colorado
man. Chimu: Eten *men* 'to swell.' Choco: Catio *bari* 'grow.' Cuna

243

pule, pelo 'all.' Itonama *amaniato*. Malibu: Chimila *muni* 'abound.'
Misumalpan: Miskito *bani* 'each.' Paez: Guambiana *minu*. Rama *bain*.
Talamanca: Tirub *pir(-kru)* 'all.' Tarascan *vini-ni* 'be full.' Timucua
mine 'large.' Yanoama: Yanomam, Yanomamï *prəwa* 'large.'
Penutian MANY.   California: Yokuts *mone* 'much.' Gulf: Atakapa *mon*
'many, all.' Plateau: Lutuami *mo:ni-s* 'large.' Yukian: Wappo *mul* 'all,'
Yuki *muna* 'all,' Clear Lake *mol* 'all.'

183 MEAT₁

Macro-Panoan ANIMAL.   Guaicuru: Toba *lo* 'domestic animal.' Lengua:
Mascoy *lau* (classifier for animals in possessive construction). Lule
lo-p 'meat.' Mataco: Mataco, Chulupi *lau, -la-* (possessive classifier
for animals).
Andean MEAT.   Araucanian: Pehuenche *ilo*. Kahuapana: Jebero *-luʔ*
'flesh.'

184 MEAT₂

Macro-Ge MEAT.   Chiquito *añe*. Ge: Proto-Ge *ñĩ. Kaingan: Palmas *ni*,
Tibagi *nin*, etc. Mashakali *ñĩñ*. Puri: Coroado *eneine*.
Equatorial MEAT.   Cayuvava *ine*. Chapacura: Urupa *uenen*. Cofan *na*.
Maipuran: Wapishana *nana* 'edible,' Piapoco *naina*, Jumana *nina*.
Piaroa *añe* 'fat' (n.). Tupi: Mekens *ñena*, Kepkiriwate *o-ñon*,
Guarategaja *ki-ñena*. Yaruro *ñaa* 'fat' (n.).
Macro-Tucanoan ANIMAL.   Huari: Masaka *nj(i)æ* 'meat.' Mobima *nono*
'domesticated animal.' Nambikwara: Southern Nambikwara *nūn²*.
Puinave: Ubde-Nehern *hun*. Ticuna *ʔyne* 'body.' Tucano: Cubeo *neo*,
neau 'fat' (n.). Yuri *nai* 'meat.'

185 MEAT₃

Macro-Tucanoan MEAT.   Kaliana *mitˢa*. Maku *munči, muči*. Ticuna *mači*.
Hokan MEAT.   Achomawi *misutˢ*. Comecrudo *ewe*. Esselen *amisah* 'deer.'
Jicaque *buisis*, pus 'deer.' Pomo: Kashaya *bihše*, East Pomo *bi:še*
'meat, deer.' Salinan: San Antonio, San Miguel *maṭʰ*. Seri *ipxasi*,
ipxaš (pl.). Subtiaba: Tlappanec *uwiʔi*. Tonkawa *ʔawas*. Yana: North
Yana *basi* 'meat, body,' Yahi *bahsi*. Yuman: Diegueño *ematt*.
Additional: Uto-Aztecan: M 125 *mas 'deer.'

186 MEAT$_4$

Macro-Ge MEAT.   Caraja *adi*. Fulnio *dae*. Guato *(ma-)deu*. Kaingan:
Tibagi *de, da* 'animal.' Kamakan *dau* 'animal.'

Macro-Carib MEAT.   Andoke *itˢy*. Carib: Hishcariana *otɨ*, Wayana *i-ote*
'game,' Waiwai *-oti* (possessive classifier for meat). Uitoto: Uitoto
ičira, Muinane *uatɨ*.

187 MOON$_1$

Macro-Ge MOON.   Erikbatsa *boto*. Ge: Cayapo *putua*, Apinage *putwaru*,
etc.

Macro-Carib MOON.   Andoke *pody*. Uitoto: Ocaina *fodjoome, podomo*.

188 MOON$_2$

Macro-Tucanoan MOON.   Auake *ataʔp, ata(m)*. Kaliana *tabu, tapo*.
Puinave: Curiariai *tamē* 'star.' Ticuna *tawø-make* (literally 'sun pale').

Chibchan-Paezan MOON.   Aruak: Bintucua *tima* 'moon, month.' Barbacoa:
Colorado *tˢabo* 'star.' Chibcha: Tunebo *sibu-ara*. Chimu: Eten *sam,
šiam* 'sun.' Motilon *tubi*. Talamanca: Borunca *tabe, tebe*, Cabecar
sibo. Cf. Antioquia: Nutabe *tebu-na* 'night.'

189 MOSQUITO

Macro-Ge MOSQUITO.   Botocudo *pitaŋ, pøtã*. Caraja *badi, bedi* 'bee.'
Ge: Apinage *puræ*. Puri: Coroado *putaŋ* 'bee.' Yabuti *porunka*.

Macro-Tucanoan MOSQUITO.   Kaliana *pələ*. Maku *mbule* 'pium.'
Puinave *pəlod* 'pium.'

Chibchan-Paezan WASP.   Aruak: Bintucua *bun*. Chibcha: Tunebo, Manare
ipare. Cuna *pulu*. Rama: Guatuso *poro*. Talamanca: Tirub *woro*. Cf.
Xinca· Chiquimulilla *hurux*. (C)

190 MOUSE

Andean MOUSE.   Quechua: Yanacocha *ukuš*. Zaparo *kaširikia*.

Chibchan-Paezan BAT.   Chibcha: Boncota *kuaixea*. Guaymi: Chumulu
guik, Gualaca *guiga*. Lenca: Guajiquero *gyiza*. Paez [quize]. Xinca:
Yupultepec *kysse*.

191 MOUTH$_1$

Macro-Panoan SAY.   Lule *je*. Moseten *ji* 'tell.' Panoan: Proto-Panoan **joʔi*.

Equatorial MOUTH.   Otomaco *jo.* Yaruro *jaoo.*
Macro-Tucanoan MOUTH.   Iranshe *ia?a.* Nambikwara: Proto-Nambikwara
*jou:. Yuri *ia.*
Andean CALL.   Araucanian: Pehuenche [ghuy] 'name' (n.). Leco *ja* 'say.'
Patagon: Patagon *jew-en,* Tehuelche *jo, jon* 'name' (n.). Yamana *ji, ja*
'say.'
Hokan MOUTH.   Subtiaba: Subtiaba *d-a:u:,* Tlappanec *r-aū?.* Yuman:
Cocopa *ija,* Yavapai *ja?,* Akwa'ala *ja,* etc. Yurumangui *jo(-ima)*
'saliva' (*ima* = 'water').

192 MOUTH₂

Macro-Ge MOUTH.   Bororo *ogwa* 'lip, mouth.' Botocudo *dⁱakie* 'chin.'
Caraja *zuuka* 'lip.' Fulnio *dⁱuči.* Ge: Apinage *jakoa,akwa,* Krenje
ajkwa, Suya *jako* 'chin.' Kaingan: Came *jenku,* Catarina *ñaky.*
Kamakan: Meniens *jego* 'beard.' Mashakali *ñikoi.* Opaie *e-ka.* (Many
forms have a prefix *ja-* or the like. Cf. Chiquito *ai* 'mouth.')
Macro-Panoan MOUTH.   Charruan: Charrua *ex,* Chana *hek.* Guaicuru:
Toba *ka* 'lip, chin,' Mbaya *aka* 'chin,' Mocovi *aka* 'chin, beard.' Lule
ka. Mataco: Choroti *ak* 'chin,' Nocten *kax.* Panoan: Proto-Panoan
*kʷiša 'lip, mouth, border,' **koi* 'chin, jaw,' Cashinahua *kə-, kəš-*
'mouth, border,' Cashibo *kwə-* 'mouth,' Chacobo *kə-* 'lips, border' (all
instrumental prefixes). Tacanan: Proto-Tacanan **kwatˢa,* Tacana *ekeke*
'lip.'
Macro-Carib MOUTH.   Bora: Miranya Oira Assu-Tapuya *ma-ɣyo,* Faai
me-kuai 'chin,' Imihita *(meex-)kaa* 'beard.' Uitoto: Uitoto *(ama-)əko*
'beard,' Coeruna *koæ,* Orejon *hoe.*

193 NARROW

Chibchan-Paezan NARROW.   Chimu: Eten *šanku.* Talamanca: Estrella
tˢine-kra 'small,' Cabecar *tˢina-ra* 'small.' Warrau *sanuk* 'narrow,
small.'
Central Amerind SMALL.   Kiowa-Tanoan: Kiowa *sjā-n.* Oto-Mangue: R
258 **(Y)(n)(H)si(?)(n).*

194 NAVEL

Equatorial NAVEL.   Arawa: Yamamadi *æ-thubori.* Cofan *tʰo?pa* 'belly.'
Guamo *tife* 'heart.' Jibaro: Zamora *atape* 'heart.' Maipuran: Wapishana
tuba 'belly,' Atoroi *tub* 'belly,' Baniva *čiabo* 'belly.' Trumai *taf, tøf.*

Macro-Tucanoan NAVEL.   Huari: Huari, Masaka *tapa* 'belly.' Mobima *dimmo-*. Puinave: Curiariai *te(e)ba* 'umbilical cord,' Hubde *tøøm*, Yehubde *toptep* 'guts,' Puinave *ok-tep* 'guts.' Tucano: Curetu *toomu-kø*, Wanana *t'omea*, Coto *tapwi*, Amaguaje *tapue* 'belly.' Yuri *toobi*.

195 NEAR

Andean UP TO.   Leco *kam* 'for, toward.' Patagon: Ona *kammai* 'as far as.' Quechua *-kama* 'as far as, up to, close to.' Zaparo *kame* 'hither.'

Penutian NEAR.   California: Yokuts *ʔamat^s* 'approach'; Costanoan: Rumsien *hamatka*, Santa Clara *amatka*. Chinook *-gəm-* (verb prefix). Oregon: Siuslaw *xumš* 'approach.' Cf. Plateau: Nez Perce *kimtam*.

196 NECK

Macro-Ge NECK.   Bororo: Otuke *ikio*. Kamakan: Meniens *inkio*.

Central Amerind NECK.   Kiowa-Tanoan: Kiowa *k'o-l;* Tanoan: Taos *k'ɔo-*, San Ildefonso *k'e*, Isleta *k'oa*, etc. Oto-Mangue: R 125 **ka(n)* 'neck, throat.' Uto-Aztecan: M 303b **ku*.

Penutian NECK.   California: Maidu **k'uji*. Gulf: Atakapa *koʔi* 'neck, throat'; Chitimacha *k'e*.

197 NIGHT₁

Macro-Panoan NIGHT.   Moseten *jomoi* 'become night.' Panoan: Macro-Panoan **jamɨ*.

Chibchan-Paezan NIGHT.   Barbacoa: Colorado *aama* 'shadow.' Itonama *jumani*. Mura: Matanawi *jamāru*. Paez: Guambiana *jem*. Warrau *ima*. (P)

198 NIGHT₂

Hokan NIGHT.   Achomawi *mahiksa*. Chimariko *hi-mokni, hi-mok* 'evening.' Salinan: San Antonio *smak^{h}ai*. Seri *iʔamok*.

Penutian DARK.   California: Maidu *jamaji* 'shadow.' Gulf: Natchez *majuk* 'dark, night'; Muskogean: Hitchiti *močusta* 'get dark,' Creek *jomuške*. Mexican: Mixe-Zoque: Sayula *amuxik* 'shadow'; Mayan: Quiché *mux* 'shadow,' Kekchí *mux* 'become cloudy.' Plateau: Klamath *mʔaj* 'shadow,' Molala *muka* 'night.'

199 NIGHT₃

Hokan NIGHT.   Comecrudo *patotiau*. Jicaque *puiste*. Salinan: San Antonio

mašitama 'shadow.' Subtiaba: Tlappanec *miša* 'shadow.' Yana: Central,
North Yana *basii*, Yahi *bahsi*.

Almosan-Keresiouan NIGHT.   Algic: Algonquian: Blackfoot -*sipi* 'during
the night.' Keresan *zaipə* 'shadow.' Mosan: Quileute *ši:p*. Siouan-
Yuchi: Siouan: Proto-Siouan **sepi*, Quapaw *psi*, Biloxi *upofi* (*f* < **s*),
Osage *opathe* 'evening'; Yuchi *ispi*. (With the Siouan metathesized
forms, compare Proto-Keresan **biši* 'be dark'.)

200 NIGHT₄

Equatorial NIGHT.   Cofan *kose, kuse*. Jibaro: Aguaruna, Zamora, Shuara
kaši. Timote: Mocochi *kisi*.

Chibchan-Paezan YESTERDAY.   Antioquia: Nutabe *ma-kasa* 'early
morning.' Barbacoa: Cayapa *kisi, kiši*, Colorado *kisi*. Lenca: Chilanga
kʼus-kʼašba 'night.' Paez: Paez *kos* 'night,' Panikita *kuskaja*. Paya
keča. Warrau *kahe*.

201 NOSE

Macro-Ge NOSE.   Kamakan: Cotoxo *nihieko, niiko*. Mashakali: Mashakali
nitˢikoe, Capoxo, Kumanasho *nišikoi*, etc.

Macro-Panoan NOSE.   Guaicuru: Mocovi *niih*. Lule *nus*. Mataco: Choroti
nus, Macca *inex*. Vilela *nihim*.

Andean NOSE.   Alakaluf: Alakaluf *noł*, Kaueskar *nouš*. Aymara *nasa*.
Gennaken *anneč*. Kahuapana: Kahuapana *netok, načik*, Jebero *nøček*.
Zaparo *nahuka*.

202 OLD

Macro-Panoan OLD.   Lule *ano* 'become old.' Panoan: Macro-Panoan **ʔani*
'big.' Tacanan: Tacana *anu* 'old woman,' Chama *ano* 'grandmother.'

Macro-Carib OLD.   Uitoto: Ocaina *onaa* 'older.' Yagua: Yameo *año*.

203 ONE₁

Macro-Panoan ONE.   Guaicuru: Guachi *tamak*. Lengua *tama*.

Macro-Carib ONE.   Bora *tˢanere, thanere* (Tessmann). Carib: Proto-
Hianocoto **teñi*. Uitoto: Uitoto *dane, dama* 'alone,' Nonuya *daamu*,
Miranya Carapana Tapuya [zähzähma]. Yagua: Peba *tomeulaj*.

204 ONE₂

Macro-Tucanoan ONE.   Auake *kiuana*. Nambikwara: Northern Nambikwara

kanã:ka. Tucano: Waikina *kanoa,* Wanana *kilia,* Hehenawa *kwina-ro* (cf.
pika-ro 'two'). Cf. Iranshe *kə̃tapwi, kula-pa* 'other side.'

Penutian ONE.   California: Miwok: Central Sierra *kenge,* Marin *kene;*
Wintun *ketet.* Chinook *ext.* Tsimshian *k'al.* Yukian: Wappo *o-kɛl* 'be
lonesome.'

205 PAIN

Macro-Carib BAD.   Carib: Hishcariana *anhi* 'evil' (n.), Surinam *anɨ:ikɨ*
'sickness,' Aparai *t-one.* Uitoto: Orejon *ana* 'devil,' Nonuya *hoani.*
Yagua: Peba *juno* 'devil,' Yameo *ana* 'pain.'

Andean PAIN.   Patagon: Manekenkn *anonia.* Quechua: Santiagueño *nana*
'pain, to hurt,' Cochabamba *nana* 'to hurt.' Zaparo: Arabela *no:* 'to
hurt.'

206 PENIS

Equatorial PENIS.   Tupi: Guaraní *t-ako* 'groins, hips,' Abanee *t-ako*
'vagina,' etc. Zamuco: Chamacoco *os-axa,* Tumraha *p-axa.*

Macro-Tucanoan PENIS.   Maku *koi.* Puinave: Curiariai *oeɣi.* Yuri *uke.*

207 PERSON

Macro-Panoan MAN.   Lengua: Angaite *kea.* Mataco: Choroti *kihi,*
Payagua *ako,* Choropi *-kaja* 'husband.'

Andean PERSON.   Leco *čaja* 'people.' Zaparo: Zaparo, Arabela *kaja,*
Iquito *kaaja* 'man.'

208 RAIN

Macro-Panoan WATER.   Lengua: Mascoy *na(-thwatkʲi)* 'bathe, wash.' Lule
na- (instrumental prefix) 'action with water.' Mataco: Mataco *nax*
'bathe,' Vejoz *nain* 'bathe.' Moseten *oñi.* Panoan: Proto-Panoan **na-ši*
'bathe,' **inɨ* 'water,' Cashinahua *nə-, no-* 'action with water.' Tacanan:
Proto-Tacanan **e-na,* Cavineña *neʔi,* Tacana *nai.*

Macro-Carib RAIN.   Uitoto: Uitoto *hanoj* 'water,' Ocaina *now(h)ə,*
Orejone *ainoe,* Nonuya *no(h)owi.* Yagua: Yagua *nahua* 'river,' Yameo
naʔa 'rainy season,' Peba *nowa* 'river.'

209 RED

Macro-Carib RED.   Andoke [peaih]. Carib: Chayma *t-api-re,* Galibi *t-apide,* etc.

Equatorial RED.   Maipuran: Piapoco *eβe-ri*, Uainuma *eba-ri*, Curipaco
ewa(-dali). Otomaco *pipi*. Tupi: Proto-Tupi **ubi* 'green.' Yuracare
bubu-si.

210 RIVER₁

Central Amerind RIVER.   Oto-Mangue: R 163 **(h)kʷe(n)*. Uto-Aztecan:
M 177 **mel* 'flow,' Hopi *məːna* 'river.'

Penutian RIVER.   California: Yokuts: Calavera *pollej;* Wintun: Noema *pel-
tepum;* Miwok: Lake Miwok *polpol* 'lake,' Central Sierra Miwok
polloku 'lake.' Chinook *emat^l* 'bay.' Gulf: Natchez *ʔapal;* Muskogean:
Alabama *pahni*. Mexican: Mayan: Mam *palu* 'sea,' Quiché *palau* 'sea,'
Kekchí *palau* 'sea, lake,' etc. Oregon: Miluk *paɬt* 'sea,' Coos *balimis*
'sea.' Yukian: Coast Yuki *mel*, Huchnom *mol*.

Cf. WATER₁.

211 RIVER₂

Macro-Ge RAIN.   Chiquito *taa*. Ge: Apinage *inta*, Karaho *ta*, Cherente *tā*,
etc. Kaingan (general) *ta*. Mashakali: Macuni *taeŋ*, Hahahay *te*,
Patasho *tiaŋ* 'water.' Opaie *ox-ata*. Puri: Coropo *tẽin* 'water.'

Macro-Carib RIVER.   Andoke *otõa*. Bora *tee*. Uitoto: Ocaina *tjaau, tiahe*.

Andean RIVER.   Leco *dua* 'water, river,' *ndowa* 'water.' Mayna *towa*
'water.' Cf. Sabela: Auca *oõdõ*.

Chibchan-Paezan WATER.   Chibcha: Margua *dia*, Boncota *ria*, etc.
Guaymi: Gualaca *ti*, Murire *či*. Misumalpan: Miskito *li, laja*,
Matagalpa, Cacaopera *li*. Paya *tia*. Rama: Guatuso, Guetar *ti*.
Talamanca: Tirub *di*, Terraba *ti, di*, etc. Tarascan *it'i*. (C)

212 ROAD₁

Macro-Carib ROAD.   Uitoto: Ocaina *naahon*. Yagua: Yagua *nɔn*, Peba *nou*.

Macro-Tucanoan ROAD.   Puinave: Querari *nãmã*. Ticuna *nama*. Yuri
nemo.

Andean ROAD.   Patagon: Tehuelche, Teuesh *nooma*, Tsoneka *noma*.
Quechua: Santiagueño *ñan*, Ecuadorean *ñambi*. Sabela: Auca *-dõ*
(suffix, phonetically *nõ*).

Penutian GO.   California: Maidu *nen* 'travel.' Gulf: Atakapa *non*.

213 ROAD₂

Equatorial ROAD.   Timote: Cuica *pa.* Tupi: Proto-Tupi **pe, *ape,* Arikem
pa, paa.

Central Amerind ROAD.   Kiowa-Tanoan: Tanoan: Taos *p'ĩẽ,* Hopi Tewa
p'o. Uto-Aztecan: M 350 **po.*

Penutian ROAD.   California: Maidu *bo, ben* 'to step.' Gulf: Natchez *be*
'go' (pl. subject). Mexican: Mayan: Proto-Mayan **be,* Quiché *be* 'go,'
Kekchí *-be-* 'go' (auxiliary), Jacaltec *b'eji* 'walk,' etc.

Cf. Chibchan-Paezan COME₁.

214 ROOT

Equatorial ROOT.   Coche *tabotaha.* Cofan *t'afa.* Guahibo: Cuiva *tabu.*
Zamuco: Ayoré *taposi.* Cf. Jibaro: Aguaruna *čapik* 'rope.'

Andean ROOT.   Aymara *sapʰi* (borrowing from Quechua?). Patagon: Ona
sape 'rope.' Quechua (general) *sapi.*

215 ROUND

Andean ROUND.   Araucanian *monkoll.* Kahuapana: Jebero *mungapiʎi.*
Patagon: Tsoneka *muarie.* Quechua: Cochabamba *moloq'u.*

Chibchan-Paezan EGG.   Allentiac *muru* 'testicle.' Xinca: Chiquimulilla
muuru.

Hokan ROUND.   Comecrudo *pawapel.* Tequistlatec *apelote?.* Tonkawa
pilaw.

Penutian EGG.   California: Maidu *p'ala* 'testicle.' Mexican: Mayan:
Quiché *mol, bolox* 'round,' Kekchí *mol,* Tzotzil *balbal* 'round.'
Plateau: Lutuami *napal,* Klamath *napl.* Zuni *mo?le.*

216 SALIVA

Equatorial SALIVA.   Guahibo: Guahibo *ione,* Cuiva *one.* Tupi: Proto-Tupi
*eni.

Andean SALIVA.   Aymara: Lupaca *wiʎi* 'to spit.' Cholona *olle.*

217 SAY₁

Macro-Ge SPEAK.   Guato *m-utə.* Kaingan: Dalbergia *tadn ~ tu* 'tell,'
Tibagi *to* 'say.' Mashakali: Capoxo *atai.*

Equatorial SAY.   Jibaro: Shuara *ti ~ ta,* Aguaruna *ti.* Kandoshi *taa.*

251

Maipuran: Amuesha *ot,* Cabere *ita* 'talk,' Piapoco *tani* 'talk,' Maypure
tura 'talk.' Uro: Puquina *ata.* Yuracare *ta.*

Andean SAY.   Kahuapana: Jebero *tu, itu.* Leco *du* 'speak.' Zaparo *ati.*

Chibchan-Paezan SING.   Chibcha [ty]. Talamanca: Terraba *ti.* (C)

Hokan SAY.   Achomawi *t-* (quotative, third person). Chumash *-ti-* (verbal
action), *ti* 'name.' Salinan: San Miguel *ṭeʔ* 'tell.' Subtiaba: Tlappanec
na-ʔta 'he speaks.' Yana *tii* 'say,' (quotative). Washo *id.*

218 SAY₂

Penutian SAY.   Chinook *kʷɬ* 'tell.' Yukian: Wappo *kal, kel.*

Almosan-Keresiouan SPEAK.   Algic: Algonquian: Proto-Algonquian
*kelaw; Wiyot *he:l* 'say.' Caddoan: Caddo *kan-* (quotative). Iroquoian:
Mohawk *-kar-* 'story,' Oneida *-kalatu-* 'tell a story,' Cherokee *kaka:raʔ*
'story.' Kutenai *kn-* 'think about.' Mosan: Chemakuan: Quileute *kul*
'have an idea'; Salish: Songish, Musqueam *qʷəl,* Squamish *kʷal*
'answer,' etc. Siouan-Yuchi: Siouan: Mandan *kina* 'tell.'

219 SAY₃

Hokan SAY.   Chimariko *-go:-, -ko:-* 'talk.' Coahuilteco *ka:.* Comecrudo
kiwa. Pomo: East Pomo *ga(-nuk)* 'speak.' Seri *kee, kaʔ.* Tequistlatec
ko. Yana *ga-* (verbal activity; found in a number of verb stems, e.g. *ga-
ja:* 'to talk').

Almosan-Keresiouan SAY.   Algic: Yurok *hegol* (*h* < *zero), *hego:, hego:s*
'shout,' Wiyot *a:γ.* Caddoan: Wichita *-kaʔ* (quotative). Iroquoian:
Seneca *ka* ~ *kæ* 'story' (but cf. Mohawk *kar* 'story' and SAY₂ above).
Kutenai *kei, -ki-.* Mosan: Chemakuan: Chemakum *ku* 'speak,'
Quileute *ku;* Wakashan: Bella Bella *-kʲ-* 'says'; Salish: Thompson *-oko:*
(quotative), Upper Chehalis *-ače* (quotative), Shuswap *-okʷe*
(quotative). Siouan-Yuchi: Siouan: Mandan *kaʔɛhɛ* (quotative); Yuchi
kɛ.

220 SEE₁

Macro-Carib SEE.   Carib: Wayana *ene,* Waiwai *enə,* Motilon *anu* 'eye,'
Surinam *o:nu* 'eye,' etc. Uitoto: Muinane *ono* 'know.' Yagua: Yagua
nuwa:tø 'mirror,' Yameo *nutē* 'look at.'

Equatorial SEE.   Kariri *ne.* Maipuran: Campa *nie, uni.*

Central Amerind SEE.   Oto-Mangue: R 345 **ni(n)* 'see, know, look at,
hear.' Uto-Aztecan: M 366 **ne* 'see.' Cf. Kiowa *dū* 'seek.'

Penutian SEE.   Gulf: Tunica *niju* 'think'; Atakapa *ini* 'search'; Muskogean:
Choctaw *nowa*. Mexican: Tzeltal, Tzotzil, Kekchí, etc., *na* 'know,'
Kekchí (Stoll) *nau* 'know.' Yukian: Yuki, Wappo *naw.*

Almosan-Keresiouan SEE.   Algic: Algonquian: Proto–Central Algonquian
*ne:w, Yurok *new.* Iroquoian: Cherokee *ni* 'look.' Siouan-Yuchi:
Siouan: Ofo *i-newa-,* Catawba *nī.*

221 SEE₂

Macro-Panoan SEE.   Guaicuru: Mocovi *avana.* Mataco: Mataco, Choroti,
Chunupi *wen.* Panoan: Proto-Panoan **ʔoī,* Panobo *uiñ* 'look at.'

Macro-Carib KNOW.   Carib: Motilon *wano* 'I know.' Uitoto *uiño* 'learn.'

Penutian SEE.   California: Wintun: South Wintu *wini.* Gulf: Atakapa *wine*
'find'; Tunica *wenu* 'find'; Natchez *eł.* Mexican: Mayan: Proto-Mayan
*il, Huastec *wal* 'eye'; Mixe-Zoque: Mixe *vihn* 'eye.'

222 SEE₃

Macro-Ge SEE.   Botocudo *pip, pim.* Caraja *bie.* Chiquito *ipa* 'know.' Ge:
Kraho *pu* ~ *pupun,* Krenje *pupua.* Kaingan: Dalbergia, Tibagi *ve.*
Mashakali *pe-*

Macro-Panoan SEE.   Lengua: Mascoy *wi(-taiji).* Moseten *ve.* Panoan:
Proto-Panoan **βi-ro* 'eye,' **βi-* 'face, eye, surface.' Tacanan: Proto-
Tacanan **ba* 'look at.'

223 SEED₁

Andean SEED.   Quechua: Cochabamba, Wanka *muhu,* Junin *muju,*
Ecuadorean *muju* 'fruit.' Sabela *mo.* Yamana: Yamana *amaia* 'berries,'
Yahgan *amaɣan.* Zaparo: Andoa *imio.*

Chibchan-Paezan SEED.   Misumalpan: Miskito *ma* 'seed, fruit.' Yanoama:
Yanomamï, Sanema *ma,* Yanomam *mak.* Cf. Misumalpan: Sumu *makka*
'seed, fruit' (in which, however, *-kka* is probably a suffix) and Chibcha
uba 'flower.' (C)

Cf. CHILD₂.

224 SEED₂

Macro-Ge SEED.   Caraja *idʕi* (Davis), *teʔ.* Ge: Proto-Ge **zi.*

Macro-Panoan SEED.   Lule [zu] *t'u.* Mataco: Vejoz *łoi,* Choroti *ło,* Macca
t'oi. Panoan: Proto-Panoan **iŝi.* Tacanan: Chama, Huarayo *eso.*

Hokan SEED.   Pomo: North Pomo *so:,* Kashaya *ʔiso.* Seri *is* 'fruit.'

Subtiaba: Subtiaba *iši* 'grain of corn, corn,' Tlappanec *iššu* 'grain of corn, corn.' Yuman: Cocopa *jes*, Walapai *jatˢ*, Havasupai *ijatˢ*, etc.

Penutian SEED.   Gulf: Tunica *uxsa;* Atakapa *otˢ*. Mexican: Mixe-Zoque: Tetontepec *hiʔkš* 'fruit.'

Almosan-Keresiouan SEED.   Iroquoian: Seneca *dˁi:ja*. Keresan: Santa Ana *(hi:-)ẓa(-ni)*. Siouan-Yuchi: Proto-Siouan (M) **su, *šu* 'seed, grain.' (KS)

225 SEEK

Macro-Ge SEEK.   Botocudo *pe, pen*. Ge: Kraho *pwǝm* 'want.' Kaingan: Tibagi *penoa, penoi*. Opaie *pino* 'wish.'

Andean LOVE.   Kahuapana *apenurave* 'I love,' *apenotu* 'lover.' Zaparo: Zaparo *pani* 'want,' Andoa *pani* 'desire.'

226 SHINE

Andean SUN.   Aymara: Aymara, Lupaca *lupi*. Catacao *nap*. Cholona: Cholona *nem* 'day,' Hivito *nim, ñim, ngim*. Quechua: Cochabamba, etc. *ʎupʰi* 'shine.' Yamana: Yamana *løm*, Yahgan *løm, løn*. Zaparo: Iquito *janamia, nunami, inami* 'fire.'

Penutian SHINE.   Gulf: Atakapa *lam;* Natchez *lem*. Mexican: Mixe-Zoque: Zoque *neʔm;* Mayan: Yucatec *lemba* 'shine, lightning,' Tzotzil *lemlaˑyet* 'lighten,' Mam *lemlohe*. Plateau: Klamath *wlʔeplʔ* 'lightning.' Zuni *lomo* 'flash, burn brightly.'

227 SHORT

Equatorial SMALL.   Kandoshi: Kandoshi *kania-ši* 'near,' Murato *kania-či* 'young.' Maipuran: Amuesha *kuñič*. Tupi: Maue *kūnīī*, Arikem *kenin*, Siriono *akē* 'child.'

Andean SHORT.   Cholona *kunču* 'small.' Itucale *kuøinexi*. Patagon: Tsoneka *koneke*, Teuesh *koončenken* 'small.'

228 SHOULDER

Hokan SHOULDER.   Achomawi *tala* 'shoulder blade.' Salinan: San Antonio *tatal, itaʔl*. Yana: North Yana *dul* 'neck.'

Almosan-Keresiouan SHOULDER.   Algic: Algonquian: Shawnee *telja*. Mosan: Salish: Nisqualli *talakʷ*, Siciatl *salaq-ǝn*, Songish *tˀɛlawˀ* 'wing.' (AM)

229 SING

Macro-Carib DANCE.   Uitoto *se*. Yagua: Yameo *seje*.

Hokan SING.   Achomawi *e:s*. Seri *k-oos*. Subtiaba: Tlappanec *na-ʔsja* 'dance.' Tequistlatec *šow*. Yuman: Tipai *šijaw*, Kahwan *suja:-t*.

230 SIT₁

Macro-Ge SIT.   Botocudo *nep*. Caraja *nɔ̃*. Ge: Proto-Ge *ñĩ, *ñĩr*. Kaingan: Came *nin*, Dalbergia *nɛ*, Guarapurava *ni*. Kamakan *one* (imperative). Mashakali *ñĩm*.

Macro-Panoan SIT.   Guaicuru: Abipone *añi*. Lule [aany] 'stoop.' Mataco: Enimaga *aneho*. Tacanan: Proto-Tacanan *ani*.

Macro-Tucanoan BE.   Mobima *en(-na)*. Puinave: Ubde-Nehern, Papury *nii* 'be, live.' Ticuna *niʔĩ*. Tucano *nii* 'be' (*estar*).

231 SIT₂

Hokan SIT.   Achomawi: Atsugewi *we-* 'by sitting on.' Chimariko *-wo-, wa-* 'by sitting.' Subtiaba *t-a:u* (*t* = factitive). Yana *wa*. Yuman: Tonto *oa*, Walapai *ua*, Kiliwa *ouau, huwa*.

Almosan-Keresiouan SIT.   Caddoan: Pawnee *wi* 'seated,' Caddo *ʔawi* 'sitting.' Keresan: Proto-Keresan *ʔu* 'dwell.' Siouan-Yuchi: Siouan: Catawba *waʔ*. (KS)

232 SIT₃

Andean SIT.   Alakaluf *sakkar, šakar*. Cholona *a-tg-an* 'be seated.' Kahuapana *zukør*. Leco *seča*. Quechua: Caraz *ta:ki*. Yamana: Yahgan [ytakona].

Almosan-Keresiouan SIT.   Algic: Algonquian: Shawnee *ateki* 'it sits there'; Yurok *t˚ek*. Mosan; Wakashan· Nootka, Nitinat *t'iqʷ-ił*; Chcmakuan. Chemakum *t'aq*. (AM)

233 SKIN₁

Macro-Ge SKIN.   Caraja *takɔ*. Chiquito *i-taki-s*. Mashakali: Macuni *točai*.

Andean SKIN.   Kahuapana *ytek* 'lip.' Leco *bu-suče*. Patagon: Patagon [zog] *t˚og*, Tsoneka *sug* 'hide,' Tehuelche *zek*. Zaparo *t˚okwe*.

Additional: Macro-Panoan: Mataco: Mataco *t'ah*, Chulupi *tax, tox*.

234 SKIN₂

Hokan SKIN. Chimariko *hi-pxaǰi* 'skin, bark.' Chumash: Santa Ynez *paχ*,
Santa Barbara *pax*. Seri *-biłʔ*. Washo *basi* 'to skin, flay.'
Penutian BARK. Chinook *pxa* 'older bark.' Gulf: Natchez *habeš, ebeš;*
Muskogean: Alabama *afakči*. Mexican: Mayan: Yucatec *boš*, Pokomchi
pas. Plateau: Yakima *psa*, North Sahaptin *pǝx* 'skin,' Nez Perce *pekt*
'fish skin.' Tsimshian *mas*.
Almosan-Keresiouan SKIN. Keresan: Proto-Keresan **pisčanani*. Siouan-
Yuchi: Siouan: Catawba *pis*. (KS)

235 SLEEP₁

Macro-Ge SLEEP. Bororo: Bororo *anu*, Umotina *unori* (n.), *inǝtu* (v.).
Caraja *rōrō*. Chiquito *ano*. Ge: Proto-Ge **nō, *nōr* 'lie.' Kaingan:
Guarapurava *nor*, Tibagi *nan* 'lie down,' *nang-ja* 'bed' ('lie down' +
instrument), Dalbergia *nǝ* 'lie.' Kamakan *ha-nun* 'bed.'
Macro-Carib SLEEP. Uitoto: Uitoto *inu*, Coeruna *ko-ina*, Ocaina *ønu*.
Yagua *nɛ* 'hammock.'
Equatorial SLEEP. Cofan *anan-je*, *ʔãnã*. Piaroa: Saliba *ainaa*. Tupi:
Guaraní *añeno* 'lie down,' Guayaki *ñeno*.
Penutian LIE DOWN. Gulf: Atakapa *ni:* (sing. subject); Tunica *na, no:*
'lay down'; Natchez *nu:* 'sleep,' *newa* 'be sleepy.' Mexican: Mixe-
Zoque: Zoque *ǝŋ* 'sleep.' Yukian: Wappo *hin* 'sleep,' Coast Yuki *in*
'sleep.' Cf. California: Costanoan: Mutsun *one* 'sit down.'

236 SLEEP₂

Equatorial SLEEP. Jibaro: Aguaruna *kana*. Timote *keun*.
Macro-Tucanoan SLEEP. Canichana *xana*. Tucano: Tucano *kani*, Desana
kane, etc.

237 SMALL

Macro-Carib CHILD. Bora: Miranya *mæni*, Imihita *mene* 'child, son.'
Carib: Proto-Hianocoto **mure*, Apiaca *moni*, Bakairí *imeri* 'small.'
Macro-Tucanoan SMALL. Mobima *-mo* (diminutive). Puinave: Papury
-me, Ubde-Nehern *-ma* (diminutive). Tucano: Yahuna *meni* 'child.' Cf.
Nambikwara: Proto-Nambikwara **mǝitˢ* 'child,' Sabane *mais*, Southern
Nambikwara *wēt*, *wēs*.
Almosan-Keresiouan CHILD. Algic: Algonquian: Blackfoot *man-* 'young,'

256

Cheyenne *emonae* 'he is young.' Mosan: Wakashan: Kwakiutl *m'ən*
'young of animals'; Salish: Squamish *mən'*, Twana *bədə* (*b* < **m*,
d < **n*). (AM)
Additional: Uto-Aztecan: M 86 **mal*, **ma* 'child.'

238 SMELL₁

Hokan SMELL.   Chimariko *mičxu* 'stink.' Karok *imšakara* 'smell'
(transitive). Pomo: North Pomo, etc. *miše* 'stink,' Southeast Pomo
mxe- 'stink.' Salinan: San Antonio *me:s.* Shasta *ku-matik'-ik* 'it
stinks.' Tonkawa *moskoj* 'stink.'
Penutian DIRTY.   California: Miwok: Bodega *?umučče* 'smell'; Costanoan:
Mutsun, San Juan Bautista *muns* 'dirt.' Gulf: Natchez *mis-* 'stink.'
Mexican: Totonac *(ša-)mas(-ni?)* 'rotten.' Oregon: Yakonan
mət'ant'inst. Tsimshian *ma?tks* 'dirty, slimy.' Cf. Mexican: Huave *ne-
ameeč* 'devil'; Chinook *masači* 'bad'; Oregon: Siuslaw *mik'a* 'bad.'
Almosan-Keresiouan SMELL.   Algic: Algonquian: Proto–Central
Algonquian **mat*, **mat'i*; **mi:s*, **mit* 'excrement,' **mači* 'bad.'
Iroquoian: Cherokee *ga-wasɔ̄gɔ̄.* Keresan: Santa Ana, etc. *busU* 'have
an odor.' Kutenai *mat'* 'dirty.' Mosan: Wakashan: Kwakiutl *me:s*, *m'əs*
'bad,' *-?məs*, *-?ms* 'useless part of,' Nootka *misa,mač* 'dirty';
Chemakuan: Chemakum *masa*, Quileute *basi?* 'bad,' *bas* 'dirty.'

239 SMELL₂

Macro-Ge SMELL.   Bororo *ko* 'stink' (n.), *ko* (v.). Botocudo *kui*
'fragrance.'
Hokan SMELL.   Chimariko *xa.* Seri *k'ee* 'stink.' Yuman: Campo *xʷi*,
Cocopa *xʷix.*
Penutian SMELL.   Chinook *-kux.* Oregon: Alsea *hkʲ-.* Yukian: Wappo *kuh*
'stink.'
Almosan-Keresiouan SMELL.   Iroquoian: Seneca *kē* 'stink.' Keresan:
Acoma *k'ui* 'be spoiled.' Siouan-Yuchi: Siouan: Santee *kuka* 'be
rotten,' Catawba *hake:.* Cf. Caddoan: Pawnee *kaha:r* 'stink.' (KS)
Additional: Uto-Aztecan: M 390 **?uk*, **hukʷ* 'smell' (transitive), "but
Proto-Numic **?akʷi*, or even **?ekʷi*, does not fit."

240 SNAKE₁

Macro-Ge SNAKE.   Ge: Proto-Ge **kangā.* Mashakali *kānā(not').* Opaie
kuni. Puri: Coropo *kañun.*

Macro-Carib SNAKE.   Andoke *kono* 'rope.' Carib: Palmella *okon* (Carib generally *okoj, okej).* Uitoto: Uitoto *konega* 'rope,' Nonuya *konahɔ* 'rope.' Yagua *koli, koni.*
Andean SNAKE.   Itucale *axkanu.* Sechura: Sec *kon-mpar.* Zaparo: Zaparo *kono,* Iquito *kuni.*
Chibchan-Paezan WORM.   Rama: Guatuso *karan.* Tarascan *karha-si.* (C)
Penutian SNAKE.   Gulf: Muskogean: Koasati, Hitchiti *šinti,* Choctaw *sint,* Creek *četto.* Mexican: Mayan: Kekchí *kʾanti,* Tzeltal *čan,* Tzotzil *čon,* Yucatec *kan.* Oregon: Alsea *kʲinaq.* Plateau: Molala *kwala.*

241 SNAKE₂

Equatorial ROPE.   Maipuran: Arawak [tomy], Chontaquiro *tumuti,* Bare *isemo.* Tupi: Proto-Tupi *tˢam.*
Macro-Tucanoan SNAKE.   Nambikwara: Proto-Nambikwara *tʾep.* Puinave: Hubde *čop, toop, teop* 'worm,' Puinave *čeb.* Ticuna aʔtape.
Chibchan-Paezan SNAKE.   Aruak: Kagaba *ta(k)bi.* Chimu: Eten *tˢuvat.* Cuitlatec *nømi* 'worm.' Choco: Nonama *toma,* Waunana *tama,* etc. Jirajara *tub.* Talamanca: Borunca *tebek, tabek.* Warrau *huba.*

242 SOUR

Hokan BITTER.   Chimariko *qoijo-in* 'sour.' Karok *ʔuːx.* Pomo: East Pomo *b-iko* (*b-* is an adjective prefix). Salinan: San Miguel *t-iek* 'animal's gall,' San Antonio *t-erk* 'animal's gall. Shasta *ičʾaj.* Subtiaba *g-iːko, g-iːka* 'liver,' *m-iːka* 'sour.' Tequistlatec *aggua, -gwa* 'gall.' Tonkawa *ʔixʔex.* Washo *tˢ-iga-l* 'kidney.' Yana *kʾai* 'be bitter.' Yuman: Yuma *xkʷak,* Walapai *hak,* Havasupai *ahaː,* Akwa'ala *l-axaː.*
Penutian SOUR.   California: Maidu: South Maidu *oho;* Wintun: Colouse *aka* 'bitter.' Gulf: Atakapa *ox* 'sharp,' Tunica *kaji.* Mexican: Mayan: Yucatec, etc. *ka(-il)* 'bitter.'

243 STAR₁

Macro-Ge STAR.   Chiquito *oši* 'flame.' Ge: Chavante *wašia,* Cherente *waši.* Mashakali: Mashakali *aši,* Macuni *asi, sai.* Oti *ašo* 'fire.'
Macro-Panoan MOON.   Guaicuru: Guachi *oes* 'sun.' Panoan: Proto-Panoan *ʔoši̇.
Macro-Tucanoan MOON.   Auixiri *esa, øsa.* Tucano: Wanana *se, sī* 'sun, moon,' Waikina *axsē.*

Central Amerind STAR.   Oto-Mangue: R 280 *(n)(h)se(h)(n)*. Uto-
Aztecan: M 413 *su, *tˢu* ("some forms come from *so, *tˢo").
Hokan DAY.   Achomawi: Atsugewi *asi:ji*. Chimariko *asi*. Esselen *asi* 'sun.'
Seri *šax*. Yurumangui *siaa* 'heaven.'

244 STAR₂

Chibchan-Paezan BURN.   Choco: Catio *besia* 'shine, burn.' Barbacoa:
Cayapa *bextˢu* 'fried.' Paez [apaz] 'burn' (transitive). (P)
Hokan STAR.   Salinan: San Antonio *maša-lak* 'morning star' (cf. Jicaque
lak-sak 'sun,' a compound in which *lak* = 'glow' and *sak* = 'sun').
Yuman: Kiliwa *mesi*, Walapai *hamsi*, etc.
Penutian STAR.   Gulf: Chitimacha *paasta;* Muskogean: Choctaw *fičik*.
Mexican: Mixe-Zoque: Zoque *matˢa*, Texistepec *batˢʼa*, Tetontepec
maaxtˢ.
Additional: Uto-Aztecan: M 268b, M 268c *metˢa, *meja*, etc. Keresiouan:
Keres *maṣa* 'light' (n.).
Cf. LIGHT.

245 STONE₁

Macro-Ge MOUNTAIN.   Ge: Krenje *akrã* 'hill,' Cayapo *krãi*. Kaingan:
Catarina *kren*, Tibagi *krin*, etc. Kamakan: Cotoxo *kere, kri*.
Andean STONE.   Alakaluf *kiella, čella*. Araucanian *kura*. Aymara:
Aymara *kʼala*, Jaqaru *qala* 'rock.' Itucale *axeri*.

246 STONE₂

Andean STONE.   Alakaluf: Kaueskar *atak*. Gennaken: Gennaken *atuk*
'mountain,' Pehuelche *atek, atak*. Mayna *tiokn*. Sabela *dika*.
Chibchan-Paczan STONE.   Allentiac *toko*. Atacama *tokʼ-na* 'to stone.'
Chimu: Eten *čax* 'iron.' Guaymi: Chumulu *tukila* 'mountain.' Jirajara
dox. Paez: Guambiana *šux*. Tarascan *tˢaka-pu*.
Hokan FLINT.   Chimariko *qa:ku* 'arrowpoint.' Karok *šak* 'arrowpoint.'
Pomo: East Pomo *xaga* 'knife.' Salinan: San Miguel *išak, išik* 'knife,'
asakʼa. Yana *haga, xaga* 'flint, arrowpoint.'
Almosan-Keresiouan STONE.   Caddoan: Caddo *siiko*, Adai *ekseka*.
Keresan: Santa Ana *hi-sgai* 'knife.' (KS)

247 STRONG

Equatorial WILD.   Guahibo: Guayabero *polala*. Kariri *apru*. Yuracare *pare*.

Macro-Tucanoan STRONG.   Canichana *bere, bele* 'strength.' Iranshe *pwita* 'strong, hard.' Ticuna *pora*. Tucano: Siona *puin* 'be strong.'

248 SUN₁

Macro-Ge SUN.   Bororo *ari* 'moon.' Kaingan: Came *eri*, Apucarana *āra*, etc.

Macro-Panoan SUN.   Guaicuru: Toba *ala*, Komlek *olo* 'zenith,' Guachi *oalete* 'moon,' Toba *lon* 'kindle,' Mocovi *alon* 'burn.' Lengua: Mascoy *aleu* 'burn (transitive), shine,' *p-eltin* 'moon.' Lule *ale* 'burn' (intransitive), *alit*. Mataco: Choroti *wela*, Enimaga *wal*. Vilela *olo*.

Macro-Carib FIRE.   Carib: Trio *ole-ole* 'flame,' Crichana *iri(-ipo)* 'fire-place,' Surinam *t-u:ri* 'torch,' etc. Uitoto *ole*. Yagua: Yameo *ole*.

Equatorial SUN.   Maipuran: Cayeri *eri*, Piapoco *eeri, eri*, Apolista *uri* 'star.' Otomaco *ura* 'moon.' (MA)

Macro-Tucanoan SUN.   Capixana *varuvaru*. Catuquina: Catuquina *waɫja* 'moon,' Parawa *wadia* 'moon.' Iranshe *ireʔ*. Mobima *il-* 'dry in sun' (transitive). Puinave: Tiquie *uero*, Yehubde *werho* 'moon,' Querari *uidn* 'moon.'

Chibchan-Paezan DAY.   Choco: Catio *una* 'shine.' Chimu: Eten *inen* 'light.' Jirajara: Ayoman *iñ* 'sun.' Paez *en*. Timucua [inny]. (P)

Hokan SUN.   Chimariko *alla, ala*. Comecrudo *al*. Karankawa *auil* 'moon.' Pomo: East Pomo *la:* 'sun, moon,' North, Central Pomo *da* 'sun.' Salinan *naʔ*. Yuman: Yuma *ña*, Tipai *ña:*, Kiliwa *inja:*, etc.

249 SUN₂

Macro-Tucanoan SUN.   Auixiri *akroak*. Canichana *kol, koxli, korli* 'day.' Huari *ikirinæ* 'day.' Koaia *akori* 'moon.' Maku *kele,kelia* 'day.' Natu *kra-sulo*. Puinave *kəlod, ked, korlot* 'star.' Uman *kari*.

Andean SUN.   Alakaluf *kala* 'day.' Aymara *kʰana* 'light' (n.). Cholona *kenna* 'stars.' Itucale *hanuna*. Kahuapana: Jebero *ukli* 'day, light.' Patagon: Patagon *kenek, kerren* 'day,' *kolaš, kunaš* 'star' (probably diminutive), Hongote *kekar*, Ona *kren* 'moon.' Quechua: Ancash *xunax* 'day.'

Chibchan-Paezan KINDLE.   Chibcha: Chibcha *b-gena(-suka)*, Manare *okina-no.* Misumalpan: Miskito *klau-an.* Rama *kunkani* 'light' (n.). (C)

250 SUN₃

Chibchan-Paezan DAY.   Choco: Sambu *ibaru* 'month,' Citara *ibare.* Tarascan *piri-tani* 'lighten' (v.), *piri-rasi* 'luminous.' Xinca: Yupultepec, Chiquimulilla, etc. *pari* 'day, sun.'

Penutian SUN.   Gulf: Muskogean: Choctaw *pala* 'light (n.), shine.' Oregon: Kalapuya *ampiun.* Tsimshian *pialst, bials* 'star.' Yukian: Huchnom *pilaṭ,* Coast Yuki *pilɛt.* (California: Wintun: Colouse *pellar* is probably a borrowing from Yuki.)

251 SUN₄

Chibchan-Paezan FIRE.   Barbacoa: Colorado *tehe* 'firewood.' Chimu: Eten *tok* 'stove.' Jirajara: Jirajara *dueg,* Ayoman *dug.* Timucua *toka.* Warrau *doki-a* 'burn' (intransitive). (P)

Penutian SUN.   California: Costanoan: Monterey *tuš* 'day,' Santa Cruz *tuhe* 'day'; Wintun: Sacramento River *tuku.* Gulf: Tunica *tahč̓i.* Mexican: Mixe-Zoque: Sierra Popoluca *tˢok* 'shine,' Sayula *taʔkš* 'shine'; Totonac: Papantla *tuxkaket* 'light' (n.). Oregon: Siuslaw *tˢxaju:wi.* Tsimshian *tˢius.* Zuni *jatokka.* Cf. BURN.

252 SWALLOW

Penutian SWALLOW.   California: Yokuts *me:k̓i, mik̓²-is* 'throat.' Chinook *mokue, -mo:k-* 'throat.' Yukian: Huchnom *meka* 'drink,' Coast Yuki *mekup* 'throat.'

Almosan-Keresiouan SWALLOW.   Algic: Yurok *mik̓olum.* Kutenai *uʔmqoɫ.* Mosan: Wakashan: Kwakiutl *mək;* Salish: Pentlatch *məkwəm,* Nısqualli *omikalekʷ.* Cf. Algonquian: Cheyenne *na-mha-az* 'I swallow.' (AM)

253 TESTICLE

Macro-Ge EGG.   Bororo: Bororo *ba* 'egg, testicle,' Umotina *ba.* Puri: Coroado *paki.*

Macro-Panoan EGG.   Moseten [buisc] *buiš* 'yoke.' Panoan: Proto-Panoan **βači.*

Macro-Carib TESTICLE.   Uitoto: Coeruna *ka-moesse* 'penis,' Miranya

Carapana Tapuya *ga-moto* 'penis.' Yagua: Yagua *si-mase*, Yameo *wi-miasel*.

254 THIN

Macro-Ge SMALL. Botocudo *kuǰi*. Kaingan: Ingain *kutui*, Catarina *kaičidn*.

Equatorial THIN. Chapacura: Quitemo *kuči*. Maipuran: Arawak *kitˢke* 'narrow.' Uro: Caranga *kos*. (A)

Hokan NARROW. Seri *kosot*. Tequistlatec *guʔušu*.

Penutian SMALL. Proto-California Penutian **kut* 'little.' Chinook: Wishram *kˀatˢ*. Mexican: Huave *kičeeč;* Totonac *aktˢu;* Mayan: Pokomchi *kˀisa*, Tzotzil *kočol* 'weak.' Plateau: Klamath *kˀečča*. Yukian: Wappo *kutˀija*.

255 THROAT

Hokan THROAT. Salinan: San Antonio *p-e:nikˀa*. Tequistlatec *nukˀ* 'swallow.'

Penutian THROAT. Gulf: Muskogean: Proto-Muskogean **nukkwi* 'neck'; Natchez *noč*, *naxts*. Mexican: Huave *o-nik* 'neck'; Mayan: Chorti *nukˀ* 'swallow,' Huastec *nukˀ*. Plateau: Klamath *nawg*, North Sahaptin *nuqˀwaš*.

256 TONGUE₁

Macro-Carib TONGUE. Bora: Bora *mee-nixigua*, Imihita *me-nehekoa*. Carib: Proto-Hianacoto **-iñiiko*. Cf. Yagua *onesi*, *ɔneči*.

Macro-Tucanoan TONGUE. Catuquina: Catuquina *noɤo*, Parawa *noko*. Puinave: Hubde *noked(n)*, Papury *noken*, Puinave *rok*, *lok*.

Chibchan-Paezan TONGUE. Barbacoa: Cayapa *nīska*, *nihka*, Colorado *nika*. Betoi *ineka*. Cf. Allentiac *nanak*, but also Allentiac *nanat*, Millcayac *nanat*. (P)

257 TONGUE₂

Macro-Ge TONGUE. Chiquito: Chiquito *otu*, Churapa *i-juto* 'my tongue.' Ge: Krenje *joto*, Kraho *i-jɔʔto*.

Macro-Tucanoan TONGUE. Capixana *tau*. Kaliana *k-ā:tū*. Muniche *tø(ng)*. Yuri *otæ*.

258 TONGUE₃

Macro-Ge LICK.   Botocudo *numeraŋ*. Kaingan: Aweikoma *nemindaŋ*.

Equatorial TONGUE.   Cayuvava *i-ne*. Jibaro: Shuara *iñe*, Gualaquiza *iñei*,
Aguaruna *inei-inei*. Kariri: Kariri *ñunu*, Sapuya [nunuh]. Maipuran:
Kustenau *nu-nei*, Cauishana, Ipurina, Machiguenga *-nene*, Wapishana
u-nenu, Toyeri *wu-onu*. Otomaco: Otomaco *jonna*, Taparita *jonan*.
Piaroa: Piaroa *ne*, Saliba *nene*. Trumai *a-no*. Tupi: Tupi, Guaraní
ñẽʔẽ, Apichum *o-njon*.

Macro-Tucanoan LICK.   Catuquina: Catauisi *no* 'tongue.' Puinave: Ubde-
Nehern *nemmei*, Papury *nemøi*. Tucano *nene*.

Central Amerind TONGUE.   Kiowa-Tanoan: Kiowa *dẽ*. Uto-Aztecan: M
441a **neni*.

259 TREE₁

Macro-Carib FOREST.   Carib: Surinam *itu*, Apiaca *itua*, etc. Uitoto:
Uitoto *atikø*, *xatike*, Coeruna *atˢaitto*. Yagua *toha*, *to:*, *tɔx*.

Equatorial TREE.   Esmeralda *tate*. Kariri: Dzubucua *dˢi* 'wood,' Kamaru
tˢi 'firewood.' Maipuran: Mehinacu, Waura, Yaulapiti *ada*, Arawak
adda, Mandauaca, Uainuma *a:ta*, etc. Otomaco *andu*. Trumai *dei* 'tree,
wood.' Yaruro *ando*.

Central Amerind TREE.   Kiowa-Tanoan: Tanoan: Tewa *te*, Taos *tuɬo-na*.
Uto-Aztecan: M 309 **tua* 'oak tree.' Azteco-Tanoan: WT 91 **tu;* no
forms given.

Penutian TREE.   California: Maidu *də* 'bushes.' Chinook *-te:* (in
compounds). Gulf: Atakapa *te-* (in *te-waš* 'leaf'); Natchez *dˢu:;*
Muskogean: Choctaw *iti*, Alabama *ito:*, Creek *ito*. Mexican: Mayan:
Proto-Mayan **teʔ*. Zuni *ta*.

260 TREE₂

Macro-Carib TREE.   Bora: Miranya *i-mæ*, Miranya Oira Assu-Tapuya
ymaana. Uitoto: Uitoto *amena*, Ocaina *amuunna*, Orejone *anaina*.
Yagua *ne:nɔ*, *nɨɨnu*.

Andean TREE.   Itucale *enenga* 'firewood.' Kahuapana: Kahuapana *nala*,
Jebero *nala* 'wood.' Zaparo: Iquito *nan*, *nana*. Cf. Gennaken: Pehuelche
alan 'wood.'

261 TREE₃

Chibchan-Paezan TREE.   Andaqui *sa-kani-fi* 'forked stick.' Aruak: Kagaba *kalli*, Guamaca, Bintucua *kann*. Chibcha: Chibcha *tse-ganny-ka* 'crutch,' Margua *kar(-kua)*. Guaymi: Muoi *kan* 'wood.' Itonama *kana* 'pole.' Motilon: Dobocubi *kañ* 'bamboo.' Rama *kat*. Talamanca: Bribri *kar*.

Penutian TREE.   Chinook *ičkan* 'wood.' Tsimshian ɢ*an*. Yukian: Wappo *hol*, Clear Lake *hol* 'wood,' Huchnom, Yuki *ol*. Cf. Mexican: Huave *šiəl*.

262 TWO

Macro-Tucanoan TWO.   Catuquina *upaua*. Nambikwara: Northern Nambikwara *pʔá:n*, Sabane *paʔlin*. Puinave: Hubde *mbeere*, Puinave *mbee*, *be*. Ticuna *peia*. Tucano: Yahuna *ipo*, Tucano *pia-na*, Waikina *pia-ro*, etc.

Andean TWO.   Araucanian *epu*. Aymara *paja*. Cholona *ip*. Gennaken: Pehuelche *pe-č* (cf. *ge-č* 'three'). Yamana: Yahgan *i-pai* 'we two,' *-pai*, *-pa*, *-pi* (nominal dual).

Chibchan-Paezan TWO.   Aruak: Atanque, Bintucua *moga*. Atacama *poja*. Barbacoa: Colorado *palu*, *paluga*, Cayapa *paʎu*. Chibcha: Tegria, Manare *bukai*, Pedraza *bukuaj*, etc. Chimu: Mochica *paš*. Cuna *po*. Guaymi: Move *bokoloro* 'twin.' Malibu: Chimila *muxuna*. Misumalpan: Matagalpa *buju*, Cacaopera *muɣɣu*. Mura *mukui*. Paez: Guambiana *paj*. Paya *pok*. Rama *puksak*, *pukakba* 'twin.' Talamanca: Tirub *pugda*, Estrella, Chiripo *bor*, Cabecar *bur*.

Penutian TWO.   California: Wintun *palo-l* (*l* dual as in pronouns); Maidu *pene*. Gulf: Atakapa *happalst*, *-pe* (deduced from 'ten' = 'hands two'); Chitimacha *ʔupa*. Mexican: Huave *apool* 'snap in two.' Tsimshian *məla* 'both.' Yukian: Yuki *-ope*, Wappo *hopi*, *pʔala* 'twins.'

Additional: Oto-Mangue: R 222 **(h)kʷa(h)(n)* 'two.'

263 VAGINA

Equatorial VAGINA.   Guahibo *petu*. Kandoshi *apčir-ič* 'vulva.' Maipuran: Goajiro *piero*, Wachipairi *ped*, Toyeri *apuit*. Uro: Uro, Caranga *piši* 'vulva.'

Hokan VAGINA.   Karok *vi:θ*. Tequistlatec *la-bešu*. Washo *d-i:bis*.

Additional: Uto-Aztecan: M 449 'vagina' (no reconstruction), Hopi *mosinga* 'clitoris,' Papago *muus* 'vagina.'

264 WATER₁

Macro-Carib WATER.   Bora: Muinane *maaño* 'wet.' Uitoto: Uitoto *(h)iman(i)* 'river,' Ocaina *maanu* 'river, sea.'

Macro-Tucanoan WATER.   Iranshe *mana*. Kaliana *inam, nam*. Maku *na²me* 'water, river, rain.'

Chibchan-Paezan DRINK.   Allentiac: Allentiac *maña*, Millcayac *mañe*. Chimu: Eten *man* 'eat, drink.' Jirajara: Jirajara *mangi*, Ayoman *mambi*, Gayon *manvi*. Cf. Choco: Catio *mimbu* 'swallow.' (P)

Additional: Almosan-Keresiouan: Proto-Siouan **m-ni*.
Cf. RIVER₁.

265 WATER₂

Macro-Ge WATER.   Bororo: Bororo *poba*, Umotina *po* 'river.' Caraja *beæ*, *beai* 'drink.' Guato *ma-vei* 'rain.' Mashakali: Capoxo *vui* 'rain.' Opaie *poe* 'lake.' Oti *beia* 'rain.' Puri: Coroado *ba* 'drink.' Cf. Botocudo *muniã-po* 'rain,' *muniã* 'water.'

Macro-Tucanoan WET.   Mobima *poi* 'to wet.' Puinave: Ubde-Nehern, Papury *puui* 'to wet.' Tucano *pu* 'become wet,' *puu* 'make wet.'

Chibchan-Paezan WATER.   Atacama *k²epi-pui* 'tear' (*k²epi* = 'eye'). Barbacoa: Cayapa *pi*, Colorado *pi* 'water, river,' Cuaiquer *pi* 'river.' Choco: Catio *ba* 'liquid, sap.' Cuna *apojoa* 'moisten.' Mura: Mura *pe* 'water, river,' Matanawi *api* 'water, river.' Paez: Paez *afi* 'clear water,' Guambiana, Totoro *pi*, Moguex *pii*. Rama *s-ba* 'wet.' Timucua *ibi* 'river.'

Central Amerind WATER.   Kiowa-Tanoan: Kiowa *p²ɔ* 'stream'; Tanoan: Tewa *p²o*, Taos *p²o(-one)*, Isleta *p²ãide*. Oto-Mangue: R 234 **(n)(H)kʷa(h)(²)(n)*. Uto-Aztecan: M 455a **pa*.

Penutian RAIN.   California: Miwok: Marin, Lake Miwok *u:pa;* Maidu *bai*. Gulf: Natchez *joba* (v.); Muskogean: Hitchiti *obæ* (v.), Choctaw *ombe*. Mexican: Mayan: Huastec *a:b*.

266 WHITE₁

Macro-Panoan WHITE.   Lule *po*. Mataco: Macca *fo*. Vilela *ope, obe*.

Equatorial WHITE.   Cayuvava *ja-pora-xa*. Maipuran: Achagua *paraj*, Bare *balini*, Wapishana *barak*. Tupi: Pawate *epeira* 'cleanse,' Arikem *ta-puari* 'clean.' Yuracare *bolo-si*. Zamuco: Zamuco *pororo*, Chamacoco *poro*.

Macro-Tucanoan WHITE.   Canichana *bara, bala*. Capixana *pan-æræ*. Catuquina [parany]. Nambikwara: Proto-Nambikwara **pa:n*. Tucano: Desana *bure, boleri*, Chiranga *bole*.

Chibchan-Paezan CLEAN.   Andaqui [fanszu-za] 'cleanse.' Atacama *palan* 'cleanse.' Barbacoa: Colorado *pura* 'cleanse.' Paez *finde* (Paez *nd* < **r*). Warrau *bere*. (P)

Cf. WHITE₂.

267 WHITE₂

Hokan WHITE.   Chumash: Santa Cruz *pupu*. Comecrudo *pepok*. Jicaque *pek*. Karankawa *peka*. Tequistlatec *afuhga*. Washo *dal-popoi*.

Almosan-Keresiouan WHITE.   Algic: Algonquian: Cree, Natick *pahke* 'clean.' Mosan: Salish: Coeur d'Alene *peq*, Kalispel *paq*, etc. (AM)

Cf. WHITE₁.

268 WIND (n.)

Macro-Ge WIND.   Caraja *kɨhɨ*. Ge: Macro-Ge **kok*. Kaingan: Southern Kaingan *kaka*, Tibagi *kanka*, etc.

Andean WIND.   Cholona: Cholona *kaz, kas, kaš*, Hivito *koktom*. Itucale *køxøana*. Patagon: Tsoneka *kučen*, Tehuelche *koošen, kosen*.

Chibchan-Paezan WIND.   Barbacoa: Colorado *kiši*. Chimu: Eten *kus*. Paez *keis*. (P)

269 WING

Hokan WING.   Chumash: Santa Ynez *qa:m, qap* 'feather,' Santa Cruz, San Luis Obispo *s-kama*. Comecrudo *xam* 'feather, bird.' Cotoname *komiom* 'bird.' Karankawa *hamdolak* 'feather.' Karok *xip*. Shasta *čop-ha* 'bird.' Seri *kap*. Tequistlatec *k-kap* 'to fly.' Yurumangui *a-ikan*. Yuman: Cochimi *guan* 'wing, feather.' Cf. Coahuilteco *jam* 'bird, to fly.'

Penutian WING.   California: Yokuts *k'aps-aj* 'shoulder.' Mexican: Mayan (general) *kob* 'arm, shoulder,' Huastec *okob* 'arm, wing.' Yukian: Yuki *kap*, Wappo *kupɛ, kapɛ?* 'feather.'

Almosan-Keresiouan WING.   Keresan: Proto-Keresan **t'a:pɪ*. Mosan:

Wakashan: Nootka *kam*. Siouan-Yuchi: Siouan: Catawba *hi-čip* (Speck).

270   WISH (v.)

Macro-Ge SEEK.   Bororo *emaru*. Botocudo *moru* 'love.' Fulnio *-ma* 'seeking.' Kamakan *mã*.

Macro-Panoan WISH.   Guaicuru: Toba *ama* 'masturbate,' Mocovi *aman* 'masturbate.' Lengua *min(-jeji)*. Lule *mai*. Mataco: Nocten *umin*, Payagua *mai*, Choroti *emi* 'dear.' Moseten *maje*.

Andean WISH.   Aymara: Aymara *muna* 'love,' Jaqaru *muna*. Cholona *men*. Kahuapana: Jebero *malealk* 'ask.' Patagon: Ona *maniel-en*. Quechua: Cochabamba, Santiagueño *muna*. Sabela *mẽ*.

Chibchan-Paezan WISH.   Andaqui *miña-za* 'I sought.' Barbacoa: Colorado *munai-jo* 'love,' *muna-ha* 'wish.' Timucua *mani, manta, mani-no* 'think.' Cf. Warrau *obone* 'think.' (P)

Hokan LIKE.   Chimariko *miʔinan*. Karok *ʔi:mnih* 'love.' Pomo: East Pomo *mara*.

Penutian WISH.   California: Miwok: Central Sierra *menna* 'try,' Lake Miwok *menaw* ~ *minaw* 'try'; Wintun: Patwin *meina* 'try' (probable borrowing from Miwok). Gulf: Tunica *me* 'seek'; Natchez *mai* 'love.' Oregon: Takelma *mi:li:* 'love.' Tsimshian *ba:l* 'try.'

Almosan-Keresiouan WISH.   Algic: Algonquian: Shawnee *menw-* 'prefer, like,' Fox *menw* 'enjoy.' Keresan: Laguna *amuu* 'love.' Mosan: Wakashan: Nootka *ma:na* 'try, test'; Salish: Lkungen *aməna* 'hunt,' Thompson *-mamən* (desiderative). Siouan-Yuchi: Siouan: Catawba *muʔe*.

271 WOMAN₁

Equatorial WOMAN   Coche *šima, čima*. Timote: Maripu *timua* 'girl.' Zamuco: Tumraha *timičarne*, Chamacoco *tybičarne, tymičarne*.

Macro-Tucanoan WOMAN.   Iranshe *nãmiʔi*. Puinave: Querari *nẽ(m)-bid* 'daughter' (*bid* = 'small'). Tucano: Tucano *nomio*, Coto *tomio*, Amaguaje *nomio, romio*, Siona *romi* (forms without initial *n-* are usual in Western Tucanoan).

Andean WOMAN.   Araucanian: Araucanian *domo* 'woman, female,' Pehuenche *zomo, domo* 'woman, female.' Gennaken *-tˢəm* 'female.' Patagon: Tehuelche *čame, semoe* 'female,' *tˢamen* 'female of animals.' Zaparo: Zaparo *itomo, itiumu*, Iquito *tem*.

272 WOMAN₂

Macro-Panoan WOMAN. Charruan: Charrua *čalo-na* 'girl' (*na* = 'child').
Lengua: Sanapana *kilaua*, Angaite *kelaa*. Lule *kila* 'girl,' *kili-p*
'female.'
Equatorial WOMAN. Guahibo *kvantua* 'first wife.' Timote: Cuica *kneu*
'female.' Tupi: Proto-Tupi **kujã*, Kamayura, etc. *kunja*. Yuracare *igūn*
'girl.'

273 WOMAN₃

Chibchan-Paezan WOMAN. Barbacoa: Colorado *sona*, Cayapa *suna*
'wife.' Chimu: Eten *sønaŋ* 'wife.' Jirajara: Ayoman [senha] 'woman,
wife.' Lenca: Chilanga *suŋ*.
Central Amerind WOMAN. Kiowa-Tanoan: Tanoan: Taos *łiw-*, Isleta *łiu-*,
Jemez *tjo*. Oto-Mangue: R 340 **(Y)(n)su(h)n* 'woman, daughter,
mother.' Uto-Aztecan: M 470 (no reconstruction; "most of the forms
reflect something like **su, *sun, *so, *son*").
Penutian WOMAN. California: Miwok: Central Sierra Miwok *ʔoša:*
'wife.' Mexican: Mayan (general) *-iš-* 'female,' Huastec *ušum* 'woman,
wife.' Plateau: North Sahaptian *ašam*.

274 WOOD₁

Macro-Tucanoan FIRE. Koaia *i*. Yuri *ii*.
Chibchan-Paezan WOOD. Allentiac: Allentiac *eje*, Millcayac *eje* 'tree.'
Barbacoa: Cuaiquer *ii*. Choco: Catio *oi* 'forest,' Chami *ea* 'forest,'
Citara [elle] *eje* 'forest.' Motilon *ee* 'candle.' Mura: Mura *ii, iji*, Mura-
Piraha *ie*, Matanawi *i* 'firewood.' Paez: Paez *uʔj*, Moguex *oi-t*.
Timucua *aje* 'forest, tree, wood.'
Hokan WOOD. Esselen *ii*. Yana *ʔi(-na)*. Yuman: Cocopa *i:* 'wood, tree,'
Walapai *i:ʔi:* 'wood, tree, etc.'
Almosan-Keresiouan TREE. Iroquoian: Seneca *-jē-*. Siouan-Yuchi: Proto-
Siouan **jā;* Yuchi *ja*. (KS)

275 WOOD₂

Macro-Ge WOOD. Kaingan: Came *ka* 'wood, stick,' Catarina *ko*
'firewood, tree,' Apucarana *ka* 'tree,' etc. Mashakali: Mashakali,
Capoxo *ke*. Puri: Coroado *ke* 'wood, fire.'
Chibchan-Paezan FIREWOOD. Antioquia: Nutabe *ki-a* 'fire,' Catio *ki(-ra)*

'fire.' Aruak: Guamaca *ge* 'fire,' Bintucua *gei* 'tree, fire,' Atanque *gie* 'tree, fire.' Chibcha: Chibcha *kie* 'tree.' Guaymi: Chumulu, Gualaca, Changuena *ke*. Motilon: Motilon *ka* 'tree.' Paez: Paez *eki, e?kx^j,* Moguex *eki-t*. Cf. Barbacoa: Cayapa *či* 'tree,' and Itonama *či* 'classifier for trees.'

Hokan WOOD. Achomawi: Atsugewi *ahwi*. Chimariko *ho?eu* 'board.' Pomo: North, Central Pomo *haj*, Kashaya *?ahaj*, Northeast Pomo *?aha:*, etc. Shasta *?akka:(h)a*. Tequistlatec *?okø*.

276 WORK₁ (v.)

Equatorial WORK. Guahibo *xana*. Maipuran: Toyeri *ekka, ega*. Zamuco: Tumraha *t-axho*.

Andean MAKE. Araucanian *ka*. Leco *kia, kian* 'created.' Sabela: Sabela *kæi* 'do!,' Auca *kæ*. Zaparo *aki* 'done.'

Chibchan-Paezan MAKE. Barbacoa: Colorado, Cayapa *ke* 'make,' (derivational element for denominative verbs). Chibcha [ky]. Chimu *-ko* 'causative.' Cuitlatec *-gi* (transitivizer). Misumalpan: Miskito *-ka* (ending for all transitive verbs). Paez *ki*. Paya *kaa*. Timucua *iki-no*. Xinca: Yupultepec *ka*.

Penutian MAKE. California: Maidu *kə* 'make, put.' Gulf: Atakapa *ka*. Mexican: Mayan: Yucatec *kah*. Plateau: North Sahaptin, Nez Perce *ku* 'do.'

Almosan-Keresiouan MAKE. Algic: Algonquian: Blackfoot *-ka-* (inanimate object), Cree *ke* (inanimate object); Wiyot *ga*. Keresan: Santa Ana *kuja* 'do.' Siouan-Yuchi: Proto-Siouan **kax;* Yuchi *k²a . . . kɔ* 'work.'

277 WORK₂ (v.)

Macro Ge WORK. Bororo: Umotina *pthi*. Botocudo [py]. Ge: Krenje *pĩ, opi*, Crengez *api*.

Macro-Tucanoan MAKE. Catuquina: Canamari *bu* 'do!' Puinave: Tiquie *beei* 'work,' Papury *bøæi* 'work, make.' Tucano: Wanana *ve*, Tucano *wee*.

278 YELLOW₁

Equatorial RED. Cayuvava *titibɔ* 'blood.' Guahibo *t'obia*. Kandoshi *čobiapi*. Maipuran: Baniva *tewari* 'yellow,' Manao *taweti*. Piaroa: Piaroa *toahe, tuahe*, Saliba *duva*. Trumai *t'omate*. Tupi: Tembe *taua*

269

'yellow,' Oyampi *tawa* 'yellow,' Arikem *taboro* 'yellow.' Yuracare *tebe* 'blood,' *tebetebesi*.

Chibchan-Paezan YELLOW.   Aruak: Guamaca *tamukuega*. Chibcha: Chibcha *tib-*, Tegria *tam-airo*, Uncasica *tamo-ja*, etc. Chimu: Eten *tˢaːm*. Mura: Matanawi *tomā* 'blue.' Tarascan *tˢipan-be-ti*.

279 YELLOW₂

Central Amerind YELLOW.   Kiowa-Tanoan: Tanoan: Isleta *tˢʔu*, San Ildefonso *tˢʔe*, Taos *tˢʔul-wi*. Oto-Mangue: R 245 **(n)si* 'yellow, white, bright.' Uto-Aztecan: M 476 **si*, **tˢi* 'yellow.'

Almosan-Keresiouan YELLOW.   Iroquoian: Seneca *dˀi(-t-kwar)* 'bile.' Siouan-Yuchi: Siouan: Proto-Siouan (C) **ri*, Hidatsa *tˢi*, Dakota *zi*, Biloxi, Tutelo *si*, Ofo *fi*, etc.; Yuchi *ti*. (KS)

280 YESTERDAY

Macro-Ge YESTERDAY.   Caraja *kenau, kanau*. Chiquito *kañi*.

Equatorial YESTERDAY.   Cofan *kānī*. Guahibo *kanibi*. Cf. Guamo *čuna* 'evening.'

Macro-Tucanoan YESTERDAY.   Auake *a(x)koan*. Iranshe *ionitie-kanā* (*ionitie* = 'other'). Kaliana *ōākai*. Nambikwara: Proto-Nambikwara **kanaC* (final consonant *-C* varies; not reconstructed). Puinave: Tiquie *čan*. Tucano: Tucano, Sara, Waikina, etc. *kane*.

281 YOUNG

Macro-Ge CHILD.   Bororo: Otuke *kaoro* 'boy.' Ge: Proto-Ge **kra*, Cherente *kedæ*, Acroamirim *kutæ*, Apinage *kræ*, etc. Kaingan: Southern Kaingan *kræ* 'son.' Kamakan: Kamakan *kraniŋ*, Masacara *kra, kræ*. Mashakali: Macuni *ia-kuto*. Puri: Coroado *krikra* 'small.'

Equatorial NEW.   Maipuran: Toyeri *-ket* (diminutive). Timote *akotˢ*. Trumai *axos, axus* 'young, child.' Uro: Caranga *kˀaata* 'raw,' Chipaya *kaata-ža* 'raw.'

Chapter 5

Grammatical Evidence for Amerind

This chapter presents grammatical evidence for the validity of both Amerind as a whole and the stocks set forth in Chapter 3. The separation of lexical evidence and grammatical evidence is of course to some extent arbitrary. It is no doubt clear that the etymology of a word like 'house' belongs in the lexicon, whereas a marker of durative aspect that appears everywhere as a bound element in the verbal complex should be treated as grammatical. On the other hand, because of the process of grammaticization, especially in a family of considerable historical depth like Amerind, a particular etymon may appear in some languages as lexical and in others as grammatical. For example, some Andean languages have a dual marker that would generally be deemed a grammatical element, yet this dual marker clearly derives from the general Amerind word for 'two' (and has indeed been included in the Amerind etymological dictionary). This and other such items are cross-referenced to the dictionary at appropriate points. However, in general, I have put most of these occurrences in the lexicon rather than here on the principle that since this is a historically oriented work, each item should be classified by its earliest ascertainable function, and lexical items often develop grammatical functions, whereas the reverse process is quite rare. An example from English might be the use of 'isms' and 'ologies' as free forms abstracted from their bound derivational usage.

In trying to present an organized review of purely grammatical elements, I have followed the same principle so far as possible, given that grammatical items themselves change function in the course of their historical development. Third-person pronouns, for example, commonly develop from distance demonstratives, and in many languages they function in both ways. Because the demonstrative appears to be the earlier use, I classify these pronouns as demonstratives.

This basic principle has still another application. When we find, for example, one first-person pronoun in virtually all stocks of Amerind and another confined to a single stock, the latter pronoun is assumed to be a later innovation. Hence its description follows that of the older and more widespread element.

The general order of exposition is as follows: personal pronouns, demonstratives, and reflexives (items 1–27); pronominal and nominal categories of number, gender, and case (28–57); nominal derivatives from other nouns and from verbs (58–65); participial and other adjective formants (66–69); verbal categories (tense-mood, voice, and other derivational categories such as causatives; 70–99); and finally negation and interrogatives (100–107). The stocks are presented in the same south–north order used in the two preceding chapters.

In connection with the first topic to be considered, personal pronouns, we might usefully begin by summarizing some of the material presented in Chapter 2. First, we saw that Amerind appears to have had a system of four persons, first, second, third, and inclusive, which were in principle indifferent to number although the inclusive pronoun (first in association with second) was by its very nature dual. Various subgroups developed markers that, when added to the original elements, pluralized them. But none of these 'pluralizers' is broadly enough distributed to suggest its existence in Proto-Amerind. In fact, in many Amerind languages *n-*, for example, at least in certain uses as a first-person marker, is indifferent to number or has secondarily differentiated into singular and plural by vowel alternation.

A pluralized first-person pronoun is normally exclusive if there is an inclusive-exclusive distinction. Inclusive person, however, becomes an inclusive first-person plural. This plural, as we shall see, is the highly probable source in certain instances of a general first-person plural.

We also saw in Chapter 2 that the pronominal system was probably ergative. Though there is no evidence for this assumption in the noun, it is particularly clear in the two almost universally distributed elements of the first-person pronoun, *n* and *i*. Of these, *n* was probably used for independent pronouns, nominal possessives, and the subject of transitive verbs, whereas *i* was used ergatively for the object of transitive verbs and the subject of intransitive verbs, including nouns and adjectives used statively in predication.

272

1. First-person *n* was thoroughly discussed in Chapter 2, and need not be gone into here. It will be recalled that it occurs in all 11 Amerind stocks.

2. Though first-person *i* was also discussed in Chapter 2, essentially only South American occurrences were given there, so a more complete review is in order.

MACRO-GE. Bororo has *i(-nno)* first-person singular independent pronoun (cf. *cě(-nno)* 'we,' etc.) and *i-* first-person singular possessive, subject or object of verb. As object, *i-* may be suffixed. It can also be used with postpositions (e.g. *i-po* 'with me'). In general in what follows it will be assumed that a pronominal element, if used as a possessive, can also be used with prepositions or postpositions. Similar uses are reported in other languages, e.g. the Bororo group, but information is very incomplete; Umotina has *ija* as first-person singular independent pronoun, and *i-* as first-person singular verb subject and possessive (palatalizing). Chiquito has *i-* (palatalizing) as first-person singular possessive and verb subject. In Fulnio, nouns and verbs fall into two classes: in one, *i-* is prefixed as a possessive or verb subject; in the other, it is zero, but initial *t, d,* and *k* are palatalized. In Krenje (Ge), *i-* (sometimes followed by a nasal element) occurs as a possessive and as a subject of stative verbs, e.g. *i-k ʾin* 'I am ugly,' but not as a subject of active verbs, whether transitive or intransitive. In Kraho (the other best-described Ge language), *i-* is a first-person singular possessive, the subject of intransitive verbs, and the object of transitives in certain verb classes (the facts are too complex to be treated here in detail). Examples are *i-tyk* 'I died' and *ka i-pupu* 'thou seest me.' Kaingan has Aweikoma *i, ig,* first-person singular independent pronouns, and Palmas *i, ig,* first-person singular pronouns, possessives, and verb subjects or objects (preceding the verb in all cases and treated as unbound elements). In Coroado (Puri), only the independent pronouns are recorded; here *i-n* 'I,' when compared with *a-n* 'thou,' shows that the indicator of the first-person pronoun is *i.* For other Macro-Ge languages grammatical data are very sparse or completely lacking.

MACRO-PANOAN. The Charruan language Guenoa has [y-ti] as the first-person singular independent pronoun. (Since *-ti* is suffixed to all independent pronouns, the analysis is clear.) It also has *i-* as a verb subject. In the sparse word list on which our knowledge of Charrua proper rests, we have *i-mau* 'ear,' *i-xou* 'eye,' and *i-neu* 'son.' Since body parts and kinship terms occur only in possessed form in these languages, and the most common response is to give first-person singular forms, the *i-* in these words is in all probability the first-person singular possessive. The Lengua language Mascoy has *e-* as the first-person singular possessive. The Guaicuru subgroup in general has *i-* as the first-person singular possessive and the object of transitive verbs. In Vejoz and other dialects of Mataco, *i-* occurs as the first-person possessive; Vejoz has *ij(-am)* as the first-person singular possessive independent pronoun, and Payagua has *ja-* 'my' and *j(-am)* 'I.' (I am not quite sure of the analysis of the *j(-am).*) Enimaga, which is genetically the most distant from Mataco proper, has *ji-* 'my.' The *i-* of Mataco palatalizes, as indicated in the discussion in Chapter 2. Moseten, which seems to have no bound pronouns, has *je* 'I.' For Proto-Panoan, Shell reconstructs *$*?i$* as the first-person singular independent pronoun. In Tacanan, the first-person singular independent pronoun is based on *e-*, with different suffixes in the singular and plural; there are no bound forms. I find no evidence of *i* as a first-person marker in Lule and the closely related Vilela.

MACRO-CARIB. In the Bora language Muinane, the basic first-person possessive is *ta-;* however, prefixing it to a noun with an initial alveolar consonant palatalizes it. This strongly suggests that *ta-* is an innovation prefixed to a former first-person possessive form that palatalizes. In the Carib languages generally, *i-* is the first-person singular possessive, the subject of intransitive verbs, and the object of verb forms in which a third person acts on the first person. In Yagua, the facts parallel those in Muinane. The first-person possessive and verb subject is *ra-*, followed by a palatalizing element more extensive in its workings than the *ta-* of Muinane. These data are reported by Powlison (1962). The earlier, or possibly dialectally different, material of Tessman (1930) gives *dea-* as the first-person possessive, suggesting that *ra-* < *da*.

EQUATORIAL has Esmeralda *je-*, first-person singular independent pronoun, *e-*, first-person singular possessive; Kandoshi *i-*, first-person singular possessive, *ija, ij*, first-person plural independent pronouns; Oyampi, in the Tupian group, *je*, first-person singular independent pronoun, *e-*, first-person singular possessive; Yuracare *i-*, first-person singular subject of statives and reflexives (e.g. *suñe-i* 'I am a man'); and Ayoré, of the Zamuco group, *i-*, first-person singular possessive.

The MACRO-TUCANOAN stock has Capixana *ja-*, Catuquina *i-*, and Tiquie (Puinave) *ja-*, all first-person singular verb subjects. In the Tucano subgroup, we have Desana *-ji* and Wanana *jii*, first-person singular verb objects, and Bara *ji*, first-person singular possessive.

In ANDEAN, we find Araucanian *l-i*, first-person singular subjunctive, *j(-u)*, first-person dual possessive verb subject (*u* is dual), *i(-ñ)*, first-person plural verb subject (*ñ* is plural); Ona and Tehuelche, in the Patagon group, *ja,* first-person singular independent pronoun, *(j)i-kuwa,* first-person plural independent pronoun, *ji-,* first-person singular possessive, *i-,* verb subject (e.g. *i-m-joško* 'I thee hear'); Jaqaru (Aymara) *i(-ma),* first person acts on second person; Yamana proper *hi-,* first-person possessive, and in the same group, Yahgan *i-tapan* 'myself,' *i-matagu-aki* 'that which was given to me,' *i(-pai),* first-person dual independent pronoun (see TWO in the Amerind dictionary); and finally, Quechua *-j,* first-person singular possessive, *-j(-ku),* first-person plural exclusive present subjunctive (cf. *-n-ku,* 'they'; see *n-* as third person, item 15).

For CHIBCHAN-PAEZAN, Paezan has Colorado of the Barbacoa group with *i,* first-person singular pronoun. In Chibchan, we find Chibcha *i-,* first-person singular possessive and verb subject before initial alveolar stems; Cuitlatec *-i,* first-person singular possessive; and, in Misumalpan, Cacaopera *-i,* first-person singular verb subject, Miskito *-i,* first-person singular and first-person plural possessive.

CENTRAL AMERIND has Proto-Uto-Aztecan **i-ne-,* first-person singular possessive, **i-ta(-me),* first-person plural possessive; and Hopi (also Uto-Aztecan) *ʔi,* first-person singular possessive. In Oto-Mangue, we find Chinantec *-j,* first-person object in bipersonal forms.

HOKAN has Achomawi *i,* first-person singular possessive; Chumash *-i,* first-person verb object and possessive, and *i-* 'first-person singular acts on second or third singular'; Comecrudo *-i-,* first-person singular verb subject; Southeast Pomo *ʔi-,* first-person possessive before some non-descending-generation kin terms; Seri *ʔe,* first-person independent pronoun and *ʔi-,* first-person possessive (cf. *i-* third person non-glottalized). Tlappanec (Subtiaba) has many first-person singular possessive suffixes glottalized versus third person (cf. Seri). Other Hokan examples are Chontal (Tequistlatec) article + *i, j,* in first-person possessive (e.g. *la-i-igur* 'my house' [Highland Chontal]); Tonkawa *ʔ-,* first-person subject in past tense declarative (cf. glottalization in Seri, Tlappanec, Yuman); Washo *(m-)i-* 'first person acts on second person'; Yana *(ǰ-)i-,* first-person singular possessive (Sapir's analysis), *mau-s-i* 'I am about to . . .'; and Yuman *ʔ-, ʔi-,* first-person possessive with some ascending-generation kin terms.

PENUTIAN has Atakapa *hi-, i-,* first-person singular verb objects, Tunica *ʔi-,* first-person singular verb object and possessive, Yuki *i:,* first-person singular object independent pronoun, and Wappo *i:,* first-person singular verb object. This pronoun is apparently found only in the Yuki-Gulf subgroup of Penutian.

275

3. In addition to *n* and *i*, whose Amerind status is obvious, there are other first-person forms to be considered. These are all more recent innovations that serve to mark off certain subgroupings. Some have basically plural functions, thereby confining *n* in particular to singular uses. Here we consider three occurrences of first-person *m;* each may be regarded as an independent innovation for reasons set forth below.

The first occurrence is in Auake, Kaliana, and Maku, which form a subgroup of MACRO-TUCANOAN. One piece of evidence for the subgroup's validity is the agreement of Kaliana and Auake in both first- and second-person singular pronouns (on the latter, see item 10, below), unlike the rest of Macro-Tucanoan. The first-person pronouns are Kaliana *mē(-be)* and Auake *mai(-kiete)*.

Second, there are several examples of first-person *m* forms in widely separated CHIBCHAN-PAEZAN languages. In the Paezan group, we find Itonama -*mo*, first-person singular and plural verb object; Chimu *moiñ* 'I,' *mæ(-ič)* 'we,' and *maiño* 'my'; Warrau *ma-*, *me-*, *m-*, first-person singular possessives; and Catio (in the Chocoan subgroup) *mya, myra,* first-person singular pronouns. This form is mainly Paezan; the only Chibchan example is Cuitlatec *mɨmɨ* 'I' and -*mɨ,* first-person singular possessive and verb subject.

The third occurrence of first-person *m* is in PENUTIAN, where it is mainly plural. In California Penutian, we find in Yokuts, which has only freestanding pronouns, *mak$^{?}$*, first-person dual inclusive, and *mai*, first-person plural inclusive subject pronouns, and *makwa* and *maiwa* as corresponding object pronouns. In Costanoan, Kroeber cites Rumsien *mak,* first-person plural subject pronoun, and Arroyo de la Cuesta gives Mutsun [mac-se], first-person plural. Miwok also has *m* first-person plural forms (e.g. Coastal Miwok *ma:* 'we') as well as -*m, me*, first-person plural subject of verbs in all the dialects. In addition, *m* is the singular first-person subject in certain verb forms, specifically Kroeber's "second subjunctive." Farther north there is Takelma (Oregon) with -*am* as a first-person plural object marker in the verb (in alienable possessives -*da-m*, in which -*da* is a marker that appears in other possessives), and as the subject in certain tenses combined with other analyzable elements. All of these are plural. Tsimshian has -*m* as the first-person plural subject of intransitive verbs. For Yuki, Kroeber gives *mi:*, first-person plural inclusive. As can be seen from the examples, the meaning is predominantly plural. In languages like Yokuts and Yuki, with an inclusive-exclusive distinction, the *m* form is inclusive, and this may have been its original function. All of the languages cited also have *m* in the second person.

4. In MACRO-PANOAN, the Moseten first-person plural independent pronoun is [izuñ], and Lule has [cen] as the first-person plural imperative subject and as a possessive. This adds to the evidence for a Macro-Panoan family in which Moseten is a link between the Lule-Vilela group on the one hand and the Pano-Tacana group on the other.

5. As noted, the MACRO-TUCANOAN language most closely related to Ticuna is the extinct Yuri. One piece of evidence of this relationship is the close resemblance between their first-person plural independent pronouns, Ticuna *to* and Yuri *too.*

6. The predominant second-person pronoun in Amerind, as discussed in Chapter 2, is *m-;* it appears in every stock. Alongside *m,* numerous second-person pronominal forms in *p* and *b* were cited in Chapter 2, particularly in EQUATORIAL and CHIBCHAN-PAEZAN. Whether these forms are all related I am not certain, but given the frequent alternations in Amerind languages between nasals and non-nasals, it is probable that most of the non-nasal forms belong here. Consider, for example, that both *bV* and *mV* are cited for Bribri in the Talamanca subgroup of Chibchan.

7. A second-person singular prefixed *a-* was also discussed in Chapter 2. Besides sporadic occurrences elsewhere, it is characteristic of the MACRO-GE, MACRO-PANOAN, and MACRO-CARIB languages (here Carib only) as a second-person singular possessive and verb subject. Its occurrence in the same pattern along with two other innovations, namely, the use of first-person *i* in these functions (elsewhere, as we have seen, usually object) and the suppletive alternation of *i-* and *t-* in the third person (see items 12 and 13), as well as the palatalizing effect in the third person, constitutes strong evidence for the existence of Ge-Pano-Carib as a higher-level unit within Amerind.

8. In ANDEAN, we may note the agreement between Quechua *kam,* second-person singular independent pronoun, and Gennaken *kemu,* Aymara *huma,* and Kahuapana *kem, huma, køma.* In Sec, a sparsely documented Northern Andean language, we have in Spruce's material [ubran cuma] 'how are you?' (cited in Buchwald 1918), which may contain the second-person singular pronoun under discussion.

9. The second-person pronoun *i* is found in a number of EQUA-TORIAL languages. In the Timote group, Cuica has [ih] as the second-person singular independent pronoun. In Saliba (Piaroan), in the second-

277

person singular imperative, verbs with initial subject markers replace the final vowel with -i. In Yaruro, the second-person singular independent pronoun is i (Crévaux 1882: 261). In Murato of the Kandoshi group, the second-person plural possessive in a fragmentary paradigm is a prefixed i- and suffixed -ni; because no other plural possessives are given, it seems plausible that -ni is here a plural marker. Otomaco has i as the second-person singular independent pronoun. The San José dialect of Guamo, a member of the Arawakan group, has aska-i as its second-person singular independent pronoun. (That this is the correct analysis is shown by comparison with the first-person singular form, aska-te.) Finally, i- is common as a second-person plural marker of the verb subject or of the noun possessive in the Maipuran group.

10. As we saw under item 3, Kaliana and Auake belong to a group of particularly closely related languages within MACRO-TUCANOAN. Parallel to the first-person singular forms cited there are second-person singular pronouns, e.g. Kaliana ka(-be) and Auake kai(-kiete). Irvine Davis (1966) reconstructs Proto-Ge *ka as the second-person singular pronoun. With this we may compare Erikbatsa ikia, Bororo aki, and Coroado ga elsewhere in MACRO-GE. At the extremes of the CHIBCHAN-PAEZAN distribution are Allentiac and Millcayac ka as second-person singular independent pronouns in the south, and in the north, Xinca with ka-, second-person singular possessive (the plural is the same with suffixed -aj), and (na-)ka, independent pronoun (cf. ne-n 'I'); and Tarascan -ke(-ni) 'first-person singular acts on second-person singular.'

11. One important indication of the validity of ALMOSAN-KERE-SIOUAN is the widespread occurrence of s as a second-person marker. Starting with Almosan, we note in Algic, Yurok -s as the second-person singular imperative and Wiyot -s- as the second-person singular verb object. In Algonquian, there is a whole series of bipersonal forms. As reconstructed by Bloomfield (1925), Proto-Central-Algonquian contained *θ, conjectured to be a voiceless interdental lateral. One of the correspondences Haas (1958b) found in her Algic comparisons is Wiyot s and Yurok s. The Central Algonquian forms are *-θe(-ne) 'first-person singular acts on second-person singular' (also found with the same meaning in Arapaho -eθeni). A series of verbal conjunctive forms contain *-eθ- and are characterized by Bloomfield as having at least one addressee as object. Examples are *-eθ-k 'third-person singular acts on second-person singular,' *eθ-aan 'first-person plural acts on second-person singular,' and a whole series of similar forms.

In other branches of Almosan, we find Kutenai -*is* as the second-person singular object and *(ne:)-s* as the second-person singular possessive. In the Wakashan family, there is Kwakiutl *so:* as the second-person singular independent pronoun, -*əs* as the second-person singular verb subject, and -*səq* 'second-person singular acts on third-person singular.' It is also quite likely that -*ns* 'first-person singular inclusive subject' is to be analyzed as -*n* 'first person' + *s* 'second person.' There is also Nootka *so:wa*, second-person singular independent pronoun (cf. *ne:wa* 'we'), and *qo:s,* second-person plural subject of the conditional (cf. *qo:n,* the corresponding first-person plural subject). A third Wakashan language, Bella Bella, has -*us*, second-person singular possessive, and -*(a)so, -(a)s*, second-person singular or plural verb subject. In Salishan, I have found only *is*- 'thy' in the genetically rather isolated Tillamook.

In the Keresiouan branch of Almosan-Keresiouan, *s* is widely represented. In the Keresan language Santa Ana, the singular independent pronoun is *(hi-)ṣu* (cf. *(hi-)nu* 'I'). Caddoan, Wichita, Pawnee, and other related languages have -*s*- as the second-person singular subject; in northern Caddoan languages, -*s* is the second-person singular object. In Northern Iroquoian languages, -*s*- is generally the second-person singular subject. This resemblance between Iroquoian and Caddoan was pointed out by Chafe (1973). In Siouan, *s* is the second-person singular subject in an important class of irregular verbs. An example is Chiwere *le* 'to go,' *haǰe* 'I go,' *s-le* 'thou goest,' *hī-le* 'he, she, it goes.' Finally, in Yuchi, *so*- is the second-person singular possessive and indirect object. Thus the second-person *s* occurs in every branch of Keresiouan.

We now come to the third-person elements. It is well known that these elements normally derive from demonstratives, usually distance demonstratives. Moreover, once this happens they may continue to be used as demonstratives, thus having a double function. For this reason, demonstratives are treated along with third-person markers, in presumed chronological order.

12. Probably the oldest item of this group is *i*-. The reason for this assumption is that it is almost always bound and pronominal in function rather than being either a pure demonstrative or a demonstrative with pronominal functions. Since the alternation of *i*- with *t*- as a characteristic of MACRO-GE, MACRO-PANOAN, and CARIB was discussed in Chapter 2, the data regarding *i* in these languages need not be repeated. To what was said there

it should be added for Macro-Ge that *i*- also occurs in Caraja as a third-person singular possessive.

In EQUATORIAL, *i*- occurs in Tupian, e.g. in Guaraní as the third-person singular possessive and as the subject of stative verbs, in Arikem as the verb subject and object and as the independent pronoun *i(-an)* (cf. *a-an* 'thou'), and in Wirafed and Oyampi as the possessive. In Cayuvava, it is one of the variants of the third-person singular possessive as a prefix occurring in combination with a number of suffixes. The *i*- singular masculine of Arawakan, to be discussed later, may be this same element in a specialized function. If so, then the *i*- of Macro-Tucanoan belongs here also.

For Kandoshi, I have noted in Tuggy (1966) such examples as *čoma* 'bathe' (intransitive), *i-čoma* 'bathe another.' In Jibaro, clearly related to Kandoshi, a parallel example is *meitiatsan* 'bathe' (intransitive), *i-meitatsian* 'bathe someone.' In the Maipuran languages Moxo and Baure, *i* similarly occurs as a transitivizer. (This development in third-person pronouns is discussed in more detail with regard to Chibchan.)

Third-person *i* is particularly common in CHIBCHAN-PAEZAN. In the Paezan group, it occurs in petrified form as the third-person object in Paez itself and in Warrau. In these, and similar cases in the Chibchan group to be cited below, the *i*- has first become an indefinite object, e.g. Cuna *i-makka* 'make something,' when the object is not mentioned. Later, it comes to be used even when the object is identified. In Cuna, it is still productive in the sense that we get contrasts like *kaa* 'to shine' (in general), *i-kaa* 'to light up a place.' A further instance in Paezan is Itonama *i*-, described as an unspecified object. In Atacama, *ia* is the third-person independent pronoun; the third-person meaning of *i*- is even clearer in the possessive pronoun *i-saja* 'his, her,' compared with *ah-saja* 'my.' In the Colorado group, we find Cayapa *ja* as the third-person independent pronoun, with the plural *ja(-la)*.

In Chibchan, besides the aforementioned example of Cuna, Guamaca, in the Aruak subgroup, has *i*- third-person singular possessive. In the Guaymi subgroup, Guaymi, Move, Murire, Muoi, etc., all have *ja* as the third-person singular independent pronoun. In the Talamanca languages, Lehmann's (1920: 285) description of the Bribri usage of *i* shows it to be exactly the same: "When no object is mentioned the verb has *i-;* this is also found in Rama where also *i*- before the noun indicates a general form *i-ñut* 'his, her face' = face in general." (In these developments to indefiniteness on both the noun and the verb, we will find a complete typological parallel in the *m*- demonstrative, discussed under item 14.) With regard to the use of *i*- before a noun, we may compare Chibcha proper [y-ba] 'blood,' [y-ta] 'hand,' etc., in which the same *i-* appears as both indefinite and generalizing, as in Lehmann's Rama example. (With the former, compare Murire *bea*, Estrella [Talamanca] *pe* 'blood,' etc.) Also in the Talamanca group, we find Borunca *i* and *iæ*, third-person singular independent pronouns, and *j-*, the third-person singular possessive. The Rama language, in addition to the possessive and generalizing uses, has *i* and *ja:* as third-person singular independent pronouns and *ja* as the independent possessive pronoun. In Guatuso, *i* functions as the third-person singular independent pronoun and as prefixed possessive.

In Lenca, we find Guajiquero *i(-na)* 'he, she' (cf. *u(-na)* 'I' and *am(-na)* 'thou'), and once more in Chilanga, we find *i-* as a prefix used with an indefinite object, as well as *i(-no)*, third-person singular independent pronoun, and *i:-*, possessive and oblique third-person singular. Finally, in two other Chibchan groups, there are Cuitlatec *i-* as a definite article (a common development of third-person demonstratives) and Tarascan *i-* 'this, that, he.'

A presumably independent development of *i-* as transitivizer is found in Moseten of the MACRO-PANOAN group.

In CENTRAL AMERIND, there are scattered occurrences in all three branches. In Oto-Mangue, we find Chinantec *ʔi* as a third-person independent pronoun; in Tanoan, Santa Clara and Tewa have *ʔiʔ* 'he, she, it' and *ʔi-winuh* 'he stood up'; and in Uto-Aztecan, Mono *ʔi-hi* is an independent third-person singular nearby demonstrative.

Third-person *i-* has a far more restricted distribution than first-person *n* and *i* and second-person *m*. This is, of course, a commonly observed diachronic phenomenon (found, for example, in Indo-European). Third-person pronouns are, in general, less stable than first- and second-person pronouns, being constantly replaced by new demonstrative elements.

13. One of these demonstratives has already been mentioned, namely, the *t-* that in some Macro-Ge, Macro-Panoan, and Carib languages has become an alternant of *i-* (mainly as the third-person singular possessive and as the verb subject before stems beginning with a vowel). The *t* marker also occurs widely as a third-person pronominal element independently of *i*. Typologically parallel to the development of *i-* in Arawakan and Tucanoan as a masculine marker (item 39) are developments of *t-* in a number of MACRO-GE languages. The clearest instance is probably Chiquito, where, in addition to the *i-* prefix that marks the third person in general, there is a -*tii* suffix for the masculine singular, opposed—contrary to the usual rules of marking theory—to a zero feminine, e.g. *i-poo-s-tii* 'his house,' *i-poo-s* 'her house.' Here -*s* is an old definiteness marker that also appears as an ab-

solutive on the noun in isolation, e.g. *poo-s* 'house' (cf. *a-poo* 'thy house'). In Kaingan, this *t* contrasts with a feminine *s* that has undergone various phonological developments, e.g. Aweikoma *ti* 'he,' *si* 'she'; Caraja *ti* 'he,' *tiki* 'she.' Fulnio also has a feminine marker *sa* (see item 38). Elsewhere in Macro-Ge, *t* simply occurs as a general third-person pronoun, e.g. Cherente (Ge) *ta* 'he, she,' Coroado *ti* 'he, she, it,' and Fulnio *t-* as the subject of intransitive and the object of transitive verbs.

A parallel development of gender markers has occurred in MACRO-PANOAN, where we find Moseten with a *-t* suffix to mark masculine nouns and *-s* as a suffix for the feminine, as in Kaingan. A partly similar development has taken place in Mascoy, where the prefix *ja-t-* is found on masculine nouns and *ja-m-* on non-masculine. Elsewhere the *t* forms denote the general third person. Bound forms already mentioned in Chapter 2 are not repeated here. In Lule, *tita* is the third-person singular pronoun, with plural *teoto*, and *te* is a demonstrative, 'this.' In Vilela, *te-* is the third-person singular possessive, and *t-* is a relative pronoun. Charrua, Guana, and Chana all have *-t* for the third-person singular possessive. In Mataco, *ta, tah,* functions as a remote demonstrative and relative pronoun.

In addition to the forms from Carib proper mentioned in Chapter 2, MACRO-CARIB has Uitoto *da* and Muinane *daa* in the Uitoto group; Andoke *dja;* and Yameo *are, ara,* and *ranum* as demonstratives, with first-, second-, and third-person deixis, respectively. There is comparative evidence that *r* < **d*. The last form, *ranum,* functions also as the third-person singular pronoun.

In ANDEAN, Ona (Patagon) *ta* functions as the third-person independent pronoun for both singular and plural. In the form *-t-*, it appears as the third-person singular object, as in *i-t-josko* 'I-it-hear'; there is also *d-* 'his, her.' In the closely related Tehuelche, *t-* is the third-person singular and plural possessive. As in Ona, it is also employed as a third-person singular object. In Araucanian, *teje* 'that' is used as a third-person singular pronoun. In Jaqaru, the verb suffix *-ta-ma* indicates third person acting on second person.

All MACRO-TUCANOAN *t* forms seem to occur as unbound demonstratives. We may cite from Tucanoan, Tucano *too* 'there,' *toho* 'that'; Yupua *ti* 'this'; Nadobo (Puinave) *tøg* 'that'; Canamari (in the Catuquina group) *tu* 'there'; and Kaliana *atu* 'there.'

For HOKAN, *t-* absolutives in Subtiaba, Washo, and Salinan were cited in Chapter 2. Possibly the Achomawi verb infinitive formation with prefixed *d-* belongs here, e.g. from *a:m* 'eat,' *d-a:m-i* 'to eat.'

As for ALMOSAN-KERESIOUAN, in the Chapter 2 discussion of *t-* as a third-person marker and absolutive, the possibility was advanced that the "linking *-t-*" of the Algic languages, which occurs before vowel stems when person markers precede, originated in this function by a process similar to that in Carib and Mataco.

14. The other widespread Amerind demonstrative and third-person marker is *m*, which often takes the form *ma* or *mo*. In MACRO-GE, it occurs in the Ge subgroup, e.g. Kradaho *me*, Northern Cayapo *amu, ama*; in the Puri subgroup, e.g. Coroado *man*, Coropo *mam*; and in Bororo proper *ema*, all third-person singular independent pronouns. Chiquito has *manu* 'that.' In Guato, almost all nouns are cited with an initial *ma-*, which thus appears to be stage III article (often called absolutive in the literature of Amerind languages). That *ma-* is a formative is shown by the variant recordings for 'fire' *(ma-)ta* (Martius 1867) and *ko-ta* (Schmidt 1905; but also *(ma-)ta* in Schmidt 1942).

In MACRO-PANOAN, there are similar forms, e.g. Moseten *mo* 'that, he'; Lule *mima* 'he, she, it,' with the plural *meoto* (cf. the forms in item 13), and in Tacanan, Tacana *me(-sa)* as the third-person singular pronoun, Chama *ma* 'that.'

In MACRO-CARIB, Carib proper *mo* is the common basis of third-person singular pronouns, e.g. Arara *mo*, Barama *moko* 'he, she,' *moro* 'it,' Galibi *moe*. It is also sometimes the basis for distance demonstratives, e.g. Tamanaco *more* 'there,' Waiwai *moro* 'that one,' Pauishana *men* 'those.' Outside of Carib, we find Uitoto *imua* 'that,' *imaki* 'those.'

Except for the striking case of Guaraní (EQUATORIAL) *amo* 'that,' I have not found *m* forms in South America outside of Ge-Pano-Carib.

In CENTRAL AMERIND, the term we are considering may be the source of the Proto-Uto-Aztecan reflexive pronoun **mo*, reconstructed by Langacker (1976: 47), which shows a remarkable resemblance to the Taos forms in Kiowa-Tanoan. In both instances, some of the forms vary for person and number, but the basic member is *mo-*, as shown below.

Person (singular)	Proto-Uto-Aztecan	Taos	Person (plural)	Proto-Uto-Aztecan	Taos
First	*ne	tā-	First	*ta-	kimā/kimo
Second	*e	ā-	Second	*mo-	māmā/māmo
Third	*mo-	mo-	Third	*mo-	ʔimā/ʔimo

Moreover, Taos has dual forms that are identical to the non-reflexives. Note the agreement in the third-person singular, which is evidently the starting point of an analogic spread. Proto-Uto-Aztecan **ne-* and **ta-* are easily identifiable with the non-reflexive first-person singular and plural, respectively. Similarly, the Taos first-person singular, *tā*, is identical with the indirect object form and similar to the subject pronoun, *ti*, when the object belongs to either the first or the third of the three genders of the Taos noun, and *ā* is identical to the second-person singular subject of intransitive verbs. In addition, Taos has adopted *-mo-* for all persons and numbers for reflexive possession, e.g. in the first gender *ʔān-* 'my,' but *ʔān-mo-* 'my own' (reflexive). The spread of a third-person reflexive to other persons has a typological parallel in Slavic and elsewhere.

The *m* as demonstrative and third-person pronoun is likewise found in PENUTIAN. In California Penutian, it occurs in Nisenan (Maidu) *mi*, third-person singular pronoun, and *mo:* 'that one' and *mɨ* 'this, that' in Shipley's description. In Bodega (Miwok), there is *maa* 'that.' In Mexican Penutian, Totonac has *ama* as the distance demonstrative, and in Yuki-Gulf, we find Atakapa *ma*, a distance demonstrative, and Chitimacha *ma* 'there.'

Turning now to ALMOSAN-KERESIOUAN, recall the brief discussion in Chapter 2 of the coincidence of the Algic impersonal possessor *m-* (particularly common in terms for body parts and often surviving in petrified form lexically incorporated in the noun) with a similar prefixed *m-* for body-part terms in Salish. We can see that typologically this is parallel to what has happened to the third-person *i-* in Chibchan. As we noted, Lehmann points to two developments in Rama. One concerns nouns in which the form with a formerly definite possessor becomes first an indefinite possessor and then general in meaning so that it becomes incorporated in the noun, as in Chibchan proper. The second development concerns the verb, in which the indefinite object comes to be used whenever the transitive verb does not have a specified object. If this usage spreads to the contexts in which an overt object is specified, it becomes a general mark of transitivity.

This second development also occurs in Salish with regard to *-m*, as is clear from Boas's (1929) Thompson River Salish forms *χwei-m* 'he is looking' when no object is specified, as against *χwei* when an object is named. We may probably compare with this the Kwakiutl (Wakashan) suffix *-əm*, which forms the passive of verbs that take the instrumental. The meaning is evidently 'someone is struck by him.' The same element probably occurs in the form *-am-* as reconstructed by Bloomfield for Proto-Central-Algonquian. Transitive verbs with inanimate objects have this ending in the third person, followed by *-w* and the usual third-person endings, as illustrated by Bloomfield's item 134: *waapant-am-wa* 'he looks at it' (1946: 99).

15. We now come to a number of other third-person and/or demonstrative markers of more restricted distribution. One of these is *n*, which is widespread in ANDEAN. Starting in the extreme south, there is Yahgan -*n*, which is suffixed to possessed nouns in the genitive construction. This may reasonably be conjectured to be a fossilized third-person form of the 'man his-house' type of construction common in languages in which the nominal possessor precedes the noun possessed. In fact, in Ona (Patagon) *n*- is the third-person singular possessive and *on* is the independent third-person singular pronoun. In Quechua, we have -*n* as the third-person singular possessive. In Zaparoan, there are Zaparo *no*, *noi*, third-person singular independent pronouns, Arabela *na*-, third-person singular possessive, and Andoa *noa* and Iquito *nuu*, both third-person singular independent pronouns. In Jebero, we find -*no*, -*nan*, as third-person singular possessives and the demonstrative *nana* 'that.' In Kahuapana, *nana* is the third-person singular independent pronoun. In the Northern Andean group, Leco has *on* as a third-person singular independent pronoun, a form similar to that of Ona, and in Cholana, the only language of the group for which there is any detailed description, there is, interestingly, a system of initial consonant mutation in which the nasal alternant indicates a third-person singular possessor. An example is the stem -*kot* 'water,' with the three singular possessed forms *a-kot* 'my water,' *mi-kot* 'thy water,' and *ŋot* 'his, her water.'

An *n* demonstrative is also fairly widely distributed in EQUATORIAL. Within Arawakan, there are occurrences in Maipuran (e.g. Amuesha *ña* 'he,' Paraujano *nia*, third-person singular independent pronoun, and *n*- possessive, and Chiriana *ne*, third-person singular independent pronoun); in Uro (e.g. Chipaya *ni*, third-person singular independent pronoun); and in Chapacura (e.g Itene *na*-, singular verb subject, and -*n*, singular verb object). Note also Cayuvava *ñe* 'there'; in the Jibaro group, Huambisa *nu* 'that' and Aguaruna *nu*, *nii*, third-person singular independent pronouns; Yuracare *na*, third-person singular independent pronoun and distance demonstrative; and Cuica (Timote) *na*, third-person singular independent pronoun.

16. A demonstrative *p* is fairly widespread, occurring in MACRO-PANOAN, ANDEAN, and HOKAN. In the first of these, we may note Mataco *pa* 'that,' which probably also occurs in the remote-past-tense marker *pa-nete*-. In the closely related Chulupi, *pa*- has become an article. There are also Vilela -*p*, third-person singular possessive, and Tacana *pa*-, third-person object. For ANDEAN, we have Quechua *paj*, third-person sin-

gular independent pronoun; Aymara -pa, third-person singular possessive; Araucanian -pe, third-person singular verb subject; and Cholona pe 'that.'

HOKAN examples are Karok paj 'that' and pa- used as an article; Chimariko pa(-mut) 'that' (cf. ma-mut 'thou'); East Pomo ba 'that'; San Luis Obispo (Chumash) pa-k 'that' (cf. si-k 'this'); San Antonio (Salinan) pa 'that,' pe- 'that, the'; Diegueño (Yuman) puu, third-person singular independent pronoun; and Coahuilteco pa, simply described as a demonstrative, po:, a singular animate demonstrative, and pi, a demonstrative referring to something immediately preceding. The very common sound symbolism i/a 'near/far,' together with the use of pa to indicate the past tense (cf. Mataco pa-nete above), suggests that pa is a distance demonstrative.

17. A third-person pronoun and distance demonstrative a is common in CHIBCHAN-PAEZAN. In the Paezan branch Warrau a- is the third-person singular possessive, as well as a distance demonstrative. There is also a in Paez itself. The dictionary gives this as the third-person singular of the verb 'to be,' but the sentences in which it occurs suggest rather a demonstrative that can be used as a copula. In Chibcha, a- is the third-person singular possessive and verb subject, and [a-sy] is the third-person singular independent pronoun and distance demonstrative. In Duit, which is closely related to Chibcha, a- is 'he, his' in the only existing document (it is probably the feminine form also). In Motilon, a- is the third-person singular subject. In Aruak, we find Kagaba a-, third-person singular possessive pronoun; and Cuna a- 'that,' a(-ti), third-person and demonstrative pronoun 'that,' and a-, third-person singular possessive (plural a-mal). In Misumalpan, there are Cacaopera -a, third-person singular verb subject (plural -a-wali), and Miskito -a, third-person verb subject. Paya a- is the third-person possessive (cf. ari 'this' and ata 'that'). In the Chilanga dialect of Lenca, a:- is the third-person plural possessive, a:-nani-, the third-person plural verb subject. Finally, in Xinca, a- is the third-person subject of intransitive verbs and of the imperative.

18. In the Almosan branch of ALMOSAN-KERESIOUAN, we find a widespread third-person marker -s, usually without distinction of number or with an additional marker to indicate plurality. It is general in Salish. Examples, from Shuswap, are -as, third-person singular possessive (plural -as-wit), and -s, subject of singular transitive verbs (with the same plural marker, -wit). In Wakashan, Bella Bella has -s as the third-person possessive. In Quileute, a Chemakuan language, what is probably historically the same element has become specialized, with -s representing a non-

feminine third-person singular verb subject, and also serving as an oblique indefinite third-person article. The *-s* in the oblique feminine plural article *-as* is probably the same element. In Kutenai, *-es* is the general third-person possessive. The only Algic occurrence seems to be in Yurok, where *-s* can be suffixed to a variety of words in a sentence as an enclitic denoting a third-person subject. We also find *-s-* in the verb complex, indicating the third-person object of a transitive verb.

19. As noted in Chapter 2, there appears to have been in Amerind, as evidenced by the striking agreement of Carib and Algonquian, a prefix *k-* that was perhaps originally a first-person dual inclusive (as it still is in some Carib languages). In both Algonquian and Carib, it is also used in bipersonal verbs to indicate the first person acting on the second, or vice versa. Its fundamental meaning, therefore, appears to have been in speaking of the first person in association with second person. This usage of what is called the "inclusive person" appears in a number of areas around the world. With a pluralizer, it becomes the first-person plural inclusive, often contrasting with an exclusive form built on the first-person singular. From here its diachronic development is often to the first-person plural inclusive as such, evolving in some instances to the first-person plural, and in the case of Amerind, in which plurality in the pronoun is often not marked in certain categories or absent altogether, it becomes a general first-person pronoun. Hortatives are necessarily first-person inclusives, and such usages occasionally arise. A development to second person is much rarer than to first person. Nevertheless, it occurs in Algic. Algonquian has retained a clear indication of the *k-*'s origin as first-person dual inclusive. Although there are separate additional markers for other uses, first person in association with the second is the common element in all occurrences of *k-* (see Hockett 1966 for a similar analysis of Algonquian *k-*). These developments are illustrated in what follows.

In ANDEAN, starting from the south, Gennaken has *-ki* as the first-person singular possessive, and both *kia* and *kua* are recorded as first-person singular independent pronouns. In the Quechuan dialect of Callejon de Huaylas, we find *kiki* 'I myself.' Perhaps also the widely occurring first-person plural exclusive pronoun (*naqa-)yku* (cf. *nuqa* 'I'; these forms are Bolivian Quechua) belongs here. In Zaparoan, there are Zaparo *kui* 'I,' *-ku,* *-ko* 'my,' *ka(-na)* 'we' (exclusive); Arabela *ki-* 'my,' *ka-na* 'our' (exclusive); Iquito *kii* 'I,' *ki-*, first-person singular verb subject; and Andoa *kua* 'I.' (The plural exclusive forms with *-na* involve a plural pronominal element discussed in item 30.) Forms similar to Zaparoan are found in Itucale: *kanø* 'I,' *kax-* 'my,' *kanakanø* 'we,' *kanax-* 'our.' In Kahuapana, we find *kua* 'I,' *-uk* 'my'; in Jebero (a member of the same group), *koa, kwa* 'I' and *-ok* 'my'; and in Mayna, hortatory *-ke* 'let us.' Cholona has *ok* 'I,' *ki-* 'our,' and Leco has *kui* for the first-person plural verb subject pronoun.

In MACRO-CARIB, in addition to the *k-* forms of Carib proper denoting the first-person dual inclusive, the first-person plural inclusive as possessive or the verb subject, and the first-person acting on the second (or vice versa in bipersonal verbs), we find Uitoto *koko,* first-person dual pronoun, and *kaj,* first-person plural pronoun.

In CENTRAL AMERIND, *k-* forms occur in both Oto-Mangue and Kiowa-Tanoan. For Oto-Mangue, Rensch cites, under no. 123, South Pame (Otomian) *kakh,* Mazahua *gɔ, kɔ,* and numerous other Otomian first-person plural inclusive pronouns, and Amuzgo first-person singular and first-person plural inclusive and exclusive forms as deriving from **hka.* In Kiowa-Tanoan, Taos has *ki-* as the first-person plural possessive and verb subject.

In HOKAN, *k* forms are common as first-person singular or plural pronouns. The Yurumangui *k-* prefix, followed by various vowels, is the first-person singular possessive and the verb subject. In Jicaque, *-kʰ* is the first-person plural verb subject. In Tonkawa, *ge-* is the first-person singular object. Maratino *ko* is probably the first-person plural inclusive pronoun. In Cochimi, a Yuman language, we find *ka-* 'my.' In Salinan, we have San Miguel *ka* 'we' and San Antonio *kak* 'we.' In Chumash, the first-person bound forms are *k-* for singular, *kis-* for dual, and *ki-* for plural. In Yana, *(ni-)gi* is 'we, us, our,' and *(wa-)gi* denotes the second-person singular acting on the first-person plural. Finally, we have Pomo *ke-* 'my' and Karok *ki-n* 'we.'

First-person *k* is also frequent in PENUTIAN. In California Penutian, *ka* is common as a bound form for the first-person singular, both in Costanoan and in Miwok. Yokuts *makʔ,* first-person dual inclusive, is perhaps to be analyzed as *ma-* 'thou' + *-kʔ* 'I.' Farther north, in Plateau Penutian, Klamath *gew* is an unbound form for the first-person singular possessive. In the Yuki-Gulf group, Chitimacha has a variety of *-k* forms for the first person, including *-k,* first-person singular verb subject, and *-ki-,* first-person object. In Mexican Penutian, Papantla (Totonac) has a number of first-person forms of this sort, including the first-person singular and plural independent pronouns *kit* and *kin,* respectively. In Mayan, *ka-* 'our' is found in Kekchí, Uspantec, and elsewhere, and *ka-* is 'my' in Chontal.

For ALMOSAN-KERESIOUAN, the Algic second-person singular

forms, and specifically, the Algonquian second-person singular and inclusive forms, have already been mentioned. Wiyot also has a first-person sub-junctive -*ak,* and Yurok has a first-person subject -*k²,* which may reflect the more usual developments of inclusive *k-.* In Keresiouan, Iroquois has *k-,* first person, and a similar *k-* is found in all the Caddoan languages, an agreement that Chafe (1979: 229) found striking. Wyandot *kw-,* a general first-person plural inclusive marker, and even more remarkably *kj-* in one of the conjugations for the first-person dual inclusive (= *ki*) seem to support the argument for first-person dual inclusive as the form's original meaning.

20. One inclusive pronoun appears to be restricted to KERESIOUAN. Chafe (1964, no. 35) equates Iroquoian *(k-)ō,* first-person singular acts on second person, with Proto-Siouan **ū,* first-person dual inclusive pronoun. To this we can add Yuchi *ō,* first-person plural inclusive verb subject.

21. Another inclusive pronoun of restricted distribution occurs in PENUTIAN. In Yuki-Gulf, it is found in Yuki *u:s,* first-person plural in-clusive independent pronoun, Huchnom *us,* first-person plural independent pronoun, Wappo *²isi,* first-person plural, Chitimacha *²uš,* first-person plu-ral, and Atakapa -*iš,* first-person plural object. So far as I can tell, it does not occur in California Penutian, but farther north we have Klamath (Pla-teau) *²is* for second person acting on first-person singular, and in Oregon Penutian, Coos -*ais* for second person acting on first person and Alsea *s-,* first-person object of imperatives.

A possibly related set of forms is found in CHIBCHAN-PAEZAN. In Paezan are found Itonama *se²,* first-person plural exclusive subject, and Col-orado -*s,* Cayapa -*sai,* -*šai,* all first-person plural hortatory. In Chibchan, Rama has *sa-, su-, s-,* first-person plural subject, and in Guatuso, we find a first-person plural -*s.* Since an alternative first-person plural consists of the first-person singular plus a plural marker (a common way of forming ex-clusive plurals) -*s* is quite possibly inclusive. I am inclined to think that the Penutian and Chibchan developments are independent.

22. Several distance demonstratives, of which *m* and *t* are the most widely distributed, have been seen in many languages, particularly in their functions as third-person pronouns. One may well ask, then, whether a can-didate for near demonstratives can be found in Proto-Amerind. The most likely is *k.* It should be borne in mind that near demonstratives frequently become far demonstratives over time. Thus, in MACRO-GE, we find Caraja *kua* 'this' and Kamakan *kue* 'that.' In Ge proper, Cherente *kua, kū,* and Kraho *ke* are third-person singular independent pronouns. In EQUA-

TORIAL, one may cite Tupian Guarayo *koo* 'this' and Guaraní *ko* 'this'; in Uro, we have Puquina *ko* 'this, that,' and in the Timote group, we find Mocochi *kiu* 'that.' For MACRO-TUCANOAN, it was noted that Auake, Kaliana, and Maku form a distinct subgroup. One of the points of agreement is Auake *ki?a* and Maku *ki* 'this.' Finally, we have these HOKAN examples: Chontal *(hi-)kija* 'this,' *(hi-)ka?a* 'that'; Jicaque *kone* 'this,' *ki?a* 'here'; Subtiaba *kagi* 'this'; Cochimi (Yuman) *khu* 'this'; Santa Ynez (Chumash) *kai, ka:*, and San Buenaventura (also Chumash) *kaki*, both meaning 'this.' Farther north, we find Atsugewi *k'e* 'here,' Achomawi and Atsugewi *-k-* 'hither,' and Karok *?o:k* 'here.'

23. Another demonstrative, found only in South America, shows predominantly near-deixis, but may originally have been a place expression meaning 'here.' In the Ge subgroup of MACRO-GE, we find Cayapo *niai* 'this' and Suya *ni* 'this,' and in Bororo, *nĩ* 'hither,' *noni* 'there (near you).' In the Panoan branch of MACRO-PANOAN, we have Arazaire *nina* 'here,' Marinahua *nino* 'here,' and Chacobo *nia* 'here,' *naa* 'this.' Guaicuru and Mataco both have *na* 'here.' In MACRO-CARIB, the Carib group has Hishcariana *en, eni* 'this,' Waiwai *oni* 'this,' Galibi *ini* 'this,' Wayana *ine* 'he, she,' and Carib *ani* 'here.' For CHIBCHAN-PAEZAN, we have these Paezan examples: Paez *ana* 'this,' Colorado (Barbacoa) *ne* 'he, she,' and Choco *nan* 'that.'

24. There is an *h-* demonstrative that seems to be confined to MACRO-PANOAN. A Panoan example is Chacobo *ha* 'that, he, she.' Vilela has *he* 'this,' Moseten *hoi* 'this,' Lengua *hoi, aha* 'there,' and Guenoa (Charruan) *h-*, third-person possessive. In Tacanan, we find Tacana *hi* 'that,' and Chama *hikiohi* 'here' (near speaker), *hikiak^wa* 'there (near you),' and *hok^wama-* 'there (distant).'

We now consider reflexives and reciprocals.

25. A reflexive *t* occurs as part of the Ge-Pano-Carib pronominal pattern in the Bororo group of MACRO-GE, where *tu-*, third-person reflexive possessive, contrasts with *u-*, non-reflexive, whereas in Carib proper, *t-* is general as a reflexive. With these we can compare in MACRO-PANOAN Tacana *-ti*, a reflexive marker on the verb. There are some instances of reflexive *t* or *d* in EQUATORIAL. One is Kariri *di-, d-* (before consonants and vowels, respectively), expressing a reflexive possessive. Yuracare has a reflexive suffix *-ta, -to* on verbs, and in Tupian, Arikem *ta-* is the third-person reflexive object. It is quite possible that these reflexive uses of *t-* may

be specializations of the common third person and distance demonstrative *t-* (item 13).

26. Reciprocals are often connected with sociatives and coordinators meaning 'with, and.' On this basis we can connect the following as the same etymon occurring in all three branches of CENTRAL AMERIND. For Oto-Mangue, Rensch (no. 348) reconstructs *(ʔ)ne(h)* glossed as 'with, and.' With this we can compare Uto-Aztecan **na*, reciprocal, posited by Langacker (1976: 47), and Kiowa *nɔ* 'and, and then, that' (conjunction).

27. There is a widespread reciprocal *p* in PENUTIAN. In California Penutian, we find Miwok *-pure*, Costanoan *-pu*, and Wintun *-pura*, all reciprocals suffixed to verbs. In Yuki-Gulf, Wappo has *pa-, po-*, reciprocals prefixed to verbs, and Yuki has *-p* as a reflexive added to pronouns, e.g. *ki-p* 'himself.' In Mexican Penutian, there is Yucatec (Mayan) *-ba;* in Plateau Penutian, Nez Perce *-p;* and in Oregon Penutian, Takelma *p-*, all expressing the reflexive.

Since many pronominal interrogatives are connected with sentence interrogation and verb categories, they are better left to the discussion of those elements. At this point, we will confine ourselves to those categories, such as number and gender, that are common to pronouns and nouns. The question of number, however, is problematical. It is probable that in Proto-Amerind both pronouns and nouns were indifferent to number, since on the whole we find markers of very restricted distribution. What does seem quite certain is that Proto-Amerind did not have a dual (except of course the inclusive pronoun discussed under item 19). Some language groups, however, developed a dual. Andean, for example, has a dual based on the Amerind word for 'two.' (See that entry in the Amerind dictionary.)

28. In MACRO-CARIB, Uitoto proper has developed a pronominal dual *-ko*, found both in the independent pronouns and suffixed to verbs as a pronominal subject. To this corresponds *-xo* in Ocaina, another language of the Uitoto group. With these we may compare the words for 'two' in a number of Carib languages, e.g. Surinam *oko*, Galibi *oko*, Maiongom *ako*. More widespread are such Carib forms for 'two' as Hishcariana *asa-ko*, Arara *ta-g*, and Nahugua *ata-ke*, which may contain the same morpheme in suffixed form.

29. A HOKAN *s* dual is discussed in Sapir and Swadesh's Yana dictionary (1960) under *ux-si* 'two.' Note that cognates of *ux* 'two' are found elsewhere in Hokan, but *-si* is redundant in Yana and occurs there only in

this word. In Chumash independent pronouns, a dual -*š*- appears from the comparison *ki-š-ku* 'we two' and *pi-š-ku* 'you two,' with the corresponding plurals *ki-ku* and *pi-ku*. Beeler (1976: 256) notes that *iš-* also occurs in Santa Barbara, another Chumash language, in *iš-kom* 'two.' In Washo, -*ši* appears as a dual in both pronouns and nouns. The Esselen plural of the independent pronouns in -*š* or -*č* may have originated from the dual, as suggested by comparing its *leš* 'we' with Washo's *leš* 'we' (dual exclusive). We may extend the comparison to Karok *iθ-*, a dual subject of verbs. In Chontal, the numbers two through five take the suffix -*ši* when used with animates. A typological parallel in Indo-European is the spread of the original Slavic dual ending for masculine animates from two to three, four, and five when used with numerals in Russian and other Slavic languages.

Several PENUTIAN languages have duals that may belong here. Maidu has a suffix -*sa* in the dual of pronouns. In Oregon Penutian, Coos prefixes *kwi-s-* 'let us two' to verbs, which can be compared to the plural cohortative *kwi-n-*. Finally, in Yuki-Gulf, Wappo has a first-person dual pronoun *i:-si:*, in which the initial part may be the widespread first-person *i* and *si:* would then be a dual.

30. Plurality is very common in Amerind pronouns and nouns, and for that matter verbs (singular versus plural action). Grammaticization of the word for 'people' in MACRO-CARIB as a plural is exemplified in the Macro-Carib etymology PEOPLE in Chapter 3. Most other plurals are similarly confined to single subgroups and are probably relatively recent innovations.

The use of *n-* for plurals is one of the few instances of a form found in more than one subgroup. It is particularly frequent as a pronominal plural, especially in the third person, from which it may have spread analogically. It is basically South American.

In EQUATORIAL, Arawakan languages commonly have -*na* or -*n* as the third-person plural possessive and as the verb subject. In Kandoshi, -*ana* is the third-person plural noun object. In the Jibaro group, Aguaruna has -*na*, -*ina* to indicate a plural subject of a verb. Saliba (Piaroa) uses *ña* (possibly < *na*) as a plural marker in demonstratives, e.g. *hi-ña-te* 'those,' in which *hi* is the demonstrative, -*te* is a plural used widely in the language, and *ña* is presumably an old plural marker to which the more recent and productive one has been added, a common process.

Analogous forms are found in MACRO-TUCANOAN. Among these are Tiquie (Puinave) *na:* 'they, their,' and *na* for the plural of demonstratives and nouns; Nadobo (also Puinave) *ana* 'the others'; and Canichana *-na* nominal plural. (All of these examples are human.) In Ticuna, we find *na-*, third-person plural possessive, and *nyʔū*, third-person plural independent pronoun.

For ANDEAN, we have already noted (item 19) the occurrence of a pronominal plural *-na* in Itucale and Zaparoan (e.g. Zaparo *ka-na* 'we'). In the Kahuapana group, as reported by Tessmann, Jebero *-na* is a third-person pluralizer: *-nøn* 'his, her,' *-nøn-na* 'their.' Elsewhere in Andean, there is no special relation to the third person. In Yamana, Yahgan, and Araucanian, *-n* occurs as the plural of independent pronouns in all three persons (e.g. Yamana *sa* 'thou,' *san* 'you').

What is apparently the same element also appears in the Chibchan branch of CHIBCHAN-PAEZAN. In Aruak, we find Kagaba *nas* 'I,' *nas-an* 'we,' *ma* 'thou,' *ma-in* 'ye'; in Guaymi, Move *nu-n* 'we,' *mu-n* 'you'; in Talamanca, Terraba *ši-n* 'we' (inclusive), *fa* 'thou,' *fa-in* 'you,' *kue* 'he, she,' *kue-in* 'they'; and in Lenca, Membreno *ina* 'he, she,' *ana-nan* 'they,' *amna* 'thou,' *amna-n* 'you.'

31. The only other plural of wide distribution is *m*. It is found in MACRO-GE. Ge examples include Krenje *ʔaj-* 'thy,' *me-ʔaj* 'your,' *h-* 'his, her,' *me-h-* 'their' and Kraho *wa* 'I,' *wa-me* 'we.' Chiquito *-ma* is a pluralizer of the third-person masculine possessive and a verb subject. Bororo has nominal plurals *-do-gue* for non-humans and *-ma-gue* for humans (where *ma-* may be a personal plural to which *-gue* has been added as a recent formation).

In CENTRAL AMERIND, we find two occurrences in Oto-Mangue. One is Ixcatec *suwa* 'he, she, that,' *suwa-ma* 'they.' The other is in Chiapanec, where intransitive verbs have *-me* and a plural subject. For similar forms marking the object of transitive verbs, Lehmann (1920) conjectures that *-me* was originally animate and *-mo* inanimate. A third possible example occurs in the San José del Sitio dialect of Otomi, which has the suffixed possessive pronouns *-go* 'my' and *go-bē* 'our' (exclusive). The exclusive is normally the plural form of the first-person singular. In Uto-Aztecan, *-me* is the most common noun plural. Similar forms are found in Kiowa-Tanoan. In Taos, the names of animals are pluralized with the suffix *-nemā* (versus *na* for the singular). Harrington's dictionary of Kiowa (1928: 15) gives a number of examples of *-mɔ̃* as a plural.

Examples are also found in PENUTIAN. In Costanoan, *-ma* is a nominal animate plural, and in the dialect of San José, it combines in either order with the -*k* plural (cf. item 32), -*k-ma* or -*ma-k*, or it occurs independently as -*ma*. Farther north, in Plateau Penutian, -*ma* and -*me* are plurals in North Sahaptin and Nez Perce, and in Chinook -*ma* is a collective. In Yuki-Gulf, we find Yuki -*am*, collective, and -*jam*, -*am*, to indicate plurality in the verb. With this we compare Atakapa -*m*, which also indicates plurality in the verb, and Chitimacha -*ma*, which is both a verbal and an adjectival plural.

32. As in Costanoan, a -*k* plural occurs in Miwok. Here -*k* or -*ko* is a pluralizer on the second-person independent pronoun (singular *mi*, plural *mi-ko*) and an animate plural with demonstratives (e.g. Northern Sierra Miwok *nekko* 'these'). The -*k* is also common throughout Miwok as an independent and bound third-person plural, affixed both to nouns as a possessive and to verbs as a subject or an object. Elsewhere in PENUTIAN, we find in Yuki-Gulf, Chitimacha with -*ka* as a plural on substantives and verbs, and Atakapa with -*k* for both the plural subject of verbs, e.g. 'lie down' *nok* (plural), *ni:* (singular), and for the plurals of independent pronouns, e.g. *na-k* 'you,' *ša-k* 'they.' In Creek, a Muskogean language, a few nouns indicating persons and a limited group of adjectives have a plural in -*aki* or -*agi*.

With these Penutian forms, we can probably connect some ALMOSAN-KERESIOUAN forms, such as the common Central and Eastern Algonquian -*aki* for the animate plural and Caddoan Wichita -*ak*- to indicate the plural object of a verb. As can be seen, the -*k* plural is almost always personal and/or animate, a pattern that strengthens the case for their relationship.

33. A plural in -*l* or -*r* is found in MACRO-PANOAN and CHIBCHAN-PAEZAN. All the Macro-Panoan examples have -*l*. In Mataco, -*el* is a plural on all independent pronouns and on nouns. With this we may compare Lule *mi-l*, the second-person plural independent pronoun, and the use of -*l* as a personal plural, e.g. *kwe-l* 'children.' In all the languages of the Guaicuru group, -*lV* occurs as a third-person plural for noun possessives and as a verb subject. An example is Mocovi *i-taa* 'his, her father,' *le-taa* 'their father.' In the Lengua group, the Mascoy second- and third-person plural pronoun *k*ʲ*el* may belong here; the corresponding singular forms, however, are entirely different.

Both -*l* and -*r* plurals are common in CHIBCHAN-PAEZAN. In Paezan, we find Guambiana, Guanaca, and Totoro with the noun plurals

-ele, -el, and *-le,* respectively, and Guambiana also has the third-person plural independent pronoun *re-jle* (singular *ri*). In Barbacoan, we have Colorado *-la* for nominal and pronominal plurals, also occurring in the closely related Cayapa for pronominal and verbal plurals. In Choco, Catio has *-ra* for nominal and pronominal plurals. In the Guaymi group of Chibchan, Move, Muoi, and Guaymi proper have *-ri* and Murire has *-re* for the pronominal plural. In Talamanca, we find Bribri *-r* for the nominal plural and Borunca [-roh] for the plural of independent pronouns in all three persons. In Misumalpan, Cacaopera has *-ambi-ra, -bi-ra,* for the second-person plural verb subject, compared with *p* as a general second-person marker. Elsewhere in Chibchan, we find Xinca *-li* for nominal and pronominal plurals, and Paya *-ri, -r,* for markers of a plural verb subject.

34. We come now to a series of plurals that seem to be confined to single stocks of Amerind. One of these is MACRO-PANOAN *-to,* seen in Lule *teoto, meoto* 'they' (the initial elements are demonstratives, as discussed in items 13 and 14). In Panoan proper we find it, for example, in the Chacobo second- and third-person independent pronouns *ma-to* and *ha-to* (singulars *ma* and *ha*). Identical forms are found in Tacanan, e.g. Chama *ma-to* and *ha-to*. A single occurrence in MACRO-GE (possibly a borrowing) is Fulnio *i-to,* third-person plural pronoun formed from the singular.

35. Another MACRO-PANOAN plural, *-bo* for the plural of personal nouns, is found in the names of many Panoan ethnic groups, e.g. Conibo, Shipibo. A closely related form occurs in Tacanan, e.g. Chama *ha-bu* (singular *ha*). (Chama *ha-bu* is in free variation with *ha-to,* mentioned in the preceding item.) Guaicuru has a similar form for the plural of demonstratives, e.g. Mocovi and Toba *eda* 'this,' *eda-va* 'these.'

36. There is a *w-* plural that seems to be restricted to HOKAN. Southeast Pomo uses *w-* for a plural action and *-wa* for an unspecified actor (cf. 'they' as impersonal in English and other languages). In Washo, we find a *-w* pronominal plural, as in *mi-w* 'you' and *-u,* which when added to numerals above three indicates human reference. Karok prefixes *va-* to a noun for an impersonal owner, and *-va* is optionally suffixed to verbs for pluralization. In Chimariko, *-wa* forms plurals of the first- and second-person pronouns, e.g. *nout* 'I,' *noutawa* 'we.' In North Yana, *-wi* is a collective plural and *-wa-* a passive (third-person plural or impersonal subjects are common sources of passives). In the Achomawi languages, *-wi* is a plural, especially in tribal names (cf. Achomawi, Atsugewi), and in Atsugewi, *waʔ*

forms the third-person plural subject in a number of verb classes. In Tonkawa, we find *we-*, *w-*, for a plural object, and *-wesʔ*, suffixed to person markers for a plural subject (cf. *neʔs* for a dual in the same function).

37. Finally, we may mention an *-ɬ* plural that is confined to ALMOSAN. In Algic, Yurok expresses the third-person plural verb subject by *-Vɬ*, the vowel here depending on the verb class. Yurok also has *-ep-aɬ* denoting the third-person plural acting on the first-person singular. In Kutenai, *ʔaɬ* is the nominal plural, and *-aɬa-* pluralizes first-person forms. In Wakashan, Nootka uses *-ʔaɬ* to indicate a plural subject. In Chemakum, the second-person singular subject of intransitive verbs is *-etˢ*, and the second-person plural is *-etˢaɬ*. In the Quileute imperative *-xʷ* expresses a singular subject, as contrasted with the plural *-axoɬ*.

The next topic is nominal classifiers, including sex-gender markers and numeral classifiers. It is quite clear that Proto-Amerind had no systems of this sort. We consider sex gender first. (For an example of a grammaticized form of the word for 'woman' becoming a feminine marker, see the Hokan etymology for WIFE in Chapter 3.)

38. In the discussion of the *t* demonstrative (item 13), I spoke of the process by which a demonstrative, originally not distinguishing sex gender, becomes specialized as masculine, e.g. Chiquito *-tii*. Either, as in Chiquito, the non-masculine remains as zero, or a new non-masculine or specifically feminine develops. A feminine *s* arose through this process in at least two MACRO-GE languages. One is Fulnio, with a feminine suffix *-sa* used not only to form nouns, as in *i-ka* 'my son,' *i-ka-sa* 'my daughter,' but also to form a set of feminine singular independent pronouns in all three persons. The other Macro-Ge example is Kaingan, where we find a feminine third-person singular pronoun *si* contrasting with the masculine singular *ti*. In MACRO-PANOAN, which shows a number of indications of a special relationship with Macro-Ge, a parallel instance is found in the Moseten noun suffixes *-s* (feminine) and *-t* (masculine).

39. A vowel contrast for gender that basically takes the form *i* masculine, *u* feminine is found in both EQUATORIAL and MACROTUCANOAN, and is one important piece of evidence of the special relationship between the two groups. In Equatorial, Maipuran has a widespread contrast of this type, sometimes as independent pronouns, e.g. Wapishana *i* 'he,' *u* 'she,' and sometimes as a prefixed possessive and/or verb subject. Occasionally other vowels occur (particularly *o* or *a* as feminine), but *i/u* is

the predominant pattern in this group. In Arawakan, the suffix *i-* is masculine throughout the Arawa subgroup, contrasted, however, with *-ni* as feminine. In Jibaro, there is a clear lexical indication of this contrast in *hiči* 'grandfather,' *hiča* 'grandmother.' As noted above, *a* is sometimes the feminine in Maipuran. In Otomaco, we find *duriri* 'son,' *daore* 'daughter.' The Zamuco subgroup has a whole series of gender markers. There are separate plural forms for nouns, and different suffixes in each verb tense for gender and number. In some instances, these suffixes differ greatly for masculine and feminine, but in the cases of minimal vowel contrast, the vowels go in the expected direction. The clearest example is the recent past tense, where we find *-iz* as the masculine singular subject and *-az* as the corresponding feminine. Another example is the genitive, which suffixes *-tie* for masculine nouns and *-tae* for feminine. The Timote subgroup has prefixed gender articles; the most common are *ka-, kas-,* for the masculine and *ku-, ku-s,* for the feminine. Here the vowel of the masculine is deviant, but there is a masculine variant *kiu-* found in *kiu-kšoj* 'boy, uncle.' There are further instances in Equatorial in which we find the vowels conforming to the pattern, but with additional consonantal elements. One is Guahibo *-ni/-wa,* found, for example, in the third-person and demonstrative pronouns *arrapo-ni, arrapo-wa,* but also in nouns. Finally, in Saliba, masculine *-ndi* and feminine *-ku* are suffixed to nouns. Note the identity of Saliba *-ku* with the feminine article of Timote.

In MACRO-TUCANOAN, vowel contrasts for gender are found in the Tucano and Puinave subgroups. The most common pattern in Tucano is *e/o,* as in Tucano proper *pakke* 'father,' *pakko* 'mother,' and in the indefinite article based on the number 'one,' *nike* for the masculine, *niko* for the feminine (and *nika* for inanimates). Pioje has *i* for the masculine, as for example in adjectives that use the suffixes *-kī* to modify masculine nouns and *-kō* to modify feminines. Here, as frequently elsewhere, gender markers are also found as verb suffixes for the subject, and as demonstratives and third-person pronouns. In Pioje, the demonstrative 'this' is reported to have the variants *-ku, -ko,* and *-kō* in the feminine. Compare these with Timote and Saliba in Equatorial. In Puinave, Papury suffixes *-ji* for the masculine of animals; from Puinave proper, we have examples such as *nau-ne* 'he is handsome,' *nau-ju* 'she is pretty'; and in Ubde-Nehern the demonstrative 'that' is *nep* in the masculine, *nip* or *nap* in the feminine. Our examples in this case are necessarily scattered because of our fragmentary knowledge of the grammatical structure of languages of the Puinave group.

Note the parallelism in diachronic process between this gender indication and the preceding one. The two most common third-person markers, *t*
(item 13) and *i* (item 12), have become specialized as masculine markers in
particular subgroups and have thus given rise to the sex-gender systems described in items 38 and 39, respectively.

40. Along with gender classification, whether sex or not, the most
common type of noun classification involves numerical classifiers in which
a numeral is preceded or followed by one of a set of elements that vary with
the shape or other properties of the item counted. I have discussed elsewhere
(Greenberg 1972) the process by which one of the classifiers, usually that
for large round objects, tends to become the general classifier and to replace
all other classifiers. Once it is found on all nouns, it ceases to be a numeral
classifier and becomes merely a petrified element either on some numerals
or on nouns where, as a marker of mere nominality, it may assume a new
function in deriving nouns from verbs. Such elements characteristically become lexicalized on nouns in a very sporadic way, so that they may appear on certain nouns in one language yet be absent on obvious cognates
in closely related languages, or may even be in free variation in the same
language.

In its later stages, this process is very similar to the one by which old
demonstratives become stage III articles or indefinite pronouns. (Compare
the Mosan developments of the Amerind demonstrative *m,* item 14.) Haas,
in her Algic comparisons, freely compares forms with and without *m-* in the
constituent stocks. We will encounter a similar phenomenon later in regard
to Penutian *-s* (item 64).

For now, we are concerned with an element in CHIBCHAN-PAEZAN
that may be reconstructed as *-kwa,* and that has the primary classificatory
meaning of 'large round object' in those languages in which there is still
a functioning system of numeral classifiers, e.g. Bribri in the Talamanca
group. (Examples of Chibchan-Paezan etymologies with and without *-kwa*
are given in Chapter 3; e.g. Chibcha proper *up-kwa* 'eye' and Rama *up* 'eye,
fruit, round thing.')

We begin in Argentina with Millcayac, a member of the Paezan branch.
Here *-gwe* regularly derives nouns from verbs, e.g. *čeri* 'to give,' *čeri-gwe*
'gift'; *pi-na* 'to die,' *pi-gwe* 'death.' In Chimu, *-k* forms verbal nouns. That
-k is an independent formative is shown by the fact that it does not occur
when the noun is in the genitive. In Paez, many nouns end in *-kue.* A comparative example, which shows that it is a suffix, is Colorado (Barbacoa)
pičo 'bird' and the related Paez form *viča-kue.* The Barbacoa languages as a

group show a suffix -ka on numerals, but in Colorado, these are in free variation with forms without -ka, e.g. man ~ manka 'one,' palu ~ paluka 'two.' Warrau seems to show a lone survival of this pattern in isa-ka 'one.' That -ka is a formative is shown by the much less frequently used variant isa-ta.

Among Chibchan languages, Chibcha proper has a suffix, -kwa or -gwa, that appears particularly on round objects, e.g. up-kwa 'eye,' pči-gwa 'hole,' fa-gwa 'star,' but on other nouns also, e.g. [kypkua] 'place.' In Motilon, many nouns have the ending -kwa, which is also found in the numeral te-kwa 'four.' In the Aruak subgroup, -kwa and -gwa appear on numerals, e.g. Kagaba maigwa 'three,' kugwa 'six,' abi-kwa 'eight.' That -kwa, -gwa, is a formative is further shown by mai-lluī 'three times,' as compared with mai-gwa 'three.' In Cuna, -kwa is often used with numerals. Thus both po and po-kwa have been recorded for 'two.' As described by Holmer (1947), Cuna -kwa is particularly common for round objects and in agent nouns formed from verbs, e.g. ape-kwa 'bather.' Its origin in the general numeral classifier, outside of its use with numerals, is shown most convincingly in the term pi-kwa 'how many?' In the Guaymi group, -kwa appears in words for round objects, e.g. Norteño o-kwa 'eye.' The Talamanca group has a fully functional set of classifiers, of which the most important is kuo. According to Lehmann (1920, 1: 277), in Bribri it "indicates in general fruits, round objects, and similar things." In the Rama group, the element takes the form -ku. An example is Guatuso fisi-ku 'eye,' compared with fisi-len 'eyelid' and fisi-iisa 'eyelashes.' Probably Xinca -ka, -k (alternating with -ha after vowels), which forms verbal nouns, belongs here. Examples from Maldonado (1897) are giri 'to grind,' giri-k 'grindstone'; taju 'put on the head,' taju-k 'hat'; and epeɫe 'to fear,' eple-k 'a fearful thing.' Finally Swadesh, in his Tarascan dictionary (1969), cites -kwa as a suffix expressing condition, action, or instrument in deriving nouns from verbs, e.g. ika-ra 'to plant,' ɩka-kwa 'a plant'; o- 'to cover,' o-kwa 'a mantle.' It also occurs frequently in words for round objects not derived from verbs, e.g. ura-kwa 'coin,' ija-hča-kwa 'pillow,' [hozqua] 'star.' Foster (1969: 158) notes a special connection with numeral classifiers, suggesting that -kwa is added as a substantivizer to what is probably a more recent system of classifiers, e.g. tʰamu-ɩču-kwa 'four flat, thin objects,' tanim-era-kwa 'three round objects.' Elsewhere (p. 84) she notes that a great many nouns occur with this suffix.

There is no evidence for a case system in Proto-Amerind in the sense of a system with overt markers for both the grammatical cases (e.g. nominative, accusative, genitive) and the local cases (e.g. locative, ablative). But the existence of what looks like an ergative system for pronouns suggests there may have been a case system for nouns. In any event, we do find a few examples of grammatical cases that have developed in individual subgroups or languages. There are also postpositions, usually for spatial reference, a few of which have a breadth of distribution that suggests they are Proto-Amerind.

41. Several CHIBCHAN-PAEZAN languages have what appears to be a related set of topicalizers or subject markers. A topicalizer *-te,* as in *an-te* 'as for me,' is found in Cuna (Holmer 1952). In the Talamanca group, Bribri *-to* and Chiripo *-te* are described as subject markers. All these languages are Chibchan. In Paezan, Catio, a Choco language, uses the suffixes *-ba, -ra,* and *-ta* as subject markers. Of these *-ta* is said to be frequently used with intransitive verbs.

42. An accusative marker *-s* occurs in PENUTIAN. In California Penutian, Costanoan has an accusative *-se.* In Wintun, *-s* is used to indicate the accusative of first- and second-person pronouns, *-t* of the others. This system is remarkably like that of Yuki, which has *-s* for the second person only, and *-t* for all other pronouns. In Oregon Penutian, Alsea has a general accusative *-s.* In Plateau, Klamath *-ʔas, -s,* is compulsory with pronouns, usual with nouns pertaining to humans, and less so with animals and things. These data, along with the exclusive occurrence of *-s* with personal pronouns in Wintun and Yuki, suggest that it was once used primarily for humans and has spread in some instances.

43. In ANDEAN, both Aymara and the closely related Jaqaru have the dative ending *-taki,* which may be compared to Leco *-čiki.* The Jaqaru formative includes in its uses the expression of purpose.

44. It is well known that datives of verbal nouns are an important (probably the most important) source of infinitives (cf. English 'to'). Developments of this sort occur in CHIBCHAN-PAEZAN, where a suffixed *-ja, -je,* or the like commonly functions as an indirect object or forms infinitives with verb roots. Beginning with Paezan, Allentiac and the closely related Millcayac have a dative *-je.* In Paez, *ia* is used both as a postposition for 'to, for' and as an element to form infinitives from verbs, e.g. *fis-ia* 'to write.' In Jirajara, *-ja* and *-je* express motion toward a place. In the Choco group, Catio *-ja* forms infinitives. In Chibchan, Tunebo of the Chibcha subgroup forms the infinitive with *-aja.* In the Guaymi subgroup, Move marks the indirect object with *-je,* and in the Talamanca subgroup, Bribri with *-ia.* Finally Miskito, in the Misumalpan group, forms the infinitive with *-ja.*

45. We now come to an affix, -k, whose primary meaning is probably 'motion toward.' Using a term common in Finno-Ugric studies, we may call it an "allative." On the one hand, it may be identical in expression to the dative, as is true of the Finnish allative and the Jirajara example in the preceding item. On the other hand, expressions meaning 'motion toward' often also indicate, or are historically related to, locations, as in present-day English 'where?,' which has taken on the meaning of the obsolete 'whither?' Examples of what I believe to be this -k affix are found in the Amerind dictionary entry ABOVE₂, which also includes variants without it. Adverbs are the graveyard of prepositions and much else. On this basis, in addition to the subgroups cited below, -k also formerly existed in MACRO-GE and MACRO-TUCANOAN, and can be claimed in all likelihood as Proto-Amerind.

Examples are found in both branches of CHIBCHAN-PAEZAN. In Paezan, Chimu has -ek 'to,' and all locative postpositions end in -k. Note also sio 'that' and sio-k 'there.' In Chibchan, we find Cuna -ki, -kine 'in, at, by'; Rama -ki 'in, on'; and Miskito (Misumalpan) -k, -ku, for the manner or direction of travel, e.g. awala-k 'by river.'

In HOKAN, we find a -k suffix on both nouns and verbs in Yuman languages meaning motion toward or location in. Other examples are Seri ʔak, ak, as a locative; Salinan ke-, k-, as a locative before pronominal affixes; Esselen ki-ki 'where is he?'; Yana -ki 'hither' and gi as a locative and objective particle; Washo -uk, -buk (in verbs of motion) 'toward a place'; Karok -ak ~ -k as a locative; Shasta and Atsugewi, -k to indicate motion toward; Achomawi -gu suffixed to verbal nouns to express purpose and -ig- (in the verbal complex) 'hither'; Chimariko hu-ak-ta 'come' (cf. hu-am-ta 'go'); and Comecrudo -ak as a directional in adverbs, e.g. pesen 'shoulder,' pesn-ak 'backward.' Perhaps Tonkawa ʔok 'when, as if' also belongs here.

In PENUTIAN, we have, in California Penutian, Maidu -k 'toward,' and Wintu -ke in he-ke 'where?' (cf. he-noni 'why?'). In Oregon Penutian, Siuslaw has ta:-k 'here,' sqa:k 'there,' či:k 'where?,' and Alsea has k- as a locative on nouns and verbs. Chinook has -k 'on.' In Yuki-Gulf, we find Natchez -kʰ 'at,' Atakapa -kin, -ki, -ke, Chitimacha -(n)ki 'at, in,' and Yuki -kʔil 'toward.' A Mexican Penutian example is Totonac k- 'in.'

Both branches of ALMOSAN-KERESIOUAN supply examples. In Algic, we have Wiyot -okʷ 'in' and Yurok -ik 'in'; and in Keresiouan, Pawnee (Caddoan) has kijah 'in,' and Seneca (Iroquoian) has -keh 'in.'

It is clear, from these examples, that the locative element can occur in the verbal complex to indicate action at or toward, and that the same affix may even be used with both verbs and nouns. In a later section on verbal derivation, we will examine instances in which a directional affix seems predominantly verbal and may in fact be a grammaticization of a verb of motion.

46. We now consider an -*m* suffix that in virtually all occurrences means to rest in place rather than motion. I consider it distinct from the grammaticizations of the verb (see GO₁ in Chapter 4). It occurs in all three groups of Ge-Pano-Carib. In MACRO-GE, we have Kaingan -*ma* as a dative. In MACRO-PANOAN, Tacanan has Chama -*me* 'location' and Lule -*ma* 'in'; Charruan has Chana *re-ma* 'where?' (*re-* occurs in a whole series of interrogatives); and Lengua has Mascoy -*me* 'in,' used with nouns and adverbs of place. In MACRO-CARIB, we find Yameo (Yagua) -*me, ma* 'at, in.' (Cf. Uitoto -*mo* for the allative.)

PENUTIAN examples are found in California Penutian, where Costanoan has San José -*mo, -mu* 'in,' and San Juan Bautista -*me* 'in'; Miwok has -*m, -mu* 'in'; and Maidu has *mo:m* 'there' (cf. *mo:* 'that'). In Oregon Penutian, we find Alsea -*əm* 'place,' *kʲi-m* 'there'; Coos -*əm* as a suffix in nouns of place; and Takelma *me* 'here.' Tsimshian has -*əm, -am*, locative. And in Yuki-Gulf, there are Wappo *ma-* 'in' (verb prefix), Yuki -*am, -m* 'in,' and Creek (Muskogean) *i-ama* 'here.'

47. An *n* locative occurs in a number of branches of Amerind. It is frequently preceded by the *m-* interrogative (item 103) with the meaning 'where?' In a few instances it has an instrumental meaning. In many languages the same case expresses both instrument and place. The transition is easy, as can be seen from such English expressions as 'to burn on the fire,' which expresses the same act as 'to burn by fire,' and the synonymy of 'to go on foot' and 'to go by foot.'

For EQUATORIAL, we have Cofan *(ma-)ñi* 'where?' In ANDEAN, Yamana has Yahgan with -*n* as a locative; Aymara has -*ana* as a locative and -*na* as a locative in an adverb; Quechua has -*n* as an instrumental; and Jebero has -*n* as an instrumental. In CHIBCHAN-PAEZAN, we find, in Paezan, Paez *(ma-)neh* 'where?,' and Cayapa (Barbacoa) *mu-ng* 'where?' In Chibchan, Aruak has Kagaba *ma-ni* 'where?,' and Misumalpan has Matagalpa *ma-n* 'where?' For PENUTIAN, we find, in California, Central Sierra Miwok *mi-nni* 'where?,' and Patwin (Wintun) *(me-)na* 'where?' Plateau has North Sahaptin *(mə-)na* 'where?' and Nez Percè *(mi-)ne* 'where.' In Yuki-Gulf, we find two Muskogean examples, Choctaw *(ma-)na* 'when?' and Chickasaw *(ma-)no* 'where?'

48. Another locative that is fairly widely attested is -pV. In EQUA-TORIAL, it appears in the Tupian languages Guaraní -pe 'in,' Arikem -pi 'in,' and Guayaki -pe 'in,' and in Timote -be 'toward.' In MACRO-TUCANOAN, we find Tucano -pe 'in' and Iranshe -pa 'place.' ANDEAN has Yahgan -pi 'in'; Ona, Tehuelche -pi 'in'; and Quechua -pi 'in.' Finally, for CENTRAL AMERIND, we have Proto-Oto-Mangue (Rensch no. 191) *kʷa 'here, there, where?'; Proto-Uto-Aztecan (Longacre) *-pa(-n) as a locative; and Kiowa -ba, -bɔ 'in.'

49. There is a suffix -tV that functions in most Amerind groups as a locative or instrumental, but is ablative in Andean. Whether the forms found in different subgroups are all etymologically connected is not certain. In Andean and Penutian they may be separate independent innovations. MACRO-PANOAN has Lule -ta 'through, in,' Vilela -at 'in,' and Moseten če 'in, about' (< *te, cf. t ~ či in the masculine suffix). In ANDEAN, we find Jaqaru (Aymara) -tʰa as exchange, from, for (separatives); Quechua (man-)ta (ablative; man is locative; see the Andean etymology INSIDE); and Cholona -te 'from' (separative). In the Paezan branch of CHIBCHAN-PAEZAN, we have Allentiac -ta for a movement to or from, the closely related Millcayac with -ta suffixed to verb stems to form the supine; and Catio (Choco) with -de for the locative. In Chibchan, we find Move, of the Guaymi group, -te 'in.' Finally, there are these PENUTIAN examples. For California, Maidu di 'in' and Wintu -ti as in anken-ti 'behind' and other locative adverbs; for Plateau, Klamath di 'place of.'

50. An allative confined to MACRO-PANOAN appears in: Moseten -ve; Vilela be; and in the Tacanan group, Tacana -βe and Chama -wa, all with the general meaning 'toward.'

51. Even more restricted within MACRO-PANOAN are Lule -le 'to-ward,' also 'if, when'; Vilela -le 'in, toward'; and Guenoa (retan-)le 'for what?' (cf. retaut 'what?'). This item is cited here because the Charruan languages have traditionally been considered genetic isolates.

We now consider a number of "sociatives," that is, adpositions with the general meaning range of English 'with' used for instrument, accompani-ment, and so forth. Each has a restricted distribution.

52. One sociative appears in MACRO-TUCANOAN; Tucano and other Tucanoan languages have a form mena 'with, having,' which is probably cognate with Ticuna mãʔã 'with.' We may perhaps compare this with the EQUATORIAL language Saliba mane 'around' (Latin gloss circum).

53. In CHIBCHAN-PAEZAN, there is a general sociative prefix that

has specialized uses in the expression of kin relationships. For Paezan, Pittier de Fabrega (1907: 330) notes that in Paez "the prefix *pe* . . . can be considered as indicating duality *pe-niiš*, 'son and father' or 'mother and daughter'; *pe-tam* 'male and female.'" With this we compare Barbacoan Colorado *pe-* 'with, in the company of.' Allentiac and Chimu both have a whole series of kin terms with initial *p-*, e.g. Allentiac *pera* 'older brother,' *pia* 'father,' *penne* 'mother,' *pekete* 'aunt,' *pete* 'parent'; Yunca *pani* 'man's sister,' *pani* 'son,' *i-pas* 'her male cousin,' *i-pa* 'his female cousin.' In Chibchan, Tarascan has *pi-* 'to be joined, together, similar' and *pipi, pire* 'man's older brother.' In far-off Klamath, of Plateau PENUTIAN, kin terms have a prefixed *p-*. (Cf. also the Amerind dictionary entry BROTHER.) A connection with the Amerind word for 'two' is possible and is not incompatible with its kinship usage, as is strikingly shown by the Paez examples. Note also that *p-* is always a prefix, even though postpositions dominate in Amerind languages.

54. A PENUTIAN form with basically associative meaning is found in two California Penutian languages, Maidu *k'an* 'with' and Wintun *xun* 'together'; in Tsimshian *qan* 'and'; in Chinook *gəm* 'near'; and in two Yuki-Gulf languages, Chitimacha *kan* 'like, almost like,' Atakapa *han* 'almost.'

55. A sociative with *ł* occurs in the Almosan branch of ALMOSAN-KERESIOUAN. It is found in Algic, where Wiyot *-ł* is an instrumental noun suffix; in Mosan, where Thompson River Salish uses *-əł* 'and' with people and Tillamook has *-wał* 'in company with'; and in Kutenai, where we find *-mał* 'in company with.'

56. Finally, mention should be made of a special resemblance within ALMOSAN between Algonquian and Kwakiutl. Bloomfield (1941) devotes an entire article to the Algonquian stem *i:t* 'fellow,' and Boas, in his grammar of Kwakiutl (1947), discusses a suffix *o:t*, which he glosses the same way—'fellow.' A Kwakiutl example is *go:kula* 'to live in a house,' *go:kul-o:t* 'housemate.' Semantically similar examples are adduced by Bloomfield, e.g. 'fellow chief' from 'chief' or 'to be a chief.' Though the Algonquian examples involve an initial stem rather than a suffix, the resemblance between the two is reinforced by certain phonological factors. Bloomfield cites *wi:t*, in which *w-* is said to be a frozen form of the third-person possessive, and notes (p. 296): "It is safe to say that PA *wi:t* figures as a root . . . in a number of formations, some of them quite archaic." Compare this with Boas (1947: 335), where *-wət* is given as a variant of *-o:t*. This formative is necessarily suffixed in Kwakiutl, which has only suffixes.

57. A widespread sociative is found in MACRO-PANOAN that generally has the shape *-ja,* meaning 'with.' It occurs in Moseten, Lule, and Panoan, among others. In Moseten, the related meaning 'having' occurs in formatives like *p^hen-ja-t* 'married man' (from 'wife' + 'having' + masculine marker). Similar is Mataco *-jo.* Pelleschi (1896–97) gives the example [ciequa] 'wife,' [ciequa-jo] 'to have a wife, be married.' In all probability the Mocovi (Guaicuru) verb *ija* 'to accompany' belongs here and possibly also Cavineña (Tacanan) *ja* 'against.' On the shift of meaning, compare English 'to fight with.'

We now come to the general topic of nominal derivation. Before proceeding to nominal derivation from verbs, let us deal briefly with the process of noun-noun derivation, specifically diminutives and augmentatives. Consonant alternation as a method of forming diminutives is fairly common in North America, but I am not certain, without detailed investigation, to what extent it is an areal and to what extent a genetic phenomenon. It is therefore excluded from the present study. In the Amerind dictionary entry SMALL there are examples of a suffixed *-mV* that has been grammaticized as a diminutive in some languages. Similar examples, all under SMALL, will be found in the Chapter 3 etymologies for MACRO-GE, EQUATORIAL, and ALMOSAN-KERESIOUAN.

58. In dealing with nominal derivation from verbs, we begin with items of more specific meaning and then move to infinitives, verbal nouns, and so forth. The first item to be considered is a derivational element found in ANDEAN that indicates place or instrument (the close connection between the two was mentioned earlier, in the discussion of case). An example is Gennaken *iakłu-we* 'mirror,' derived from the verb *iakłe* 'to look' plus *-we* (place, instrument). The term can be regarded as meaning either the place in which one sees an image or the means by which it is seen. The suffix also occurs in Patagonian, e.g. Tehuelche *-we* (instrument), in Araucanian *-we* (place or instrument), and in Aymara *-wi* 'place.'

59. A similar derivational suffix is found in KERESIOUAN. Cherokee, which forms the Southern branch of Iroquoian, suffixes *-sdi* to form nouns of instrument. In the Keresan subgroup, we find *-stɪ.* In Davis's Santa Ana examples, the ambiguity between place and instrument is found in a number of instances, e.g. *ʔaiča-stɪ* 'mattress, mat' from a verb meaning 'to cover.'

60. In both Equatorial and Macro-Tucanoan languages, the suffixes *-re, -ri* form agent nouns from verbs. In EQUATORIAL, we have Ayoré

(Zamuco) -ore; Kariri -ri; and Toyeri (Maipuran) -eri acompanied by a prefix e-. In MACRO-TUCANOAN, there are Canichana -ri, and, in Puinave, Ubde-Nehern -re (agent, active participle).

61. I have found only one other general formant of nouns from verbs common to two or more Amerind subgroups. This is -n(V), which derives infinitives and verbal nouns from verb stems. In ANDEAN, we find, in the Patagon subgroup, Ona, Tehuelche -n; Araucanian -n; Quechua -na; and in Zaparoan, Zaparo -no, Andoa -nu. The suffix occurs also in CHIBCHAN-PAEZAN. In Paezan, we have Itonama -na, ne; Cayapa (Barbacoa) -nu; and Timucua -ni. In Chibchan, Tarascan has -ni. These are once more basically infinitive markers. A similar -n occurs in HOKAN, and shows the characteristics of stage III articles, which often—because of their function as a general marker of nominality—form verbal nouns. Historically, then, it may not be related to forms from other branches of Amerind. In Yurumangui, -na is a general noun formant, as is Esselen -nex, -no, suffixed to nouns, e.g. iwa-no 'house.' For Tonkawa, Hoijer (1960) lists an -n as an "infinitive verb suffix," but it also derives nouns from verbs with other than infinitival meaning (e.g. čo:l 'defecate,' čo:lan 'excrement') and appears on numerous nouns for which there is no verb as a derivational source. Moshinsky (1974) lists an absolutive -n in Southeast Pomo that forms nouns from verbs. This seems to be close semantically to the Andean and Chibchan examples already cited. In PENUTIAN, a few languages form infinitives and verbal nouns in this way: California Penutian has Maidu -n and Yokuts -n; in Yuki-Gulf, there is Atakapa -en (cf. item 65).

62. In CENTRAL AMERIND, Langacker (1977: 47) reconstructs Proto-Uto-Aztecan *-wa as an abstract nominalizer, and comments (p. 120): "There is a decent amount of evidence for reconstructing the single proto-form *wa 'one' for PUA, e.g. i-wa 'this one.'" With these we compare Rensch's Proto-Oto-Mangue no. 392, *(ʔ)wa(h)(n) 'that one, oneself, the same.' In the Kiowa-Tanoan branch, Taos has -waʔi (plural -waʔina), which is suffixed to the absolutive form of the noun whenever it occurs with a possessive prefix, e.g. puj-ena 'friend,' ʔan-puj-waʔi 'my friend,' as it were 'my friend that-one.' It seems therefore equatable with the aforementioned Uto-Aztecan and Oto-Mangue forms.

63. Of very limited distribution in ANDEAN is Kaueskar -kar, which forms nouns from verbs but is also a general marker of nominality on many nouns. With this we may compare, in Patagonian, Ona -kar, found in ma-kar 'yours' (really 'your-thing') and doubtless the same word as [carro] in

Tehuelche, glossed in Spanish as 'toda madera.' With this we may possibly connect Quechua *k²ara* 'skin,' since historically the words for 'skin' and 'body' are often related or homonymous. I cite this here because Kaueskar, listed as a separate stock by Loukotka, is, as noted elsewhere, hardly more than a dialect of Alakaluf, which in turn has generally been classified as unrelated to Patagonian (and, of course, to Quechua).

64. The element *-s*, historically a stage III article in PENUTIAN, has as a basic or even exclusive function in certain languages the formation of verbal nouns. Elsewhere I have discussed it in detail as a diachronic typological parallel to Nilo-Saharan *k-* (Greenberg 1981: 110–11). In California Penutian, it appears in Costanoan, Miwok, Wintun, and Yokuts. In Costanoan, it is a common noun ending, and we have the characteristic feature of dialectal occurrence or non-occurrence in the same lexical item (e.g. San José, Santa Clara *tuxi* 'day,' compared with San Juan Bautista *tuxi-s* with the same meaning). Kroeber (1904) mentions *-s* in Coastal Miwok as a nominal marker of the absolute or the subjective in the noun. In Wintun, *-s* is universally productive in forming verbal nouns, e.g. *hara* 'go,' *hara-s* 'act of going.' In Yokuts, we find Gashowu *mik²i* 'swallow,' *mik²i-š* 'throat.' Gashowu *š* corresponds to *s* in other Yokuts dialects. Farther north, in Plateau Penutian, Klamath *-s* is described as fossilized on most nouns. A comparative example is Klamath *loloks*, Yakima (also Plateau) *eloks*, and Tsimshian *lok*, all meaning 'fire.' In Oregon Penutian, Alsea has *-s* as a general nominalizer, and it is also common in Coos, where in addition to forming verbal nouns (e.g. *waa* 'to speak,' *waa-s* 'speech'), Frachtenberg notes (1922: 326) that "*-s* was the general suffix indicating nouns and . . . all nominal suffixes in *-s* eventually go back to this nominal suffix." In Takelma, another Oregon Penutian language, Sapir (1922: 225) describes *-s* as a nominal derivational element "in a fairly considerable number of words." The same element also appears in Yuki-Gulf. In Wappo, *-s* is a general nominal and adjective formant, and *-st* and *-št* are very common noun formants in Atakapa, particularly from verbs. This is presumably a complex element (cf. Coos), but *-š* occurs particularly often in eastern Atakapa dialects as an infinitive.

65. In Chapter 2, Algonquian *-an-*, which is suffixed to body parts, was compared to Salish *-n*. A probably related example is found in Keresan, in which numerous nouns, including body-part expressions, end in *-ani* or *-ini*. That this is a formative is shown both by its frequency and by the occurrence of incorporated and independent forms of the same stem, e.g.

Santa Ana *-sdi* in *ha-sdiʔni* 'foot.' It is thus ALMOSAN-KERESIOUAN
in its distribution. But it may not be restricted to that subfamily. It could
very well be the same *-an* found widely as a variant in the word for 'hand,'
makan or the like, and evidently derived from *maka* 'give' (see HAND (1)
in the Amerind dictionary). It may also occur in the common noun formative *-an* of the PENUTIAN language Totonac (e.g. *makan* 'hand'). If these
connections are valid, an old petrified Amerind affix has once more become
productive in Almosan-Keresiouan (see also item 61).

66. We now consider adjectival and participial formants. I have encountered only one of these in more than one subgroup of Amerind. This
is *-k*, found in MACRO-PANOAN and HOKAN. In Macro-Panoan, we find
the Mataco suffix *-ek* that forms active and passive participial nouns from
verbs, as in *čukʷan* 'to study,' *čukʷen-ek* 'student'; *ten* 'to sing,' *ten-ek*
'song.' It also occurs in Lengua, where it forms adjectives from stative
verbs, e.g. Mascoy *tasi* 'to be good,' *tasi-k* 'good.' Examples from Tacanan
are Cavineña *aja* 'to make,' *aja-ke* 'that which he makes,' and *biso-ja* 'to be
ashamed,' *bisoa-ki* 'ashamed.' Similar instances occur in Panoan, e.g. Conibo *pi* 'to sit,' *pi-ki* 'that which is seated.' In Hokan, Subtiaba *gi-* and
Tlappanec *k-* form passive past participles, and Seri *k-* forms adjectives.
In Esselen, almost all adjectives end in *-ki*, and in Tonkawa *-k* added to the
third person forms a participial to which first- and second-person markers
may be prefixed when appropriate. An example of this formation is *jakpa-
ne-k* 'you having struck him.' In Pomo, *k-* forms adjectives.

67. An adjective formant *m-* is found in Subtiaba, Tlappanec, and
other HOKAN languages. An example from Comecrudo (Coahuiltecan) is
meskan 'distant,' *maketiau* 'heavy.' In Yuman languages (e.g. Diegueño),
there is a subordinate *-m* that is parallel in its functions to the participial *-k*
of Tonkawa treated in the preceding item.

68. A suffixed *-ma* that forms past participles in EQUATORIAL languages is probably not related to the preceding formant. In Guayaki, a Tupian language, it is described as indicating the completion of a process in
the present, e.g. *pui-ma* 'having become heavy.' A similar suffix is found in
the Jibaro-Kandoshi group, e.g. Kandoshi *ipaana* 'to conceive,' *ipaana-ma*
'pregnant.' In Jibaro, *-ma* forms passive participles, e.g. *apar-* 'to cook,'
apar-ma 'cooked.'

69. A suffix of the same general meaning as the preceding one is found
in CHIBCHAN-PAEZAN. A Paezan example is Warrau *-naː*, and from

Chibchan, we have, in the Aruak subgroup, Kagaba *akpei-ne* 'opened' and, in the Misumalpan subgroup, Sumu *-na* and Miskito *-an,* both markers of passive past participles.

We turn now to verb inflection, taking as our first topic mood and tense together, since they are often difficult to separate. They are considered here under four rubrics: (1) present, durative, and habitual; (2) past; (3) future, optative, and desiderative; and (4) imperative.

70. A sibilant suffix, usually *-s,* occurs in both Penutian and Almosan-Keresiouan. Its meaning is most frequently given as continuative, occasionally as present. In PENUTIAN, we find in California Penutian, Patwin (Wintun) *-s* for the present tense; in Plateau, Sahaptin *-š²* for the continuative and Nez Perce *-s* for the present-perfect; in Oregon, Siuslaw *-i:s, -u:s,* for the durative; and in Yuki-Gulf, Yuki *-is* and Chitimacha *-iš* for the continuative. In ALMOSAN-KERESIOUAN, in Wakashan, there is Kwakiutl *-əs, -s,* for continually; and in Salish, we find Upper Chehalis *s-* for the continuative. In Keresiouan, Chafe (1979: 228) posits *-s,* perhaps with an associated glottal stop, as indicating the imperfective or progressive in both Caddoan and Iroquoian. To these we may add Acoma (Keresan) *-sə,* described by Miller (1965: 129) as indicating the continuative, repetitive, and habitual.

71. A suffixed *-i* to mark the present or the durative is found in MACRO-CARIB and CHIBCHAN-PAEZAN. In Macusi, a Carib language, *-i* is described by Goeje (1946: 5) as marking an "indefinite tense that indicates the present in particular," and Goeje notes that it also occurs in the Carib languages Kaliana, Accawai, Oyana, and Trio. We may compare this with, in the Bora group, Muinane *-ʔi* for the durative or the progressive, and in the Yagua group, Yameo *-i* for the progressive. In Paezan, Catio, a Chocoan language, indicates the present tense by *-i,* and Warrau forms a "gerund" by *-i* that is actually a present participle, e.g. *naxoro-i* 'eating.' In Chibchan, the main verb endings in Kagaba, an Aruak language, are *-i, -li, -ni, -hi,* and *-ši,* described as progressive markers. Cuna has *-i* as a present marker. In the Rama group, we have *-i* for the present in Rama proper and a number of verbs in Guatuso that form the present tense with *-e* or *-i.* In Misumalpan, the Miskito verb forms the present participle in *-i.*

72. In the Talamanca group of CHIBCHAN, Bribri has a durative *-ke,* which may be compared with Xinca *-ki-.*

73. In Wappo, a Yuki-Gulf language of PENUTIAN, we find a con-

trast -*a* (durative) / -*i* (punctual), which may be compared with Coos (Oregon Penutian) -*at* / -*it* with the same functions. This same -*a* / -*i* pattern is found in Quileute, a Wakashan language of ALMOSAN. It may be more widespread. Final vowels are particularly susceptible to phonetic change, and aspect markers themselves are not very stable over time.

74. An iterative-habitual *t* is found in two HOKAN subgroups. East Pomo has *t^h*- for intermittent action and Salinan has -*t*-, -*te*-, iterative plurals in nouns and verbs. The same element is found in PENUTIAN, where Wappo -*tɛ* marks plurality and iteration in verbs, as does Miwok -*ti*. There is also Maidu -*to*, glossed as 'repeatedly, reciprocally, plural object.'

75. In ANDEAN, an *n* forms the present in some Patagon languages, e.g. Tehuelche -*n*, to which we may compare Cholana -*n*- (present) and Jebero *na*- (recently). Quechua -*n*-, which occurs in almost all of the present inflections of the verb, probably belongs here also.

76. In the Oregon branch of PENUTIAN, Takelma *(a)l*- is described as continuative. In Plateau, we find Nez Perce -*la*- for the durative, and Chinook uses -*l*- for a repeated action. With these may be connected, in California Penutian, Yaudanchi (Yokuts) -*ad*- for the durative if, as seems possible, -*ad*- < *-*al*-.

77. Coming now to indicators of past time or completion, MACRO-PANOAN and HOKAN agree in having a past-tense marker *n*. For Panoan, Prost (1962) cites Chacobo -*ni* 'a long time ago,' which may be compared to Tacana -*na* indicating the remote past, Lule [-ny], the recent past, and Mataco -*ne*, the past. In Hokan, Achomawi expresses the distant past by -*n*-, Atsugewi by -*ʔn*-. In Subtiaba and Tlappanec, *ni*- indicates the perfective durative, and in North Yana, -*ʔna*, -*ʔn*, marks the remote past. We may also mention Cayapo, a Ge language, which has a suffix -*na* for the present or recent past. Since detailed grammars are scarce within the MACRO-GE group, the suffix may quite possibly occur elsewhere.

78. Another past indicator in MACRO-PANOAN is found in Lule -*ate* (remote past); Vilela *ete*, an adverb indicating completed act; Tacana -*tia* (immediate past), -*ba*, -*tiba* (past); and Mataco *pa-nte* (remote past). In the last example, *pa*-, a distance demonstrative, seems to add a nuance of remoteness (see item 16); compare *ma-te* for the recent past in the same language, which also contains the *ma*- demonstrative discussed in item 14. Other examples are Chacobo (Panoan) *ʔita* for an action taken yesterday, and Mascoy (Lengua) *athta* for the past. In addition, we find Moseten *at* + verb

+ *te* to indicate the perfect, *at* + verb + *ike* for the pluperfect. With these we may compare Kraho (GE) *itɛ* (a free form that precedes the verb) for the past tense.

79. In northernmost CHIBCHAN, Tarascan past-tense *-š-* (Foster 1969: 62) can be connected with *-aš* for the past in Chilanga, a dialect of Lenca.

80. The following etymology represents a past-tense marker in HOKAN: Yurumangui *iba*, Coahuilteco *pa-*, Tequistlatec *-pa*, Salinan *be-*, Pomo *(hi)ba*, Karok *-ʔipa* ~ *pa-* (near past), and Shasta *pʔ-* (distant past, habitual past). The marker probably also occurs in Salinan *-iwa-š*, which when suffixed to nouns means 'that which was formerly,' e.g. *noqš* 'head,' *noqš-iwa-š* 'skull.' The last element, *-š*, is a common noun formant in Chumash. The agreement in a form **ipa* among Yurumangui in the extreme south, Coahuilteco in the middle, and Karok in the far north is striking.

81. Several instances in which grammaticized forms of the verb 'to wish' serve as future markers will be found in the etymologies in Chapters 3 and 4. In MACRO-TUCANOAN, Ubde-Nehern, a Puinavean language, has a future marker, *-te*, that probably corresponds to Ticuna *ta* with the same meaning. With this we may compare, in CENTRAL AMERIND, Chiapanec (Oto-Mangue) *-ta* and Kiowa (Kiowa-Tanoan) *-da*, *-tʔ*, both indicators of future tense.

82. In MACRO-PANOAN, Tacana *-ha* for the desiderative is probably related to Abipone (Guaicuru) *ihe* 'to wish,' and these may be compared to Opaie *-he* 'to wish' in MACRO-GE.

83. In MACRO-PANOAN, Chacobo *-no* (desiderative) and Shipibo *-nõ* (purposive), in the Panoan group, may be compared to Lule *-no* (desiderative).

84. A set of forms in *s* or *š* expressing the future or the optative occurs in HOKAN. These include Seri *s-*, future; Chumash *-saʔ*, future; Salinan of San Antonio *-še*, desiderative; Proto-Pomo **ix*, **iš*, optative; Washo *-aša*, desiderative or future (Kroeber), *-ašaʔ*, imminent future (Jacobsen); Yana *-si(ʔ)i*, future; and Karok *-aviš*, *-eš*, *-haš*, future.

85. Another HOKAN element, of more restricted distribution, is found in Santa Ynez and Santa Barbara (both Chumash) *sili-*, desiderative, and Esselen *čili-*, optative or imperative. These languages doubtless belong to the same subgroup of Hokan. They are included here for the benefit of those who still doubt the validity of a Hokan group.

86. Of the hortatives and imperatives in Amerind, to which we now turn, the first, *pV-*, might perhaps have been treated under inclusive pronouns. I believe, however, that its earliest meaning was the hortative 'let us . . . ,' which easily develops into an inclusive pronoun, dual or plural. Its wide distribution suggests that it is Proto-Amerind. In MACRO-GE, it appears in Ge proper, e.g. Kraho *pa-*, first-person dual inclusive possessive and verb subject, and in Bororo *pa-*, first-person plural inclusive. In MACRO-PANOAN, it occurs in Panoan proper, e.g. Chacobo *-pa*, polite imperative; Tacana *pa-*, optative; Lule *-pe*, plural imperative; and Vilela *pa-* 'let us . . . ,' *-p*, third-person hortative. In ANDEAN, we find it in Araucanian *-pe*, third-person hortative, and in Aymara *-pa-n*, third-person hortative (the *n-* here is an Andean third-person marker; see item 15). In Jaqaru, a language closely related to Aymara, there is *-pʰa*, third-person hortative. It also occurs in the Zaparoan subgroup, where we have Andoa *pa-*, first-person dual inclusive possessive, and Iquito *-pa*, first-person inclusive hortative. In CHIBCHAN-PAEZAN, Miskito (Misumalpan) *-pi*, first-person plural imperative may be compared to Chilanga (Lenca) *-bi*, first-person plural verb subject. Some instances of Chibchan *p* as a second-person plural imperative, listed in Chapter 2 as variants of *m* (see item 6), may actually belong here.

From the California branch of PENUTIAN, we may cite Maidu *pe*, exhortative, Patwin (Wintun) *bu*, first-person plural exhortative, and Miwok *pa-* "indirective" (i.e., to get someone else to do something). An exhortative *baʔ* occurs in Takelma, an Oregon Penutian language. In Yuki-Gulf, Muskogean in general has forms in *p* for the first-person plural, e.g. Hitchiti *pu-*, *po-*, first-person plural subject, *pu-*, first-person plural object; and Creek *po(-mi)* 'we' (cf. *či(-mi)* 'thou'). In KERESIOUAN, Keresan has a hortative *p-*, thus conforming to the general Amerind pattern. If Iroquoian, which has no labials, has undergone the change *p > kw*, as posited by Chafe, we may equate the *p* forms with the first-person plural pronouns of Northern Iroquoian languages, particularly Wyandot *kwa-*, first-person plural inclusive.

87. It is quite possible that Proto-Amerind, like so many other languages, used the verb stem as an imperative. A small number of imperative formations are found in individual subgroups. One instance occurs in CHIBCHAN-PAEZAN, where we find Warrau *-u*, second-person singular, Chibcha *-u*, second-person singular, and Paya *-u*, second-person singular (also used suppletively as second-person plural).

88. Another imperative formative occurs in HOKAN, where we have Yurumangui -*i*, Salinan -*i*-, Washo -*je*, Karok -*i*, and Yana -*ʔi*. Perhaps the Tonkawa hortatory enclitic *ʔe:* belongs here too.

89. Another HOKAN imperative, noted by Sapir (1917b), is represented by Subtiaba -*la*, -*l*; Esselen -*la*, which according to Kroeber (1904) is future or optative; Santa Barbara (Chumash) -*la*, andative imperative; and Tequistlatec -*laʔ*.

90. Also in HOKAN, Crawford (1976) notes the resemblance of the Seri imperative *ka*- to Yuman Cocopa *k*- and Mohave *k*-. With these we can compare Yurumangui *k*-, Salinan *k*-, and Washo *gə*-. In the Yahi dialect of Yana, there is -*ga*, but it is a suffix, not a prefix like the others.

91. Another set of imperatives occurs in KERESIOUAN. Wichita, a Caddoan language, prefixes *hi*-, *i*-, which is conditional when used with a subordinate and imperative elsewhere. In Keresan, *ʔi-ma* is an irregular imperative of the verb 'to come.' This form may be related to the *i*- of Northern Iroquoian, which does not have a specific imperative meaning and is prefixed only to a verb form that would be monosyllabic without it. Such monosyllables would be most frequently imperatives of verbs with monosyllabic roots, as in the Keresan example.

92. In considering derivational voice formation in the verb, we may note that it is common in languages for causatives to function also as both transitivizers and denominatives. ANDEAN examples are Yahgan *u:*-, *tu:*-, causative; Araucanian -*tu*-, denominative or causative reversive; and, in the Zaparoan group, Zaparo -*tə* and Shimigae -*te*, both causative. From the Almosan branch of ALMOSAN-KERESIOUAN, we have the Algic examples of Wiyot -*at*, transitivizer, Yurok -*et*, -*ət*, transitivizers (cf. Robins 1958: 32), as in *wejew*- 'be woven,' *wejewet*- 'to weave,' and Blackfoot (Algonquian) -*at*, transitivizer (Uhlenbeck 1938: 135–36). In Mosan, we have Kwakiutl (Wakashan) -*d*, a transitivizer after locative suffixes; Salish -*t*, transitivizer, and Kutenai -*ʔnt* 'action by hand' (in which, according to Boas, the -*t* is a transitivizer). In Keresan, there is a -*tu* that makes actions out of statives, e.g. *mʔeʔɛ:* 'be frozen,' *mʔe-tu* 'freeze.' In Iroquoian, Seneca has a causative -*ʔt*, -*st*; in the second form, the -*s* is probably also causative (see item 94).

93. A causative *m* occurs in two South American stocks. In MACRO-PANOAN, we find it in Panoan, e.g. Chacobo -*ma* and Cashibo -*mi*. In Tacanan, there are Tacana -*me* and Chama -*mee*. In Lengua, it is found in Mascoy -*me*. Chulupi, a Mataco language, has -*am*, -*em*, -*um*; and Lule has

a prefix *me-*. In EQUATORIAL, the causative *m-* is found throughout Tupian in the form *mbo-* ~ *mo-*. It occurs in some Arawakan languages as a suffix, e.g. Baure (Maipuran) *i* ~ *mo*, in which the choice is morphologically determined (on *i*, see item 12). Finally, Aguaruna, a language of the Jibaro group, has a verb *ma* ~ *m* 'to do,' which forms denominatives, e.g. *tumaš* 'a comb,' *tumaš-ma* 'to comb.'

94. In ALMOSAN-KERESIOUAN, a causative *-s* is found in Salish, Quileute, and Wiyot. These are all Almosan languages. In addition, in Northern Iroquoian the Seneca suffix *-st* seems to show the fusion of two causative elements, a not uncommon development (see item 92). Since *-s* also occurs as a third-person singular pronoun in Almosan-Keresiouan—including Salish and Quileute—the causative in those two languages may in fact have originated from the pronoun by the process described in items 12 for *i* and 14 for *m*.

95. A causative *-n* is found in PENUTIAN. Examples are Miwok (California) *-ne*, Takelma (Oregon) *-(a)n*, and Tsimshian *-ǝn*.

It has been seen that one source of transitivizers and causatives is a third-person object pronoun. Another is verbs with the general meaning 'make, work, do.' Examples are given in the etymologies in Chapters 3 and 4 (see, for instance, the Chibchan entries for WORK$_1$ in the Amerind dictionary).

96. In MACRO-PANOAN, Lule *-ki* is intransitive and reflexive. This can be compared with Chacobo *-ki*, intransitivizer, and Cashibo *-aka*, reflexive; both are in the Panoan subgroup.

97. In ANDEAN, Yahgan *mu-* for the reflexive is probably cognate with Araucanian *-m* for the passive and *-am* for the impersonal.

98. In MACRO-CARIB, there is a common Carib root that takes two forms. Chayma, Cumanogoto *wače*, and Kaliana *vase* represent one, and Chayma, Cumanogoto, Macusi *weči*, Accawai *weiǰi* represent the other. Although in both cases the basic meaning is 'to be,' the first variants are also used as auxiliaries to form the present, and the second ones, for the past. (For further discussion, see Goeje 1946: 24.) There is a striking agreement here with Yameo, a language of the Yagua subgroup of Macro-Carib, which suffixes *-weša* to form a past tense.

99. In a number of HOKAN languages, there is a contrast between *m* 'direction toward' and *k* 'direction away.' The first might have been included in the Amerind dictionary under GO$_1$, its usual meaning, but in a few lan-

guages it means 'come.' Likewise, the *k* could have been entered under GO$_4$. Both are included here because in Hokan they often form a contrasting pair and because their usage is wider than 'go to . . .' and 'come from . . .' as grammaticized components of the verb complex to express direction of action. In Chimariko, there is a direct contrast between *ho-am-ta* 'go' and *hu-ak-ta* 'come.' Crawford (1976: 308) compares, under the entry 'away,' Yuman *-m* with Washo *imiʔ, imi, im* 'out, out from.' In Yana, *-ma-* means 'there, from there,' and *-ki* 'hither.' In Karok, there is an adverb *k-uːk* 'hither,' contrasting with *m-uːk* 'by means of.' (The close relation between place and instrument was discussed in item 47.) In Shasta, *-k-* indicates motion toward, and *-m-* motion from; Atsugewi has *-k-* for motion toward but apparently lacks the *-m-*. In Achomawi, we have the full contrast: *-m-* is action away from and *-g-* is action toward. In the Coahuiltecan group, *-m* occurs as a suffix on verbs indicating action away, e.g. Coahuilteco *pepola-m* 'pour out,' *pexpola-m* 'throw into water,' *aiwama-m* 'I go there' (note also *wam-kiu* 'I come from,' and compare with both the Quinigua verb *wame* 'go').

We now come to negation and interrogation, items of wider, often sentential scope, although they may be syntactically or morphologically connected with the verb.

100. A negative with *k* is found in three Amerind subgroups. In MACRO-GE, we have Cayapo (Ge) *ked*, Bororo *ka*, Caraja *ko, koŋ*, Guato *egu*, and Kamacan *ki*. In CENTRAL AMERIND, we may cite Proto-Uto-Aztecan **ka, *kai* (Miller no. 306), and Proto-Oto-Mangue **ku* (Rensch no. 136). In HOKAN, we find Yurumangui *k-, ka-;* Jicaque *kua;* Cocopa (Yuman) *k-*, a privative, as in *k-maːm* 'blind'; Salinan *k* + possessive marker + verb; East Pomo *kuji* 'no,' *kʰu* 'not'; Yana *kuu-;* Karok *-k;* and in the Coahuiltecan subgroup, Coahuilteco *axam* 'not,' Comecrudo *kam* 'not,' and Karankawa *kom* 'not.'

101. An *m* negative is found in MACRO-PANOAN. In Panoan we have Chacobo and Cashibo *ma;* and in Tacanan we find Tacana *-ama* 'without' and Chama *-ama* ~ *-ma* 'without.' Examples from other Macro-Panoan families are Vilela *ama-dubbe, ama-rop, ama-dop* 'there is not'; Lengua: Mascoy *mo;* Mataco: Chulupi *ampa* 'there is not' (*pa* is a demonstrative and article).

102. There are two common interrogatives in Amerind. The first usually has an initial *k-*, as the following examples indicate. In ANDEAN, we find Yahgan *kunna* 'who?,' *kana* 'where?'; Tehuelche (Patagon) *keme*

'who?,' *kenaš* 'when?,' *kienai* 'where?'; Araucanian *kam* 'how?'; Aymara *kuna* 'what?,' *kamisa* 'how?'; and Iquito (Zaparoan) *kanə:ka* 'who?' In CHIBCHAN-PAEZAN, Totoro, of the Paez subgroup, has *kin* 'who?' and Paez proper has *kīh* 'what?' Catio, a Choco language, has *kai*. In HOKAN, Yurumangui has *ku* 'where?'; Seri *kiʔ* 'who?'; Tlappanec *gwana* 'when?'; Walapai (Yuman) *ka* 'who?'; and Santa Barbara (Chumash) *kenu* 'why?' In the Pomo subgroup, we find North Pomo *kʾo* 'what?,' Central Pomo *kʾowa* 'what?,' and East Pomo *kia* 'who?' Other Hokan examples are Shasta *kura* 'where?,' Achomawi *ki:* 'who?,' and Coahuilteco *ka* 'who?' Finally, in PENUTIAN, we find Klamath (Plateau) *ka* 'who?,' Alsea (Oregon) *qau* 'who?,' Tsimshian *gu* 'who?,' and Tunica (Yuki-Gulf) *ka-ku* 'who?' (and *ka-* in other interrogatives).

103. The second commonly found interrogative is illustrated in the following examples. In MACRO-GE, it is found in Krenje (Ge) *menɔ* 'who?' and Botocudo *mina* 'who?' EQUATORIAL examples are Guayaki *ma, mae* 'what?, how?,' Guaraní *mbaʔe* 'who?,' Guajajara *mɔn* 'who?,' and Uruku *mome* 'where is?' (all Tupi languages); Toyeri (Maipuran) *me-jo* 'where?'; and Cofan *ma-ñi* 'where?' Saliba (Piaroa) has interrogatives in *uma-, eme-*, e.g. *ume-kena* 'when?' Also in Equatorial are Maripu (Timote) *manub* 'in which direction,' Yuracare *ama-se* 'whence?,' and Kandoshi *maja* 'what?' In CHIBCHAN-PAEZAN, the Paezan branch has Paez *maneh* 'when?,' *manzos* 'how often?'; Guambiana *mu* 'who?'; Cayapa (Barbacoa) *maa, muŋ* 'who' and Colorado (also Barbacoa) *mo, moa* 'who?'; Allentiac *mem, men* 'who?'; and Catio (Choco) *mai* 'where?' In Chibchan, we find Kagaba (Aruak) *mai* 'who?,' *mani* 'where?,' and Matagalpa (Misumalpan) *man* 'where?' For PENUTIAN, we can cite, in California Penutian, Central Sierra Miwok *mitan* 'when?,' *minni* 'who?,' San José (Costanoan) *mani* 'where?,' and Patwin (Wintun) *mena* 'where?' Plateau has North Sahaptin *me:n, mna* 'where?,' and Oregon, Siuslaw *minč* 'when?' and Alsea *mis* 'when?' In Yuki-Gulf, we find two Muskogean examples: Choctaw *mana, mat* 'when?' and Chickasaw *mano* 'where?' Many of the words cited above contain a locative *n* (see item 47).

104. The following interrogative is apparently restricted to MACRO-CARIB. In the Carib languages, we have Macusi *onoŋ* 'which?,' *ane* 'who?,' and Surinam *iine* 'which?'; in the Uitoto group, Uitoto *nine* 'where?' and Muinane *nino* 'where?,' *nirui* 'why?,' *nə* 'what?'; in Yagua, Yameo *na* 'who?,' *nen, nun* 'what?'; and in Bora, Miranya *ine* 'what?'

105. Of even more restricted distribution is the following interroga-

tive, apparently limited to the Chibchan branch of CHIBCHAN-PAEZAN: Chibcha *fi(-kwa)* 'how many?'; Cuna *pii(-kwa)* (on *-kwa*, see item 40), *pia* 'where?'; Bribri (Talamanca) *bi-k* 'how many?'; Paya *pia* 'which?, where?'

106. In PENUTIAN, we find the following interrogative. In California Penutian, Central Sierra Miwok has *tinnə* 'what?' In Plateau, we find North Sahaptin *tunn* 'what?' and Nez Perce *ʔitu* 'what?' In Oregon, there is Siuslaw *tɔn* 'what?' We also have Chinook *tan* 'what?'; and, in Mexican Penutian, Totonac *tu* 'what?,' Mam (Mayan) *titi* 'what?,' and Zoque (Mixe-Zoque) *tija* 'what?'

107. Finally, we consider a system that does not easily lend itself to categorization. Containing three members in its fullest form, it is found in a number of ALMOSAN-KERESIOUAN languages. It occurs in the most complete form (or at least has been most fully described) in Quileute, a member of the Chemakuan branch of Mosan (Andrade 1933: especially pp. 180ff and pp. 219ff, to which the reader is referred for a full discussion). Andrade identifies two sets of three elements, which he calls "formal bases" and "applicative classifiers," with obvious phonetic and semantic similarities.

The formal bases are *aʔ-*, *he-*, and *o-*. They are always initial and occur on both nouns and verbs. Every noun with a postpositive morpheme must begin with one of the three. By a postpositive morpheme is meant one that can never be initial and might indeed be called a suffix except that it usually has a quite concrete meaning. Such postpositives are a feature of a number of languages in the area and may exist by the side of free forms with the same meaning. A Quileute example is *-disčʔ-* 'hat,' always bound and often part of a large complex. The form *tsʔigapus* is a free morpheme meaning 'hat,' but we also find *o:-disčʔ-it*, in which the postpositive base is preceded by a formal base and followed by *-it*, a common noun formant.

With regard to the meaning of the formal bases, *o-* refers to objects or actions that can be confined to more or less definite places; hence almost all body parts begin with this form. The second, *he-*, involves actions directed toward specific objects, and when used with nouns usually forms terms for artifacts with a specific purpose, e.g. *he-ʔčʔexat* 'fishing line.' The *aʔ-* base is the most vague and is the unmarked member, used whenever neither of the other two is appropriate.

The applicative classifiers are *-a*, *-i*, and *-o*. They are suffixed to verb stems and are always followed by other inflectional elements. Every verb must have one of these classifiers; hence they divide verbs into three classes.

The -o is affixed when an action is applied to a definite location or to a particular part or portion of an object. The -i denotes an action directed toward a specific person or object rather than at a particular point in space. The -a is unmarked and tends to be durative. Andrade also points to the existence of a Quileute verb o- 'to be in a place.'

In Kwakiutl, of the Wakashan subgroup of Mosan, there is a clear use of o- to mark location in the contrast between -xsd- 'behind, tail end,' which occurs as a bound form in compounds and elsewhere, and the noun o:-xsde? 'the hind end' (cf. also o?jo: 'the middle'). This construction is obviously similar to that of Quileute. In Salish, the third branch of Mosan, Squamish has a rare prefix ?i-, with three stems in p, whose meaning can reasonably be described as instrumental, e.g. 'hold something (in the hand, by means of the hand)' (Kuipers 1967: 118).

Moving to the Algic branch of Almosan, we find in Yurok a set of three preverbal particles, ?o, ni, and ?i, whose scope appears to be sentential (Robins 1958: 102). It appears that Yurok ?o corresponds to Quileute -o, and Yurok ?i to Quileute -i. Robins describes the Yurok preverbal particles as being basically locative but having a number of metaphorical uses. Many of his examples suggest that ?o is generally restricted to expressing location within something, e.g. 'there is a lot of dust in the house,' 'I hid the door in the forest.' The ?i seems more indefinite in location, e.g. 'I saw it rolling about there.' In Cheyenne, often considered to be a genetically distant branch of Algonquian, there is an o- prefixed to verbs. For example, when prefixed to the verb meaning 'to eat' it is translated as 'the eating, when there is eating.' The last example is from Petter (1952).

Various aspects of the system we have been describing are found in the Keresiouan subgroups Keresan, Iroquoian, Siouan, and Yuchi. In Santa Ana Keresan, there is a prefix ?u- that derives nouns from verbs, but sometimes occurs without a corresponding verb. Since Santa Ana has no o, u is a reasonable phonetic correspondence. This ?u is accompanied by one of a set of noun-forming suffixes. Although according to Davis (1979), it forms action nouns, as is usual with such nominal derivatives, many of the meanings are place or instrument, often ambiguously either. Examples that indicate primarily place are ?ugujani 'seat' (cf. -guja 'to sit') and ?u:bajani 'fire place' (cf. -baja 'light a fire'). In addition, every Santa Ana verb has, after the pronominal prefixes of subject and/or object, a "thematic prefix," a, i, or u. These phonetically match the applicative classifiers of Quileute -a, -i, and -o. Their meanings are so vague that Davis does not attempt to characterize them, but there is at least one contrast—*i-ka* 'to look' versus *u-ka-ča* 'to see something'—in which *i-* matches rather well Andrade's characterization of Quileute *i-* as locationally vague as against *o-* "applied to a definite location." Even more striking is the Keresan verb *ʔu* 'to dwell,' which corresponds to Quileute *o* 'to be in a place,' mentioned earlier.

In Northern Iroquoian languages, the verb stems are preceded by vocalic elements on the basis of which Barbeau (Wyandot), and Boas (Oneida), among others, have classified the verbs into conjugations. In contrast to Keresan and Quileute, however, Iroquoian languages have four affixes: *a, i, e* or *ē,* and *o* or *ō.* Once more they are so highly lexicalized that no attempt is made to specify their meaning and in Chafe's grammar of Seneca (1963), they are included in the stem. A closer lexical study might show correlations of meaning with the other languages mentioned. It is, however, striking that we once more have a set of vowels that are clearly, from a historical point of view, not part of the stem.

There is also a parallel between the Iroquoian noun and the initial *o* of Quileute and *ʔu* of Santa Ana. A prefix *ʔo* occurs with many stems (for Seneca, see Chafe 1963: 18). In form, it is a neuter object prefix, but it gives the noun specific meaning, e.g. *kasnɔ́* 'bark,' *ʔosnɔ́* 'the bark.' For a number of stems, this is the only form that occurs, e.g. *ʔonḗɔ̃́ʔ* 'corn.' The most remarkable agreement with Quileute is in its well-known occurrence in place names. Numerous examples may be found in Beauchamp (1906), a work on aboriginal place names of New York, e.g. *o-quaʔ-ga* 'the place of hulled corn soup' (p. 28), *o-noγ-sa-daʔ-go* 'where buried things are dug up' (p. 32), *on-o-wa-da-geγ* 'white clay' or 'muddy place' (p. 53), *o-gahʔ-gwaahʔ-geh* 'residence of the sunfish' (p. 66).

An even more striking case of parallelism occurs in Siouan languages. In Mandan, Kennard (1936: 15) describes *o-* as a general locative and nominalizer. With certain verbs of motion, it indicates the place where the action took place, e.g. *o-ni* 'footprint' (= 'where he walked'). In Dorsey and Swanton (1912: 68), we find Biloxi *o-, u-* defined as "a prefix indicating that the action is performed inside of a given area." In Crow, according to Lowie (1941: 9), *i:-* prefixed to verbs indicates instrument, e.g. *i:-o:xaxuk* 'by it they pierced it.' The nouns are then indicated by separate words, e.g. 'knee,' 'arrow,' meaning 'they pierced his knee with an arrow.' In Dakota, *a-* prefixed to verbs expresses action on, *o-* an action inside, and *i-* an action with some definite object in view, often an instrument. In addition, the Dakota prefix *o-* on a noun is a definitizer. Williamson (1902: vii) reports that "*o* prefixed to a verb makes it a verbal noun with about the same effect as prefixing the definite article in English." This closely parallels what Chafe says about Seneca *ʔo*. In Winnebago, these same elements occur with an initial *h-*, i.e. *ha* 'on,' *hi* 'with, by means of,' *ho* 'in.' It will be recalled that the Quileute formal bases, which function as prefixes, are *aʔ, he, o*. It is easy to see how by analogical change the *h* would be lost. Evidently in Winnebago, analogy has worked in the other direction, with all having *h-*. The correspondence between such closely related languages as Dakota and Winnebago is so clear that they must have a common origin, and Quileute gives a starting point for the Winnebago *h-* forms.

The interrelatedness of these systems is confirmed by the evidence of Yuchi, the language generally considered to be genetically closest to Siouan. Here we have as verb prefixes *hi-*, instrumental (cf. Quileute *he*) and *a-* for a static location. Moreover, Yuchi has two sets of subject pronouns, usually marked by vowel differences, e.g. *d-i-*, *d-o-*, for the first-person singular. Wagner (1934: 328) gives the example *d-i-adɛ* 'I hunt (with no definite aim in mind),' *d-o-adɛ* 'I hunt (for a certain animal).' Here the resemblance to the Santa Ana Keresan example with *i-* 'to look (in general)' versus *u-* 'to see something' is quite exact.

The network of agreements sketched in this section clearly cannot have resulted from a series of accidents. It may be conjectured that fuller investigation will reveal still other points of contact among Almosan-Keresiouan languages.

Chapter 6

The Na-Dene Problem

What is here called the Na-Dene problem is the question of whether Haida, clearly the most distant from the other languages of the group, belongs to the Na-Dene family at all. Within the family as traditionally formulated, the subgroups are clear; Eyak, Tlingit, and Haida are progressively more remote from the Athabaskan group, which contains such languages as Apache, Navajo, Tanaina, and Chipewyan:

I   HAIDA: Haida
II CONTINENTAL NA-DENE
   A TLINGIT: Tlingit
   B ATHABASKAN-EYAK
      1 EYAK: Eyak
      2 ATHABASKAN: Apache, Navajo, etc.

In an important paper published in 1915, Sapir, taking up the suggestions of Boas and others,* presented systematic evidence that Haida is a member of the Na-Dene family. In recent years, however, doubts about this connection have grown. Robert Levine, in a detailed examination of Sapir's paper, has sought to refute the affiliation of Haida with Na-Dene (1979). This refutation has apparently been generally accepted by specialists in these languages, except probably Heinz-Jürgen Pinnow. Michael Krauss, whose leading position in the field is based on extensive contributions, has accepted it as final: "We owe it to Levine in a recent paper for debunking once and for all the claim that Haida has been demonstrated to be genetically related to Tlingit" (1979: 841).

*For a discussion of the early history of the Na-Dene hypothesis, see Krauss (1964).

Levine's paper is addressed specifically to Sapir's evidence, both grammatical and lexical. The lexical evidence consists of 98 etymologies involving either Athabaskan and Tlingit, Athabaskan and Haida, or all three. It should be noted that Sapir's presentation not only omits Eyak, for which little evidence was then available, but presents only etymologies in which Athabaskan figures. Hence any important resemblances between Tlingit and Haida, to the exclusion of Athabaskan, would not appear in Sapir's etymologies.

Pinnow (1966) is the only other systematic source for Na-Dene etymologies. Although his book includes Eyak data, it presents only etymologies involving Tlingit. As a result, any etymologies that involve Eyak and Haida alone will not be found in either source.

Even overlooking Pinnow's etymological work and the new linguistic data that have been accumulated since Sapir wrote his paper, it must be acknowledged that Sapir did not present all of the evidence available in his day. Still, let us see how his evidence fares in the face of Levine's attack.

Of Sapir's 98 etymologies, 38 exclude Haida, that is, they compare only Athabaskan and Tlingit and hence are irrelevant to this discussion. (Levine's count of 39 seems to be in error.) This leaves us with 60 comparisons that include Haida, of which 30 are between Haida and Athabaskan only and 30 involve all three languages. I do not wish to reproduce the entire Sapir list here since his publication is readily available. But as a guide to the following discussion, I will give Sapir's numbers for the comparisons involving Haida. Those involving Athabaskan and Haida only are 3, 7, 9, 13, 14, 15, 16, 17, 21, 23, 28, 29, 34, 37, 38, 41, 42, 44, 50, 53, 61, 67, 70, 73, 77, 80, 83, 84, 87, and 96. Those involving all three languages are 1, 4, 5, 10, 11, 12, 18, 19, 22, 25, 31, 33, 40, 45, 48, 51, 59, 60, 62, 64, 65, 68, 69, 74, 78, 82, 89, 93, 95, and 98.

Levine adduces eight reasons for rejecting an etymology. Unfortunately, he does not identify by Sapir's numbers those he rejects on the first of his criteria, the most important one, since it involves the largest number of disallowed items. He merely gives the overall total, and I have therefore had to make my own judgments, which in a few cases may disagree with his.

The first reason that Levine gives for rejecting etymologies is the following. Sapir assumed a basic consonant-vowel (CV) structure for the root in Na-Dene and believed the final consonants that sometimes appear to be ancient affixes whose meaning cannot be recovered. He therefore included $CV:CVC$ comparisons as well as $CVC_1:CVC_2$ sets. Levine rejects etymologies based on this assumption, which would increase our chances of accepting accidental resemblances as true cognates. Within Athabaskan, however, there is a great deal of variation in final consonants. Those of the prefixes also often involve different and varying reflexes. Indeed, only stem-initial consonants have been reconstructed by Hoijer and Krauss; the final consonants of Athabaskan stems have never been reconstructed. Regarding vowels, Hoijer (1960: 963) states: "Vowels have been little studied comparatively, but it is evident that the development of these sounds is completely variable, even between languages otherwise very much alike."

Hence it does not seem reasonable to reject all etymologies involving variability in final consonants. Probably a number of these are valid and a number are not, but perhaps we cannot tell which are correct. At any rate, Levine eliminates 13 unspecified comparisons involving Haida on that criterion. In fact I was hard put to discover 13 examples conforming to the first criterion. I assume these to be 17, 42, 50, 53, 59, 61, 62, 64, 69, 70, 74, 77, and 84. Eight of these (17, 42, 50, 53, 61, 70, 77, and 84) involve only Athabaskan and Haida (AH), and the other five (59, 62, 64, 69, and 74) involve Athabaskan, Tlingit, and Haida (ATH).*

Levine's second criterion for rejection is what he calls "overresemblance": because the languages are so remotely related, and cognates so few, he is highly suspicious of pairs that are too similar. But in my experience, even languages that are very distantly related are sure to have very close resemblances in a few instances, either because of sounds that have been conservative or because of parallel sound changes of certain very common and expected sorts. Thus between contemporary English and Hittite,[†] two distant Indo-European cousins, we find the following: English 'water' = Hittite *watar*; English 'up' = Hittite *up-*, a verb meaning 'to raise'; and English 'eat' = Hittite *et-*. All are accepted cognates. At any rate, Levine eliminates six etymologies whose members evince a pronounced similarity. Of these, numbers 80 and 83 are AH and 11, 33, 59, and 78, ATH. I have assumed above that number 59 was excluded in the first group because of the difference in final consonants between Haida *sil* 'to steam' and Tlingit *si:t*

---

*Because Levine does not begin numbering his rejection criteria until his second (which he therefore calls his first), my numbers for his criteria will be one greater than his; for example, what I refer to as Levine's fifth category he calls his fourth.

[†]Hittite is so different from the rest of Indo-European that some linguists have made it a separate branch coordinate with the rest of the family. This is the so-called Indo-Hittite hypothesis, which is no longer in general favor but still has a few adherents (e.g. Edgar Sturtevant, Warren Cowgill). On balance, I believe it is probably correct.

'to cook.' It is included in the second group because of its identity with Athabaskan *sil* 'steam,' *-sil* 'to steam.'

Next Levine eliminates six etymologies simply because changed ideas about Athabaskan reconstruction have destroyed their validity. These are Sapir's 38 and 80 (AH) and 4, 19, 25, and 69 (ATH). Of these, 69 was previously eliminated under the first criterion, and 80 under the second. He then eliminates two others, 73 (AH) and 74 (ATH), on the grounds of changes in Sapir's own thinking about Na-Dene reconstruction. I have already assumed 74 to be eliminated under the first criterion.

The fifth (Levine's fourth) ground for eliminating etymologies is unique correspondences, found in 44 and 73 (AH) and 45 and 59 (ATH). Of these, 59 has already been eliminated twice, and 73 was eliminated under the previous criterion. The rejection here of number 59 (the word for 'steam') strengthens the case for its rejection under the first criterion. But in Chapter 1 I have given reasons for retaining cognates involving unique correspondences if they are strong on other grounds. One of the above, number 45, involves Athabaskan *m*, Haida *w*, and Tlingit *w*. In Krauss's reconstruction of Athabaskan (1964), **w* replaces Sapir's, and later Hoijer's, **m*. The consonants thus become identical. It is always a good sign if reconstruction makes forms converge backward in time toward greater resemblance.

The sixth basis for rejection is what Levine calls "serious misanalysis of grammatical forms." In this category, for the first time he rejects numbers 3 and 16 (AH) and 98 (ATH). The seventh criterion (Levine's sixth), "incorrect gloss," involves a single item, number 69 (already eliminated under the first and third criteria). Here Levine contends that the Haida form Sapir glosses as 'back of' really appears to mean 'downward motion.' This could easily be glossed as 'under' in English, as in "He put it under the table." The Athabaskan forms are *t'a* 'tail' and *t'a-ŋ* 'backward,' and Tlingit has *t'a* 'behind.' Actually, even if the original translation of the Haida item is wrong, 'behind' and 'under' can reasonably be seen as related, as in the two vulgar English words for 'buttocks,' 'bottom' and 'behind,' and more elegantly in Latin, in Martial 8.26.7, *cum captivos ageret sub curribus Indos.* Here, though the Latin word *sub* usually means 'underneath,' the reading is 'behind': "when he drags the captive Indians behind the chariots."

The eighth, and last, of Levine's reasons is unreported correspondences, that is, correspondences Sapir either did not list (11 and 15) or incorrectly transcribed (25). "These additional correspondences erode the apparent simplicity of the relations between Na-Dene vowels as Sapir presents them" (Levine 1979: 164). Of these etymologies, 15 is AH; 11 and 25 (also eliminated by Levine's first and third criteria, respectively) are ATH.

Let us assume that all Levine's eliminations are correct. It apparently never occurred to him or to those who have accepted his results to ask what etymologies remain, and what this group signifies. Those who have kept score during the foregoing discussion realize that of the 30 Athabaskan-Haida comparisons, 14 still stand, namely, 7, 9, 13, 14, 21, 23, 28, 29, 34, 37, 41, 67, 87, and 96. Among three-way comparisons, 17 of 30 survive all attacks. Of these, 1, 5, 10, 12, 18, 22, 31, 40, 48, 51, 60, 65, 68, 82, 89, 93, and 95 are also found in Eyak, so that there is four-way agreement. This fact is particularly significant, as has been shown in the explanation of methodology (Chapter 1). That there should be a number of resemblances between two languages A and B and other resemblances between B and C might be dismissed as a proof of relationship among the three, but that the resemblances should so often be the same cannot be so easily shrugged off. We have here once again the multiplication of probabilities.

The significance of 17 three-way resemblances can be put into perspective by a comparison with a linguistic family about which there is no reasonable doubt, namely, Indo-European. In one respect, of course, the odds greatly favor Indo-European: in contrast to Na-Dene, with its handful of specialists, Indo-European has been studied intensively for more than a century by a substantial portion of the linguistic community. As a consequence, we have a comparative dictionary for every branch of Indo-European, but no such dictionary exists for Athabaskan.

Let us take Albanian and Armenian as instances of two isolated Indo-European languages comparable to Tlingit and Haida, and Celtic as a group with a fairly large number of distinct languages comparable to Athabaskan. Celtic probably has greater internal differentiation than Athabaskan; moreover, I have accepted occurrence in any Celtic language, ancient or modern, as sufficient for inclusion in the following study. Except where otherwise indicated, the Celtic citation is from Old Irish, by far the best-known early form and in fact the earliest attested.

Using the standard Indo-European comparative dictionary of Walde and Pokorny (1927), arranged by Indo-European roots, I began this study by looking up every Albanian item listed in the index. Then when I found, for instance, Albanian birë 'mouth' under the Indo-European root bher (3), I searched the rest of the bher (3) section to see if there were both Armenian and Celtic entries. By this procedure, I found the 37 etymologies listed in

Table 10. In the table, Walde-Pokorny's phonetic transcriptions of Albanian are replaced with present-day standard orthography based on the literary language—the southern dialect, Tosk, though where relevant a few Gheg (northern dialect) forms are cited. The Armenian cited is Classical Armenian, which is based on documents that go back as far as 15 centuries. Armenian has two *l* sounds; the barred form, *ł*, was probably velar or velarized and has become a voiced velar fricative in the modern language. Albanian likewise has two *l* sounds, *l* having a palatal quality and *ll* a velar quality. Both languages also have two *r* sounds, a tapped sound, transcribed as *r* in both languages, and a rolled sound, transcribed as *ř* in Armenian and as *rr* in Albanian. Finally, Armenian and Celtic verb forms are cited in the first-person singular of the present indicative, which usually ends in -*Vm* in both languages.

Let us apply some of Levine's criteria to these 37 etymologies and see which will survive the test. Under his first rubric, Levine eliminated all instances in which a CV form in one language is compared with a CVC form in another, or a CVC_1 form with a CVC_2. Most Indo-European roots, however, are CVC or CCVC, with certain limited initial clusters. Indo-Europeanists universally allow certain extensions called *root determinatives*, which are additional consonants whose meaning cannot be determined. These often differ from language to language, and certain roots have a fairly large number of such additions. In fact, one eminent Indo-Europeanist, Émile Benveniste, has developed a theory of the Indo-European root on this basis, reducing all roots to the pattern CVC. In addition, many roots appear sporadically with or without a prefixed *s-*, the so-called *s*-movable.

Since the probability of purely accidental resemblance is much greater when we compare CV with CVC, or CVC_1 with CVC_2, I have allowed as legitimate all instances in which there are at least two consonants in common. Thus Walde-Pokorny's comparison of an Albanian form *sqVl* and an Armenian form *qVl* + *k* is allowed because they have two consonants (*q* and *l*) in common. This is obviously more than fair to Levine.

I have not used semantic criteria to eliminate cognates, as Levine does, because they are rather vague. Still, mutatis mutandis, Levine would surely reject, on semantic grounds, the relationship of Armenian 'far' with Celtic 'in front of, for' and a few other comparisons that I have allowed. So two criteria for eliminating cognates, derived from Levine with the modifications specified above, are being applied: (1) only one consonant reconstructed as the same and (2) unique correspondences.

Note that Levine's requirement that all correspondences be recurrent, that is, occur in two or more etymologies, has a chain effect. If an etymology is rejected because it contains a non-recurrent correspondence, then any other correspondence found in the same word will be irrelevant, since it occurs in an invalid etymology. In applying this test, where there is agreement in only two of the three consonants, I have considered only those two. In number 16, for example, only the correspondences for *q* and *l* are considered. Further, I have disregarded vowels. Proto-Indo-European's intricate system of morphologically and phonologically conditioned vowel alternations, *Ablaut,* causes complications. Often one language has generalized one vowel of a given alternation by analogy, while another language has generalized a different vowel. Later changes have further obscured the correspondences. In addition, I have treated the two *l* sounds of Albanian and Armenian as equivalent, and likewise the two *r* sounds, since in each case they have arisen from a single origin by internal changes.

Only a half dozen etymologies survive this test: 1, 2, 3, 18, 22, and 23 (disregarding the *j* in Albanian *mjal*). To discuss all 37 etymologies, and the reasons for their general acceptance by Indo-Europeanists, would be interesting but would take us too far from the point.

Many of the Indo-European reconstructions, it will be noted, have alternative forms. This is because they seem to go back to highly similar, but not identical, originals. An example is number 21, in which the Proto-Indo-European form has an *h* in parentheses. The reason for this is that Sanskrit *mahant-* 'large' would require an aspirate, which is not found in Greek *megas* 'large' or elsewhere. In other instances, in forms with initial vowels, Armenian sometimes has *h* (as in number 10, *hum* 'raw'), sometimes nothing (as in 22, *amb*). With the development of laryngeal theory, William Austin (1942) sought to explain the initial h in Armenian as a survival of one of the ancestral laryngeals. We see, then, that such instances are treated by Indo-Europeanists not as etymologies—much less relationships—to be rejected, but as problems to be solved.

In this chapter, only lexical evidence has been discussed, since I believe this to be sufficient. If there were only three branches of Indo-European, and these were known only in their modern forms (Old Armenian and Old Irish have been used here), some linguists might speak of an Indo-European problem as they do a Na-Dene problem. In spite of all the talk of "phylum linguistics," the two main branches of Na-Dene are no more distant from each other than the branches of Indo-European are from one another. I do not say

Table 10. Albanian-Armenian-Celtic Cognates and Their Proto-Indo-European Roots

Albanian	Armenian	Celtic	Proto-Indo-European
1 *ballë* 'forehead'; *balash* 'horse with white spot on forehead'	*bal* 'white spot on a horse's forehead'	*ball* 'spot'	*bhel (1)*
2 *barrë* 'load'	*ber-em* 'carry'	*bir-u* 'carry'	*bher*
3 *birë* 'hole'	*beran* 'mouth'	*bern* 'hole' (MI)	*bher (3)*
4 *dhi* 'goat'	*ezn* 'ox'	*ag* 'cow'	*ago-*
5 *dhjetë* 'ten'	*tasn* 'ten'	*deich* 'ten'	*dek^{ʷ}m̥*
6 *djalë* 'child'	*dalar* 'green, fresh'	*dail* 'leaf' (W)	*dhāl, dhel?*
7 *dorë* 'hand'	*dzeṙn* 'arm'	*gort* 'cornfield'; *gorz* (B) 'hedge, fence'	*gher (4)*
8 *dru* 'tree'	*tram* 'firm'	*derucc* 'acorn'	*derew(o)-*
9 *du* 'two'	*erku* 'two'	*dau* 'two'	*dwōu*
10 *ëmblë* 'sweet'; *t-ëmblë* 'gall'	*hum* 'raw'	*om* 'raw'	*omo*
11 *emër* 'name'; *emën* (Gheg) 'name'	*anun* 'name'	*ain m-* 'name' [a]	*en(o)men-, (o)nomen, nōmen-, $_c$n$_{(o)}$men-*
12 *gjanj* 'hunt, pursue'	*gan* 'blows, stick'	*gon-im* 'wound, kill'	*g^{ʷ}hen*
13 *gjashtë* 'six'	*vets'* 'six'	*sē* 'six'; *chwech* (W) 'six'	*s(u)ek^{ˠ}s, ᵕek^{ˠ}s*
14 *gjerb* 'sip'	*arbi* 'drink'	*srub* 'snout' (MI)	*srebh*
15 *gjumë* 'sleep' (n.)	*k'un* 'sleep' (n.)	*suan* 'sleep' (n.)	*suepno-*
16 *halë* 'fishbone, pine needle, splinter, awn'	*č'elk'-em* 'split'	*scailim* 'release, destroy, dismantle' (MI)	*(s)qel*
17 *harr* 'weed out, prune'	*k'or-em* 'scratch'	*scaraim* 'separate'	*(s)ǩer*
18 *im* 'my'; *mua* 'I'	*im* 'my'	*mē* 'me'	*me-*
19 *lig* 'bad'	*atkat* 'poor, few'	*liach* 'miserable, unfortunate'	*leig, leiq*
20 *llërë* 'forearm'	*otn* 'forearm'	*elin* 'elbow' (W)	*o-lina*
21 *madh* 'good'	*mets* 'large'	*mag-* 'large' (MI; in compounds)	*meg^ˠ(h)*
22 *mbi, mbë* 'near, on'	*amb-* 'about' (in compounds)	*ambi-* 'around' (G)	*ambhi, m̥bhi*
23 *mjal* 'honey'	*meḷr* 'honey'	*mil* 'honey'	*melit*
24 *motër* 'sister'	*mayr* 'mother'	*mathir* 'mother'	*māter*
25 *për* 'for, about, on, by, because of'	*heri* 'far' (< *per-o* 'on the other side')	**eri* 'in front of, for' (Proto-Celtic)	*per-*
26 *plot* 'full'	*li* 'full'	*lia* 'more'	*plē-*
27 *qeth* 'cut hair, shear'	*k'er'-em* 'take off, skin, peel'	*scrissid* 'scraper, graving tool'	*sk^{ˠ}ere-t*
28 *quanj* 'to name'; *quh-em* 'be called'	*lu* 'informed'	*cloth* 'fame'	*k^{ˠ}leu*
29 *shatë* 'seven'	*evt'n* 'seven'	*secht n-* 'seven' [a]	*septm̥*

30 *(kä)-ta* 'these'	*-d* 'the'	*(ua)-d* '(from) it'	*to-, ta*
31 *ti* 'thou'	*du* 'thou'	*tü* 'thou'	*tü*
32 *tre* 'three'	*ere-k* 'three'	*tri* 'three'	*trei*
33 *verrë* 'alder tree'	*geran* 'log, beam'	*gwern* 'alder, mast'	*wer-nā*
34 *vjehërr* 'father-in-law'	*skesur* 'father-in-law'	*chwegr* 'father-in-law' (w)	*swekʷuro-*
35 *vjell* 'vomit'	*gel-um* 'turn'	*fill-im* 'bend'	*wel*
36 *zjarr* 'fire, heat'	*jer* 'warmth'	*grith* 'sun, heat' (MI)	*gʷʰher-*
37 *zonjë* 'lady, wife'	*ken* 'woman'	*ben* 'woman'	*gʷenā*

NOTE: In the Celtic column, B is Breton, G is Gaulish, MI is Middle Irish, and W is Welsh.

[a] *m-* or *n-* is the usual way of symbolizing that, in the Celtic system of initial consonant mutation, the next word has the nasal form, indicating that the preceding word formerly ended in a nasal consonant.

nearer because of several factors that do make the Indo-European comparisons more difficult, namely, the common occurrence of biconsonantal and triconsonantal roots and the fact that both Albanian and Armenian have considerable bodies of loanwords that reduce the amount of inherited material.

The point is that one must not be rigorous in the sense of being as restrictive as possible, or assume that only one process—regular sound change—is at work in the evolution of languages when many processes are known to be operative. The point is to take into account what we know about diachronic processes. The numerous "near-misses" found where there is a valid classification, as against where there is not, themselves represent non-random phenomena. We need explanations of non-random linguistic phenomena, and here they are at hand in terms of well-attested facts of linguistic history.

Chapter 7

Conclusions and Overview

This volume has been concerned primarily with the evidence for the validity of a genetic unit, Amerind, embracing the vast majority of New World languages. The only languages excluded are those belonging to the Na-Dene and Eskimo-Aleut families. The preceding chapter examined the now widely held view that Haida, the most distant language genetically, is not to be included in Na-Dene. It confined itself to Sapir's data, although the evidence could have been buttressed considerably by the use of more recent materials. It also sought to show that even after Levine's unreasonable attack (1979), what survives is a body of evidence superior to that which could be adduced under similar restrictions for the affinity of Albanian, Celtic, and Armenian, all three universally recognized as valid members of the Indo-European family of languages.

The remaining family, Eskimo-Aleut, whose internal unity is not at present a matter of dispute, is affiliated with various groups in northern Asia and Europe, especially (but not exclusively) Uralic, Indo-European, and Chukotian. Rasmus Rask, one of the founders of comparative linguistics, espoused a genetic connection between Uralic and Eskimo. Eskimo-Aleut's affinity with Chukchee-Koryak and Kamchadal has been repeatedly noted since the early 1800's.

In the nineteenth century, the unity of Ural-Altaic was generally accepted, though it is now greeted with great skepticism. In the last half century or so, G. J. Ramstedt, Roy A. Miller, and others have presented evidence for the inclusion of Korean and Japanese in Altaic. These are but a few of the mostly pairwise connections that have been suggested from time to time.

About 10 years ago I carried out a general survey of these languages and others having possible connections with one or more of them, using as controls several other groups, such as Ket (an isolated language in Siberia), Dravidian, and some language families of Africa. My conclusion was that there is indeed a family of languages, for which the name "Eurasiatic" is suggested, composed of the following nine groups:

Indo-European	Japanese
Uralic-Yukaghir	Ainu
Altaic (i.e. Turkic,	Gilyak
Mongolic, Tungusic)	Chukotian
Korean	Eskimo-Aleut

Of these, Korean, Japanese, and Ainu probably form a subgroup. Neither Japanese nor Korean has been included in Altaic; neither is likely to be an Altaic language in the traditional sense. On the face of it, for example, Mongolic is far closer to Turkic than either is to Japanese or Korean. That Korean is widely accepted as Altaic probably results from the historical accident that Ramstedt, the most prominent proponent of the notion, was an Altaicist who also worked on Korean. Had he been a Uralicist, he would very likely have hypothesized that Korean was a Uralic language.

Evidence for the validity of the Eurasiatic family as outlined will be presented in my forthcoming book. The possibility that other languages or groups might also belong to the family remains to be thoroughly investigated.

Regarding the origins of Na-Dene, the only serious hypothesis thus far advanced connects it with Sino-Tibetan (see Sapir 1925a and Shafer 1952, 1957). In Shafer's publications, only Athabaskan is compared with Sino-Tibetan, which others have proposed is related to Ket. The Sapir-Shafer hypothesis clearly requires investigation in a broader classificational context. As matters stand, there is virtually no likelihood that any two of the three native American language groups, Amerind, Na-Dene, and Eskimo-Aleut—much less all three together—form a valid linguistic unit.

A considerable number of historical hypotheses emerge from the present and the forthcoming volumes. Of these, the most fundamental bears on the question of the peopling of the Americas. The earliest human skeletal remains found in the Americas belong to the late Pleistocene epoch, and these all belong to our own species, *Homo sapiens sapiens*. This skeletal record contrasts in both respects with the Old World paleontological record.

Furthermore, the pre-Columbian population was physiologically similar to that of Asia, and the existence of a Bering land bridge, at various geologically recent periods, is well established. These considerations, along with the linguistic factors adduced earlier, point to the settlement of the Americas from Asia by three major migrations. Strictly speaking, because language groups can become extinct without leaving any trace, the linguistic evidence suggests a *minimum* of three migrations.

The oldest must be represented linguistically by Amerind, since that group covers a far more extensive territory than the others, centers to the south of them, and shows far greater internal linguistic differentiation. It may plausibly be connected with the Paleo-Indian (Clovis) culture, which dates back at least 11,000–12,000 years and has left both physical and artifactual remains (Haynes 1982).

The Na-Dene group was probably the second to arrive. Its peripheral geographical position and less-deep internal linguistic differentiation suggest that it entered the western hemisphere later than Amerind. The general location and internal classification of the Na-Dene languages suggest a place of original differentiation in the coastal or insular areas of eastern Alaska and northern British Columbia; the spread of the Athabaskans to western interior Canada, with outliers in Washington, Oregon, and the American Southwest, must be comparatively recent. The case for a northwestern location of the ancestral Athabaskan speakers is strengthened by the fact that the northern languages have the greatest diversity. In an article originally published in 1936, Sapir points to the greater dialect cleavage of northern Athabaskan as decisive evidence for this location (1963: 213–14). Dell Hymes (1960: 23) and more recently Krauss (1973: 904) assert that the original homeland of the Athabaskans was in or near Alaska. Krauss cites as evidence the fact that the greatest divergence is found within the Athabaskan languages of Alaska. The coming of the Na-Dene people may perhaps be linked to the appearance of an archaeologic culture later than the Clovis culture, namely, Paleo-Arctic or Beringian, dated 7,000–10,000 B.P. (West 1981).

The Eskimo-Aleut migration was probably the most recent, but its age relative to that of the Na-Dene is subject to considerable uncertainty. Eskimo itself is divided into Yuit and Inuit, with a sharp boundary between the two on the west coast of Alaska. Everything north and east of Unalakleet is Inuit, extending through Alaska and Canada to Greenland. The other branch, Yuit, consists of Siberian Eskimo, Central Alaskan Eskimo, and Pacific Coast Alaskan Eskimo. One form of Siberian Eskimo, Sirenik, is so different from the rest of Eskimo that it may form a separate branch, distinct from both Inuit and Yuit. If this hypothesis is correct, there is a possibility that Proto-Eskimo was spoken on the western side of the Bering Strait. However, the geographical location of Aleut rather suggests southwestern Alaska as the ancestral homeland, with Siberian Eskimo a reverse movement, perhaps earliest in the case of the speakers of Sirenik.

Based on the close similarity of all forms of Inuit, its identification with the relatively recent Thule culture is generally accepted. The Thule culture existed substantially less than one millennium ago. The much older Anangula culture, dated 8,500–10,000 B.P., is thus at least as ancient as the Beringian. Named after a site in the eastern Aleutian Islands, it has been identified by W. S. Laughlin (1980) with ancestral Aleut. This correlation is plausible if by Aleut we mean the earliest stage of Eskimo-Aleut, continued *in situ* by the Aleuts while the ancestors of the Eskimos migrated to the east and north.

The linguistic evidence that Eskimo-Aleut is the most recent of the three migrations rests on the following considerations. First, Eskimo-Aleut linguistic differentiation is significantly less than that of Na-Dene. One indication of this fact is the universal acceptance of the relationship of Eskimo to Aleut as against the rejection by many linguists of the Na-Dene affiliation of Haida, genetically the most distant language of that group. Second, Eskimo and Aleut have geographic positions even more peripheral in the Americas than those of the Na-Dene branches; Eskimo is also spoken in Siberia. Finally, we may adduce the position of Eskimo-Aleut as the easternmost extension of the vast Eurasiatic family; it is the only New World family with clear Old World connections.

Although we have presented linguistic criteria to establish a relative chronology of the three migrations, we have considered only archaeological correlations as a source for an absolute chronology. The only comparable linguistic method available is glottochronology, whose reliability has been the subject of increasing skepticism since the 1960's. Nevertheless, it will be considered here.

For a glottochronological study of the Amerind family, we must compare pairs of languages, with each member of a pair affiliated with a different substock. Swadesh, in his later publications (1959, 1962), gives some relevant results. In order to take into account the "dregs" factor, however, that is, the deceleration of the rate of word loss as the common vocabulary is confined increasingly to more stable items (see Appendix A), he carries out certain fairly arbitrary manipulations. But the data on which these manipulations depend, that is, the length of the word list and the percentage of adjudged cognates, are not given. Moreover, at this distance of separation the probable error becomes large, and a difference of judgment regarding even one cognate will produce a difference of from a half to a full millennium. Swadesh himself did not consider the method reliable for periods of more than 8,000 years.

Swadesh (1958) provides the only list of relevant pairs of Amerind languages, along with information about the size of the vocabulary list and the proportion of cognates. The pairs are Quechua-Tarascan, Tarascan-Zuni, Miskito-Yahgan, and Miskito-Moseten, with 6.5 millennia of divergence for the first pair and 7.0 for the others. All the comparisons are based on lists of fewer than 100 words, with an assumed retention rate of .86 per millennium. If we apply the Joos function, described in Appendix A, but map it into the interval .86–1.00 rather than .80–1.00 (the rate originally assumed by Joos on the basis of a 200-word list), Swadesh's 7,000 B.P. dates are increased to 9,000 B.P.

Because among other considerations, Swadesh tended to see more cognates than most, I believe that even these dates are too recent. A date of 10,000 B.P. or 11,000 B.P. does not seem unreasonable. But if we are to consider glottochronology seriously in dating Amerind, we should use full 200-word lists from a number of lexically well-attested languages in different branches of Amerind.

With regard to Na-Dene, we are somewhat better off. In an excellent review of the problem, which takes into account both previous studies and his own data, Krauss (1973: 950–53) proposes that the split between Athabaskan-Eyak and Tlingit occurred about 5,000 B.P. We should probably add 1,000 or even 2,000 years to that date to account for the earlier separation of Haida from the rest of Na-Dene. A date of 7,000 B.P. agrees reasonably well with that of the Beringian culture.

Finally, regarding the origins of Eskimo-Aleut, Robert McGhee (1976) notes in his review of previous glottochronological work that estimates have ranged from 3,000 B.P. to 6,000 B.P. Even 6,000 B.P. falls two to four millennia short of the date of the Anangula culture. In sum, the relative dates of the Na-Dene and Eskimo-Aleut migrations are less certain than the inference that both are later than the Amerind migration.

335

The foregoing theory of the settling of the Americas by three waves of migrants receives important confirmation from its close coincidence with two other lines of evidence, serological and dental (see Greenberg, Turner & Zegura 1985). I became aware of the results of these other areas of investigation only after the main lines of the classification presented here were well established. Christy Turner and Stephen Zegura also arrived at their conclusions independently of the linguistic evidence. Of the two, Turner's dental evidence appears to be more secure than Zegura's serological data. Even regarding the serological data, plausible alternatives are very few, and they generally suggest either an Amerind–Na-Dene–Eskimo-Aleut trichotomy or an Eskimo-Aleut–Amerind dichotomy, within which Na-Dene is considered part of Amerind. An as-yet-unpublished study by Robert C. Williams on the distribution of immunoglobulin G, designed expressly to test the three-migration hypothesis, provides strong support for that theory.

The foregoing is the most basic of the historical conclusions that follow from the linguistic evidence presented in this volume, but of course there are many others. For example, the assignment of the Timucua language of Florida to the Paezan branch of Chibchan-Paezan (with its nearest relatives in Venezuela) suggests that the Timucuas came to Florida from northern South America via the Caribbean. Another instance has to do with the Yuki-Wappo languages, which are found in California but belong to the large Gulf subgroup of Penutian. Since all the other Gulf languages are found in the southeastern United States, we may posit a migration from that region to California. William Elmendorff (1968) estimates that Yuki separated from Wappo about 2,000 years ago; hence the migration of the Proto-Yukian speakers to California is probably at least as old as 2,000 B.P.

If the results presented in this volume and in the companion volume on Eurasiatic are valid, our classification of the world's languages, based on genetic criteria, undergoes considerable simplification. Together with the conclusions of other investigators, such as Paul Benedict's about Southeast Asia, my results lead to the assumption of a quite limited number of major stocks, as shown in Table 11. Austroasiatic and Austro-Thai can probably be included in a single Austric stock. This grouping was originally proposed by Wilhelm Schmidt (1906) but needs restatement in important respects in light of Benedict's work. Unaware of the Kadai group of languages, to which Thai belongs, Schmidt classified Thai as Sino-Tibetan.

To these major stocks we must add a number of isolated languages,

336

Table 11. The World's Major Linguistic Families

KHOISAN	DRAVIDIAN
NIGER-KORDOFANIAN	SINO-TIBETAN
NILO-SAHARAN	AUSTROASIATIC
AFRO-ASIATIC	AUSTRO-THAI
NORTH CAUCASIAN[a]	INDO-PACIFIC
KHARTVELIAN (SOUTH	AUSTRALIAN
CAUCASIAN)[b]	NA-DENE
EURASIATIC	AMERIND

[a]Embraces most of the languages of the Caucasus.
[b]Consists of Georgian and its closest relatives.

such as Basque, Ket, Burushaski, and the extinct non–Indo-European languages known from ancient Near East records: Sumerian, Hurrian-Vannic, Hattic, and Elamite.

At this level of classification what is now required is a comparison of all these groupings to see if still deeper groupings can be discerned. Some revision of earlier work in the light of such a broader evidential base may also prove necessary. Several plausible hypotheses have already been presented in the literature. I have tentatively formulated others, but it would be premature to state them until all possibilities have been given equal consideration. The ultimate goal is a comprehensive classification of what is very likely a single language family. The implications of such a classification for the origin and history of our species would, of course, be very great.

Appendixes

Appendix A

A Generalization of Glottochronology to n Languages

With a large proportion of the vocabulary recoverable by comparison even after a great lapse of time, it becomes possible to compare genetically defined groups of languages with other, similar groups to arrive at still deeper classifications.* The general mathematical model outlined below shows how multilateral comparison increases the proportion of recoverable vocabulary as the number of languages compared increases. In fact, multilateral comparison is an even better tool than an examination of the model might suggest, for the "semantic criterion" is applied strictly in glottochronology; in a standard list of 100 or 200 basic words, only those pairs that are the "best translation" of a given item are counted as cognates. But because semantic change, like other processes of change, has a cumulative effect over time, many more cognates are in fact recoverable even when they have undergone semantic shifts. An example is the so-called *Hund*-dog phenomenon. In English, the word 'hound,' cognate with German *Hund,* still exists but does not appear in a glotto-chronological comparison.

The theory behind glottochronology is that if we take a list of, say, 200 basic words (and such a list has been devised), the rates of retention of words on this list in their original meanings over a given time period will be reasonably similar in historically independent cases. By examining a number of documented cases, a retention rate variously calculated at .80–.85 for 1,000 years has been ascertained (with a probable error based on the variability among the test cases); the value .80 is the one used here. If, after 1,000 years, 80 percent of the wordlist has been retained, then in the next 1,000 years 80 percent of what is left will be retained, so that the rate of retention of the original vocabulary is .80 × .80 or .64 (.80²). In general, if t is the number of millennia, the retention rate is the exponential function $.80^t$.

If we now compare two languages that have a common origin, each replacing vocabulary independently at this rate, then after t millennia the common vocabulary

---

*All calculations in Appendix A and Appendix B were carried out on an HP 11C and all the programs were written by myself. I am indebted to James A. Fox for independently carrying out all the calculations in Appendix A and those in Tables B.1–B.24 (as well as the generating function in Appendix B), using BASIC as his programming language.

Appendix A

Table A.1. Recoverable Vocabulary Based on the Joos Function

	Number of languages				
Years	2	3	4	5	6
1,000	.648	.882	.959	.985	.994
2,000	.440	.700	.835	.906	.945
3,000	.310	.542	.693	.788	.851
4,000	.226	.420	.563	.666	.740
5,000	.168	.328	.456	.555	.631
6,000	.128	.259	.370	.461	.534
7,000	.100	.207	.302	.383	.451
8,000	.079	.167	.248	.319	.381
9,000	.063	.136	.206	.268	.323
10,000	.051	.112	.171	.226	.274
20,000	.010	.023	.038	.053	.068

	Number of languages				
Years	7	8	9	10	20
1,000	.998	.999	1.000	1.000	1.000
2,000	.967	.979	.987	.991	1.000
3,000	.892	.921	.941	.955	.995
4,000	.794	.834	.865	.889	.976
5,000	.690	.737	.775	.806	.937
6,000	.594	.643	.683	.717	.883
7,000	.508	.556	.597	.632	.819
8,000	.433	.479	.519	.554	.751
9,000	.371	.413	.450	.484	.683
10,000	.318	.356	.391	.422	.618
20,000	.083	.096	.110	.122	.220

will be $.80^t \times .80^t$ or $.80^{2t}$. All glottochronological calculations made hitherto are based on this formula (with the constant varying, as indicated, from .80 to .85). It is possible, however, to generalize from two to n languages. Suppose, to take the simplest case, that n is three. Call the languages A, B, and C. Then, after t millennia, the original vocabulary falls into 2^3, or eight parts. First, there is the vocabulary not found in any of the three languages. Let us call this the *unrecoverable vocabulary*. Then, we have the vocabulary surviving in A but not in B or C, in B but not in A or C, and in C but not in A or B. This vocabulary, which cannot be recovered by comparison, is the *submerged vocabulary*. The fifth, sixth, and seventh parts are the vocabulary surviving in two languages, that is, A and B, A and C, and B and C. Finally, as the eighth class, we will have the vocabulary surviving in all three languages, A, B, and C.

Note that the division of the original vocabulary into eight parts for $n = 3$ is

$$\binom{3}{0} = 1 + \binom{3}{1} \text{ (i.e. 3 words taken 1 at a time)} = 3 + \binom{3}{2}$$

$$\text{(i.e. 3 words taken 2 at a time, or } 3 \times 2 / 1 \times 2) = 3 + \binom{3}{3} = 1,$$

342

Table A.2. Recoverable Vocabulary Based on a Homogeneous Replacement Rate

	Number of languages				
Years	2	3	4	5	6
1,000	.640	.896	.973	.993	1.000
2,000	.410	.705	.864	.940	.975
3,000	.262	.518	.705	.827	.901
4,000	.168	.366	.541	.679	.781
5,000	.107	.252	.397	.528	.685
6,000	.068	.170	.282	.393	.495
7,000	.044	.114	.196	.283	.369
8,000	.028	.075	.134	.198	.266
9,000	.018	.049	.090	.136	.187
10,000	.011	.032	.060	.093	.129
20,000	.000	.000	.001	.001	.002

	Number of languages				
Years	7	8	9	10	20
1,000	1.000	1.000	1.000	1.000	1.000
2,000	.989	.996	.998	.999	1.000
3,000	.945	.970	.984	.991	1.000
4,000	.854	.903	.937	.959	1.000
5,000	.726	.796	.849	.889	.996
6,000	.585	.662	.728	.782	.981
7,000	.450	.525	.593	.653	.943
8,000	.333	.399	.461	.519	.872
9,000	.258	.293	.345	.396	.770
10,000	.168	.209	.250	.293	.649
20,000	.003	.004	.005	.006	.022

so that $1 + 3 + 3 + 1 = 8$. But this is simply the well-known binomial expansion for the special case $n = 3$, for which the general formula is the following:

$$1 = p^n + np^{n-1}q + (n/2)p^{n-2}q^2 \ldots npq^{n-1} + q^n$$

If we take p as the retained vocabulary and q as the replaced vocabulary, then npq^{n-1} represents the submerged vocabulary and q^n the unrecoverable vocabulary. The vocabulary recoverable by comparison, then, is the total vocabulary minus the sum of the last two terms, i.e. $1 - (npq^{n-1} + q^n)$. Clearly, as the number of languages n increases, more and more of the lost vocabulary becomes merely submerged, and more and more submerged vocabulary becomes recoverable by survival in the additional languages.

Another relevant factor can be included in the calculation. We have assumed that all the items on the vocabulary list are equally stable. But this assumption is clearly improbable. If languages have been separated for, say, 5,000 years, what they still have in common will generally be the more stable elements. Hence a smaller proportion of items should be lost in the next 1,000 years than in the previous 1,000

343

years. In other words, we have a constantly decelerating rate of vocabulary loss. Failure to take this so-called dregs effect into account results in an underestimation of the retention rate.

A proposal to deal with the dregs effect is found in Joos (1964). The proposal is to split the standard list into eight sublists according to a normal frequency distribution. The empirically ascertained rate of .80 for 1,000 years is then the sum of 2 percent of the list with r (retention rate) = .96; 7 percent with r = .93; 17 percent with r = .89; 24 percent with r = .84; 24 percent with r = .78; 17 percent with r = .71; 7 percent with r = .63; and 2 percent with r = .54.

The binomial theorem can be combined with the Joos function into a function that takes account of both variables, the number of languages, n, and the time in millennia, t. To illustrate, I give the first two terms of the function for five languages after 3,000 years (i.e. $n = 5$, $t = 3$):

$$1 - \left\{(.02 \times [5 \times .96^3 \times .04^4 + .04^5]) + \right.$$
$$\left. (.07 \times [5 \times .93^3 \times .07^4 + .07^5]) + \ldots\right\}$$

Table A.1 shows the proportion of vocabulary expected to be recovered for two to ten languages after periods of 1,000 years to 10,000 years, as calculated by the Joos function. The retention rates for 20,000 years and for 20 languages are shown to give a sense of the expected outcomes after still longer periods of time and with larger numbers of languages. In Table A.2, the expected proportion of recoverable vocabulary without compensating for the dregs effect is calculated for purposes of comparison.

Appendix B

The Mathematical Bases
of Subgrouping

The term "mathematics of subgrouping" is here restricted to the lexicon and is based on glottochronological assumptions. The model is in a sense a purely formal one, in which we investigate the consequences of extending the glottochronological model to more than two languages. Both the usual homogeneous retention rate of .80 per 1,000 years and the more complex, but empirically much more realistic, inhomogeneous retention rate proposed by Joos (described in Appendix A) are employed. The comparison shows that the clarity of evidence bearing on subgrouping problems varies both with the specific subgrouping and with the time period involved.

For this purpose, the four-language case has been investigated in considerable detail. Four appeared to be the minimum number needed to provide some insight into the problems involved without the use of an elaborate program on a large computer. But the general approach is promising, I think, and should be extended to more complex cases.

For reasons to be set forth in the final section, the method illustrated here is being advocated not as a practical way to carry out subgrouping even relatively small numbers of languages, but rather as an explanation of how and why certain difficulties arise. Furthermore, it will indicate how those difficulties can to some degree be overcome in practice through methods that transcend the limitations of glottochronology, at least under the usual assumptions.

The results in Tables B.1–B.24 represent in abbreviated form the actual work performed: more time periods were investigated, the three-language case was also studied in detail, and the calculations were carried out to five places rather than three as presented here. The data in the tables, however, should be sufficient to represent the general pattern of these distributions. (All the tables to this appendix appear at the end of the text, beginning on p. 353.)

Tables B.1–B.24 each have two parts, labeled A and B. The data in part A are based on a homogeneous rate of change and those in part B on the inhomogeneous Joos rate. The columns represent a time variable, which we will call p; p represents the number of years a given language group existed before certain splits occurred. The rows represent a second time period, designated by the variable q, following such splits. Both p and q are expressed in millennia. Thus $p = 2$, $q = 5$ means that a given group was 2,000 years old when it split, and that 5,000 years have elapsed since that split occurred.

Each table is labeled with a four-letter sequence, an arrow, and a second four-letter sequence. The first sequence refers to the expected surface distribution of cognates, and the second to the true, or underlying, classification. These sequences refer to single cases, in most instances representative of a number of cases that have the same results. These cases will be explained later, and the results, which give a fully detailed labeling for each table, are to be found in Table B.25.

Four languages can be classified in 14 ways, as follows:

1. aaab	4. abbb	7. abba	10. abca	13. abcc
2. aaba	5. aabb	8. aabc	11. abbc	14. abcd
3. abaa	6. abab	9. abac	12. abcb	

These sequences fall into four isomorphic sets: 1–4, 5–7, 8–13, and 14. (Two or more classifications are isomorphic if each can be converted into one of the others simply by reordering the languages.) In Tables B.1–B.24, *aaab*, *aabb*, *aabc*, and *abcd* have been chosen as symbols for these four sets.

As an example of how these tables are to be read, consider the entry in Table B.1, part A, for column 4, row 2, namely, .107. Since this is an A subtable, it assumes a homogeneous retention rate of .80 per 1,000 years. On this assumption, in a subgroup with the configuration *aabb*, the expected proportion of cognates of the pattern *aaaa*—that is, with all four languages agreeing—would be close to 11 percent if the ancestral language of *aa* first split from that of *bb* after 3,000 years as a single language, and a_1 has since been diverging from a_2, and b_1 from b_2 for 1,000 years.

Should we be interested in what the proportion of other distributions of cognates is to be expected for $p = 3$, $q = 1$ with the same underlying classification of *aabb*, we cannot determine this directly, but we can easily derive it by examining the other tables with the underlying pattern *aabb*. In doing so, we must note that certain different surface distributions of cognates with the same true underlying classification will give the same results and will therefore not require separate tables. If the true subgrouping is *aabb*, for example, the surface distribution of cognates *aabc* and *abcc* will be the same for any value of the variables p and q. In both instances we have agreement in the cognates in the languages of one branch of the *aabb* classification and disagreement in the other. To get the total distribution for given values of p and q and the same underlying classification, we consult Table B.25, which contains the full set of cognate distributions for the true classification *aabb* found in Tables B.1–B.6. For fixed p and q, the formula $B_1 + (4 \times B_2) + B_3 + (2 \times B_4) + (4 \times B_5) + B_6$ (where B_1 represents the value in Table B.1, B_2 represents the value in Table B.2, etc.) should account for all the cognate distributions and will in fact add up to 1.00, plus or minus up to .002 because of rounding errors.

Just as the sequence to the left of the arrow in each of the first 24 tables can stand for a multiplicity of cognate distributions, so too the sequence to the right can stand for a multiplicity of language classifications with the same properties. The number of distinct tables is thus further reduced.

Several further simplifications have been made to keep the study within reasonable bounds and presentable in two dimensions. One of these may be called the assumption of "equal branching": for true classification *aabb*, it is assumed that the periods *p* and *q* are equal, and in all cases it is assumed that the four languages are contemporary (see the accompanying figure). It is assumed that $p_1 = p_2$ and that $q_1 = q_2 = q_3 = q_4$. Otherwise, we would have four different variables with three degrees of freedom—vastly increasing the number of cases. As p_1 or p_2 approaches 0, we have the isomorphic classifications *aabc* and *abcc*, respectively. In general, then, it is possible to consider the degree of ramification as a continuous rather than a discrete function, but this possibility is not pursued here.

A further simplifying assumption is that a maximum of two time periods is involved. For true classification *abcd*, there is only a single period, since there is no branching subsequent to the initial divergence. Hence in Tables B.21–B.24, although conformity with the other tables is maintained by retaining two dimensions, the actual single time period is the sum of the values for the rows and columns: thus column 3, row 3 (2,000 + 2,000), column 2, row 4 (1,000 + 3,000), and column 4, row 1 (3,000 + 1,000) all refer to the distribution of cognates after 4,000 years.

Table B.25 gives the full set of cognate distributions and true classifications for Tables B.1–B.24. It is unnecessary to list variant isomorphic classifications on the right side of the arrow; whenever we have two languages forming one branch and two forming another, we can always understand them as *aabb*, and the same is true for *aabc*, *aaab*, and *abcd*. The last is of course the limiting case of an isomorphic group with only one member.

Table B.26 contains the generating functions for Tables B.1–B.24. Looking once again at the figure, we see that there are in all six time periods involved: p_1, p_2, q_1, q_2, q_3, and q_4. In any of these periods there is an independent retention of

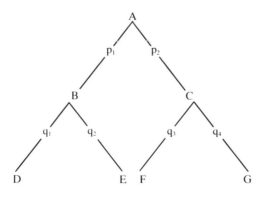

Equal branching

cognates. For A subtables, the retention rate is $.8^p$, where p is the length of the period in thousands of years. In other words, the function is exponential. During any given period there is a corresponding cognate loss of $1 - .8^p$. Each period involves changes independent of those occurring in each of the others, and a certain proportion of the vocabulary with which it begins is retained or lost as a function of its length. For each period, there are exactly two possibilities for a given item, retention or loss. In this instance, since there are six periods, the number of possible combinations is 2^6, or 64. Let us call these possibilities *genotypes*. But the number of surface cognate distribution patterns, or *phenotypes,* is far smaller than 64. In fact these will generally be the sum of a whole series of genotypes.

Consider the classification *aabb* once more. A phenotypic distribution of cognates *aabb* is the sum of three genotypes. In one of these, words are replaced in one branch during period p_1 but not in q_1 and q_2, whereas in the other branch they are retained during p_2, q_3, and q_4. Hence their proportion is

$$(1 - .8^{p_1}) (.8^{p_2}) (.8^{q_1}) (.8^{q_2}) (.8^{q_3}) (.8^{q_4}).$$

Given the assumption of equal branching, by which $p_1 = p_2$ and $q_1 = q_2 = q_3 = q_4$, this function becomes

$$(1 - .8^p) (.8^p)(.8^{4q}).$$

In a second genotype, words are replaced in p_2 but not in any other period. Given $p_1 = p_2$, this function is the same as the preceding one. Finally, there is the genotype in which some words are lost in both p_1 and p_2 but unchanged in q_1, q_2, q_3, and q_4; or, after simplifications resulting from the equal-branching assumption, $(1 - .8^p)^2 (.8^{4q})$. The phenotype subsumes all the foregoing, hence including three genotypes.

For the inhomogeneous retention rate, the same general formula holds; however, in place of $.8^p$, for example, we have $.02 \times (.96^p) + .07 \times (.93^p) + \ldots$ (see Appendix A).

By the process just described, all the generating functions can be stated in terms of $f(p,q)$, where p and q are the two successive time periods, or $f(p)$, where only one time period occurs (for classification *abcd*). All are exponential functions; they can be simplified by letting $x = .8^p$ and $y = .8^q$ in both the homogeneous retention function and the correspondingly more complex expression based on the Joos function for the inhomogeneous rate.

These generating functions are set forth in Table B.26. Tables B.1 and B.15, B.2 and B.17, and B.5 and B.19 have the same generating functions.

A number of the properties of the tables can be derived from these functions. For example, when $p = 0$ and $q = 0$ (or for Tables B.21–B.24, when $p = 0$), we have a period before differentiation has begun; hence all words in the list are identical (*aaaa*), and other distributions equal 0. For any number n, $n^0 = 1$, so that using the homogeneous retention rate, with surface distribution *aaaa* (Tables B.1, B.7, B.15, and B.21), the sum of the non-exponential coefficients is 1, whereas for the others it is 0 (similarly for the Joos function).

We are essentially interested in the properties of the distributions of values in Tables B.1–B.24, especially in terms of maxima, minima, and rates of increase and decrease of the time periods. Our observations will help to explain why certain subgroupings are more difficult to arrive at under certain conditions than under others. In Table B.1(A), for example, when $p = 2$ and $q = 3$, $r = .028$. The time periods, p and q, are expressed, as always, in thousands of years; occurrences of given distributions are indicated by r.

The 48 subtables fall into seven categories of distributional properties. The first category consists of those subtables with a surface cognate distribution *aaaa*: Tables B.1, B.7, B.15, and B.21, with true classifications *aabb*, *aabc*, *aaab*, and *abcd*, respectively. These of course stand for other distributions also, as set forth in Table B.25. The tables of this type show a monotonic decrease in r from the value 1 when $p = 0$ and $q = 0$ to a limit of 0 as p and q approach infinity. A monotonic decrease occurs when for fixed p, the greater the value of q, the smaller the value of r, and for fixed q, the greater the value of p, the smaller the value of r.

However, the rate at which r approaches 0 varies from table to table. As a measure of this variation we can take, for some fixed value p, the value of q at which r reaches .1 between its upper limit, 1, and its lower limit, 0. For the fixed value, we have chosen $p = 1$, i.e. 1,000 years. The smaller the value of q at which $r = .1$, the more rapidly the decrease occurs. Because only Table B.21 represents a single time period, 1 is added to the value of q for each of the other 23 tables.

The values of q in millennia, according to the measure just described, are given for three categories in Table B.27. As shown in Table B.26, two tables—B.1 and B.15—have the same generating function; hence they have the same values for q. As we can see in Table B.27, the decrease is less rapid for the inhomogeneous rates of the Part B column. This variance is due to the "dregs effect." Since the items that remain as time passes are the more stable ones, and their rate of replacement in ensuing periods is lower, there is a deceleration. Note also that as the internal diversity of the true classification increases, the deceleration is more pronounced. In other words, with greater diversity the proportion of agreement in cognates across all the languages decreases more rapidly. The longer the time period, then, the more difficult it is to discern the relatedness of languages from lexical counts; but if a relationship can be seen, subgrouping is obviously easier.

The opposite difficulty develops with true internal diversity over long time periods. In the second category, those cases with surface cognates of the pattern *abcd* (Tables B.6, B.14, B.20, and B.24, with true classifications *aabb*, *aabc*, *aaab*, and *abcd*, respectively), there is a monotonic increase of r from 0 at $p = 0$, $q = 0$, to 1 as a limit as p and q approach infinity. For fixed p, then, the greater the value of q, the greater the value of r; and for fixed q, the greater the value of p, the greater the value of r.

We can measure the rate of increase by fixing p at 1 (1,000 years), and determining the value of q for which r has increased to the midpoint, .5. As before, we add 1 to each value, except for that of Table B.24, which shows true classification *abcd*, to make the results comparable. The greater the value, the longer it takes to reach the midpoint and hence the slower the rate of replacement. The results set forth in Table B.28 appear in order of increasing internal diversity of the true classification. Another way to demonstrate the same hierarchy is to compare the values of r in the relevant tables for $p = 10$, $q = 10$ (Table B.29).

Tables B.28 and B.29 make it clear that, as expected, the part B values have a slower rate of increase; that is, they reach .5 after a longer period of time, and after a very long period (Table B.29), their values are smaller. Furthermore, the greater the internal diversity of the true classification, the more rapid the increase of r. After long periods of time, the greater the internal true diversity, the more it will appear that the true classification is *abcd*—that is, that no internal subgrouping is possible. This is in fact the case where the separation is considerable; thus in Indo-European such higher-level groupings as Italo-Celtic are controversial. A similar problem in Amerind is that of Ge-Pano-Carib. The data in Tables B.28 and B.29 suggest that such intermediate groupings may well exist but will be increasingly difficult as time passes to distinguish from classifications in which all the groups are coordinate, like *abcd* in the four-language case.

In the third category are the cases in which the surface distribution of cognates coincides with the true classification, namely, Table B.3, *aabb;* Table B.11, *aabc;* Table B.16, *aaab;* and Table B.24, *abcd.* Note that Table B.24 has already been included in category 2, since it has true classification *abcd.* It is included here because it is being considered from a different point of view; however, as a member of this group, it requires special treatment. In Table B.24, with true classification *abcd,* r has the limit 1 as p, the only time variable, approaches infinity. As can be seen by comparing parts A and B, the rate at which r approaches 1 is lower for the inhomogeneous rates of change (part B). This is another example of the dregs effect.

For the other three tables in this category, r approaches 1 as a limit as p approaches infinity and q approaches 0. Since infinity is not a specific number, for any finite value of p the limit 1—a situation in which the surface distribution always coincides with the true classification—will never be reached. For each finite value of p, as q approaches 0, the limit of r will be less than 1. The larger the value of p, the initial period, the closer this limit is to 1, theoretically reaching 1 when p is equal to infinity. The data for these tables are presented in Table B.30.

In general the inhomogeneous values (part B) shown in Table B.30 are greater than the homogeneous values (part A). This effect becomes proportionately more powerful—as measured, for example, by their ratios—as q, the second time period, increases. The values of course decrease as the time of divergence from the common ancestor increases. We have once more the dregs effect. What remains is the most stable portion of the vocabulary.

The other main effect discernible in Table B.30 is that the greater the internal diversity, the higher the value of the limit p for a given q. This reaches a climax in Table B.24 (not shown in Table B.30, for which the limit also is 1). An examination of these tables (B.3, B.11, B.16, B.24) will show the same phenomenon: the greater the internal diversity, the greater the proportion of surface cognate distributions that coincide with the true classification. The reason for this is that languages with greater internal diversity belonging to different branches diverge earlier and hence have longer periods of separate development, thus increasing the surface distribution of cognates that reflect membership in different groupings in the classification. An important corollary is that the possibility of detecting the true classification based on surface distribution of cognates varies with the classification itself.

We have considered three categories up to now, those types with surface pattern *aaaa,* those with surface *abcd,* and those in which the surface distribution coincides with the true classification. The remaining four categories differ from the first three in that they all have upper limits, or maxima, less than 1. The minimum for each is of course 0, and p and q are also 0. Before divergence, we have what is theoretically a single language: the true classification is *aaaa,* with a value for r of 1, so that the value of every other distribution is necessarily 0.

The fourth category comprises all those cases for which the maximum occurs when $p = 0$ and q has some value between 0 and 1. It contains two subtypes. The first, represented by Tables B.2, B.9, and B.17, includes those instances in which the distribution of cognates differs for only one of the four languages from the true classification. In Table B.2 (*aaab* → *aabb*), for example, only the third language differs. In the second subtype, represented by Tables B.5, B.12, B.13, and B.19, two languages differ in their cognate distribution from the underlying classification—for example, Table B.12 (*abcc* → *aabc*), in which the second and third languages differ.

In Table B.31, both the value of q for which the maximum occurs and the maximum of r are given. As noted above, these maxima all occur when $p = 0$.

The fifth category is exemplified by Tables B.4 and B.18, each of which is a separate subtype. Exactly two of the four languages grouped together in the surface cognate distribution are grouped together in the true classification. For the other two languages the cognates disagree, even though the languages are grouped together. In Table B.4 (*aabc* → *aabb*), the first two languages agree in being grouped together; the second two are not grouped together in the cognate distribution but *are* in the classification. In Table B.18 (*abbc* → *aaab*), the second and third languages are grouped together in both the cognate distribution and the classification, while the first language is not grouped with them in the cognates but is in the classification. In category 5 the maximum occurs as p approaches infinity, not 0 as in category 4. Table B.32 gives the values of q for which the maximum value of r occurs as p approaches infinity.

Category 6 is represented by Tables B.8 and B.10, which have identical maxima. The distribution of cognates contains two pairs of languages, not necessarily discrete, such that the true classification puts both members of one pair in the same group but divides the two members of the other pair. For example, Table B.8 (*aabb* → *aabc*) includes one pair, *aa,* that belongs to the same group both in the distribution of cognates and in the underlying classification. For the third and fourth items, the classification assigns to separate groups languages that belong to the same group in the cognate distribution. In Table B.10 (*aaba* → *aabc*), one of the isomorphic cases is *aaab* → *aabc*. In this instance, the first two languages agree in both cognate distribution and linguistic classification. The second and third languages agree in cognate distribution but belong to different linguistic groups. The maximum is reached by p in this group when $q = 0$. These maxima of p, with $q = 0$, and the values of the maxima themselves are found in Table B.33.

The seventh, and last, category contains those distributions in which the true classification is *abcd*, so that there is neither subdividing nor a second time variable. Any distribution of cognates (except *aaaa* and *abcd*, which have already been discussed) is represented. Hence the cognate distributions of either two or three languages agree (e.g. *aabc* → *abcd*, represented by Table B.23, or *aaab* → *abcd*, represented by Table B.22). The two cases have different maxima. In Table B.34, the value of *p* and the maximum *r* for this value are given for each of the two subtypes.

The relative clarity of subgrouping, as reflected in the extent to which the cognate distributions and the valid underlying classification correspond, varies with a number of factors: (1) the relative and absolute values of the time periods, (2) the classifications themselves, and (3) the assumption of a homogeneous or an inhomogeneous retention rate for the vocabulary. Although the details of Joos's assumptions have not been investigated in regard to their empirical validity, an inhomogeneous rate—which generally makes subgrouping more difficult—is doubtless closer to reality.

The real situation, however, is not as difficult as these considerations seem to suggest. To begin with, glottochronology is an extremely weak method, even for evaluating lexical evidence for subgrouping. One weakness is that, as currently practiced, it uses only pairwise percentages, so that items of wide distribution are weighted the same as those diagnostically more valuable ones of narrow distribution. The mathematical method described in this appendix would in principle overcome this limitation, but its application to a large number of languages and time periods would be exceedingly complex.

A further weakness of glottochronological theory is even more difficult to overcome. The theory is essentially a binary one in that it posits only two discrete values, cognacy and non-cognacy. But in reality cognates of closely related languages often reflect common phonological, derivational, and semantic innovations that support a notion of gradations of cognacy to which it is difficult, or perhaps impossible, to assign numerical values. Common semantic change may well simply remove an item from the list, and thus the item will not figure in classification at all. Further evidence from morphological systems often provides evidence of common innovations of highly idiosyncratic, and hence strongly probative, value.

Add to these weaknesses the problem of highly unequal documentation of vocabulary from different languages and it becomes apparent that the pairwise counting of cognates is in practice a very ineffectual method. It succeeds where genetic relatedness is obvious anyway and fails in more subtle cases, where only a fuller marshaling of the evidence can give a decisive answer. The fact remains that the theory of the distribution of vocabulary resemblances in relation to linguistic classification under varying assumptions is a topic of theoretic interest.

Table B.1. *aaaa* → *aabb*

Years following splits (*q*)	Years before splits (*p*)					
	250	1,000	2,000	3,000	5,000	10,000
	A. HOMOGENEOUS RATE OF CHANGE					
250	.716	.512	.328	.210	.086	.009
1,000	.366	.262	.168	.107	.044	.005
2,000	.150	.107	.069	.044	.018	.002
3,000	.061	.044	.028	.018	.007	.001
5,000	.010	.007	.005	.003	.001	.000
10,000	.000	.000	.000	.000	.000	.000
	B. INHOMOGENEOUS RATE OF CHANGE					
250	.710	.509	.335	.225	.108	.023
1,000	.365	.262	.172	.116	.056	.012
2,000	.158	.113	.074	.050	.024	.005
3,000	.071	.051	.034	.023	.011	.002
5,000	.016	.012	.008	.005	.002	.001
10,000	.001	.001	.000	.000	.000	.000

Table B.2. *aaab* → *aabb*

Years following splits (*q*)	Years before splits (*p*)					
	250	1,000	2,000	3,000	5,000	10,000
	A. HOMOGENEOUS RATE OF CHANGE					
250	.041	.030	.019	.012	.005	.001
1,000	.092	.066	.042	.027	.011	.001
2,000	.084	.060	.039	.025	.010	.001
3,000	.059	.042	.027	.017	.007	.001
5,000	.021	.015	.010	.006	.003	.000
10,000	.001	.001	.000	.000	.000	.000
	B. INHOMOGENEOUS RATE OF CHANGE					
250	.042	.030	.020	.013	.006	.001
1,000	.091	.066	.043	.029	.014	.003
2,000	.085	.061	.040	.027	.013	.003
3,000	.063	.045	.030	.020	.010	.002
5,000	.028	.020	.013	.009	.004	.001
10,000	.004	.003	.002	.001	.001	.000

Table B.3. *aabb* → *aabb*

Years following splits (q)	Years before splits (p)					
	250	1,000	2,000	3,000	5,000	10,000
A. HOMOGENEOUS RATE OF CHANGE						
250	.084	.288	.472	.590	.714	.791
1,000	.043	.147	.242	.302	.366	.405
2,000	.018	.060	.099	.124	.150	.166
3,000	.007	.025	.041	.051	.061	.068
5,000	.001	.004	.007	.009	.010	.011
10,000	.000	.000	.000	.000	.000	.000
B. INHOMOGENEOUS RATE OF CHANGE						
250	.086	.287	.461	.571	.688	.773
1,000	.044	.147	.237	.294	.354	.398
2,000	.019	.064	.102	.127	.153	.172
3,000	.009	.029	.046	.057	.069	.078
5,000	.002	.007	.011	.013	.016	.018
10,000	.000	.000	.000	.001	.001	.001

Table B.4. *aabc* → *aabb*

Years following splits (q)	Years before splits (p)					
	250	1,000	2,000	3,000	5,000	10,000
A. HOMOGENEOUS RATE OF CHANGE						
250	.012	.036	.057	.070	.085	.093
1,000	.047	.099	.147	.177	.208	.228
2,000	.073	.121	.165	.192	.222	.240
3,000	.076	.109	.140	.159	.179	.192
5,000	.054	.066	.076	.083	.091	.095
10,000	.009	.010	.010	.011	.011	.011
B. INHOMOGENEOUS RATE OF CHANGE						
250	.013	.036	.057	.070	.084	.094
1,000	.048	.099	.144	.173	.203	.225
2,000	.073	.121	.163	.190	.218	.238
3,000	.077	.113	.144	.163	.184	.199
5,000	.061	.077	.091	.099	.109	.115
10,000	.020	.022	.024	.025	.026	.027

Table B.5. *abac → aabb*

Years following splits (q)	Years before splits (p)					
	250	1,000	2,000	3,000	5,000	10,000
A. HOMOGENEOUS RATE OF CHANGE						
250	.002	.002	.001	.001	.000	.000
1,000	.023	.016	.010	.007	.003	.000
2,000	.047	.034	.022	.014	.006	.001
3,000	.056	.040	.026	.016	.007	.001
5,000	.043	.031	.020	.013	.005	.001
10,000	.008	.006	.004	.002	.001	.000
B. INHOMOGENEOUS RATE OF CHANGE						
250	.002	.002	.001	.001	.000	.000
1,000	.023	.016	.011	.007	.003	.001
2,000	.046	.033	.022	.015	.007	.001
3,000	.055	.040	.026	.018	.008	.002
5,000	.048	.035	.023	.015	.007	.002
10,000	.018	.013	.008	.006	.003	.001

Table B.6. *abcd → aabb*

Years following splits (q)	Years before splits (p)					
	250	1,000	2,000	3,000	5,000	10,000
A. HOMOGENEOUS RATE OF CHANGE						
250	.001	.005	.007	.008	.010	.011
1,000	.038	.064	.088	.103	.119	.128
2,000	.159	.213	.262	.293	.326	.346
3,000	.321	.385	.442	.479	.518	.540
5,000	.623	.672	.722	.746	.776	.794
10,000	.944	.954	.962	.967	.973	.977
B. INHOMOGENEOUS RATE OF CHANGE						
250	.002	.005	.007	.009	.010	.011
1,000	.038	.064	.087	.101	.116	.127
2,000	.151	.203	.249	.277	.308	.330
3,000	.294	.356	.411	.445	.481	.508
5,000	.554	.609	.656	.686	.718	.741
10,000	.874	.894	.911	.922	.933	.942

Table B.7. $aaaa \rightarrow aabc$

Years following splits (q)	Years before splits (p)					
	250	1,000	2,000	3,000	5,000	10,000
A. HOMOGENEOUS RATE OF CHANGE						
250	.677	.410	.210	.107	.028	.001
1,000	.346	.210	.107	.055	.014	.001
2,000	.142	.086	.044	.023	.006	.000
3,000	.058	.035	.018	.009	.002	.000
5,000	.010	.006	.003	.002	.000	.000
10,000	.000	.000	.000	.000	.000	.000
B. INHOMOGENEOUS RATE OF CHANGE						
250	.671	.407	.217	.119	.040	.004
1,000	.345	.210	.112	.161	.020	.002
2,000	.149	.090	.048	.027	.009	.001
3,000	.067	.041	.022	.012	.004	.000
5,000	.015	.009	.005	.003	.001	.000
10,000	.001	.000	.000	.000	.000	.000

Table B.8. $aabb \rightarrow aabc$

Years following splits (q)	Years before splits (p)					
	250	1,000	2,000	3,000	5,000	10,000
A. HOMOGENEOUS RATE OF CHANGE						
250	.039	.102	.118	.102	.058	.008
1,000	.020	.052	.060	.052	.030	.004
2,000	.008	.021	.025	.021	.012	.002
3,000	.003	.009	.010	.009	.005	.001
5,000	.001	.001	.001	.001	.001	.000
10,000	.000	.000	.000	.000	.000	.000
B. INHOMOGENEOUS RATE OF CHANGE						
250	.039	.102	.118	.105	.068	.019
1,000	.020	.052	.061	.054	.035	.010
2,000	.009	.023	.026	.023	.015	.004
3,000	.004	.010	.012	.011	.007	.002
5,000	.001	.002	.003	.002	.000	.000
10,000	.000	.000	.000	.000	.001	.000

Table B.9. abbb → aabc

Years following splits (q)	Years before splits (p)					
	250	1,000	2,000	3,000	5,000	10,000
A. HOMOGENEOUS RATE OF CHANGE						
250	.039	.023	.012	.006	.002	.000
1,000	.087	.052	.027	.014	.004	.000
2,000	.080	.048	.025	.013	.003	.000
3,000	.055	.034	.017	.009	.002	.000
5,000	.020	.012	.006	.003	.001	.000
10,000	.001	.001	.000	.000	.000	.000
B. INHOMOGENEOUS RATE OF CHANGE						
250	.039	.024	.013	.007	.002	.000
1,000	.086	.052	.028	.015	.005	.000
2,000	.081	.049	.026	.014	.005	.000
3,000	.059	.036	.019	.011	.004	.000
5,000	.027	.016	.009	.005	.002	.000
10,000	.003	.002	.001	.001	.000	.000

Table B.10. aaba → aabc

Years following splits (q)	Years before splits (p)					
	250	1,000	2,000	3,000	5,000	10,000
A. HOMOGENEOUS RATE OF CHANGE						
250	.080	.132	.137	.114	.063	.009
1,000	.111	.118	.102	.079	.041	.005
2,000	.093	.082	.063	.046	.022	.003
3,000	.062	.051	.037	.026	.012	.000
5,000	.022	.017	.011	.008	.003	.000
10,000	.001	.001	.000	.000	.000	.000
B. INHOMOGENEOUS RATE OF CHANGE						
250	.081	.132	.137	.119	.074	.020
1,000	.112	.118	.104	.083	.049	.013
2,000	.094	.084	.066	.050	.028	.007
3,000	.067	.055	.041	.030	.016	.004
5,000	.029	.023	.016	.011	.006	.001
10,000	.004	.003	.002	.001	.001	.000

Table B.11. *aabc* → *aabc*

Years following splits (*q*)	Years before splits (*p*)					
	250	1,000	2,000	3,000	5,000	10,000
	A. HOMOGENEOUS RATE OF CHANGE					
250	.019	.119	.293	.456	.683	.867
1,000	.051	.142	.268	.374	.515	.624
2,000	.074	.138	.214	.273	.347	.402
3,000	.077	.117	.160	.192	.231	.258
5,000	.054	.067	.080	.089	.099	.106
10,000	.009	.010	.011	.011	.011	.011
	B. INHOMOGENEOUS RATE OF CHANGE					
250	.020	.119	.283	.430	.635	.829
1,000	.051	.142	.261	.358	.487	.603
2,000	.074	.139	.213	.270	.340	.402
3,000	.078	.121	.166	.199	.239	.272
5,000	.061	.079	.096	.108	.121	.132
10,000	.020	.023	.024	.026	.027	.028

Table B.12. *abcc* → *aabc*

Years following splits (*q*)	Years before splits (*p*)					
	250	1,000	2,000	3,000	5,000	10,000
	A. HOMOGENEOUS RATE OF CHANGE					
250	.007	.013	.015	.012	.007	.001
1,000	.033	.043	.041	.033	.018	.002
2,000	.057	.058	.050	.038	.019	.003
3,000	.062	.057	.045	.033	.016	.002
5,000	.046	.037	.027	.019	.013	.001
10,000	.008	.006	.004	.003	.001	.000
	B. INHOMOGENEOUS RATE OF CHANGE					
250	.007	.014	.015	.013	.008	.002
1,000	.033	.043	.041	.034	.021	.006
2,000	.056	.058	.050	.040	.023	.006
3,000	.062	.058	.047	.036	.020	.005
5,000	.051	.043	.032	.024	.013	.003
10,000	.018	.014	.009	.007	.003	.001

Table B.13. *abcb → aabc*

Years following splits (q)	Years before splits (p)					
	250	1,000	2,000	3,000	5,000	10,000
A. HOMOGENEOUS RATE OF CHANGE						
250	.005	.008	.009	.007	.004	.001
1,000	.028	.029	.026	.020	.010	.001
2,000	.052	.046	.036	.026	.012	.002
3,000	.059	.048	.035	.025	.011	.001
5,000	.045	.034	.023	.016	.007	.001
10,000	.008	.006	.004	.003	.001	.000
B. INHOMOGENEOUS RATE OF CHANGE						
250	.005	.008	.008	.007	.004	.001
1,000	.028	.029	.026	.021	.012	.003
2,000	.051	.046	.036	.027	.015	.004
3,000	.059	.049	.036	.027	.014	.003
5,000	.050	.039	.027	.019	.010	.002
10,000	.018	.013	.009	.006	.003	.001

Table B.14. *abcd → aabc*

Years following splits (q)	Years before splits (p)					
	250	1,000	2,000	3,000	5,000	10,000
A. HOMOGENEOUS RATE OF CHANGE						
250	.003	.015	.035	.055	.081	.102
1,000	.042	.095	.163	.220	.295	.352
2,000	.166	.251	.349	.423	.514	.581
3,000	.329	.421	.518	.588	.671	.730
5,000	.629	.695	.760	.805	.855	.888
10,000	.945	.957	.968	.975	.983	.988
B. INHOMOGENEOUS RATE OF CHANGE						
250	.003	.015	.035	.053	.077	.100
1,000	.043	.095	.160	.212	.280	.341
2,000	.158	.242	.333	.401	.486	.558
3,000	.302	.393	.487	.553	.632	.698
5,000	.561	.635	.706	.754	.808	.852
10,000	.876	.902	.925	.940	.956	.968

359

Table B.15. *aaaa → aaab*

Years following splits (q)	Years before splits (p)					
	250	1,000	2,000	3,000	5,000	10,000
A. HOMOGENEOUS RATE OF CHANGE						
250	.716	.512	.328	.210	.086	.009
1,000	.366	.262	.168	.107	.044	.005
2,000	.150	.107	.069	.044	.018	.002
3,000	.061	.044	.028	.018	.007	.001
5,000	.010	.007	.005	.003	.001	.000
10,000	.000	.000	.000	.000	.000	.000
B. INHOMOGENEOUS RATE OF CHANGE						
250	.710	.509	.335	.225	.108	.023
1,000	.365	.262	.172	.116	.056	.012
2,000	.158	.113	.074	.050	.024	.005
3,000	.071	.051	.034	.023	.011	.002
5,000	.016	.012	.008	.005	.002	.001
10,000	.001	.001	.000	.000	.000	.000

Table B.16. *aaab → aaab*

Years following splits (q)	Years before splits (p)					
	250	1,000	2,000	3,000	5,000	10,000
A. HOMOGENEOUS RATE OF CHANGE						
250	.130	.334	.518	.636	.760	.837
1,000	.146	.250	.344	.405	.468	.507
2,000	.112	.155	.193	.218	.244	.260
3,000	.073	.090	.106	.116	.127	.133
5,000	.025	.028	.030	.032	.034	.035
10,000	.001	.001	.001	.001	.001	.001
B. INHOMOGENEOUS RATE OF CHANGE						
250	.133	.333	.508	.618	.735	.820
1,000	.147	.250	.340	.396	.456	.500
2,000	.115	.159	.198	.223	.249	.267
3,000	.079	.099	.117	.128	.139	.148
5,000	.034	.038	.042	.045	.047	.049
10,000	.004	.004	.004	.005	.005	.005

Table B.17. *abbb* → *aaab*

Years following splits (q)	Years before splits (p)					
	250	1,000	2,000	3,000	5,000	10,000
A. HOMOGENEOUS RATE OF CHANGE						
250	.041	.030	.019	.012	.005	.001
1,000	.092	.066	.042	.027	.011	.001
2,000	.084	.060	.039	.025	.010	.001
3,000	.059	.042	.027	.017	.007	.001
5,000	.021	.015	.010	.006	.003	.000
10,000	.001	.001	.000	.000	.000	.000
B. INHOMOGENEOUS RATE OF CHANGE						
250	.042	.030	.020	.013	.006	.001
1,000	.091	.066	.043	.029	.014	.003
2,000	.085	.061	.040	.027	.013	.003
3,000	.063	.045	.030	.020	.010	.002
5,000	.028	.020	.013	.009	.004	.001
10,000	.004	.003	.002	.001	.001	.000

Table B.18. *abbc* → *aaab*

Years following splits (q)	Years before splits (p)					
	250	1,000	2,000	3,000	5,000	10,000
A. HOMOGENEOUS RATE OF CHANGE						
250	.007	.019	.030	.036	.044	.048
1,000	.036	.062	.086	.101	.117	.127
2,000	.063	.087	.109	.123	.137	.146
3,000	.069	.086	.101	.111	.121	.127
5,000	.051	.057	.063	.066	.070	.071
10,000	.009	.010	.010	.010	.010	.010
B. INHOMOGENEOUS RATE OF CHANGE						
250	.008	.020	.030	.036	.043	.048
1,000	.037	.062	.085	.099	.114	.125
2,000	.062	.086	.108	.121	.135	.145
3,000	.076	.087	.103	.112	.123	.130
5,000	.058	.065	.072	.077	.081	.085
10,000	.020	.021	.022	.022	.023	.023

Table B.19. *abcc → aaab*

Years following splits (q)	Years before splits (p)					
	250	1,000	2,000	3,000	5,000	10,000
	A. HOMOGENEOUS RATE OF CHANGE					
250	.002	.002	.001	.001	.000	.000
1,000	.023	.016	.010	.007	.003	.000
2,000	.047	.034	.022	.014	.006	.001
3,000	.056	.040	.026	.016	.007	.001
5,000	.043	.032	.020	.013	.005	.001
10,000	.008	.006	.004	.002	.001	.000
	B. INHOMOGENEOUS RATE OF CHANGE					
250	.002	.002	.001	.001	.000	.000
1,000	.023	.016	.011	.007	.003	.001
2,000	.046	.033	.022	.015	.007	.001
3,000	.055	.040	.026	.018	.008	.002
5,000	.048	.035	.023	.015	.007	.002
10,000	.018	.013	.008	.006	.003	.001

Table B.20. *abcd → aaab*

Years following splits (q)	Years before splits (p)					
	250	1,000	2,000	3,000	5,000	10,000
	A. HOMOGENEOUS RATE OF CHANGE					
250	.001	.003	.005	.006	.008	.008
1,000	.035	.055	.073	.084	.096	.103
2,000	.153	.194	.230	.254	.278	.294
3,000	.314	.362	.405	.433	.462	.480
5,000	.618	.655	.689	.710	.733	.747
10,000	.943	.950	.957	.961	.965	.968
	B. INHOMOGENEOUS RATE OF CHANGE					
250	.002	.004	.005	.007	.008	.009
1,000	.035	.055	.072	.082	.094	.102
2,000	.145	.184	.219	.240	.263	.280
3,000	.287	.334	.375	.400	.428	.448
5,000	.548	.589	.625	.647	.671	.689
10,000	.872	.887	.900	.908	.916	.923

Table B.21. *aaaa → abcd*

Years following splits (q)	Years before splits (p)					
	250	1,000	2,000	3,000	5,000	10,000
A. HOMOGENEOUS RATE OF CHANGE						
250	.640	.328	.134	.055	.009	.000
1,000	.328	.168	.069	.028	.005	.000
2,000	.134	.068	.028	.012	.002	.000
3,000	.055	.028	.012	.005	.001	.000
5,000	.009	.005	.002	.001	.000	.000
10,000	.000	.000	.000	.000	.000	.000
B. INHOMOGENEOUS RATE OF CHANGE						
250	.636	.330	.144	.066	.015	.001
1,000	.330	.177	.080	.038	.009	.000
2,000	.144	.080	.038	.018	.005	.000
3,000	.066	.038	.018	.009	.003	.000
5,000	.015	.009	.005	.003	.001	.000
10,000	.001	.000	.000	.000	.000	.000

Table B.22. *aaab → abcd*

Years following splits (q)	Years before splits (p)					
	250	1,000	2,000	3,000	5,000	10,000
A. HOMOGENEOUS RATE OF CHANGE						
250	.076	.105	.088	.059	.021	.001
1,000	.105	.094	.065	.041	.013	.001
2,000	.088	.065	.041	.024	.007	.000
3,000	.059	.041	.024	.013	.004	.000
5,000	.021	.013	.007	.004	.001	.000
10,000	.001	.001	.000	.000	.000	.000
B. INHOMOGENEOUS RATE OF CHANGE						
250	.076	.105	.090	.064	.028	.004
1,000	.105	.096	.070	.048	.021	.003
2,000	.090	.070	.048	.032	.014	.002
3,000	.064	.048	.032	.021	.009	.001
5,000	.028	.021	.014	.009	.004	.001
10,000	.004	.003	.002	.001	.001	.000

363

Table B.23. *aabc → abcd*

Years following splits (q)	Years before splits (p)					
	250	1,000	2,000	3,000	5,000	10,000
A. HOMOGENEOUS RATE OF CHANGE						
250	.009	.034	.057	.062	.046	.008
1,000	.034	.053	.062	.058	.037	.006
2,000	.057	.062	.058	.049	.027	.004
3,000	.062	.058	.049	.037	.019	.003
5,000	.046	.037	.027	.019	.009	.001
10,000	.008	.006	.004	.003	.001	.000
B. INHOMOGENEOUS RATE OF CHANGE						
250	.009	.034	.056	.062	.052	.019
1,000	.034	.052	.062	.061	.046	.016
2,000	.056	.062	.061	.054	.038	.013
3,000	.062	.061	.054	.046	.031	.010
5,000	.052	.046	.038	.031	.020	.006
10,000	.019	.016	.013	.010	.006	.002

Table B.24. *abcd → abcd*

Years following splits (q)	Years before splits (p)					
	250	1,000	2,000	3,000	5,000	10,000
A. HOMOGENEOUS RATE OF CHANGE						
250	.004	.047	.173	.337	.634	.946
1,000	.047	.136	.295	.459	.718	.961
2,000	.173	.295	.459	.603	.804	.974
3,000	.337	.459	.603	.718	.867	.983
5,000	.634	.718	.804	.867	.940	.993
10,000	.946	.961	.974	.983	.993	.999
B. INHOMOGENEOUS RATE OF CHANGE						
250	.005	.046	.161	.303	.559	.874
1,000	.046	.128	.267	.407	.633	.895
2,000	.161	.267	.407	.531	.715	.917
3,000	.303	.407	.531	.633	.778	.935
5,000	.559	.633	.715	.778	.866	.958
10,000	.874	.895	.917	.935	.958	.985

Table B.25. Cognate Distributions and True Classifications for Tables B.1–B.24

Table number	Distribution → true classification	Table number	Distribution → true classification
B.1	aaaa → aabb	B.14	abcd → aabc
B.2	aaab, aaba, abaa, abbb → aabb	B.15	aaaa → aaab
B.3	aabb → aabb	B.16	aaab → aaab
B.4	aabc, abcc → aabb	B.17	abbb, abaa, aaba → aaab
B.5	abac, abcb, abca, abbc → aabb	B.18	abbc, aabc, abac → aaab
B.6	abcd → aabb	B.19	abcc, abca, abcb → aaab
B.7	aaaa → aabc	B.20	abcd → aaab
B.8	aabb → aabc	B.21	aaaa → abcd
B.9	abbb, abaa → aabc	B.22	aaab, abbb, abaa, aaba → abcd
B.10	aaba, aaab → aabc	B.23	aabc, abcc, abac, abbc, abca,
B.11	aabc → aabc		abcb → abcd
B.12	abcc → aabc	B.24	abcd → abcd
B.13	abcb, abbc, abca, abac → aabc		

NOTE: Types *abab* and *abba* should not occur when *aabb* or *abca* is the true classification, and types *aabb*, *abab*, and *abbd* should not occur with true classification *aaab* or *abcd*, a fact that led Gleason (1959) to exclude certain classifications. These variants could, however, occur by semantic change.

Table B.26. Generating Functions for Tables B.1–B.24

Table number	Function
B.1	x^2y^4
B.2	$x^2y^3 - x^2y^4$
B.3	$y^4 - x^2y^4$
B.4	$2x^2y^4 - 2x^2y^3 + y^2 - y^4$
B.5	$x^2y^2 - 2x^2y^3 + x^2y^4$
B.6	$1 - 4x^2y^4 + 8x^2y^3 - 4x^2y^2 + y^4 - 2y^2$
B.7	x^3y^4
B.8	$x^2y^4 - x^3y^4$
B.9	$x^3y^3 - x^3y^4$
B.10	$x^2y^3 - x^3y^4$
B.11	$y^3 \quad 2x^2y^3 - x^2y^4 + 2x^3y^4$
B.12	$x^2y^2 - x^2y^4 - 2x^3y^3 + 2x^3y^4$
B.13	$x^2y^2 - x^2y^3 - x^3y^3 + x^3y^4$
B.14	$1 - 4x^3y^4 + x^2y^4 + 4x^3y^3 + 4x^2y^3 - 5x^2y^2 - y^2$
B.15	x^2y^4 (= Table B.1)
B.16	$y^3 - x^2y^4$
B.17	$x^2y^3 - x^2y^4$ (= Table B.2)
B.18	$x^2y^4 - x^2y^3 + y^2 - y^3$
B.19	$x^2y^2 - 2x^2y^3 + x^2y^4$ (= Table B.5)
B.20	$1 - 3x^2y^4 + 6x^2y^3 - 3x^2y^2 - 3y^2 + 2y^3$
B.21	x^4
B.22	$x^3 - x^4$
B.23	$x^2 - 2x^3 + x^4$
B.24	$1 - 6x^2 + 8x^3 - 3x^4$

Table B.27. Data for Tables B.1, B.7, B.15, and B.21

Table number	A. Homogeneous rate	B. Inhomogeneous rate	True classification
B.1, B.15	3.080	3.151	aabb, aaab
B.7	2.900	2.980	aabc
B.21	2.550	2.710	abcd

Table B.28. Data for Tables B.6, B.14, B.20, and B.24

Table number	A. Homogeneous rate	B. Inhomogeneous rate	True classification
B.20	4.85	5.22	aaab
B.6	4.71	5.04	aabb
B.14	4.50	4.79	aabc
B.24	4.27	4.73	abcd

Table B.29. Data for Tables B.6, B.14, B.20, and B.24
($p = 10, q = 10$)

Table number	A. Homogeneous rate	B. Inhomogeneous rate	True classification
B.20	.968	.923	aaab
B.6	.977	.942	aabb
B.14	.988	.968	aabc
B.24	.999	.985	abcd

Table B.30. Data for Tables B.3, B.11, and B.16

Years following splits (q)	Table 3 (aabb)		Table 16 (aaab)		Table 11 (aabc)	
	A. Hom. rate	B. Inhom. rate	A. Hom. rate	B. Inhom. rate	A. Hom. rate	B. Inhom. rate
250	.800	.796	.846	.843	.894	.892
1,000	.410	.410	.512	.512	.640	.640
2,000	.168	.177	.262	.272	.410	.420
3,000	.069	.080	.134	.150	.262	.282
5,000	.012	.018	.035	.050	.107	.136
10,000	.000	.001	.001	.005	.012	.028

Table B.31. Data for Tables B.2, B.9, and B.17 and Tables B.5, B.12, B.13, and B.19

Table number	A. Homogeneous rate		B. Inhomogeneous rate	
	q	max r	q	max r
B.2, B.9, B.17	1.29	.105	1.30	.105
B.5, B.12, B.13, B.19	3.11	.063	3.32	.063

Table B.32. Data for Tables B.4 and B.18

Table number	A. Homogeneous rate		B. Inhomogeneous rate	
	q	max r	q	max r
B.4	1.56	.250	1.58	.250
B.18	1.82	.148	1.86	.148

Table B.33. Data for Tables B.8 and B.10

Table number	A. Homogeneous rate		B. Inhomogeneous rate	
	p	max r	p	max r
B.8, B.10	1.82	.148	1.06	.148

Table B.34. Data for Tables B.22 and B.23

Table number	A. Homogeneous rate		B. Inhomogeneous rate	
	p	max r	p	max r
B.23	3.11	.063	3.32	.062
B.22	1.29	.106	1.30	.105

Appendix C

Distribution of the Amerind Etymologies

This appendix presents two tables summarizing the distribution of the 329 etymologies given in Chapters 4 and 5 that are found in two or more of the 11 Amerind stocks. Table C.1 shows the distribution of all 281 Amerind etymologies listed in the dictionary; the entry numbers correspond exactly with the order of presentation there. The numbers in Table C.2, which covers the grammatical etymologies in Chapter 5, correspond to the item numbers in that chapter. In both tables the data are tabulated in north–south order under the following abbreviations:

AK	Almosan-Keresiouan	MT	Macro-Tucanoan
P	Penutian	E	Equatorial
H	Hokan	MC	Macro-Carib
CA	Central Amerind	MP	Macro-Panoan
CP	Chibchan-Paezan	MG	Macro-Ge
AN	Andean		

Parenthetical entries indicate uncertainty about an item's relationship to the rest of the etymology (e.g., the item in question may occur in only one subgroup of the stock, or in only a few languages).

Table C.1. Distribution of the Etymologies in Chapter 4

Chap. 4 no.	AK	P	H	CA	CP	AN	MT	E	MC	MP	MG
1					X				X		X
2	X	X	X		X		X		X	X	X
3						X		X			
4					X				X		
5					X		X	X			
6		X		(X)		X					
7			X		X	X		X	X	X	X
8	X	X									
9			X						X		X
10	X						X				X
11	X	X	X		X			X		X	X
12						X			X	X	
13				(X)				X			X
14	X			X			X	X	(X)	X	
15	X								X	X	
16		X						X			X
17			X								X
18	X									X	
19			X					X			
20		X	X				X				
21								X		X	X
22	X	X		X	X	X					
23							X	X			
24	X			(X)				X			
25			X			X	X				
26						X				X	X
27	X	X	X	(X)			X				
28		X	X	X						X	
29							X	X		X	X
30	X	X			X	X	X	X			X
31						X		X	X		
32			X						X	X	X
33	X	X		X	X	X	X		X	X	X
34							X			X	
35	X	X	X		X	X				X	X
36				X	X						
37		X	X			X	X				
38	X		X			X				X	X
39			X	X			X	X			X
40		X				X		X	X		

Table C.1. Distribution of the Etymologies in Chapter 4 *(cont.)*

Chap. 4 no.	AK	P	H	CA	CP	AN	MT	E	MC	MP	MG
41	X			X	X		X	X		X	
42		X		X						X	X
43		X	X	X		X			X		X
44								X			X
45		X	X		X						
46							X				X
47	X	X	X								
48			X		X						
49		X	X		X				X		
50	X	X	X			X	X	X		X	X
51	X	X									
52	X	X	X								
53	(X)	X	X	X	X	X	X	X	X	X	X
54	X	X	X				X	X			
55		X		(X)		X			X		
56	(X)	X	X	X	X	X				X	
57						X			X	X	X
58		X		X							
59	X	X					X	X		X	X
60						X			X		
61				(X)	X	X				X	X
62		X					X	X			
63				X			X		X	X	X
64		X	X	(X)		X					
65	X	X			X			X			
66	X		X		X					X	X
67				X	X	X		X		X	X
68		X		X	X						
69	X			(X)	X	X			X		
70	X	X	X		X						
71			X			X					
72	X	X	X			X	X		X	X	X
73		X	X			X				X	
74				(X)	X	X	X			X	
75						X				X	
76	X	X			X			X			
77					X					X	
78	X			X							
79			X	(X)	X	X	X	X		X	X
80						X		X			

Table C.1. Distribution of the Etymologies in Chapter 4 *(cont.)*

Chap. 4 no.	AK	P	H	CA	CP	AN	MT	E	MC	MP	MG
81				X					X		X
82	X			X	X			X			
83			X				X			X	
84		X				X					
85	X	X					X	X			X
86			X		X						
87	X	X	X			X	X	X		X	X
88						X		X			
89		X	X								
90		X	X			X	X	X			
91						X			X		
92				X	X						
93							X	X			
94						X		X			
95	X				X			X			
96	X	X	X								X
97		X		X			X	X	X		
98	X	X					X			X	
99						X	X				X
100						X	X				
101		X			X			X			
102	X		X		X						X
103	X			(X)			X				
104			X	X			X	X	X	X	X
105	X										X
106		X			X			X			X
107			X								X
108		X	X			X		X	X		
109				X	X	X	X		X	X	X
110			X					X	X		X
111									X	X	
112	X			X	X					X	X
113									X		X
114		X				X	X				
115					X	X					X
116	X	X								X	
117	X	X	X				X				X
118		X	X				X	X			X
119					X			X			
120		X	X	X			X	X	X	X	X

Table C.1. Distribution of the Etymologies in Chapter 4 *(cont.)*

Chap. 4 no.	AK	P	H	CA	CP	AN	MT	E	MC	MP	MG
121	X	X	X							X	
122	X				X			X		X	
123				(X)	X		X				X
124							X				X
125	X	X	X	X							
126	X	X		X	X	X	X	X		X	X
127									X		X
128	X	X	X	X	X						
129		X				X				X	
130	(X)		X		(X)			X		X	
131	(X)		X	(X)	X		X	X			
132					X		X		X		
133	X					X		X			
134									X	X	X
135			X			X					
136	X		X								
137	X	X	X	X	X	X	X	X		X	X
138	X						X			X	X
139			X		X	X			X		X
140		X	X	X	X			X	X		
141	X				X						
142						X		X			
143								X			X
144	X									X	X
145		X		(X)	X						
146						X	X				
147			X								X
148			X				X				
149	X									X	X
150	X	X	X			X					
151			X				X				
152	X	X									
153	X			X	X	X		X	(X)	X	
154			X				X	X			X
155			X		X			X	X		X
156		X			X		X	X		X	
157		X	X	(X)	X						
158	X	X									
159	X	X	X	X			X	X		X	X
160	X	X		(X)		X					

Table C.1. Distribution of the Etymologies in Chapter 4 *(cont.)*

Chap. 4 no.	AK	P	H	CA	CP	AN	MT	E	MC	MP	MG
161				(X)	X	X					
162								X			X
163				X			X	X			
164			X						X		
165		X		X			X	X	X	X	X
166		X	X	(X)	X		X				
167								X	X	X	
168	(X)		X		X			X			
169					X			X			
170		X			X		X		X		X
171	X	X	X		X						
172					X					X	X
173	X		X								
174		X	X								
175	X		X	X					X	X	X
176		X		(X)	X						
177		X	X								
178			X			X					
179		X						X			X
180						X			X		X
181			X		X						
182		X			X						
183						X				X	
184							X	X			X
185			X	(X)			X				
186									X		X
187									X		X
188					X		X				
189					X		X				X
190					X	X					
191			X			X	X	X		X	
192									X	X	X
193				X	X						
194							X	X			
195		X				X					
196		X		X							X
197					X					X	
198		X	X								
199	X		X								
200					X			X			

Table C.1. Distribution of the Etymologies in Chapter 4 *(cont.)*

Chap. 4 no.	AK	P	H	CA	CP	AN	MT	E	MC	MP	MG
201						X				X	X
202									X	X	
203									X	X	
204		X					X				
205						X			X		
206							X	X			
207						X				X	
208									X	X	
209								X	X		
210		X		X							
211					X	X			X		X
212		X				X	X		X		
213		X		X				X			
214						X		X			
215		X	X		X	X					
216						X		X			
217		X			X	X		X			X
218	X	X									
219	X		X								
220	X	X		X				X	X		
221		X							X	X	
222										X	X
223					X	X					
224	X	X	X							X	X
225						X					X
226		X				X					
227						X		X			
228	X		X								
229		X							X		
230							X			X	X
231	X		X								
232	X					X					
233						X				(X)	X
234	X	X	X								
235		X						X	X		X
236							X	X			
237	X			(X)			X		X		
238	X	X	X								
239	X	X	X	(X)							X
240		X			X	X			X		X

Table C.1. Distribution of the Etymologies in Chapter 4 *(cont.)*

Chap. 4 no.	AK	P	H	CA	CP	AN	MT	E	MC	MP	MG
241					X		X	X			
242		X	X								
243			X	X			X			X	X
244		X	X	(X)	X						
245						X					X
246	X		X		X	X					
247							X	X			
248			X		X		X	X	X	X	X
249					X	X	X				
250		X			X						
251		X			X						
252	X	X									
253									X	X	X
254		X	X					X			X
255		X	X								
256					X		X		X		
257							X				X
258				X			X	X			X
259		X		X				X	X		
260						X			X		
261		X			X			•			
262		X		(X)	X	X	X				
263			X	(X)				X			
264	(X)				X		X		X		
265		X		X	X		X				X
266					X		X	X		X	
267	X		X								
268					X	X					X
269	X	X	X								
270	X	X	X		X	X				X	X
271						X	X	X			
272								X		X	
273		X		X	X						
274	X		X		X		X				
275			X		X						X
276	X	X			X	X		X			
277							X	X			X
278					X			X			
279	X			X							
280							X	X			X
281								X			X

Table C.2. Distribution of the Amerind Etymologies in Chapter 5

Chap. 5 no.	AK	P	H	CA	CP	AN	MT	E	MC	MP	MG
1	X	X	X	X	X	X	X	X	X	X	X
2		X	X	X	X	X	X	X	X	X	X
3		X			X		X				
6	X	X	X	X	X	X	X	X	X	X	X
7									X	X	X
10					X		X				X
12				X	X			X	X	X	X
13	X		X			X	X		X	X	X
14	X	X		X					X	X	X
15						X		X			
16			X			X				X	
19	X	X	X	X		X			X		
21		X			(X)						
22			X				X	X			X
23					X				X	X	X
25								X	X	X	X
29		X	X								
30					X	X	X	X			
31		X		X							X
32	X	X									
33					X					X	
34										X	(X)
38										X	X
39						X	X				
45	X	X	X		X	X					X
46		X							X	X	X
47		X			X	X		X			
48			X			X	X	X			
49		X			X	X				X	
52							X	X			
53		X			X						
60							X	X			
61		X	X		X	X					
66			X							X	
70	X	X									
71					X				X		
73	X	X									
74		X	X								
77			X							X	X
78										X	X

Table C.2. Distribution of the Amerind Etymologies in Chapter 5

Chap. 5 no.	AK	P	H	CA	CP	AN	MT	E	MC	MP	MG
81				X			X				
82										X	X
86	X	X			X	X				X	X
92	X					X					
93								X		X	
100			X	X							X
102		X	X		X	X					
103		X			X			X			X

Appendix D

Summary of the Classification

The languages of the New World, as demonstrated in the text, fall into three distinct and independent families: (1) Eskimo-Aleut (part of the Eurasiatic family), (2) Na-Dene, and (3) Amerind. The following classification lists all the New World languages mentioned in the book, illustrating the genetic relationships posited.

The classification of Amerind that follows may seem, in two respects, to depart from that implied by the foregoing chapters: it lists six basic Amerind stocks, rather than the 11 discussed consistently in text (but see p. 60, which explains the aggregating of the 11 into six); and it follows, for purely genetic reasons, a generally north-to-south progression, whereas the etymologies in text pursue, for purely practical reasons, a south-to-north progression (the seeming disparity is of no consequence).

In a few instances groups that have been treated separately in the etymologies (for historical reasons) are here joined in a higher-level grouping. For example, Yukian and Gulf are cited separately in the etymologies in Chapters 3 and 4 because they have traditionally been thought to have no special relationship to each other. I consider them both members of a single group, which I call Yuki-Gulf. Moreover, it is not even apparent that Yukian is its most divergent member, despite its enormous geographic separation from the remainder of the group. Similarly, a Ritwan group is posited in the classification (following Sapir), though Wiyot and Yurok have been cited independently in the etymologies.

Group names are in capital letters: BORORO is a group, Bororo is a specific language. In the Amerind classification, when no further subgrouping is apparent, the subgroups are ordered alphabetically within each group, as are the languages within each subgroup.

378

ESKIMO-ALEUT

I ALEUT: Aleut
II ESKIMO
  A YUIT: Central Alaskan Eskimo, Pacific Coast Alaskan Eskimo, Siberian
    Eskimo, Sirenik
  B INUIT: North Alaskan Eskimo, Canadian Eskimo, Greenlandic Eskimo

NA-DENE

I HAIDA: Haida
II CONTINENTAL NA-DENE
  A TLINGIT: Tlingit
  B ATHABASKAN-EYAK
    1 EYAK: Eyak
    2 ATHABASKAN: Tanaina, Chipewyan, Apache, Navajo, etc.

AMERIND

I NORTHERN AMERIND
A ALMOSAN-KERESIOUAN
  1 ALMOSAN
    a ALGIC
      (1) ALGONQUIAN: Abenaki, Arapaho, Beothuk, Blackfoot,
        Cheyenne, Chippewa, Cree, Delaware, Fox, Gros Ventre,
        Kickapoo, Kowilth, Menomini, Miami, Micmac, Mohegan,
        Montagnais, Munsee, Natick, Northern Arapaho, Ojibwa,
        Potowotami, Shawnee
      (2) RITWAN
        (a) WIYOT: Wishosk, Wiyot
        (b) YUROK: Yurok
    b KUTENAI: Kutenai
    c MOSAN
      (1) CHEMAKUAN: Chemakum, Quileute
      (2) SALISH: Bella Coola, Chilliwak, Coeur d'Alene, Columbian,
        Cowichan, Kalispel, Lillooet, Lkungen, Musqueam, Nisqualli,
        Nootsack, Pentlatch, Shuswap, Siciatl, Snanaimuk, Snohomish,
        Songish, Spokane, Squamish, Thompson, Tillamook, Twana,
        Upper Chehalis
      (3) WAKASHAN: Bella Bella, Kwakiutl, Nitinat, Nootka
  2 KERESIOUAN
    a CADDOAN: Adai, Arikara, Caddo, Kitsai, Pawnee, Wichita
    b IROQUOIAN: Cherokee, Huron, Mohawk, Onandaga, Oneida, Seneca,
      Tuscarora, Wyandot

    c KERESAN: Acoma, Keres, Laguna, Santa Ana, Santo Domingo

    d SIOUAN-YUCHI

      (1) YUCHI: Yuchi

      (2) SIOUAN: Assiniboin, Biloxi, Catawba, Chiwere, Crow, Dakota, Hidatsa, Mandan, Ofo, Osage, Quapaw, Santee, Teton, Tutelo, Winnebago, Woccon

B PENUTIAN

  1 CALIFORNIA

    a MAIDU: Maidu, Nisenan, Northeast Maidu, South Maidu

    b MIWOK-COSTANOAN

      (1) COSTANOAN: Monterey, Mutsun, Rumsien, San Francisco, San José, San Juan Bautista, Santa Clara, Santa Cruz, Soledad

      (2) MIWOK: Bodega, Central Sierra Miwok, Coastal Miwok, Lake Miwok, Marin Miwok, Northern Sierra Miwok, Plains Miwok, Southern Sierra Miwok, Tuolumne, Western Miwok

    c WINTUN: Colouse, Kope, Noema, Nomlaki, North Wintu, Patwin, Sacramento River, South Wintu, West Wintu, Wintu

    d YOKUTS: Calavera, Gashowu, Yaudanchi, Yawelmani, Yokuts

  2 CHINOOK: Chinook, Wasco, Wishram

  3 MEXICAN

    a HUAVE: Huave

    b MAYAN: Aguacatec, Chol, Chontal, Chorti, Huastec, Ixil, Jacaltec, Kakchiquel, Kekchí, Mam, Maya, Pokomchi, Quiché, Tzeltal, Tzotzil, Tzutuhil, Uspantec, Yucatec

    c MIXE-ZOQUE: Ayutla, Mixe, Oluta, Sayula, Sierra Popoluca, Tetontepec, Texistepec, Western Mixe, Zoque

    d TOTONAC: Papantla, Tepehua, Totonac

  4 OREGON: Alsea, Coos, Iakon, Kalapuya, Lower Umpqua, Miluk, Siuslaw, Takelma, Yakonan

  5 PLATEAU: Cayuse, Klamath, Lutuami, Modoc, Molala, Nez Perce, North Sahaptin, Sahaptin, Yakima

  6 TSIMSHIAN: Nass, Tsimshian

  7 YUKI-GULF

    a ATAKAPA: Atakapa

    b CHITIMACHA: Chitimacha

    c MUSKOGEAN: Alabama, Apalachee, Chickasaw, Choctaw, Creek, Hitchiti, Koasati, Mikasuki, Muskokee

    d NATCHEZ: Natchez

    e TUNICA: Tunica

    f YUKIAN: Clear Lake Yuki, Coast Yuki, Huchnom, Wappo, Yuki

  8 ZUNI: Zuni

C HOKAN

  1 NUCLEAR HOKAN

    a NORTHERN

     (1) KAROK-SHASTA
- (a) KAROK: Arra-Arra, Karok
- (b) CHIMARIKO: Chimariko
- (c) SHASTA-ACHOMAWI
  - I SHASTA: Konomihu, Shasta
  - II ACHOMAWI: Achomawi, Atsugewi

     (2) YANA: Central Yana, North Yana, South Yana, Yahi

     (3) POMO: Central Pomo, Clear Lake, East Pomo, Kashaya, North Pomo, Northeast Pomo, South Pomo, Southeast Pomo, Southwest Pomo

   b WASHO: Washo

   c ESSELEN-YUMAN

     (1) ESSELEN: Esselen

     (2) YUMAN: Akwa'ala, Campo, Cochimi, Cochiti, Cocopa, Diegueño, Havasupai, Kahwan, Kiliwa, Maricopa, Mohave, Tipai, Tonto, Walapai, Yavapai, Yuma

   d SALINAN-SERI

     (1) SALINAN: San Antonio, San Miguel

     (2) CHUMASH: La Purisima, San Buenaventura, San Luis Obispo, Santa Barbara, Santa Cruz, Santa Rosa, Santa Ynez

     (3) SERI: Seri

   e WAICURI: Waicuri

   f MARATINO: Maratino

   g QUINIGUA: Quinigua

   h TEQUISTLATEC: Tequistlatec (= Chontal)

  2 COAHUILTECAN

   a TONKAWA: Tonkawa

   b NUCLEAR COAHUILTECAN

     (1) COAHUILTECO: Coahuilteco

     (2) COTONAME: Cotoname

     (3) COMECRUDO: Comecrudo

   c KARANKAWA: Karankawa

  3 SUBTIABA: Subtiaba, Tlappanec

  4 JICAQUE: Jicaque

  5 YURUMANGUI: Yurumangui

II CENTRAL AMERIND

A KIOWA-TANOAN

  1 KIOWA: Kiowa

  2 TANOAN: Hopi Tewa, Isleta, Jemez, Piro, San Ildefonso, San Juan, Santa Clara, Taos, Tewa, Towa

B OTO-MANGUE: Azmugo, Chiapanec, Chinantec, Ixcatec, Mangue, Mazahua, Mixtec, Otomi, Pame, Popoloca, Zapotec

C UTO-AZTECAN: Cora, Hopi, Huichol, Mejicano Azteco, Mono, Nahuatl, Opata, Papago, Pima, Shoshone, Southern Paiute, Tarahumara, Varohio, Yaqui

III CHIBCHAN-PAEZAN
  A CHIBCHAN
    1 CUITLATEC: Cuitlatec
    2 LENCA: Chilanga, Guajiquero, Intibucat, Membreno, Opatoro, Similaton
    3 NUCLEAR CHIBCHAN
      a ANTIOQUIA: Katio, Nutabe
      b ARUAK: Atanque, Bintucua, Guamaca, Kagaba, Tairona
      c CHIBCHA: Boncota, Chibcha, Duit, Manare, Margua, Pedraza,
        Sinsiga, Tegria, Tunebo, Uncasica
      d CUNA: Cueva, Cuna
      e GUAYMI: Changuena, Chumulu, Gualaca, Guaymi, Move, Muoi,
        Murire, Norteño, Penomeño, Sabanero
      f MALIBU: Chimila
      g MISUMALPAN: Cacaopera, Matagalpa, Miskito, Sumu, Tawaska,
        Ulua
      h MOTILON: Barira, Dobocubi, Motilon
      i RAMA: Corobisi, Guatuso, Guetar, Rama
      j TALAMANCA: Borunca, Bribri, Cabecar, Chiripo, Estrella, Terraba,
        Tiribi, Tirub, Viceyta
    4 PAYA: Paya
    5 TARASCAN: Tarascan
    6 XINCA: Chiquimulilla, Jutiapa, Sinacatan, Xinca, Yupultepec
    7 YANOAMA: Sanema, Shiriana, Yanam, Yanoam, Yanomam, Yanomamï
  B PAEZAN
    1 ALLENTIAC: Allentiac, Millcayac
    2 ATACAMA: Atacama
    3 BETOI: Betoi
    4 CHIMU: Chimu, Eten, Mochica
    5 ITONAMA: Itonama
    6 JIRAJARA: Ayoman, Gayon, Jirajara
    7 MURA: Matanawi, Mura, Mura-Piraha
    8 NUCLEAR PAEZAN
      a ANDAQUI: Andaqui
      b BARBACOA: Cara, Cayapa, Colorado, Cuaiquer
      c CHOCO: Andagueda, Baudo, Catio, Chami, Choco, Citara, Darien,
        Empera, Napipi, Nonama, Saija, Sambu, Tado, Tucura, Uribe,
        Waunana
      d PAEZ: Coconuco, Guambiana, Guanaca, Moguex, Paez, Panikita,
        Totoro
    9 TIMUCUA: Tawasa, Timucua
    10 WARRAU: Warrau
IV ANDEAN
  A AYMARA: Aymara, Jaqaru, Lupaca
  B ITUCALE-SABELA

     1 ITUCALE: Itucale
     2 MAYNA: Mayna
     3 SABELA: Auca, Sabela, Tuwituwey
  C KAHUAPANA-ZAPARO
     1 KAHUAPANA: Jebero, Kahuapana, Tschaahui
     2 ZAPARO: Andoa, Arabela, Iquito, Shimigae, Zaparo
  D NORTHERN
     1 CATACAO: Catacao, Colan
     2 CHOLONA: Cholona, Hivito
     3 CULLI: Culli
     4 LECO: Leco
     5 SECHURA: Sec, Sechura
  E QUECHUA: Ancash, Caraz, Chinchaysuyu, Cochabamba, Ecuadorean, Huanacucho, Huanuco, Junin, Junin-Huanca, Lamisto, Santiagueño, Wanka, Yanacocha
  F SOUTHERN
     1 ALAKALUF: Alakaluf, Kaueskar
     2 ARAUCANIAN: Araucanian, Mapuche, Moluche, Pehuenche
     3 GENNAKEN: Gennaken, Pehuelche
     4 PATAGON: Hongote, Manekenkn, Ona, Patagon, Tehuelche, Teuesh, Tsoneka
     5 YAMANA: Yahgan, Yamana
V EQUATORIAL-TUCANOAN
  A MACRO-TUCANOAN
     1 AUIXIRI: Auixiri
     2 CANICHANA: Canichana
     3 CAPIXANA: Capixana
     4 CATUQUINA: Bendiapa, Canamari, Catauisi, Catuquina, Parawa
     5 GAMELLA: Gamella
     6 HUARI: Huari, Masaka
     7 IRANSHE: Iranshe
     8 KALIANA-MAKU
        a AUAKE: Auake
        b KALIANA. Kaliana
        c MAKU: Maku
     9 KOAIA: Koaia
    10 MOBIMA: Mobima
    11 MUNICHE: Muniche
    12 NAMBIKWARA: Mamainde, Nambikwara, Northern Nambikwara, Sabane, Southern Nambikwara
    13 NATU: Natu
    14 PANKARURU: Pankaruru
    15 PUINAVE: Curiariai, Dou, Hubde, Macu-Papury, Marahan, Nadobo, Papury, Parana Boaboa, Puinave, Querari, Tiquie, Ubde-Nehern, Yehubde

16 SHUKURU: Shukuru
17 TICUNA-YURI
   a TICUNA: Ticuna
   b YURI: Yuri
18 TUCANO: Amaguaje, Bahukiwa, Bara, Buhagana, Chiranga, Coreguaje, Coto, Cubeo, Curetu, Desana, Dyurema, Dyurumawa, Erulia, Hehenawa, Palanoa, Pioje, Piojeuti, Sara, Siona, Tama, Tsoloa, Tucano, Tuyuka, Tuyulu, Uaiana, Uasona, Waikina, Wanana, Wiriana, Yahuna, Yeba, Yupua
19 UMAN: Uman
B EQUATORIAL
  1 MACRO-ARAWAKAN
    a GUAHIBO: Churuya, Cuiva, Guahibo, Guayabero
    b KATEMBRI: Katembri
    c OTOMACO: Otomaco, Taparita
    d TINIGUA: Pamigua, Tinigua
    e ARAWAKAN
      (1) ARAWA: Culino, Jarua, Paumari, Yamamadi
      (2) MAIPURAN: Achagua, Adzaneni, Amarakaeri, Amuesha, Anauya, Apolista, Apurina, Araicu, Arawak, Atoroi, Baniva, Bare, Baure, Black Carib, Cabere, Campa, Canamari, Carutana, Cauishana, Cayeri, Chamicuro, Chana, Chiriana, Chontaquiro, Curipaco, Goajiro, Guana, Guinau, Ignaciano, Ipurina, Island Carib, Jumana, Kariay, Karif, Karro, Karutana, Kozarini, Kuniba, Kustenau, Machiguenga, Manao, Mandauaca, Mapidiana, Marawa, Mashco, Maypure, Mehinacu, Moxo, Palicur, Paraujano, Paresi, Passe, Piapoco, Piro, Resigaro, Siusi, Tariana, Terena, Tereno, Toyeri, Uainuma, Uarakena, Wachipairi, Wapishana, Waura, Yaulapiti, Yavitero, Yucuna
      (3) CHAPACURA: Abitana, Chapacura, Itene, Kitemoka, Mure, Pawumwa, Quitemo, Tora, Urupa, Wanyam, Yaru, Yuva
      (4) GUAMO: San José, Santa Rosa
      (5) URO: Callahuaya, Caranga, Chipaya, Puquina, Uro
  2 CAYUVAVA: Cayuvava
  3 COCHE: Coche
  4 JIBARO-KANDOSHI
    a COFAN: Cofan
    b ESMERALDA: Esmeralda
    c JIBARO: Aguaruna, Gualaquiza, Huambisa, Jibaro, Shuara, Upano, Zamora
    d KANDOSHI: Kandoshi, Murato, Shapra
    e YARURO: Yaruro
  5 KARIRI-TUPI
    a KARIRI: Dzubucua, Kamaru, Kariri, Sapuya

    b TUPI: Abanee, Amniapa, Apichum, Arara, Arikem, Awety, Chiriguano, Cocama, Digüt, Emerillon, Guajajara, Guaraní, Guarategaja, Guarayo, Guayaki, Kabishiana, Kamayura, Kawahib, Kepkiriwate, Kuruaya, Makurape, Manitsawa, Maue, Mekens, Mondé, Mundurucu, Oyampi, Pawate, Purubora, Ramarama, Sanamaika, Sheta, Shipaya, Siriono, Tapute, Tembe, Tupari, Tupi, Uruku, Wirafed, Yuruna

  6 PIAROA: Macu, Piaroa, Saliba

  7 TARUMA: Taruma

  8 TIMOTE: Cuica, Maguri, Maripu, Mocochi, Timote

  9 TRUMAI: Trumai

10 TUSHA: Tusha

11 YURACARE: Yuracare

12 ZAMUCO: Ayoré, Chamacoco, Ebidoso, Guaranoco, Siracua, Tumraha, Zamuco

VI GE-PANO-CARIB

A MACRO-CARIB

  1 ANDOKE: Andoke

  2 BORA-UITOTO

    a BORA: Bora, Faai, Imihita, Miranya, Miranya Oira Assu-Tapuya, Muinane

    b UITOTO: Andoquero, Coeruna, Erare, Miranya Carapana Tapuya, Muinane, Nonuya, Ocaina, Orejone, Uitoto, Uitoto-Kaimo

  3 CARIB: Accawai, Apalai, Aparai, Apiaca, Arara, Arekuna, Azumara, Bakairí, Barama River, Carib, Carijona, Cariniaco, Chayma, Crichana, Cumanogoto, Diau, Galibi, Gimanoto, Guaque, Hianacoto, Hishcariana, Jaricuna, Kaliana, Macusi, Maiongom, Maquiritare, Motilon, Nahugua, Northern Wayana, Opone, Oyana, Palmella, Pariri, Pauishana, Pemon, Pimenteira, Roucouyenne, Surinam, Tamanaco, Taulipang, Trio, Waiwai, Wayana, Yabarana

  4 KUKURA: Kukura

  5 YAGUA: Masamae Yameo, Peba, Yagua, Yameo

B MACRO-PANOAN

  1 CHARRUAN. Chana, Charrua, Guenoa

  2 LENGUA: Angaite, Guana, Kaskiha, Lengua, Mascoy, Sanapana

  3 LULE-VILELA

    a LULE: Lule

    b VILELA: Vilela

  4 MATACO-GUAICURU

    a GUAICURU: Abipone, Caduveo, Guachi, Guaicuru, Komlek, Mbaya, Mocovi, Pilaga, Toba, Toba-Guazu

    b MATACO: Ashluslay, Choropi, Choroti, Chulupi, Chunupi, Churupi, Enimaga, Macca, Mataco, Nocten, Payagua, Suhin, Towothli, Vejoz

  5 MOSETEN: Moseten

6 PANO-TACANA

  a PANOAN: Amahuaca, Arazaire, Capanahua, Caripuna, Cashibo, Cashinahua, Cazinaua, Chacobo, Conibo, Culino, Marinahua, Mayoruna, Nocaman, Panobo, Shipibo

  b TACANAN: Arasa, Cavineña, Chama, Guarayo, Guariza, Huarayo, Reyesano, Tacana, Tiatinagua

C MACRO-GE

  1 BORORO: Bororo, Koraveka, Otuke, Umotina

  2 BOTOCUDO: Botocudo

  3 CARAJA: Caraja

  4 CHIQUITO: Chiquito, Churapa

  5 ERIKBATSA: Erikbatsa

  6 FULNIO: Fulnio

  7 GE-KAINGAN

    a KAINGAN: Apucarana, Aweikoma, Bugre, Came, Catarina, Dalbergia, Guarapuava, Ingain, Kaingan, Palmas, Serra do Chagu, Southern Kaingan, Tibagi

    b GE: Acroamirim, Apinage, Aponegicran, Cayapo, Chavante, Cherente, Chicriaba, Crengez, Geico, Gorotire, Ishikrin, Kadurukre, Karaho, Kradaho, Kraho, Krenje, Northern Cayapo, Northern Karaho, Ramkokamekran, Sakamekran, Southern Cayapo, Suya

  8 GUATO: Guato

  9 KAMAKAN: Cotoxo, Kamakan, Masacara, Meniens

  10 MASHAKALI: Capoxo, Hahahay, Kumanasho, Macuni, Malali, Mashakali, Monachobm, Monosho, Patasho

  11 OPAIE: Guachi, Opaie

  12 OTI: Oti

  13 PURI: Coroado, Coropo, Puri

  14 YABUTI: Arikapu, Mashubi, Yabuti

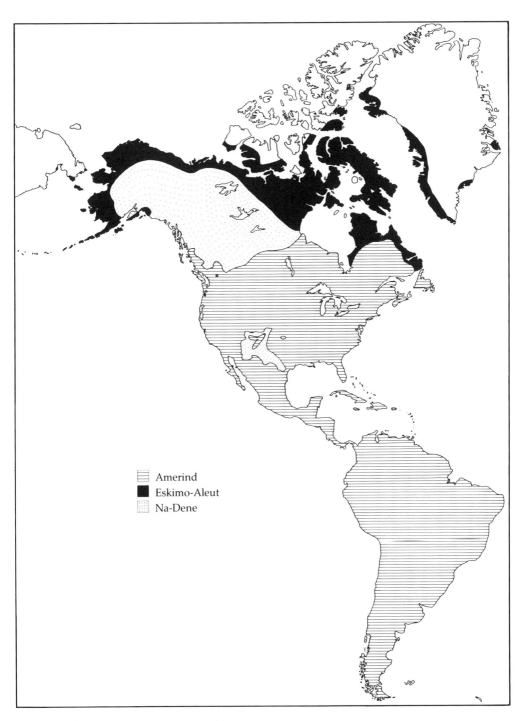

Amerind
Eskimo-Aleut
Na-Dene

Language families of the New World

387

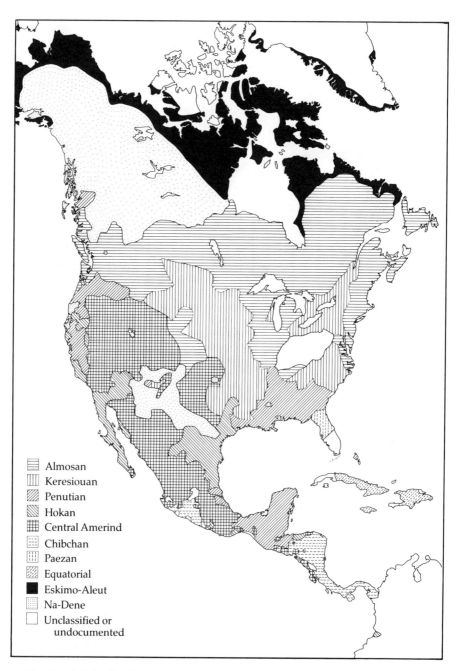

The legend reads:

Almosan
Keresiouan
Penutian
Hokan
Central Amerind
Chibchan
Paezan
Equatorial
Eskimo-Aleut
Na-Dene
Unclassified or undocumented

The Amerind family, North and Central America

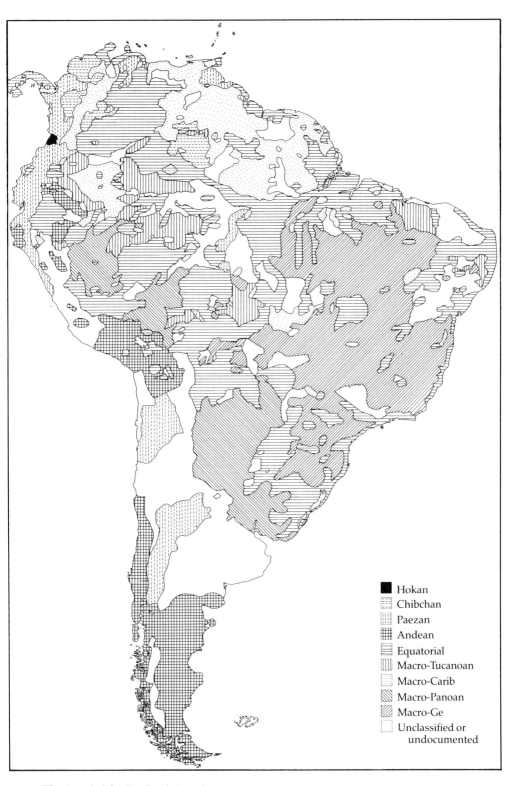

Hokan

Chibchan

Paezan

Andean

Equatorial

Macro-Tucanoan

Macro-Carib

Macro-Panoan

Macro-Ge

Unclassified or
undocumented

The Amerind family, South America

References Cited

References Cited

The following abbreviations are used in the References:

AA   *American Anthropologist.* Washington, D.C.: American Anthropological Association.

CTIL   *Current Trends in Linguistics*, 14 vols., ed. Thomas A. Sebeok. 1963–76. The Hague: Mouton.

HS   *Hokan Studies*, eds. Margaret Langdon and Shirley Silver. 1976. The Hague: Mouton.

IJAL   *International Journal of American Linguistics.* Chicago: University of Chicago Press.

JSA   *Journal de la Société des Américanistes.* Paris.

LNA   *The Languages of Native America*, ed. Lyle Campbell and Marianne Mithun. 1979. Austin: University of Texas Press.

UCPAAE *University of California Publications in American Archeology and Ethnology.* Berkeley: University of California.

UCPL   *University of California Publications in Linguistics.* Berkeley: University of California.

Achinstein, Peter. 1977. "History and Philosophy of Science: A Reply to Cohen," in Frederic Suppe, ed., *The Structure of Scientific Theories*, 2d ed. Urbana: University of Illinois Press, 350–60.

Allen, Louis. 1931. "Siouan and Iroquoian," *IJAL* 6:185–93.

Allen, W. S. 1953. "Relationship in Comparative Linguistics," *Transactions of the Philological Society*, 52–108.

Andrade, Manuel J. 1933. "Quileute," in *Handbook of American Indian Languages*, vol. 3, ed. Franz Boas. New York: Columbia University Press, 149–292.

Austin, William M. 1942. "Is Armenian an Anatolian Language?," *Language* 18:22–25.

References Cited

Beauchamp, William M. 1906. *Aboriginal Place Names of New York.* New York State Education Department, New York State Museum, Bulletin 108.

Beeler, M. S. 1976. "Barbareño Chumash: A Farrago," in *HS.*

Benedict, Paul K. 1976. "Sino-Tibetan: Another Look," *Journal of the American Oriental Society* 96:167–97.

Bibolotti, Benigno. 1917. *Moseteno Vocabulary and Treatises.* Evanston, Ill.: Northwestern University.

Bloomfield, Leonard. 1925. "On the Sound System of Central Algonquian," *Language* 1:130–56.

———. 1941. "Proto-Algonquian -i:t- 'fellow,'" *Language* 17:292–97.

———. 1946. "Algonquian," in *Linguistic Structures of Native America.* Viking Fund Publications in Anthropology 6:85–129.

Boas, Franz. 1929. "Classification of American Indian Languages," *Language* 5:1–7.

———. 1947. "Kwakiutl Grammar with a Glossary of Suffixes," ed. Helene Boas Yampolsky and Zellig S. Harris, *Transactions of the American Philosophical Society* 37:201–377.

Bopp, Franz. 1854. "Über das Albanische in seinen verwandschiftlichen Beziehungen," *Akademie der Wissenschaften Berlin, Abhandlungen Phil.-Hist. Klasse,* 459–549.

Bosswood, J. 1973. "Evidence for the Inclusion of Arikpatsa in the Macro-Ge Phylum," in *Serie Linguistica Miscellanea.* Brazil: Summer Institute of Linguistics.

Bouquiaux, Luc. 1967. "Le Système des classes nominales dans quelques langues (birom, ganawuri, anaguta, irigwe, kaje, rukuba, appartenant au groupe 'Plateau' (Nigeria centrale))," in *Colloque internationale sur la classification nominale dans les langues negro-africaines, Aix, France, 1967.* Paris: Éditions du Centre National de la Recherche Scientifique, Sciences Humaines.

Brockelmann, Carl. 1908. *Kurzgefasste vergleichende Grammatik der semitischen Sprachen.* Berlin: Reuther & Reichard.

Brugmann, Karl. 1886. *Grundriss der vergleichenden Grammatik der indogermanischen Sprachen,* vol. 1. Strassburg: Trübner.

———. 1902. *Kurze vergleichende Grammatik der indogermanischen Sprachen,* vol. 1. Strassburg: Trübner.

Buchwald, Otto von. 1918. "Migraciones sudamericanas," *Boletín de la Sociedad Ecuatoriana de Estudios Históricos Americanos* (Quito) 1:227–36.

Campbell, Lyle. 1977. *Quichean Linguistic Prehistory.* Berkeley: University of California Press.

Campbell, Lyle, and Marianne Mithun, eds. 1979. *The Languages of Native America: Historical and Comparative Assessment.* Austin: University of Texas Press.

Capell, A. 1939–40. "The Classification of Languages in North and Northwest Australia," *Oceania* 10:241–72, 404–33.

———. 1941–43. "Languages of Arnhem Land, North Australia," 2 parts, *Oceania* 12:364–92; 13:24–50.

Chafe, Wallace L. 1963. *Handbook of the Seneca Language.* Albany: New York
 State Museum, Bulletin 388.
———. 1964. "Another Look at Siouan and Iroquoian," *AA* 66:852–62.
———. 1973. "Siouan, Iroquoian and Caddoan," in *CTIL*, vol. 10.
———. 1979. "Caddoan," in *LNA*.
Christinat, Jean-Louis. 1963. "Mission ethnographique chez les indiens Erigpactsa
 (Mato Grosso)," *Bulletin de la Société Suisse des Américanistes* (Geneva)
 25:3–33.
Crawford, James M. 1979. "Timucua and Yuchi: Two Language Isolates of the
 Southeast," in *LNA*.
Crawford, Judith G. 1976. "Seri and Yuman," in *HS*.
Crévaux, J. 1882. "Vocabulaire de la langue yaroura," in J. Crévaux, P. Sagot, and
 L. Adam, *Grammaires et vocabulaires roucouyenne, arouagé, piapoco et d'au-
 tres langues,* Paris: Maisonneuve, 260–61.
Curr, Edward M. 1886–87. *The Australian Race.* Melbourne: Ferres.
Darnell, Regna, and Joel Sherzer. 1971. "Areal Linguistics in North America:
 A Historical Perspective," *IJAL* 37:20–28.
Darwin, Charles. 1871. *The Descent of Man and Selection in Relation to Sex.* Lon-
 don: Murray.
Davis, Irvine. 1966. "Comparative Je Phonology," *Estudios Lingüísticos*
 1.2:10–24.
———. 1968. "Some Macro-Je Relationships," *IJAL* 34:42–47.
———. 1979. "The Kiowa-Tanoan, Keresan, and Zuni Languages," in *LNA*.
Delbrück, Berthold. 1880. *Einleitung in das Sprachstudium,* 4th ed. Leipzig:
 Breitkopf & Haertel.
Dempwolff, Otto. 1934–37. *Induktiver Aufbau eines indonesischen Wortschatzes,*
 2 vols. Berlin: Reimer.
Dixon, Roland B. 1913. "New Linguistic Families in California," *AA* 15:647–55.
Dixon, Roland B., and Alfred L. Kroeber. 1913. "Relationships of Indian Languages
 in California," *Science,* n.s. 37:225.
Dorsey, James Owen, and John R. Swanton. 1912. *A Dictionary of the Biloxi and
 Ofo Languages. Bureau of American Ethnology Bulletin* 47.
Durbin, Marshall. 1973. "Proto-Hianacoto: Guaque-Carijona-Hianacoto-Umaua,"
 IJAL 39:22–31.
Dyen, Isidore. 1959. Review of Joseph Greenberg, 'Essays in Linguistics,' *Language*
 35:527–52.
Elmendorff, William W. 1968. "Lexical and Cultural Change in Yukian," *Anthropo-
 logical Linguistics* 10.7:1–41.
Fodor, István. 1966. *The Problems in the Classification of the African Languages.*
 Budapest: Hungarian Academy of Sciences.
Forrest, R. A. D. 1950. "The Ju-Sheng Tone in Pekingese," *Bulletin of the School of
 Oriental and African Studies,* 443–47.
Foster, Mary LeCron. 1969. *The Tarascan Language.* Berkeley: University of Cali-
 fornia Press.

Fox, James Allan. 1978. "Proto-Mayan Accent, Morpheme Structure Conditions, and Velar Innovations," Ph.D. dissertation, University of Chicago.

Frachtenberg, Leo J. 1922. "Coos," in *Bureau of American Ethnology Bulletin* 40.2:297–429.

Freeland, Lucy S. 1930. "The Relationship of Mixe to the Penutian Family," *IJAL* 6:28–36.

Gabelentz, Georg von der. 1891. *Die Sprachwissenschaft.* Leipzig: Weigel.

Gallatin, Albert. 1836. "A Synopsis of the Indian Tribes Within the United States East of the Rocky Mountains," *Transactions and Collections of the American Antiquarian Society* (Cambridge, Mass.) 2:1–422.

Gatschet, Albert S. 1876. *Zwölf Sprachen aus dem Südwesten Amerikas.* Berlin: Böhlau.

Girard, Victor. 1971. *Proto-Takanan Phonology.* Berkeley: University of California Press.

Gleason, Henry Allen. 1955. *Workbook in Descriptive Linguistics.* New York: Holt.

———. 1959. "Counting and Calculating for Historical Reconstruction," *Anthropological Linguistics* 1.2:21–32.

Goeje, Claudius Henricus de. 1946. "Études linguistiques caraïbes," part 2, *Verhandelingen der Koninklijke Akademie van Wetenschappen, Afdeeling Letterkunde* (Amsterdam) 49.2.

Greenberg, Joseph H. 1953. "Historical Linguistics and Unwritten Languages," in A. L. Kroeber, ed., *Anthropology Today.* Chicago: University of Chicago Press.

———. 1957. *Essays in Linguistics.* Chicago: University of Chicago Press.

———. 1960. "The General Classification of Central and South American Languages," in Anthony Wallace, ed., *Men and Cultures: Selected Papers of the 5th International Congress of Anthropological and Ethnological Sciences, 1956.* Philadelphia: University of Pennsylvania Press, 791–94.

———. 1963. *The Languages of Africa.* Bloomington: Indiana University Press.

———. 1972. "Numeral Classifiers and Substantival Number," *Working Papers in Language Universals* (Stanford University) 9:1–40.

———. 1978. "How Does a Language Acquire Gender Markers?," in J. H. Greenberg, ed., *Universals of Human Language,* vol. 3. Stanford, Calif.: Stanford University Press.

———. 1979. "The Classification of American Indian Languages," in Ralph E. Cooley et al., eds., *Papers of the 1978 Mid-America Linguistics Conference at Oklahoma.*

———. 1981. "Nilo-Saharan Movable *k*- as a Stage III Article (with a Penutian Parallel)," *Journal of African Languages and Linguistics* 3:105–12.

———. Forthcoming. *Indo-European and Its Closest Relatives: The Eurasiatic Language Family.* Stanford, Calif.: Stanford University Press.

Greenberg, Joseph H., Christy G. Turner, and Stephen Zegura. 1985. "Convergence of Evidence for the Peopling of the Americas," *Collegium Antropologicum* (Zagreb) 9,*1*:33–42.

Gregersen, Edgar A. 1977. *Language in Africa.* New York: Gordon & Breach.

Gursky, Karl-Heinz. 1965. *Zur Frage der historischen Stellung der Yuki-Sprachfamilie. Abhandlung der Völkerkundlichen Arbeitsgemeinschaft* (Hanover) 8.

Guthrie, Malcolm. 1967. *Comparative Bantu: An Introduction to the Comparative Linguistics and Prehistory of Bantu Languages*, vol. 1. Farnborough, Eng.: Gregg Press.

Haas, Mary R. 1951. "The Proto-Gulf Words for 'water' (with Notes on Siouan-Yuchi)," *IJAL* 18:238–40.

———. 1952. "The Proto-Gulf Words for 'land' (with a Note on Proto-Siouan)," *IJAL* 18:238–40.

———. 1956. "Natchez and the Muskogean Languages," *Language* 32:61–72.

———. 1958a. "A New Linguistic Relationship in North America: Algonkian and the Gulf Languages," *Southwestern Journal of Anthropology* 14:231–64.

———. 1958b. "Algonkian-Ritwan: The End of a Controversy," *IJAL* 24:159–73.

———. 1960. "Some Genetic Affiliations of Algonkian," in Stanley Diamond, ed., *Culture in History*, New York: Columbia University Press.

———. 1965. "Is Kutenai Related to Algonkian?," *Canadian Journal of Linguistics* 10:77–92.

Hale, Kenneth. 1962. "Jemez and Kiowa Correspondences in Reference to Kiowa-Tanoan," *IJAL* 28:1–5.

———. 1967. "Toward a Reconstruction of Kiowa-Tanoan Phonology," *IJAL* 33:112–20.

Harrington, J. P. 1928. *Vocabulary of the Kiowa Language. Bureau of American Ethnology Bulletin* 84.

Haynes, Vance. 1982. "Were Clovis Progenitors in Beringia?," in D. Hopkins et al., eds., *Paleoecology of Beringia*. New York: Academic Press.

Henry, Jules. 1939. "The Linguistic Position of the Ashluslay Indians," *IJAL* 10:86–91.

Herrero, Andrés. 1834. *Doctrina y Oraciones Cristianas en lengua Mosetena. . . .* Rome: Imprenta de Propaganda.

Hewson, John. 1968. "Beothuk and Algonkian: Evidence Old and New," *IJAL* 34:85–93.

Hockett, Charles F. 1957. "Central Algonquian Vocabulary: Stems in /k-/," *IJAL* 23:247–68.

———. 1966. "What Algonquian Is Really Like," *IJAL* 32:59–73.

Hoijer, Harry. 1960. "Athapaskan Languages of the Pacific Coast," in Stanley Diamond, ed., *Culture in History.* New York: Columbia University Press.

Holmer, Nils M. 1947. *Critical and Comparative Grammar of the Cuna Language.* Gothenburg: Etnografiska museet.

———. 1952. *Ethno-linguistic Cuna Dictionary.* Gothenburg: *Etnologiska Studier,* vol. 29.

Hymes, Dell. 1960. "Lexicostatistics So Far," *Current Anthropology* 1:3–44.

Jacobsen, William H., Jr. 1958. "Washo and Karok: An Approach to Comparative Hokan," *IJAL* 24:195–213.

Jespersen, Otto. 1922. *Language: Its Nature, Origin and Development*. London: Allen & Unwin.

Joos, Martin. 1964. "Glottochronology with Retention Rate Homogeneity," in *Proceedings of the Ninth International Congress of Linguists*. London: Mouton.

Kennard, Edward A. 1936. "Mandan Grammar," *IJAL* 9:1–43.

Key, Mary Ritchie. 1968. *Comparative Tacanan Phonology with Cavineña Phonology and Notes on Pano-Tacanan Relationship*. The Hague: Mouton.

———. 1979. *The Grouping of South American Indian Languages*. Tübingen: Gunter Narr.

Krauss, Michael E. 1964. "Proto-Athapaskan-Eyak and the Problem of Na-Dene, 1: Phonology," *IJAL* 31:18–28.

———. 1973. "Na-Dene," in *CTIL*, vol. 10.

———. 1979. "Na-Dene and Eskimo-Aleut," in *LNA*.

Kroeber, Alfred R. 1904. "The Languages of the Coast of California South of San Francisco," *UCPAAE* 2:29–80.

———. 1906. "The Yokuts and Yuki Languages," in *Boas Anniversary Volume*. New York: Stechert.

———. 1906–7. "Shoshonean Dialects of California," *UCPAAE* 4:65–165.

———. 1909. "The Bannock and Shoshone Languages," *AA* 11:266–77.

———. 1910. "The Chumash and Costanoan Languages," *UCPAAE* 9:259–63.

———. 1915. "Serian, Tequistlatecan, and Hokan," *UCPAAE* 11:279–90.

Kuipers, Aert H. 1967. *The Squamish Language*. The Hague: Mouton.

———. 1970. "Towards a Salish Etymological Dictionary," *Lingua* 26:46–72.

Lafone y Quevedo, Samuel Alexander. 1901–2. "Los Indianos Mosetens y su lengua," *Anales de la Sociedad Científica Argentina*, vols. 52–54.

Lamb, Sydney M. 1959. "Some Proposals for Linguistic Taxonomy," *Anthropological Linguistics* 1.2:33–49.

Lane, George S. 1968. "The Beech Argument: A Re-evaluation of the Linguistic Evidence," *Zeitschrift für vergleichende Sprachforschung*, n.f. 81:198–202.

Langacker, Ronald W. 1976. *Non-Distinct Arguments in Uto-Aztecan. UCPL*, Vol. 82.

———. 1977. *Studies in Uto-Aztecan Grammar*, vol. 1: *An Overview of Uto-Aztecan Grammar*. Dallas: Summer Institute of Linguistics.

Langdon, Margaret. 1979. "Some Thoughts on Hokan with Particular Reference to Pomoan and Yuman," in *LNA*.

Latham, Robert G. 1846. "Miscellaneous Contributions to the Ethnography of North America," *Proceedings of the Philological Society* (London) 2:31–50.

———. 1860. *Opuscula: Essays Chiefly Philological and Ethnographical*. London: Williams & Norgate.

Laughlin, W. S. 1980. *Aleuts: Survivors of the Bering Land Bridge*. New York: Holt, Rinehart.

Lehmann, Walter. 1915. "Über die Stellung und Verwandschaft der Subtiaba-Sprache der Pazifischen Küste Nicaraguas und über die Sprache von Tapachula in Südchiapas," *Zeitschrift für Ethnologie* 47:1–34.

———. 1920. *Zentral Amerika*, 2 vols. Berlin: Reimer.

Lemle, Miriam. 1971. "Internal Classification of the Tupi-Guarani Family," in David Bendor-Samuel, ed., *Tupi Studies I*. Norman, Okla.: Summer Institute of Linguistics.

Levine, Robert D. 1979. "Haida and Na-Dene: A New Look at the Evidence," *IJAL* 45:157–70.

Longacre, Robert. 1967. "Systemic Comparison and Reconstruction," in McQuown (1967), cited below.

———, ed. 1968. "Comparative Reconstruction of Indigenous Languages," in *CTIL*, vol. 4.

Loukotka, Čestmír. 1931. "La familia lingüística Mashakali," *Revista del Instituto de Etnología de la Universidad Nacional de Tucumán* 2:21–47.

———. 1932. "La familia lingüística Kamakan del Brasil," *Revista del Instituto de Etnología de la Universidad Nacional de Tucumán* 2:493–524.

———. 1937. "La familia lingüística Coroado," *JSA* 29:157–214.

———. 1968. *Classification of South American Indian Languages*, ed. Johannes Wilbert. Los Angeles: Latin American Center, University of California.

Lounsbury, Floyd. 1958. Personal communication.

Lowie, Robert H. 1941. *The Crow Language: Grammatical Sketch and Analyzed Text. UCPAAE* 39.

Maldonado, Jhoan de Paz. 1897. "Relación del pueblo de Sant-Andres Xunxi," *Relaciones Geográficas de Indias* (Madrid) 3:149–54.

Martius, Karl Friedrich Philipp von. 1867. *Beiträge zur Ethnographie und Sprachenkunde Amerikas, zumal Brasiliens*, 2 vols. Leipzig: Fleischer.

Mason, John Alden. 1950. "The Languages of South American Indians," in Julian H. Steward, ed., *Handbook of South American Indians. Bureau of American Ethnology Bulletin* 143, vol. 6:157–317.

Matteson, Esther, et al. 1972. *Comparative Studies in Amerindian Languages*. The Hague: Mouton.

Matthews, G. Hubert. 1958. "Handbook of Siouan Languages," Ph.D. dissertation, University of Pennsylvania.

McGhee, Robert. 1976. "Parsimony Isn't Everything: An Alternative View of Eskaleutian Linguistics and Prehistory," *Canadian Archaeological Association Bulletin* 8:60–81.

McLendon, Sally. 1964. "Northern Hokan (b) and (c): A Comparison of Eastern Pomo and Yana," in William Bright, ed., *Studies in California Linguistics*. Berkeley: University of California Press.

———. 1973. *Proto Pomo*. Berkeley: University of California Press.

McQuown, Norman A. 1942. "Una posible síntesis lingüística Macro-Mayance," in R. P. Gamboa, ed., *Mayas y Olmecas*. Mexico City: Sociedad Mexicana de Anthropológia.

———. 1955. "The Indigenous Languages of Latin America," *AA* n.s. 57:501–70.

———, ed. 1967. *Handbook of Middle American Indians* (gen. ed. Robert Wauchope), Vol. 5: *Linguistics*. Austin: University of Texas Press.

Meillet, Antoine. 1934. *Introduction à l'étude comparative des langues indo-européenes*. Paris: Hachette.

Meinhof, Carl. 1910. *Grundriss einer Lautlehre der Bantusprachen,* 2d revised and expanded ed. Berlin: Reimer.

———. 1932. *Introduction to the Phonology of Bantu Languages.* Berlin: Reimer/ Vohsen.

Michelson, Truman. 1915. "Rejoinder to Sapir," *AA* n.s. 17:194–98.

———. 1938. "Algonquian Notes," *IJAL* 9:103–12.

Miller, Roy Andrew. 1971. *Japanese and the Other Altaic Languages.* Chicago: University of Chicago Press.

Miller, Wick R. 1965. *Acoma Grammar and Texts.* Berkeley: University of California Press.

———. 1967. *Uto-Aztecan Cognate Sets.* Berkeley: University of California Press.

Miller, Wick R., and Irvine Davis. 1963. "Proto-Keresan Phonology," *IJAL* 29:310–30.

Moshinsky, Julius. 1974. *A Grammar of Southeastern Pomo.* UCPL 72.

Newman, Paul. 1970. "Historical Sound Laws in Hausa and in Dera (Kanakuru)," *Journal of West African Languages* 7:39–51.

Newman, Stanley S. 1964. "Comparison of Zuni and California Penutian," *IJAL* 30:1–13.

Olson, Ronald D. 1964. "Mayan Affinities with Chipaya of Bolivia, 1: Correspondences," *IJAL* 30:313–24.

———. 1965. "Mayan Affinities with Chipaya of Bolivia, 2: Cognates," *IJAL* 31:29–38.

Oltrogge, David F. 1977. "Proto Jicaque-Subtiaba-Tequistlateco: A Comparative Reconstruction," in *Two Studies in Middle American Comparative Linguistics.* Austin: University of Texas Press.

Peeke, Catherine. 1973. *Preliminary Grammar of Auca.* Norman, Okla.: Summer Institute of Linguistics.

Pelleschi, Juan. 1896–97. "Los Indios Matacos y su lengua," *Boletín del Instituto Geográfico Argentino* (Buenos Aires) 17:559–62.

Petter, Rodolphe. 1952. *Cheyenne Grammar.* Newton, Kans.: Mennonite Publication Office.

Pinnow, Heinz-Jürgen. 1966. *Grundzüge einer historischen Lautlehre des Tlingit: Ein Versuch.* Wiesbaden: Otto Harrassowitz.

Pitkin, Harvey, and William Shipley. 1958. "Comparative Survey of California Penutian," *IJAL* 24:174–88.

Pittier de Fabrega, Henri François. 1907. "Ethnographic and Linguistic Notes on the Páez Indians of Tierra Adentro, Cauca, Colombia," *Memoirs of the American Anthropological Association* 1. 5:301–57.

Powell, John Wesley. 1891. "Indian Linguistic Families North of Mexico," *Bureau of American Ethnography Report* 7:7–139.

Powlison, Paul S. 1962. "Palatalization Portmanteaus in Yagua (Peba-Yaguan)," *Word* 18:280–99.

Price, R. David. 1978. "The Nambiquara Linguistic Family," *Anthropological Linguistics* 20.1:14–37.

Prost, Gilbert R. 1962. "Signaling of Transitive and Intransitive in Chacobo (Pano)," *IJAL* 28:108–18.

Radin, Paul. 1916. "On the Relationship of Huave and Mixe," *AA* 18:411–21.

———. 1919. "The Genetic Relationship of North American Indian Languages," *UCPAAE* 14:489–502.

———. 1924. "The Relationship of Maya to Zoque-Huave," *JSA* 16:317–24.

Ramstedt, G. J. 1928. "Remarks on the Korean Language," *Mémoires de la Société Finno-Ougrienne* 58:441–53.

Reichard, Gladys A. 1925. "Wiyot Grammar and Texts," *UCPAAE* 22:1–215.

Rensch, Calvin Ross. 1976. *Comparative Otomanguean Phonology.* Bloomington: Indiana University Press.

Rivet, Paul. 1911a. "La famille linguistique peba," *JSA* 8:173–206.

———. 1911b. "Affinités du Miranya," *JSA* 8:117–52.

———. 1925. "La langue arda ou une plaisante méprise," *Proceedings of the 21st International Congress of Americanists,* vol. 2. Wiesbaden: Lessing.

———. 1942. "Un dialecte Hoka colombien: le yurumangí," *JSA* 34:1–59.

Robins, R. H. 1958. *The Yurok Language.* Berkeley: University of California Press.

Rona, José Pedro. 1964. *Nuevos elementos acerca de la lengua Charrua.* Montevideo: Departamento de Lingüística, Universidad de la República.

Rood, David S. 1973. "Swadesh's Keres-Caddo Comparisons," *IJAL* 39:189–90.

Sapir, Edward. 1913. "Wiyot and Yurok, Algonkin Languages of California," *AA* n.s. 17:188–94.

———. 1915. "The Na-Dene Languages: A Preliminary Report," *AA* n.s. 17:534–58.

———. 1917a. Review of Benigno Bibolotti, 'Moseteno Vocabulary and Treatises,' *IJAL* 1:183–84.

———. 1917b. "The Position of Yana in the Hokan Stock," *UCPAAE* 13:1–34.

———. 1920. "Hokan and Coahuiltecan Languages," *IJAL* 1:280–90.

———. 1921. "A Characteristic Penutian Form of Stem," *IJAL* 2:58–67.

———. 1922. "The Takelma Language of Southwestern Oregon," in Franz Boas, ed., *Handbook of American Indian Languages. Bureau of American Ethnology Bulletin* 40.2:1–296.

———. 1925a. "The Similarity of Chinese and Indian Languages," *Science* 62 (Oct. 16), no. 1607, xii.

———. 1925b. "The Hokan Affinities of the Subtiaba in Nicaragua," *AA* 27:402–35, 491–527.

———. 1929. "Central and North American Languages," *Encyclopaedia Britannica,* 14th ed., vol. 5.

———. 1963. *Selected Writings of Edward Sapir,* ed. David Mandelbaum. Berkeley: University of California Press.

Sapir, Edward, and Morris Swadesh. 1970. *Yana Dictionary.* Berkeley: University of California Press.

Schachter, Paul. 1971. "The Present State of African Linguistics," in *CTIL,* vol. 7.

Schmidt, Max. 1905. *Indianerstudien in Zentralbrasilien.* Berlin.

———. 1942. "Resultados de mi tercera expedicíon a los Guatos efectuada en el año de 1928," *Revista de la Sociedad Científica del Paraguay* (Asuncíon) 5.6:41–75.

Schmidt, Wilhelm. 1906. *Die Mon-Khmer Völker, ein Bindeglied zwischen Völkern Zentralasiens und Austronesiens.* Braunschweig: Vieweg.

Sebeok, Thomas A., ed. 1973. *Current Trends in Linguistics,* vol. 10: *Linguistics in North America.* The Hague: Mouton.

Shafer, Robert. 1952. "Athapaskan and Sino-Tibetan," *IJAL* 18:12–19.

———. 1957. "A Note on Athapaskan and Sino-Tibetan," *IJAL* 23:116–17.

Shell, Olive. 1965. "Pano Reconstruction," Ph.D. dissertation, University of Pennsylvania.

Shipley, William. 1957. "Some Yukian-Penutian Lexical Resemblances," *IJAL* 23:269–74.

Siebert, Frank T., Jr. 1941. "Certain Proto-Algonquian Consonant Clusters," *Language* 17:298–303.

———. 1975. "Resurrecting Virginia Algonquian from the Dead: The Reconstituted and Historical Phonology of Powhatan," in James J. Crawford, ed., *Studies in Southeastern Indian Languages,* Athens: University of Georgia Press, 258–453.

Silver, Shirley. 1964. "Shasta and Karok: A Binary Comparison," in William Bright, ed., *Studies in Californian Linguistics.* Berkeley: University of California Press.

Speck, Frank G. 1934. *Catawba Texts.* New York: Columbia University Press.

Sturtevant, Edgar H. 1942. *The Indo-Hittite Laryngeals.* Baltimore: Linguistic Society of America.

Suárez, Jorge. 1969. "Moseten and Pano-Tacanan," *Anthropological Linguistics* 11.9:255–66.

Susnik, Branislava. 1968. *Chulupi: esbozo gramatical analítico.* Asunción: Museo Etnográfico Andrés Barbero.

Swadesh, Morris. 1953a. "Mosan, I: A Problem of Remote Common Origin," *IJAL* 19:26–44.

———. 1953b. "Mosan, II: Comparative Vocabulary," *IJAL* 19:223–36.

———. 1954. "Perspectives and Problems of Amerindian Comparative Linguistics," *Word* 10:306–32.

———. 1958. "Some New Glottochronological Dates for Amerindian Linguistic Groups," in *Proceedings of the Thirty-Second International Congress of Americanists, 1956.* Copenhagen: Munksgaard.

———. 1959. *Mapas de Clasificación Lingüística de México y de las Américas.* Cuadernos del Instituto de Historia, Serie Anthropológia 8. Mexico City: University of Mexico.

———. 1962. "Afinidades de las Amerindias," in *Proceedings of the Thirty-Fourth International Congress of Americanists, 1960.* Horn-Wien: Berger.

———. 1967. "Linguistic Classification in the Southwest," in Dell Hymes and William Bittle, eds., *Studies in Southwestern Ethnolinguistics.* The Hague: Mouton.

————. 1969. *Elementos del Tarasco antiguo*. Mexico City: University of Mexico.

Swadesh, Morris, and Joseph Greenberg. 1953. "Jicaque as a Hokan Language," *IJAL* 19:216–22.

Szemerényi, Oswald J. L. 1970. *Einführung in die vergleichende Sprachwissenschaft*. Darmstadt: Wissenschaftliche Buchgesellschaft.

Szinnyei, Joszef. 1910. *Finnisch-Ugrische Sprachwissenschaft*. Leipzig: Goeschen.

Taylor, Alan H. 1982. Review of Lyle Campbell and Marianne Mithun, eds., 'The Languages of Native America,' *Language* 50:440–43.

Taylor, Allan R. 1963. "Comparative Caddoan," *IJAL* 29:113–31.

Tessmann, Gunter. 1930. *Die Indianer Nordost-Perus*. Hamburg.

Tovar, Antonio. 1961. *Catálogo de las lenguas de América del Sur*. Buenos Aires: Editorial Sudamericana.

Tuggy, Juan. 1966. *Vocabulario Candoshi de Loreto*. Peru: Summer Institute of Linguistics.

Uhle, Max. 1890. "Verwandschaft und Wanderungen der Tschibtscha," in *Proceedings of the 7th International Congress of Americanists*. Berlin: Kühl.

Uhlenbeck, Christianus Cornelius. 1938. "A Concise Blackfoot Grammar," *Verhandelingen der Koninklijke Akademie van Wetenschappen, Afdeeling Letterkunde* (Amsterdam) n.s. 41.

Ultan, Russell. 1964. "Proto-Maiduan Phonology," *IJAL* 30:355–70.

Wagner, Gunter. 1934. "Yuchi," in Franz Boas, ed., *Handbook of American Indian Languages*, vol. 3. New York: Columbia University Press.

Walde, Alois, and Julius Pokorny. 1927. *Vergleichendes Wörterbuch der indogermanischen Sprachen*, 3 vols. Berlin: De Gruyter.

Welmers, William. 1973. *African Language Structures*. Berkeley: University of California Press.

West, F. H. 1981. *The Archaeology of Beringia*. New York: Columbia University Press.

Whorf, Benjamin, and George L. Trager. 1937. "The Relationship of Uto-Aztecan and Tanoan," *AA* 39:609–24.

Wilbur, Terence H., ed. 1977. *The Lautgesetz-Controversy: A Documentation (1885–1886)*. Amsterdam: Benjamin.

Williams, Robert C., et al. Forthcoming. "GM Allotypes in Native Americans: Evidence for Three Distinct Migrations Across the Bering Land Bridge," *American Journal of Physical Anthropology*.

Williamson, John P. 1902. *An English-Dakota Dictionary*. New York: American Tract Society.

Wolff, Hans. 1950–51. "Comparative Siouan," *IJAL* 16:61–66, 113–21, 160–78; 17:197–204.

Wurm, Stephen A. 1972. *Languages of Australia and Tasmania*. The Hague: Mouton.

Indexes

Index to the Amerind Etymologies

The following is an alphabetical index of the more than 1,890 lexical etymologies listed in Chapters 3 and 4 in support of the Amerind family and its branches. For practical reasons, the 107 grammatical traits discussed in Chapter 5 are not included. Each etymology is identified by its semantic gloss and the group or groups to which it is assigned, followed by the page number(s) on which that etymology appears. Thus, the entry "Arrive, AK, P: 166, 146," means that the Almosan-Keresiouan etymology for "Arrive" is to be found on p. 166 and the Penutian etymology on p. 146. The Amerind dictionary entries are separately indexed. The following abbreviations are used:

AK	Almosan-Keresiouan	H	Hokan
AM	Amerind	MC	Macro-Carib
AN	Andean	MG	Macro-Ge
CA	Central Amerind	MP	Macro-Panoan
CP	Chibchan-Paezan	MT	Macro-Tucanoan
E	Equatorial	P	Penutian

411

413

Index of Language Names

The following list contains the names of all the New World languages and language groups mentioned in the text. A few groups that are no longer considered valid (e.g. Andean-Equatorial) appear in the index but not in the classification. Language groups are in capital letters: PUINAVE is a group; Puinave is a language. When a group comprises a single language of the same name, the entry is shown as Aleut (ALEUT). An "f" following a page number indicates a separate entry on the following page; an "ff" indicates separate entries on the following two pages. "Passim" is used for clumps of four or more references that fall within five pages of each other: 181, 186, 187, 192 qualifies for 181–92 passim; 181, 187, 192 does not.

Index of Language Names

Central Yana, 133–42 passim, 210, 218, 222, 233, 242, 248, 381
Chacobo, 50, 75, 184, 187f, 227, 237, 246, 290, 295, 310–15 passim, 386
Chama, 50, 75ff, 185, 188, 190, 202, 212, 221, 248, 253, 283, 290, 295, 302f, 313, 315, 386
Chamacoco, 51, 85–92 passim, 185, 200, 205, 214, 228f, 236, 249, 266f, 385
Chami, 109–22 passim, 182, 198, 214, 226, 231, 235, 268, 382
Chamicuro, 88, 90f, 223, 384
Chana (CHARRUAN), 74–77 passim, 207, 221, 232, 246, 282, 302, 385
Chana (MAIPURAN), 210, 384
Changuena, 107, 109, 116, 269, 382
Chapacura, 51, 85–91 passim, 191, 213, 238, 384
CHAPACURA, 51, 83–93 passim, 188–213 passim, 219–27 passim, 234–44 passim, 262, 285, 384
Charrua, 74f, 184, 202f, 207, 221, 238, 246, 268, 273, 282, 385
CHARRUAN, 50, 74f, 77, 184, 202f, 207, 221, 232, 238, 246, 268, 273, 282, 290, 302f, 385
Chavante, 69–73 passim, 196, 217, 222, 225, 241, 243, 258, 386
Chayma, 79–83 passim, 198, 202, 219f, 226, 235, 243, 249, 314, 385
CHEMAKUAN, 41, 163–90 passim, 205, 218f, 232–38 passim, 252, 255, 257, 286, 317, 379
Chemakum, 166–78 passim, 184, 186, 190, 205, 232ff, 238, 252, 255, 257, 296, 379
Cherente, 73, 194, 197, 218f, 221, 230, 250, 258, 270, 282, 289, 386
Cherokee, 165–78 passim, 184, 227, 241, 252f, 257, 305, 379
Cheyenne, 57, 168–79 passim, 196, 198, 216, 226, 232, 257, 261, 318, 379
Chiapanec, 124, 293, 311, 381
Chibcha, 52, 106–22 passim, 183, 193, 196, 206, 210, 215, 224–34 passim, 252f, 260–70 passim, 280, 286, 298f, 312, 317, 382
CHIBCHA, 106–22 passim, 183, 185, 193, 196, 204, 206–53 passim, 260–80 passim, 286, 298ff, 312, 317, 382
CHIBCHAN, 39, 52, 61, 84, 106–22 pas-

sim, 183, 185, 208ff, 212, 224–58 passim, 275–317 passim, 382
CHIBCHAN-PAEZAN, 52, 58ff, 61, 106–22, 182–317 passim, 336, 382
Chickasaw, 150–59 passim, 182, 213, 302, 316, 380
Chicriaba, 73, 225, 243, 386
Chilanga, 109–22 passim, 183, 204–12 passim, 240, 248, 268, 281, 286, 311f, 382
Chilliwak, 240, 379
Chimariko (CHIMARIKO), 41, 53, 58, 131–42 passim, 184–90 passim, 197, 201–60 passim, 267, 269, 286, 295, 301, 315, 381
Chimila, 52, 108–22 passim, 182–93 passim, 206, 208f, 232, 240, 244, 264, 382
Chimu, 58, 108–19 passim, 183, 193, 229, 243, 269, 276, 298, 301, 304, 382
CHIMU, 106–22 passim, 182f, 193f, 198, 204, 206, 215, 220, 227–32 passim, 238–46 passim, 258–70 passim, 276, 298, 301, 304, 382
Chinantec, 53, 275, 281, 381
Chinchaysuyu, 102f, 105f, 200, 215, 217, 383
Chinook, 53, 55, 146–62 passim, 191, 202, 226–33 passim, 247–64 passim, 294, 301, 304, 310, 317, 380
CHINOOK, 41, 53, 55, 58, 143–62 passim, 191, 202, 226–36 passim, 247–64 passim, 294, 301, 304, 310, 317, 380
Chipaya, 85–93 passim, 187, 202–9 passim, 219, 236, 270, 285, 384
Chipewyan, 321, 379
Chippewa, 168f, 174, 379
Chiquimulilla, 109–22 passim, 184f, 206, 209, 227, 245, 251, 261, 382
Chiquito, 44f, 48, 67–73 passim, 182, 184, 193, 196f, 202, 204, 212, 221, 223, 225, 237–62 passim, 270, 273, 281, 283, 293, 296, 386
CHIQUITO, 44f, 48, 66–73 passim, 182, 184, 193–204 passim, 212, 221, 223, 225, 237–62 passim, 270, 273, 281, 283, 293, 296, 386
Chiranga, 235, 266, 384
Chiriana, 191, 285, 384
Chiriguano, 89, 385
Chiripo, 108–19 passim, 193, 196, 264, 300, 382

418

General Index

Fox, James Allan, 144
Freeland, Lucy, 143

Gabelentz, Georg von der, 18
Gender markers, 281–82, 296–98
Genetic classification: and regular sound correspondences, 2–3, 6–13, 19–22; and valid genetic units, 4; relationships vs. classifications, 4–5, 7; comparative resemblances, 5f; reconstructions, 8–10, 12–13, 18–19, 32, 33–34, 36; recurrences vs. correspondences, 10–16 passim, 33–34; morphophonemic alterations and analogies, 13–14; cognates, 19–22, 346–52 passim; and glottochronology, 25n, 27–28, 334–35, 341–44, 345, 352; comparison of isolated languages, 325–30; of languages worldwide, 336–37; mathematics of subgrouping, 345–67
Girard, Victor, 73
Gleason, Henry A., 10
Glottochronology, 25n, 27–28, 334–35, 341–44, 345, 352
Goeje, C. H. de, 78
Granberry, Julian, 107
Gregersen, Edgar, 3
Grimm's law, 11
Gursky, Karl-Heinz, 143
Guthrie, Malcolm, 15–16

Haas, Mary R., 40, 56, 144, 163ff
Habitual mood, 310
Hale, Kenneth, 123
Hanson, Norwood R., 7
Harrington, J. P., 40, 42, 123
Henry, Jules, 73
Hockett, Charles, 55, 163
Hoenigswald, Henry, 35
Hoijer, Harry, 10, 323f
Hortative mood, 311ff
Hrozný, Bedrich, 36

Imperatives, 312–13
Infinitives, 282, 300, 306
Instrumental case, 302f
Interrogatives, 302, 315–17

Jacobsen, William H., 132
Jespersen, Otto, 18, 34

Joos, Martin, 28
Joos function, 342, 344

Key, Mary R., 39, 50, 73f
Krauss, Michael, 321, 323f, 335
Kroeber, Alfred, 3, 25, 40, 42, 46, 131, 143, 164
Kuipers, Aert, 57, 165

Lafone y Quevedo, S. A., 73
Lamb, Sydney, 3, 43
Latham, Robert G., 163
Laughlin, W. S., 134
Lehmann, Walter, 46–47, 107, 131
Lemle, Miriam, 84
Levine, Robert D., 9, 43, 321–27 passim
Loanwords, 19–22
Locative case, 301–3
Loukotka, Čestmír, 38f, 44, 64f, 74, 78, 84, 93, 99, 107
Lounsbury, Floyd, 45, 66

Martius, Karl von, 64
Mason, J. A., 39
Matteson, Esther, 39
McGhee, Robert, 335
McLendon, Sally, 132
McQuown, Norman A., 39, 143
Meillet, Antoine, 30, 32f
Meinhof, Carl, 17, 23, 31
Metathesis, 8, 15
Meyer, Gustav, 33
Michelson, Truman, 49, 56
Miller, Roy A., 331
Miller, Wick R., 123f, 165
Mood (verbs), 309–14, 318

Na-Dene problem, 40, 321–25
Negation, 315
Neo-Grammarians, 3, 7, 11, 15, 17, 30f
Newman, Paul, 3
Newman, Stanley, 42, 144
Nouns: affixes, 46–48, 56–57; number, 291; plurals, 292, 295, 297; gender markers, 296–98; numerical classifiers, 298–99; case system, 299–303; sociatives, 303–5; diminutives, 305; formation from verbs, 305–8, 314, 318ff; formal bases, 317
Numerical classifiers, 298–99

General Index

Olson, Ronald D., 84
Oltrogge, David F., 132
Optative mood, 311ff

Peeke, Catherine, 99
Pinnow, Heinz-Jürgen, 321f
Pitkin, Harvey, 144
Plurals: noun, 292, 295, 297; pronoun, 292–96
Powell, J. W., 39–40, 131
Price, R. David, 93
Pronouns: affixes, 44–58; inclusive vs. exclusive, 56, 287–89, 312; 1st person, 273–77, 287–89; 2d person, 277–79, 288f, 312; 3d person, 279–87, 314; demonstratives, 279–90 passim, 288–90; gender markers, 281–82, 296–98; reflexives and reciprocals, 290–91; plurality, 292–96
Purposive mood, 311

Radin, Paul, 42, 143
Ramstedt, G. J., 331f
Rask, Rasmus, 331
Reciprocals, 291
Reconstruction, 8–10, 12–13, 18–19, 32ff, 36, 43
Reflexives, 290–91
Reichard, Gladys, 163
Rensch, Calvin, 16, 123f
Ritschl, Friedrich, 35
Rivet, Paul, 78, 83, 107
Rona, José, 74
Rood, David, 163

Sapir, Edward, 12; Na-Dene hypothesis, 9, 321–25 passim; on classification of Amerind, 40–49 passim, 54f, 57, 131, 143, 163f
Saussure, Ferdinand de, 12, 19
Schachter, Paul, 2, 17, 23, 31
Schleicher, August, 18, 31f, 34f
Schmidt, Wilhelm, 336

Schulze, G., 12
Shafer, Robert, 332
Shell, Olive, 50, 73
Shipley, William, 40, 143f
Siebert, Frank T., 165
Silver, Shirley, 132
Sociatives, 303–5
Sound comparisons, 2–3, 6–13, 19–22
Sound laws, 8, 10, 17f, 30–31
Sturtevant, Edgar, 18
Suárez, Jorge, 73
Subject markers, 300
Swadesh, Morris, 38, 54, 131, 163, 335
Synchronic resemblances, 5–6
Szinnyei, Joszef, 17

Taylor, Allan R., 43
Teeter, Karl, 163
Tense: present, 309–10; past, 310–11, 314; future, 311
Tovar, Antonio, 31
Trager, George, 40, 123ff
Turner, Christy, 43n, 336

Uhle, Max, 107
Ural-Altaic languages, 331–32

Verbs: infinitives, 282, 300, 306; mood and tense, 309–14, 318; imperatives, 312–13; causatives, 313–14; transitivizers, 313–14; intransitives, 314; and motion, 314–15, 318f; applicative classifiers, 317–20
Verner's law, 11, 13, 36

Welmers, William, 1–2
Whorf, Benjamin, 40, 123f
Wilbur, Terence H., 30
Williams, Robert C., 336
Wolff, Hans, 165
Word sandhi, 14
Wurm, Stephen, 29

Zegura, Stephen, 43, 336

438